Time Series Models, Causality and Exogeneity

Foundations of Probability, Econometrics and Economic Games

Editors: Omar F. Hamouda, *Professor of Economics, York University, Canada*
and J.C.R. Rowley, *Professor of Economics, McGill University, Canada*

This major new series reprints in book form a selection of the most important and influential articles on probability, econometrics and economic games which cumulatively have had a major impact on the development of modern economics.

A distinctive feature of the series is the detailed general introduction to each volume which discusses the criteria for selection and locates the articles in the context of the development of the literature. There is also an individual introduction to each volume. This editorial structure will make each collection an invaluable resource both for teaching and research.

The series will include the classic articles in addition to the most recent and influential articles in the field. By combining classic material with articles at the frontiers of modern research, the editors have prepared a series that will be indispensable to any serious scholar or student with an interest in econometrics and economic games.

Volume 1.	Expected Utility, Fair Gambles and Rational Choice
Volume 2.	Paradoxes, Ambiguity and Rationality
Volume 3.	Economic Games, Bargaining and Solutions
Volume 4.	Probability Concepts, Dialogue and Beliefs
Volume 5.	Statistical Foundations for Econometrics
Volume 6.	Econometric Exploration and Diagnosis
Volume 7.	The Probability Approach to Simultaneous Equations
Volume 8.	Time Series Models, Causality and Exogeneity
Volume 9.	The Reappraisal of Econometrics
Volume 10.	Discrete and Continuous Systems, Cointegration and Chaos

Wherever possible, the articles in these volumes have been reproduced as originally published using facsimile reproduction, inclusive of footnotes and pagination to facilitate ease of reference.

For a list of all Edward Elgar published titles visit our site on the World Wide Web at http://www.e-elgar.co.uk

Time Series Models, Causality and Exogeneity

Edited by

Omar F. Hamouda

Professor of Economics
York University, Canada

and

J.C.R. Rowley

Professor of Economics
McGill University, Canada

FOUNDATIONS OF PROBABILITY, ECONOMETRICS AND ECONOMIC GAMES

An Elgar Reference Collection
Cheltenham, UK • Lyme, US

Published by
Edward Elgar Publishing Limited
8 Lansdown Place
Cheltenham
Glos GL50 2HU
UK

Edward Elgar Publishing Company, Inc.
1 Pinnacle Hill Road
Lyme
NH 03768
US

A catalogue record for this book is available from the British Library.

Library of Congress Cataloguing in Publication Data
The Foundations of probability, econometrics, and economic games /
edited by Omar F. Hamouda and J.C.R. Rowley.
A collection of journal articles published by various authors between 1937–1996, with an introduction to each volume by the editors.
Includes bibliographical references.
Contents: v. 1. Expected utility, fair gambles, and rational choice — v. 2. Paradoxes, ambiguity, and rationality — v. 3. Economic games, bargaining, and solutions — v. 4. Probability concepts, dialogue, and beliefs — v. 5. Statistical foundations for econometrics — v. 6. Econometric exploration and diagnosis — v. 7. The probability approach to simultaneous equations — v. 8. Time series models, causality, and exogeneity — v. 9. The reappraisal of econometrics — v. 10. Discrete and continuous systems, cointegration, and chaos.
1. Econometrics. 2. Econometric models. 3. Probabilities.
I. Hamouda, O.F. II. Rowley, J.C.R.
HB139.F678 1997
330'.01'5195—dc21 96–54038
CIP

ISBN 1 85898 440 8
1 85898 370 3 (10 title set)

Printed and bound in Great Britain by
Hartnolls Limited, Bodmin, Cornwall

Contents

Acknowledgements

The editors and publishers wish to thank the authors and the following publishers who have kindly given permission for the use of copyright material.

American Economic Association for article: Christopher A. Sims (1972), 'Money, Income, and Causality', *American Economic Review*, **LXII** (4), September, 540–52.

American Geophysical Union for articles: Keith William Hipel, Angus Ian McLeod and William C. Lennox (1977), 'Advances in Box–Jenkins Modeling, I: Model Construction', *Water Resources Research*, **13** (3), June, 567–75; Keith William Hipel, Angus Ian McLeod and William C. Lennox (1977), 'Advances in Box–Jenkins Modeling, II: Applications', *Water Resources Research*, **13** (3), June, 577–86.

American Statistical Association for article: Gregory C. Chow and Richard E. Levitan (1969), 'Spectral Properties of Non-Stationary Systems of Linear Stochastic Difference Equations', *Journal of the American Statistical Association*, **64** (326), June, 581–90; G.C. Tiao and G.E.P. Box (1975), 'Intervention Analysis with Applications to Economic and Environmental Problems', *Journal of the American Statistical Association*, **70** (329), March, 70–79; G.C. Tiao and G.E.P. Box (1981), 'Modeling Multiple Time Series with Applications', *Journal of the American Statistical Association*, **76** (376), December, 802–16.

Biometrika Trustees for articles: M.G. Kendall (1994), 'On Autoregressive Time Series', *Biometrika*, **XXXIII** (II), August, 105–22; J. Wise (1955), 'The Autocorrelation Function and the Spectral Density Function', *Biometrika*, **42**, 151–9.

Blackwell Publishers Ltd for articles: I. Adelman (1960), 'Business Cycles: Endogenous or Stochastic?', *Economic Journal*, **LXX** (280), December, 783–96; C.W.J. Granger and M.J. Morris (1976), 'Time Series Modelling and Interpretation', *Journal of the Royal Statistical Society*, **139** (2), 246–57; Robin Rowley and Renuka Jain (1986), 'Sims on Causality: An Illustration of Soft Econometrics', *Scottish Journal of Political Economy*, **33** (2), May, 171–81.

Duke University Press for article: Thomas F. Cargill (1974), 'Early Applications of Spectral Methods to Economic Time Series', *History of Political Economy*, **6**, 1–16.

Econometric Society for articles: Eugen Slutzky (1937), 'The Summation of Random Causes as the Source of Cyclic Processes', *Econometrica*, **5** (2), April, 105–46; Irma Adelman and Frank L. Adelman (1959), 'The Dynamic Properties of the Klein–Goldberger Model', *Econometrica*, **27** (4), October, 596–625; Robert H. Strotz and H.O.A. Wold (1960),

'Recursive vs. Non Recursive Systems: An Attempt at Synthesis', *Econometrica*, **28** (2), April, 417–27; C.W.J. Granger (1966), 'The Typical Spectral Shape of an Economic Variable', *Econometrica*, **34** (1), January, 150–61; C.W.J. Granger (1969), 'Investigating Causal Relations by Econometric Models and Cross-Spectral Methods', *Econometrica*, **37** (3), July, 424–38; Robert F. Engle, David F. Hendry and Jean-Francois Richard (1983), 'Exogeneity', *Econometrica*, **51** (2), March, 277–304.

Economic Research Service, U.S. Department of Agriculture for article: Roger K. Conway, P.A.V.B. Swamy, John F. Yanagida and Peter von zur Muehlen (1984), 'The Impossibility of Causality Testing', *Agricultural Economics Research*, **36** (3), Summer, 1–19.

Elsevier Science B.V. for articles: C.W.J. Granger (1980), 'Testing for Causality: A Personal Viewpoint', *Journal of Economic Dynamics and Control*, **2** (4), November, 329–52; Edward C. Prescott (1986), 'Theory Ahead of Business Cycle Measurement', *Federal Reserve Bank of Minneapolis Quarterly Review*, **10**, Fall, 9–22.

Elsevier Science S.A. for articles: M.B. Priestley (1988), 'Current Developments in Time Series Modelling', *Journal of Econometrics*, **37** (1), 67–86; Arnold Zellner (1988), 'Causality and Causal Laws in Economics', *Journal of Econometrics*, **39** (1), September, 7–21.

Federal Reserve Bank of Minneapolis for article: Thomas J. Sargent (1979), 'Estimating Vector Autoregressions Using Methods not Based on Explicit Economic Theories', *Federal Reserve Bank of Minneapolis Quarterly Review*, **3** (3), Summer, 8–15.

International Economic Review for article: A.C. Harvey (1978), 'Linear Regression in the Frequency Domain', *International Economic Review*, **19** (2), June, 507–12.

National Bureau of Economic Research, Inc. for article: Robert F. Engle (1976), 'Interpreting Spectral Analyses in Terms of Time-Domain Models', *Annals of Economic and Social Measurement*, **5** (1), Winter, 89–109.

Oxford University Press for article: Kevin D. Hoover (1995), 'Facts and Artifacts: Calibration and the Empirical Assessment of Real-Business-Cycle Models', *Oxford Economic Papers*, **47** (1), January, 24–44.

Taylor & Francis Ltd for article: O.D. Anderson (1976), 'The Backshift Operator in Time Series Analysis', *International Journal of Mathematical Education in Science and Technology*, **7** (2), May, 235–41.

University of Chicago Press for article: Mark W. Watson (1993), 'Measures of Fit for Calibrated Models', *Journal of Political Economy*, **101** (6), December, 1011–41.

Every effort has been made to trace all the copyright holders but if any have been inadvertently overlooked the publishers will be pleased to make the necessary arrangement at the first opportunity.

In addition the publishers wish to thank the Library of the London School of Economics and Political Science and the Marshall Library, Cambridge University, for their assistance in obtaining these articles.

General Introduction to the Series

Omar F. Hamouda and J.C.R. Rowley

The meaningful intrusion of mathematics and statistics into economics and other social sciences began in the final decades of the last century, encouraged by the emergence of marginalist economic theories after the 1870s and by the slow transformation of statistics when correlation and regression were accepted as basic ingredients of research, comprehensive data were collected, and the interplay of abstract reasoning and empirical investigation became fashionable. In the 1940s and later, this intrusion widened as econometrics acquired a probabilistic framework and as dynamic, stochastic and general-equilibrium models were developed. Now almost all economists – in research centres, universities, business, government and other locations – must face up to the need for sufficient knowledge of (and experience with) some standard mathematical techniques and various aspects of probability, including distribution functions, parametric summaries, estimation and statistical inference.

With growing familiarity, economists have also started to recognize other significant aspects of research, not least the heroic assumptions of models, weak integration of successive empirical findings in relation to some systematic paths of confirmation, validation and refutation (loosely expressed as 'progress' in empirical knowledge of economic phenomena), haphazard awareness of methodological issues, and the fundamental awkwardness of characterizing economic behaviour, options and beliefs with simple models having excessively precise ingredients. Consideration of these additional aspects has resulted in a growing interest in non-standard mathematics (fuzzy sets, for example), inferential robustness, ambiguity and vagueness, the clarification of paradoxes by drawing on recent experiments in cognitive science, and meta-analytical appreciation of cumulative research beyond the confines of more conventional interests.

In collecting the papers reproduced in the ten volumes of this series, we tried to provide a valuable resource for economists, one that is quite comprehensive and does not promote any particular view – other than the need to read widely, beyond a few economic journals and common textbooks. We include both sophisticated technical papers and surveys aimed at a wider audience, hoping to make various treatments of economic theory and econometrics accessible to a heterogeneous audience. Some important papers have already been included in earlier collections, confirming their recognition by other observers. We supplement them with papers of historical significance, some descriptive accounts that are not widely known to economists (because they may appear in 'remote' statistical or educational journals), and a few critical appraisals that directly question the appropriateness of popular conventions and normal practices. Occasionally, in order to manage the task of representing a wide range of literature, we cite excluded papers that are reproduced in some other useful collections which are issued by Elgar. These collections are usually cited in new introductions prepared for the separate volumes of the series. The reader of the current collection meets alternative perspectives, unresolved conflicts and plain mistakes as well as clear statements of standard matters relating to expected utility, economic games, probabilistic dialogue, econometric estimation and calibration, discrete linear time-series methods (and their extensions to both continuous and chaotic systems), and both static and sequential forms of statistical inference.

Each volume seems useful by itself but most readers might gain by 'dipping' into several of them. Certainly our collection involves duplication within individual volumes (for example, when we include both 'algebraic' and 'geometric' accounts of econometric estimation or some partially-overlapping descriptions of utility) and a few historical treatments that have been supplanted in recent textbooks. The latter encourages awareness of the historical paths by which economists came to accept current approaches and techniques, while a limited degree of duplication is useful if different perspectives enhance the clarification of technical demands, fundamental ingredients and incompleteness or if our potential readers come from very different backgrounds in terms of their technical skills and commitment to the areas being discussed. These features reveal strong prejudice to be identified with the value of mathematical sophistication, benefits of knowing major historical connections, and need for effective communiction with a wide audience, deficient in mathematical skills but interested in (or concerned about) the implications of technical research and its spillovers to relevant issues or professional acceptance.

Our recognition of the substantial benefits of mathematical skills is qualified in two important respects, which are identified with the need for validation and the hazard of confusing economics merely with applied mathematics. Here it seems useful to recall Marshall's account of a pro-realistic approach to economic research,

> I went more and more on the rules: (1) Use mathematics as a shorthand language rather than as an engine of enquiry. (2) Keep to them until you have done. (3) Translate into English. (4) Then illustrate by examples that are important in real life. (5) Burn the mathematics. (6) If you can't succeed in (4) burn (3). (Marshall, 1906)

Even with ten volumes, we could not give sufficient attention to realistic examples that would illustrate the application of expected utility, game concepts, probability notions and econometrics. This is an unfortunate omission since the usefulness of these elements is not demonstrated but rather has to be presumed as an act of faith, which may be difficult for readers overwhelmed by a plethora of strange symbols, mathematical theorems, apparent remoteness from real economic phenomena, and difficulties of interpretation.

As Samuelson noted in his Presidential Address to the American Economic Association (1961),

> if economists spend more and more of their time on highly technical mathematics and statistics, they must not be surprised if the intelligent man of affairs comes to ignore this part of their activities.

Knight also reminded an earlier generation of economists that the interpretability of abstract theory and deductions drawn from them should be a primary concern,

> the makers and users of economic analysis have in general still to be made to see that deductions from theory are necessary, not because literally true ... but only if they bear a certain relation to

literal truth and if all who work with them constantly bear in mind what that relation is. ... [In] a field where the relations between theory and practice do not come instinctively to the minds of the users of both, the supplementation of theory by works of interpretation becomes indispensable. (Knight, 1921)

Perhaps some future collections of 'applied' and interpretative papers will remove these deficiencies by showing how actual choices, evaluations and inferences can be reconciled with the abstractions revealed in the papers that we have reproduced. Then we may satisfy Marshall's sensible demand for a clearer demonstration of 'relevance' for economic (and econometric) theory, while resisting a full commitment to his fifth rule.

The second qualification reflects clear hazards of excessive formalization, over-optimistic precision, and restrictions on the normal choice for effective modes of communication by confusing economics with applied mathematics. Hicks noted such hazards when he reviewed an early textbook on econometrics,

Our mathematician will not have become an economist until he has learned that there are vital things in economics which are not applied mathematics; and that there is much else which could be stated mathematically but which anyone with a sense of mathematical elegance would prefer to state in prose. (Hicks, 1942)

Our selections do not give full expression to strong views about the vagueness of most economic situations, the potential subjectivity of relevant data, or the common incidence of severe measurement errors that plague empirical research. We have tried to deal with these troublesome matters elsewhere.

The volumes in our collection are entitled: (1) Expected Utility, Fair Gambles and Rational Choice, (2) Paradoxes, Ambiguity and Rationality, (3) Economic Games, Bargaining and Solutions, (4) Probability Concepts, Dialogue and Beliefs, (5) Statistical Foundations for Econometrics, (6) Econometric Exploration and Diagnosis, (7) The Probability Approach to Simultaneous Equations, (8) Time Series Models, Causality and Exogeneity, (9) The Reappraisal of Econometrics, and (10) Discrete and Continuous Systems, Cointegration and Chaos. Connections among contents of the ten volumes are indicated by arrows and integers in the two flow diagrams given below (Figures 1 and 2). The double arrows for econometrics provide a linkage between the two diagrams. Clearly it is difficult to characterize so many papers without compression and a modest degree of distortion. Thus we could not 'find room' for rationality, evidence, strategic competition, rules, solution concepts and other important elements in the summary offered by the diagrams. Nevertheless the arrows reveal sufficient linkages between many elements, relative to the economic context and the mathematical representations of bargaining, rational choice and dynamic macroeconomic theories (historically associated with cobweb phenomena or multiplier-accelerator interaction).

In choosing papers for inclusion, we sought to encourage cross-fertilization across 'fields' in economics and between the social sciences and both experimental and mathematical disciplines. Historically, academic economists have tended to compartmentalize their activities and, despite an occasional use of analogies from biology or physics, have ignored many valuable treatments of similar material by non-economists. We offer connections with this wider literature when convenient survey papers are available. Also the introductions to individual volumes cite a few additional sources – both recent and classical

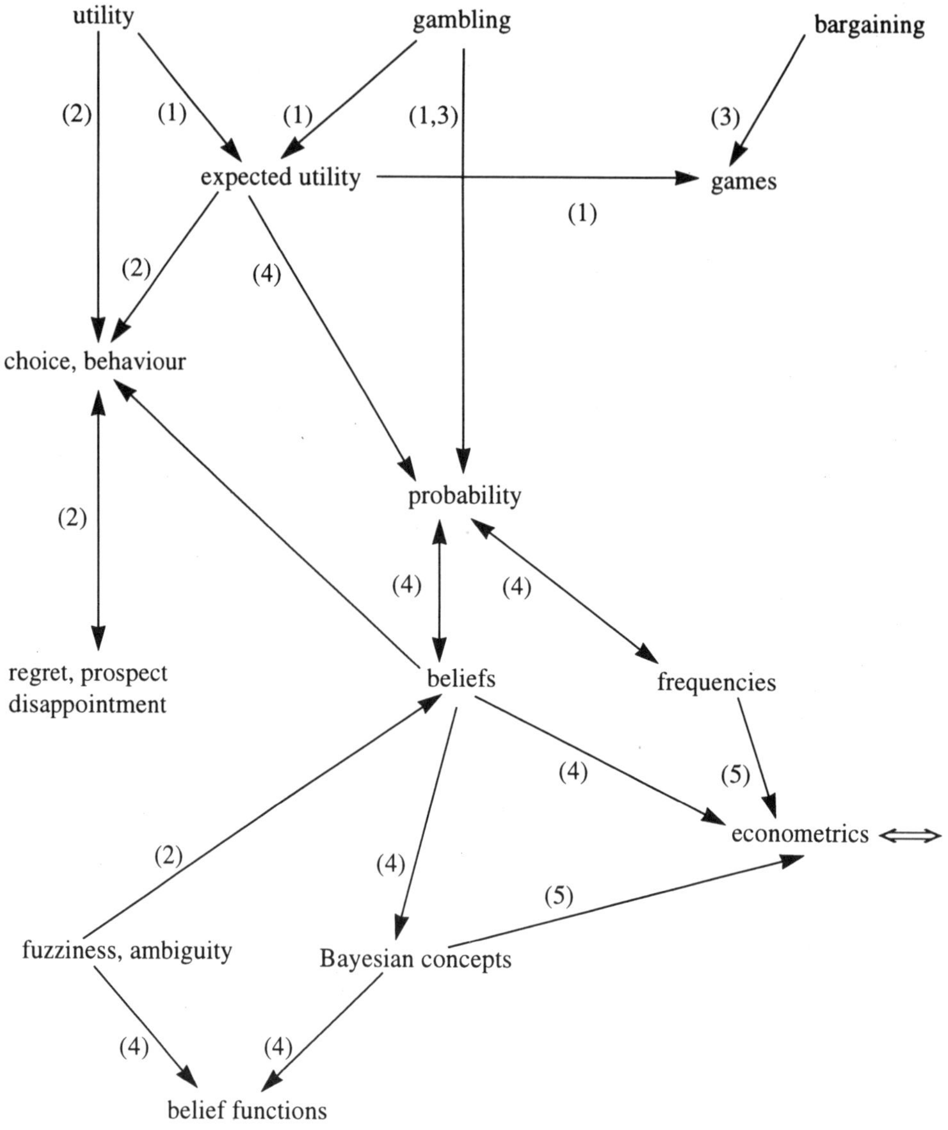

Figure 1 Tentative connections (I)

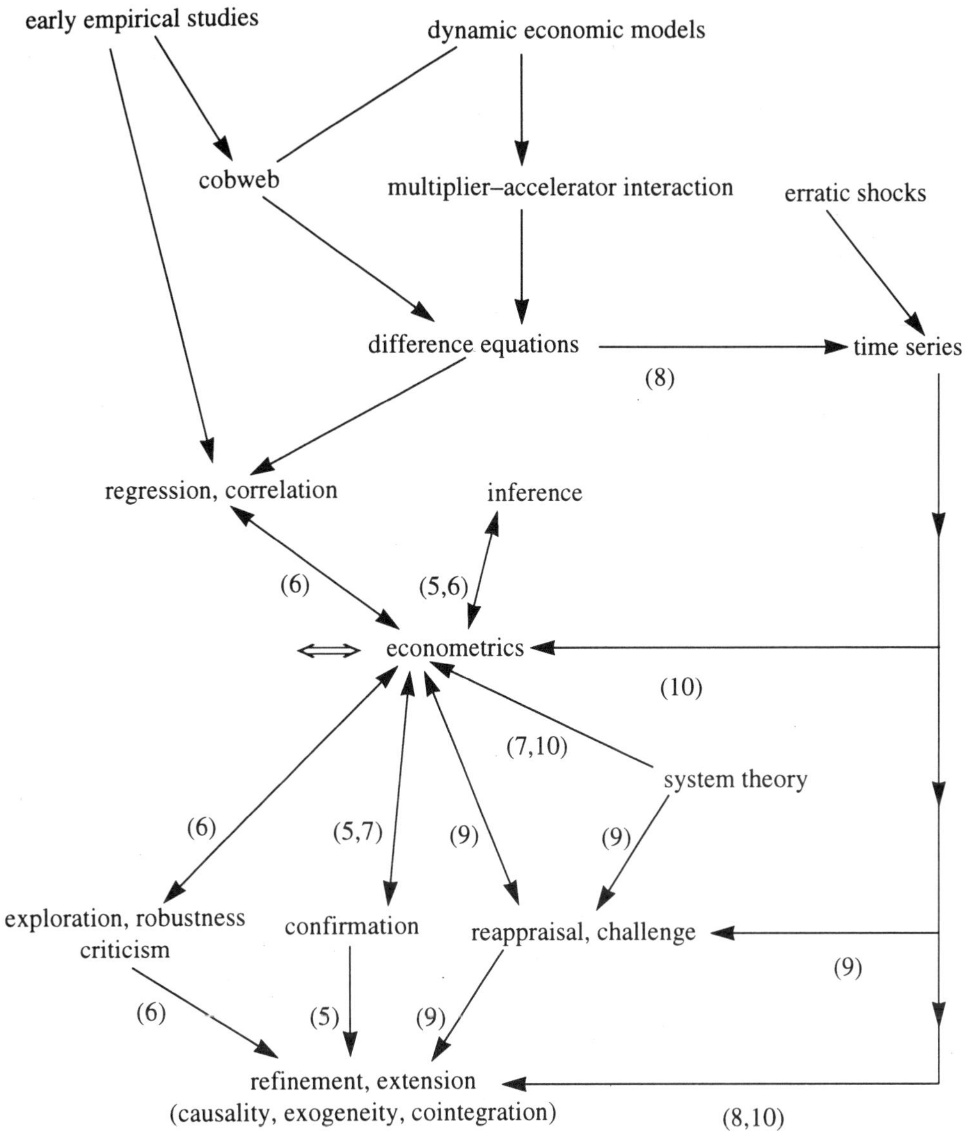

Figure 2 Tentative connections (II)

treatments – that should be actively pursued. This potential widening of interests is consistent with the general reason for our production of this new series – we wanted to give potential readers a strong encouragement to 'pause for thought' and find additional stimulus from the papers that we offer. The anticipated audience includes students wanting a ready access to basic references, new researchers seeking to 'stretch' themselves, and more mature researchers discovering gaps in their appreciation of particular areas. All of these groups will, for example, find papers that can initiate more awareness of newer fashions (ambiguity, chaos, calibration, cognitive biases, cointegration, dialogue, encompassing, game solutions, intransitive or irrational preferences, long memory, rational belief functions, regret and prospect, robust criticism, and specification searches) and some major features of earlier literature.

An apology is offered to all authors who feel slighted by the non-inclusion of their papers. Hopefully, they will enjoy considering how we will have to alter the choices of papers when we repeat this exercise, in twenty years or so, in the light of the evolution of economic theory, statistics and econometrics! Clearly the rapid development of both computational software and cognitive experimentation will transform economic theory and econometric practice, reflecting more awareness of methodological issues and fertile challenges to the conventional frameworks for analysis.

Bibliography

Hamouda, O.F., and J.C.R. Rowley (1988), *Expectations, Equilibrium and Dynamics* (New York: St Martin's Press).

Hamouda, O.F., and J.C.R. Rowley (1996), *Probability and Economics* (London: Routledge).

Hicks, J.R. (1942), 'Review', *Economic Journal*, 350–52.

Knight, F.H. (1921), *Risk, Uncertainty and Profit* (Boston: Houghton Mifflin).

Marshall, A. (1906), Letter to Bowley. Reprinted in A.C. Pigou (1953), *Alfred Marshall and Current Thought*, Chapter 1 (London: Macmillan).

Introduction: *Time Series, Causality and Exogeneity*

Omar F. Hamouda and J.C.R. Rowley

The practical range of econometrics has frequently been divided between situations in which econometric theory, earlier empirical findings and basic institutional knowledge are sufficient to guide the specification of major functional relationships (or 'structure') and other situations in which the contributions of these elements are more modest. It is convenient (but quite misleading) to identify much of the latter 'non-structural econometrics' with exploratory time-series analysis, while 'structural econometrics' is restricted to the familiar framework of regression models, in which prior information can be combined with formal parametric tests and simple residual analysis to confirm the initial structural specifications and add quantitative estimates for the various linkages expressed within them. In the last three or four decades, with a rapid growth of computational facilities and development of some appropriate 'friendly' software, the practical range of structural econometrics has widened to include searches for specification through exploratory, sequential research in which tentative or incomplete structural content at each stage of a sequence of stages is modified – as determined by subjective reactions to diagnostic statistics, forecasting performance, and other empirical checks.

Increasingly, conventional structural econometrics and time-series analysis have been separated as two alternative methods of approaching the exploration of economic phenomena with both real and simulated data. This partial separation is unfortunate since it understates the fundamental interactions between the methods, their shared statistical bases, and frequent complementarity. It seems better to view various approaches to the data analysis as part of a collective package, from which econometricians can pick the technical ingredients that fit the particular context of their research efforts, as influenced by (a) the availability and reliability of structural information, (b) the frequency, coverage, duration and perceived accuracy of data, (c) the relative stability of the economic phenomena being explored, in the light of any institutional and behavioural changes producing structural changes in either the actions of economic agents or the data recording their outcomes, (d) capacities for computation, and (e) the various purposes of the researchers and their clients in undertaking any analyses, the usual constraints on their completion, and facilities for the communication of empirical findings. This comprehensive list of determinants is unlikely to be satisfactorily reduced to a simple choice between structural regression models and the time-series alternatives.

Indeed time-series analysis and simulation have a long history of contribution to both quantitative and qualitative economics, dating back to the instructive mimic-cycle controversies of seventy years ago, and even beyond those controversies to the potential characterizations and tentative explorations of major economic circles whenever time-series data of sufficient duration were available to our predecessors. Current economic theory is also deeply concerned with time-series patterns, which underlie the fashionable edifice of 'rational' (or consistent) conditional expectations, various notions of real business cycles, parametric calibration and other challenges to estimation, temporal causality, and dominant rhetorical language for addressing any evaluations and judgement of the rival theoretical perceptions. Thus the true structural nature of econometrics, if associated with a strong reliance on economic theory and institutions, must have some important elements which cannot be clearly expressed by either a particular choice of variables to be included in the structural regression models or quantitative constraints on the size of corresponding regression coefficients. In important respects, time-series analysis can be structural and has often carried a structural significance in the clarification of economic phenomena, their effective display and simulation, major data adjustments and their technical consequences, the representation of primary qualitative features, and tests of the perceived rationality of economic agents over time.

In the five parts of this collection of reprinted papers, we try to illustrate some important aspects of time-series analysis for economists and to give basic references for their technical features. Relevant aspects are also illustrated in several sections of Volume 9, *The Reappraisal of Econometrics*, and throughout Volume 10, *Discrete and Continuous Systems: Cointegration and Chaos*, which together reveal the enhanced menu of novel time-series specifications that emerged in recent years for use by economic theorists, 'quantitative economists' (King, 1995) and econometricians. Additional technical information is contained in the references cited below and in the Elgar collection on *Time Series* (Harvey). Contact with this burgeoning literature will, we hope, establish how drastically both economic theory and econometrics have been transformed by the intrusion of rediscovered or new time-series ingredients in modelling procedures.

Part I focuses attention on two episodes in the history of economics, both of which markedly affected the interpretation of empirical evidence and established the hazards of linking such evidence with a strong imputation of causal influences. By the first two decades of this century, prominent economists were beginning to associate crude patterns of cyclical fluctuations with their potential determinants – by plotting simple graphs of economic time series and by locating the occurrence of prior shocks which could explain, by their timing and magnitude, the severity and qualitative features of such fluctuations. Visual inspection and *ad hoc* indications of correlation gave support for causal hypotheses. Although the empirical periodogram of Schuster and others was being developed for separating economic cycles with different frequencies (in a Fourier decomposition), there was no foundation for any probability-based tests and the essential concepts of ergodicity and stationarity for time series (as a realization of basic random processes) were undiscovered, although the 'law of large numbers' might be routinely cited in connection with (momentary) risky investments, insurance and banking by Pigou and other economists (influenced by the contemporary descriptions to be found in the successful statistical textbooks of Bowley and Yule, for example).

In this situation, simulations of Slutsky and Yule involving linear difference equations and the summation of random shocks, with no direct economic meaning, demonstrated wave-like phenomena which resembled patterns found in economic time series. These 'mimic cycles', which were arbitrary and initially without any structural foundation, undermined any identification of principal causes for most economic fluctuations by mere visual inspection and timing. Linear mathematical operations (associated with difference equations and summation) and erratic random shocks produced the desired patterns without involving any economic explanation! Later this awkward finding undermined the evaluation of deterministic multiplier-accelerator models of the Hansen–Samuelson type (Samuelson, 1939, 1959) solely in terms of a perceived relationship between the numerical values of a few structural parameters (representing the marginal propensity to consume and the accelerator coefficient, for example) and the dynamic stability or growth characteristics of such models. There is something profoundly disturbing about leaving major qualitative dynamics to be determined by 'external' non-systematic disturbances rather than by those 'internal' factors which can be linked more clearly to the visible activities of economic agents. For econometricians, the advocacy of a major role for external shocks weakened most support for a strong reliance on those parametric constraints which could produce dampened or explosive fluctuations in the absence of equation errors (shocks), and it provoked alternative arguments in favour of systemic regime shifts, as found in the theoretical approach of Hicks (1950) to cycles.

In the 1920s, Yule and Slutsky established the notions of linear summation and autoregressive schemes for random disturbances, although the mathematics of stationary random processes, linear extrapolation, filtering, and flexible periodicity were not clarified until a decade later through the efforts of Khinchin, Kolmogorov and Wiener, and their followers. Understanding of a convenient linkage between all stationary autoregressive schemes and their moving-average representations (at least in linear systems) emerged from Wold's doctoral thesis at the end of the 1930s – an important turning point for a greater appreciation of many technical aspects of time-series analysis. Access to the principal features of these historical developments is possible from the citations given by Wold (1954b) and Yaglom (1962).

Our first paper in Part I is an English translation of the paper by Slutsky that appeared in an early issue of *Econometrica*, after Frisch had launched a wider appreciation of impulse and propagation effects for economic cycles (the interplay of internal and external factors) in 1933. [Reprints of Frisch's contribution and some other historically-important treatments of cyclical growth are conveniently available in the papers assembled by Gordon and Klein (1966) for the American Economic Association.] Slutsky focuses special attention on the possible connection between irregular or random disturbances and 'a system of more or less regular waves', and on the empirical validation of any causal mechanisms for economic phenomena from time-series data. He suggests that the presence of waves of definite orders 'will always remain a fact begging for explanation' and, for the first time, demonstrates the practical value of simulative experimentation as a means of exploring potential causal connections.

A Presidential Address to the Royal Statistical Society by Yule, which also deals with the inferential imprecision of 'non-sense correlations' among time-series data, is reprinted in the Elgar collection on *The History of Econometrics* (Darnell, Vol. I). Yule (1926: 2) reminded his audience of the confusion of causality with correlation, noting 'it is fairly familiar that we sometimes obtain between quantities varying with the time ... quite high correlations to which we cannot attach any physical significance whatever, although under the ordinary test the correlation would be held to be certainly "significant",' a reminder that seems just as important today with the rapid expansion of computational software and economic data, and the comon preoccupation with tests of temporal causality as identified in Part IV!

Simulative experimentation is also the basic ingredient of other papers (Chapters 2 and 3) reprinted in Part I. With a vigorous growth of economy-wide modelling in the 1950s, interest among applied econometricians shifted away from the fine details of estimators' distributional properties to the conditional simulation of consequences which might stem from hypothetical changes in economic policies. Large models seemed to be incapable of replicating diverse cyclical patterns, as revealed by the chronologies of the National Bureau of Economic Research (NBER), and other dynamic adjustments despite the use of structural information to guide their construction and initial evaluation. The endogenous content of fitted models failed to meet this empirical standard of generating some persistent fluctuations in the long run. The possible flaw in replication attracted new 'solutions' such as a reliance on 'tender-loving-care corrections' or 'stochastic simulation' to rejuvenate such fluctuations – solutions which quickly became common features of econometric forecasting processes. Stochastic simulation procedures introduce supplementary erratic shocks to any estimated equations in generating time paths for conditional forecasts, clearly influenced by earlier Slutsky–Yule–Frisch explorations, clarifying comments of Haavelmo (1940), and contents of the two papers reprinted here. The subsequent (enhanced and widened) results of dynamic 'solutions' for large-scale econometric modelling are clearly illustrated in various technical papers in the conference report of Hickman (1972), while those in Guetzkow (1962) and Naylor (1969) demonstrate a growing sophistication (and more areas of application) of simulative experiments and computation during the 1950s and 1960s.

The interaction of simultaneous-equation models (SEM) and their time-series counterparts (TSA) was also clarified by the discovery of alternative representations of the SEM – initiated by Tinbergen, Haavelmo and other researchers at the Cowles Commission in the 1940s – demonstrated in Tinbergen (1940) and Hurwicz (1944) by arithmetical elimination of contemporaneous and endogenous variables from the basic equations of the structural form to obtain 'deduced' or 'reduced' time-series equations for each endogenous variable of a linear dynamical system – that is, autoregressive equations with common parameters and composite moving-average errors. The dynamic properties and estimates of such alternative (final form) representations were subsequently appraised by Quenouille (1957), Goldberger (1959), and Theil and Boot (1962) – being rediscovered by Zellner and Palm (1974), Wallis (1977) and others, three decades after their first appearance and half a century after the controversies raised by Slutsky and Yule! But then, attention was to be focused on the parametric constraints imposed on time-series representations by structural-form specifications rather than on the severity of inferential criticisms from earlier times. Technical issues affecting model parameters, consistent estimation and probability-based testing replaced guides to specification and adverse forecasting evaluations in econometric dialogue.

The SEMTSA connection suffers from an excessive dependence on the ability of economists to provide a sufficient amount of structural information to specify the complete structural-form equations, a strong requirement when most econometric research is exploratory and economic theories incomplete. Moreover, as recognized by the Adelmans, such content may not be expressed in terms of either parameters or the choice of explanatory variables. The referential NBER chronologies and other standards of evaluation might serve another purpose – namely to guide the 'calibration' of parameters of linear difference equations (ARIMA processes), rather than estimation, so that the simulations of such equations display qualitative features which are identified by such standards. Thus time-series models can be separated from the primary SEMTSA on two principal grounds. First, the familiar SEM format exaggerates and distorts the contributions of *a priori* economic theory to empirical research (Sargent and Sims, 1977). Second, a myopic preoccupation with this format may have diverted attention away from our knowledge of cyclical characteristics and some appropriate sources of dynamic 'structural' information – as expressed by relative variations, smoothness, procyclicality and other qualitative relationships, for example.

Such criticisms emerged when the 'rational-expectations' (RE) challenges to any structural autonomy in SEM (Lucas, 1972, 1976) weakened the academic status of large econometric models and encouraged the emergence of radically different perspectives on the exploration and display of business cycles, including a stronger commitment to equilibrium and external shocks. In Part II, we reprint three papers which reflect the shift towards calibration and 'quantitative economics'. These papers can be supplemented by King (1995) and Eichenbaum (1991, 1996), which contain valuable accounts of this development and some of the unresolved technical issues raised by it, while the various contributions to Lucas (1981) and Lucas and Sargent (1981) illustrate the evolution of RE methodology and recent equilibrium cycles theories, including attempts to estimate dynamic RE econometric models. The radical advocacy of qualitative NBER patterns is strongly expressed too by Kydland and Prescott (1990). Part II is completed by a terse historical account linking Slutsky–Yule controversies, the shift towards calibration methods, and other forms of data adjustment which can distort causal inferences. Here we identify yet another area in which time-series smoothing mislead economists in their searches for cyclical components of different frequencies.

Technical aspects of time-series analysis are the focus of papers contained in Part III. There are many excellent textbooks on estimation, identification and intervention modelling for linear TSA – those of Box and Jenkins, Chatfield, Fuller, Hannan, Harvey, Kendall, Nelson, and Priestley have influenced students and many economic researchers over the last four decades – and the associated mathematics of stochastic processes. We have chosen eight papers to illustrate the exploration of time-series data and a short introduction to the backshift or lag operator, which is often used in this context. These papers deal with various means of representing dynamic phenomena by both single and multiple equations of the autoregressive type with moving average errors (ARMA models), adjustments seeking to achieve stationarity (through transformations or differencing of data) or recognize changes that can be expressed as interventions, diagnostic statistics, and many elements of interpretation, forecasting and qualification. They mainly stress linear and discrete models, usually with constant parameters and normally-distributed errors. More information on the particular demands of non-linear and continuous models for economic time series is provided in Volume 10, *Discrete and Continuous Systems, Cointegration and Chaos*. Such extensions involve important changes in emphasis, especially in regard to predictability, freedom from starting values, fragile stability, asymmetry, and irreverse time paths – as we make clear in Volume 10.

The paper of Kendall (Chapter 8) offers a simple introduction to Yule–Walker equations (first discussed by Walker in 1931) for estimating autoregressive models of known size (stochastic difference equations) from empirical correlograms. The asymptotic properties of the corresponding parametric estimates were established by Mann and Wald (1943), while Stone (1949) warned of the 'extreme inefficiency of long-term predictions from autoregressive schemes' as noted earlier by both Yule and Kendall. The AR schemes offer a convenient framework for updating successive predictions, and they enjoy widespread acceptance (despite such dire warnings) among business firms for the provision of routine short-term 'non-structural' predictions, sometimes combined with estimates from alternative sources and 'anticipations' (Granger, 1989; Nelson, 1973).

The repeated use of Yule–Walker equations for ARMA models of differing size is a common means for choosing among these models, with plots of estimates for the autocorrelation, partial and inverse autocorrelation functions (ACF, PACF, IACF) becoming a standard feature of both econometric and time-series software. Alternative means of identification, the related aspects of model adequacy, and other technical matters of model construction, exploration and validation are described for single equations in the two papers of Hippel, McLeod and Lennox (Chapters 9 and 10), while those of Box and Tiao (Chapters 12 and 13) extend discussion to multiple equations and simple changes that can be expressed as 'interventions', giving useful illustrations as well as mathematical and statistical results.

The remaining three papers take up other significant aspects of applied time-series analysis. Granger and Morris (Chapter 14) appraise the impact of composite processes, in which 'aggregate' time series are generated by the sum of stochastic ingredients, each associated with separate time-series features; Priestley (Chapter 15) considers the estimation and identification of a collection of 'state-dependent' and other non-linear models; and Sargent (Chapter 16) offers a partisan appreciation of vector autoregressive modelling, which has emerged as a considerable rival of structural models in simulative experiments of macroeconomic developments.

Aggregation of economic time series can occur in two distinct ways. First, many macroeconomic variables or industrial averages can be viewed as weighted sums of elements with diverse historical experience. Their collective representation is usually a more complex process than those associated with individual components – the sum of several AR(1)-generated variables may produce an ARMA-generated composite, for example. Second, aggregation can occur over time, as when annual or quarterly data are used to explore dynamic phenomena affected by shorter-term (daily, monthly) shocks. The time intervals for data and economic decisions differ so the specification of generating mixed time-series processes might need to reflect the presence of temporal aggregation, measurement errors, and a critical distinction of flow and stock variables for such processes (Rowley and Trivedi, 1975, ch. 5). The intrusion of additional moving-average ingredients seems to be ubiquitous here, as noted by Granger and Morris. Important changes of time-series characteristics due to aggregation or smoothing have been recognized for more than half a century by economists and statisticians. Initially, this recognition stemmed from attempts to de-seasonalize or de-trend economic data and other pragmatic transformations of data in the 1930s, such as variate differencing (Tintner, 1940, 1952). A later revival of interest from different perspectives is signalled by Quenouille (1958) and Working (1960), and by the practical requirements of estimating parameters for differential equation systems with independent stochastic errors from discrete data (Phillips, 1959; Durbin, 1961).

The substantial use of vector autoregressions (VAR) is relatively new. Its origins stem from responses to a forceful rational-expectations challenge of support for the SEM, which was directed at the weak bases for structural autonomy of most structural forms and the non-availability of sufficient *a priori* parametric constraints for specifying these forms. VAR can also reflect some correlative notions for co-movements within the NBER chronologies for economic fluctuations, including a dependence on latent factors (Sargent and Sims, 1977) and Bayesian priors. Their recent prominence is clearly established by Sims (1980) and many simulative VAR experiments reported in the *Federal Reserve Bank of Minneapolis Quarterly Review* and elsewhere, but not without resistance and qualification (Malinvaud, 1984). The inclusion of the paper by Sargent illustrates some technical aspects of this literature, while empirical studies reported by various Federal Reserve banks in their research-based journals point to a few prominent applications, using involving the generation of conditional predictions.

One major source of criticism for the basic probability constraints of the SEM is the *a priori* characterization of variables in terms of their presumed connections with the equation errors of structural forms, that is, the separation of endogenous from predetermined variables as introduced at the Cowles Commission. Underlying this separation is a fundamental problem of identifying, representing or exploring the principal causal dependencies which link economic phenomena, while avoiding the confusion of correlation with causality and retaining a probabilistic framework. The treatment of this problem and any appraisal of the SEM approach to it again link the provision of 'structural' information and actual time-series characteristics, and raise deeper philosophical issues and interest in the degree of acceptable approximation. Our selection of reprinted papers in Part IV seeks to indicate various attempts of economists to deal with dynamic causality and exogeneity, ranging from advocacy of statistical procedures and tests to guide causal modelling, to an identification of regression with the fundamental nature of dynamic economic models, which might effectively be clarified with patterns of causal 'arrows', as used in cobweb models and later displayed by Tinbergen (1940), for example. The substantial content of these attempts is far removed from the cavalier language which arbitrarily separates those variables 'determined within' or 'explained by' a group of given equations from other variables 'determined outside' them, often merely for theoretical convenience in limiting the size of models – cursory language which detracts from an evaluation of the distributional properties for parametric estimates but, unfortunately, still found in econometric textbooks!

Any discussions of causality, endogeneity, exogeneity and predetermination should also not presume that firm controllability is a common attribute of exogenous variables – thus sensible appraisals of potential impacts for any policy interventions must be qualified by realistic behavioural constraints, and the actual ability of SEM and other modelling procedures to guide policy-making is limited. Such restrictions were stressed by Orcutt (1952) after the SEM began to be fashionable. He reacted to two important aspects of 'causality', autonomy, and conditional predictions in the probability-based framework of SEM, as found in (a) a preliminary classification of *all* measured variables, according to their presumed statistical independence relative to equation errors, and (b) strong support given to consistent estimation of structural parameters rather than reduced-form ones. The probability-based classification of variables is presented by Koopmans (1950), for whom the prior distinction between endogenous and predetermined variables is affected by a desire to obtain consistent and asymptotically unbiased estimates, while the choice between alternative forms is explored in a partisan fashion by Marschak (1953) in terms of relative autonomy and the consequences for conditional predictions of future time paths experienced by targeted endogenous variables when 'policy consists in changing those elements of the structure and those exogenous variables that are under the policy-maker's control' and where the hazards of parametric instabilities can undermine the validity of corresponding estimates. The probability-based classification also underlies new concepts of completeness and identification in the SEM, while causal ordering can be discussed with reference to associated (block) hierarchies and decompositions for classes of variables as demonstrated in Simon (1953), Fisher (1965) and other papers reproduced in Ando *et al.* (1963). The particular selections for Part IV shift attention partially away from this framework and towards alternative bases for dynamic specification, a much greater reliance on testing for potential causality or exogeneity rather than *a priori* constructs, and wider notions of exogeneity which retain probability elements.

The first stochastic difference equations for economic data emerged from cobweb theory and sequence or process analysis in the 1930s. In these contexts, any causal influences could be readily identified within flow diagrams of unilateral linkages among variables through time, sometimes associated with the calculation of numerical 'path coefficients' (Wright, 1934) to suggest relative strengths of particular influences. Models contained functional relations which were essentially sequential or recursive rather than interdependent, asymmetric rather than symmetric. The joint probability laws of the SEM are compatible with the intrusion of supplemental random effects in such models only if the laws preserve these features. Instead the usual probability approach to the SEM invokes a symmetry and interdependence among endogenous variables, and thus attracts interpretations of mutual causality. Resistance to these interpretations was pursued by Wold, who sought to maintain the earlier asymmetry and unilateral causality as well as the attractiveness of least-squares estimates. Within the SEM, his views of sequential analysis (Wold, 1949, 1953) require the structural forms to be recursive in a statistical sense – each equation needs a single endogenous or LHS variable of interest, there should be a definite 'triangular' structure for current endogenous variables, and contemporaneous equation errors must be small, irregular and mutually uncorrelated – so the system reflects a 'cause-and-effect' situation, roughly compatible with each regression equation being an irreversible conditional expectation and yielding unbiased least-squares estimates when multicollinearity is absent. Also small deviations from this situation, or specification errors, can be explored with 'proximity theorems' (Wold and Faxér, 1957) from which formal conditions for small asymptotic biases of least-squares estimates can be established.

The causal aspects of this perspective were refined throughout two decades, as found in Wold (1954a, 1956, 1964, 1974) and a Strotz–Wold collaboration offered here. The latter accepts a concept of causality 'intended to that of the everyday usage in the laboratory and emphasizes the notion of control' for construction of economic theory in non-experimental situations, and it seeks to explore grounds for a synthesis of recursive and interdependent perspectives from the acceptance of this concept as a referential standard, with dynamic equations representing adjustments toward equilibrium situations. More radical suggestions are attributable to Granger, Sims, Caines, Haugh and Pierce who later replaced the asymmetry of economic theories by a greater reliance on pragmatic testing to confirm temporal causality and exogeneity in multiple time-series structures. We have reproduced two papers by Granger (Chapter 20) and Sims (Chapter 18) here. They retained a notion of block recursivity among variables of linear dynamic structures for determining exogeneity but added some exploratory processes using conventional tests of significance. A survey of the underpinnings for such processes is provided by Pierce and Haugh (1977), while Caines and Chan (1975) illustrate the similar developments of engineers for exploration of feedback mechanisms. Strong resistance to causality testing is clear from Feige and Pearce (1979), Jacobs, Leamer and Ward (1979) and the reproduced papers of Rowley and Jain (Chapter 19) and of Conway *et al.* (Chapter 21), while Newbold (1978) clarifies distortions affecting such testing when measurement errors occur. However, the continuing interest in causal testing is illustrated by Granger (1982, 1988), Geweke (1984), and the reproduced paper of Zellner (Chapter 22). An identification of causality with the statistical linkage of exogenous and endogenous variables permits some ambiguities. The final paper of Part IV by Engle, Hendry and Richard (Chapter 23) seeks to resolve these by qualifying, extending and illustrating various concepts of exogeneity for econometricians.

Modern time-series analysis is a fusion of two traditions, one based on the use of stochastic difference equations and autocorrelations and another drawing on the Fourier decomposition with sine waves of different frequencies. For stationary series, these traditions merge with a recognition that autocorrelation functions (from the 'time domain') and spectral density functions (from the 'frequency domain') are Fourier transform pairs – so the traditions yield two alternative but complementary methods of representing and identifying stationary time-series processes, as first demonstrated for linear continuous processes by Wiener and Khintchin in the 1930s, and later extended to discrete ones. Stochastic features stem from the addition of erratic shocks to difference equations and similar changes to amplitudes and phases for the frequency or spectral approach. In Part V, we indicate several aspects of spectral methods to estimation and causality, as well as some attempts to recognize and deal with the inherent non-stationarity of many economic phenomena.

The early history of spectral methods is sketched by Cargill (Chapter 25), while realistic elements of business cycles, multiplier–accelerator interaction, and trend removal are acknowledged by Granger (Chapter 24) and by Chow and Levitan (Chapter 28) to the extent that they affect formulae for spectral densities and estimation. Other papers by Wise (Chapter 27), Engle (Chapter 29) and Harvey (Chapter 30) consider basic interactions and cross-fertilization of the two alternative domains, and Granger (Chapter 26) uses both to suggest how we might explore causality. Their efforts can be supplemented by reference to the many textbooks that extol the spectral approaches to estimation, identification and interpretation of both economic and non-economic time series – such as Bloomfield (1976), Brillinger (1975), Fuller (1976), Gottman (1981), Hannan (1960, 1970), and Nerlove, Grether and Carvalho (1979), as well as those cited above, for example.

Bibliography

Ando, A., F.M. Fisher and H.A. Simon (1963), *Essays on the Structure of Social Science Models* (Cambridge, MA: The MIT Press).

Bloomfield, P. (1976), *Fourier Analysis of Time Series: An Introduction* (New York: Wiley).

Box, G.E.P. and G.M. Jenkins (1970), *Time Series Analysis* (San Francisco: Holden-Day).

Brillinger, D.R. (1975), *Time Series: Data Analysis and Theory* (New York: Holt, Rinehart and Winston).

Caines, P.E. and C.W. Chan (1975), 'Feedback Between Stationary Processes', *IEEE Transactions*

on Automatic Control, **20** (4): 498–508.
Darnell, A.C. (ed) (1994), *The History of Econometrics* (Aldershot: Edward Elgar).
Durbin, J. (1961), 'Efficient Fitting of Linear Models for Continuous Stationary Time Series From Discrete Data', *Bulletin de l'Institut International de Statistique*, **38**: 273–81.
Eichenbaum, M. (1991), 'Technology Shocks and the Business Cycle', *Economic Perspectives, Federal Reserve Bank of Chicago*, **15** (2): 14–31.
Eichenbaum, M. (1966), 'Some Comments on the Role of Econometrics in Economic Theory', *Economic Perspectives, Federal Reserve Bank of Chicago*, **20** (1): 22–31.
Feige, E.L. and D.K. Pearce (1979), 'The Casual Causal Relationship Between Money and Income: Some Caveats for Time Series Analysis', *The Review of Economics and Statistics*, **61** (4): 521–33.
Fisher, F.M. (1965), 'Dynamic Structure and Estimation in Economy-Wide Econometric Models', in (eds) J.S. Duesenberry, G. Fromm, L.R. Klein and E. Kuh, *The Brookings Quarterly Econometric Model of the United States* (Amsterdam: North-Holland), ch. 15.
Fuller, W.A. (1976), *Introduction to Statistical Time Series* (New York: Wiley).
Geweke, J. (1984), 'Inference and Causality in Economic Time Series Models', in (eds) Z. Griliches and M. Intriligator, *Handbook of Econometrics* (Amsterdam: North-Holland), Vol. 2, ch. 19.
Goldberger, A.S. (1959), *Impact Multipliers and Dynamic Properties of the Klein–Goldberger Model* (Amsterdam: North-Holland).
Gordon, R.A. and L.R. Klein (eds) (1966), *Readings in Business Cycles* (London: George Allen and Unwin).
Gottman, J.M. (1981), *Time-Series Analysis* (Cambridge: Cambridge University Press).
Granger, C.W.J. (1982), 'Generating Mechanisms, Models, and Causality', in (ed.) W. Hildenbrand, *Advances in Econometrics* (Cambridge: Cambridge University Press), ch. 8.
Granger, C.W.J. (1988), 'Some Recent Developments in a Concept of Causality', *Journal of Econometrics*, **39**: 199–211.
Granger, C.W.J. (1989), *Forecasting in Business and Economics* (New York: Academic Press), second edition.
Guetzkow, H. (ed.) (1962), *Simulation in Social Science: Readings* (Englewood Cliffs, NJ: Prentice-Hall).
Haavelmo, T. (1940), 'The Inadequacy of Testing Dynamic Theory by Comparing Theoretical Solutions and Observed Cycles', *Econometrica*, **8** (4): 312–21.
Hannan, E.J. (1960), *Time Series Analysis* (London: Methuen).
Hannan, E.J. (1970), *Multiple Time Series* (New York: Wiley).
Harvey, A. (ed.) (1994), *Time Series* (Aldershot: Edward Elgar).
Hickman, B.G. (ed.) (1972), *Econometric Models of Cyclical Behavior* (New York: Columbia University Press for NBER), two volumes.
Hicks, J.R. (1950), *A Contribution to the Theory of the Trade Cycle* (Oxford: Clarendon Press).
Hurwicz, L. (1944), 'Stochastic Models of Economic Fluctuations', *Econometrica*, **12** (2): 114–24.
Jacobs, R.L., E.E. Leamer and M.P. Ward (1979), 'Difficulties with Testing for Causation', *Economic Inquiry*, **17**: 401–13.
King, R.G. (1995), 'Quantitative Theory and Econometrics', *Federal Reserve Bank of Richmond Economic Quarterly*, **81** (3): 53–105.
Koopmans, T.C. (1950), 'When is an Equation System Complete for Statistical Purposes?', in (ed.) T.C. Koopmans, *Statistical Inference in Dynamic Economic Models* (New York: Wiley), ch. XVII.
Kydland, F.E. and E.C. Prescott (1990), 'Business Cycles: Real Facts and a Monetary Myth', *Quarterly Review, Federal Reserve Bank of Minneapolis*, Spring, 3–18.
Lucas, R.E. (1972), 'Econometric Testing of the Natural Rate Hypothesis', in (ed.) O. Eckstein, *The Econometrics of Price Determination* (Washington, DC: Board of Governors of the Federal Reserve System), 50–59.
Lucas, R.E. (1976), 'Econometric Policy Evaluation: A Critique', in (eds) K. Brunner and A. Meltzer, *The Phillips Curve and Labor Markets* (Amsterdam: North Holland), 19–46.
Lucas, R.E. (1981), *Studies in Business-Cycle Theory* (Cambridge, MA: MIT Press).
Lucas, R.E. and T.J. Sargent (eds) (1981), *Rational Expectations and Econometric Practice* (Minneapolis: University of Minneapolis Press).

Malinvaud, E. (1984), 'Forecasting and Conditional Projection Using Realistic Prior Distributions – Comment', *Econometric Reviews*, **3**: 113–17.

Mann, H.B. and A. Wald (1944), 'On the Statistical Treatment of Linear Stochastic Difference Equations', *Econometrica*, **11** (3&4): 173–220.

Marschak, J. (1953), 'Economic Measurements for Policy and Prediction', in (eds) W.C. Hood and T.C. Koopmans, *Studies in Econometric Method* (New York: Wiley), ch. 1.

Naylor, T.H. (ed.) (1969), *The Design of Computer Simulation Experiments* (Durham, NC: Duke University Press).

Nelson, C.R. (1973), *Applied Time Series Analysis for Managerial Forecasting* (San Francisco: Holden-Day).

Nerlove, M., D.M. Grether and J. Carvalho (1979), *Analysis of Economic Time Series* (New York: Academic Press).

Newbold, P. (1978), 'Feedback Induced by Measurement Errors', *International Economic Review*, **19** (3): 787–91.

Orcutt, G.H. (1952), 'Toward Partial Redirection of Econometrics', *Review of Economics and Statistics*, **34** (3): 195–213, including Comments by T.C. Koopmans, J. Tinbergen and N. Georgescu Roegen.

Phillips, A.W. (1959), 'The Estimation of Parameters in Systems of Stochastic Differential Equations', *Biometrika*, **46**: 67–76.

Pierce, D.A. and L.D. Haugh (1977), 'Causality in Temporal Systems: Characterizations and a Survey', *Journal of Econometrics*, **5**: 265–93.

Quenouille, M.H. (1957), *The Analysis of Multiple Time-Series* (London: Griffin). Reviewed by A. Zellner (1959), *Journal of Farm Economics*, **41**: 682–4.

Quenouille, M.H. (1958), 'Discrete Autoregressive Schemes With Varying Time-Intervals', *Metrika*, **1** (1): 21–7.

Rowley, J.C.R. and P.K. Trivedi (1975), *Econometrics of Investment* (London: Wiley).

Samuelson, P.A. (1939), 'A Synthesis of the Principle of Acceleration and the Multiplier', *Journal of Political Economy*, **47**: 786–97.

Samuelson, P.A. (1959), 'Alvin Hansen and the Interactions Between the Multiplier Analysis and the Principle of Acceleration', *Review of Economics and Statistics*, **31**: 183–4.

Sargent, T.J. and C.A. Sims (1977), 'Modeling Without Pretending to Have Too Much *A Priori* Economic Theory', in (ed.) C.A. Sims, *New Methods in Business Cycle Research: Proceedings From a Conference* (Minneapolis: Federal Reserve Bank of Minneapolis).

Simon, H.A. (1953), 'Causal Ordering and Identifiability', in (eds) W.C. Hood and T.C. Koopmans, *Studies in Econometric Method* (New York: Wiley), ch. 3.

Sims, C.A. (1980), 'Macroeconomics and Reality', *Econometrica*, **48**: 1–48.

Stone, J.R.N. (1949), 'Prediction from Autoregressive Schemes and Linear Stochastic Difference Equations', *Econometrica*, **17** (Suppl.): 29.

Theil, H. and J.C.G. Boot (1962), 'The Final Form of Econometric Equation Systems', *Review of the International Statistical Institute*, **30**: 136–52.

Tinbergen, J. (1940), 'Econometric Business Cycle Research', *Review of Economic Studies*, **7**: 73–90.

Tintner, G. (1940), *The Variate Difference Method* (Bloomington, Ind.: Principia Press).

Tintner, G. (1952), *Econometrics* (New York: Wiley), ch. 11.

Wallis, K.F. (1977), 'Multiple Time Series Analysis and the Final Form of Econometric Models', *Econometrica*, **45**: 1481–97.

Wold, H. (1949), 'Statistical Estimation of Economic Relationships', *Econometrica*, **17** (Suppl.): 1–22.

Wold, H. (1953), *Demand Analysis: A Study in Econometrics* (New York: Wiley).

Wold, H. (1954a), 'Causality and Econometrics', *Econometrica*, **22** (2): 162–77.

Wold, H. (1954b), *A Study in the Analysis of Stationary Time Series* (Stockholm: Almqvist and Wiksell).

Wold, H. (1956), 'Causal Inference From Observational Data: A Review of Ends and Means', *Journal of the Royal Statistical Society*, **A119** (Part 1): 28–61.

Wold, H. (1964), 'The Approach of Model Building: Crossroads of Probability Theory, Statistics, and the Theory of Knowledge' and 'On the Definition and Meaning of Causal Concepts', in *Model Building in the Human Sciences* (Monaco: Editions Sciences Humaines).

Wold, H. (1974), 'Causal Flows With Latent Variables', *European Economic Review*, **5**: 67–86.

Wold, H. and P. Faxér (1957), 'On the Specification Error in Regression Analysis', *Annals of Mathematical Statistics*, **28** (1): 265–7.

Working, H. (1960), 'Note on the Correlation of First Differences of Averages in a Random Chain', *Econometrica*, **28** (4): 916–18.

Wright, S. (1934), 'The Method of Path Coefficients', *Annals of Mathematical Statistics*, **5**: 161–215.

Yaglom, A.M. (1962), *An Introduction to the Theory of Stationary Random Functions* (Englewood Cliffs, NJ: Prentice-Hall). Based on a survey essay in a Russian journal in 1952.

Zellner, A. and F. Palm (1974), 'Time Series Analysis and Simultaneous Equation Econometric Models', *Journal of Econometrics*, **2** (1): 17–54.

Part I
Mimic Cycles and Simulation

[1]

THE SUMMATION OF RANDOM CAUSES AS THE SOURCE OF CYCLIC PROCESSES*

By Eugen Slutzky

I. SCOPE OF THE INVESTIGATION

Almost all of the phenomena of economic life, like many other processes, social, meteorological, and others, occur in sequences of rising and falling movements, like waves. Just as waves following each other on the sea do not repeat each other perfectly, so economic cycles never repeat earlier ones exactly either in duration or in amplitude. Nevertheless, in both cases, it is almost always possible to detect, even in the multitude of individual peculiarities of the phenomena, marks of certain approximate uniformities and regularities. The eye of the observer instinctively discovers on waves of a certain order other smaller waves, so that the idea of harmonic analysis, viz., that of the possibility of expressing the irregularities of the form and the spacing of the waves by means of the summation of regular sinusoidal fluctuations, presents itself to the mind almost spontaneously. If the results of the analysis happen sometimes not to be completely satisfactory, the discrepancies usually will be interpreted as casual deviations superposed on the regular waves. If the analyses of the first and of the second halves of a series give considerably divergent results (such as, for example, were found by Schuster while analyzing sunspot periodicity),[1] it is, even then, possible to find the solution without giving up the basic concept. Such a discrepancy may be the result of the interference of certain factors checking the continuous movement of the process and substituting for the former regularity a new one which sometimes may

* Professor Eugen Slutzky's paper of 1927, "The Summation of Random Causes as the Source of Cyclic Processes," *Problems of Economic Conditions*, ed. by The Conjuncture Institute, Moskva (Moscow), Vol. 3, No. 1, 1927, has in a sense become classic in the field of time-series analysis. While it does not give a complete theory of the time shape that is to be expected when a given linear operator is applied to a random (auto-non-correlated) series, it has given us a number of penetrating and suggestive ideas on this question. It has been, and will no doubt continue to be, highly stimulating for further research on this vast and—not least for business-cycle analysis—most important problem. Unfortunately Professor Slutzky's paper so far has been available only in Russian (with a brief English summary). Some years ago Professor Henry Schultz had the original article translated into English by Mr. Eugene Prostov, and suggested that it be published in Econometrica. At the request of the Editor Professor Slutzky has prepared for our Journal a revised English version with which he has incorporated also a number of important results obtained after 1927.—Editor.

[1] Arthur Schuster, "On the Periodicities of Sunspots," *Phil. Trans.*, Series A, Vol. 206, 1906, p. 76.

even happen to be of the same type as the former one. Empirical series are, unfortunately, seldom long enough to enable one definitely to prove or to refute such an hypothesis. Without dwelling on the history of complicated disputes concerning the above-mentioned problem, I will mention only two circumstances as the starting points for the present investigation—one, so to speak, in the field of chance, the other in the field of strict regularity.

One usually takes the analysis of the periodogram of the series as the basis for the discovery of hidden periodicities. Having obtained from the periodogram the values of the squares of the amplitudes of the sinusoids, calculated by the method of least squares for waves of varying length, we ask whether there is a method of determining those waves which do not arise from chance. Schuster apparently has discovered a suitable method;[2] but we must give up his criterion when we remember that among his assumptions is that of independence of the successive observations. As a general rule we find that the terms of an empirical series are not independent but correlated and at times correlated very closely. This circumstance, as is known, may very perceptibly heighten the oscillation of the derived characteristics of the series, and it is quite conceivable that waves satisfying Schuster's criterion would in fact be casual—just simulating the presence of a strict regularity.[3] Thus we are led to our basic problem: is it possible that a definite structure of a connection between random fluctuations could form them into a system of more or less regular waves? Many laws of physics and biology are based on chance, among them such laws as the second law of thermodynamics and Mendel's laws. But heretofore we have known how regularities could be derived from a chaos of disconnected elements because of the very disconnectedness. In our case we wish to consider the rise of regularity from series of chaotically-random elements because of certain connections imposed upon them.

Suppose we are inclined to believe in the reality of the strict periodicity of a business cycle, such, for example, as the eight-year period postulated by Moore.[4] Then we should encounter another difficulty. Wherein lies the source of the regularity? What is the mechanism of

[2] A. Schuster, "On the Investigation of Hidden Periodicities, etc.," *Terrestrial Magnetism*, Vol. 3, 1898.

[3] The further development of Schuster's methods, which we find in his extremely valuable paper, "The Periodogram of the Magnetic Declination as Obtained from the Records of the Greenwich Observatory during the Years 1871–1895," *Trans. of the Cambridge Philos. Soc.*, Vol. 18, 1900, p. 107, seems to overcome this difficulty. Because it is rather unfinished in mathematical respects, however, the influence of this paper seems not to have been comparable to its importance.

[4] H. L. Moore, *Generating Economic Cycles*, New York, 1923.

causality which, decade after decade, reproduces the same sinusoidal wave which rises and falls on the surface of the social ocean with the regularity of day and night. It is natural that even now, as centuries ago, the eyes of the investigators are raised to the celestial luminaries searching in them for an explanation of human affairs. One can dauntlessly admit one's right to make bold hypotheses, but still should not one try to find out other ways?[5] What means of explanation, however, would be left to us if we decided to give up the hypothesis of the superposition of regular waves complicated only by purely random components? The presence of waves of definite orders, the long waves embracing decades, shorter cycles from approximately five to ten years in length, and finally the very short waves, will always remain a fact begging for explanation. The approximate regularity of the periods is sometimes so distinctly apparent that it, also, cannot be passed by without notice. Thus, in short, *the undulatory character of the processes and the approximate regularity of the waves* are the two facts for which we shall try to find a possible source in random causes combining themselves in their common effect.

The method of the work is a combination of induction and deduction. It was possible to investigate by the deductive method only a few aspects of the problem. Generally speaking, the theory of chance waves is almost entirely a matter of the future. For the sake of this future theory one cannot be too lavish with experiments: it is experiment that shows us totally unexpected facts, thus pointing out problems which otherwise would hardly fall within the field of the investigator.[6]

II. COHERENT SERIES OF CONSEQUENCES OF RANDOM CAUSES AND THEIR MODELS

There are two kinds of chance series: (1) those in which the probability of the appearance, in a given place in the series, of a certain value of the variable, depends on previous or subsequent values of the variable, and (2) those in which it does not. In this way we distinguish

[5] A similar viewpoint is found in the remarkable work of G. U. Yule, "Why Do We Sometimes Get Nonsense-Correlations between Time Series?" *Journal of the Royal Statistical Society*, Vol. 89, 1926. This work approaches our theme rather closely.

[6] The following exposition is based on a large amount of calculation. The author expresses special gratitude to his long-time collaborator, E. N. Pomeranzeva-Ilyinskaya and also to O. V. Gordon, N. F. Rein, M. A. Smirnova and E. V. Luneyeva. The calculations were carefully checked, almost all work having been independently performed by two individuals. It is very unlikely that undetected errors are sufficiently significant to affect to any perceptible degree our final conclusions. A few errors, detected in the course of time in Tables I, III, and IX of the original paper, are noted at the end of this paper, and an error in Figure 7, B_4, has been corrected when it was re-drawn.

between *coherent*[7] and *incoherent* (or random) series. The terms of the series of this second kind are not correlated. In series in which there is correlation between terms, one of the most important characteristics is the value of the coefficient of correlation between terms, considered as a function of the distance between the terms correlated. We shall call it the *correlational function* of the corresponding series and shall limit our investigation to those cases in which the distribution of probabilities remains constant. The coefficient of correlation, then, is exclusively determined by the distance between the terms and not by their place in the series. The coefficient of correlation of each member with itself (r_0) will equal unity, and its coefficient of correlation (r_t) with the tth member following will necessarily equal its coefficient (r_{-t}) with the tth member preceding.

Any concrete instance of an experimentally obtained chance series we shall regard as a *model* of empirical processes which are structurally similar to it. As the basis of the present investigation we take three models of purely random series and call them the first, second, and third basic series. These series are based on the results obtained by the People's Commissariate of Finance in drawing the numbers of a government lottery loan. For the first basic series, we used the last digits of the numbers drawn; for the second basic series, we substituted 0 for each even digit and 1 for each odd digit; the third basic series was obtained in the same way as the second, but from another set of numbers drawn.[8]

Let us pass to the coherent series. Their origin may be extremely varied, but it seems probable that an especially prominent role is played in nature by the process of *moving summation* with weights of one kind or another; by this process coherent series are obtained from other coherent series or from incoherent series. For example, let causes $\cdots x_{i-2}, x_{i-1}, x_i, \cdots$ produce the consequences $\cdots y_{i-2}, y_{i-1}, y_i, \cdots$, where the magnitude of each consequence is determined by the influence, not of one, but of a number of the preceding causes, as for instance, the size of a crop is determined, not by one day's rainfall, but by many. If the influence of causes in retrospective order is expressed by the weights $A_0, A_1, A_2, \cdots A_{n-1}$, then we shall have

$$(1)\quad \begin{cases} y_i = A_0x_i + A_1x_{i-1} + \cdots + A_{n-1}x_{i-(n-1)}, \\ y_{i-1} = \qquad\quad A_0x_{i-1} + \cdots + A_{n-2}x_{i-(n-1)} + A_{n-1}x_{i-n}, \\ \cdots\cdots\cdots\cdots\cdots\cdots\cdots\cdots \end{cases}$$

[7] I venture to propose this name because it seems to me that it truly expresses what is intended, namely, the existence of some connection between the elements or parts of a thing (for example, of a series), but not a connection between this thing as a whole and another.

[8] The tables giving these series and seven others derived from them will be found in the original paper (*loc. cit.*, pp. 57–64) and are not repeated here.

Each of two adjacent consequences has one particular cause of its own, and $(n-1)$ causes in common with the other consequence. Because the consequences possess causes in common there appears between them a correlation even though the series of causes are incoherent. When all the weights are equal (*simple* moving summation) the coefficient of correlation expresses the share of the common causes in the total number of independent causes on which the consequences

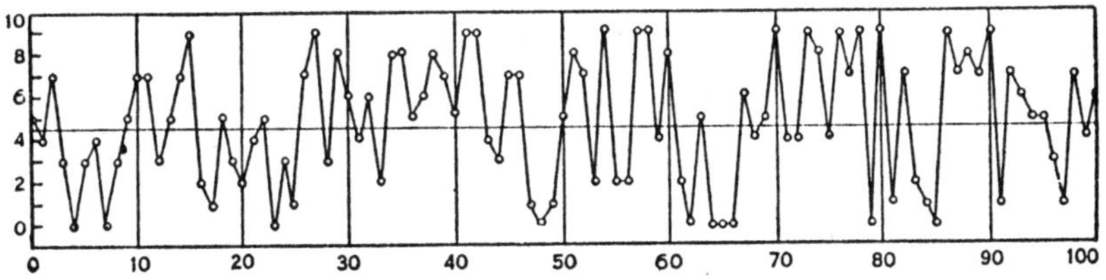

FIGURE 1.—The first 100 terms of the first basic series.

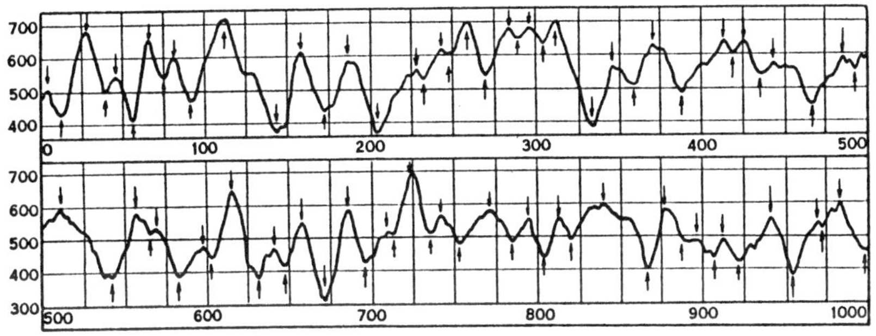

FIGURE 2.—The first 1000 terms of Model II.

depend (as has long been known from the theory of the experiment of Darbishire); then

$$r_0 = 1, r_1 = r_{-1} = \frac{n-1}{n}, r_2 = r_{-2} = \frac{n-2}{n}, \quad \cdots, r_{n-1} = r_{-(n-1)} = \frac{1}{n},$$

further coefficients being equal to zero. By taking a ten-item moving summation of the first basic series, Model I was obtained.[9] A small section of Model I is plotted in Figure 3 with an index[10] of the English

[9] In addition, 5 was added to each sum. This does not change the properties of the series. Neither does it make any difference as to the method of numbering consequences in comparison with the scheme used in formula (1). At the outset of the work, it seemed to be technically more convenient to give the consequence the same number as the earliest cause and not the latest. Thus, for example, for Model I,

$$y_0 = x_0 + x_1 + x_2 + \cdots + x^9 + 5.$$

[10] Dr. Dorothy S. Thomas, "Quarterly Index of British Cycles," in W. L. Thorp, *Business Annals*, New York, 1926, p. 28.

business cycles for 1855–1877 in juxtaposition—an initial graphic demonstration of the possible effects of the summation of unconnected causes.

In turn the consequences become causes. Taking a ten-item moving summation of Model I, we obtained the 1000 numbers of Model II. Performing a two-item moving summation twelve times in succession on the third basic series,[11] we obtained the 1000 numbers of Model IVa. First and second differences of Model IVa give Models IVb and IVc respectively (See Figure 4). Furthermore, the application of scheme (1) to the second basic series gives[12] Model III if the weights used are

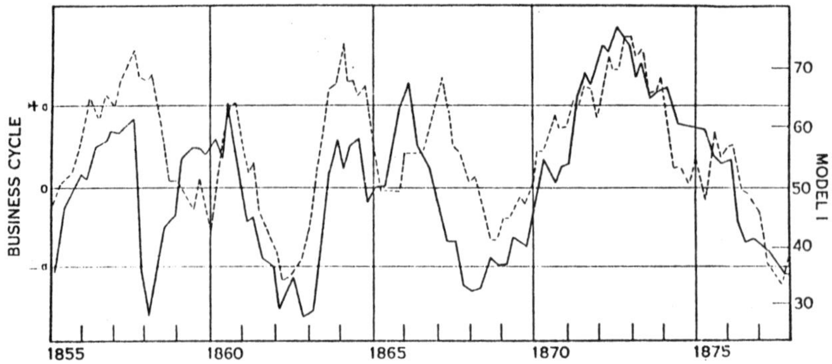

FIGURE 3.————An index of English business cycles from 1855 to 1877; scale on the left side. ---------Terms 20 to 145 of Model I; scale on the right side.

10^4 times the ordinates of the Gaussian curve taken at intervals of 0.1σ. Because this model was very smooth it appeared sufficient to use only the 180 even members out of the 360 items (see Figure 11 under the numbers 0, 2, 4, · · · 358). Model IIIa—the last one—is 10^4

[11] It actually was computed by applying the scheme (1) to the third basic series with the weights 1, 12, 66, 220, 495, 792, 924, 792, · · · , 12, 1, because s-fold simple summation of two items is equivalent, as can be shown easily, to direct summation with the weights $C_0^s, C_1^s, C_2^s, \cdots, C_s^s$, (where C_k^s is the number of combinations of s things taken k at a time.

[12] The exact values of Model III could be obtained by multiplying the corresponding items of the basic series by the exact values of the function $10^4 \exp\{-\frac{1}{2}(0.1t)^2\}/\sqrt{2\pi}$, for integral values of t. This function was the basis of obtaining the 4th differences of Model III. Approximate values of Model III were found by using a set of weights composed of 95 numbers corresponding to the values of the above function for integral values of t from -47 to $+47$, with the numbers less than 1 rounded off to the nearest tenth and numbers greater than 1 to whole units. The numbers of the basic series were written on a ribbon which we slid along the column of weights. Inasmuch as the basic series consisted of zeros and ones, all of the computations were plain additions. For Model IVa, a ribbon with holes in the place of unities was constructed.

times the 4th differences of the numbers of Model III from the 7th to the 97th.[13]

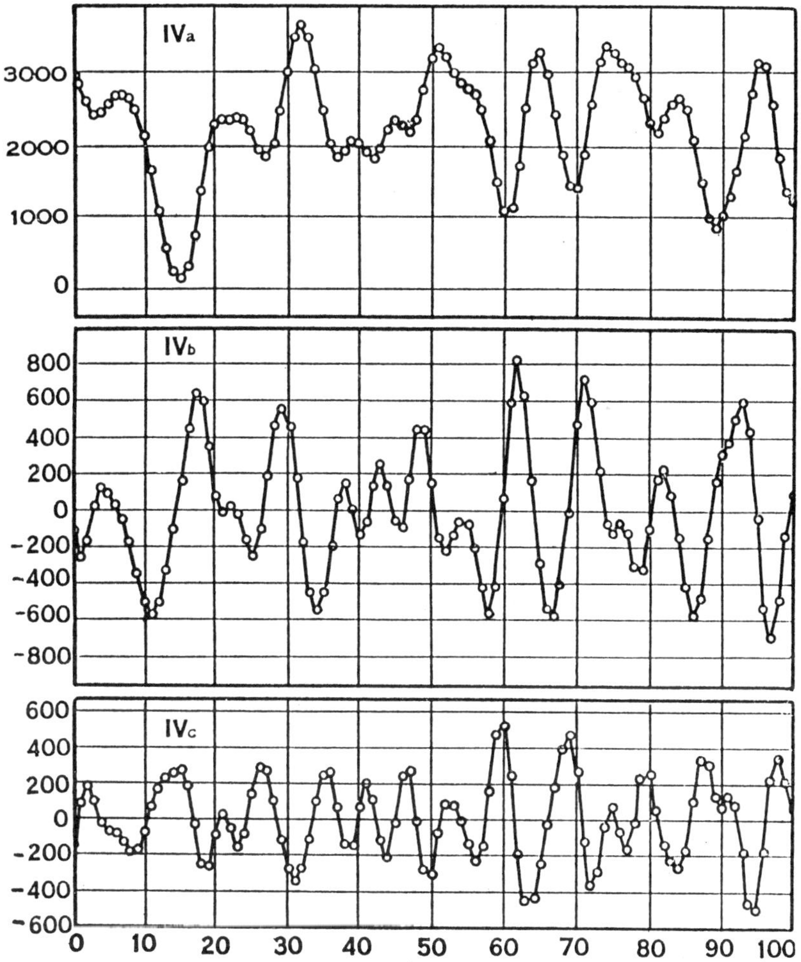

FIGURE 4.—The first 100 terms of Models IVa, IVb, and IVc.

We could not be satisfied by a smaller number of models because it was necessary to observe their various properties and to have illustra-

[13] For the calculation of these differences the accuracy with which we determined the items of Model III was not sufficient, so the following method was used: It is easy to see that the *n*th order differences of the items of the series obtained by scheme (1) are equivalent to those computed by the same scheme but applying weights equal to the differences of the original weights (keeping in mind that the series of original weights is extended at both ends with zeros).

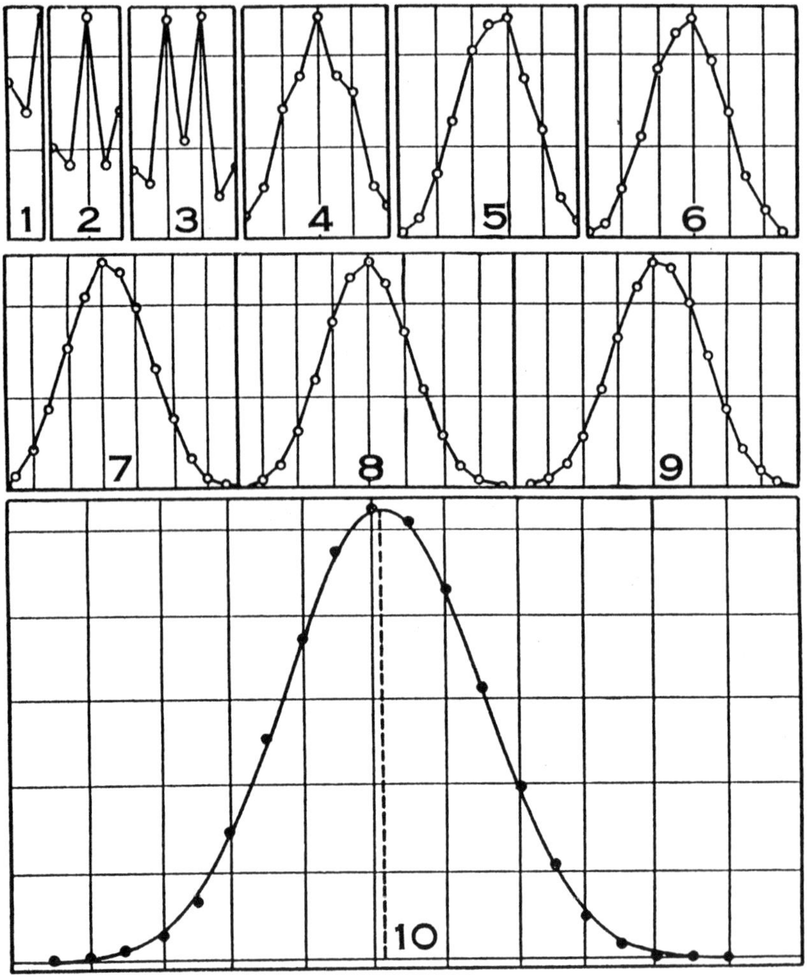

FIGURE 5.—An example of the crossing of random weights. The weights of the causes for each of 10 successive summations are shown, i.e., $A_k'^{(1)}$, $A_k'^{(2)}$, $\cdots$, $A_k'^{(10)}$. See Appendix, Section 1.

With the help of S. Pineto's *Tables de logarithmes vulgaires a dix decimales*, St. Petersburg, 1871, the values of the function

$$\exp\{-\tfrac{1}{2}(0.1t)^2\}/\sqrt{2\pi}$$

were obtained to ten decimal places for integral values of t from 0 to 44; this series was completed by using Sheppard's tables, and the differences of the entire series up to and including the 4th differences were taken. Multiplying the latter by 10^8 and expressing the result in integers, we obtained weights with the help of which—and by using scheme (1)—the values of $10^4\,\Delta^4 y_{III}$ were obtained from the second basic series.

tions for the elucidation of the different aspects of the problem. We could not aspire to imitate nature in forming a set of weights; still, in the course of the work, we have come across an exceptionally curious circumstance. First, each multifold simple summation of n items at a time gives a set of weights which approaches the Gaussian curve as a limit. In the Appendix, Section 1, there is given the instance of a tenfold summation of three items at a time with the weights chosen absolutely at random for each successive summation. The ten con-

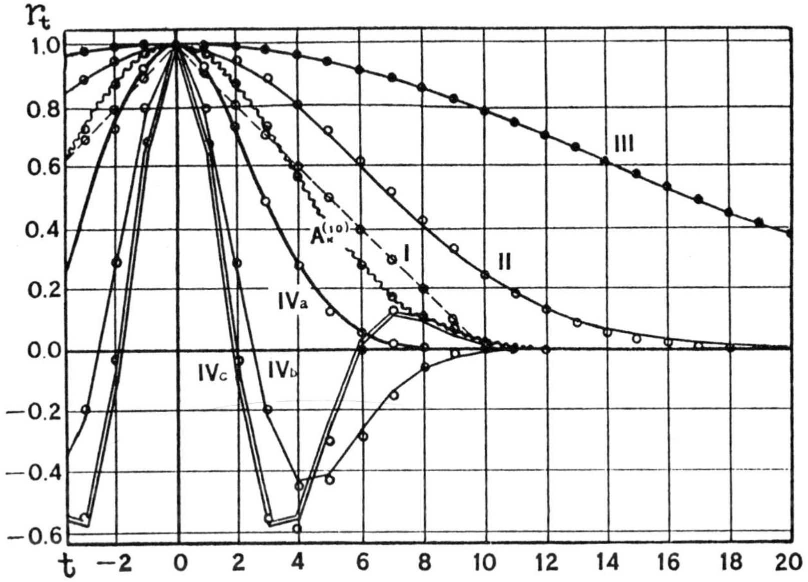

FIGURE 6.—oooo The correlational functions of Models I–IVc, and of the scheme of the crossing of the chance weights ($A_k'^{(10)}$).

Corresponding Gaussian curves and the reduced differences of the ordinates of the Gaussian curve.

secutive sets of weights are depicted in Figure 5. It is easily seen how they gradually become more and more like the Gaussian curve, and for the tenth summation the weights approach the Gaussian curve very closely.

This is far from being a chance result. From further considerations (Appendix, Section 1) we find that we have here actually encountered a law which, under certain conditions, must necessarily realize itself in the chaos of random entanglements and crossings of endless numbers of series of causes and consequences. The problem is specially important for the reason that the correlational function of a derived series is defined entirely by the respective weights-function. It is possible to prove (see Appendix, Sections 1, 2, and 3) that if the series of weights follows the Gaussian curve, the correlational function of the resulting consequence series is capable of being expressed by a similar curve with a greater or smaller degree of approximation. For the series of consequences proportionate to the increments of the cause—that is, the differences of order k of the series of causes—the correlational function can be represented by the series of the differences (of order $2k$) of the ordinates of the Gaussian curve. It could not be by chance that the correlational function of all of our models, with the exception of the most elementary one (Model I), belong to one of the two types mentioned (see Figure 6). No exception is found in the correlational

TABLE 1

Distance between terms	Correlation coefficients with random weights	Ordinates of Gaussian curve	Differences
t	r_t	R_t	$r_t - R_t$
0	1.000	1.000	0.000
1	0.965	0.965	0.000
2	0.868	0.866	+0.002
3	0.727	0.723	+0.004
4	0.567	0.562	+0.005
5	0.410	0.407	+0.003
6	0.275	0.274	+0.001
7	0.171	0.171	0.000
8	0.097	0.100	−0.003
9	0.051	0.054	−0.003
10	0.024	0.027	−0.003
11	0.011	0.013	−0.002
12	0.004	0.006	−0.002
13	0.001	0.002	−0.001
14	0.000	0.001	−0.001

function for the series of consequences of the 10th order obtained in the course of the crossing of the random weights in the example mentioned above. The values of these correlation coefficients (r_t), together with the ordinates of the corresponding Gaussian curve (R_t), are given in Table 1 (for the calculation see Appendix, Section 2).

III. THE UNDULATORY CHARACTER OF CHANCE SERIES; GRADUALITY AND FLUENCY AS TENDENCIES

Our models, representing several sets of experiments, give an inductive proof of our first thesis, namely, *that the summation of random causes may be the source of cyclic, or undulatory processes.*[14] It is, however

[14] The definition of the business cycle as being a process (not necessarily periodic) characterized by successive rises and falls, is given by *W. C. Mitchell* in Introduction to *W. L. Thorp, Business Annals*, New York, 1926, pp. 32–33.

not difficult to determine the reason why it must be so inevitably. We shall first observe a series of independent values of a random variable. If, for the sake of simplicity, we assume that the distribution of probabilities does not change, then, for the entire series, there will exist a certain horizontal level such that the probabilities of obtaining a value either above or below it would be equal. The probability that a value, which has just passed from the positive deviation region to the negative, will remain below at the subsequent trial is $\frac{1}{2}$; the probability that it will remain below two times in succession is $\frac{1}{4}$; three times $\frac{1}{8}$; and so on. Thus the probability that the values will remain for a long time above the level or below the level is quite negligible. It is, therefore, practically certain that, for a somewhat long series, the values will pass many times from the positive deviations to the negative and vice versa. Let us designate as a *half-wave* a portion of the series in which the deviation does not change sign. Thus, for 1000 numbers of the third basic series we find 540 half-waves (instead of the theoretically expected 500). Taking from this number the first 512 half-waves we find among them a number of half-waves of the length 1,2, etc. In Table 2 the actual (n_i') and theoretical[15] (n_i) frequencies for half-waves of various lengths are shown. That the observed series is consistent with the theoretical series can be found by the calculation of the χ^2 criterion of goodness of fit.[16]

TABLE 2

Length of half-wave	Actual frequency	Theoretical frequency
i	n'_i	n_i
1	261	256
2	137	128
3	65	64
4	29	32
5	14	16
6	4	8
7	1	4
8 and more	1	4
Total	512	512

If a variable can have more than two values and if, in a certain interval of a more or less considerable length, it happens to remain above

[15] L. von Bortkiewicz, *Die Iterationen*, 1917, Formel 75, p. 99.

[16] We find, indeed,

$$\chi^2 = \sum \frac{(n_i' - n_i)^2}{n_i} = 7.78,$$

the corresponding probability being $P = 0.35$; see *Tables for Statisticians and Biometricians*, ed. by K. Pearson, Part I, Table XII.

(or below) its general level, then in that interval it will have a temporary level about which it almost certainly will oscillate. Thus on the waves of one order there appear superimposed waves of another order.

The unconnected random waves are usually called irregular zigzags. A correlation between the items of a series deprives the waves of this characteristic and introduces into their rising and falling movements an element of *graduality*. In order to make the reasoning more concrete, let us consider a series obtained from an incoherent series by means of a ten-item moving summation. Our Model I will be used as the example. Any items of this model separated from each other by more than 9 intervals (as, for example, the values $y_0, y_{10}, y_{20}, \cdots$) are not correlated with each other and consequently form waves of the above considered type, i.e., irregular zigzags. But if we consider the entire series, we shall certainly find gradual transitions from the maximum point of a wave to its minimum and vice versa, since the correlation between neighboring items of the series makes small differences between them more probable than large ones. This we find to be true for all of our models.

We must distinguish between the *graduality* of the transitions and their *fluency*. We could speak about the absence of the latter property if a state of things existed where there would be an equal probability for either a rise or a fall after a rise as well as after a fall. If fluency were missing we should obtain waves covered by zigzags such as we find in Model I (see Figure 3).

For example, we have for Model I,

$$
\begin{aligned}
y_0 &= 5 + x_0 + x_1 + x_2 + \cdots + x_9, \\
y_1 &= 5 + x_1 + x_2 + \cdots + x_9 + x_{10}, \\
y_2 &= 5 + x_2 + \cdots + x_9 + x_{10} + x_{11}, \\
&\cdots\cdots\cdots\cdots\cdots\cdots\cdots\cdots
\end{aligned}
$$

from which we obtain

$$
\begin{aligned}
\Delta y_0 &= y_1 - y_0 = x_{10} - x_0, \\
\Delta y_1 &= y_2 - y_1 = x_{11} - x_1, \\
&\cdots\cdots\cdots\cdots
\end{aligned}
$$

Thus we see that the adjacent first differences do not have any causes in common, and hence are not correlated. The same applies to differences which are further apart, with the exception of such as $y_1 - y_0 = x_{10} - x_0$ and $y_{11} - y_{10} = x_{20} - x_{10}$. The series of differences is almost incoherent and hence the waves will be covered by chaotically irregular zigzags such as we find in Model I.

Let us assume further that adjacent differences are positively correlated. Then, in all probability, after a rise another rise will occur, after a fall a further fall; a steep rise will have the *tendency* to continue-with the same steepness, a moderate one with the same moderateness. So small sections of a wave will tend to be straight lines; and the greater the coefficient of correlation between adjacent differences the closer the sections approximate straight lines.[17]

Correlation between second differences plays an analogous role. The greater this correlation coefficient, the greater the tendency toward the preservation of the constancy of the second differences. Over more or less considerably long intervals a series with approximately constant second differences will tend to approximate a second-degree parabola as all "good" curves do. In Table 3 are given, for Models, I, II, and III, the values of the correlation coefficients between the adjacent items of the series (r_1), between the adjacent first differences ($r_1^{(1,1)}$), and between the adjacent second differences ($r_1^{(2,2)}$). The coefficients were calculated by the formulas of the Appendix, Section 1. As we go from the first basic series to Model I and then to Models II and III, we find progressive changes in their graphic appearance (see Figures, 3, 2, 8, and 11 respectively). These changes are produced at first by the introduction and then by the growth of graduality and of fluency in the movements of the respective chance waves. The growth of the degree of correlation between items (or between their differences) as we go from the first basic series to Model I, etc. (see Table 3) corresponds to the changes in the graphic appearance of our series.

TABLE 3

Model	Coefficient of correlation between:		
	Terms	First differences	Second differences
	r_1	$r_1^{(1,1)}$	$r_1^{(2,2)}$
I	0.9	0.0	−0.5
II	0.985	0.85	0.0
III	0.9975	0.9925	0.9876

IV. EMPIRICAL EVIDENCE OF THE APPROXIMATE REGULARITY OF CHANCE WAVES

Our first thesis, that is, the demonstration of the possibility of the appearance of undulatory processes of a more or less fluent character as the result of the summation of random causes, may be considered

[17] The term *tendency* is used here in a strict sense. To each equation of regression (giving the value of the conditional mathematical expectation of a variable as a function of some other variable) there corresponds an approximate equation between the variables themselves. The closer to unity the absolute value of the coefficient of correlation lies, the greater is the probability that this functional relationship will be maintained within the limits of the desired accuracy; i.e., the stronger will be the *tendency*.

as practically proved. However, our second thesis, that is, the demonstration of *the approximate regularity of the waves*, offers considerably greater difficulties. Again we shall begin with the inductive method.

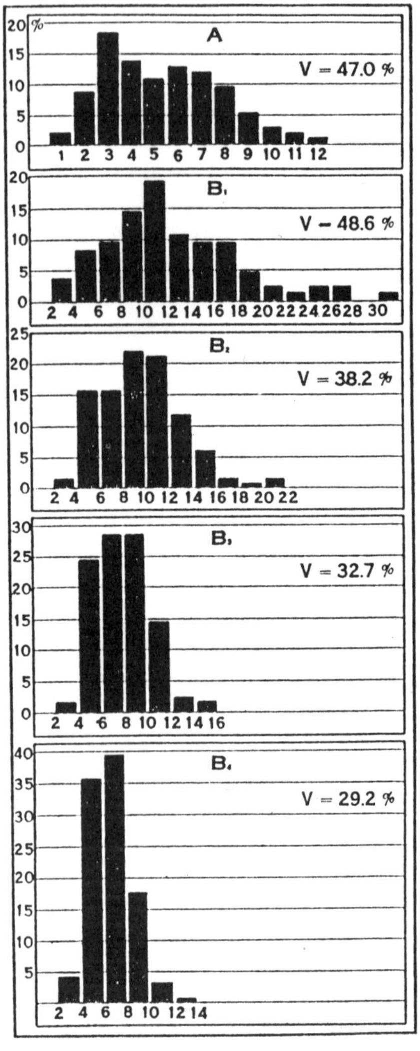

FIGURE 7.—The frequency distributions of the lengths of waves and half-waves: A, Business cycles of 12 countries, not including England (Mitchell); B_1 to B_4, Models II, IVa, IVb, and IVc respectively.

In Figure 2 are plotted 1000 points of Model II; a continuous line has been passed through them, which, because of the small scale, seems to be a comparatively fluent curve. One can distinguish on the curve waves of different orders—even down to insignificant zigzags, of which a number are not apparent on the graph because of their minuteness. The maxima and minima having been listed, together with the length of their half-waves and amplitudes, we have found that, since an empirically descriptive point of view, in its very nature, permits only approximate solutions,[18] it was legitimate to draw a boundary between waves and *ripples:* maxima and minima with amplitudes of ten units or less being discarded as ripples. The remaining maxima and minima are indicated by arrows in Figure 2. The distribution of the lengths of the 83 half-waves for Model II is given graphically in Figure 7 (B_1). Figure 7 includes the distribution (A) of the lengths of 93 cycles of economic life for 12 countries outside of England, as given by Mitchell.[19] The coefficient of variation for the latter is 47.0%[20] as compared to 48.6% for Model II. Thus we find variation of the same degree in the two distributions. The distributions for Models IVa, IVb, and IVc are also shown in Figure 7. The average lengths of waves are 9.23, 7.36 and 6.15, while the coefficients of variation are 38.2%, 32.7% and 29.2% respectively. In general appearance these last three distributions are similar to the first two, although the last three have less variation, in spite of the fact that for Models IV, a, b, and c, the data are taken without discarding the ripples. Our models being based on some a priori schemes, it appears quite likely that some day it will be possible to calculate the mathematical expectation and variability of the distances between maxima and minima. In this respect, therefore, the chance waves in coherent series must be subject to some kind of regularity, the regularity of this type being observed even in the chaotic zigzags of purely random series.[21]

We are interested, however, in a different aspect of the problem. The attempt of Mitchell to deny the periodicity of business cycles is a result of his tendency to stick to a purely descriptive point of view. The means of description which he uses and which we tried to imitate for our models are far too crude. If we try to apply the same method to a sum of two or three sinusoids the result would be approximately the same. Those investigators of economic life are right who believe in their acumen and instinct and subscribe to at least an approximate correctness in the concept of the periodicity of business cycles. Let us

[18] Cf. E. Husserl, *Ideen zu einer reinen Phänomenologie und phänomenologischen Philosophie,* Halle a.d.S., 1922, § 74: *Deskriptive und exakte Wissenschaften,* p. 138–139.

[19] W. L. Thorp, *Business Annals,* Introduction by W. C. Mitchell, p. 58.

[20] *Ibid.*

[21] Cf. L. von. Bortkiewicz, *Die Iterationen,* 1917.

again examine Model II (Figure 2). In many places there are, apparently, large waves with massive outlines as well as smaller waves lying, as it were, over them; sometimes these are detached from them, sometimes they are almost completely merged into them. For example, at the beginning of Figure 2, three waves of nearly equal length are apparent, that is, from the first to the third minimum, from the third to the fifth, and from the fifth to the sixth. Upon these waves smaller

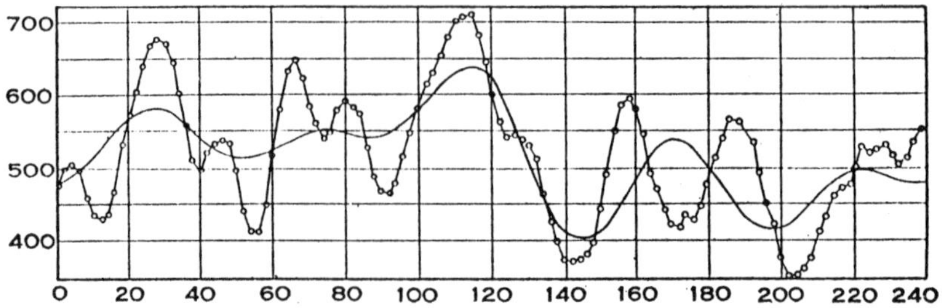

FIGURE 8.—o-o-o The first 120 even terms of Model II. ——— Sum of the first five harmonics of Fourier series: $y=518.14-20.98\cos(2\pi t/240)+50.02\sin(2\pi t/240)+17.30\cos(2\pi t/120)-3.16\sin(2\pi t/120)-10.93\cos(2\pi t/80)+35.66\sin(2\pi t/80)+17.18\cos(2\pi t/60)-21.92\sin(2\pi t/60)-38.53\cos(2\pi t/48)-3.65\sin(2\pi t/48)$.

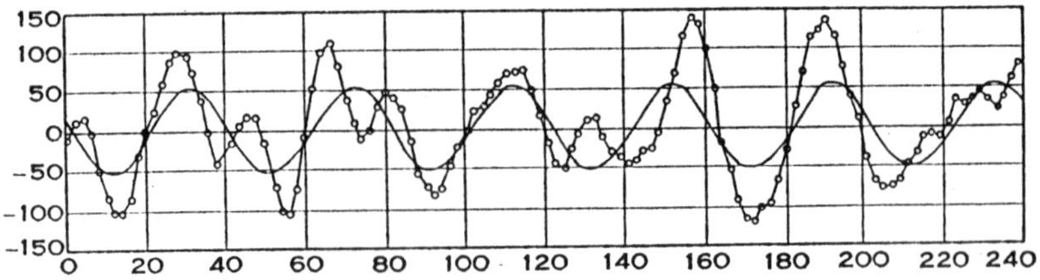

FIGURE 9.—o-o-o The deviations of Model II from the sum of the first five harmonics of Fourier series. ——— 6th sinusoid: $y=12.98\cos(2\pi t/40)-51.50\sin(2\pi t/40)$.

ones can be seen having also approximately equal dimensions. A careful examination of the graphs of our models will disclose to the reader a number of places where the approximate equality of the length of the waves is readily apparent. If we had a much shorter series, such as a series offered by the ordinary statistics of economic life with its small number of waves, we should be tempted to consider the sequence as strictly periodic, that is, as composed of a few regular harmonic fluctuations complicated by some insignificant casual fluctuations. For instance, let us consider two sections of Model II, lying one directly above the other in Figure 2, namely, the section from item 100 to item 250 and the one from 600 to 750. The similarity between the waves in these sections is apparent.

The accuracy of the above deduction is limited by the imperfection of a visual impression. To eliminate this shortcoming, let us analyze one or two sections of our models harmonically by means of Fourier's analysis. This has been done for a section of 240 points of Model II and the 360 points of Model III. Because of the great fluency of these series it was sufficient to use only the even-numbered ordinates (i.e., 0, 2, · · · 238, and 0, 2, · · · 358, respectively), thus saving some computation. The results for the 120 points of Model II are shown in Figures 8, 9 and 10, those for the 180 points of Model III in Figures 11 and 12.

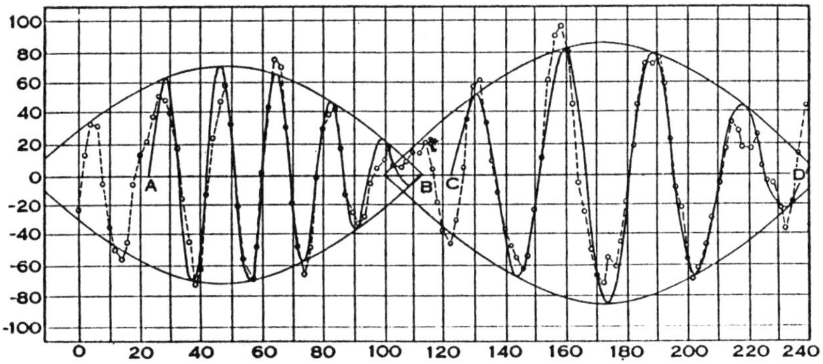

FIGURE 10.—o-o-o The deviations of Model II from the sum of six harmonics.

$$A\text{———}B\colon y_I = 71 \sin \frac{2\pi}{264}(t + 18) \sin \frac{2\pi}{18}(t - 24).$$

$$C\text{———}D\colon y_{II}\ 85 \sin \frac{2\pi}{288}(t - 100) \sin \frac{2\pi}{14\frac{2}{3}}(t - 122\tfrac{1}{3})$$

First let us consider Model II. In Figure 8 the sum of the first five sinusoids of the Fourier series are shown, while in Figure 9 the deviations from that sum are shown together with the sixth sinusoid. It is known, of course, that practically any given curve can be represented by a sum of a series of sinusoids provided a large enough number of terms is taken. It is not for every empirical series, however, that we can obtain such a significant correspondence and such a sharply expressed periodicity with a comparatively small number of harmonics. The approximately regular waves which were apparent even in the crude series are much more distinct now when they are isolated by deducting the sum of the first five harmonics. Of course, we cannot assert that the rest of Model II would follow the same periodicity, but, for our purposes, it is sufficient that successive waves should maintain an approximate equality of length for six periods. This hardly can be considered to be a chance occurrence; the explanation of such an effect must be found in the mechanism of the connection of the random values.

The deviations from the sum of six harmonics are plotted in Figure 10 together with the corresponding fluent curves. These curves are obtained as interference waves of two sinusoids with equal amplitudes and approximately equal periods. In other words, such a curve can be represented as the product of two sinusoids or as a sinusoid with an amplitude also changing along a sinusoid. These *bending sinusoids*

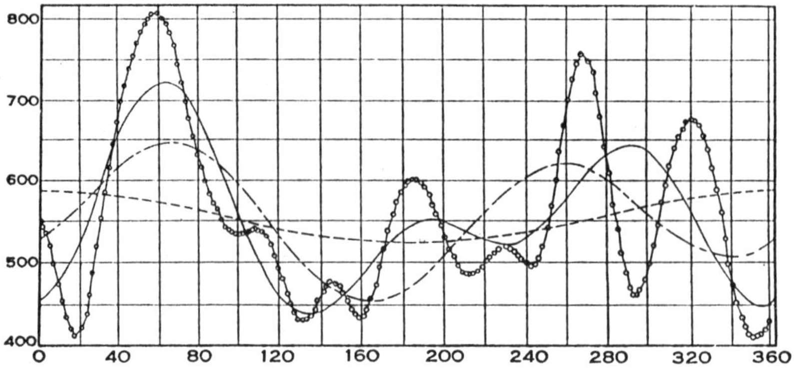

FIGURE 11.—o-o-o The first 180 even terms of Model III. ----$y_I = 554.8 + 31.79 \cos(2\pi t/360) + 3.40 \sin(2\pi t/360)$. ------ $y_{II} = y_I - 58.82 \cos(2\pi t/180) + 46.63 \sin(2\pi t/180)$. ———— $y_{III} = y_{II} - 75.36 \cos(2\pi t/120) + 0.61 \sin(2\pi t/120)$.

separate on the graph the regions which place our empirical series in a definite *regime*.[22] Over a large part of the first region the regime is maintained for three or four periods with a correspondence that is much greater than could reasonably be expected between an analytical curve and a random series. At the beginning and end of a region the regime is broken. The point where a bending sinusoid cuts the axis of abscissas is the *critical point*. After this point a regime is replaced by another regime of the same type, but having different parameters. Throughout the greater part of the second region, as in the first, the regime is quite well sustained.[23]

[22] The term *regime* has been borrowed for the purposes of theoretical statistics from hydrography by N. S. Tchetverikov. See his work: "Relation of the Price of Wheat to the Size of the Crop," *The Problems of Economic Conditions*, Vol. 1, Issue 1, Moscow, 1925, p. 83.

[23] The parameters of a regime,

$$y = A \sin[(360°/L)(x - a)] \sin[(360°/l)(x - b)]$$

are easy to determine by means of graphical construction after a few trials. It is also possible to make corrections, using the method of least squares, but in our case we did not think it necessary.

If a result like the foregoing is not due to chance, a much better proof could be expected from an analysis of Model III for which the correlation between the elements is greater than for Model II. In Figure 11 the even-numbered points from 0 to 358 of Model III are plotted together with the first harmonic of the Fourier series, the sum of the first two, and the sum of the first three sinusoids. Instead of the six sinusoids needed for Model II, only three are here necessary for our purposes. The deviations from these are shown in Figure 12. Three regions are apparent with a change of regimes at the critical

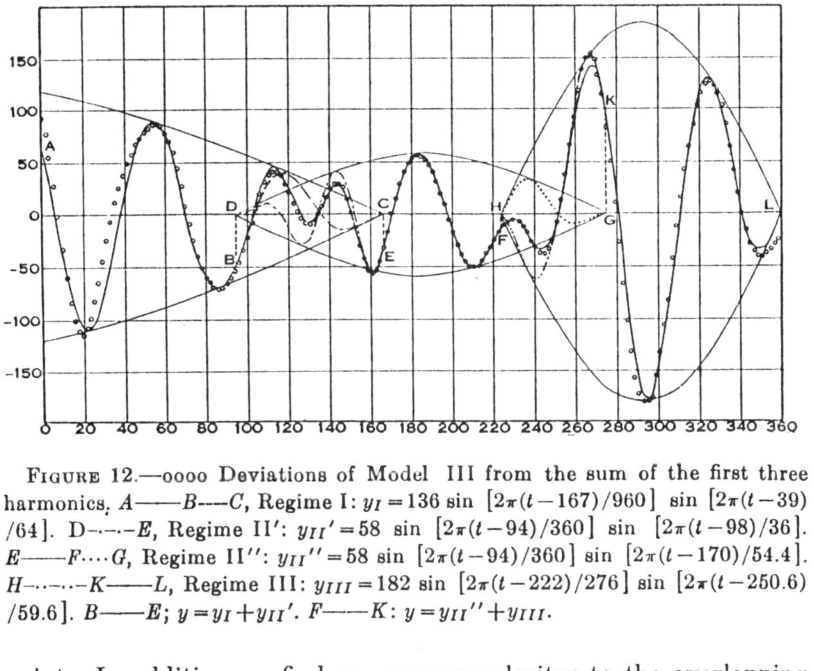

FIGURE 12.—oooo Deviations of Model III from the sum of the first three harmonics. *A*——*B*----*C*, Regime I: $y_I = 136 \sin [2\pi(t-167)/960] \sin [2\pi(t-39)/64]$. D-.-.-*E*, Regime II′: $y_{II}' = 58 \sin [2\pi(t-94)/360] \sin [2\pi(t-98)/36]$. *E*——*F*····*G*, Regime II″: $y_{II}'' = 58 \sin [2\pi(t-94)/360] \sin [2\pi(t-170)/54.4]$. *H*-..-..-*K*——*L*, Regime III: $y_{III} = 182 \sin [2\pi(t-222)/276] \sin [2\pi(t-250.6)/59.6]$. *B*——*E*; $y = y_I + y_{II}'$. *F*——*K*: $y = y_{II}'' + y_{III}$.

points. In addition we find one more regularity: to the overlapping parts of the said regions corresponds every time the partial superposition of the regimes, i.e., the algebraical addition of the respective curves.

Let us try now to summarize our observations in the following tentative and hypothetical manner:

The summation of random causes generates a cyclical series which tends to imitate for a number of cycles a harmonic series of a relatively small number of sine curves. After a more or less considerable number of periods every regime becomes disarranged, the transition to another regime occurring sometimes rather gradually, sometimes more or less abruptly, around certain critical points.

V. THE TENDENCY TO SINUSOIDAL FORM

In addition to the tendencies towards graduality and fluency (that is towards linear and parabolic forms for small sections) we find a third tendency, namely, the tendency toward a sinusoidal form.

Let $y_i, y_{i+1}, y_{i+2}, \cdots$ be the ordinates of a sinusoid. Then it is always true that

$$\Delta^2 y_i = -a y_{i+1}, \qquad (2)$$

where $\Delta^2 y_i = (y_{i+2} - y_{i+1}) - (y_{i+1} - y_i)$, that is, the ith second difference of the series.

Conversely, it can easily be proved that the function defined by an equation of the form (2) in case $0 < a < 4$ must be a sinusoid.[24] Now, if there is a high correlation between the second differences ($\Delta^2 y_i$) and the ordinates (y_{i+1}) of a series, then equation (2) will be approximately true and there will exist a tendency toward a sinusoidal form in the series. The closer the correlation coefficient between $\Delta^2 y_i$ and y_{i+1}, denoted by us by $r_1^{(2,0)}$, is to -1, the more pronounced (or strong) is the tendency to a sinusoidal form.

A tendency toward either linear or parabolic forms cannot appear in a very large section of a coherent series because it would disrupt its cyclic character. The accumulation of deviations necessarily destroys every linear or parabolic regime even though the respective correlations are very high. After a regime is disrupted the new section will have a new, let us say a parabolic, regime (i.e., a regime of parabolas with different parameters). This process continues throughout the entire series, so that each coherent series of the type considered here is patched together out of a number of parabolas with variable parameters whose variations generally cannot be foreseen.

A sinusoidal regime is also bound to disrupt gradually, this being a property which distinguishes every tendency from an exact law. But under favorable conditions the sinusoidal tendency can be maintained over a number of waves without contradicting the basic property of a coherent series. In order to obtain a result of this kind it is necessary that the respective correlations be sufficiently high. But, as a matter of fact, $r_1^{(2,0)}$ for Model II is approximately the same as for Model I (-0.315 and -0.316), while Model III with its great smoothness has an $r_1^{(2,0)}$ less than that of Model IVa (-0.578 as compared to -0.599). It seems, however, to be very probable that this criterion is insufficient just because we have to deal here not with one sinusoid but with a whole series of sinusoids having different periods. Equation (2), of

[24] The condition $0 < a < 4$ is always satisfied in our case since $a = 2\ (1 - r_1)$ where r_1 is a correlation coefficient between the adjacent terms of the series (between y_i and y_{i+1}). See Appendix, Section 4.

course, is true only for a single sinusoid and cannot be applied to a sum of sinusoids.

To find an instance more apt to illustrate the tendency in question, let us consider the differences of various orders for Model III, the series best adapted for such purposes. If a curve is represented by a sum of sinusoids, then the differences of all orders are sums of sinusoids having waves of the same periods as the curve. The higher the order of the difference, the more pronounced are the shorter periods, since the differencing process weights the shorter periods as against the longer ones. Thus, by applying the formulas of the Appendix, Section 1, we find

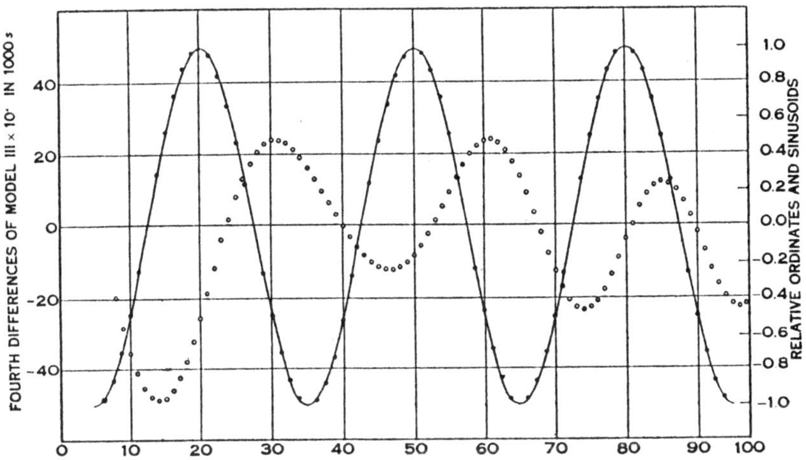

FIGURE 13.—oooo The fourth differences of Model III $\times 10^4$. —·—·— Their relative ordinates, together with the sinusoid.

that the coefficients of correlation, $r_1^{(2,0)}$, for Model III itself, and for its first, second, third, and fourth differences, are -0.5781, -0.7756, -0.8462, -0.8830, and -0.9057, respectively. The following considerations will show us to what extent the simple sinusoidal regime is maintained at least over small portions of the last series.

Let us determine the highest (or lowest) point of a typical wave (A or B, respectively, in Figure 14) as the apex of a second-degree parabola which passes through the three highest (or the three lowest) points of the wave. Then, let us draw a horizontal line bisecting the distance between the highest and lowest points of the wave. Further, let us denote the point where this horizontal line crosses the straight line joining the two points between which the horizontal line passes as C. This point divides AB into two quarter-waves, AC and BC. For each of these, let us make the following construction: Dividing the base line DC (D having the same abscissa as A) into six equal parts, we obtain seven points corresponding to 0°, 15°, 30°, 45°, 60°, 75°, and 90°. At the five central points construct perpendiculars and extend them to the parabola fitted to the three empirical points (interpolated according to Newton's formula). These perpendiculars are the ordinates of an empirical half-wave and, if we divide through by the maximum ordinate AD, we obtain the relative ordinates y_{15}, y_{30}, y_{45}, y_{60}, and y_{75}. If our wave is a sinusoid, these relative ordinates will equal the sines of 15°, 30°, 45°, 60°, and 75°, respectively. The empirical relative ordinates for the 12 quarter-waves of $\Delta^4{}_{v_{III}}$ are shown by black dots around the regular sinusoid of Figure 13, while the relative ordinates of the first, second, etc., quarters of every empirical wave are shown on the first,

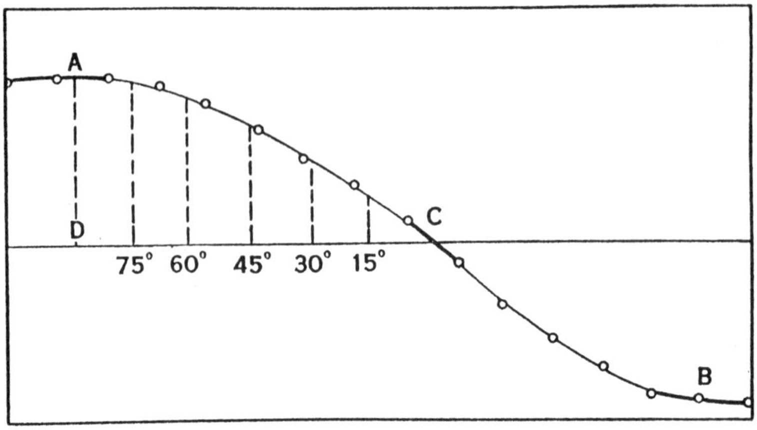

FIGURE 14.—A Scheme for Calculation of the Relative Ordinates.

second, etc., quarters of the sinusoid. The points can hardly be distinguished from the curve. Thus the tendency to a sinusoidal form is shown rather distinctly. If we compute the arithmetic averages of the relative ordinates having the same abscissa (e.g., $\bar{y}_{15} = 1/12(y_{15}^{(1)} + y_{15}^{(2)} + \cdots + y_{15}^{(12)})$ and compare them with the corresponding sines (e.g., sin 15°), we shall see that the deviations are less than ½ in the second decimal place (see Table 4). The agreement is, therefore, close enough

TABLE 4

Phase-angle (α)	15°	30°	45°	60°	75°
$\bar{y}_\alpha$	0.258	0.496	0.703	0.863	0.964
Sin α	0.259	0.500	0.707	0.866	0.966
Deviations	−0.001	−0.004	−0.004	−0.003	−0.002

to be considered as the clear manifestation of the tendency toward a sinusoidal form, and thus displays once more the ability of chance waves to simulate regular harmonic oscillations.

VI. ON THE PSEUDO-PERIODIC CHARACTER OF THE EMPIRICAL CORRELATIONAL FUNCTION[25]

As a further illustration of the sinusoidal tendency, I shall consider here a chance series satisfying, to a rather high degree of approximation, the equation

$$\Delta^4 z_i - p\Delta^2 z_{i+1} - q z_{i+2} = 0, \tag{3}$$

corresponding, if treated as a precise one, to the sum of two sinusoids.

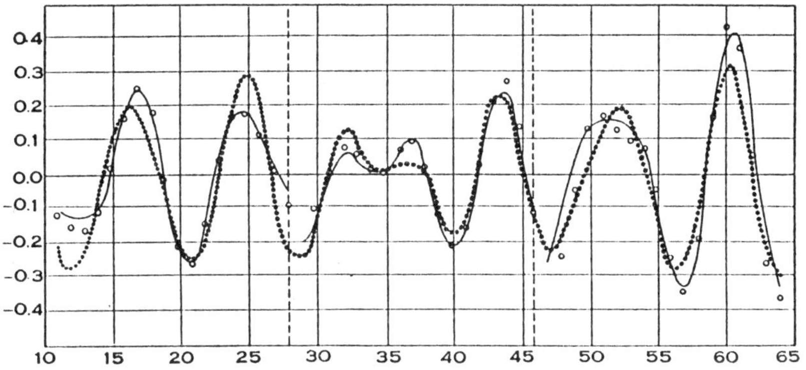

FIGURE 15.— o o o o The reduced empirical correlation function of Model IVc. ——— Sum of two sinusoids, separately for each of three intervals. ..... Sum of three sinusoids.

Let us denote the series in question by the symbols

$$\rho'_{11}, \rho'_{12}, \cdots, \rho'_{64},$$

the values of ρ'_t (see Figure 15) being given by the equation

$$\rho'_t = \sqrt{\frac{128 - t}{128}}\,\rho_t, \tag{4}$$

where ρ_t is the empirical correlation coefficient between the terms (y_i, y_{i+t}) of the series made up by 128 items of Model IVc. As the values of ρ_t have been calculated from very different numbers of items varying from 117 (that is, $128-11$) to 64 (that is, $128-64$), the reduction

[25] Eugen Slutzky, "On the Standard Error of the Correlation Coefficient in the Case of Homogenous Coherent Chance Series" (in Russian, with English summary). Transactions of the Conjuncture Institute, Vol. 2, 1929, pp. 94–98, 154.

by (4) has been thought useful in order to bring the respective standard deviations to approximate equality.

Before going further, the following remarks will be made. Let y_0, y_1, $\cdots$ be a stationary chance series. This implies that the mathematical expectation, $E(y_i)$, is a constant, that the standard deviation, σ, is a constant, and that the correlation coefficient, r_t, between y_i and y_{i+t}, is a function of t only. Then, putting, without loss of generality, $E(y_i)=0$, we shall have $\sigma^2=E(y_i^2)$ and $r_t=E(y_iy_{i+t})/\sigma^2$. This being the *theoretical* correlation coefficient, let us suppose that $r_t=0$ if $t>\omega$. Then the correlation coefficient, r'_u, between the empirical correlation coefficients, ρ_t and ρ_{t+u}, will be given by the equation

$$r'_u = r(\rho_t, \rho_{t+u}) = \frac{\sum_{-\omega}^{\omega} r_t r_{t+u}}{\sum_{-\omega}^{\omega} r_t^2}, \tag{5}$$

this formula being approximately correct if it be supposed (1) that ρ_t and ρ_{t+u} are calculated from the same number of values, n; (2) that n is sufficiently large; and (3) that $t>2\omega$, $n-t>\omega$, and $u>0$.[26]

Let us suppose now that the values of r'_u calculated from (5) may be held to be approximately true for the series of the reduced correlation coefficients (ρ'_{11}, ρ'_{12}, $\cdots$ ρ'_{64}) defined above. Then we have to consider the following problem:

The series given (ρ'_t) being a chance series, there can exist no periodicity in the strict sense of the word. Its cyclical character being, however, obvious (see Figure 15), it may be asked whether the law of its composition from simple harmonics cannot be detected when its correlational function is known.

Let us try to solve this problem to the first approximation by supposing that our series can be duly approximated by the sum of two sinusoids with constant periods and varying amplitudes and phases. To this end, let us find the parameters of the regression equation which can be written in the form

$$\Delta^4\rho'_u = p\Delta^2\rho'_{u+1} + q\rho'_{u+2} + \epsilon, \tag{6}$$

ϵ being the "error," and p and q being determined by the method of least squares. If we denote the correlation coefficients between the pairs of values

$$(\Delta^4\rho'_u, \Delta^2\rho'_{u+1}), (\Delta^4\rho'_u, \rho'_{u+2}), (\Delta^2\rho'_{u+1}, \rho'_{u+2}),$$

by r_{12}, r_{13}, r_{23} respectively, then, using the formulae (43)–(44) (Appendix, Section 1), we obtain

[26] Cf. Slutzky, *loc. cit.* in note 25, pp. 91–94.

$$(7) \qquad r_{12} = \frac{\Delta^6 r'_{-3}}{\sqrt{\Delta^8 r'_{-4}\Delta^4 r'_{-2}}}\,; \quad r_{13} = \frac{\Delta^4 r'_{-2}}{\sqrt{\Delta^8 r'_{-4}}}\,; \quad r_{23} = \frac{\Delta^2 r'_{-1}}{\sqrt{\Delta^4 r'_{-2}}},$$

where r'_{-u} $(=r'_u)$ is the correlation coefficient defined by the equation (5). These values are

$$r'_{-4} = r'_4 = -\ 0.761{,}874{,}30,$$
$$r'_{-3} = r'_3 = -\ 0.618{,}465{,}96,$$
$$r'_{-2} = r'_2 = -\ 0.013{,}793{,}10,$$
$$r'_{-1} = r'_1 = -\ 0.689{,}655{,}17,$$

whence, using (7),

$$r_{12} = 0.945{,}847, \quad r_{13} = 0.760{,}844, \quad r_{23} = -\ 0.919{,}999.$$

Then, by the well-known formula of linear regression, we obtain

$$p = -\ 1.419{,}386, \quad q = -\ 0.425{,}828,$$

the multiple correlation coefficient, between $\Delta^4\rho_u$ on the one hand, and $\Delta^2\rho_{u+1}$ and ρ_{u+2} on the other, being $r_{1.23}=0.986$. The correlation is thus very high and so it is quite reasonable to omit ϵ in (6) and to treat the resulting approximate equation according to the rules of the calculus of finite differences. We find thus that the solution of this equation is the sum of two sinusoids with the periods

$$L_1 = 9.40, \quad L_2 = 6.04.$$

Let us, then, divide our series $(\rho'_{11}, \rho'_{12}, \cdots \rho'_{64})$ into three parts, of 18 items each, and let us find, for each part separately, two sinusoids with the periods $L_1=9, L_2=6$, these being the whole numbers nearest to the theoretical values just obtained. We find the results given in Table 5.

TABLE 5

	Part I		Part II		Part III	
	$L_1=9$	$L_2=6$	$L_1=9$	$L_2=6$	$L_1=9$	$L_2=6$
Amplitude	0.19790	0.07820	0.12614	0.12527	0.29123	0.13340
Phase	231°37′	52°39′	218°2′	295°2′	270°52′	2°33′

A glance at Fig. 15 shows that the theoretical curves fit the empirical points very satisfactorily and it seems fairly certain that, if we had included one or two sinusoids more, we could have obtained a quite satisfactory fit, even if treating our empirical series as a whole. This can be proved by the fact that the sum of three sinusoids

$$\begin{aligned} z = {} & 0.1893 \sin\left[(360°/8.80)t - 47°3'\right] \\ & + 0.1000 \sin\left[(360°/7.14)t + 168°24'\right] \\ & + 0.0794 \sin\left[(360°/5.87)t - 76°3'\right], \end{aligned}$$

though found by rather a rough graphical estimate, fits our empirical curve in a fairly satisfactory manner.[27]

VII. THE LAW OF THE SINUSOIDAL LIMIT

Many tendencies dealt with rather empirically in the preceding discussion will be more clearly understood, and their significance more fully appreciated, if we take into consideration the following propositions.[28]

THEOREM A: (*The Law of the Sinusoidal Limit*)

Let $y_1, y_2, \cdots$ *be a chance series fulfilling the conditions,*

$$E(y_i) = 0, \quad E(y_i^2) = \sigma^2 = f(n),$$

$$\frac{E(y_i y_{i+t})}{E(y_i^2)} = r_t = \phi(t, n),$$

where n is a parameter specifying the series as a whole, and $f(n)$ *and* $\phi(t, n)$ *are independent of i. If, furthermore, the correlation coefficient,* r_1, *between* y_i *and* y_{i+1}, *satisfies the condition*

$$|r_1| \leqq c < 1, \qquad (n \to \infty),$$

and the correlation coefficient between $\Delta^2 y_i$ *and* y_{i+1}, *that is,* ρ_1, *is such that*

$$\lim \rho_1 = -1, \qquad (n \to \infty),$$

then (1) ϵ *and* η *being taken arbitrarily small and s arbitrarily large, there will exist a number,* n_0, *such that for every* $n > n_0$, *the probability, that the absolute values of the deviations of* $y_i, y_{i+1}, \cdots y_{i+s}$ *from a certain sinusoid will not exceed* $\epsilon\sigma$, *will be* $>1-\eta$; *(2) the period of this sinusoid will be determined by the equation*

$$\cos(2\pi/L) = r_1;$$

(3) the number of the periods in the interval $(i, i+s)$ *will be arbitrarily large provided s and n be taken large enough.*

This proposition (for its proof see Appendix, Section 4) would be of no interest could we not give at least a single instance of a chance series satisfying the conditions of Theorem *A*. This is done by

[27] The above illustration seems to throw some light on the difficulties connected with the idea of a correlation periodogram. Cf. Dinsmore Alter, "A Group or Correlation Periodogram," etc., *Monthly Weather Review*, Vol. 55, No. 6, June, 1927, pp. 263–266; Sir Gilbert Walker, "On Periodicity in Series of Related Terms," *Proc. Royal Soc.*, Ser. A, Vol. 131, No. A 818, 1931, pp. 518–532.

[28] E. Slutsky, "Sur un théorème limite relatif aux séries des quantités éventuelles," *Comptes Rendus*, Paris, t. 185, seance du 4 Juli, 1927, p. 169.

THEOREM B: Let $x_1, x_2, \cdots$ be a random series fulfilling the conditions

$$E(x_i) = 0,\ E(x_i^2) = \sigma_x^2 = \text{const.},\ E(x_i x_j) = 0, \qquad (i \neq j).$$

Now, if we put

$$x_i^{(1)} = x_i + x_{i-1},\ x_i^{(2)} = x_i^{(1)} + x_{i-1}^{(1)},\ \cdots,$$

$$x_i^{(n)} = x_i^{(n-1)} + x_{i-1}^{(n-1)},$$

and

$$y_i = \Delta^m x_i^{(n)},$$

then the series $y_1, y_2, \cdots$ will tend to obey the law of the sinusoidal limit, provided m and n be increasing indefinitely and m/n = constant (for the proof see Appendix, Section 4).

Both propositions can be generalized to the case of a chance series practically coinciding, not with one sinusoid, but with the sum of a certain number of sinusoids.[29] In every case, however, the practical coincidence (and it is a very essential character of the series under consideration) does not extend itself to the series as a whole, the respective sinusoids of closest fit being different for different partial series. This is plainly evident for the chance series of Theorem B, for, s being arbitrarily large and n and m being sufficiently large, the values y_i and y_{i+t} will be wholly independent of each other as soon as $t > m + n + 1$, whence it follows that the phases and the amplitudes of the sinusoids practically coincident with the partial series, $y_i, y_{i+1}, \cdots y_{i+s}$, and $y_{i+t+s}, y_{i+t+s+1}, \cdots y_{i+t+2s}$, respectively, will also be independent of each other provided $t > m + n + 1$.

The following considerations will show us the same problem from a somewhat different standpoint. Let us suppose a certain mechanism is being subjected to damped vibrations of a periodic character and to casual disturbances accumulating energy just sufficient to counterbalance the damping.[30] Then the movement of the system could be regarded as consisting of the two parts: of the vibrations determined by the initial conditions at some given moment, and of the vibrations generated by the disturbances that have occurred since. As soon as the first part has been nearly extinguished by the damping process after due lapse of time, the actual vibrations will be reduced practically to the second part, that is, to the accumulated consequences of the chance

[29] V. Romanovsky, "Sur la loi sinusoidale limite," *Rend. d. Circ. mat. di Palermo*, Vol. 56, Fasc. 1, 1932, pp. 82–111; V. Romanovsky, "Sur une generalisation de la loi sinusoidal limite," *Rend d. Circ. mat. di Palermo*, Vol. 57, Fasc. 1, pp. 130–136; cf. Sir Gilbert Walker, *op. cit.*, in note 27.

[30] Cf. G. Udney Yule, "On a Method of Investigating Periodicities in Disturbed Series with Special Reference to Wolfer's Sunspot Numbers," *Phil. Trans. Roy. Soc. of London*, Ser. A. Vol. 226, 1927, pp. 267–298.

causes. The latter, after a due time, being again reduced to a value not different practically from zero, the vibrations will consist of the disturbances accumulated during the second interval of time and so on. It is evident that the vibrations ultimately will have the character of a chance function, the described process being a particular instance of the summation of random causes. Should the disturbances be small enough, there would exist an arbitrarily large, but finite, number, L_0, such that the resulting process would be practically coincident, in every interval of the length, $L \leqq L_0$, with a certain periodic (or nearly periodic) function, obeying thus the law of the sinusoidal limit.

Analogous considerations may be applied to the motion of planetary, or star systems, the innumerable cosmic influences being considered as casual disturbances. The paths of the planets, if regarded during billions of years, should be considered, therefore, as chance functions, but if we do not wish to go beyond thousands of years their approximate representation must be taken as not casual.

The chance functions of the type just considered appearing on the one end of the scale, and the random functions on the other, there evidently must exist all possible intermediate gradations between these extremes. The ability of the coherent chance series to simulate the periodic, or the nearly periodic, functions, seems thus to be definitely demonstrated.

It remains for us to try to clear up theoretically the remarkable property of some specimens of chance series, which do not belong to the extreme classes of their type, of being approximately representable by a small number of sinusoids, over a shorter or longer interval.

It is well known that every empirical series consisting of a finite number of terms ($N=2n$ or $2n+1$) can be represented precisely by a finite Fourier series, that is by the sum of a finite number (n) of sinusoids. Further, it is plainly evident, the series under consideration being chance series and the coefficients of the Fourier expansion,

$$y_t = A_0 + \sum_1^n A_k \cos(2\pi kt/N) + \sum_1^n B_k \sin(2\pi kt/N),$$

that is, the values $A_0, A_1, \cdots A_n$, and $B_0, B_1, \cdots B_n$, being linear functions of $y_1, y_2, \cdots y_n$, that the variables A_k and B_k will also be chance variables. Their mathematical expectations, standard deviations, and the correlation coefficients between them can be easily obtained.[31] Denoting by R_k^2 the intensity of the kth harmonic, that is,

[31] E. Slutsky, "Alcuni applicazioni di coefficienti di Fourier al analizo di sequenze eventuali coherenti stazionarii," *Giorn. d. Istituto Italiano degli Attuari*, Vol. 5, No. 4, 1934; see also E. Slutsky, "Sur l'extension de la theorie de periodogrammes aux suites des quantités dependentes." *Compte Rendus*, t. 189, seance du 4 novembre, 1929, p. 722.

the square of its amplitude, we shall have

$$R_k^2 = A_k^2 + B_k^2,$$

and

$$(8)\quad \begin{aligned} E(R_k^2) &= (4\sigma_y^2/N)\left[1 + 2\sum_1^{N-1} r_t \cos(2\pi kt/N)\right] \\ &\quad - (8\sigma_y^2/N^2)\sum_1^{N-1} tr_t \cos(2\pi kt/N), \end{aligned}$$

whence, for the case of a random series, we obtain at once the formula of Schuster,

$$(9)\quad E(R_k^2) = 4\sigma_y^2/N,$$

the probability distribution being the same in both cases,

$$(10)\quad P(R_k^2 > Z^2) = \exp\left[-Z^2/E(R_k^2)\right].$$

Let us suppose the m intensities happening to have the largest values in some given case are those with the indices: $\alpha, \beta, \cdots \mu$ and let

$$\tfrac{1}{2}(R_\alpha^2 + R_\beta^2 + \cdots + R_\mu^2) = ps^2,$$

s^2 being the square of the empirical standard deviation and p the coefficient measuring the degree of approximation reached in the given case by means of m harmonics. By taking account of (8), (9), and (10), we see at once that, in the case of a random series, the indices $\alpha, \beta, \cdots \mu$ are able to assume any values with equal probability but that in the case of a coherent series those having the largest values of $E(R_k^2)$ will be the most probable. As half of the sum of the intensities is equal to the square of the empirical standard deviation (Parceval's theorem), it is but natural that the coherent chance series, in many cases at least, may be represented—the degree of approximation being the same—by a smaller number of harmonics than the random series.

It can be proved further (under suppositions of a not very restrictive character) that the correlation coefficients between the intensities belonging to the same interval, as well as between those belonging to the adjacent intervals, are quantities of the order $1/N^2$, and that the standard deviation of the intensity, σ_{R^2}, tends to be equal to its probable value, $E(R_k^2)$. Whence it is evident that the indices of the harmonics which happen to be the most suited for the representation of the series in a certain interval must also be practically independent of the indices of the "best" harmonics in adjacent intervals, the length of these intervals being sufficiently large. The larger the probable value of the intensity the larger also must be the extent of its casual variation. These are properties quite consistent with a considerable degree of regularity—as well as with the abrupt changes of the "regimes" determined by studying the empirical series dealt with in the foregoing pages.

Appendix

MATHEMATICAL NOTES OF THE THEORY OF RANDOM WAVES

1. Let $x_0, x_1, \cdots x_i, \cdots$ be a random series, that is, a series of chance values independent of each other. Let this be our basic series and let it be considered as a model of incoherent series of random causes. Denoting by the symbol E the mathematical expectation, let us suppose that

$$E(x_i) = 0,\ E(x_i^2) = \sigma_x^2 = \text{const.};\ E(x_i x_j) = 0, \qquad (i \neq j). \tag{1}$$

From the basic incoherent series of causes let us construct a coherent series of "consequences," $\cdots y_{i-2}, y_{i-1}, y_i, \cdots$, by the scheme

$$y_i = \sum_{k=0}^{n-1} A_k x_{i-k}, \tag{2}$$

where the quantities A_k are constants.[32] Then, by using (1) and (2), it can easily be shown that

$$E(y_i) = 0, \tag{3}$$

$$E(y_i^2) = \sigma_y^2 = \sigma_x^2 \sum_{k=0}^{n-1} A_k^2, \tag{4}$$

$$E(y_i y_{i+t}) = \sigma_x^2 \sum_{k=0}^{(n-1)-t} A_k A_{k+t}. \tag{5}$$

Since equations (4) and (5) do not depend on i, the coefficient of correlation between y_i and y_{i-t}, that is, r_t, is also independent of i, and we have

$$r_t = \frac{\sum_{k=0}^{(n-1)-t} A_k A_{k+t}}{\sum_{k=0}^{n-1} A_k^2}, \tag{6}$$

from which it immediately follows that

$$r_0 = 1;\ r_t = r_{-t};\ r_t = 0,\ (t \geqq n). \tag{7}$$

The process of moving summation can be repeated. As before, let us take $\cdots x_{i-2}, x_{i-1}, x_i, \cdots$ as the basic series underlying the conditions

[32] Cf. Prof. Birger Meidell's valuable investigation of the analogous cumulative processes in his paper, "Über periodische und angenäherte Beharrungszustände," *Skandinavisk Aktuarietidskrift*, 1926, p. 172.

(1). Then on performing an s-fold moving summation we obtain the following successive consequence series:

$$(8)\qquad \begin{aligned} x_i^{(1)} &= \sum_{k=0}^{n-1} \alpha_k^{(1)} x_{i-k}; \quad x_i^{(2)} = \sum_{k=0}^{n-1} \alpha_k^{(2)} x_{i-k}^{(1)}; \cdots \\ x_i^{(s)} &= \sum_{k=0}^{n-1} \alpha_k^{(s)} x_{i-k}^{(s-1)}. \end{aligned}$$

After the s-fold summation we have an expression of type (2) with $y_i = x_i^{(s)}$. Hence, if we take $n=2$ and $\alpha_k^{(j)}=1$, it can easily be shown that

$$(9)\qquad y_i = x_i^{(s)} = \sum_{k=0}^{s} C_k^s x_{i-k}.$$

If we put

$$(10)\qquad \phi(t) = \frac{1}{\sqrt{2\pi}} \exp\left(-\tfrac{1}{2}t^2\right),$$

we can, by the use of well-known transformations, obtain the approximate expression (which we write for an *even* s)

$$(11)\qquad y_i = D \sum_{k=0}^{s} x_{i-k}\phi\left(\frac{k - s/2}{\sqrt{s/4}}\right),$$

D being a coefficient, the value of which need not concern us here.

It is very remarkable that a similar result will always be obtained for s sufficiently great, whatever be the weights used, provided it is supposed (1) that the weights are not negative, (2) that they remain constant at every given stage of the process, and (3) that the summation does not tend to degenerate into a mere repetition of the same values, which would be the case should all $\alpha_k^{(s)}$ but one tend to approach 0; (the sum of the weights is supposed, without loss of generality, to be constant).

To prove this, let us remark first that the result of the s-fold summation given by (8) can evidently be obtained by a similar s-fold summation with the weights

$$p_0^{(j)}, p_1^{(j)}, \cdots, p_{n-1}^{(j)}, \qquad (j = 1, 2, \cdots, s),$$

where

$$p_k^{(j)} = \frac{\alpha_k^{(j)}}{m_j}, \qquad m_j = \sum_{k=0}^{n-1} \alpha_k^{(j)},$$

if we multiply the resulting weights by the proportionality factor $m_1 \cdot m_2 \cdot \cdots \cdot m_s$.

Now to prove our proposition we shall use the following analogy (kindly suggested to the author by Prof. A. Khinchin).

Let $z_1, z_2, \cdots z_s$ be a set of random variables whose possible values are $0, 1, 2, \cdots, n-1$, the respective probabilities being $p_0^{(j)}, p_1^{(j)}, \cdots p_{n-1}^{(j)}, (j=1, 2, \cdots s)$. Then it is easy to see that the probability of the equation

$$k = z_1 + z_2 + \cdots + z_s \tag{12}$$

must be equal to the coefficient of x^k in the expansion of

$$\prod_{j=1}^{s} (p_0^{(j)} + p_1^{(j)}x + p_2^{(j)}x^2 + \cdots + p_{n-1}^{(j)}x^{n-1}). \tag{13}$$

On the other hand, it can be proved that the same coefficient, multiplied by $m_1 \cdot m_2 \cdot \cdots \cdot m_s$, will be equal to the coefficient A_k in the equation (2) obtained by an s-fold summation according to the scheme (8) with the weights

$$m_j p_0^{(j)}, m_j p_1^{(j)}, \cdots, m_j p_{n-1}^{(j)}, \qquad (j = 1, 2, \cdots, s).$$

This is easily seen for $s=2$ and the result can be generalized by mathematical induction from s to $s+1$.

This analogy leads us to the following considerations. Let us put

$$\left\{\begin{aligned} a_j &= E(z_j) = \sum_{k=0}^{n-1} kp_k^{(j)}, \\ b_j &= E[(z_j - a_j)^2] = \sum_{k=0}^{n-1} (k - a_j)^2 p_k^{(j)}, \\ c_j &= E[|z_j - a_j|^g] = \sum_{k=0}^{n-1} |k - a_j|^g p_k^{(j)}, \qquad (g > 2). \end{aligned}\right. \tag{14}$$

It is evident that $b_j=0$ only if every $(k-a_j)^2p_k^{(j)}=0$ for $k=0, 1, 2, \cdots (n-1)$, and that this is possible only when every $p_k^{(j)}$ but one is equal to zero, the exceptional p being 1, in which case the values $x_k^{(j)}$ are merely repetitions of the values $x_k^{(j-1)}$.

This case being excluded, we shall have, on the average at least,

$$(1/s)\sum_1^s b_i > \epsilon > 0; \tag{15}$$

whence

$$\frac{\left[\sum_1^s c_i\right]^2}{\left[\sum_1^s b_i\right]^g} < \frac{\left[(1/s)\sum_1^s c_i\right]^2}{s^{g-2}\epsilon^g} \to 0. \tag{16}$$

But this is the well known Liapounoff's condition, under which the probability distribution of the sum $z_1+z_2+\cdots+z_s$, that is, the distribution of the coefficients A_k, tends to the normal law.[33]

Let us put, for instance,

$$\alpha_0^{(j)} = \alpha_1^{(j)} = \cdots = \alpha_{n-1}^{(j)} = 1, \qquad (j = 1, 2, \cdots, s).$$

Then we obtain

$$m_j = \sum_{k=0}^{n-1} \alpha_k^{(j)} = n,$$

$$m_1 m_2 \cdots m_s = n^s, \tag{17}$$

$$p_k^{(j)} = 1/n,$$

for

$$j = 1, 2, \cdots, s, \quad \text{and} \quad k = 0, 1, \cdots, n-1;$$

and

$$a_j = E(z_j) = \sum_{k=0}^{n-1} k p_k^{(j)} = (n-1)/2,$$

$$b_j = E[(z_j - a_j)^2] = (1/n)\left\{\sum_{k=0}^{n-1} k^2 - n a_j^2\right\} = (n^2-1)/12. \tag{18}$$

Whence

$$k_0 = E(k) = E\left[\sum_1^s z_j\right] = s(n-1)/2, \tag{19}$$

and

$$\sigma_k = \sqrt{s b_j} = \sqrt{s(n^2-1)/12}. \tag{20}$$

As s tends towards ∞, the value of A_k will thus approach a limit, which enables us to write, for s large but finite, the following approximate equations:[34]

[33] It is evident that, since Liapounoff's theorem is a proposition about the limit properties of certain integrals and not of the individual ordinates, the above demonstration must be interpreted also in the same sense. For many cases, however, for example, in the case of the illustration below, the additional conditions are satisfied under which the values of the variables A_k themselves are tending toward the ordinates of the Gaussian curve.

Cf. Liapounoff, "Nouvelle forme du théorème sur la limite de probabilité," *Memoires de l'Academie de science de St.-Petersbourg*, serie 8, Vol. 12, No. 5.

R. von Mises, *Vorlesungen aus dem Gebiete der Angewandten Mathematik*, Bd. I *Wahrscheinlichkeitsrechnung und ihre Anwendungen*, 1931, p. 200–212.

R. von Mises, "Generalizzazione di un teorema sulla probabilità della somma di un numero illimitato di variabili casuali," *Giornale dell'Istituto Italiano degli Attuari*, Anno 5, N4, p. 483–495.

[34] This result coincides with that given in the first edition of this memoir in 1927; it was supplied to the author by the courtesy of Prof. A. Khinchin who derived it by the application of the well-known Cauchy theorem to the evaluation of the coefficient of x^k in the expansion of

$$(1 + x + x^2 + \cdots + x^{n-1})^s.$$

I am sorry that the calculations are too long to be reproduced here.

$$(21)\qquad A_k \overset{a}{=} n^s\sqrt{6/\pi s(n^2-1)}\exp\{-6(k-k_0)^2/s(n^2-1)\}.$$

For the general case, we shall give here the following illustration Let the weights for a set of successive summations be certain random numbers. For this purpose, let us choose consecutive groups of three numbers from the first basic series (Column 2, Table I, Appendix II). For the first moving summation the weights will be $\alpha_0^{(1)}=5$, $\alpha_1^{(1)}=4$, $\alpha_2^{(1)}=7$; for the second $\alpha_0^{(2)}=3$, $\alpha_1^{(2)}=0$, $\alpha_2^{(2)}=3$, etc. Performing the substitutions indicated by formula (8) we obtain the resulting weights corresponding to A_k of formula (2), $A_k^{(1)}=\alpha_k^{(1)}$, $A_k^{(2)}$, $A_k^{(3)}$, $\cdots$ $A_k^{(10)}$. For each given s, we divide the weights by the largest $A_k^{(s)}$ to obtain the relative weights, $A'^{(s)}_k$ (see Table VIII, Appendix II, of the original paper, and Figure 5). The series of quantities $A'^{(10)}_k$ does not differ greatly from the Gaussian curve obtained by putting[35]

$$(22)\qquad B'^{(10)}_k = 1004\exp\{-\tfrac{1}{2}[(k-9.26)/2.67]^2\}.$$

2. The coefficients of correlation between the terms of a coherent series are, in many cases, easy to obtain by using formula (6). For a simple moving summation of n equally weighted items at a time, we have $A_0=A_1=\cdots=A_{n-1}=1$. It is easy to see that

$$(23)\qquad \begin{cases} r_t = (n-|t|)/n, & (|t|\leqq n)\\ r_t = 0, & (|t|\geqq n).\end{cases}$$

From formulas (4), (5), (9) and the properties of $\overset{s}{C}_k$, we find for the s-fold moving summation of two terms, that is, $(n=2)$, that

$$(24)\qquad \sigma_y^2 = \sigma_x^2[1+(\overset{s}{C}_1)^2+(\overset{s}{C}_2)^2+\cdots+(\overset{s}{C}_{s-1})^2+1] = \sigma_x^2\overset{2s}{C}_s,$$

and

$$(25)\qquad E(y_iy_{i+t}) = \sigma_x^2[\overset{s}{C}_0\overset{s}{C}_t+\overset{s}{C}_1\overset{s}{C}_{t+1}+\cdots+\overset{s}{C}_{s-t}\overset{s}{C}_s] = \sigma_x^2\overset{2s}{C}_{s-t}.$$

Hence

$$(26)\qquad r_t = \overset{2s}{C}_{s-t}/\overset{2s}{C}_s = \frac{s(s-1)\cdots(s-t+1)}{(s+1)(s+2)\cdots(s+t)}.$$

Consider another case. Let us form, from a basic series, a coherent series by the scheme:

[35] Let us pass a second degree parabola through $A_0'^{(10)}$, $A_1'^{(10)}$, $A_2'^{(10)}$; another through $A_2'^{(10)}$, $A_3'^{(10)}$, $A_4'^{(10)}$; etc. Denote the area of this figure by S, its maximum ordinate by y_0, and the abscissa bisecting the area by k_0. Then, in the Gaussian equation

$$B'^{(10)}_k = [S/\sigma\sqrt{2\pi}]\exp\{-\tfrac{1}{2}[(k-k_0)/\sigma]^2\},$$

all of the parameters are known, since

$$k_0 = 9.26,\quad y_0 = S/\sigma\sqrt{2\pi} = 1004,$$

and hence

$$\sigma = S/y_0\sqrt{2\pi} = 2.67$$

$$y_i = D\sum_{k=0}^{2k_0} x_{i-k}\phi[(k-k_0)/\sigma], \tag{27}$$

where $\phi(t)$ is given by formula (10), D is a constant, and k_0 is a number large enough so that $\phi(t)$ can be neglected for $|t| > k_0/\sigma$. Then, from (6), the coefficient of correlation is

$$r_t = \frac{\sum_{k=0}^{2k_0-t} \phi[(k-k_0)/\sigma]\phi[(k-k_0+t)/\sigma]}{\sum_{k=0}^{2k_0} \{\phi[(k-k_0)/\sigma]\}^2}. \tag{28}$$

If σ is sufficiently large we can substitute integrals for the summations in (28). Inserting $z = k - k_0$, we then obtain the approximation formula

$$r_t = \frac{\int_{-\infty}^{+\infty} \exp\left[-\tfrac{1}{2}\frac{z^2+(z+t)^2}{\sigma^2}\right]dz}{\int_{-\infty}^{+\infty} \exp\left[-\frac{z^2}{\sigma^2}\right]dz} \tag{29}$$

$$= \exp(-t^2/4\sigma^2) = \frac{\phi(t/\sigma\sqrt{2})}{\phi(0)}.$$

Inasmuch as Model III is formed by the scheme of formula (27), with $D = 10^4$, $k_0 = 48$, and $\sigma = 10$, we can calculate the correlation function by formula (29). The values for $[\phi(t/\sqrt{200})]/\phi(0)$, $(t = 0, 1, 2, \cdots)$, were calculated with the aid of Sheppard's tables.[36] The symbol $R_{t(III)}$, instead of $r_{t(III)}$, indicates that an approximate, and not an exact, formula was used in the calculation.

Model IVa was obtained by a 12-fold moving summation of two items; therefore, its correlation function, $r_{t(IVa)}$, is obtained by using formula (26), which, if we consider (11), gives $R_{t(IVa)} = \phi(t/\sqrt{6})/\phi(0)$. The discrepancies between the two results are rather small. The correspondence between $r_{t(IVb)}$ and $R_{t(IVb)}$ is somewhat less, as is also that between $r_{t(IVc)}$ and $R_{t(IVc)}$. Both sets were computed by formula (45) (see next paragraph), but for the calculation of $r_{t(IVb)}$ and $r_{t(IVc)}$ the actual values of $r_{t(IVa)}$ were used as the base, while for $R_{t(IVb)}$ and $R_{t(IVc)}$ the approximate values of $R_{t(IVa)}$, obtained by the Gaussian formula, were used. Even here the discrepancies are not very great when regarded from the same point of view (see Figure 6).

[36] *Tables for Statisticians and Biometricians*, ed. by K. Pearson, Cambridge, 1914, Table II.

Finally, for Model II, corresponding to the scheme

$$(30) \qquad y_i = x_i^{(2)} = \sum_{k=0}^{18} A_k^{(2)} x_{i+k} + 50,$$

$$(A_k^{(2)} = 1, 2, \cdots, 9, 10, 9, \cdots, 2, 1),$$

the coefficients of correlation can be obtained directly from formula (6). It is worth noting that, even in this case, a good approximation, $R_{t(II)}$, can be obtained by the use of the Gaussian curve, the equation being

$$(31) \qquad R_{t(II)} = \exp\left[-\tfrac{1}{2}(t/5.954)^2\right],$$

where $\sigma = 5.954$ was obtained by equating the areas of the Gaussian curve and of the empirical curve, and the computations were carried through with the help of Simpson's rule (see Figure 6).

A few more words may be said about the correlational function for the weights, $A'_k{}^{(10)}$, of our example of the crossing of random weights (see Section 2 of the text, Appendix, Section 1, and Figure 6). The exact values of the coefficients of correlation (r_t) were found by formula (6), while approximate values (R_t) were obtained from the equation

$$(32) \qquad R_t = \exp\left[-\tfrac{1}{2}(t/3.727)^2\right],$$

which was obtained in the same manner as was equation (31). Both the exact and approximate values are given in Table 1 (see also Figure 6). Also, let us note that, from the equation of the Gaussian curve which approximates the weights, $A'_k{}^{(10)}$ (see formula (22) above), it is possible to find an approximate expression for the coefficients of correlation by using formula (29). An expression analogous to (32) would be obtained, but instead of $\sigma = 3.727$, we would have $\sigma = 3.776$. The correlation coefficients are only slightly less accurate than those found from formula (32), the deviations are all of one sign, and none is greater than 0.009.

Let us make one more observation. If a chance variable $y_i = u_i + v_i$, where u_i is a coherent series and v_i is a random series, it is easy to show that

$$(33) \qquad E(y_i y_{i+t}) = E(u_i u_{i+t}),$$

$$(34) \qquad (Ey_i^2) = \sigma_u^2 + \sigma_v^2,$$

$$(35) \qquad r_{y_i, y_{i+t}} = \frac{r_{u_i, u_{i+t}}}{1 + (\sigma_v^2/\sigma_u^2)},$$

where $E(u_i)$ and $E(v_i)$ are taken equal to zero.

If $r_{u_i, u_{i+t}}$ lies along the Gaussian curve, then $r_{y_i, y_{i+t}}$ will lie along a similar curve with ordinates proportionally reduced, except that r_0 will, as formerly, equal unity; the *chapeau de gendarme* has taken on the spike of the *budenovka* (a Soviet military cap). It is to be expected that this figure and the analogous figures for the correlation function of the differences (formula (45) of the following paragraph) will be encountered in the investigation of empirical series.[37]

3. Let us now investigate the differences of various orders of the series y_i, i.e., $\Delta^\alpha y_i$, $\Delta^\beta y_i$, and their coefficients of correlation.[38] As before, let

$$E(y_i) = 0;\ E(y_i^2) = \sigma_y^2 = \text{constant};\ E(y_i y_{i+t})/\sigma_y^2 = r_t, \tag{36}$$

where r_t is supposed to be independent of i. Let us introduce the notation

$$r_t^{(\alpha,\beta)} = r_{\Delta^\alpha y_i \Delta^\beta y_{i+t}}, \qquad (\alpha \geqq \beta); \tag{37}$$

and, in particular,

$$r_t^{(\alpha,\alpha)} = r_{\Delta^\alpha y_i \Delta^\alpha y_{i+t}} \qquad r_t^{(\alpha,0)} = r_{\Delta^\alpha y_i, y_{i+t}}. \tag{38}$$

By using the equality

$$C_k^{2\alpha} = C_{\alpha-k}^{\alpha} C_0^{\alpha} + C_{\alpha-(k-1)}^{\alpha} C_1^{\alpha} + \cdots + C_{\alpha-1}^{\alpha} C_{k-1}^{\alpha} + C_{\alpha}^{\alpha} C_k^{\alpha}, \tag{39}$$

it can be shown that

$$\begin{aligned} \sigma_{\Delta^\alpha y_i}^2 &= E[(\Delta^\alpha y_i)^2] = E[(C_\alpha^\alpha y_{i+\alpha} - C_{\alpha-1}^\alpha y_{i+\alpha-1} + C_{\alpha-2}^\alpha y_{i+\alpha-2} \\ &\quad - \cdots + (-1)^\alpha C_0^\alpha y_i)^2] = (-1)^\alpha \Delta^{2\alpha} r_{-\alpha} \sigma_y^2. \end{aligned} \tag{40}$$

From (40), by using the equality,

$$C_k^{\alpha+\beta} = C_{\alpha-k}^{\alpha} C_0^{\beta} + C_{\alpha-k+1}^{\alpha} C_1^{\beta} + \cdots + C_{\alpha-1}^{\alpha} C_{k-1}^{\beta} + C_k^{\beta}, \tag{41}$$

we obtain

$$E[\Delta^\alpha y_i \Delta^\beta y_{i+t}] = (-)^\alpha \Delta^{\alpha+\beta} r_{t-\alpha} \sigma_y^2, \qquad (\alpha \geqq \beta), \tag{42}$$

and from this we have

$$r_t^{(\alpha,\beta)} = \frac{(-1)^\alpha \Delta^{\alpha+\beta} r_{t-\alpha}}{\sqrt{(-1)^{\alpha+\beta} \Delta^{2\alpha} r_{-\alpha} \Delta^{2\beta} r_{-\beta}}}. \tag{43}$$

In the same manner we obtain

$$r_t^{(\alpha,0)} = \frac{(-1)^\alpha \Delta^\alpha r_{t-\alpha}}{\sqrt{(-1)^\alpha \Delta^{2\alpha} r_{-\alpha}}}, \tag{44}$$

37 Cf. Figure 19 of Yule, "Why Do We Sometimes Get Nonsense-Correlations · · · ," *loc. cit.*, p. 43.

38 Cf. O. Anderson, "Über ein neues Verfahren bei Anwendung der 'Variate-Difference' Methode," *Biometrika*, Vol. 15, 1923, pp. 142 ff.

and, as a special case of formula (43), we have

$$r_t^{(\alpha,\alpha)} = \frac{\Delta^{2\alpha} r_{t-\alpha}}{\Delta^{2\alpha} r_{-\alpha}}. \tag{45}$$

By this formula and by (26) the correlation coefficients for Models IV*b* and IV*c* have been computed.

4. Let us now prove Theorem A (see Section VII above). The regression coefficient of $\Delta^2 y_i$ on y_{i+1} being

$$E(\Delta^2 y_i \cdot y_{i+1})/\sigma_y^2 = -2(1 - r_1),$$

we obtain the approximate equation

$$\Delta^2 y_i \overset{a}{=} -2(1 - r_1) y_{i+1}.$$

Whence

$$y_{i+2} \overset{a}{=} 2 r_1 y_{i+1} - y_i, \tag{46}$$

the errors of both equations being evidently identical. If we denote this error by α_2 and put $\beta_2 = \alpha_2/\sigma_y$, we may apply the well-known formula of correlation theory and thus obtain

$$E(\beta_2^2) = E(\Delta^2 y_i)(1 - \rho_1^2)/\sigma_y^2 = (1 - \rho_1^2)(6 - 8r_1 + 2r_2). \tag{47}$$

Now, under the suppositions of Theorem A,

$$\lim_{n \to \infty} \beta_2^2 = 0;$$

whence, applying Tchebycheff's theorem, we see that β_2 has the stochastical limit $E(\beta_2) = 0$, $(n \to \infty)$; that is, ϵ and η being arbitrarily small, the probability

$$P\{ |\beta_2| > \epsilon \} < \eta,$$

provided n is sufficiently large.

On the other hand, if we put

$$y_{i+2} = 2r_1 y_{i+1} - y_i + \alpha_2,$$
$$y_{i+3} = 2r_1 y_{i+2} - y_{i+1} + \alpha_3,$$
$$\cdots\cdots\cdots\cdots$$
$$y_{i+s} = 2r_1 y_{i+s-1} - y_{i+s-2} + \alpha_s;$$

and if we insert y_{i+2} in the second equation of this system, y_{i+3} in the third, and so on, we obtain, after reduction,

$$y_{i+s} = C_1 y_{i+1} + C_2 y_i + \lambda_s \sigma_y, \tag{48}$$

where

(49) $$\lambda_s = a_0\beta_s + a_1\beta_{s-1} + \cdots + a_{s-2}\beta_2,$$

the values $a_0, a_1, \cdots a_{s+2}$, being determined by the conditions

(50) $$\begin{cases} a_0 = 1, \quad a_1 = 2r_1, \\ a_{k+2} = 2r_1 a_{k+1} - a_k. \end{cases}$$

This equation is identical with

(51) $$y_{i+2} = 2r_1 y_{i+1} - y_i,$$

that is, with (46) considered as a precise equation. The solution of (51) or (50) can be obtained easily. We find

(52) $$y_t = A \cos (2\pi t/L) + B \sin (2\pi t/L),$$

and

(53) $$a_k = C \cos (2\pi k/L) + D \sin (2\pi k/L),$$

where we have put

(54) $$\cos (2\pi/L) = r_1,$$

L being the period of the respective sinusoid. It is evident that, under the assumptions of Theorem A, ($|r_1| \leqq \lambda < 1$), we shall have

(55) $$L \leqq 2\pi/\text{arc} \cos \lambda = H = \text{constant}.$$

Two sinusoids must now be considered. The first, which will be denoted by S_1, is determined by (51), or (52), and the initial points y_i, y_{i+1}. It is evident that $C_1 y_{i+1} + C_2 y_i$ in (48) is the ordinate of S_1 which could be obtained in this form from (51) by successive substitutions. The deviation of the actual value of y_{i+s} from S_1 is $\lambda_s \sigma_y$ as given by (48) and (49), the coefficients a_k being the ordinates of the second sinusoid (S_2) determined by (50) or (53), and the initial values $a_0 = 1$, $a_1 = 2r_1$. But, if we put, in (53), $k = 0$, and then $k = 1$, we obtain

$$C = 1, \quad D = r_1/\sqrt{1 - r_1^2}.$$

Hence the amplitude of S_2 is

$$\sqrt{C^2 + D^2} = 1/\sqrt{1 - r_1^2} \leqq 1/\sqrt{1 - \lambda^2} = K = \text{constant}.$$

$$C = 1, \quad D = r_1/\sqrt{1 - r_1^2}.$$

Thus, taking into account that every a_k in (49) has an upper limit $\leqq\sqrt{C^2+D^2}$, $(n\to\infty)$ and remembering the theorems of my *Metron* memoir[39] we conclude that λ_s has the stochastical limit $=0$ and that, ϵ and η being arbitrarily small and s arbitrarily large, the probability that the conditions

$$\lambda_2 < \epsilon, \lambda_3 < \epsilon, \cdots, \lambda_s < \epsilon,$$

are simultaneously satisfied will be $>1-\eta$ provided n is sufficiently large. The formulas (54) and (55) complete the proof.

To prove theorem B, we may proceed here as follows: It is seen by (43) and (45) that the correlation coefficient between y_i and y_{i+1} is

$$r_1 = r_1^{(m,m)} = \frac{\Delta^{2m} r_{-m+1}}{\Delta^{2m} r_{-m}}, \tag{56}$$

and the correlation coefficient between $\Delta^2 y_i$ and y_{i+1} is given by

$$\rho_1 = r_1^{(m+2,m)} = \frac{(-1)^m \Delta^{2m+m} r_{-(m+1)}}{\sqrt{\Delta^{2(m+2)} r_{-(m+2)} \Delta^{2m} r_{-m}}}, \tag{57}$$

where, using (26) we must put

$$r_t = \frac{C_{n-t}^{2n}}{C_n^{2n}}.$$

On the other hand, r_{-t} being equal to r_t, it can easily be seen that

$$C_n^{2n} \Delta^{2m} r_{-m} = \sum_{k=0}^{2m} (-1)^k C_k^{2m} C_{n-m+k}^{2n} = A_{n+m}, \tag{58}$$

where A_{n+m} is the coefficient of x^{n+m} in the expansion of $(1+x)^{2n}(1-x)^{2m}$. Applying Cauchy's theorem we have

$$A_{n+m} \frac{1}{2\pi i} \int_{|1|} \frac{(1+x)^{2n}(1-x)^{2m}}{x^{n+m+1}} dx.$$

If we put $x=e^{i\phi}$, we obtain, after reduction,

$$A_{n+m} = [(-1)^m 2^{2(n+m)}/\pi] \int_0^\pi \cos^{2n}\phi \sin^{2m}\phi \, d\phi.$$

[39] E. Slutzky, "Über Stochastische Asymptoten und Grenzwerte," *Metron*, Vol. 5, N. 3, 1925, pp. 61–64.

Hence

$$(59) \quad A_{n+m} = \frac{(-1)^m 2^{n+m} 1\cdot 3 \cdots (2n-1)\cdot 1\cdot 3 \cdots (2m-1)}{1\cdot 2\cdot 3 \cdots (n+m)}.$$

Thus we obtain, by (58),

$$(60) \qquad \Delta^{2m} r_{-m} = \frac{(-1)^m 2^m 1\cdot 3 \cdots (2m-1)}{(n+1)(n+2)\cdots(n+m)}.$$

If we notice that

$$\Delta^{2m+2} r_{-(m+1)} = \Delta^{2m} r_{-(m+1)} - 2\Delta^{2m} r_{-m} + \Delta^{2m} r_{-(m-1)},$$

where, evidently,

$$\Delta^{2m} r_{-(m+1)} = \Delta^{2m} r_{-(m-1)},$$

we get

$$\begin{aligned} \Delta^{2m} r_{-m+1} &= \tfrac{1}{2}\Delta^{2(m+1)} r_{-(m+1)} + \Delta^{2m} r_{-m} \\ (61) \qquad &= \frac{(-1)^m 2^m 1\cdot 3 \cdots (2m-1)(n-m)}{(n+1)(n+2)\cdots(n+m+1)}, \end{aligned}$$

so that, by (56), (57), (60), and (61), we obtain

$$(62) \qquad r_1 = (n-m)/(n+m+1)$$

and[40]

$$(63) \qquad \rho_1 = -\sqrt{\frac{(2m+1)(n+m+2)}{(2m+3)(n+m+1)}}.$$

Now, it is evident that, n/m being constant,

$$r_1 < \frac{n/m - 1}{n/m + 1} < 1$$

and

$$\rho_1 \to -1, \qquad (n \to \infty),$$

which proves Theorem B.

CORRECTIONS OF BASIC DATA

The tables of figures which contain the series used in the present investigation are to be found in the original paper (*loc. cit.*, pp. 57–64). As the preparation of them has involved a great deal of time and labor

[40] To apply this formula in the case of No. V, we should notice that Model III is approximately equivalent to the series (y_1) of Theorem B, with $n = 400$.

and as it may be expected that someone will make use of them for the purpose of analogous studies, we give here correct readings for the *errata* found after the figures had been published. (Those relating to Table VI are immaterial and are omitted here.)

Table	Column					
	1	2	6	7	8	10
I	300				−453	
	418			−361		
	637				332	
	638			− 10	461	
	639		1367	451	295	
	807			255		
	819				211	
	820			496	−252	
	821		2290	244	−488	
	971				− 99	
	972			263	− 98	
	973		2134	165	−186	
III	23	− 4551				
	72	−20219				
IX	9		0.0007			
	11					0.0059
	13					0.0001
	14					0.0000

Eugen Slutzky

Mathematical Institute of the Moscow State University
Moscow, U.S.S.R.

[2]

Econometrica, Vol. 27, 4 (October 1959)

THE DYNAMIC PROPERTIES OF THE KLEIN-GOLDBERGER MODEL

BY IRMA ADELMAN AND FRANK L. ADELMAN*

The authors examine the dynamic properties of the Klein-Goldberger model of the United States economy by extrapolating the exogenous variables and solving the equations on the IBM 650 for one hundred years. In this process no indication was found of oscillatory behavior. The introduction of random impulses of a reasonable order of magnitude, however, generates cycles which are comparable in their properties to those of the United States economy.

1. INTRODUCTION

ONE OF THE MOST vexing of the unsolved problems of dynamic economic analysis is that of constructing a model which will reproduce adequately the cyclical behavior of a modern industrial community. None of the schemes so far advanced have (yet) offered a satisfactory endogenous explanation of the persistent business fluctuations so characteristic of Western capitalism. It is true that there exist theories which lead to oscillatory movements, but, except under very special assumptions, these swings either die down, or else they are explosive in nature.[1] In the latter case, appeal is usually made to externally imposed constraints in order to limit the fluctuations of the system,[2] while, in the former case, exogenous shocks must be introduced from time to time to rejuvenate the cyclical movement.[3] Since recourse to either of these devices is rather artificial, it is of interest to seek a more satisfactory mechanism for the internal generation of a persistent cyclical process.

While it is desirable for an economic model (or any other model, for that matter) to be as simple as possible, it is almost certain that an adequate explanation of the business cycle cannot be found through approaches as idealized as those usually suggested. It may be of interest, therefore, to examine, from this point of view, the most complicated econometric description of the United States published in recent years—the 1955 forecast-

* The authors are, respectively, Acting Assistant Professor of Economics at Stanford University and physicist at the Livermore branch of the University of California Lawrence Radiation Laboratory. They are grateful to the Computation Division of the Radiation Laboratory for the use of their facilities. Also, they wish to express their appreciation to Arthur Goldberger for his helpful discussion of this paper.

1 P. A. Samuelson, "The Interaction of the Accelerator and the Multiplier," *Review of Economic Statistics*, vol. XXI (1939), pp. 75–78.

2 J. R. Hicks, *A Contribution to the Theory of the Trade Cycle* (Oxford, 1939.)

3 R. Frisch, "Propagation Problems and Impulse Problems in Dynamic Economics," *Economic Essays in Honor of Gustav Cassel* (London, 1933), pp. 171–205.

ing scheme of Klein and Goldberger.[4] This structure, which consists of 25 difference equations[5] in a corresponding number of endogenous variables, is nonlinear in character, and includes lags up to the fifth order. By its very nature it constitutes a description of a dynamic world, rather than a portrayal of comparative statics. Not only are the endogenous variables in each period functions of exogenous inputs, but also of lagged endogenous quantities and of stock variables. Thus, even if all the exogenous magnitudes were held constant, the economy represented by these equations would still vary with time.

But, while this model has been applied to yearly projections of economic activity in this country with some success, its dynamic properties have been analyzed only under highly simplifying assumptions.[5a] In particular, it would be interesting to find out whether this construct really offers an endogenous explanation of a persistent cyclical process. We should like to learn whether the system is stable when subjected to single exogenous shocks, what oscillations (if any) accompany the return to the equilibrium path, and what is the reponse of the model to repeated external and internal shocks.

The purpose of this paper, then, is to investigate these issues in some detail. There are perhaps two major reasons which indicate why this work has not previously been done. First of all, the fact that Klein and Goldberger used observed quantities as inputs for their annual forecasts, rather than values generated by the model from earlier data, prevented them from studying, at the same time, the type of dynamic paths which would be traversed by the system in the absence of external interference. Secondly, the complexity of the model requires the use of modern high-speed computers for the long-run solution of the system in a reasonable length of time. Since the problem is about the right size for the IBM 650 calculator, and since the appropriate computing facilities exist at the University of California Radiation Laboratory, we programmed the equations for that machine.

2. THE MODEL

The Klein-Goldberger econometric model of the United States[6] is a system of 25 difference equations in as many endogenous variables. Some

[4] L. R. Klein and A. S. Goldberger, *An Econometric Model of the United States, 1929–1952* (Amsterdam, 1955).

[5] Including 5 tax equations.

[5a] In the December, 1957 meeting of the Econometric Society, A. S. Goldberger and J. Cornwall presented the results of their (independent) investigations of their respective linearized versions of the Klein-Goldberger model. (The abstracts appear in *Econometrica*, vol. 26 (1958), pp. 620, 621.) At the same meeting one of us (I.A.) gave a discussion paper on these studies, including in it the material of Sections I–V of the present paper.

[6] For an excellent, more detailed description of this model, see C. F. Christ, "Aggregate Econometric Models," *American Economic Review*, vol. XLVI (1956), pp. 385–408.

of the equations are accounting identities, while others, behavioral in nature, were derived from statistical fits to empirical data. Generally speaking, each equation describes some significant feature of the economy. The real sector of the model includes, in addition to the usual consumption and investment relationships, a production function, a corporate profits equation, and a corporate savings function. Also taken into account are private employee compensation, farm income, imports,and depreciation. The monetary sector consists of two liquid asset functions, two interest rate equations, a wage adjustment relationship, and an agricultural price equation. There are also five tax equations, which represent the impact of government tax policies upon the economy, and five accounting identities. Of the exogenous variables, the most important (aside from time) are government expenditures, population size, and the distribution of the labor force among the several sectors of the economy. All these equations are given in Appendix A, together with the definitions of the symbols used.

For this study of the Klein-Goldberger system several changes were introduced into the most recent Klein-Goldberger model, some for convenience and some for consistency or logic. First, whenever the standard error of estimate of a regression coefficient was more than twice as large as the coefficient itself, we dropped the corresponding term from the equations. The justification for so high a level of significance is that, for our purposes, we felt it less serious an error to ascribe to a zero coefficient a nonzero value than to ignore a regression coefficient which has an economic existence. The alterations made in accordance with this criterion are indicated in Appendix B, Section 1. In principle, of course, one should correct the equations for these omissions. However, since we were not interested in accurate prediction, but, rather, in the dynamic performance of the model, we felt that the required modifications were small[7] and would not add to the value of the study.

A second departure from the original system was to delete the import equation. This was done because, during the sample period, the calculated quantities of imports constituted a poor approximation to the values observed.[8] After imports had been dropped from the list of endogenous variables, it seemed reasonable also to omit both imports and exports from the model. For, since both would now be exogenous, and since their difference contributes only a small amount to GNP, it is difficult to see how their exclusion could alter the dynamic character of the system.

A modification of quite another sort was made in the form of the tax equations. Since those given by Klein and Goldberger were not intended

[7] Indeed, in all cases, the quantitative changes which would have been required lay within the standard errors of the constants to be altered.

[8] Cf. Klein-Goldberger, *op. cit.*, p. 95 and Figure 29, p. 102.

to be applicable for more than a few years,[9] we had to re-estimate all the tax relationships. Therefore, at the suggestion of A. Goldberger,[10] we adopted a new set of tax functions, which assumed that the tax policies of 1952, interpreted as relationships between real variables, would continue indefinitely into the future. These are incorporated into the tax equations which appear in Appendix B.1.

We were also forced to alter the interest rate equations. Since the excess bank reserves, R_t, are taken as exogenous, the short term interest rate $(i_S)_t$ and the long term rate $(i_L)_t$ can both be computed without reference to the rest of the system. With the small values of R_t typical of the postwar period, it is evident from the short-term interest rate equation [Eq. (15)] that $(i_S)_t$ will double (roughly) every decade. And yet there is no restoring force within the system to keep this quantity at a reasonable value! Similarly, $(i_L)_t$ will, ultimately, become equal to about $0.7(i_S)_t$. In view of the fact that such a projection would eventually result in economic nonsense, we decided to suppress the interest rate equations and to fix (arbitrarily) the short term rate at 2.5% and the long term rate at 3.5%.

Lastly, the agricultural price equation was re-evaluated, using only the postwar data. The reason for this alteration was the admittedly unsatisfactory behavior of the form used by Klein and Goldberger.[11]

We were still not in a position to follow the long-term development of this system, however, as it was necessary to extrapolate the exogenous variables far into the future. This was done, in some instances, by fitting a least-squares straight line to the postwar data. But, in the case of governmental expenditures, the discontinuity because of the Korean War and the subsequent intensification of military preparedness, imparted a trend to the postwar data much steeper than could reasonably be expected to continue. Therefore, we estimated the rate of increase of government expenditures by fitting a straight line to both the prewar and the postwar points, omitting only those of 1951 and 1952. The level was chosen to coincide, more or less, with that of those latter two years. With this procedure we found that our extrapolation leads to numbers which appear to be consistent with current experience.

On the other hand, agricultural subsidy income and the number of farm operators have a declining trend. For these quantities it seemed more appropriate to use a fit of the form

$$X = a + \frac{b}{t - \alpha},$$

in order that they never become negative. Finally, since there was no obvious

[9] Klein-Goldberger, *op. cit.*, pp. 96–102.

[10] Private communication.

[11] Klein-Goldberger, *op. cit.*, p. IX and Fig. 31, p. 105.

trend, during the postwar period, for the index of hours worked and the index of farm exports, both were taken as constant. The extrapolations of all the exogenous quantities appear in Appendix B. 2. The initial values of the lagged variables are listed in Appendix B. 3.

3. CALCULATIONAL PROCEDURE

The modified Klein-Goldberger model to be investigated thus consists of a set of 22 simultaneous equations in a corresponding number of endogenous variables. What we must do in order to evaluate the magnitudes of the endogenous variables for the year t is to insert into these equations the values for the $(t-1)$st and preceding years, as required, along with appropriate exogenous numbers, and solve the equations simultaneously. Using the newly found endogenous quantities for the tth year plus the required exogenous magnitudes, we can then solve the system for the endogenous variables of the $(t+1)$st period. This process is continued until we have traveled sufficiently far into the future to satisfy our curiosity.

At first glance the system we wish to analyze would appear to be highly nonlinear. The substitution of $q = 1/p$ as a variable, however, instead of the price level p itself, leaves us with only a single nonlinear equation (18), the wage and salary identity. Of course, it is much easier to solve a set of simultaneous *linear* equations than it is to evaluate a nonlinear system. For this reason it was decided to "linearize"[12] (18), and then to utilize a successive approximation procedure to find the solution of the nonlinear set to the desired degree of accuracy. Our criteria for an acceptable solution were that the value of each variable appearing in the nonlinear equation must differ from its previous approximation by less than 1/2% and that the original form of that equation also be satisfied to that accuracy. Since convergence was quite rapid, even when the initial guess was poor, our criteria appear to be sufficiently stringent to assure convergence to the economically relevant solution of the system (in case there is more than one solution).

Before actually programming the equations for the IBM 650, however, it was possible, by appropriate algebraic substitutions, to reduce the 22 equations down to a set of four simultaneous equations in four unknowns. The investment relation (2) could be evaluated from exogenous and lagged data, while the equations remaining after the completion of the algebra could be solved *seriatim* as soon as the answers to the first five were available. This procedure was advantageous, if not actually necessary, because the computation time required for the solution of a simultaneous linear system by matrix inversion is proportional to the cube of the rank of the matrix.

[12] To do this, we wrote the equation in terms of differences from initial (extrapolated) guesses, which must be consistent with the integral form of the equation.

After all the preceding considerations were taken into account, it turned out that neither memory space nor running time was a serious limitation on the use of the IBM 650. Therefore, the problem was coded for the machine in a straightforward manner. As a matter of interest, the computations for one year could be made during an operating time of about one minute.[13]

4. THE DYNAMIC NATURE OF THE MODEL

Now, we are finally in a position to study some of the problems raised in the Introduction. First of all, what is the dynamic nature of the Klein-Goldberger model? That is, what sort of time path will these equations generate in the absence of additional external constraints or shocks? A priori, it is conceivable that the long-run extrapolation of this short-run

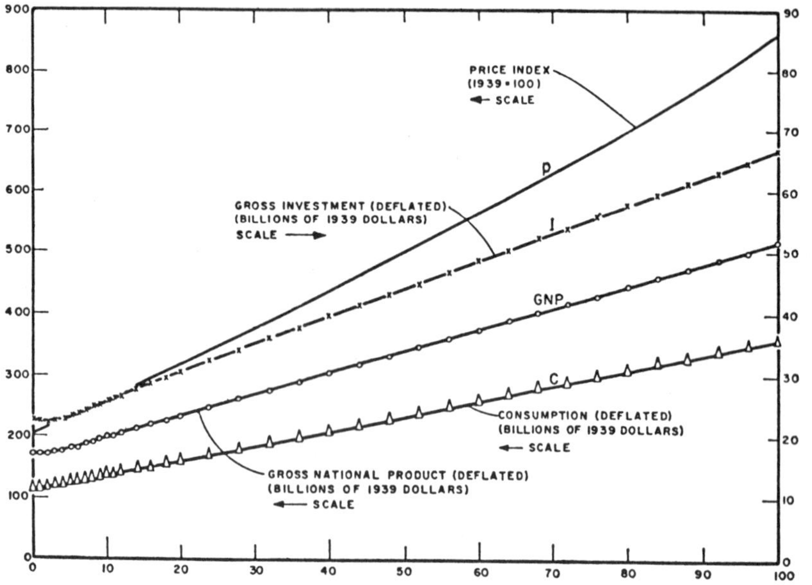

KLEIN-GOLDBERGER TIME PATHS
FIGURE 1

predictive system will indicate that the economy so described is subject to a business cycle more or less analogous to that observed in modern industrialized societies. On the other hand, it is also possible that this model cannot offer even a qualitative picture of the economic growth process in the real world.

[13] The actual time depends on the number of iterations required for convergence; in the linear part of the time path, the first guess is adequate.

Our first machine data decided the issue unequivocally. After a brief "settling-down" period, the system is quite monotonic and essentially linear. These is no hint whatever of any internally generated business cycle, and, indeed, even in the first few years, the shock of start-up is not sufficient to induce more than a single turning point in any variable. Of course, since most of the exogenous trends are fitted by straight lines, it is not surprising that the overall character of the solution is linear, rather than, say, quadratic, but the absence of oscillations is less obvious (a priori) and more significant.

The time paths of several of the more important quantities are depicted in Figure 1. The several curves in Figure 1 represent the projections of the price index and of the real values of GNP, consumer expenditures, and gross private investment, respectively. The approximate behavior of the rest of the variables may be inferred from the information in Table I.[14]

In an attempt to see whether the qualitative properties of the solution are at all sensitive to the starting conditions, we reduced the magnitudes of all but seven[15] of the initial values of the real quantities by 10 per cent. The results of this calculation possessed the same general character as had been observed previously. As might have been anticipated, the new ordinates were invariably lower, and, except for corporate savings, the slopes of the curves tended to be the same or smaller. The linearity was even more marked with the reduced inputs; indeed, only two variables showed any turning points at all. These were corporate savings and corporate surplus, both of which were actually negative for several periods. Since, in view of these results, it was felt that small variations in our input would not lead to significant differences in the *nature* of our solution, a more detailed investigation of the influence of initial values upon the operation of the model was postponed to a future date.

The implications of these results are quite clear. Since the economic variables in the Klein-Goldberger model grow almost linearly with time, it is apparent that this scheme does not contain an intrinsic explanation of a persistent oscillatory process. That is, the complete lack of even a broad hint of cyclical behavior in the absence of shocks precludes the application of the Klein-Goldberger analysis to economies in which oscillations are presumed to develop spontaneously. The conclusions one may draw from this observation lie anywhere between the two extreme positions which follow. On the one hand, if one wishes to retain the hypothesis that periodic cumulative movements are self-generated in the course of the growth

[14] The authors will be happy to furnish, upon request, the detailed results of their computations.

[15] The ones excluded were N_W, h, N_E, N_F, N_G, N, N_P (for explanation of symbols, see Appendix A).

TABLE I

BEHAVIOR OF KLEIN-GOLDBERGER MODEL THROUGH TIME

Variable* \ (years)	24 (first year)	30	60	90	120
$Y+T+D$	171.5	186.0	291.1	396.3	501.5
$\Delta(Y+T+D)$	.294	3.42	3.51	3.51	3.51
C	115.1	125.1	199.3	273.9	348.7
ΔC	.015	2.42	2.48	2.49	2.49
W_1	80.6	86.7	137.5	188.4	239.3
ΔW_1	—.046	1.64	1.70	1.70	1.70
A_1	9.0	9.5	12.6	15.9	19.2
ΔA_1	.008	.100	.108	.109	.110
I	22.9	24.0	37.9	51.5	64.9
ΔI	—.289	.434	.455	.450	.448
K	45.9	65.3	163.0	260.8	357.1
ΔK	3.75	3.05	3.24	3.23	3.20
D	18.5	21.0	34.6	48.2	62.2
ΔD	.396	.429	.458	.452	.448
P_C	14.9	15.4	22.5	29.6	36.8
ΔP_C	—.454	.245	.233	.237	.240
P	33.1	33.8	44.3	54.7	65.3
ΔP	—.667	.361	.343	.349	.353
S_P	.44	.57	2.17	2.85	3.16
ΔS_P	—.192	.082	.032	.015	.007
B	.63	2.96	48.80	125.71	216.51
ΔB	.250	.65	2.20	2.86	3.16
N_W	54.2	53.6	64.7	75.7	86.9
ΔN_W	—1.06	.352	.365	.370	.373
L_1	70.5	71.7	80.6	89.6	98.7
ΔL_1	.037	.288	.299	.301	.301
L_2	40.8	45.9	79.4	112.7	146.0
ΔL_2	1.40	1.00	1.12	1.11	1.11
w	344	443	1043	1817	2776
Δw	15.9	17.3	22.9	29.0	35.2
p	206	238	412	604	825
Δp	4.1	5.8	6.0	6.9	7.9
p_A	318	363	604	871	1179
Δp_A	5.7	8.1	8.3	9.6	11.0
T	14.5	15.8	25.5	35.3	45.0
ΔT	.028	.315	.324	.324	.324
T_W	7.6	9.0	19.2	29.3	39.5
ΔT_W	.069	.329	.338	.339	.339
T_A	.47	.49	.65	.82	.99
ΔT_A	.0003	.0050	.0055	.0056	.0056
T_C	9.4	9.6	12.9	16.0	19.3
ΔT_C	—.204	.110	.105	.108	.108
T_P	12.9	13.2	19.4	26.0	32.8
ΔT_P	—.268	.198	.212	.225	.231

* For any quantity Q, $\Delta Q = Q_{t+1} - Q_t$.

process in a realistic economy, one may contend that the Klein-Goldberger model is fundamentally inadequate, and hence that it is inapplicable to further business cycle theory. On the other hand, one may hold that, to the extent that the behavior of this system constitutes a valid qualitative approximation to that of a modern capitalist society, the observed solution of the Klein-Goldberger equations implies that one must look elsewhere for the origin of business fluctuations. Under the latter assumptions, cyclical analysis would be limited to an investigation of the reaction of the economic system to various perturbations. And, since the Klein-Goldberger model does present a more or less detailed description of the interactions among the various sectors of the economy, it could itself be utilized in the examination of the mechanism of response to shocks. Actually, as we shall see, exploitation of the latter alternative can prove extremely profitable.

5. STABILITY OF THE SYSTEM

It is apparent from the preceding discussion that, under ordinary conditions, the Klein-Goldberger model is non-oscillatory in nature. It remains to be seen whether the economy described by this system is stable under large exogenous displacements.

In order to study this point, we solved the equations as in the preceding section, until the system was essentially on its long-run equilibrium path (about 8 years). Then, in the ninth period, we suddenly reduced the real magnitude of federal outlays from its extrapolated level of 37.5 to the much lower figure of 10; in the succeeding years government expenditures were returned to the values they would have had in the absence of external interference.

While it is obvious that such a discontinuity in an exogenous variable is basically equivalent to a change in initial conditions, it is equally obvious that the response of a dynamic system to large displacements may be quite different from its behavior under small perturbations.[16]

Figure 2 presents some of the calculated results of this extremely severe shock to the economy.[17] As is evident from these curves, the community was immediately thrown into a very deep depression by the sudden drop in federal outlays. The restoration of a normal governmental budget during the following year alleviated the situation only slightly, but, by the second year after the dip, the business world had more than recovered. The

[16] E.g., consider a marble trapped in a horizontal saucer. If the disturbance is not large enough to cause the marble to cross the saucer rim, the system is stable. However, once the marble crosses the rim, it will not return to the saucer without the application of external forces. See also, P. A. Samuelson, *Foundations of Economic Analysis* (Harvard, 1953), pp. 200–262.

[17] More data are, of course, available for this case, and will be provided upon request.

next period saw the return of national income, farm receipts, and total employment to their pre-shock trends. However, it was not until the fourth year after the disturbance that real private employee compensation achieved its unperturbed level, as the price index rose more rapidly than the wage rate. Meanwhile, possibly as a result of the fact that consumer expenditures lagged yet another period, there was a mild business recession

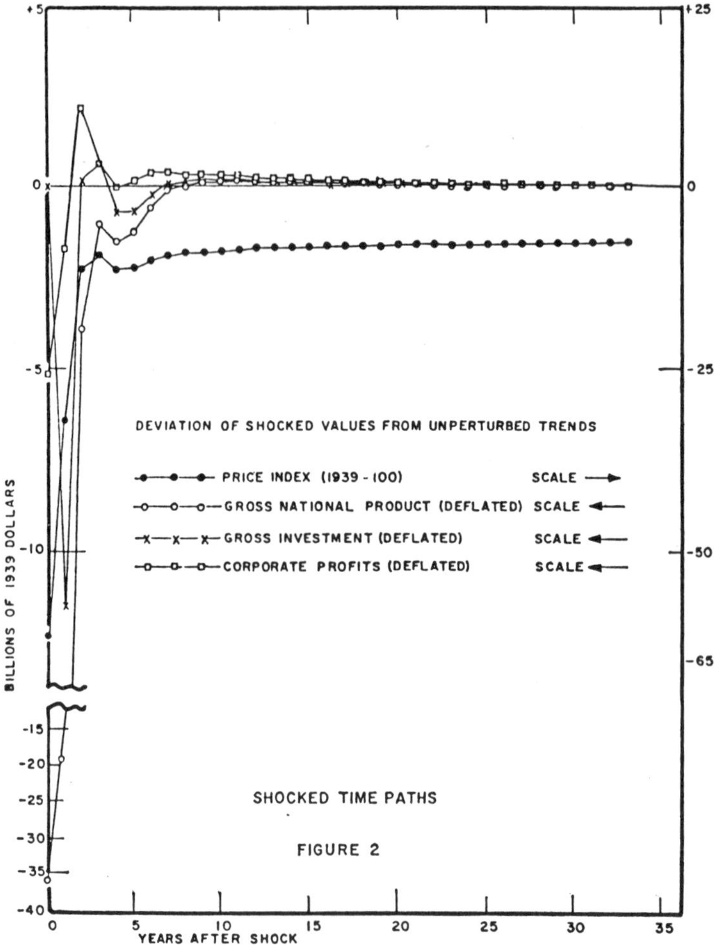

SHOCKED TIME PATHS

FIGURE 2

in the fourth year, the effects of which were felt throughout the rest of the economy for the next two periods. The subsequent boom reached its peak (with respect to its unperturbed trend) about eight years later, and then tapered off extremely slowly over an additional 22 years or so. While calculations were not continued beyond this point, it appears that, after this 34 year cycle, the economy has essentially returned to its basic equilibrium path, except for the price and wage indices[18] and for the cumulative corporate surplus (all of which remained lower).

While the details of the response of a Klein-Goldberger economy to a strong shock will depend on the nature of the perturbation, it would appear likely from this calculation that even a very strong shock will not permanently distort the long-run path of the economy. In other words, the Klein-Goldberger system is stable. Nevertheless, a sharp disturbance does suffice to create a business cycle of depth comparable to that which one would expect in an actual economy under a corresponding inpulse. And, while the duration of the cyclical movement is much longer than that normally observed in practice, it is probable that the later stages of such a cycle, if it really existed, would be obscured by the intervention of new exogenous shocks.

6. INTRODUCTION OF RANDOM SHOCKS

So far, we have studied the dynamic properties of the Klein-Goldberger system by treating it as if it were composed of a set of exact functional relationships. That is to say, we have abstracted from the random elements which are inherent in the statistical specification of the equations. Furthermore, we have used smooth extrapolation procedures for predicting the magnitudes of the exogenous variables. We saw that under those assumptions the Klein-Goldberger equations are inadequate as an explanation of the cyclical behavior of our economy.

We cannot yet assess the validity of the Klein-Goldberger equations, however, as a representation of the United States economy over a long period of time because we must still analyze the time path of their system under the impact of random shocks.[19] After all, as was pointed out by Haavelmo,[20] a model which differs from empirical fact by comparatively small and nonsystematic external factors may still be useful. It is therefore of great interest to see whether or not the introduction of relatively minor uncorrelated perturbations into the Klein-Goldberger structure will generate cyclical fluctuations analogous to those observed in practice.

With these considerations in mind, we exposed the Klein-Goldberger system to two distinct varieties of random impulses. First of all, random

[18] The real wage rate, however, does return to its equilibrium trend by the end of the cycle.

[19] The idea that economic fluctuations may be due to random shocks was first suggested in 1927 by E. Slutzky, "The Summation of Random Causes as the Source of Cyclical Processes," translated into English in *Econometrica*, Vol. 5 (1937), pp. 105 ff. It was also suggested independently by R. Frisch, *op. cit.*

[20] T. Haavelmo, "The Inadequacy of Testing Dynamic Theory by Comparing Theoretical Solutions and Observed Cycles," *Econometrica*, Vol. 8 (1940), p. 312.

shocks were superimposed upon the extrapolated values of the exogenous quantities (shocks of type I). Secondly, random perturbations were introduced instead into each of the empirically fitted Klein-Goldberger equations (shocks of type II). In addition we made a set of calculations in which both kinds of disturbances were present.

7. SHOCKS OF TYPE I

Shocks of type I arise logically whenever exogenous quantities are projected in a smooth manner over long periods of time, for, while it is convenient to extrapolate these variables in a continuous fashion, even a cursory glance at the data over a period of a few years shows that these magnitudes tend to jump more or less erratically with respect to any smooth curve one might draw. It is, of course, obvious that a system that incorporates such statistical fluctuations may not be completely satisfactory for quantitative purposes. On the other hand, it may still prove fruitful to compare with economic experience the frequency of occurrence and the amplitudes of whatever cycles may arise.

We shall therefore modify our method of extrapolation of the exogenous variables in order to see what effects these random perturbations may have. For this purpose we define the value of an exogenous variable y_t at time t as its trend value $\bar{\bar{y}}_t$ plus the shock term δy_t, and assume that δy_t has a Gaussian distribution[21] with a mean of zero. In order that the shocks inflicted upon the system be of a more or less realistic magnitude at all times, we evaluate the standard deviation of δy_t over that portion of the data for which our least squares fit was made,[22] and, for our subsequent calculations, we maintain the ratio of the standard deviation of δy_t to y_{t-1} at a value independent of time. It is interesting to note that these standard deviations (see Appendix B. 4) are, in general, quite small; in fact, only three of them exceed 10 per cent of the trend value of the corresponding variable.

In examining the behavior of the twelve exogenous variables[23] over the sample period, it becomes evident that there exists a high degree of correlation between the long- and the short-term interest rates, and between the size of government payrolls and the number of government em-

[21] This assumption also underlies the principle of least squares fits.

[22] It will be recalled that we used data from 1946–1952 for our least squares extrapolations of all exogenous variables except government expenditures, G; for G, data for 1929–1940 and 1946–1950 were used.

[23] These variables, it will be recalled, are the short-term i_S and long term interest rates i_L, the index of hours worked h, government employee compensation W_2, government expenditures G, the index of agricultural exports F_A, agricultural subsidies A_2 and five population and labor force variables (N_P, N, N_E, N_F, and N_G).

ployees.[24] It is therefore appropriate to assume that these pairs of variables move together and that the determination of a shock on one variable of each pair automatically sets the size of the corresponding shock on the other. Hence we are left with a set of ten random exogenous shocks, whose magnitudes and signs are to be established.

The technique employed for this purpose was to divide the normal curve of error into 100 regions of equal area. To each region we assigned both the normal deviate associated with the midpoint of its interval and a previously unassigned integer between 00 and 99, inclusive. Then selecting a two-digit random number, we effectively chose at random a specific region of the Gaussian distribution and the corresponding normal deviate. Multiplying this deviate by the standard deviation of δy_t, we found the magnitude and direction of a shock on the variable y at time t. Since the selection of an interval in this manner was thus purely random, and since all intervals defined the same area under the curve, this method produced a normally distributed[25] *random* shock upon the variable in question. By repeating this

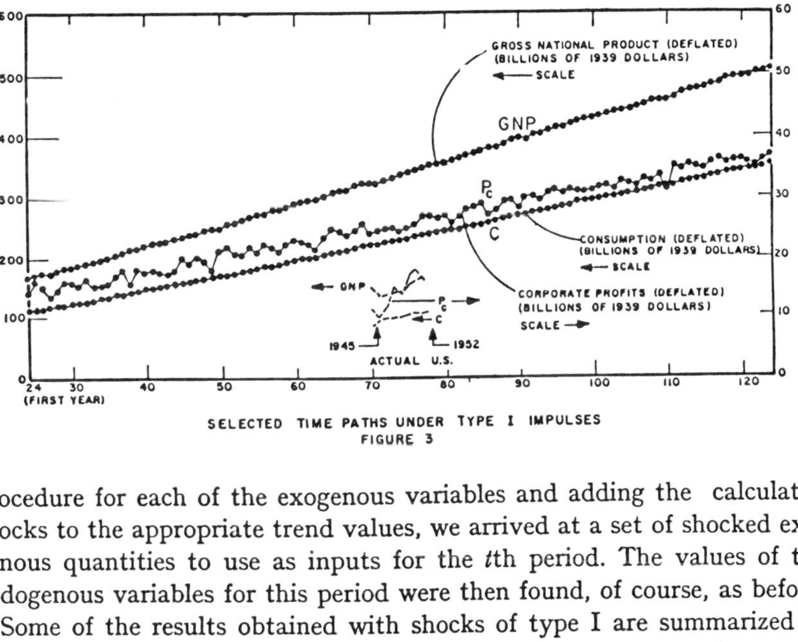

SELECTED TIME PATHS UNDER TYPE I IMPULSES
FIGURE 3

procedure for each of the exogenous variables and adding the calculated shocks to the appropriate trend values, we arrived at a set of shocked exogenous quantities to use as inputs for the *t*th period. The values of the endogenous variables for this period were then found, of course, as before.

Some of the results obtained with shocks of type I are summarized in Figure 3. The solid lines in this graph portray the computed time paths

[24] The correlation coefficient between government payrolls W_2 and government expenditures G for the sample years 1946–52 is 0.97 and that between the interest rates is 0.89.

[25] Since we have divided the normal curve into discrete intervals, we actually have only a (good) approximation to a normal distribution.

of GNP, consumption, and corporate profits, while the dotted lines represent actual time paths of these variables for the postwar portion of the sample period.[26] From this figure, it would seem that the introduction of forces of type I into the model generates 3 to 4 year swings in the variables of the system. However, the same graph also reveals that the average amplitude of the "cycles" induced by random shock on exogenous quantities is unrealistically small. It would appear, then, that type I perturbations of reasonable magnitude superimposed upon the Klein-Goldberger model will not produce the sort of cyclical behavior observed in the actual economy. We shall therefore proceed to see whether shocks of type II will prove more promising.

8. SHOCKS OF TYPE II

To understand the origin of shocks of type II, one should recall that, in the process of fitting their empirical data, Klein and Goldberger endowed each of their behavioral equations with a random error term.[27] At least three sources of irregularity could produce this term. In the first place, simplifying assumptions are inevitable whenever one wishes to construct a concrete model of a realistic economy. Some of these abstractions are made for convenience, others because the precise equations of motion of an economic system are not yet known. Variables which in practice exert a direct influence upon the solution may be suppressed from several of the equations, made exogenous, or omitted entirely; similarly, relationships which are an integral part of the description may be lost in the process of approximation. Moreover, in predictive models, inherently nonlinear relationships are often treated in a linear approximation for the sake of expediency. In view of these considerations, it is reasonable to expect that the inexactness of the functional form of the Klein-Goldberger equations as a representation of the economic behavior of our society contributes to the size of the random error term.

Secondly, even if the Klein-Goldberger relationships did have a functional form derived from indisputable theory, the fact that the coefficients are based upon empirical data would imply a random error term, as a result of the usual sampling fluctuations. These include, for example, the uncertainty of the degree to which the sample is representative of the universe, as well as the changes in accounting practices, coverage, and reporting techniques which generally occur in the collection of data over a long period of time.

[26] The data for the actual time paths are taken from Klein-Goldberger, *op. cit.*, pp. 131–133.

[27] This is standard econometric procedure; cf. Klein-Goldberger, *op. cit.*, pp. 42–46.

A third potential contributor to the size of shocks of type II is of quite a different character. It arises from the possibility that some of the economic relationships which compose the Klein-Goldberger system may *never* be valid as exact equations. This situation will result if the aggregation of microeconomic quantities into macroeconomic variables is not a legitimate procedure. For example, if the value of total consumption depends upon the distribution of income as well as on its magnitude, a precise macroeconomic relationship between overall consumption and aggregate income will not exist. A similar effect, which will also be reflected in the size of the random error term, would occur if decision functions are probabilistic rather than single-valued.

It is therefore evident from the above discussion that the residuals of the several empirically fitted equations included in the Klein-Goldberger model can be attributed to a number of different types of irregularity. Since there would appear to be no a priori correlation among the many individual sources of fluctuation, the random error terms can be assumed for all practical purposes to be distributed in a Gaussian manner. We therefore postulate that each error term is distributed normally about a mean of zero, and we evaluate its standard deviation, just as in the case of shocks of type I, from the standard errors observed for the sample period (see Appendix B. 5).

In order to introduce perturbations of type II into the Klein-Goldberger model, we added a random error term to the right-hand side of each of the original non-definitional relationships.[28] Then the same process of algebraic substitution which was used in the simplification of the unshocked system was applied to this new group of equations. These operations left us with a set of equations in which the several error terms appear as parameters, analogous to the exogenous and the lagged variables. Once the sizes and directions of these endogenous shocks are determined (by the selection of two-digit random numbers, as in the case of type I impulses), the system is solved as before. A similar procedure can be used to investigate the behavior of the Klein-Goldberger equations when both shocks of type I and shocks of type II are present simultaneously.

Some of the results of the computation with shocks of type II are plotted in Figure 4. As in Figure 3, the solid lines represent the calculated behavior of GNP, consumption, and corporate profits, respectively, while the dotted lines depict the time paths traversed by the same quantities during the postwar period in the United States.[26] As before, we see that the shocked Klein-Goldberger system produces oscillatory movements with periods of 3 to 4 years. But, unlike the behavior of the model under the action of forces

[28] The equations involved are (1) – (8) and (10) – (13) of Appendix A.

of type I, the swings generated here compare favorably in magnitude with those experienced by the United States economy after World War II. Thus, the superposition of impulses of type II upon the Klein-Goldberger equations leads to cycles whose gross properties are reasonably realistic.

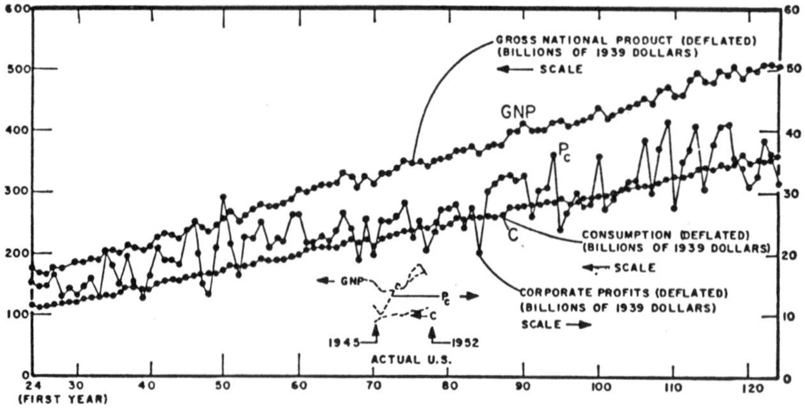

SELECTED TIME PATHS UNDER TYPE II IMPULSES
FIGURE 4

Since the effects of shocks of type II are much larger than those of type I disturbances, the same statement can be made for a system in which both kinds of perturbations are present. And, in view of the fact that, on a priori grounds, either type of shock may be present in an actual economy, it would seem appropriate to carry out our more detailed analysis for the case in which both forces are present.

9. ANALYSIS OF COMPUTED CYCLES

It is encouraging, of course, to find that the amplitudes and the periods of the oscillations observed in this model are roughly the same as those which are found in practice. But, this much agreement is merely a necessary condition for an adequate simulation of the cyclical fluctuations of a real industrial economy. We must investigate further to find out whether or not a shocked version of the Klein-Goldberger system really produces business cycles in the technical sense.[29] Specifically, how nearly all-pervasive are the cumulative movements which arise? How are the various oscillations correlated? Is there any consistent phase relationship among the

[29] R. A. Gordon, for example, defines business cycles in the following manner: "Business cycles consist of recurring alternations of expansion and contraction in aggregate economic activity, the alternating movements in each direction being self-reinforcing and pervading virtually all parts of the economy." *Business Fluctuations* (Harpers, 1952), p. 214.

several economic series? Do the time paths of the individual variables of the model correspond to those observed in the United States economy? In other words, if a business cycle analyst were asked whether or not the results of a shocked Klein-Goldberger computation could reasonably represent a United States-type economy, how would he respond?

To answer these questions we shall apply to the data techniques developed by the National Bureau of Economic Research (NBER)[30] for the analysis of business cycles.

One property of cyclical fluctuations in an industrial economy is a marked tendency for a clustering of peaks and troughs of individual economic time series about particular reference dates. It is, in fact, precisely this characteristic of business cycles that Burns and Mitchell use as their criterion for the dating of turning points in the United States economy.[31] And, inasmuch as the oscillations in the Klein-Goldberger model occur in response to random (i.e., noncorrelated) perturbations, a study of the simultaneity of occurrence of peaks (and troughs) will provide us with quite a stringent test of the validity of the model.

As in the normal NBER procedure,[32] we first date the specific cycles;[33] i.e., we determine all the turning points of each of the several time series. Then, to establish the reference dates[33] for the turning points of the *overall* business cycle, we examine the data for bunching (in time) of specific cycle peaks and troughs.[34]

Table II is a summary of some of the relevant characteristics of the business cycles observed in our shocked Klein-Goldberger economy. In examining this table, one should recall that intervals and dates can have

[30] The methods and results of the NBER work are summarized in A. F. Burns and W. C. Mitchell, *Measuring Business Cycles* (National Bureau, 1946) and in W. C. Mitchell, *What Happens During Business Cycles* (National Bureau, 1951).

[31] Mitchell, *op. cit.*, pp. 10–11.

[32] See Burns and Mitchell, *op. cit.*, Ch. 2.

[33] In the rest of this paper we will need the definitions of several quantities prevalent in the literature of business cycles. See, for example, Mitchell, *op. cit.*, pp. 9–11, or Gordon, *op. cit.*, p. 232.

(1) Reference dates are those dates which mark the turning points of overall business activity in the economy.

(2) A reference cycle of an economic variable V represents the behavior of V between the reference dates marking two consecutive minima of overall business activity.

(3) A specific cycle of V represents the behavior of V between the dates marking two consecutive minima of V itself.

[34] Our procedure corresponds to that of the NBER (cf. Mitchell, *op. cit.*, pp. 10–12). As a basis for establishing the reference dates we used all the Klein-Goldberger endogenous quantities except the 5 tax variables. A reference peak (trough) was said to occur (in our data) during any year in which the modal number of specific cycle peaks occurs, provided that at least 10 peaks (troughs) are found in a two-year period which includes the model year.

TABLE II
REFERENCE DATING FOR SHOCKED KLEIN-GOLDBERGER MODEL

Reference Dates		Elapsed Time (Years)		Number of Series at Peaks Which:			Number of Series at Troughs Which:		
Trough (T)	Peak(P)	T→P	P→T	Lag One Year	Coin-cide	Lead One Year	Lag One Year	Coin-cide	Lead One Year
–	27	–	2	–	–	–	–	–	–
29	31	2	1	2	8	6	1	6	4
32	37	5	1	1	8	5	4	7	4
38	42	4	1	1	10	0	1	13	1
43	45	2	1	2	7	4	0	10	0
46	51	5	2	2	11	1	3	8	3
53	54	1	2	4	12	1	2	10	4
56	59	3	1	1	10	1	1	11	4
60	63	3	1	2	7	6	4	6	2
64	68	4	2	6	6	3	5	7	1
70	72	2	1	2	7	3	1	13	1
73	74	1	1	2	9	1	2	8	2
75	77	2	1	2	8	4	0	10	2
78	79	1	1	2	8	2	3	9	3
80	83	3	2	2	12	1	1	7	3
85	86	1	2	4	12	2	2	11	2
88	90	2	1	2	12	2	1	11	4
91	94	3	2	3	10	1	3	11	3
96	98	2	4	5	8	3	1	9	3
102	106	4	1	3	12	2	3	10	2
107	109	2	1	4	9	1	5	11	2
110	113	3	1	2	11	4	5	7	1
114	116	2	1	5	7	4	3	13	0
117	119	2	1	1	8	8	4	9	3
120	–	–	–	–	–	–	–	–	–
Totals		59	34	60	212	65	55	217	54
Average per cycle		2.56	1.48	2.61	9.22	2.82	2.39	9.43	2.34
Percent of Specific Cycles Represented		–	–	14.5	51.2	15.7	13.3	52.4	13.0

significance only to the nearest year, inasmuch as the Klein-Goldberger computation was made on a year-to-year basis. The first two columns give the reference dates for the peaks and troughs, respectively. Since one can identify 23 complete business cycles (measured either from trough to trough or from peak to peak) occurring in the 93 years included in our calculation, the average length of a cycle is 4.0 years. This result is in startling agreement with the 4 year post-World War II cycles in the United States economy, as well as with the mean length of American peacetime business cycles since 1854.[35]

The Klein-Goldberger cycles are broken down, in columns 3 and 4, to indicate the duration of the expansion and contraction phases of each cycle. The average expansion covered 2.6 years, while the normal contraction occupied only 1.5. The agreement with the observed figures for the United States (2.1 and 1.8, respectively)[36] is surprisingly good when one considers the fact that the length of a single business cycle stage in our Klein-Goldberger computation can be estimated only to an integral number of years.

The validity of this comparison of United States and Klein-Goldberger business cycles is dependent, of course, upon the degree of reliability with which the reference dates have been determined. One criterion which can be used is the extent to which specific cycle peaks (troughs) tend to cluster at times coincident with the maxima (minima) of the overall business cycles. In our Klein-Goldberger data, 51 per cent of the individual series, on the average, have maxima coincident with an upper turning point of general business activity, and 52 per cent have minima which coincide with a reference trough. The corresponding figures for the United States economy are 58 per cent and 52 per cent respectively.[36] In addition, the proportions of specific cycles which lead or lag the business cycle in our computed data is quite similar to the analogous figure[37] for the United States economy. Our numbers are given in the last line of Table II.

All in all, it would appear that there is a remarkable correspondence between the characteristics of fluctuations generated by the superposition of random shocks upon the Klein-Goldberger system and those of the business cycles which actually occur in the United States economy. The resemblance is not restricted to qualitative parallelism, but is, indeed,

[35] Computed from the NBER dating for the period 1854–1949, reproduced in Gordon, *op. cit.*, p. 216. We omitted from our averages the Civil War cycle and those corresponding to the two World Wars.

[36] These percentages were estimated from Chart 3 (pp. 16–17) of G. H. Moore, *Statistical Indicators of Cyclical Revivals and Recessions* (National Bureau Occasional Paper 31, 1950). Moore's graph was presented on a monthly basis and included the years 1885–1940.

[37] Mitchell, *op. cit.*, Table 15, pp. 154–155, Table 16, pp. 159–167, and Table 42, pp. 312–325.

TABLE III

COMPARISON OF KLEIN-GOLDBERGER AND NBER SPECIFIC CYCLES

Variable	Frequencies and Other Properties at Peaks								Frequencies and Other Properties at Troughs								Remarks
	One Year Lead	Coincide	One Year Lag	Other	K-G Classification	NBER Classification	K-G Index of Conformity (%)	NBER Index of Conformity (%)	One Year Lead	Coincide	One Year Lag	Other	K-G Classification	NBER Classification	K-G Index of Conformity (%)	NBER Index of Conformity (%)	Remarks
$Y+T+D$	1	21	1	1	Coincident	Coincident	+100	*+100	2	21	0	1	Coincident	Coincident	+92	*+50	
Y	1	21	1	1	Coincident	Coincident	+100	*+100	1	22	0	1	Coincident	Coincident	+100	*+50	
C	1	8	3	0	Coincident	Coincident	+100	*+100	5	5	1	1	Leading-Coincident	Coincident	−17	*+50	
I	4	20	0	3	Coincident	Coincident	+100	*+100	0	23	1	3	Coincident	Coincident	+100	*+100	
W_1	2	10	3	2	Coincident	Coincident	+83	*+100	1	10	3	3	Coincident	Concident	+8	*+50	
A_1	6	8	7	7	Irregular	Coincident	−4	+60	8	5	5	10	Irregular	Coincident	−33	+12	
P	4	19	0	4	Coincident	Coincident	+91	—	0	22	1	4	Coincident	Coincident	+100	—	
N_W	4	18	2	2	Coincident	Coincident	+91	+100	3	19	2	2	Coincident	Coincident	+100	+100	
P_C	4	20	0	4	Coincident	Coincident	+100	*+100	3	20	1	4	Coincident	Coincident	+92	*+100	
S_P	4	16	0	4	Coincident	Coincident	+83	+100	0	17	4	3	Coincident	Coincident	+100	+50	
B	0	5	1	1	Coincident	—	+100	—	1	5	1	0	Coincident	—	−42	—	
K	1	9	6	0	Coincident	—	+87	—	0	11	3	1	Coincident	—	+33	—	
D	10	6	3	6	Leading	—	+22	—	10	7	4	5	Leading	—	−25	—	
L_1	14	4	5	3	Leading	—	+13	—	5	6	9	5	Lagging-Irregular	—	+8	—	
L_2	4	15	0	4	Coincident	—	−65	—	2	17	3	1	Coincident	—	−83	—	Inverse
p	3	17	2	0	Coincident	Coincident	+100	+64	0	20	2	0	Coincident	Coincident	+83	+82	
p_A	4	17	2	5	Coincident	Coincident	+100	+50	6	14	4	4	Coincident	Coincident	+42	+60	
w	0	1	9	1	Lagging	Lagging	+83	+100	0	4	7	0	Lagging	Coincident	−67	−50	
w/p	2	17	1	5	Coincident	—	−74	—	0	21	0	4	Coincident	—	−100	—	Inverse
K/Y	4	19	1	4	Coincident	—	−100	—	5	19	1	3	Coincident	—	−100	—	Inverse

quantitative, in the sense that the duration of the cycle, the relative length of the expansion and contraction phases, and the degree of clustering of peaks and troughs are all in numerical agreement (within the accuracy of measurement) with empirical evidence. Therefore, we shall study the Klein-Goldberger cycles in more detail.

Table III summarizes, for the shocked Klein-Goldberger model, some of the significant features of the specific cycle patterns observed in the endogenous variables. As can be seen from columns 6, 7, 14, and 15, the segregation of the Klein-Goldberger economic variables into leading, coincident, and lagging series is quite similar to the division of the analogous quantities in the United States economy by the NBER. (Columns 2 – 5 and 10 – 13 give the data which lead to our grouping; the NBER separation into categories is taken from Mitchell.[37]) Of the 20 series listed, 12 are classified as coincident series at both peaks and troughs. These are gross national product ($Y + T + D$), national income Y, gross investment I, private employee compensation W_1, non-wage non-farm income P, employment N_W, corporate profits P_C, corporate savings S_P, corporate surplus B, capital stock K, the general price index p, and the index of agricultural prices p_A. In addition, consumption C coincides at peaks, but has a tendency to lead at troughs. All of these results are in accord with NBER experience (when available), except that the United States specific cycles for consumption coincide, rather than lead at the troughs.

Three additional variables (corporate liquid assets L_2, real wages w/p, and the capital-output ratio K/Y) are in inverse coincidence with the business cycle, in the sense that their troughs tend to occur at reference peaks and vice versa. Unfortunately, we were unable to find the identical items among the NBER data; however, on both theoretical and empirical grounds, these inverse relationships are eminently reasonable. As far as L_2 is concerned, for example, both transactions demand and investment opportunities are reduced as business activity falls and therefore liquid surpluses should begin to accumulate.[38] Indeed, the NBER has some experimental data to support the proposition that the cash component of L_2, at least, tends to rise as the downturn develops (and vice versa).[39]

With respect to the capital-output ratio, it too should fall in times of expansion and climb during a contraction. From a theoretical point of view, as shown by Duesenberry,[40] a non-decreasing capital-output ratio during a business expansion would imply a rising marginal efficiency of investment. But the marginal efficiency of investment cannot increase unless

[38] An excellent description of this process can be found in Gordon, *op. cit.*, p. 270–271.

[39] Mitchell, *op. cit.*, p. 148.

[40] J. S. Duesenberry, *Business Cycles and Economic Growth* (McGraw-Hill, 1958), p. 112.

the capital-output ratio drops. Therefore, the capital-output ratio must fall during the boom phase. Furthermore, the time required for the formation and depletion of the capital stock exceeds the time lag inherent in the production of consumer goods; this too implies that the capital-output ratio will move in a direction opposite to that of the general level of economic activity.

With regard to w/p, both Marshall[41] and Keynes[42] suggested that real wages tend to vary inversely with the level of output and employment. This theorem, which has been thoroughly discussed in the literature,[43] is consistent with our observations. In addition, experimental data concerning the movement of real wages in industrial economies,[44] while somewhat inconclusive, tend to confirm the calculated inverse behavior of this variable.

Of the remaining four quantities, the NBER considers farm income A_1 to concur with the general business cycle and money wage rates w to coincide at troughs and to lag at peaks. We, on the other hand, find the former series to be irregular and the latter to lag everywhere. But, as is evident from Table III, the NBER data for agricultural incomes do not show a very high degree of conformity to the overall business cycle (especially at the troughs), and farm output itself (in real terms) tends to have a higher correlation with metereological cycles than with business cycles.[45] For wages, the disagreement between the behavior of the shocked Klein-Goldberger model at the troughs and the NBER analysis may simply be a reflection of the fact that the Klein-Goldberger equations do not appear to allow enough interaction between unemployment and wage rates.[46]

41 A. Marshall, *Principles of Economics*, 8th ed. (Macmillan, 1947), p. 620.

42 J. M. Keynes, *The General Theory of Employment, Interest and Money* (Harcourt Brace, 1935), p. 10.

43 See, e.g., J. T. Dunlop, "The Movement of Real and Money Wage Rates," *Economic Journal*, Vol. 48 (1938), pp. 413–34; L. Tarshis, "Changes in Real and Money Wages," *Economic Journal*, Vol. 49 (1939), pp. 150–154; R. Ruggles, "The Relative Movements of Real and Money Wage Rates," *Quarterly Journal of Economics*, Vol. 55 (1940), pp. 130–149; S. C. Tsiang, *The Variations of Real Wages and Profit Margins in Relation to the Trade Cycle* (London, 1947), pp. 10–12; and K. W. Rotschild, *The Theory of Wages* (New York, 1956), pp. 128–131.

44 Roughly speaking, statistical evidence seems to support the proposition if we take account of *product wages* (i.e., money wages deflated by an index of wholesale prices) (see Tsiang, *op. cit.*, Ch. III) and to undermine it if we consider money wages deflated by a cost of living index (see Dunlop, *op. cit.*, and Tarshis, *op. cit.*). It should be noted that the deflator used for real wages in our computations is the implicit deflator for GNP, and therefore that our (w/p) is closer to the product wage rate than to the measure of real wages analyzed by Dunlop and Tarshis.

45 Mitchell, *op. cit.*, p. 56 and Gordon, *op. cit.*, pp. 347–350.

46 D. Creamer and M. Bernstein, *Behavior of Wage Rates During Business Cycles* (National Bureau Occasional Paper 34) applied the NBER method to British and American statistics and found an average lag of wages behind general business activity of about 7 months at the major turning points, and longer for the minor ones.

In our study personal liquid assets L_1 tend to lead at peaks and to lag somewhat irregularly at troughs. We have not encountered comparable NBER series. However, one might attribute a lead in personal liquidity at a peak to the de facto financing of the last stages of the boom by dishoarding on the part of overoptimistic consumers, and the lag at a trough to the satisfaction of pent-up demand in the light of renewed income prospects.

Finally, depreciation D leads, in our calculations, at both troughs and peaks. While Fabricant[47] has found that depreciation charges tend to show much less cyclical fluctuation than corporate gross income or physical output, our computations do not exhibit this behavior. But, it should be noted that, first of all, the Klein-Goldberger depreciation is deflated and more complicated than that of Fabricant, and, secondly, that Fabricant's data cover only the first fourteen years immediately following World War I. We feel, therefore, that existing empirical work is inconclusive on this point, especially in view of the complex nature of any realistic measure of depreciation.

Columns 8 – 9 and 16 – 17 of Table III present the indices of conformity[48] of the specific cycles to the expansions and contractions of the business cycles of both the Klein-Goldberger data and the NBER statistics.[49] These indices measure the correlation between the direction of movements in the individual series which comprise the business cycle and that of the overall economic fluctuations which result. In evaluating the data, one should note that those NBER indices which are preceded by an asterisk in the table are based upon only four complete cycles and therefore that they can assume no numerical values other than 0, $\pm$ 50, and $\pm$ 100. While, by definition, an index of + 100 denotes perfect concurrence in direction of specific cycles with the general business cycle for all four cycles, an index of + 50 for these data states merely that, in exactly three out of the four cases examined, the series expanded during the reference expansion (or contracted during the reference contraction).

As can be seen from this table, there is reasonably good agreement

[47] S. Fabricant, *Capital Consumption and Adjustment* (NBER, 1938), p. 197.

[48] The index of conformity of a set of specific cycles to the expansion of the overall business cycle is the percentage of conforming movements minus the percentage of non-conforming movements. A conforming movement occurs when the value of the variable at a reference peak is higher than its value at the preceding trough. If the two values are equal, the movement does not contribute to the index (although it is counted as an event in computing the percentages). A non-conforming movement is a movement opposite in direction to a conforming movement. The index of conformity to reference contractions is defined in an analogous manner.

[49] The NBER data are taken from Mitchell, *op. cit.*, Table 15, pp. 154–155, Table 16, pp. 159–167, and Table 42, pp. 312–325.

between the Klein-Goldberger indices of conformity and those of the NBER, especially during expansions.[50] A major discrepancy appears, however, in agricultural incomes A_1, where the tendency for irregular behavior of the Klein-Goldberger series observed in the classification process is confirmed by the low values of the conformity indices; the NBER conformity is somewhat higher. We also find that the Klein-Goldberger total payrolls W_1 do not conform as well to business contractions as the NBER data would suggest they should. This is probably due primarily to the failure of money wages w to contract sufficiently in the model. This tendency for rigidity in money wages during contractions, however, is confirmed in the NBER data. Finally, Klein-Goldberger consumption C appears to have little or no tendency to fall during business contractions. This behavior, which agrees with post-World War II United States experience, may be due to the fact that a strong upward trend in consumption expenditures (and in the economic variables in general) has been built into our extrapolation of the Klein-Goldberger model. It is, however, conceivable that there exists a real difference in consumption patterns since World War II, as compared with the prewar era (from which the NBER data were taken). Such a shift would be reflected, at least partially, in the Klein-Goldberger statistical fits.

Generally speaking, then, the specific cycles generated in the Klein-Goldberger model by random shocks thus bear an obvious resemblance to those of cycles found in the United States economy. The division of the Klein-Goldberger data into leading, lagging, and coincident series is almost identical to that of the NBER (when available), and is in accord with theoretical expectations. Similarly, the indices of conformity to the business cycle are reasonably consistent with those given by Mitchell[51] for the United States economy.

10. CONCLUSIONS

Our investigation into the dynamic nature of the econometric model of Klein and Goldberger suggests that their equations do not offer an immediate explanation of an internally generated cyclical process. For, in the absence of perturbations, the time paths of the economic variables are monotonic and essentially linear in character. Furthermore, the behavior of the model is remarkably stable, as evidenced by the fact that

[50] In an economy with a prevalent upward trend, conformity to expansions is more regular than conformity to contractions. Therefore, for the Klein-Goldberger data, a conformity index of +60 to expansions is fairly low. However, since the rising trend also tends to weaken the conformity to expansion of series with inverted timing, a conformity —60 to expansions is high.

[51] Mitchell, *op. cit.*, pp. 154–55, 159–167, and 312–325.

the solution resumes its unperturbed equilibrium growth trend even after a strong exogenous disturbance.

On the other hand, when random shocks of a realistic order of magnitude are superimposed upon the original form of the Klein-Goldberger equations, the cyclical fluctuations which result are remarkably similar to those described by the NBER as characterizing the United States economy. The average duration of a cycle, the mean length of the expansion and contraction phases, and the degree of clustering of individual peaks and troughs around reference dates all agree with the corresponding data for the United States economy. Furthermore, the lead-lag relationships of the endogenous variables included in the model and the indices of conformity of the specific series to the overall business cycle also resemble closely the analogous features of our society. All in all, it would appear that the shocked Klein-Goldberger model approximates the behavior of the United States economy rather well.

In view of these results, it is not unreasonable to suggest that the gross characteristics of the interactions among the real variables described in the Klein-Goldberger equations may represent good approximations to the behavioral relationships in a practical economy. There are, of course, a number of significant defects in the detailed workings of the Klein-Goldberger system. For example, the treatment of the monetary quantities and the interconnections between them and the real sector both need improvement. Nevertheless, the representation would seem to offer a good working basis for the investigation of cyclical fluctuations, especially if the deficiencies mentioned above are corrected.

But, the behavior of the Klein-Goldberger system under random perturbations is also suggestive from another point of view. Ever since the path-breaking article of Frisch on the propagation of business cycles, the possibility that the cyclical movements observed in a capitalistic society are actually due to random shocks has been seriously considered by business cycle theorists. The results we have found in this study tend to support this possibility. For, the agreement between the data obtained by imposing uncorrelated perturbations upon a model which is otherwise non-oscillatory in character is certainly consistent with the hypothesis that the economic fluctuations experienced in modern, highly developed societies are indeed due to random impulses.

Of course, these random impulses are not necessarily synonymous with an exogenous theory of the business cycle. For, as we saw in Section 8 above, it was primarily shocks of type II which led to agreement between the cyclical behavior of the model and that of the United States economy. And, the reader will recall, these shocks may reflect inexactness in the model, statistical inaccuracies in the fits, or inherent randomness in the decision functions of the economic units themselves. While none of these factors is, strictly speaking, endogenous to the particular Klein-Goldberger system investigated, this does not imply that the type of perturbations actually responsible for the observed cyclical behavior are exogenous to economic theory in general.

In conclusion, we should like to emphasize that, while we have shown that the shocked Klein-Goldberger model offers excellent agreement with economic fact, we have not proved either that the Klein-Goldberger model itself is a good representation of the basic interactions among the several sectors of our economy or that random shocks are the prime cause of business cycles. In view of the remarkable quantitative correspondence with reality, however, we are very tempted to suggest that the second of these hypotheses is true and that, in addition, the Klein-Goldberger system is, except for the deficiencies discussed, not very far wrong.

Berkeley, California

APPENDIX A

1. Explanation of Symbols

$Y + T + D$	Gross national product, 1939 dollars
C	Consumer expenditures, 1939 dollars
I	Gross private domestic capital formation, 1939 dollars
G	Government expenditures for goods and services, 1939 dollars
p	Price index of gross national product, 1939: 100
F_E	Exports of goods and services, 1939 dollars
F_I	Imports of goods and services, 1939 dollars
W_1	Private employee compensation, deflated
W_2	Government employee compensation, deflated
D	Capital consumption charges, 1939 dollars
P_C	Corporate profits, deflated
S_P	Corporate savings, deflated
T	Indirect taxes less subsidies, deflated
T_W	Personal and payroll taxes less transfers associated with wage and salary income, deflated
T_P	Personal and corporate taxes less transfers associated with nonwage nonfarm income, deflated
T_C	Corporate income taxes, deflated
T_A	Taxes less transfers associated with farm income, deflated
K	End-of-year stock of private capital, 1939 dollars from arbitrary origin
F_A	Index of agricultural exports, 1939: 100
p_A	Index of agricultural prices, 1939: 100
p_I	Index of prices of imports, 1939: 100
N_P	Number of persons in the United States
N	Number of persons in the labor force
N_W	Number of wage-and-salary-earners
N_G	Number of government employees
N_F	Number of farm operators
N_E	Number of nonfarm entrepreneurs

h	Index of hours worked per year, 1939: 100
w	Index of hourly wages, 1939: 122.1
P	Nonwage nonfarm income, deflated
A_1	Farm income, deflated
A_2	Government payments to farmers, deflated
i_L	Average yield on corporate bonds, per cent
i_S	Average yield on short term commercial paper, per cent
R	Excess reserves of banks as a percentage of total reserves
L_1	End-of-year liquid assets held by persons, deflated
L_2	End-of-year liquid assets held by businesses, deflated
t	Time trend, years, $t = 1$ is 1929
B	End-of-year corporate surplus, deflated, from arbitrary origin

2. Klein and Goldberger's Equations

(1)* $$C_t = -22.26 + 0.55(W_1 + W_2 - T_W)_t + 0.41(P - T_P - S_P)_t + 0.34(A_1 + A_2 - T_A)_t + 0.26C_{t-1} + 0.072(L_1)_{t-1} + 0.26(N_P)_t$$

(2)* $$I_t = -16.71 + 0.78(P - T_P + A_1 + A_2 - T_A + D)_{t-1} - 0.073K_{t-1} + 0.14(L_2)_{t-1}$$

(3)* $$(S_P)_t = -3.53 + 0.72(P_C - T_C)_t + 0.076(P_C - T_C - S_P)_{t-1} - 0.028B_{t-1}$$

(4)* $$(P_C)_t = -7.60 + 0.68P_t$$

(5)* $$D_t = 7.25 + 0.10\frac{K_t + K_{t-1}}{2} + 0.044(Y + T + D - W_2)_t$$

(6)* $$(W_1)_t = -1.40 + 0.24(Y + T + D - W_2)_t + 0.24(Y + T + D - W_2)_{t-1} + 0.29t$$

(7)* $$(Y + T + D - W_2)_t = -26.08 + 2.17[h(N_W - N_G) + N_E + N_F]_t + 0.16\frac{K_t + K_{t-1}}{2} + 2.05t$$

(8)* $$w_t - w_{t-1} = 4.11 - 0.74(N - N_W - N_E - N_F)_t + 0.52(p_{t-1} - p_{t-2}) + 0.54t$$

(9)* $$(F_I)_t = 0.32 + 0.0060(W_1 + W_2 - T_W + P - T_P + A_1 + A_2 - T_A)_t + 0.81(F_I)_{t-1}$$

(10)* $$(A_1)_t\frac{p_t}{(p_A)_t} = -0.36 + 0.054(W_1 + W_2 - T_W + P - T_P - S_P)_t\frac{p_t}{(p_A)_t} - 0.007(W_1 + W_2 - T_W + P - T_P - S_P)_{t-1}\frac{p_{t-1}}{(p_A)_{t-1}} + 0.012(F_A)_t$$

(11)* $$(p_A)_t = -131.17 + 2.32p_t$$

(12)* $$(L_1)_t = 0.14(W_1 + W_2 - T_W + P - T_P - S_P + A_1 + A_2 - T_A)_t + 76.03(i_L - 2.0)_t^{-0.84}$$

(13)* $$(L_2)_t = -0.34 + 0.26(W_1)_t - 1.02(i_S)_t - 0.26(p_t - p_{t-1}) + 0.61(L_2)_{t-1}$$

(14)* $$(i_L)_t = 2.58 + 0.44(i_S)_{t-3} + 0.26(i_S)_{t-5}$$

(15)* $$100\,\frac{(i_S)_t - (i_S)_{t-1}}{(i_S)_{t-1}} = 11.17 - 0.67R_t$$

(16) $$C_t + I_t + G_t + (F_E)_t - (F_I)_t = Y_t + T_t + D_t$$

(17) $$(W_1)_t + (W_2)_t + P_t + (A_1)_t + (A_2)_t = Y_t$$

(18) $$h_t \frac{w_t}{p_t} (N_W)_t = (W_1)_t + (W_2)_t$$

(19) $$K_t - K_{t-1} = I_t - D_t$$

(20) $$B_t - B_{t-1} = (S_P)_t$$

(21) $$T_t = 0.0924(Y + T + D)_t - \frac{275.4}{p_t}$$

(22) $$(T_W)_t = 0.1549(W_1)_t + 0.1310(W_2)_t - \frac{1398.1}{p_t}$$

(23) $$(T_C)_t = 0.4497(P_C)_t + \frac{548.2}{p_t}$$

(24) $$(T_P)_t = 0.248(P - T_C - S_P)_t + 0.2695 \frac{p_{t-1}}{p_t} (P - T_C - S_P)_{t-1} + + 0.4497(P_C)_t - \frac{1162.1}{p_t}$$

(25) $$(T_A)_t = \frac{50.0}{p_t}$$

APPENDIX B

1. The equations that, for the actual calculations, replaced their counterparts of Appendix A

(3) $$(S_P)_t = -3.53 + 0.72(P_C - T_C)_t - 0.028B_{t-1}$$

(9) $$(F_I)_t = (F_E)_t$$

(10) $$(A_1)_t \frac{p_t}{(p_A)_t} = 0.054(W_1 + W_2 - T_W + P - T_P - S_P)_t \frac{p_t}{(p_A)_t} + 0.012(F_A)_t$$

(11) $$(p_A)_t = 1.39p_t + 32.0$$

(13) $$(L_2)_t = 0.26(W_1)_t - 1.02(i_S)_t - 0.26(p_t - p_{t-1}) + 0.61(L_2)_{t-1}$$

(14) $$(i_L)_t = 3.5$$

(15) $$(i_S)_t = 2.5$$

(16) $$C_t + I_t + G_t = Y_t + T_t + D_t$$

(21) $$T_t = 0.0924(Y + T + D)_t - 1.3607$$

(22) $$(T_W)_t = 0.1549(W_1)_t + 0.131(W_2)_t - 6.9076$$

(23) $$(T_C)_t = 0.4497(P_C)_t + 2.7085$$

(24) $$(T_P)_t = 0.248(P - T_C - S_P)_t + 0.2695\frac{p_{t-1}}{p_t}(P - T_C - S_P)_{t-1} + 0.4497(P_C)_t - 5.7416$$

(25) $$(T_A)_t = 0.0512(A_1 + A_2)_t$$

2. Extrapolations

$$(W_2)_t = 1.82 + .578t$$
$$(N_E)_t = 3.70 + .118t$$
$$(N_F)_t = 4.01 + \frac{2.12}{t-15}$$
$$(N_G)_t = 2.01 + .321t$$
$$(N_P)_t = 97.39 + 2.589t$$
$$N_t = 44.53 + .964t$$
$$h_t = 1.062$$
$$G_t = 19.892 + .567t$$
$$(A_2)_t = .108 + \frac{.0746}{t-16}$$
$$(F_A)_t = 171.86$$

3. Initial values used in calculations

Endogenous Variables	1951 $(t-2)$	1952 $(t-1)$	Exogenous Variables	1952 $(t-1)$	1953 (t)
$Y+T+D$	—	172.0	h	—	1.062
C	—	111.4	W_2	15.12	15.70
W_1	—	78.65	G	—	33.5
A_1	—	7.3	A_2	0.1187	0.1173
I	—	24.3	F_A	—	171.86
K	—	41.5	N_P	—	159.6
D	—	19.35	N	—	67.63
P_C	—	16.51	N_E	—	6.53
P	—	35.17	N_F	—	4.25
S_P	—	1.9	N_G	—	9.71
B	—	.19	i_S	2.5	2.5
N_W	—	56.0	i_L	3.5	3.5
L_1	—	95.2			
L_2	—	38.1			
w	—	326.2			
p	197.5	202.4			
p_A	—	303.0			
T	—	14.51			
T_W	—	8.63			
T_A	—	.38			
T_C	—	10.14			
T_P	—	13.72			

4. Standard deviations used for Type I shocks (upon exogenous variables)

Variable	$\sigma_{\delta y_t}$	$\frac{\sigma_{\delta y_t}}{y_{t-1}}$
i_S	.512	.20
i_L	.146	.0423
h	.0185	.018
W_2	1.77	.123
G	.88	.026
A_2	.0192	.16
F_A	12.2	.071
N_P	.086	.00054
N	.125	.0018
N_E	.114	.017
N_F	.234	.055
N_G	.975	.10

5. Standard deviations used for Type II shocks (upon equations)

Variable	Equation	$\sigma_{\delta y_t}$	$\frac{\sigma_{\delta y_t}}{y_{t-1}}$
C	(1)*	.958	.0086
I	(2)*	2.946	.12
S_P	(3)	5.428	.29
P_C	(4)*	.700	.044
D	(5)*	.699	.036
W_1	(6)*	1.0325	.013
$Y+T+D$	(7)*	2.319	.013
w	(8)*	4.861	.015
A_1	(10)	.955	.13
L_1	(12)*	.017575	.00059
L_2	(13)	1.2911	.034
p_A†	(11)	15.716	.052

† Based on residuals from our re-estimated equation for p_A for the years 1946–52.

[3]

BUSINESS CYCLES—ENDOGENOUS OR STOCHASTIC?[1]

I. Introduction

The idea that the cyclical fluctuations observed in advanced industrial economies may be due to the effect of erratic, uncorrelated shocks upon an otherwise interrelated system was first suggested by Ragnar Frisch in 1933.[2] This hypothesis received a rather mixed reception. For, on the one hand, an appeal to unexplained random perturbations in order to account for a fundamental feature of the dynamics of a capitalistic economy is not particularly satisfying. This is evidently the position taken by Hicks, who states categorically in discussing Frisch's theory, " this particular hypothesis will not do." [3]

On the other hand, several studies [4] have indicated that Frisch's explanation of cyclical behaviour provides us with an extremely good approximation to the qualitative features of the actual motion of economic time series. One of the most recent of these, and the most detailed, was part of an investigation into the dynamic nature of the Klein–Goldberger econometric model of the United States economy, undertaken in 1956–58 by my husband and myself and published in the October 1959 issue of *Econometrica*.[5] In this paper we found that, in the absence of external perturbations, the time paths of the economic variables of the Klein–Goldberger equations were monotonic and essentially linear in character. Thus, their model does not offer an immediate explanation of an internally generated cyclical process. However, when random shocks of a realistic order of magnitude were superimposed upon the Klein–Goldberger system the cyclical fluctuations which resulted were remarkably similar to those described by the N.B.E.R. as characterising the United States economy. The average duration of a cycle, the mean length of the expansion and contraction phases, and the degree of clustering of individual peaks and troughs around the turning points of the general business cycle all agreed with the corre-

[1] This paper was presented at the December 1959 meeting of the Econometric Society. I am indebted to F. L. Adelman and K. J. Arrow for their valuable suggestions.

[2] R. Frisch, " Propagation and Impulse Problems in Dynamic Economics," *Economic Essays in Honour of Gustav Cassel* (London, 1933), pp. 171–205.

[3] J. R. Hicks, *A Contribution to the Theory of the Trade Cycle* (Oxford, 1950), p. 90. See also, pp. 193–195.

[4] Cf., *e.g.*, R. M. Goodwin, " Econometrics in Business Cycle Analysis," in A. H. Hansen's *Business Cycles and National Income* (New York, 1951), p. 421; E. Slutzky, " The Summation of Random Causes as the Source of the Cyclic Processes," *Econometrica*, Vol. 5 (April 1937), pp. 105–46; M. G. Kendall, *The Advanced Theory of Statistics* (London, 1946), Vol. II, pp. 400–37; and G. H. Fisher, " Some Comments on Stochastic Macro-Economic Models," *American Economic Review*, Vol. 42, June, December 1952, pp. 528–39.

[5] I. Adelman and F. L. Adelman, " The Dynamic Properties of the Klein–Goldberger Model," *Econometrica*, Vol. 27, October 1959, pp. 596–625.

sponding data for the United States. Furthermore, the lead–lag relationships of the endogenous variables included in the model and the indices of conformity of the specific series to the overall business cycle also resembled closely the analogous features of our society. All in all, the shocked Klein–Goldberger model approximated the cyclical behaviour of the United States economy extremely well.

But the fact that the shocked Klein–Goldberger model corresponds so well to economic experience does not prove either that the model itself is a good representation of the fundamental interactions among the several sectors of our economy or that random shocks are the prime cause of business cycles. For the close agreement with reality is, *a priori*, a consequence of both the model and the shocks. How much of this agreement is due to the basic structure of the underlying economic relations, and how much to the stochastic features superimposed upon the model remains to be determined.

This study is designed to shed some light upon this question. We shall proceed in the following way: First of all, in a manner analogous to that used in the previous study, we impose random, uncorrelated shocks upon a set of economic time series related only by accounting definitions, and study the oscillations which result. The degree to which these fluctuations approximate the business cycle observed in the United States economy will then be compared with the corresponding results of our Klein–Goldberger study. We will see that the superposition of shocks upon a model with minimal economic content leads to a reasonable facsimile of a business cycle. However, the approximation will be seen to be distinctly inferior to that derived from the shocked Klein–Goldberger system.

II. The Naïve Model

The simplest model of an expanding economy that one can generate is to extrapolate all the endogenous variables of the system linearly, having regard only for the accounting identities inherent in the choice of variables. To facilitate comparison with the Klein–Goldberger model, our " naïve " model was derived in the following fashion. All the variables and the accounting identities of the Klein–Goldberger model were retained. However, all the behavioural equations of the system were replaced by simple extrapolations based on least-squares fits to the post-war (1946–52) data. For consumption (C), investment (I), government expenditures (G), corporate savings (S_P), corporate profits (P_C), indirect taxes less subsidies (T), depreciation (D), private (W_1) and government (W_2) employee compensation, the number of wage and salary earners (N_W), the index of hourly wages (w) and the price index (p), simple linear fits were used. Since the short (i_S) and long-term (i_L) interest rates and the index of hours worked per year (h) exhibited no obvious trends during this period, they were taken to be constant. On the other hand, farm income (A_1), government payments to farmers (A_2) and private (L_1) and business (L_2) liquid assets all had declining trends during the sample period. For these quantities it therefore seemed more appropriate to use a fit of the form

$$X = a + \frac{b}{t - \alpha}$$

in order that they never become negative. This procedure yielded a basic set of twenty-five equations in an equal number of variables. Five of these equations are accounting definitions, while the rest express each variable as a function only of time.

In order to see what effects random perturbations may have upon this " naïve " model, a random term δy_t was then inserted into those extrapolations which replace *behavioural* equations of the Klein–Goldberger model. For this purpose the value of a variable y_t at time t was defined as its trend value, $\bar{y}_t$, plus a shock term δy_t. And y_t was assumed to have a Gaussian distribution with a mean of zero. (The resulting system of equations appears in Appendix A2.) In order that the shocks inflicted upon the system be of a realistic order of magnitude at all times, the standard deviation of δy_t was evaluated over that portion of the data for which the least-squares fit was made. And, for the subsequent calculations, the ratio of the standard deviation of δy_t to $\bar{y}_{t-1}$ was maintained at a value independent of time. It is interesting to note that these standard deviations (see Appendix A3) are, in general, quite small; in fact, only four of them exceed 10% of the trend value of the corresponding variable.

Given the size of the standard deviation, the technique employed to determine the magnitude and sign of the exogenous shock upon each variable was to divide the normal curve of error into 100 regions of equal area. To each region was assigned both the normal deviate associated with the mid-point of its interval and a previously unassigned integer between 00 and 99, inclusive. Then the selection of a two-digit random number effectively specified at random a particular region of the Gaussian distribution and its corresponding normal deviate. Multiplying this deviate by the standard deviation of δy_t, the magnitude and direction of a shock upon the variable y at time t were established. Since the selection of an interval in this manner was thus purely random, and since all intervals define the same area under the curve, this method produced a normally distributed *random* shock upon the variable in question. The repetition of this procedure for each of the variables of equations (1)–(14) yielded a series of random, normally distributed, uncorrelated shocks of realistic size.

Using this technique for the evaluation of the magnitudes and signs of the random terms, the shocked " naïve " model was solved for 100 years with the aid of an I.B.M. 650 calculator. The typical behaviour of the time series generated by this process is portrayed in Fig. 1. The solid lines in this graph describe the computed time paths of national income, investment and corporate profits, while the dotted lines represent the actual time

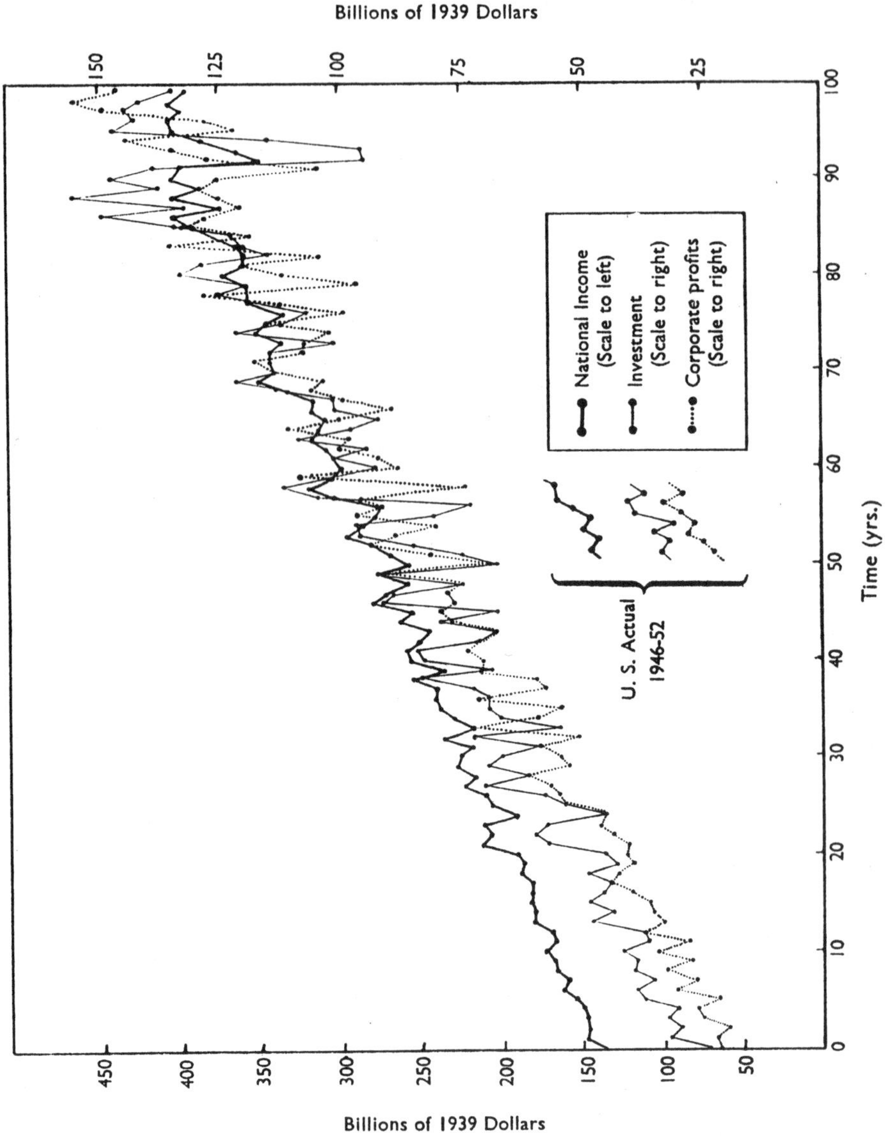
Billions of 1939 Dollars
150
125
100
75
50
25
National Income (Scale to left)
Investment (Scale to right)
Corporate profits (Scale to right)
U. S. Actual 1946-52
450
400
350
300
250
200
150
100
50
Billions of 1939 Dollars
0
10
20
30
40
50
60
70
80
90
100
Time (yrs.)

Fig. 1.

paths of the same variables during the post-war period in the United States. As apparent from this figure, under the impact of random shocks the individual variables of the system exhibit cyclical swings of more or less realistic durations and amplitudes.

The presence of qualitatively correct oscillatory movements in the individual variables of this system is but to be expected, however. This much agreement with reality is merely a *necessary* condition of an adequate simulation of the cyclical fluctuations of a real industrial economy. We must investigate further to find out whether or not the shocked version of this " naïve " model really produces business cycles in the technical sense. Specifically, how nearly all-pervasive are the cumulative movements which arise? Are the various oscillations correlated? Is there any consistent phase relationship among the several economic series? Do the time-paths of the individual variables of the model correspond to those observed in the United States economy? To answer these questions, the techniques developed by the N.B.E.R. for the analysis of business cycles were applied to the data.

One property of cyclical fluctuations in an industrial economy is a marked tendency for a clustering of peaks and troughs of individual economic time series about particular reference dates. It is, in fact, precisely this characteristic of business cycles that Burns and Mitchell [1] use as their criterion for the dating of turning-points in the United States economy. And, inasmuch as the oscillations in our model occur in response to random non-correlated perturbations, a study of the simultaneity of occurrence of peaks (and troughs) provides us with quite stringent a test of the realism of this system.

As in the normal N.B.E.R.[2] procedure, the specific cycles were dated first; *i.e.*, all the turning-points of each of the time series were determined. Then, to establish reference dates for the turning-points of the *overall* business cycles, the data were examined for bunching (in time) of specific cycle peaks and troughs. A reference peak (trough) was said to occur in our data during any year in which the modal number of specific cycle peaks occurs, provided that at least 10 peaks (troughs) are found in a 2-year period which includes the modal year.

Table I is a summary of some of the relevant characteristics observed in the shocked naïve model. The first two columns give the reference dates for the peaks and troughs, respectively. Since one can identify 20 complete business cycles (measured either from trough to trough or from peak to peak) occurring in the 90 years included in the calculation, the average length of a cycle is 4·5 years. This result is in startling agreement with the

[1] A. F. Burns and W. C. Mitchell, *Measuring Business Cycles* (National Bureau, 1946), and W. C. Mitchell, *What Happens During Business Cycles* (National Bureau, 1951), pp. 10–11.

[2] The methods and results of the N.B.E.R. are summarised in Burns and Mitchell, *op. cit.*, and in Mitchell, *op. cit.*

4-year post-Second World War cycles in the United States economy, as well as with the mean length of American peace-time business cycles since 1864.[1] The longest cycle in our data as measured from trough to trough was

TABLE I

Reference Dating for the Shocked Naïve Model

Reference dates.		Elapsed time, years.		Number of series at peaks which:			Number of series at troughs which:		
Peaks (P).	Trough (T).	$T - P$.	$P - T$.	Lead, one year.	Co-incide.	Lag, one year.	Lead, one year.	Co-incide.	Lag, one year.
11	8	3	1	4	5	2	4	6	1
22	12	10	3	1	8	3	2	7	3
28	25	3	2	0	8	3	3	8	1
33	30	3	1	4	8	3	5	6	2
39	34	5	1	3	7	2	5	7	3
41	40	1	3	2	5	5	3	7	2
47	44	3	2	3	7	2	2	8	2
50	49	1	2	3	9	2	3	7	3
53	52	1	4	1	8	2	5	7	1
61	57	4	1	3	7	2	3	8	1
63	62	1	1	2	8	8	5	8	2
72	66	6	3	5	6	1	4	7	4
75	73	2	2	4	7	4	4	5	4
78	77	1	2	2	6	5	6	7	2
82	80	2	1	4	8	1	2	8	2
85	83	2	1	4	7	3	2	10	0
87	86	1	1	3	5	5	5	6	3
89	88	1	1	5	5	5	3	6	4
91	90	1	1	6	6	3	4	7	4
96	92	4	2	2	7	4	2	8	4
—	98	—	—	—	—	—	2	7	4
TOTALS		56	34	61	137	65	74	150	57
Average per cycle		2·80	1·70	3·05	6·85	3·25	3·70	7·50	2·85
% of specific cycles represented		—	—	17·9	40·2	19·1	21·8	44·1	16·8

13 years in duration; the shortest lasted 2 years. The corresponding figures for the United States economy were 9·2 and 2·2 years respectively.

The computed cycles are broken down, in columns 3 and 4. to indicate the duration of the expansion and contraction phases of each cycle. The average expansion covered 2·8 years, while the normal contraction took 1·7. The agreement with the observed figures for the United States (2·0 and 1·8 respectively) is surprisingly good, considering the fact that, in our computations, the length of a single business-cycle stage can be estimated only to an integral number of years.

The validity of this comparison of United States and computed business cycles is dependent, of course, upon the degree of reliability with which the

[1] Computed from the N.B.E.R. dating for the period 1854–1949. We omitted from our averages the Civil War cycle and those corresponding to the two World Wars.

reference dates have been determined. One criterion which can be used is the extent to which specific cycle peaks (troughs) tend to cluster at times coincident with the turning-points of the overall business cycles. In our results 40% of the individual series, on the average, have maxima coincident with an upper turning-point of general business activity, and 44% have minima which coincide with a reference trough. The corresponding figures for the United States economy are 58 and 52%, respectively.[1] In addition, the percentage of specific cycles which lead or lag the business cycle in our computed data are 17·9 and 19·1% at the peaks, and 21·8 and 16·8% at the troughs. The analogous numbers for the United States economy lie between 13 and 16%.[1] Thus, while the computed specific cycles definitely tend to cluster at business-cycle turning-points, the degree of bunching is significantly less in the shocked naïve model than in the United States economy.

All in all, it would appear that there is a fair correspondence between the characteristics of the fluctuations generated by the superposition of random shocks upon economic time series related only through accounting definitions and the nature of the business cycles which actually occur in the United States economy. The mean duration of the cycles and the relative length of their expansion and contraction phases are in close numerical agreement with empirical evidence. The degree of bunching of peaks and troughs, however, while significant, does not approximate actual experience as closely as might be desired. We must therefore study the computed cycles in greater detail.

Table II summarises some of the significant features of the specific cycle patterns observed in the variables of the perturbed naïve model. Columns 2–5 and 10–13 give the data which lead to our grouping of the economic variables into leading, coincident and lagging series. As apparent from these columns, the number of turning-points of the specific cycles which occur in the " other " column is generally comparable to the modal number of events in the leading, coincident or lagging columns. As a result, it was generally impossible to classify the variables of the model unambiguously according to the timing of their turning-points relative to those of the reference cycle. Of the twenty variables listed in Table II, five were completely irregular in their behaviour at the turning-points of the general business cycle (see columns 6 and 14 of this table). Twelve series were classified as coincident-irregular, and one (consumption) as coincident–lagging. Only a single variable, national income (Y), tended to have peaks and troughs which coincided consistently with those of the overall reference cycle. It should be noted, though, that, as can be seen by comparing columns 6 and 14 with 7 and 15, except for the tendency towards more erratic behaviour in the computed series, the classification of the variables of

[1] These percentages were estimated from Chart 3 (pp. 16–17) of G. H. Moore, *Statistical Indicators of Cyclical Revivals and Recessions* (National Bureau Occasional Paper 31, 1950).

TABLE II

Comparison of Computed and N.B.E.R. Specific Cycles

	Properties at peaks.								Properties at troughs.								
Variable	One-year lead.	Co-incide	One-year lag.	Other.	Our classification.	N.B.E.R. classification.	Our index of conformity, %.	N.B.E.R. index of conformity.	One-year lead.	Co-incide.	One-year lag.	Other.	Our classification.	N.B.E.R. classification.	Our index of conformity, %.	N.B.E.R. index of conformity.	Remarks.
C	3	5	5	3	Coinc.–Lag	Coinc.	+ 70	+100	3	3	3	7	Irreg.	Coinc.	−80	+ 50	
I	1	11	5	12	Coinc.–Irreg.	Coinc.	+ 90	+100	4	14	3	7	Coinc.	Coinc.	+60	+100	
Sp	3	11	2	12	Coinc.–Irreg.	Coinc.	+ 40	+100	7	7	4	9	Irreg.	Coinc.	+30	+ 50	
P_C	4	6	6	15	Irreg.	Coinc.	+ 30	+100	4	12	1	13	Coinc.–Irreg.	Coinc.	+30	+100	
D	3	3	8	9	Lag–Irreg.	—	+ 40	—	5	4	8	5	Lag	—	−70	—	
W_1	1	8	4	9	Coinc.–Irreg.	Coinc.	+ 60	+100	1	7	6	8	Coinc.–Irreg.	Coinc.	0	+ 50	
N_w	6	8	3	10	Coinc.–Irreg.	Coinc.	+ 60	+100	4	8	3	12	Coinc.–Irreg.	Coinc.	−50	+100	
w	2	6	2	5	Coinc.–Irreg.	Lagging	+ 80	+100	2	6	1	5	Coinc.–Irreg.	Coinc.	−70	− 50	
p_A	3	12	4	9	Coinc.–Irreg.	Coinc.	+ 50	+ 50	2	11	6	9	Coinc.–Irreg.	Coinc.	+20	+ 60	
i_S, i_L	3	3	6	13	Irreg.	—	+ 10	—	5	4	6	10	Irreg.	—	− 5	—	
A_1	4	9	5	15	Coinc.–Irreg.	Coinc.	+ 50	+ 60	5	11	4	14	Coinc.–Irreg.	Coinc.	+40	+ 12	
L_1	2	7	8	13	Irreg.	—	+ 30	—	9	9	1	12	Irreg.	—	+20	—	
L_2	1	12	2	14	Coinc.–Irreg.	—	+ 30	—	1	10	3	14	Coinc.–Irreg.	—	+60	—	
Y	1	13	3	6	Coinc.	Coinc.	+100	+100	3	13	2	4	Coinc.	Coinc.	+60	+ 50	
P	2	13	3	12	Coinc.–Irreg.	Coinc.	+ 60	—	6	11	3	9	Coinc.–Irreg.	Coinc.	+60	—	
p	6	7	3	11	Irreg.	Coinc.	+ 40	+ 64	4	8	4	11	Coinc.–Irreg.	Coinc.	−50	+ 82	
K	0	5	3	6	Coinc.–Irreg.	—	+ 70	—	1	8	1	3	Coinc.	—	−20	—	
B	1	1	1	0	Irreg.	—	+100	—	2	1	0	0	—	—	−90	—	
K/Y	2	12	2	10	Coinc.–Irreg.	—	− 60	—	5	13	2	5	Coinc.	—	−80	—	Inverse
w/p	3	8	4	12	Coinc.–Irreg.	—	+ 20	—	4	9	4	9	Coinc.–Irreg.	—	−10	—	

the model into leading, coincident and lagging quantities is generally similar to that of the N.B.E.R.

Columns 8–9 and 16–17 of Table II present the indices of conformity of the specific cycles to the expansions and contractions of the business cycles for both the computed time series and the N.B.E.R. statistics. These indices measure the correlation between the direction of movement in the individual series and that of the overall business fluctuations. As can be seen from this table, there is fairly poor agreement between the indices of conformity of the computed series and those of the N.B.E.R., especially during contractions.

Generally speaking, then, the cycles generated by random uncorrelated shocks upon a system in which the only relationships among the variables are due to accounting procedures bear a certain amount of resemblance to the cycles found in the United States economy. The mean length of the cycles, and the average duration of prosperity and recession, agree fairly well with United States experience. On the other hand, the tendency towards a clustering of turning-points of specific cycles at reference peaks and troughs is significantly weaker in the computed cycles than it is in practice. And, in addition, the computed time series were much more erratic in their lead–lag behaviour than their counterparts in the United States economy.

III. The Klein–Goldberger Model

To help us assess these results, let us see how they compare with those obtained when the dynamic behaviour of the shocked 1954 Klein–Goldberger econometric model of the United States economy was studied in the same manner. The details of the Klein–Goldberger investigation are discussed in the October 1959 issue of *Econometrica*, and will not be given here.

Table III summarises the characteristics of the reference cycles in the shocked Klein–Goldberger economy in a form similar to that of Table I. As before, the mean duration of the computed cyclical swings (4·0 years) and the relative length of the average expansion and contraction (2·6 and 1·5 years respectively) are in close agreement with the actual data for the United States. Unlike in the shocked naïve model, however, the specific cycle peaks and troughs of the Klein–Goldberger system tend to cluster more markedly at reference turning dates: In the Klein–Goldberger calculations 51% of the specific cycle peaks and 52% of specific cycle troughs occurred at reference extrema, as compared to only 40 and 44% for the naïve model. Thus, the substitution of the economic interactions of the Klein–Goldberger system for the simple extrapolations of the naïve scheme leads to a decided improvement in the characteristics of the reference cycle.

However, for an adequate description of actual experience we must require, in addition, that the specific cycle patterns observed be realistic as

TABLE III

Reference Dating for Shocked Klein–Goldberger Model

Reference dates.		Elapsed time, years.		Number of series at peaks which:			Number of series at troughs which:		
Trough (*T*).	Peak (*P*).	*T* – *P*.	*P* – *T*.	Lag, one year.	Co-incide.	Lead, one year.	Lag, one year.	Co-incide.	Lead, one year.
—	27	—	2	—	—	—	—	—	—
29	31	2	1	2	8	6	1	6	4
32	37	5	1	1	8	5	4	7	4
38	42	4	1	1	10	0	1	13	1
43	45	2	1	2	7	4	0	10	0
46	51	5	2	2	11	1	3	8	3
53	54	1	2	4	12	1	2	10	4
56	59	3	1	1	10	1	1	11	4
60	63	3	1	2	7	6	4	6	2
64	68	4	2	6	6	3	5	7	1
70	72	2	1	2	7	3	1	13	1
73	74	1	1	2	9	1	2	8	2
75	77	2	1	2	8	4	0	10	2
78	79	1	1	2	8	2	3	9	3
80	83	3	2	2	12	1	1	7	3
85	86	1	2	4	12	2	2	11	2
88	90	2	1	2	12	2	1	11	4
91	94	3	2	3	10	1	3	11	3
96	98	2	4	5	8	3	1	9	3
102	106	4	1	3	12	2	3	10	2
107	109	2	1	4	9	1	5	11	2
110	113	3	1	2	11	4	5	7	1
114	116	2	1	5	7	4	3	13	0
117	119	2	1	1	8	8	4	9	3
120	—	—	—	—	—	—	—	—	—
TOTALS . .		59	34	60	212	65	55	217	54
Average per cycle .		2·56	1·48	2·61	9·22	2·82	2·39	9·43	2·34
% of specific cycles represented .		—	—	14·5	51·2	15·7	13·3	52·4	13·0

well. Table IV presents a comparison of the Klein–Goldberger and N.B.E.R. specific cycles, in a form analogous to that of Table II. As can be seen by comparing columns 6 and 14 of the two tables, the Klein–Goldberger model succeeds in removing the indeterminacy present in the naïve system. Only agricultural incomes (A_1) remain irregular in their pattern of behavior in the Klein–Goldberger data. But, in view of the low index of conformity reported by the N.B.E.R. for this variable, this may not be unrealistic. In addition, there is also extremely close agreement between the N.B.E.R. and the Klein–Goldberger classification of variables into leading, lagging and coincident series. Eleven Klein–Goldberger variables are classified as coincident at both peaks and troughs. These are: national income (Y), gross investment (I), private employee compensation (W_1), non-wage, non-farm income (P), employment (N_W), corporate profits (P_C), corporate savings (S_P), corporate surplus (B), capital stock (K), the

TABLE IV

Comparison of Klein–Goldberger and N.B.E.R. Specific Cycles

Variable.	Properties at peaks.								Properties at troughs.								Re-marks.
	One-year lead.	Co-incide.	One-year lag.	Other.	K.–G. classifi-cation.	N.B.E.R. classifi-cation.	K.–G. index of con-formity, %.	N.B.E.R. index of con-formity, %.	One-year lead.	Co-incide.	One-year lag.	Other.	K.–G. classifi-cation.	N.B.E.R. classifi-cation.	K.–G. index of con-formity, %.	N.B.E.R. index of con-formity, %.	
$Y+T+D$	1	21	1	1	Coinc.	Coinc.	+100	+100	2	21	0	1	Coinc.	Coinc.	+ 92	+ 50	
Y	1	21	1	1	Coinc.	Coinc.	+100	+100	1	22	0	1	Coinc.	Coinc.	+100	+ 50	
C	1	8	3	0	Coinc.	Coinc.	+100	+100	5	5	1	1	Leading–Coinc.	Coinc.	− 17	+ 50	
I	4	20	0	3	Coinc.	Coinc.	+100	+100	0	23	1	3	Coinc.	Coinc.	+100	+100	
W_1	2	10	3	2	Coinc.	Coinc.	+ 83	+100	1	10	3	3	Coinc.	Coinc.	+ 8	+ 50	
A_1	6	8	7	7	Irreg.	Coinc.	− 4	+ 60	8	5	5	10	Irreg.	Coinc.	− 33	+ 12	
P	4	19	0	4	Coinc.	Coinc.	+ 91	—	0	22	1	4	Coinc.	Coinc.	+100	—	
Nw	4	18	2	2	Coinc.	Coinc.	+ 91	+100	3	19	2	2	Coinc.	Coinc.	+100	+100	
Pc	4	20	0	4	Coinc.	Coinc.	+100	+100	3	20	1	4	Coinc.	Coinc.	+ 92	+100	
Sp	4	16	0	4	Coinc.	Coinc.	+ 83	+100	0	17	4	3	Coinc.	Coinc.	+100	+ 50	
B	0	5	1	1	Coinc.	—	+100	—	1	5	1	0	Coinc.	—	− 42	—	
K	1	9	6	0	Coinc.	—	+ 87	—	0	11	3	1	Coinc.	—	+ 33	—	
D	10	6	3	6	Leading	—	+ 22	—	10	7	4	5	Leading	—	− 25	—	
L_1	14	4	5	3	Leading	—	+ 13	—	5	6	9	5	Lagging–Irreg.	—	+ 8	—	
L_2	4	15	0	4	Coinc.	—	− 65	—	2	17	3	1	Coinc.	—	− 83	—	Inverse
p	3	17	2	0	Coinc.	Coinc.	+100	+ 64	0	20	2	0	Coinc.	Coinc.	+ 83	+ 82	
pA	4	17	2	5	Coinc.	Coinc.	+100	+ 50	6	14	4	4	Coinc.	Coinc.	+ 42	+ 60	
w	0	1	9	1	Lagging	Lagging	+ 83	+100	0	4	7	0	Lagging	Coinc.	− 67	− 50	
w/p	2	17	1	5	Coinc.	—	− 74	—	0	21	0	4	Coinc.	—	−100	—	Inverse
K/Y	4	19	1	4	Coinc.	—	−100	—	5	19	1	3	Coinc.	—	−100	—	Inverse

general price index (p) and the index of agricultural prices (p_A). Consumption (C) coincides at peaks, but has a tendency to lead at troughs. And corporate liquid assets (L_2), real wages (w/p) and the capital/output ratio (K/Y) are in inverse coincidence with the business cycle in the sense that their troughs tend to occur at reference peaks, and vice versa. All of these results are in accord with N.B.E.R. experience (when available), except that United States specific cycles for consumption coincide, rather than lead, at the troughs. In addition, as evident from columns 8–9 and 16–17 of this table, the indices of conformity calculated for the Klein–Goldberger statistics are quite consistent with those given by Mitchell for the United States economy.

Generally speaking, then, it would appear that the specific cycles generated in the Klein–Goldberger model by random shocks resemble the cycles found in the United States economy much more closely than do those of the naïve model. Since, in addition, the characteristics of the reference cycles of the Klein–Goldberger model are also more satisfactory, we conclude that the shocked Klein–Goldberger equations offer a better approximation to United States cyclical experience than does the shocked naïve model.

IV. Discussion

When the work described in this paper on a minimal stochastic model of a complex industrial economy is compared with the earlier investigation on the Klein–Goldberger system three facts stand out:

(1) a minimal stochastic model is reasonably satisfactory in simulating business fluctuations in the United States;

(2) the Klein–Goldberger equations by themselves describe a non-oscillatory economy;

(3) the superposition of random shocks upon the Klein–Goldberger system leads to an extremely close representation of the cyclical fluctuations of American business activity.

These results suggest that it is the stochastic features of the shocked Klein–Goldberger model, rather than the interactions described directly by the Klein–Goldberger equations themselves, which are responsible for the excellent agreement with reality mentioned above. We have not, of course, proved that business cycles are stochastic in origin, but it is my belief that the evidence presented here creates a strong presumption in favour of this hypothesis. This is especially significant in view of the absence (to date) of a completely satisfactory endogenous theory of business cycles.

It would also appear that there is some validity to the Klein–Goldberger description of the interactions which take place among the several sectors of the economy. That is to say, the interrelations which exist among economic units must be incorporated in a reasonable manner into any rational description of the dynamic behaviour of an industrial complex. A purely stochastic theory of cyclical fluctuations constitutes merely a first approximation to reality.

The implications for the student of business cycles are quite clear. The theorist need not explain a determinate economic path with observable oscillations at predetermined points of time. If he accepts the stochastic hypothesis he knows how and why business cycles arise: the normal perturbations upon the day-to-day operation of an economy suffice to generate a persistent oscillatory process of the observed magnitude. The primary task of the business-cycle analyst is to investigate the reaction patterns of an economic system to various shocks, for it is in this sphere of activity that his efforts are likely to be most significant.

IRMA ADELMAN

Stanford University.

APPENDIX A

1. *Explanation of Symbols*

$Y + T + D$	Gross national product, 1939 dollars
C	Consumer expenditures, 1939 dollars
I	Gross private domestic capital formation, 1939 dollars
G	Government expenditures for goods and services, 1939 dollars
p	Price index of gross national product, 1939 : 100
W_1	Private employee compensation, deflated
W_2	Government employee compensation, deflated
D	Capital consumption charges, 1939 dollars
P_C	Corporate profits, deflated
S_P	Corporate savings, deflated
T	Indirect taxes less subsidies, deflated
K	End-of-year stock of private capital, 1939 dollars from arbitrary origin
p_A	Index of agricultural prices, 1939 = 100
p_1	Index of prices of imports, 1939 = 100
N_p	Number of persons in the United States
N	Number of persons in the labor force
N_w	Number of wage-and-salary-earners
N_g	Number of government employees
N_f	Number of farm operators
N_e	Number of non-farm entrepreneurs
h	Index of hours worked per year, 1939 = 100
w	Index of hourly wages, 1939 = 122·1
P	Non-wage, non-farm income, deflated
A_1	Farm income deflated
A_2	Government payments to farmers, deflated
i_L	Average yield on corporate bonds, %
i_S	Average yield on short term commercial paper, %
L_1	End-of-year liquid assets held by persons, deflated
L_2	End-of-year liquid assets held by businesses, deflated
t	Time trend, years, $t = 2$ in 1952
B	End-of-year corporate surplus, deflated, from arbitrary origin

2. *The Naïve Model*

$$
\begin{array}{lrl}
(1) & C_t = & 111{\cdot}9 + 2{\cdot}72t + \delta_c \\
(2) & I_t = & 26{\cdot}2 + 1{\cdot}17t + \delta_I \\
(3) & S_{Pt} = & 2{\cdot}85 + 0{\cdot}20t + \delta_{Sp} \\
(4) & P_{Ct} = & 18{\cdot}53 + 1{\cdot}23t + \delta_{Pc} \\
(5) & D_t = & 18{\cdot}76 + 1{\cdot}21t + \delta_D \\
(6) & (W_1)_t = & 77{\cdot}25 + 2{\cdot}69t + \delta_{W_1} \\
(7) & (Nw)_t = & 54{\cdot}68 + 1{\cdot}13t + \delta_{N_w} \\
(8) & W_t = & 326{\cdot}8 + 17{\cdot}92t + \delta_W \\
(9) & (p_A)_t = & 305 + 7{\cdot}07t + \delta_{pa} \\
(10) & i_S = & 2{\cdot}5 + \delta_{i_S} \\
(11) & i_t = & 3{\cdot}5 + \delta_{i_S} \\
(12) & (A_1)_t = & 7{\cdot}3 + \dfrac{2{\cdot}5}{t+7} + \delta_A \\
(13) & (L_1)_t = & 92{\cdot}44 + \dfrac{16{\cdot}76}{t+7} + \delta_{L_1} \\
(14) & (L_2)_t = & 35{\cdot}88 + \dfrac{6{\cdot}69}{t+7} + \delta_{L2} \\
(15) & G_t = & 32{\cdot}933 + 0{\cdot}567t \\
(16) & (W_2)_t = & 15{\cdot}114 + 0{\cdot}578t \\
(17) & T_t = & 14{\cdot}146 + 0{\cdot}514t \\
(18) & (A_2)_t = & 0{\cdot}108 + \dfrac{0{\cdot}0746}{t+7} \\
(19) & h_t = & 1{\cdot}062 \\
(20) & Y_t = & C_t + I_t + G_t - T_t - D_t \\
(21) & P_t = & Y_t - (W_1)_t - (W_2)_t - (A_2)_t - (A_1)_t \\
(22) & p_t = & \dfrac{h_t\, w_t\, (Nw)_t}{(W_1)_t + (W_2)_t} \\
(23) & K_t = & K_{t-1} + I_t - D_t \\
(24) & B_t = & B_{t-1} + S_p
\end{array}
$$

3. *Standard Errors Used for Shocks*

Variable	% Standard deviation
C	1·07
I	9·79
S_P	61·4
P_C	9·43
D	3·97
W_1	2·41
N_w	2·89
w	1·49
p_A	7·29
i_S	20·00
i_L	14·28
A_1	10·2
L_1	3·0
L_2	3·57

Part II
Calibration

[4]

Federal Reserve Bank of Minneapolis
Quarterly Review Fall 1986

Theory Ahead of Business Cycle Measurement*

Edward C. Prescott
Adviser
Research Department
Federal Reserve Bank of Minneapolis
and Professor of Economics
University of Minnesota

Economists have long been puzzled by the observations that during peacetime industrial market economies display recurrent, large fluctuations in output and employment over relatively short time periods. Not uncommon are changes as large as 10 percent within only a couple of years. These observations are considered puzzling because the associated movements in labor's marginal product are small.

These observations should not be puzzling, for they are what standard economic theory predicts. For the United States, in fact, given people's ability and willingness to intertemporally and intratemporally substitute consumption and leisure and given the nature of the changing production possibility set, it would be puzzling if the economy did not display these large fluctuations in output and employment with little associated fluctuations in the marginal product of labor. Moreover, standard theory also correctly predicts the amplitude of these fluctuations, their serial correlation properties, and the fact that the investment component of output is about six times as volatile as the consumption component.

This perhaps surprising conclusion is the principal finding of a research program initiated by Kydland and me (1982) and extended by Kydland and me (1984), Hansen (1985a), and Bain (1985). We have computed the competitive equilibrium stochastic process for variants of the constant elasticity, stochastic growth model. The elasticities of substitution and the share parameters of the production and utility functions are restricted to those that generate the growth observations. The process governing the technology parameter is selected to be consistent with the measured technology changes for the American economy since the Korean War. We ask whether these artificial economies display fluctuations with statistical properties similar to those which the American economy has displayed in that period. They do.[1]

I view the growth model as a paradigm for macro analysis—analogous to the supply and demand construct of price theory. The elasticities of substitution and the share parameters of the growth model are analogous to the price and income elasticities of price theory. Whether or not this paradigm dominates, as I expect it will, is still an open question. But the early results indicate its power to organize our knowledge. The finding that when uncertainty in the rate of technological change is incorporated into the growth model it

*This paper was presented at a Carnegie-Rochester Conference on Public Policy and will appear in a volume of the conference proceedings. It appears here with the kind permission of Allan H. Meltzer, editor of that volume. The author thanks Finn E. Kydland for helpful discussions of the issues reviewed here, Gary D. Hansen for data series and some additional results for his growth economy, Lars G. M. Ljungqvist for expert research assistance, Bruce D. Smith and Allan H. Meltzer for comments on a preliminary draft, and the National Science Foundation and the Minneapolis Federal Reserve Bank for financial support. The views expressed herein are those of the author alone.

[1]Others [Barro (1981) and Long and Plosser (1983), for example] have argued that these fluctuations are not inconsistent with competitive theory that abstracts from monetary factors. Our finding is much stronger: standard theory predicts that the economy will display the business cycle phenomena.

displays the business cycle phenomena was both dramatic and unanticipated. I was sure that the model could not do this without some features of the payment and credit technologies.

The models constructed within this theoretical framework are necessarily highly abstract. Consequently, they are necessarily false, and statistical hypothesis testing will reject them. This does not imply, however, that nothing can be learned from such quantitative theoretical exercises. I think much has already been learned and confidently predict that much more will be learned as other features of the environment are introduced. Prime candidates for study are the effects of public finance elements, a foreign sector, and, of course, monetary factors. The research I review here is best viewed as a very promising beginning of a much larger research program.

The Business Cycle Phenomena

The use of the expression *business cycle* is unfortunate for two reasons. One is that it leads people to think in terms of a time series' business cycle component which is to be explained independently of a growth component; our research has, instead, one unifying theory of both of these. The other reason I do not like to use the expression is that it is not accurate; some systems of low-order linear stochastic difference equations with a nonoscillatory deterministic part, and therefore no cycle, display key business cycle features. (See Slutzky 1927.) I thus do not refer to business cycles, but rather to business cycle *phenomena*, which are nothing more nor less than a certain set of statistical properties of a certain set of important aggregate time series. The question I and others have considered is, Do the stochastic difference equations that are the equilibrium laws of motion for the stochastic growth display the business cycle phenomena?

More specifically, we follow Lucas (1977, p. 9) in defining the business cycle phenomena as the recurrent fluctuations of output about trend and the co-movements among other aggregate time series. Fluctuations are by definition deviations from some slowly varying path. Since this slowly varying path increases monotonically over time, we adopt the common practice of labeling it *trend*. This trend is neither a measure nor an estimate of the unconditional mean of some stochastic process. It is, rather, defined by the computational procedure used to fit the smooth curve through the data.

If the business cycle facts were sensitive to the detrending procedure employed, there would be a problem. But the key facts are not sensitive to the procedure if the trend curve is smooth. Our curve-fitting method is to take the logarithms of variables and then select the trend path $\{\tau_t\}$ which minimizes the sum of the squared deviations from a given series $\{Y_t\}$ subject to the constraint that the sum of the squared second differences not be too large. This is

$$\min_{\{\tau_t\}_{t=1}^{T}} \sum_{t=1}^{T} (Y_t - \tau_t)^2$$

subject to

$$\sum_{t=2}^{T-1} [(\tau_{t+1} - \tau_t) - (\tau_t - \tau_{t-1})]^2 \leq \mu.$$

The smaller is μ, the smoother is the trend path. If $\mu = 0$, the least squares linear time trend results. For all series, μ is picked so that the Lagrange multiplier of the constraint is 1600. This produces the right degree of smoothness in the fitted trend when the observation period is a quarter of a year. Thus, the sequence $\{\tau_t\}$ minimizes

$$\sum_{t=1}^{T} (Y_t - \tau_t)^2 + 1600 \sum_{t=2}^{T-1} [(\tau_{t-1} - \tau_t) - (\tau_t - \tau_{t-1})]^2.$$

The first-order conditions of this minimization problem are linear in Y_t and τ_t, so for every series, $\tau = AY$, where A is the same $T \times T$ matrix. The deviations from trend, also by definition, are

$$Y_t^d = Y_t - \tau_t \quad \text{for } t = 1, \ldots, T.$$

Unless otherwise stated, these are the variables used in the computation of the statistics reported here for both the United States and the growth economies.

An alternative interpretation of the procedure is that it is a high pass linear filter. The facts reported here are essentially the same if, rather than defining the deviations by $Y^d = (I - A)Y$, we filtered the Y using a high pass band filter, eliminating all frequencies of 32 quarters or greater. An advantage of our procedure is that it deals better with the ends of the sample problem and does not require a stationary time series.

To compare the behaviors of a stochastic growth economy and an actual economy, only identical statistics for the two economies are used. By definition, a *statistic* is a real valued function of the raw time series. Consequently, if a comparison is made, say, between the standard deviations of the deviations, the date t deviation for the growth economy must be the same function of the data generated by that model as the date t deviation for the American economy is of that economy's data. Our definitions of the deviations satisfy this criterion.

Figure 1 plots the logs of actual and trend output for the U.S. economy during 1947–82, and Figure 2 the corresponding percentage deviations from trend of output and hours of market employment. Output and hours clearly move up and down together with nearly the same amplitudes.

Table 1 contains the standard deviations and cross serial correlations of output and other aggregate time series for the American economy during 1954–82. Consumption appears less variable and investment more variable than output. Further, the average product of labor is procyclical but does not vary as much as output or hours.

The Growth Model

This theory and its variants build on the neoclassical growth economy of Solow (1956) and Swan (1956). In the language of Lucas (1980, p. 696), the model is a "fully articulated, artificial economic system" that can be used to generate economic time series of a set of important economic aggregates. The model assumes an aggregate production function with constant returns to scale, inputs labor n and capital k, and an output which can be allocated either to current consumption c or to investment x. If t denotes the date, $f: R^2 \rightarrow R$ the production function, and z_t a technology parameter, then the production constraint is

$$x_t + c_t \leq z_t f(k_t, n_t)$$

where $x_t, c_t, k_t, n_t \geq 0$. The model further assumes that the services provided by a unit of capital decrease geometrically at a rate $0 < \delta < 1$:

$$k_{t+1} = (1-\delta)k_t + x_t.$$

Solow completes the specification of his economy by hypothesizing that some fraction $0 < \sigma < 1$ of output is invested and the remaining fraction $1 - \sigma$ consumed and that n_t is a constant—say, $\bar{n}$—for all t. For this economy, the law of motion of capital condition on z_t is

$$k_{t+1} = (1-\delta)k_t + \sigma z_t f(k_t, \bar{n}).$$

Once the $\{z_t\}$ stochastic process is specified, the stochastic process governing capital and the other economic aggregates are determined and realizations of the stochastic process can be generated by a computer.

This structure is far from adequate for the study of the business cycle because in it neither employment nor the savings rate varies, when in fact they do. Being explicit about the economy, however, naturally leads to

Figure 1

Actual and Trend Logs of U.S. Gross National Product

Quarterly, 1947–82

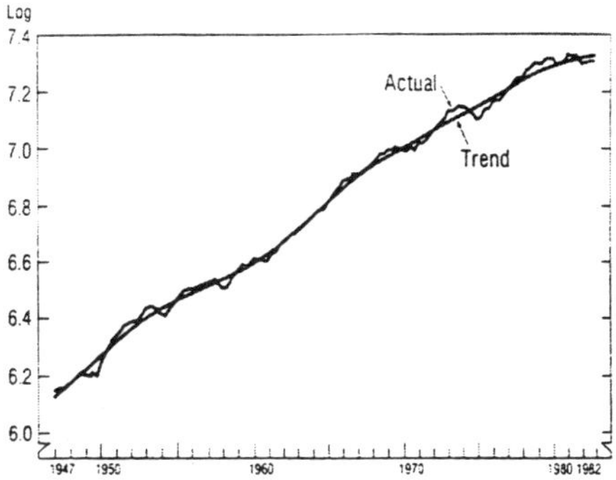

Source of basic data: Citicorp's Citibase data bank

Figure 2

Deviations From Trend of Gross National Product and Nonfarm Employee Hours in the United States

Quarterly, 1947–82

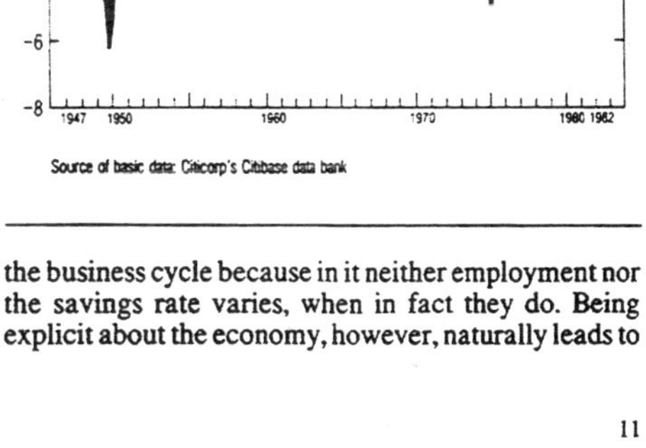

Source of basic data: Citicorp's Citibase data bank

Table 1

Cyclical Behavior of the U.S. Economy

Deviations From Trend of Key Variables, 1954:1–1982:4

Variable x	Standard Deviation	Cross Correlation of GNP With $x(t-1)$	$x(t)$	$x(t+1)$
Gross National Product	1.8%	.82	1.00	.82
Personal Consumption Expenditures				
Services	.6	.66	.72	.61
Nondurable Goods	1.2	.71	.76	.59
Fixed Investment Expenditures	5.3	.78	.89	.78
Nonresidential Investment	5.2	.54	.79	.86
Structures	4.6	.42	.62	.70
Equipment	6.0	.56	.82	.87
Capital Stocks				
Total Nonfarm Inventories	1.7	15	.48	.68
Nonresidential Structures	.4	-.20	-.03	.16
Nonresidential Equipment	1.0	.03	.23	.41
Labor Input				
Nonfarm Hours	1.7	.57	.85	.89
Average Weekly Hours in Mfg.	1.0	.76	.85	.61
Productivity (GNP/Hours)	1.0	.51	.34	-.04

Source of basic data: Citicorp's Citibase data bank

the question of what determines these variables, which are central to the cycle.

That leads to the introduction of a stand-in household with some explicit preferences. If we abstract from the labor supply decision and uncertainty (that is, $z_t = \bar{z}$ and $n_t = \bar{n}$), the standard form of the utility function is

$$\sum_{t=0}^{\infty} \beta^t u(c_t) \text{ for } 0 < \beta < 1$$

where β is the subjective time discount factor. The function $u: R_+ \rightarrow R$ is twice differentiable and concave. The commodity space for the deterministic version of this model is l_∞, infinite sequences of uniformly bounded consumptions $\{c_t\}_{t=0}^{\infty}$.

The theorems of Bewley (1972) could be applied to establish existence of a competitive equilibrium for this l_∞ commodity-space economy. That existence argument, however, does not provide an algorithm for computing the equilibria. An alternative approach is to use the competitive welfare theorems of Debreu (1954). Given local nonsaturation and no externalities, competitive equilibria are Pareto optima and, with some additional conditions that are satisfied for this economy, any Pareto optimum can be supported as a competitive equilibrium. Given a single agent and the convexity, there is a unique optimum and that optimum is the unique competitive equilibrium allocation. The advantage of this approach is that algorithms for computing solutions to concave programming problems can be used to find the competitive equilibrium allocation for this economy.

Even with the savings decision endogenous, this economy has no fluctuations. As shown by Cass (1965) and Koopmans (1965), the competitive equilibrium path converges monotonically to a unique rest point or, if z_t is growing exponentially, to a balanced growth path. There are multisector variants of this model in which the equilibrium path oscillates. (See Benhabib and Nishimura 1985 and Marimon 1984.) But I know of no multisector model which has been restricted to match observed factor shares by sector, which has a value for β consistent with observed interest rates, and which displays oscillations.

When uncertainty is introduced, the household's objective is its expected discounted utility:

$$E\{\sum_{t=0}^{\infty} \beta^t u(c_t)\}.$$

The commodity vector is now indexed by the history of shocks; that is, $\{c_t(z_1, \ldots, z_t)\}_{t=0}^{\infty}$ is the commodity point. As Brock and Mirman (1972) show, if the $\{z_t\}$ are identically distributed random variables, an optimum to the social planner's problem exists and the optimum is a stationary stochastic process with $k_{t+1} = g(k_t, z_t)$ and $c_t = c(k_t, z_t)$. As Lucas and Prescott (1971) show, for a class of economies that include this one, the social optimum is the unique competitive equilibrium allocation. They also show that for these homogeneous agent economies, the social optimum is also the unique sequence-of-markets equilibrium allocation. Consequently, there are equilibrium time-invariant functions for the wage $w_t = w(k_t, z_t)$ and the rental price of capital $r_t = r(k_t, z_t)$, where these prices are relative to the date t consumption good. Given these prices, the firm's period t problem is

$$\max_{k_t, n_t \geq 0} \{y_t - r_t k_t - w_t n_t\}$$

subject to the output constraint

$$y_t \leq z_t f(k_t, n_t).$$

The household's problem is more complicated, for it must form expectations of future prices. If a_t is its capital stock, its problem is

$$\max E \sum_{t=0}^{\infty} \beta^t u(c_t)$$

subject to

$$c_t + x_t \leq w_t \bar{n} + r_t a_t$$

$$a_{t+1} \leq (1-\delta) a_t + x_t$$

and given $a_0 - k_0$. In forming expectations, a household knows the relation between the economy's state (k_t, z_t) and prices, $w_t = w(k_t, z_t)$ and $r_t = r(k_t, z_t)$. Further, it knows the process governing the evolution of the per capita capital stock, a variable which, like prices, is taken as given.

The elements needed to define a *sequence-of-markets equilibrium* are the firm's policy functions $y(k_t, z_t)$, $n(k_t, z_t)$, and $k(k_t, z_t)$; the household's policy functions $x(a_t, k_t, z_t)$ and $c(a_t, k_t, z_t)$; a law of motion of per capita capital $k_{t+1} = g(k_t, z_t)$; and pricing functions $w(k_t, z_t)$ and $r(k_t, z_t)$. For equilibrium, then,

- The firm's policy functions must be optimal given the pricing functions.
- The household's policy functions must be optimal given the pricing functions and the law of motion of per capita capital.
- Spot markets clear; that is, for all k_t and z_t

$$\bar{n} = n(k_t, z_t)$$

$$k_t = k(k_t, z_t)$$

$$x(k_t, k_t, z_t) + c(k_t, k_t, z_t) = y(k_t, z_t).$$

(Note that the goods market must clear only when the representative household is truly representative, that is, when $a_t = k_t$.)

- Expectations are rational; that is,

$$g(k_t, z_t) = (1-\delta)k_t + x(k_t, k_t, z_t).$$

This definition still holds if the household values productive time that is allocated to nonmarket activities. Such time will be called *leisure* and denoted l_t. The productive time endowment is normalized to 1, and the household faces the constraints

$$n_t + l_t \leq 1$$

for all t. In addition, leisure is introduced as an argument of the utility function, so the household's objective becomes the maximization of

$$E \sum_{t=0}^{\infty} \beta^t u(c_t, l_t).$$

Now leisure—and therefore employment—varies in equilibrium.

The model needs one more modification: a relaxation of the assumption that the technology shocks z_t are identically and independently distributed random variables. As will be documented, they are not so distributed. Rather, they display considerable serial correlation, with their first differences nearly serially uncorrelated. To introduce high persistence, we assume

$$z_{t+1} = \rho z_t + \epsilon_{t+1}$$

where the $\{\epsilon_{t+1}\}$ are identically and independently distributed and ρ is near 1. With this modification, the recursive sequence-of-markets equilibrium definition continues to apply.

Using Data to Restrict the Growth Model

Without additional restrictions on preferences and technology, a wide variety of equilibrium processes are consistent with the growth model. The beauty of this model is that both growth and micro observations can be used to determine its production and utility functions. When they are so used, there are not many free parameters that are specific to explaining the business cycle phenomena and that cannot be measured independently of those phenomena. The key parameters of the growth model are the intertemporal and intratemporal elasticities of substitution. As Lucas (1980, p. 712) emphasizes, "On these parameters, we have a wealth of inexpensively available data from census cohort information, from panel data describing the reactions of individual households to a variety of changing market conditions, and so forth." To this list we add the secular growth observations which have the advantage of being experiments run by nature with large changes in relative prices and quantities and with idiosyncratic factors averaged out.[2] A fundamental thesis of this line of inquiry is that the measures obtained from aggregate series and those from individual panel data must be consistent. After all, the former are just the aggregates of the latter.

Secularly in the United States, capital and labor shares of output have been approximately constant, as has r, the rental price of capital. However, the nation's real wage has increased greatly—more than 100 percent since the Korean War. For these results to hold, the model's production function must be approximately Cobb-Douglas:

$$z_t f(k_t, n_t) = z_t k_t^{1-\theta} n_t^{\theta}.$$

The share parameter θ is equal to labor's share, which has been about 64 percent in the postwar period, so $\theta = 0.64$. This number is smaller than that usually obtained because we include services of consumer durables as part of output. This alternative accounting both reduces labor's share and makes it more nearly constant over the postwar period.

The artificial economy has but one type of capital, and it depreciates at rate δ. In fact, different types of capital depreciate at different rates, and the pattern of depreciation over the life of any physical asset is not constant. Kydland and I (1982, 1984) simply pick $\delta = 0.10$. With this value and an annual real interest rate of 4 percent, the steady-state capital–annual output ratio is about 2.6. That matches the ratio for the U.S. economy and also implies a steady-state investment share of output near the historically observed average. Except for parameters determining the process on the technology shock, this completely specifies the technology of the simple growth model.

A key growth observation which restricts the utility function is that leisure per capita l_t has shown virtually no secular trend while, again, the real wage has increased steadily. This implies an elasticity of substitution between consumption c_t and leisure l_t near 1. Thus, the utility function restricted to display both constant intertemporal and unit intratemporal elasticities of substitution is

$$u(c_t, l_t) = ([c_t^{1-\phi} l_t^{\phi}]^{1-\gamma} - 1)/(1 - \gamma)$$

where $1/\gamma > 0$ is the elasticity of substituting between different date composite commodities $c_t^{1-\phi} l_t^{\phi}$. This leaves γ and the subjective time discount factor β [or, equivalently, the subjective time discount rate $(1/\beta) - 1$] to be determined.

The steady-state interest rate is

$$i = (1/\beta) - 1 + \gamma(\dot{c}/c).$$

As stated previously, the average annual real interest rate is about 4 percent, and the growth rate of per capita consumption $\dot{c}/c$ has averaged nearly 2 percent. The following studies help restrict γ. Tobin and Dolde (1971) find that a γ near 1.5 is needed to match the life cycle consumption patterns of individuals. Using individual portfolio observations, Friend and Blume (1975) estimate γ to be near 2. Using aggregate stock market and consumption data, Hansen and Singleton (1983) estimate γ to be near 1. Using international data, Kehoe

[2] See Solow 1970 for a nice summary of the growth observations.

(1984) also finds a modest curvature parameter γ. All these observations make a strong case that γ is not too far from 1. Since the nature of fluctuations of the artificial economy is not very sensitive to γ, we simply set γ equal to 1. Taking the limit as $\gamma \to 1$ yields

$$u(c_t, l_t) = (1-\phi) \log c_t + \phi \log l_t.$$

This leaves β and ϕ still to be determined.

Hansen (1985b) has found that growing economies—that is, those with z_t having a multiplicative, geometrically growing factor $(1+\lambda)^t$ with $\lambda > 0$—fluctuate in essentially the same way as economies for which $\lambda = 0$. This justifies considering only the case $\lambda = 0$. If $\lambda = 0$, then the average interest rate approximately equals the subjective time discount rate.[3] Therefore, we set β equal to 0.96 per year or 0.99 per quarter.

The parameter ϕ is the leisure share parameter. Ghez and Becker (1975) find that the household allocates approximately one-third of its productive time to market activities and two-thirds to nonmarket activities. To be consistent with that, the model's parameter ϕ must be near two-thirds. This is the value assumed in our business cycle studies.

Eichenbaum, Hansen, and Singleton (1984) use aggregate data to estimate this share parameter ϕ, and they obtain a value near five-sixths. The difference between two-thirds and five-sixths is large in the business cycle context. With $\phi = 2/3$, the elasticity of labor supply with respect to a temporary change in the real wage is 2, while if $\phi = 5/6$, it is 5. This is because a 1 percent change in leisure implies a $\phi/(\phi-1)$ percent change in hours of employment.

We do not follow the Eichenbaum-Hansen-Singleton approach and treat ϕ as a free parameter because it would violate the principle that parameters cannot be specific to the phenomena being studied. What sort of science would economics be if micro studies used one share parameter and aggregate studies another?

The Nature of the Technological Change

One method of measuring technological change is to follow Solow (1957) and define it as the changes in output less the sum of the changes in labor's input times labor share and the changes in capital's input times capital share. Measuring variables in logs, this is the percentage change in the technology parameter of the Cobb-Douglas production function. For the U.S. economy between the third quarter of 1955 and the first quarter of 1984, the standard deviation of this change is 1.2 percent.[4] The serial autocorrelations of these changes are $\rho_1 = -0.21$, $\rho_2 = -0.06$, $\rho_3 = 0.04$, $\rho_4 = 0.01$, and $\rho_5 = -0.05$. To a first approximation, the process on the percentage change in the technology process is a random walk with drift plus some serially uncorrelated measurement error. This error produces the negative first-order serial correlation of the differences.

Further evidence that the random walk model is not a bad approximation is based on yearly changes. For the quarterly random walk model, the standard deviation of this change is 6.63 times the standard deviation of the quarterly change. For the U.S. data, the annual change is only 5.64 times as large as the quarterly change. This, along with the negative first-order serial correlation, suggests that the standard deviation of the persistent part of the quarterly change is closer to $5.64/6.63 = 0.85$ than to 1.2 percent. Some further evidence is the change over four-quarter periods—that is, the change from a given quarter of one year to the same quarter of the next year. For the random walk model, the standard deviation of these changes is 2 times the standard deviation of the quarterly change. A reason that the standard deviation of change might be better measured this way is that the measurement noise introduced by seasonal factors is minimized. The estimate obtained in this way is 0.95 percent. To summarize, Solow growth accounting finds that the process on the technology parameter is highly persistent with the standard deviation of change being about 0.90.[5]

The Solow estimate of the standard deviation of technological change is surely an overstatement of the variability of that parameter. There undoubtedly are non-negligible errors in measuring the inputs. Since the capital input varies slowly and its share is small, the most serious measurement problem is with the labor input. Fortunately there are two independent measures of the aggregate labor input, one constructed from a survey of employers and the other from a survey of households. Under the assumption of orthogonality of their measurement errors, a reasonable estimate of the variance of the change in hours is the covariance between the changes in the two series. Since the household survey is not used to estimate aggregate output, I

---

[3] Actually, the average interest rate is slightly lower because of risk premia. Given the value of γ and the amount of uncertainty, the average premium is only a fraction of a percent. See Mehra and Prescott 1985 for further details.

[4] I use Hansen's (1984) human capital–weighted, household hour series. The capital stock and GNP series are from Citicorp's Citibase data bank.

[5] The process $z_{t+1} = .9z_t + \epsilon_{t+1}$ is, like the random walk process, highly persistent. Kydland and I find that it and the random walk result in essentially the same fluctuations.

use the covariance between the changes in household hours and output as an estimate of the covariance between aggregate hours and output. Still using a share parameter of $\theta = 0.75$, my estimate of the standard deviation of the percentage change in z_t is the square root of $\mathrm{var}(\Delta\hat{y}) - 2\theta\,\mathrm{cov}(\Delta\hat{h}_1, \Delta\hat{y}) + \theta^2\,\mathrm{cov}(\Delta\hat{h}_1, \Delta\hat{h}_2)$, where the caret (ˆ) denotes a measured value. For the sample period my estimate is 0.763 percent. This is probably a better estimate than the one which ignores measurement error.

Still, my estimate might under- or overstate the variance of technological change. For example, the measurement of output might include significant errors. Perhaps measurement procedures result in some smoothing of the series. This would reduce the variability of the change in output and might reduce the covariance between measured hours and output.

Another possibility is that changes in hours are associated with corresponding changes in capital's utilization rate. If so, the Solow approach is inappropriate for measuring the technology shocks. To check whether this is a problem, I varied θ and found that $\theta = 0.85$ yields the smallest estimate, 0.759, as opposed to 0.763 for $\theta = 0.75$. This suggests that my estimate is not at all sensitive to variations in capital utilization rates.

To summarize, there is overwhelming evidence that technological shocks are highly persistent. But tying down the standard deviation of the technology change shocks is difficult. I estimate it as 0.763. It could very well be larger or smaller, though, given the accuracy of the measurements.

The Statistical Behavior of the Growth Models

Theory provides an equilibrium stochastic process for the growth economy studied. Our approach has been to document the similarities and differences between the statistical properties of data generated by this stochastic process and the statistical properties of American time series data. An alternative approach is to compare the paths of the growth model if the technological parameters $\{z_t\}$ were those experienced by the U.S. economy. We did not attempt this because theory's predictions of paths, unlike its predictions of the statistical properties, are sensitive to what Leamer (1983, p. 43) calls "whimsical" modeling assumptions. Another nontrivial problem is that the errors in measuring the innovations in the z_t process are as large as the innovations themselves.

The Basic Growth Model

With the standard deviation of the technology shock equal to 0.763, theory implies that the standard deviation of output will be 1.48 percent. In fact, it is 1.76 percent for the post–Korean War American economy. For the output of the artificial economy to be as variable as that, the variance of the shock must be 1.0, significantly larger than the estimate. The most important deviation from theory is the relative volatility of hours and output. Figure 3 plots a realization of the output and employment deviations from trend for the basic growth economy. A comparison of Figures 2 and 3 demonstrates clearly that, for the American economy, hours in fact vary much more than the basic growth model predicts. For the artificial economy, hours fluctuate 52 percent as much as output, whereas for the American economy, the ratio is 0.95. This difference appears too large to be a result of errors in measuring aggregate hours and output.

The Kydland-Prescott Economy

Kydland and I (1982, 1984) have modified the growth model in two important respects. First, we assume that a distributed lag of leisure and the market-produced good combine to produce the composite commodity good valued by the household. In particular,

$$u\left(c_t, \textstyle\sum_{i=0}^{\infty} \alpha_i l_{t-i}\right) = (1/3)\log c_t + (2/3)\log \textstyle\sum_{i=0}^{\infty} \alpha_i l_{t-i}$$

where $\alpha_{i+1}/\alpha_i = 1 - \eta$ for $i = 1, 2, \ldots$ and $\sum_{i=0}^{\infty} \alpha_i = 1$.

Figure 3

Deviations From Trend of GNP and Hours Worked in the Basic Growth Economy

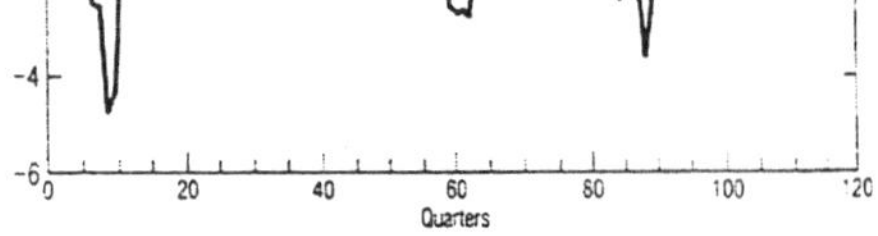

Table 2

Cyclical Behavior of the Kydland-Prescott Economy*

Variable x	Standard Deviation	Cross Correlation of GNP With $x(t-1)$	$x(t)$	$x(t+1)$
Gross National Product	1.79%	.60	1.00	.60
	(.13)	(.07)	(—)	(.07)
Consumption	.45	.47	.85	.71
	(.05)	(.05)	(.02)	(.04)
Investment	5.49	.52	.88	.78
	(.41)	(.09)	(.03)	(.03)
Inventory Stock	2.20	.14	.60	.52
	(.37)	(.14)	(.08)	(.05)
Capital Stock	.47	−.05	.02	.25
	(.07)	(.07)	(.06)	(.07)
Hours	1.23	.52	.95	.55
	(.09)	(.09)	(.01)	(.06)
Productivity (GNP/Hours)	.71	.62	.86	.56
	(.06)	(.05)	(.02)	(.10)
Real Interest Rate (Annual)	.22	.65	.60	.36
	(.03)	(.07)	(.20)	(.15)

*These are the means of 20 simulations, each of which was 116 periods long. The numbers in parentheses are standard errors.
Source: Kydland and Prescott 1984

Kydland (1983) provides justification for this preference ordering based on an unmeasured, household-specific capital stock that, like c_t and l_t, is an input in the production of the composite commodity. The economy studied has $\alpha_0 = 0.5$ and $\eta = 0.1$. This increases the variability of hours.

The second modification is to permit the workweek of capital to vary proportionally to the workweek of the household. For this economy, increases in hours do not reduce the marginal product of labor as much, so hours fluctuate more in response to technology shocks of a given size.

The statistical properties of the fluctuations for this economy are reported in Table 2. As is clear there, hours are now about 70 percent as variable as output. This eliminates much of the discrepancy between theory and measurement. If the standard deviation of the technology shock is 0.72 percent, then fluctuations in the output of this artificial economy are as large as those experienced in the U.S. economy.

A comparison of Tables 1 and 2 shows that the Kydland-Prescott economy displays the business cycle phenomena. It does not quite demonstrate, however, that there would be a puzzle if the economy did not display the business cycle phenomena. That is because the parameters α_0 and η have not been well tied down by micro observations.[6] Better measures of these parameters could either increase or decrease significantly the amount of the fluctuations accounted for by the uncertainty in the technological change.

[6]Hotz, Kydland, and Sedlacek (1985) use annual panel data to estimate α_0 and η and obtain estimates near the Kydland-Prescott assumed values.

The Hansen Indivisible Labor Economy

Labor economists have estimated labor supply elasticities and found them to be small for full-time prime-age males. (See, for example, Ashenfelter 1984.) Heckman (1984), however, finds that when movements between employment and nonemployment are considered and secondary workers are included, elasticities of labor supply are much larger. He also finds that most of the variation in aggregate hours arises from variation in the number employed rather than in the hours worked per employed person.

These are the observations that led Hansen (1985a) to explore the implication of introducing labor indivisibilities into the growth model. As shown by Rogerson (1984), if the household's consumption possibility set has nonconvexities associated with the mapping from hours of market production activities to units of labor services, there will be variations in the number employed rather than in the hours of work per employed person. In addition, the aggregate elasticity of labor supply will be much larger than the elasticity of those whose behavior is being aggregated. In this case aggregation matters, and matters greatly.

There certainly are important nonconvexities in the mapping from hours of market activities to units of labor services provided. Probably the most important nonconvexity arises from the considerable amount of time required for commuting. Other features of the environment that would make full-time workers more than twice as productive as otherwise similar half-time workers are not hard to imagine. The fact that part-time workers typically are paid less per hour than full-time workers with similar human capital endowments is consistent with the existence of important nonconvexities.

Hansen (1985a) restricts each identical household to either work $\bar{h}$ hours or be unemployed. His relation is as depicted by the horizontal lines in Figure 4. This assumption is not as extreme as it appears. If the relation were as depicted by the curved line, the behavior of the economy would be the same. The key property is an initial convex region followed by a concave region in the mapping from hours of market activity to units of labor service.

With this modification, lotteries that specify the probability of employment are traded along with market-produced goods and capital services. As before, the utility function of each individual is

$$u(c, l) = (1/3) \log c + (2/3) \log l.$$

Figure 4

Relation Between Time Allocated to Market Activity and Labor Service

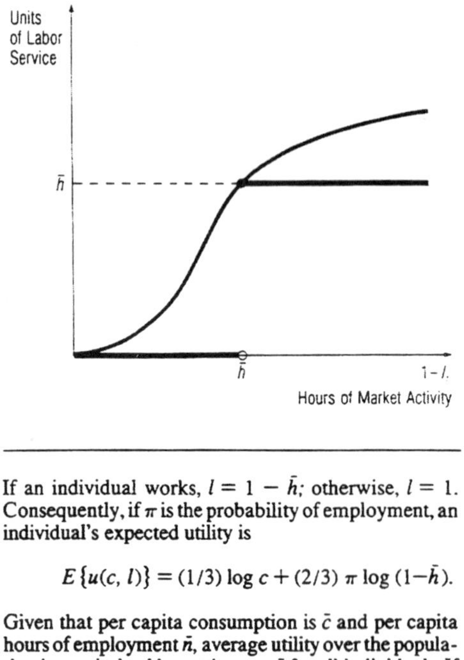

If an individual works, $l = 1 - \bar{h}$; otherwise, $l = 1$. Consequently, if π is the probability of employment, an individual's expected utility is

$$E\{u(c, l)\} = (1/3) \log c + (2/3)\ \pi \log (1-\bar{h}).$$

Given that per capita consumption is $\bar{c}$ and per capita hours of employment $\bar{n}$, average utility over the population is maximized by setting $c = \bar{c}$ for all individuals. If $\bar{l}$, which equals $1 - \pi\bar{h}$, denotes per capita leisure, then maximum per capita utility is

$$U(\bar{c}, \bar{l}) = (1/3) \log \bar{c} + (2/3) [(1-\bar{l})/\bar{h}] \log (1-\bar{h}).$$

This is the utility function which rationalizes the per capita consumption and leisure choices if each person's leisure is constrained to be either $1 - \bar{h}$ or 1. The aggregate intertemporal elasticity of substitution between different date leisures is infinity independent of the value of the elasticity for the individual (in the range where not all are employed).

Hansen (1985a) finds that if the technology shock standard deviation is 0.71, then fluctuations in output for his economy are as large as those for the American economy. Further, variability in hours is 77 percent as large as variability in output. Figure 5 shows that aggregate hours and output for his economy fluctuate together with nearly the same amplitude. These theoretical findings are the basis for my statement in the introduction that there would be a puzzle if the economy did not display the business cycle phenomena.

Empirical Labor Elasticity

One important empirical implication of a shock-to-technology theory of fluctuations is that the empirical labor elasticity of output is significantly larger than the true elasticity, which for the Cobb-Douglas production function is the labor share parameter. To see why, note that the capital stock varies little cyclically and is nearly uncorrelated with output. Consequently, the deviations almost satisfy

$$y_t = \theta h_t + z_t$$

where y_t is output, h_t hours, and z_t the technology shock. The empirical elasticity is

$$\eta = \text{cov}(h_t, y_t)/\text{var}(h_t)$$

which, because of the positive correlation between h_t and z_t, is considerably larger than the model's θ, which is 0.64. For the basic, Kydland-Prescott, and Hansen growth economies, the values of η are 1.9, 1.4, and 1.3, respectively.

Because of measurement errors, the empirical elasticity for the American economy is not well-estimated by simply computing the ratio of the covariance between hours and output and dividing by the variance of hours. The procedure I use is based on the following probability model:

$$\hat{y}_t = y_t + \epsilon_{1t}$$

$$\hat{h}_{1t} = h_t + \epsilon_{2t}$$

$$\hat{h}_{2t} = h_t + \epsilon_{3t}$$

where the caret (ˆ) denotes a measured value. The ϵ_{it} are measurement errors. Here, the $\hat{h}_{1t}$ measure of hours uses the employer survey data while the $\hat{h}_{2t}$ measure uses the household survey data. Since these are independent measures, a maintained hypothesis is that ϵ_{2t} and ϵ_{3t} are orthogonal. With this assumption, a reasonable estimate of $\text{var}(h_t)$ is the sample covariance between $\hat{h}_{1t}$ and $\hat{h}_{2t}$. Insofar as the measurement of

Figure 5

Deviations From Trend of GNP and Hours Worked in Hansen's Indivisible Labor Economy

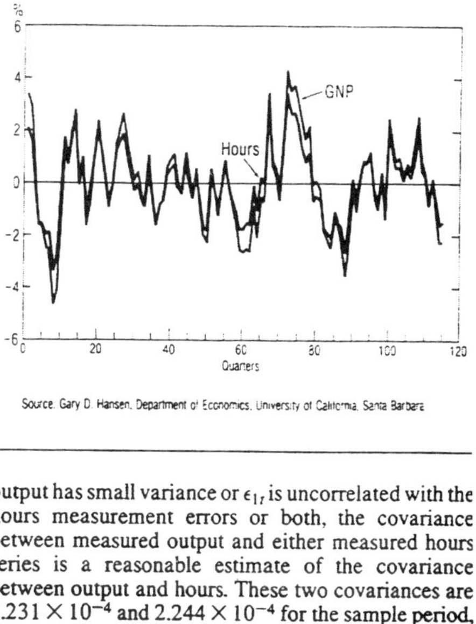

Source: Gary D. Hansen, Department of Economics, University of California, Santa Barbara

output has small variance or ϵ_{1t} is uncorrelated with the hours measurement errors or both, the covariance between measured output and either measured hours series is a reasonable estimate of the covariance between output and hours. These two covariances are 2.231×10^{-4} and 2.244×10^{-4} for the sample period, and I take the average as my estimate of $\text{cov}(h_t, y_t)$ for the American economy. My estimate of the empirical labor elasticity of output is

$$\hat{\eta} = [\text{cov}(\hat{h}_{1t}, \hat{y}_t) + \text{cov}(\hat{h}_{2t}, \hat{y}_t)]/2\ \text{cov}(\hat{h}_{1t}, \hat{h}_{2t})$$
$$= 1.1.$$

This number is considerably greater than labor's share, which is about 0.70 when services of consumer durables are not included as part of output. This number strongly supports the importance of technological shocks in accounting for business cycle fluctuations. Nevertheless, the number is smaller than those for the Kydland-Prescott and Hansen growth economies.

One possible reason for the difference between the U.S. economy and the growth model empirical labor elasticities of output is cyclical measurement errors in output. A sizable part of the investment component of output is hard to measure and therefore not included in the U.S. National Product Accounts measure of output, the gross national product (GNP). In particular, a firm's major maintenance expenditures, research and development expenditures, and investments in human capital are not included in GNP. In good times—namely, when output is above trend—firms may be more likely to undertake major repairs of a not fully depreciated asset, such as replacing the roof of a 30-year-old building which has a tax life of 35 years. Such an expenditure is counted as maintenance and therefore not included in GNP even though the new roof will provide productive services for many years. The incentive for firms to do this is tax savings: by expensing an investment rather than capitalizing it, current tax liabilities are reduced. Before 1984, when a railroad replaced its 90-pound rails, the expenditure was treated as a maintenance expense rather than an investment expenditure. If these and other types of unmeasured investment fluctuate in percentage terms more than output, as do all the measured investment components, the volatility of GNP is larger than measured. We do know that investment in rails was highly procyclical and volatile in the postwar period. A careful study is needed to determine whether the correction for currently unmeasured investment is small or large.

Another reason to expect the American economy's labor elasticity to be less than the model's is that the model shocks are perfectly neutral with respect to the consumption and investment good transformation. Persistent shocks which alter the product transformation frontier between these goods would cause variation in output and employment but not in the productivity parameters. For fluctuations so induced, the empirical labor elasticity of output would be the true elasticity. Similarly, relatively permanent changes in the taxing of capital—such as altering depreciation rates, the corporate income tax rate, or the investment tax credit rate—would all result in fluctuations in output and employment but not in the productivity parameters.

A final reason for actual labor elasticity to be less than the model's is the way imports are measured. An increase in the price of imported oil, that is, an increase in the quantity of output that must be sacrificed for a given unit of that input, has no effect on measured productivity. From the point of view of the growth model, however, an oil price increase is a negative technology shock because it results in less output, net of the exports used to pay for the imported oil, available for domestic consumption and investment. Theory predicts that such shocks will induce variations in employment and output, even though they have no effect on the aggregate production function. Therefore, insofar as they are important, they reduce the empirical labor elasticity of output.

Extensions

The growth model has been extended to provide a better representation of the technology. Kydland and I (1982) have introduced a technology with more than one construction period for new production capacity.[7] We have also introduced inventory as a factor of production. This improves the match between the model's serial correlation properties and the U.S. postwar data, but has little effect on the other statistics.

Kydland (1984) has introduced heterogeneity of labor and found that if there are transfers from high human capital people to low human capital people, theory implies that hours of the low fluctuate more than hours of the high. It also implies a lower empirical labor elasticity of output than the homogeneous household model.

Bain (1985) has studied an economy that is richer in sectoral detail. His model has manufacturing, retailing, and service-producing sectors. A key feature of the technology is that production and distribution occur sequentially. Thus there are two types of inventories—those of manufacturers' finished goods and those of final goods available for sale. With this richer detail, theory implies that different components of aggregate inventories behave in different ways, as seen in the data. It also implies that production is more volatile than final sales, an observation considered anomalous since inventories can be used to smooth production. (See, for example, Blinder 1984.)

Much has been done. But much more remains to be explored. For example, public finance considerations could be introduced and theory used to predict their implications. As mentioned above, factors which affect the rental price of capital affect employment and output, and the nature of the tax system affects the rental price of capital. Theory could be used to predict the effect of temporary increases in government expenditures such as those in the early 1950s when defense expenditures increased from less than 5 to more than 13 percent of GNP. Theory of this type could also be used to predict the effect of terms-of-trade shocks. An implication of such an exercise most likely will be that economies with persistent terms-of-trade shocks fluctu-

[7] Altug (1983) has introduced two types of capital with different gestation periods. Using formal econometric methods, she finds evidence that the model's fit is improved if plant and equipment investment are not aggregated.

ate differently than economies with transitory shocks. If so, this prediction can be tested against the observations.

Another interesting extension would be to explicitly model household production. This production often involves two people, with one specializing in market production and the other specializing in household production while having intermittent or part-time market employment. The fact that, cyclically, the employment of secondary wage earners is much more volatile than that of primary wage earners might be explained.

A final example of an interesting and not yet answered question is, How would the behavior of the Hansen indivisible labor economy change if agents did not have access to a technology to insure against random unemployment and instead had to self-insure against unemployment by holding liquid assets? In such an economy, unlike Hansen's, people would not be happy when unemployed. Their gain of more leisure would be more than offset by their loss as an insurer. Answering this question is not straightforward, because new tools for computing equilibria are needed.

Summary and Policy Implications

Economic theory implies that, given the nature of the shocks to technology and people's willingness and ability to intertemporally and intratemporally substitute, the economy will display fluctuations like those the U.S. economy displays. Theory predicts fluctuations in output of 5 percent and more from trend, with most of the fluctuation accounted for by variations in employment and virtually all the rest by the stochastic technology parameter. Theory predicts investment will be three or more times as volatile as output and consumption half as volatile. Theory predicts that deviations will display high serial correlation. In other words, theory predicts what is observed. Indeed, if the economy did not display the business cycle phenomena, there would be a puzzle.

The match between theory and observation is excellent, but far from perfect. The key deviation is that the empirical labor elasticity of output is less than predicted by theory. An important part of this deviation could very well disappear if the economic variables were measured more in conformity with theory. That is why I argue that theory is now ahead of business cycle measurement and theory should be used to obtain better measures of the key economic time series. Even with better measurement, there will likely be significant deviations from theory which can direct subsequent theoretical research. This feedback between theory and measurement is the way mature, quantitative sciences advance.

The policy implication of this research is that costly efforts at stabilization are likely to be counterproductive. Economic fluctuations are optimal responses to uncertainty in the rate of technological change. However, this does not imply that the amount of technological change is optimal or invariant to policy. The average rate of technological change varies much both over time within a country and across national economies. What is needed is an understanding of the factors that determine the average rate at which technology advances. Such a theory surely will depend on the institutional arrangements societies adopt. If policies adopted to stabilize the economy reduce the average rate of technological change, then stabilization policy is costly. To summarize, attention should be focused not on fluctuations in output but rather on determinants of the average rate of technological advance.

References

Altug, S. 1983. Gestation lags and the business cycle. Working paper, Carnegie-Mellon University.

Ashenfelter, O. 1984. Macroeconomic analyses and microeconomic analyses of labor supply. In *Essays on macroeconomic implications of financial and labor markets and political processes*, ed. K. Brunner and A. H. Meltzer. Carnegie-Rochester Conference Series on Public Policy 21: 117–55. Amsterdam: North-Holland.

Bain, I. R. M. 1985. A theory of the cyclical movements of inventory stocks. Ph.D. dissertation, University of Minnesota.

Barro, R. J. 1981. Intertemporal substitution and the business cycle. In *Supply shocks, incentives and national wealth*, ed. K. Brunner and A. H. Meltzer. Carnegie-Rochester Conference Series on Public Policy 14: 237–68. Amsterdam: North-Holland.

Benhabib, J., and Nishimura, K. 1985. Competitive equilibrium cycles. *Journal of Economic Theory* 35: 284–306.

Bewley, T. F. 1972. Existence of equilibria in economies with infinitely many commodities. *Journal of Economic Theory* 4: 514–40.

Blinder, A. S. 1984. Can the production smoothing model of inventory behavior be saved? Working paper, Princeton University.

Brock, W. A., and Mirman, L. J. 1972. Optimal economic growth and uncertainty: The discounted case. *Journal of Economic Theory* 4: 479–513.

Cass, D. 1965. Optimum growth in an aggregative model of capital accumulation. *Review of Economic Studies* 32: 233–40.

Debreu, G. 1954. Valuation equilibrium and Pareto optimum. *Proceedings of the National Academy of Science* 70: 558–92.

Eichenbaum, M. S.; Hansen, L. P.; and Singleton, K. S. 1984. A time series analysis of representative agent models of consumption and leisure choice under uncertainty. Working paper, Carnegie-Mellon University.

Friend, I., and Blume, M. E. 1975. The demand for risky assets. *American Economic Review* 65: 900–22.

Ghez, G. R., and Becker, G. S. 1975. The allocation of time and goods over the life cycle. New York: National Bureau of Economic Research.

Hansen, G. D. 1984. Fluctuations in total hours worked: A study using efficiency units. Working paper, University of Minnesota.

________. 1985a. Indivisible labor and the business cycle. *Journal of Monetary Economics* 16: 309–27.

________. 1985b. Growth and fluctuations. Working paper, University of California, Santa Barbara.

Hansen, L. P., and Singleton, K. J. 1983. Stochastic consumption, risk aversion, and the temporal behavior of asset returns. *Journal of Political Economy* 91: 249–65.

Heckman, J. 1984. Comments on the Ashenfelter and Kydland papers. In *Essays on macroeconomic implications of financial and labor markets and political processes*, ed. K. Brunner and A. H. Meltzer. Carnegie-Rochester Conference Series on Public Policy 21: 209–24. Amsterdam: North-Holland.

Hotz, V. S.; Kydland, F. E.; and Sedlacek, G. L. 1985. Intertemporal preferences and labor supply. Working paper, Carnegie-Mellon University.

Kehoe, P. J. 1984. Dynamics of the current account: Theoretical and empirical analysis. Working paper, Harvard University.

Koopmans, T. C. 1965. On the concept of optimal economic growth. In *The econometric approach to development planning*. Chicago: Rand-McNally.

Kydland, F. E. 1983. Nonseparable utility and labor supply. Working paper, Hoover Institution.

________. 1984. Labor-force heterogeneity and the business cycle. In *Essays on macroeconomic implications of financial and labor markets and political processes*, ed. K. Brunner and A. H. Meltzer. Carnegie-Rochester Conference Series on Public Policy 21: 173–208. Amsterdam: North-Holland.

Kydland, F. E., and Prescott, E. C. 1982. Time to build and aggregate fluctuations. *Econometrica* 50–70.

________. 1984. The workweek of capital and labor. Research Department Working Paper 267, Federal Reserve Bank of Minneapolis.

Leamer, E. E. 1983. Let's take the con out of econometrics. *American Economic Review* 73: 31–43.

Long, J. B., and Plosser, C. I. 1983. Real business cycles. *Journal of Political Economy* 91: 39–69.

Lucas, R. E., Jr. 1977. Understanding business cycles. In *Stabilization of the domestic and international economy*, ed. K. Brunner and A. H. Meltzer. Carnegie-Rochester Conference Series on Public Policy 5: 7–29. Amsterdam: North-Holland.

________. 1980. Methods and problems in business cycle theory. *Journal of Money, Credit and Banking* 12: 696–715. Reprinted in *Studies in business-cycle theory*, pp. 271–96. Cambridge, Mass.: MIT Press, 1981.

Lucas, R. E., Jr., and Prescott, E. C. 1971. Investment under uncertainty. *Econometrica* 39: 659–81.

Marimon, R. 1984. General equilibrium and growth under uncertainty: The turnpike property. Discussion Paper 624. Northwestern University, Center for Mathematical Studies in Economics and Management Science.

Mehra, R., and Prescott, E. C. 1985. The equity premium: A puzzle. *Journal of Monetary Economics* 15: 145–61.

Rogerson, R. D. 1984. Indivisible labor, lotteries and equilibrium. In *Topics in the theory of labor markets*, chap. 1. Ph.D. dissertation, University of Minnesota.

Slutzky, E. 1927. The summation of random causes as the source of cyclic processes. In *Problems of Economic Conditions*, ed. Conjuncture Institute, Moskva (Moskow), vol. 3, no. 1. Revised English version, 1937, in *Econometrica* 5: 105–46.

Solow, R. M. 1956. A contribution to the theory of economic growth. *Quarterly Journal of Economics* 70: 65–94.

________. 1970. *Growth theory*. Oxford: Oxford University Press.

Swan, T. W. 1956. Economic growth and capital accumulation. *Economic Record* 32: 334–61.

Tobin, J., and Dolde, W. 1971. Wealth, liquidity and consumption. In *Consumer spending and monetary policy: The linkages*. Monetary Conference Series 5: 99–146. Boston: Federal Reserve Bank of Boston.

[5]

Oxford Economic Papers 47 (1995), 24–44

FACTS AND ARTIFACTS: CALIBRATION AND THE EMPIRICAL ASSESSMENT OF REAL-BUSINESS-CYCLE MODELS

By KEVIN D. HOOVER

Department of Economics, University of California, Davis, California 95616-8578, USA

1. Whither quantitative macroeconomics?

THE RELATIONSHIP between theory and data has been, from the beginning, a central concern of the new-classical macroeconomics. This much is evident in the title of Robert E. Lucas's and Thomas J. Sargent's landmark edited volume, *Rational Expectations and Econometric Practice* (1981). With the advent of real-business-cycle models, many new classical economists have turned to calibration methods. The new classical macroeconomics is now divided between calibrators and estimators. But the debate is not a parochial one, raising, as it does, issues about the relationships of models to reality and the nature of econometrics that should be important to every school of macroeconomic thought, indeed to all applied economics. The stake in this debate is the future direction of quantitative macroeconomics. It is, therefore, critical to understand the root issues.

Lucas begins the second chapter of his *Models of Business Cycles* with the remark:

> Discussions of economic policy, if they are to be productive in any practical sense, necessarily involve *quantitative* assessments of the way proposed policies are likely to affect resource allocation and individual welfare. (Lucas 1987, p. 6; emphasis added)

This might appear to be a clarion call for econometric estimation. But appearances are deceiving. After mentioning Sumru Altug's (1989) estimation and rejection of the validity of a variant of Finn E. Kydland and Edward C. Prescott's (1982) real-business-cycle model (a model which takes up a large portion of his book), Lucas writes:

> . . . the interesting question is surely not whether [the real-business-cycle model] can be accepted as 'true' when nested within some broader class of models. Of course the model is not 'true': this much is evident from the axioms on which it is constructed. We know from the onset in an enterprise like this (I would say, in *any* effort in positive economics) that what will emerge—at *best*—is a workable approximation that is useful in answering a limited set of questions. (Lucas 1987, p. 45)

Lucas abandons not only truth but also the hitherto accepted standards of empirical economics. Models that clearly do not fit the data, he argues, may nonetheless be calibrated to provide useful quantitative guides to policy.

Calibration techniques are commonly applied to so-called 'computable general-equilibrium' models. They were imported into macroeconomics as a means of quantifying real-business-cycle models, but now have a wide range of applications. Some issues raised by calibration are common to all computable general-equilibrium models; the concern of this paper, however, is with real-business-cycle models and related macroeconomic applications; and, as will appear presently, these raise special issues. A model is calibrated when its parameters are quantified from casual empiricism or unrelated econometric studies or are chosen to guarantee that the model precisely mimics some particular feature of the historical data. For example, in Kydland and Prescott (1982), the coefficient of relative risk aversion is justified on the basis of microeconomic studies, while the free parameters of the model are set to force the model to match the variance of GNP without any attempt to find the value of empirical analogues to them.

Allan W. Gregory and Gregor W. Smith (1991, p. 3) conclude that calibration '... is beginning to predominate in the quantitative application of macro-economic models'. While indicative of the importance of the calibration methodology, Gregory and Smith's conclusion is too strong. Aside from the new classical school, few macroeconomists are staunch advocates of calibration. Within the new classical school, opinion remains divided. Even with reference to real-business-cycle models, some practitioners have insisted that calibration is at best a first step, which must be followed '... by setting down a metric (e.g. one induced by a likelihood function) and estimating parameters by finding values that make the metric attain a minimum' (Gary Hansen and Sargent 1988, p. 293).[1]

Sargent advocates estimation or what Kydland and Prescott (1991) call the 'system-of-equations approach'. Estimation has been the standard approach in macroeconometrics for over 40 years. Sargent and like-minded new classical economists modify the standard approach only in their insistence that the restrictions implied by dynamic-optimization models be integrated into the estimations. The standard of empirical assessment is the usual one: how well does the model fit the data statistically? Lucas and Kydland and Prescott reject statistical goodness of fit as a relevant standard of assessment. The issue at hand might then be summarized: who is right—Lucas and Kydland and Prescott, or Sargent?

The answer to this question is not transparent. Estimation is the *status quo*. And, although enthusiastic advocates of calibration already announce its triumph, its methodological foundations remain largely unarticulated. An uncharitable interpretation of the calibration methodology might be that the advocates of real-business-cycle models are so enamored of their creations that they would prefer to abandon commonly accepted, neutral standards of empirical evaluation (i.e. econometric hypothesis testing) to preserve their

[1] Despite the joint authorship of the last quotation, I regard Sargent and not Hansen as the preeminent proponent of the necessity of estimation, because I recall him forcefully insisting on it in his role as discussant of a paper by Thomas F. Cooley and Hansen (1989) at the Federal Reserve Bank of San Francisco's Fall Acacemic Conference; see also Manuelli and Sargent (1988, pp. 531–4).

models. This would be an *ad hoc* defensive move typical of a degenerating research program.

This interpretation is not only uncharitable, it is wrong. Presently, we shall see that Herbert Simon's (1969) *Sciences of the Artifical* provides the materials from which to construct a methodological foundation for calibration, and that calibration is compatible with a well-established approach to econometrics that is nonetheless very different from the Cowles Commission emphasis on the estimation of systems of equations. Before addressing these issues, however, it will be useful to describe the calibration methodology and its place in the history and practice of econometrics in more detail.

2. The calibration methodology

2.1. *The paradigm case*

Kydland and Prescott (1982) is the paradigm new-classical equilibrium, real-business-cycle model. It is neoclassical optimal-growth model with stochastic shocks to technology which cause the equilibrium growth path to fluctuate about its steady state.[2] Concrete functional forms are chosen to capture some general features of business cycles. Production is governed by a constant-elasticity-of-substitution production function in which inventories, fixed capital, and labor combine to generate a single homogeneous output that may either be consumed or reinvested. Fixed capital requires a finite time to be built before it becomes a useful input. The constant-relative-risk-aversion utility function is rigged to possess a high degree of intertemporal substitutability of leisure. Shocks to technology are serially correlated. Together the structure of the serial correlation of the technology shocks and the degree of intertemporal substitution in consumption and leisure choices govern the manner in which shocks are propagagated through time and the speed of convergence back towards the steady state.

Once the model is specified, the next step is to parameterize its concrete functional forms. Most of the parameters of the model are chosen from values culled from other applied econometric literatures or from general facts about national-income accounting. For example, Thomas Mayer (1960) estimated the average time to construct complete facilities to be 21 months; Robert E. Hall (1977) estimated the average time from start of projects to beginning of production to be two years. Citing these papers, but noting that consumer durable goods take considerably less time to produce, Kydland and Prescott (1982, p. 1361) assume that the paramters governing capital formation are set to imply steady construction over four quarters.[3] The values for depreciation

[2] For general descriptions of the details and varieties of real-business-cycle models see Lucas (1987), Kevin D. Hoover (1988, ch. 3), and Bennett T. McCallum (1989). Steven M. Sheffrin (1989, ch. 3, especially pp. 80, 81), gives a step-by-step recipe for constructing a prototypical real-business-cycle model.

[3] Mayer's estimates were for complete projects only, so that new equipment installed in old plants, which must have a much shorter time-to-build than 21 months, was not counted.

rates and the capital/inventory ratio are set to rough averages from the national-income accounts. Ready estimates from similar sources were not available for the remaining six paramters of the model, which include parameters governing intertemporal substitution of leisure and the shocks to technology. These were chosen by searching over possible parameter values for a combination that best reproduced certain key variances and covariances of the data. In particular, the technology shock variance was chosen in order to exactly match the variance of output in the postwar US economy.

To test the model's performance, Kydland and Prescott generate a large number of realizations of the technology shocks for 118 periods corresponding to their postwar data. They then compute the variances and covariances implied by the model for a number of important variables: output, consumption, investment, inventories, the capital stock, hours worked, productivity, and the real rate of interest.[4] These are then compared with the corresponding variances and covariances of the actual US data.[5]

Kydland and Prescott offer no formal measure of the success of their model. They do note that hours are insufficiently variable with respect to the variability of productivity to correspond accurately to the data, but otherwise they are pleased with the model's ability to mimic the second moments of the data.

Real-business-cycle models, treated in the manner of Kydland and Prescott, are a species of the genus computable (or applied) general-equilibrium models. The accepted standards for implementing computable general-equilibrium models, as codified, for example, in Ahsan Mansur and John Whalley (1984), do not appear to have been adopted in the real-business-cycle literature. For example, while some practitioners of computable general-equilibrium models engage in extensive searches of the literature in order to get some measure of the central tendency of assumed elasticities, Kydland and Prescott's (1982)

[4] In fact, it is not clear in Kydland and Prescott (1982) that these are calculated from the cross-section of a set of realizations or from a single time-series realization. In a subsequent paper that extends their results, Kydland and Prescott (1988, p. 353) are quite precise about using a cross-section of many realizations. Because they are interested only in the moments of the variables and not in particular time-series, Kydland and Prescott initialize variables to their steady-state values or, equivalently in the context of detrended data, to zero. In order to generate a time path that can be compared to the history of a particular series, it is necessary, as in Hansen and Prescott (1993), to initialize at some actual historical benchmark.

[5] Despite my referring to Kydland and Prescott's model as a growth model, the model for which they calculate the variances and covariances does not possess an exogenous source of trend growth. Thus, to make comparisons, Kydland and Prescott (1982, p. 1362) detrend the actual data using the Hodrick-Prescott filter. The particular choice of filter is not defended in any detail. Prescott (1983, p. 6) simply asserts that it produces 'about the right degree of smoothness, when fit to the logarithm of the real GNP series' without any indication by what standard rightness is to be judged. Kydland and Prescott (1990, p. 9) claim that it generates a trend close to the trend that students of business cycles would draw by hand through a plot of actual GNP. Although the Hodrick-Prescott filter is almost universally adopted in comparing real-business-cycle models to actual data, Fabio Canova (1991b) shows that the use of Hodrick-Prescott filters with different choices for the values of a key parameter or of several entirely different alternative filters radically alters the cyclical characteristics of economic data (also see Timothy Cogley and James Nason, 1993).

choice of parameterization appears almost casual. Similarly, although Kydland and Prescott report some checks on robustness, these appear to be perfunctory.[6]

In the context of computable general-equilibrium models, calibration is preferred in those cases in which, because of extensive disaggregation, the number of parameters is too large relative to the available data set to permit econometric estimation.[7] Since typical real-business-cycle models are one-good, one-agent models, there is no difficulty in estimating them using standard methods such as maximum likelihood or generalized method of moments. Indeed, since the practitioners are often interested principally in matching selected second moments, method-of-moments estimators can concentrate on the moments of interest to the exclusion of others (see Watson 1993, p. 1037).

As noted earlier, Altug (1989) estimates and rejects a close relative of Kydland and Prescott's model using maximum likelihood. The central problem of this paper can be restated: is there a case for ignoring Altug's rejection of the Kydland and Prescott model? The case must be something other than the standard one of too many parameters found in the literature on computable general-equilibrium models.

2.2. *Calibration as estimation*

Various authors have attempted to tame calibration and return it to the traditional econometric fold. Manuelli and Sargent (1988), Gregory and Smith (1990a), Canova (1991a), and Bansal *et al.* (1991) interpret calibration as a form of 'estimation by simulation'. In such a procedure, parameters are chosen, and the relevant features of the simulated output of the calibrated model are compared to the analogous features of the actual data. Such a procedure differs from standard estimation methods principally in that it allows the investigator to expand or restrict the range of features considered to be relevant.

Lucas's argument, however, is that any form of estimation is irrelevant. In their early writings, Kydland and Prescott were not in fact as explicit as Lucas about the irrelevance of estimation. They merely argued that it would be premature to apply techniques to their model, such as those developed by Lars Peter Hansen and Sargent (1980), to account for the systemic effects of rational expectations (Kydland and Prescott, 1982, p. 1369). Prescott (1983, pp. 8–11)

[6] Canova (1991a) suggests a formal methodology and provides an example in which sensitivity analysis is conducted with respect to distributions for parameter values constructed from the different values reported in unrelated studies or from *a priori* information on the practically or theoretically admissible range of parameter values.

[7] Lawrence J. Lau (1984) notices that any model that can be calibrated can also be estimated. He uses 'calibration', however, in a narrow sense. A model is calibrated when its parameters are chosen to reproduce the data of a benchmark period. Thus, parameterization on the basis of unrelated econometric studies does not count as calibration for him. Lau's usage is diametrically opposed to that of Gregory and Smith (1991) for whom calibration is only the assignment of parameter values from unrelated sources. We use 'calibration' in both Lau's and Gregory and Smith's senses. Lau and, similarly, James MacKinnon (1984) make strong pleas for estimation instead of, or in addition to, calibration, and for subjecting computable general-equilibrium models to statistical specification tests.

was more pointed: real-business-cycle models are tightly parameterized. They will almost inevitably be rejected against a weakly restricted alternative hypothesis, but such alternative hypotheses arise from the introduction of arbitrary stochastic processes and, so, are not suitable benchmarks for economic inference. 'A model may mimic the cycle well but not perfectly' (Prescott 1983, p. 10). Similarly, Kydland and Prescott (1991, p. 174) write:

> Unlike the system-of-equations approach, the model economy which better fits the data is not [necessarily?] the one used. Rather, currently established theory dictates which one is used.

The dominance of theory in the choice of models lies at the heart of the difference between estimators and calibrators. To throw the difference into high relief, one can think of estimators pursuing a competitive strategy and calibrators pursuing an adaptive strategy. Under the competitive strategy, theory proposes, estimation and testing disposes. In fine, alternative theories compete with one another for the support of the data. The adaptive strategy begins with an unrealistic model, in the sense of one that is an idealized and simplified product of the core theory. It sees how much mileage it can get out of that model. Only then does it add any complicating and more realistic feature. Unlike the competitive strategy, the aim is never to test and possibly reject the core theory, but to construct models that reproduce the economy more and more closely within the strict limits of the basic theory.

The distinction between the competitive and adaptive strategies is sharply drawn and somewhat stylized, but focuses nonetheless on a genuine difference. On the one hand, the competitive strategy is the received view of econometricians, taught in an idealized form in most econometric textbooks, even if more honored in the breach than the observance by applied economists. The competitive strategy is explicit in Gregory and Smith's (1990b) 'Calibration as Testing'. Even if in practice no theory is ever decisively rejected through a test based on an econometic estimation, the theory is nonetheless regarded as at risk and contingent—even at its core. On the other hand, the real-business-cycle modeller typically does not regard the core theory at risk in principle. Like the estimators, the calibrators wish to have a close fit between their quantified models and the actual data—at least in selected dimensions. But the failure to obtain a close fit (statistical rejection) does not provide grounds for rejecting the fundamental underlying theory. Adaptation in the face of recalcitrant data is adaptation of peripheral assumptions, not of the core. Thus, the inability of Kydland and Prescott's (1982) original real-business-cycle model to match the data prompted more complicated versions of essentially the same model that included, for example, heterogeneous labor (Kydland 1984), a banking sector (Robert G. King and Charles I. Plosser 1984), indivisible labor (Gary Hansen 1985), separate scales for straight-time and overtime work (Gary Hansen and Sargent 1988), and variable capital intensity (Kydland and Prescott 1988).

One consequence of these strategies is that esimators possess a common ground, the performance of each theoretically-based specification against actual data, on which to judge the performance of competing models. For the calibrators, however, data help discriminate only between different adaptations of the common core. The core theory itself is not questioned, so that, unintentially perhaps, the core theory becomes effectively a Lakatosian hard-core (Lakatos 1970, 1978; Blaug 1992, ch. 2). Calibration does not provide a method that could in principle decide between fundamentally different business-cycle models (e.g. real-business-cycle models or Keynesian business-cycle models) on the basis of empirical evidence derived from the calibration exercise itself.[8] Critics of real-business-cycle models who attempt such comparisons fall back either on attacking the discriminating power of calibration methods (e.g. Hartley *et al.* 1993) or on adaptations of standard econometric techniques (e.g. Canova *et al.* 1993). Kydland and Prescott are explicit in rejecting these applications of estimation techniques as missing the point of the calibration method. The aim of this paper is partly to explicate and appraise their view.[9]

2.3. *The mantel of Frisch*

Calibrators radically reject the system-of-equations approach. But Kydland and Prescott, at least, do not reject econometrics. Rather, they argue that econometrics is not coextensive with estimation; calibration is econometrics. Kydland and Prescott (1991, pp. 161, 162) point out that for Ragnar Frisch, Irving Fisher, and Joseph Shumpeter, the founders of the Econometric Society, 'econometrics' was the unification of statistics, economic theory, and mathematics. Unacknowledged by Kydland and Prescott, Mary Morgan's (1990) brilliant history of econometrics supports and elaborates their point. According to Morgan, even before the term 'econometrics' had wide currency, the econometric ideal had been to weld mathematical, deductive economics to statistical, empirical economics to provide a substitute for the experimental methods of the natural sciences appropriate to the study of society. This ideal collapsed with the rise of the system-of-equations approach in the wake of the Cowles Commission.

Kydland and Prescott point to Frisch's (1933) article, 'Propagation Problems and Impulse Response Problems in Dynamic Economics' as a precursor to both their own real-business-cycle model and to calibration methods. Frisch argues that quantitative analysis requires complete models: i.e. general-equilibrium models in a broad sense. He considers a sequence of models, starting with a very simple one, and then adding complications. He models the time-to-build feature of capital formation. He distinguishes between the impulses that start business cycles and the dynamic mechansisms that amplify and propagate them. He quantifies his models using calibration techniques. And,

[8] This is not to say that there could not be some other basis for some decision.

[9] Hoover 1994a (as well as work in progress) outlines a possible method of using econometric techniques in a way that respects the idealized nature of the core models without giving up the possibility of empirical discrimination.

precisely like Kydland and Prescott (1982), Frisch marvels at how well a very simple model can capture the features of actual data.

Although Kydland and Prescott are correct to see the affinities between Frisch's work and their own, they ignore the very real differences between Frisch and themselves. Frisch's approach is wholly macroeconomic. Frisch writes:

> In order to attack these problems on a macro-dynamic basis so as to explain the movement of the system taken in its entirety, we must deliberately disregard a considerable amount of the details of the picture. We may perhaps start by throwing all kinds of production into one variable, all consumption into another, and so on, imagining that the notions 'production', 'consumption', and on, can be measured by some sort of total indices. (1933, p. 173)

While his flight to aggregates parallels the practice of the new classical real-business-cycle model, Frisch does not suggest that this is a way station on the road to microfoundations. His article does not hint at the desirability of microfoundations, even of the pseudo-microfoundations of the representative-agent model: there is not an optimization problem to be found. Frisch appears to use calibration mainly for purposes of illustration, and not to advocate it as a preferred technique. He writes:

> At present I am guessing very roughly at these parameters, but I believe that it will be possible by appropriate statistical methods to obtain more exact information about them. I think, indeed, that the statistical determination of such structural parameters will be one of the main objectives of the economic cycle analysis of the future. (1933, p. 185)

Precisely which statistical methods are appropriate appears to be an open question.[10]

More generally, although Frisch stresses the importance of theory, there is no hint that his interpretation is limited to 'maximizing behavior subject to constraints' (Kydland and Prescott 1991, p. 164). Frisch does not define 'theory' in 'Propagation Problems . . .', but the examples he produces of theories are not of an obviously different character from the structures employed by Jan Tinbergen, Lawrence Klein, James Dusenberry, and the other 'Keynesian' macromodelers who are the special bugbears of the advocates of new-classical, real-business-cycle models.

Schumpeter (co-founder with Frisch of the Econometric Society) provides typically prolix discussions of the meaning of 'economic theory' in his magisteral *History of Economic Analysis* (1954). For Schumpeter (1954, pp. 14,

[10] Frisch's own shifting views illustrate how open a question this was for him. By 1936, he had backtracked on the desirability of estimating calibrated models. In 1938, he argued that structural estimation was impossible because of pervasive multicollinearity. In its place he proposed estimating unrestricted reduced forms (see Morgan, 1990, p. 97; also see Aldrich 1989, section 2). In this he comes much closer to Christopher Sims (1980) program of vector autoregressions without 'incredible' identifying restrictions. I am grateful to an anonymous referee for reminding me of this point. Hoover (1992) identifies Sims's program as one of three responses to the Lucas (1976) critique of policy invariance. Calibration and the systems-of-equations approach each possess a analogous response.

15), theories are, on the one hand, 'synonomous with Explanatory Hypotheses', and on the other hand, 'the sum total of the gadgets', such as '"marginal rate of substitution", "marginal productivity", "multiplier", "accelerator"', including 'stragegically useful assumptions', 'by which results may be extracted from the hypothesis'. Schumpeter concludes: 'In Mrs. Robinson's unsurpassingly felicitous phrase, economic theory is a box of tools'. Later Schumpeter defends the theoretical credentials of Wesley C. Mitchell, the subject of Tjalling Koopman's (1947) famous attack on 'Measurement without Theory':

> ... in intention as well as in fact, he was laying the foundations for a 'theory', a business cycle theory as well as a general theory of the economic process, but for a different one. (1954, p. 1166)

Kydland and Prescott (1991, p. 164) argue that the system-of-equations approach flourished in the 1950s only because economists lacked the tools to construct stochastic computable general-equilibrium models. They proclaim the death of the system-of-equations approach:

> The principal reason for the abandonment of the system-of-equations approach, however, was the advances in neoclassical theory that permitted the application of the paradigm in dynamic stochastic settings. Once the neoclassical tools needed for modeling business cycle fluctuations existed, their application to this problem and their ultimate domination over any other method was inevitable. (1991, p. 167)

This is an excessively triumphalist and whiggish history of the development of econometric thought. First, the work of Frisch and others in the 1930s provides no support for Kydland and Prescott's narrowing of the meaning of 'theory' to support such tendentious statements as: 'To summarize the Frisch view, then, econometrics is quantitative *neoclassical* theory with a basis in facts' (Kydland and Prescott 1991, p. 162; emphasis added). (A model is 'neoclassical' for Kydland and Prescott (1991, p. 164) when it is constructed from '... agents maximizing subject to constraints and market clearing'.) Second, the declaration of the death of the system-of-equations approach is premature and greatly exaggerated. Allegiance to the system-of-equations approach motivates the many efforts to interpret calibration as a form of estimation. Third, the calibration methodology is not logically connected to Kydland and Prescott's preferred theoretical framework. The example of Frisch shows that calibration can be applied to models that are not stochastic dynamic optimal-growth models. The example of Lars Peter Hansen and Sargent (1980) shows that, even those who prefer such models, can use them as the source of identification for systems of equations – refining rather than supplanting the traditional econometrics of estimation.

3. The quantification of theory

Although Kydland and Prescott overstate the degree to which Frisch and the econometrics of the 1930s foreshadowed their work, they are nonetheless correct to note many affinities. But such affinities, even if they were more complete than they turn out to be, do not amount to an argument favoring calibration over estimation. At most, they are an illicit appeal to authority. To date, no compelling defence of the calibration methodology has been offered. An interpretation of the point of calibration and an assessment of its merits can be constructed, however, from hints provided in Lucas's methodological writings of the 1970s and early 1980s.

3.1. *Models*

'Model' is a ubiquitous term in economics, and a term with a variety of meanings. One commonly speaks of an econometric model. Here one means the concrete specification of functional forms for estimation. I call these observational models. The second main class of models are evaluative or interpretive models. An obvious subclass of interpretive/evaluative models are toy models.

A toy model exists merely to illustrate or to check the coherence of principles or their interaction. An example of a toy model is the overlapping-generations model with money in its simplest incarnations. No one would think of drawing quantitative conclusions about the working of the economy from it. Instead one wants to show that models constructed on its principles reproduce certain known qualitative features of the economy and suggest other qualitative features that may not have been known or sufficiently appreciated (cf. Diamond 1984, p. 47), Were one so rash as to estimate such a model, it would surely be rejected, but that would be no reason to abandon it as a testbed for general principles.

Is there another subclass of interpretive/evaluative models, one that involves quantification? Lucas seems to think so:

> One of the functions of theoretical economics is to provide fully articulated, artificial economic systems that can serve as laboratories in which policies that would be prohibitively expensive to experiment within actual economies can be tested out at much lower cost. (Lucas 1980, p. 271)

Let us call such models benchmark models. Benchmark models must be abstract enough and precise enough to permit incontrovertible answers to the questions put to them. Therefore,

> ... insistence on the 'realism' of an economic model subverts its potential usefulness in thinking about reality. Any model that is well enough articulated to give clear answers to the questions we put to it will necessarily be artificial, abstract, patently unreal. (Lucas 1980, p. 271)

On the other hand, only models that mimic reality in important respects will be useful in analyzing actual economies.

> The more dimensions in which the model mimics the answers actual economies give to simple questions, the more we trust its answers to harder questions. This is the sense in which more 'realism' in a model is clearly preferred to less. (Lucas 1980, p. 272)

Later in the same essay, Lucas emphasizes the quantitative nature of such model building:

> Our task . . . is to write a FORTRAN program that will accept specific economic policy rules as 'input' and will generate as 'output' statistics describing the operating characteristics of time series we care about, which are predicted to result from these policies. (p. 288)

For Lucas, Kydland and Prescott's model is precisely such a program.[11]

One might interpret Lucas's remarks as making a superficial contribution to the debate over Milton Friedman's 'Methodology of Positive Economics' (1953): must the assumptions on which a theory is constructed be true or realistic or is it enough that the theory predicts 'as if' they were true? But this would be a mistake. Lucas is making a point about the architecture of models and not about the foundations of secure prediction. Lucas refers to a model as fully 'realistic' when it fully accounts for all the factors that determine the variables of interest. Lucas makes two points. Uncontroversially, he argues that toy models convey deep understanding of economic principles. More interestingly, he argues that benchmark models have an advantage over estimation. This is controversial because estimators believe that fully articulated specifications are required for accurate quantification. This is expressed in their concern for specification error, omitted variable bias, and so forth. Their view is widely shared. The point is not that estimated models are necessarily more realistic in Lucas's sense than calibrated models, nor that estimation is the only or even the most reliable way to quantify a model or its components.[12] Rather it is that any method of quantification that does not aspire to full articulation is likely to mislead. Lucas denies this, and the interesting issues are how to appraise his position, and, if his position is sustainable, how to appraise quantified benchmark models themselves.

To make this clear, consider Lucas's (1987, pp. 20–31) cost-benefit analysis of the policies to raise GNP growth and to damp the business cycle. Lucas's model considers a single representative consumer with a constant-relative-risk-aversion utility function facing an exogenous consumption stream. The model is calibrated by picking reasonable values for the mean and variance of consumption, the subjective rate of discount, and the constant coefficient of relative risk aversion. Lucas then calculates how much extra consumption consumers would require to compensate them in terms of utility for a cut in the growth of consumption and how much consumption they would be willing to give up to secure smoother consumption streams. Although the answers that Lucas seeks are quantitative, the model is not used to make predictions that might be subjected to statistical tests. Indeed, it is a striking illustration of why calibration should not be interpreted as estimation by simulation. Lucas's model is used to set upper bounds to the benefits that might conceivably be gained in the real world. Its parameters must reflect some truth about the world

[11] Kydland and Prescott do not say, however, whether it is actually written in FORTRAN.

[12] For example, to clarify a point raised by an anonymous referee, if the central bank had direct knowledge of it money supply function, that would be better than estimating it.

if it is to be useful, but they could not be easily directly estimated. In that sense, the model is unrealistic.[13]

3.2. *Artifacts*

In a footnote, Lucas (1980, p. 272, fn. 1) cites Simon's *Sciences of the Artificial* (1969) as an 'immediate ancestor' of his 'condensed' account. To uncover a more fully articulated argument for Lucas's approach to modelling, it is worth following up the reference.

For Simon, human artifacts, among which he must count economic models,

> can be thought of as a meeting point—an 'interface'...—between an 'inner' environment, the substance and organization of the artifact itself, and an 'outer' environment, the surroundings in which it operates. (Simon 1969, pp. 6, 7)

An artifact is useful, it achieves its goals, if its inner environment is appropriate to its outer environment.

The distinction between the outer and inner environments is important because there is some degree of independence between them. Clocks tell time for the outer environment. Although they may indicate the time in precisely the same way, say with identical hands on identical faces, the mechanisms of different clocks, their inner environments, may be constructed very differently. For determining when to leave to catch a plane, such differences are irrelevant. Equally, the inner environments may be isolated from all but a few key features of the outer environment. Only light entering through the lens for the short time that its shutter is open impinges on the inner environment of the camera. The remaining light is screened out by the opaque body of the camera, which is an essential part of its design.

Simon factors adaptive systems into goals, outer environments and inner environments. The relative independence of the outer and inner environments means that

> [w]e might hope to characterize the main properties of the system and its behavior without elaborating the detail of *either* the outer or the inner environments. We might look toward a science of the artificial that would depend on the relative simplicity of the interface as its primary source of abstraction and generality. (Simon 1969, p. 9)

Simon's views reinforce Lucas's discussion of models. A model is useful only if it foregoes descriptive realism and selects limited features of reality to reproduce. The assumption upon which the model is based do not matter, so long as the model succeeds in reproducing the selected features. Friedman's 'as if' methodology appears vindicated.

[13] Of course, Lucas's approach might be accepted in principle and still rejected in detail. For example, McCallum (1986, pp. 411, 412) objects to the characterization of consumption as fluctuating symmetrically about trend that is implicit in Lucas's use of a mean/variance model. If the fluctuations of consumption are better described as varying degrees of shortfall relative to the trend of potential maximum consumption, then the benefits of consumption smoothing will be considerably higher than Lucas's finds.

But this is to move too fast. The inner environment is only relatively independent of the outer environment. Adaptation has its limits.

> In a benign environment we would learn from the motor only what it had been called upon to do; in a taxing environment we would learn something about its internal structure specifically, about those aspects of the internal structure that were chiefly instrumental in limiting performance. (Simon 1969, p. 13)[14]

This is a more general statement of principles underlying Lucas's (1976) critique of macroeconometric models. A benign outer environment for econometric models is one in which policy does not change. Changes of policy produce structural breaks in estimated equations: disintegration of the inner environment of the models. Economic models must be constructed like a ship's chronometer, insulated from the outer environment so that '. . . it reacts to the pitching of the ship only in the negative sense of maintaining an invariant relation of the hands on its dial to real time, independently of the ship's motions' (Simon 1969, p. 9). Insulation in economic models is achieved by specifying functions whose parameters are invariant to policy. The independence of the inner and outer environments is not something which is true of arbitrary models; rather it must be built into models. While it may be enough in hostile environments for models to reproduce key features of the outer environment 'as if' reality was described by their inner environments, it is not enough if they can do this only in benign environments. Thus, for Lucas, the 'as if' methodology interpreted as an excuse for complacency with respect to modeling assumptions must be rejected. Simon's notion of the artifact helps justify Lucas's both rejecting realism in the sense of full articulation and at the same time, insisting that only through carefully constructing the model from invariants—tastes and technology, in Lucas's usual phrase—can the model secure the benefits of a useful abstraction and generality.

Recognizing that a model must be constructed from invariants does not itself tell us how to quantify it. The emphasis on a maintained theory or inner environment presents a generic risk for quantified idealized models (see Section 2.2 above). The risk is particularly severe for the calibration methodology with its adaptive strategy. Gregory and Smith (1991, p. 30) observe that '[s]etting parameter values (i.e. calibrating), simulating a model and comparing properties of simulations to those of data often suggests fruitful modifications of the model'. Generally, such modifications leave the essential core theory intact and attempt to better account for the divergences from the ideal, to better account for the fudge factors need to link the output of the model to the phenomenal laws. The risk, then, is that the core of the model becomes completely insulated from empirical confirmation or disconfirmation—even in the weakest senses of

[14] Haavelmo (1944, p. 28) makes a similar point in his well-known example of the failure of autonomy: the relationship between the speed of a car and the amount of throttle may be well-defined under uniform conditions, but would break down immediately the car was placed in a different setting. To understand how the car will perform on the track as well as on the road requires us to repair to the deeper principles of its operation.

those terms. Kydland and Prescott (1991, p. 171) explicitly deny that the confidence in the answers a model gives to policy questions can '. . . be resolved by computing some measure of how well the model economy mimics historical data'. Rather, '[t]he degree of confidence in the answer depends on the confidence that is placed in the economic theory being used'. Kydland and Prescott do not explain what alternative sources there might be to justify our confidence in theory; the adaptive strategy of the calibration approach almost guarantees that empirical evidence will not be among those sources.

3.3. *Quantification without history*

Calibrators of real-business-cycle models typically concentrate on matching selected second moments of variables rather than, say, matching the actual historical evolution of the modeled variables. Why? Lucas (1977, p. 218) observes that 'business cycles are all alike', not in exact detail but qualitatively. An informative test of a model's ability to capture business-cycle behavior is not, therefore, its fit to some historical time series, which is but one of many possible realizations, but rather its ability to characterize the distribution from which that realization was drawn. Lucas (1977, pp. 219, 234) advocates the test of Irma Adelman and Frank L. Adelman (1959). The Adelmans asked the question, could one distinguish data generated by simulating a model (in their case, the Klein-Goldberger macroeconometric model) from actual data describing the economy, in the absence of knowledge of which was which? The Adelmans' test compares the distribution of outcomes of the model to the actual economy. Once a close relation is established, to experiment with alternative policy rules is an easy next step. Even though government is not modelled in Kydland and Prescott's initial models, policy analysis is their ultimate goal (Kydland and Prescott, 1982, p. 1369). Concentration on the second moments of variables can be seen as the practical implementation of the Adelmans' standard: one eschews the particular realization in favor of a more general characterization of the distribution of possible outcomes.[15]

One reason, therefore, not to apply a neutral statistical test for the match between model and reality is that it is along only selected dimensions that one cares about the model's performance at all. This is completely consistent with Simon's account of artifacts. New classical economics has traditionally been skeptical about discretionary economic policies. New classical economists are, therefore, more concerned to evaluate the operating characteristics of policy rules. For this, the fit of the model to a particular historical realization is largely irrelevant, unless it assures it will also characterize the future distribution of

[15] The Adelmans themselves examine the time-series properties of a single draw, rather than the characteristics of repeated draws. This probably reflects, in part, the computational expense of simulating a large macroeconometric model with the technology of 1959. It also reflects the application of Burns and Mitchell's techniques for characterizing the repetitive features of business cycles through averaging over historical cycles all normalized to a notional cycle length. King and Plosser (1989) attempt to apply precisely Burns and Michell's techniques to outcomes generated by a real-business-cycle model.

outcomes. The implicit claim of most econometrics is that it does assure a good characterization. Probably most econometricians would reject calibration methods as coming nowhere close to providing such assurance. Substantial work remains to be done in establishing objective, comparative standards for judging competing models.

4. Aggregation and general equilibrium[16]

Whether calibrated or estimated, real-business-cycle models are idealizations along many dimensions. The most important dimension of idealization is the the models deal in aggregates while the economy is composed of individuals. After all, the distinction between microeconomics and macroeconomics is the distinction between the individual actor and the economy as a whole. All new classical economists believe that one understands macroeconomic behavior only as an outcome of individual rationality. Lucas (1987, p. 57) comes close to adopting the *Verstehen* approach of the Austrians.[17] The difficulty with this approach is that there are millions of people in the economy and it is not practical—nor is it ever likely to become practical—to model the behavior of each of them.[18] Universally, new classical economists adopt representative-agent models, in which one agent or a few types of agents, stand in for the behavior of all agents.[19] The conditions under which a single agent's behavior can accurately represent the behavior of an entire class are onerous and almost certainly never fulfilled in an actual economy.

One interpretation of the use of calibration methods in macroeconomics is that the practitioners recognize that highly aggregated theoretical models must be descriptively false, so that estimates of them are bound to fit badly in comparison to atheoretical econometric models, which are able to exploit large numbers of free parameters. The theoretical models are nonetheless to be preferred because policy evaluation is possible only within their structure. In this, they are exactly like Lucas's benchmark consumption model (see Section 3.1, above).

Calibractors appeal to microeconomic estimates of key parameters because information about individual agents is lost in the aggregatation process. Estimators, in contrast, could argue that the idealized representative-agent

[16] Aggregation and the problems it poses for macroeconomics are the subject of a voluminous literature. The present discussion is limited to a narrow set of issues most relevant to the question of idealization.

[17] For a full discussion of the relationship between new classical and Austrian economics see Hoover (1988, ch. 10).

[18] In Hoover (1984, pp. 64–6; and 1988, pp. 218–20), I refer to this as the 'Cournot problem' since it was first articulated by Augustin Cournot ([1838] 1927, p. 127).

[19] Some economists reserve the term 'representative-agent models' for models with a single, infinitely-lived agent. In a typical overlapping-generations model the new young are born at the start of every period, and the old die at the end of every period, and the model has infinitely many periods; so there are infinitely many agents. On this view, the overlapping-generations model is not a representative-agent model. I, however, regard it as one, because within any period one type of young agent and one type of old agent stand in for the enormous variety of people, and the same types are repeated period after period.

model permits better use of other information. Lars Peter Hansen and Sargent (1980, pp. 91, 92), for example, argue that the strength of their estimation method is that it accounts consistently for the interrelationships between constituent parts of the model—i.e. that is a general-equilibrium method. Calibrators respond, however, that it is precisely the importance of general equilibrium that supports their approach. Kydland and Prescott write:

> ... it is in the stage of calibration where the power of the general equilibrium approach shows up most forcefully. The insistence on internal consistency implies that parsimoniously parameterized models of the household and business sector display rich dynamic behavior through the intertemporal substitution arising from capital accumulation and from other sources. (1991, p. 170)

The trade-off between the gains and losses of the two methods is not clear cut. Lucas (1987, pp. 46, 47) and Prescott (1986, p. 15) argue that the strength of calibration is that it uses multiple sources of information, supporting the belief that it is structured around true invariants. This argument would appear to appeal to the respectable, albeit philosophically controversial view, that a theory is better supported when tested on information not used in its formulation (see Lipton 1991, ch. 8; Hoover 1994b). Unfortunately, it is not clear that calibration relies on independent information nor that it avoids estimation altogether. Parameters are sometimes chosen for calibrated business-cycle models because they mimic so-called 'stylized facts'. That the models then faithfully reproduce such facts is not independent information. Other parameters are chosen from microeconomic studies. This introduces estimation through the back door, but without any but a subjective, aesthetic metric to judge model performance.

Furthermore, since all new classical, equilibrium business-cycle models rely on the idealization of the representative agent, both calibrated and estimated versions share a common disability: using the representative-agent model in any form begs the question by assuming that aggregation does not fundamentally alter the structure of the aggregate model. Physics may provide a useful analogy. The laws that relate pressure, temperature, and volumes of gases are macrophysics. The 'ideal-gas laws' can be derived from a micromodel: gas molecules are assumed to be point masses, subject to conservation of momentum, with a distribution of velocities. An aggregate assumption is also needed: the probability of the gas molecules moving in any direction is taken to be equal.

Direct estimation of the ideal gas laws shows that they tend to break down—and must be corrected with fudge factors—when pushed to extremes. For example, under high pressures or low temperatures the ideal laws must be corrected according to van der Waals' equation. This phenomenal law, a law in macrophysics, is used to justify alterations of the micromodel: when pressures are high one must recognize that forces operate between individual molecules.

The inference of the van der Waals' force from the macrophysical behavior of gases has an analogue in the development of real-business-cycle models. Gary Hansen (1985), for example, introduces the microeconomic device of indivisible labor into a real-business cycle model, not from any direct reflection on the nature of labor markets at the level of the individual firm or worker, but as an attempt to account for the macroeconomic failure of Kydland and Prescott's (1982) model to satisfactorily reproduce the relative variabilities of hours and productivity in the aggregate data.[20] Of course, direct estimation of Kydland and Prescott's model rather than calibration may have pointed in the same direction.[21]

Despite examples of macro to micro inference analogous to the gas laws, Lucas's (1980, p. 291) more typical view is that we must build our models up from the microeconomic to the macroeconomic. Unlike gases, human society does not comprise homogeneous molecules, but rational people, each choosing constantly. To understand (*verstehen*) their behavior, one must model the individual and his situation. This insight is clearly correct, it is not clear in the least that it is adequately captured in the heroic aggregation assumptions of the representative-agent model. The analogue for physics would be to model the behavior of gases at the macrophysical level, not as derived from the aggregation of molecules of randomly distributed momenta, but as a single molecule scaled up to observable volume—a thing corresponding to nothing ever known to nature.[22]

5. Calibration and macroeconomic practice

The calibration methodology has both a wide following and a substantial opposition within the new classical school. I have attempted to give it a sympathetic reading—both in general and in its specific application to real-business-cycle models. I have concentrated on Kydland and Prescott, as its most prolific practitioners, and on Lucas, an articulate advocate. Although calibration is consistent with appealing accounts of the nature and role of models in science and economics, of their quanfication and idealization, its practical implementation in the service of real-business-cycle models with representative agents is less than compelling.

Does the calibration methodology amount to a repudiation of econometric estimation altogether? Clearly not. At some level, econometrics still helps to supply the values of the parameters of the models. Beyond that, whatever has been said in favor of calibration methods to the contrary notwithstanding, the

[20] Canova (1991b, p. 33) suggests that the particular covariance that Hansen's modification of Kydland and Prescott's model was meant to capture is an artifact of the Hodrick-Prescott filter, so that Hansen's model may be a product of misdirected effort rather than a progressive adaptation.

[21] This, rather than collegiality, may account for Kydland and Prescott's (1982, p. 1369) tolerant remark about the future utility of Lars Peter Hansen and Sargent's (1980) econometric techniques as well as for Lucas's (1987, p. 45) view that there is something to be learned from Altug's estimations of the Kydland and Prescott model—a view expressed in the midst of arguing in favour of calibration.

[22] A notable, non-new-classical attempt to derive macroeconomic behavior from microeconomic behavior with appropriate aggregation assumptions is Durlauf (1989). In a different, but related context, Stoker (1986) shows that demand systems fit the data only if distributional variables are included in the estimating equations. He takes this macroeconomic evidence as evidence for the failure of the microeconomic conditions of exact aggregation.

misgivings of econometricians such as Sargent are genuine. The calibration methodology, to date, lacks any discipline as stern as that imposed by econometric methods. For Lucas (1980, p. 288) and Prescott (1983, p. 11), the discipline of the calibration method comes from the paucity of free parameters. But one should note that theory places only loose restrictions on the values of key parameters. In practice, they are actually pinned down from econometric estimation at the microeconomic level or accounting considerations. Thus, in some sense, the calibration method would appear to be a kind of indirect estimation. Thus, although as was pointed out earlier, it would be a mistake to treat calibration as simply an alternative form of estimation, it is easy to understand why some critics interpret it that way. Even were there less flexibility in the parameterizations, the properties ascribed to the underlying components of the idealized real-business-cycle models (the agents, their utility functions, production functions, and constraints) are not subject to as convincing cross checking as the analogous components in physical models usually are. The fudge factors that account for the discrepancies between the ideal model and the data look less like van der Waals' equation than like special pleading. Above all, it is not clear on what standards competing, but contradictory, models are to be compared and adjudicated.[23] Some such standards are essential if any objective progress is to be made in economics.[24]

ACKNOWLEDGEMENTS

I thank Thomas Mayer, Kevin Salyer, Steven Sheffrin, Roy Epstein, Nancy Cartwright, Gregor Smith, Edward Prescrott, Adrian Pagan, and two anonymous referees for helpful comments on an earlier draft. The earliest version of this paper, entitled 'Calibration versus Estimation: Standards of Empirical Assessment in the New Classical Macroeconomics', was presented at the American Economic Association meetings in Washington, DC, December 1990.

[23] Prescott (1983, p. 12) seems oddly, to claim that inability of a model to account for some real events is a positive virtue—in particular, that the inability of real-business-cycle models to account for the Great Depression is a point in their favour. He writes: 'If any observation can be rationalized with some approach, then that approach is not scientific'. This seems to be a confused rendition of the respectable Popperian notion that a theory is more powerful the more things it rules out. But one must not mistake the power of a theory with its truth. Aside from issues of tractability, a theory that rationalizes only and exactly those events that actually occur, while ruling out exactly those events that do not occur is the perfect theory. In contrast, Prescott seems inadvertently to support the view that the more exceptions the better rule.

[24] Watson (1993) develops a goodness-of-fit measure for calibrated models. It takes into account that, since idealization implies differences between model and reality that may be systematic, the errors-in-variables and errors-in-equations statistical models are probably not appropriate. Also see Gregory and Smith (1991, pp. 27–8), Canova (1991a), and Hoover (1994a).

REFERENCES

ADELMAN, I. and ADELMAN, F. L. (1959). 'The Dynamic Properties of the Klein-Goldberger Model', *Econometrica*, **27**, 596–625.

ALDRICH, J. (1989). 'Autonomy', *Oxford Economic Papers*, **41**, 15–34.

ALTUG, S. (1989). 'Time-to-Build and Aggregate Fluctuations: Some New Evidence', *International Economic Review*, **30**, 889–920.

BANSAL, R. and GALLANT, R. A., HUSSEY, R., and TAUCHEN, G. (1991). 'Nonparametric Structural Estimation of Models for High-Frequency Currency Market Data', unpublished typescript.

BLAUG, M. (1992). *The Methodology of Economics: Or How Economists Explain*, Cambridge University Press, Cambridge, 2nd ed.

CANOVA, F. (1991a). 'Sensitivity Analysis and Model Evalution in Simulated Dynamic General Equilibrium Economies', unpublished typescript, Department of Economics, European University Institute, Florence, Italy.

CANOVA, F. (1991b). 'Detrending and Business Cycle Facts', unpublished typescript, Department of Economics, European University Institute, Florence, Italy.

CANOVA, F., FINN, M., and PAGAN, A. R. (1992). 'Evaluating a Real Business Cycle Model', unpublished typescript.

COGLEY, T. and NASON, J. M. (1993). 'Effects of the Hodrick-Prescott Filter on Trend and Difference Stationary Time Series: Implications for Business Cycle Research', unpublished typescript.

COOLEY, T. F. and HANSEN, G. D. (1989). 'Welfare Consequences of Monetary and Fiscal Policy', paper presented to the Federal Reserve Bank of San Francisco's Fall Academic Conference, 1 December.

COURNOT, A. [1838] (1927). *Researches into the Mathematical Principles of the Theory of Wealth*, Nathaniel T. Bacon (trans,), Macmillan, New York.

DIAMOND, P. A. (1984). *A Search-Equilibrium Approach to the Micro Foundations of Macroeconomics: The Wicksell Lectures, 1982*, MIT Press, Cambridge, MA.

DURLAUF, S. N. (1989). 'Locally Interacting Systems, Coordination Failure, and the Behavior of Aggregate Activity', unpublished typescript.

FRIEDMAN, M. (1953). 'The Methodology of Positive Economics', in *Essays in Positive Economics*, Chicago University Press, Chicago, IL.

FRISCH, R. (1933). 'Propagation Problems and Impulse Response Problems in Dynamic Economics', in *Economic Essays in Honour of Gustav Cassel: October 20th 1933*, George Allen and Unwin, London.

GREGORY, A. W. and SMITH, G. W. (1990a). 'Calibration as Estimation', *Econometric Reviews*, **9**, 57–89.

GREGORY, A. W. and SMITH, G. W. (1990b). 'Calibration as Testing: Inference in Simulated Macroeconomic Models' in *Journal of Business and Economic Statistics*, forthcoming.

GREGORY, A. W. and SMITH, G. W. (1991). 'Calibration in Macroeconomics', in G. S. Maddala and C. R. Rao (eds), *Handbook of Statistics*, **10**: *Econometics*, forthcoming.

HAAVELMO, T. (1944). 'The Probability Approach in Econometrics', *Econometrica*, **12** (supplement).

HALL, R. E. (1977). 'Investment, Interest Rates, and the Effects of Stabilization Policies' *Brookings Papers on Economic Activity*, **6**, 61–100.

HANSEN, G. D. (1985). 'Indivisible Labor and the Business Cycle', *Journal of Monetary Economics*, **16**, 309–28.

HANSEN, G. D. and PRESCOTT, E. C. (1993). 'Did Technology Shocks Cause the 1990–1991 Recession', *American Economic Review*, **83**, 280–6.

HANSEN, G. D. and SARGENT, T. J. (1988), 'Straight Time and Overtime in Equilibrium', *Journal of Monetary Economics*, **21**, 281–308.

HANSEN, L. P. and SARGENT, T. J. (1980). 'Formulating and Estimating Dynamic Linear Rational Expectations Models', in R. E. Lucas, Jr. and T. J. Sargent (eds), *Rational Expectations and Econometric Practice*, George Allen & Unwin, London, 1981.

HARTLEY, J. , SALYER, K., and SHEFFRIN, S. (1992). 'Calibration and Real Business Cycle Models: Two Unorthodox Tests', unpublished typescript.

HOOVER, K. D. (1984). 'Two Types of Monetarism', *Journal of Economic Literature*, **22**, 58–76.

HOOVER, K. D. (1988). *The New Classical Macroeconomics: A Skeptical Inquiry*, Blackwell, Oxford.

HOOVER, K. D. (1992). 'The Rational Expectations Revolution: An Assessment', *The Cato Journal*, **12**, 81–96.

HOOVER, K. D. (1994a). 'Six Queries About Idealization in an Empirical Context', *Poznan Studies in the Philosphy of Science and the Humanities*, **38**, 43–53.

HOOVER, K. D. (1994b). 'In Defence of Datamining: Some Preliminary Throughts', in K. D. Hoover and S. M. Sheffrin (eds), *Monetarism and the Methodology of Econmics: Essays in Honor of Thomas Mayer*, Elgar, Aldershot, forthcoming.

KING, R. G. and PLOSSER, C. I. (1984). 'Money, Credit and Prices in a Real Business Cycle', *American Economic Review*, **74**, 363–80.

KING, R. G. and PLOSSER, C. I. (1989). 'Real Business Cycle Models and the Test of the Adelmans', paper presented to the Federal Reserve Bank of San Francisco's Fall Academic Conference, 1 December 1989.

KOOPMANS, T. C. (1947). 'Measurement without Theory', *Review of Economics and Statistics*, **29**, 161–72.

KYDLAND, F. E. (1984). 'Labor-force Heterogeneity and the Business Cycle' in K. Brunner and A. H. Meltzer (eds), *Essays on Macroeconomic Implications of Financial and Labor Markets and Political Processes*, Carnegie-Rochester Conference Series on Public Policy, **21**.

KYDLAND, F. E. and PRESCOTT, E. C. (1982). 'Time to Build and Aggregate Fluctuations', *Econometrica*, **50**, 1345–70.

KYDLAND, F. E. and PRESCOTT, E. C. (1988). 'The Workweek of Capital and Its Cyclical Implication' *Journal of Monetary Economics*, **21**, 243–60.

KYDLAND, F. E. and PRESCOTT, E. C. (1990). 'Business Cycles: Real Facts and a Monetary Myth', *Federal Reserve Bank of Minneapolis Quartly Review*, **14**, 3–18.

KYDLAND, F. E. and PRESCOTT, E. C. (1991). 'The Econometrics of the Great Equlibrium Approach to Business Cycles', *Scandinavian Journal of Economics*, **93**, 161–78.

LAKATOS, I. (1970). 'Falsification and the Methodology of Scientific Research Programmes', in I. Lakatos and A. Musgrave (eds), *Criticism and the Growth of Knowledge*, Cambridge University Press, Cambridge.

LAKATOS, I. (1978). 'History of Science and Its Rational Reconstructions' in J. Worrall and G. Currie (eds), *The Methodology of Scientific Research Programmes: Philosphical Papers*, **1**, Cambridge University Press, Cambridge.

LAU, L. J. (1984). 'Comments', in H. E. Scarf and J. B. Shoven (eds), *Applied General Equilibrium Analysis*, Cambridge University Press, Cambridge.

LIPTON, P. (1991). *Inference to the Best Explanation*, Routlege, London.

LUCAS, R. E., JR. (1976). 'Econometric Policy Evaluaton: A Critique', in *Studies in Business-Cycle Theory*, Oxford, Blackwell, 1981.

LUCAS, R. E., JR. (1977). 'Understanding Business Cycles', in *Studies in Business-Cycle Theory*, Blackwell, Oxford, 1981.

LUCAS, R. E., JR. (1980) 'Methods and Problems in Business Cycle Theory', in *Studies in Business-Cycle Theory*, Blackwell, Oxford, 1981.

LUCAS, R. E. JR. (1986). 'Adapttive Behavior and Economic Theory', *Journal of Business*, **59**, S401–26.

LUCAS, R. E., JR. (1987), *Models of Business Cycles*, Blackwell, Oxford.

LUCAS, R. E., JR. and SARGENT, T. J. C. (eds) (1981). *Rational Expectations and Econometric Practice*, George Allen and Unwin, London.

MACKINNON, J. (1984). 'Comments', in H. E. Scarf and J. B. Shoven (eds), *Applied General Equilibrium Analysis*, Cambridge University Press, Cambridge.

MANSUR, A. and WALLEY, J. (1984). 'Numerical Specification of Applied General-equilibrium models: Estimation, Calibration, and Data', in H. E. Scarf and J. B. Shoven (eds.), *Applied General Equilibrium Analysis*, Cambridge University Press, Cambridge.

MANUELLI, R. and SARGENT, T. J. (1988). 'Models of Business Cycles: A Review Essay' *Journal of Monetary Economics*, **22**, 523–42.

MAYER, T. (1960). 'Plant and Equipment Lead Times' *Journal of Business*, **33**, 127–32.

MCCALLUM, B. T. (1986). 'On "Real" and "Sticky-Price" Theories of the Business Cycle', *Journal of Money, Credit and Banking*, **18**, 397–414.

MCCALLUM, B. T. (1989). 'Real Business Cycle Models', in R. J. Barro (ed.), *Modern Business Cycle Theory*, Blackwell, Oxford.

MORGAN, M. (1990). *The History of Econometric Ideas*, Cambridge University Press, Cambridge.

PRESCOTT, E. C. (1983). '"Can the Cycle be Reconciled with a Consistent Theory of Expectations" or A Progress Report on Business Cycle Theory', Working Paper, No. 239, Research Department, Federal Reserve Bank of Minneapolis.

PRESCOTT, E. C. (1986). 'Theory Ahead of Business Cycle Measurement', *Federal Reserve Bank of Minneapolis Quarterly Review*, **10**, 9–22.

SCHUMPETER, J. A. (1954). *History of Economic Analysis*, Oxford University Press, New York.

SHEFFRIN, S. M. (1989). *The Making of Economic Policy*, Blackwell, Oxford.

SIMON, H. A. (1969). *The Sciences of the Artificial*, MIT Press, Cambridge, MA.

SIMS, C. A. (1980). 'Macroeconomics and Reality', *Econometrica*, **48**, 1–48.

STOKER, T. M. (1986). 'Simple Tests of Distributional Effects on Macroeconomic Equations', *Journal of Political Economy*, **94**, 763–95.

WATSON, M. W. (1993). 'Measures of Fit for Calibrated Models', *Journal of Political Economy*, **101**, 1011–41.

[6]

Measures of Fit for Calibrated Models

Mark W. Watson

Northwestern University and Federal Reserve Bank of Chicago

This paper suggests a new procedure for evaluating the fit of a dynamic structural economic model. The procedure begins by augmenting the variables in the model with just enough stochastic error so that the model can exactly match the second moments of the actual data. Measures of fit for the model can then be constructed on the basis of the size of this error. The procedure is applied to a standard real business cycle model. Over the business cycle frequencies, the model must be augmented with a substantial error to match data for the postwar U.S. economy. Lower bounds on the variance of the error range from 40 percent to 60 percent of the variance in the actual data.

I. Introduction

Economists have long debated appropriate methods for assessing the empirical relevance of economic models. The standard econometric approach can be traced back to Haavelmo (1944), who argued that an economic model should be embedded within a complete probability model and analyzed using statistical methods designed for conducting inference about unknown probability distributions. In the modern literature, this approach is clearly exemplified in work such as that of L. Hansen and Sargent (1980) or McFadden (1981). However, many economic models do not provide a realistic and complete

This paper has benefited from constructive comments by many seminar participants; in particular I thank John Cochrane, Marty Eichenbaum, Jon Faust, Lars Hansen, Robert Hodrick, Robert King, and Robert Lucas. Two referees also provided valuable constructive criticism and suggestions. The first draft of this paper was written while I was visiting the University of Chicago, whose hospitality is gratefully acknowledged. This research was supported by the National Science Foundation through grants SES-89-10601 and SES-91-22463.

[*Journal of Political Economy*, 1993, vol. 101, no. 6]

probability structure for the variables under consideration. To analyze these models using standard econometric methods, they must first be augmented with additional random components. Inferences drawn from these expanded models are meaningful only to the extent that the additional random components do not mask or change the salient features of the original economic models.

Another approach, markedly different from the standard econometric approach, has become increasingly popular for evaluating dynamic macroeconomic models. This approach is clearly articulated in the work of Kydland and Prescott (1982) and Prescott (1986). In a general sense, the approach asks whether data from a real economy share certain characteristics with data generated by the artificial economy described by an economic model. There is no claim that the model explains all the characteristics of the actual data, nor is there any attempt to augment the model with additional random components to more accurately describe the data. On the one hand, the results from this approach are easier to interpret than the results from the standard econometric approach since the economic model is not complicated by additional random elements added solely for statistical convenience. On the other hand, since the economic model does not provide a complete probability structure, inference procedures lack statistical foundations and are necessarily ad hoc. For example, a researcher may determine that a model fits the data well because it implies moments for the variables under study that are "close" to the moments of the actual data, even though the metric used to determine the distance between the moments is left unspecified.

This paper is an attempt to put the latter approach on a less ad hoc foundation by developing goodness-of-fit measures for the class of dynamic econometric models whose endogenous variables follow covariance stationary processes. It is not assumed that the model accurately describes data from the actual economy; the economic model is not a null hypothesis in the statistical sense. Rather, the economic model is viewed as an approximation to the stochastic processes generating the actual data, and goodness-of-fit measures are proposed to measure the quality of this approximation. A standard device—stochastic error—is used to motivate the goodness-of-fit measures. These measures answer the question, How much random error would have to be added to the data generated by the model so that the autocovariances implied by the model + error match the autocovariances of the observed data?

The error represents the degree of abstraction of the model from the data. Since the error cannot be attributed to a data collection procedure or to a forecasting procedure, for instance, it is difficult a priori to say much about its properties. In particular, its covariance with the observed data cannot be specified by a priori reasoning. Rather than make a specific assumption about the error's covariance properties, I construct a representation that minimizes the contribution of the error in the complete model. Thus, in this sense, the error process is chosen to make the model as close to the data as possible.

Many of the ideas in this paper are close to, and were motivated by, ideas in Altug (1989) and Sargent (1989). Altug (1989) showed how a one-shock real business cycle model could be analyzed using standard dynamic econometric methods, after first augmenting each variable in the model with an idiosyncratic error. This produces a restricted version of the dynamic factor analysis or unobserved index models developed by Sargent and Sims (1977) and Geweke (1977). Sargent (1989) discusses two models of measurement error: in the first the measurement error is uncorrelated with the data generated by the model, and in the second the measurement error is uncorrelated with the sample data (see also G. Hansen and Sargent 1988). While similar in spirit, the approach taken in this paper differs from that of Altug and Sargent in two important ways. First, in this paper, the error process is not assumed to be uncorrelated with the model's artificial data or with the actual data. Rather, the correlation properties of the error process are determined by the requirement that the variance of the error is as small as possible. Second, the joint data-error process is introduced to motivate goodness-of-fit measures; it is not introduced to describe a statistical model that can be used to test statistical hypotheses, at least in the standard sense. Rather, the analysis in this paper is similar to the analysis in Campbell and Shiller (1988), Durlauf and Hall (1989), Hansen and Jagannathan (1991), and Cochrane (1992). Each of these papers uses a different approach to judge the goodness of fit of an economic model by calculating a value or an upper bound on the variance of an unobserved "noise" or a "marginal rate of substitution" or a "discount factor" in observed data.

The minimum approximation error representation developed in this paper motivates two sets of statistics that can be used to evaluate the goodness of fit of the economic model. First, like the variance of the error in a regression model, the variance of the approximation error can be used to form an R^2 measure for each variable in the model. This provides an overall measure of fit. Moreover, spectral methods can be used to calculate this R^2 measure for each frequency so that the fit can be calculated over the "business cycle," "growth," or other specific frequency bands. A second set of statistics can be constructed by using the minimum error representation to form fitted values of the variables in the economic model. These fitted values show how well the model explains specific historical episodes; for example, can a real business cycle model simultaneously explain the growth in the United States during the 1960s and the 1981–82 recession?

The paper is organized as follows. Section II develops the minimum approximation error representation and goodness-of-fit measures. Section III calculates these goodness-of-fit statistics for a standard real business cycle model using postwar U.S. macroeconomic data on output, consumption, investment, and employment. Section IV concludes the paper by providing a brief discussion of some tangential issues that arise from the analysis.

II. Measures of Fit

Consider an economic model that describes the evolution of an $n \times 1$ vector of variables $\mathbf{x}_t$. Assume that the variables have been transformed, say by first-differencing or forming ratios, so that $\mathbf{x}_t$ is covariance stationary. As a notational device, it is useful to introduce the autocovariance generating function (ACGF) of $\mathbf{x}_t$, $A_{\mathbf{x}}(z)$. This function completely summarizes the unconditional second-moment properties of the process. In what follows, "economic model" and "$A_{\mathbf{x}}(z)$" will be used interchangeably; that is, the analysis considers only the unconditional second-moment implications of the model. Nonlinearities and variation in conditional second and higher moments are ignored to help keep the problem tractable. The analysis will also ignore the unconditional first moments of $\mathbf{x}_t$; modifying the measures of fit for differences in the means of the variables is straightforward.

The empirical counterparts of $\mathbf{x}_t$ are denoted $\mathbf{y}_t$. These variables differ from $\mathbf{x}_t$ in an important way. The variables making up $\mathbf{x}_t$ correspond to the variables appearing in the theorist's simplification of reality; in a macroeconomic model they are variables such as "output," "money," and the "interest rate." The variables making up $\mathbf{y}_t$ are functions of raw data collected in a real economy; they are variables such as "per capita gross domestic product in the United States in 1987 dollars" or "U.S. M2" or "the yield on 3-month U.S. Treasury bills."

The question of interest is whether the model generates data with characteristics similar to those of the data generated by the real economy. Below, goodness-of-fit measures are proposed to help answer this question. Before I introduce these new measures, it is useful to review standard statistical goodness-of-fit measures to highlight their deficiencies for answering the question at hand.

Standard statistical goodness-of-fit measures use the size of sampling error to judge the coherence of the model with the data. They are based on the following: First, $A_{\mathbf{y}}(z)$, the population ACGF for $\mathbf{y}_t$, is unknown but can be estimated from sample data. Discrepancies between the estimator $\hat{A}_{\mathbf{y}}(z)$ and $A_{\mathbf{y}}(z)$ arise solely from sampling error in $\hat{A}_{\mathbf{y}}(z)$, and the likely size of the error can be deduced from the stochastic process that generated the sample. Now, *if* $A_{\mathbf{y}}(z) = A_{\mathbf{x}}(z)$, sampling error also accounts for the differences between $\hat{A}_{\mathbf{y}}(z)$ and $A_{\mathbf{x}}(z)$. Standard goodness-of-fit measures show how likely it is that $A_{\mathbf{y}}(z) = A_{\mathbf{x}}(z)$, on the basis of the probability that differences between $\hat{A}_{\mathbf{y}}(z)$ and $A_{\mathbf{x}}(z)$ arise solely from sampling error. If the differences between $\hat{A}_{\mathbf{y}}(z)$ and $A_{\mathbf{x}}(z)$ are so large as to be unlikely, standard measures of fit suggest that the model fits the data poorly, and vice versa if the differences between $\hat{A}_{\mathbf{y}}(z)$ and $A_{\mathbf{x}}(z)$ are not so large as to be unlikely. The key point is that the differences between $\hat{A}_{\mathbf{y}}(z)$ and $A_{\mathbf{x}}(z)$ are judged by how informative the sample is about the population moments of $\mathbf{y}_t$. This is a sensible procedure for judging the coherence of a null hypothesis, $A_{\mathbf{y}}(z) = A_{\mathbf{x}}(z)$, with the data. It is arguably less sensible when this null hypothesis is known to be false.

Rather than rely on sampling error, the measures of fit that are developed here are based on the size of the stochastic error required to reconcile the autocovariances of $\mathbf{x}_t$ with those of $\mathbf{y}_t$. In particular, let $\mathbf{u}_t$ denote an $n \times 1$ error vector; then the importance of a difference between $A_{\mathbf{x}}(z)$ and $A_{\mathbf{y}}(z)$ will be determined by asking, How much error would have to be added to $\mathbf{x}_t$ so that the autocovariances of $\mathbf{x}_t + \mathbf{u}_t$ are equal to the autocovariances of $\mathbf{y}_t$? If the variance of the required error is large, then the discrepancy between $A_{\mathbf{x}}(z)$ and $A_{\mathbf{y}}(z)$ is large, and conversely if the variance of $\mathbf{u}_t$ is small. The vector $\mathbf{u}_t$ is the approximation error in the economic model interpreted as a stochastic process. It captures the second-moment characteristics of the observed data that are not captured by the model. Loosely speaking, it is analogous to the error term in a regression in which the set of regressors is interpreted as the economic model. The economic model might be deemed a good approximation to the data if the error term is small (i.e., the R^2 of the regression is large) and might be deemed a poor approximation if the error term is large (i.e., the R^2 of the regression is small).

To be more precise, assume that $\mathbf{x}_t$ and $\mathbf{y}_t$ are jointly covariance stationary, and define the error $\mathbf{u}_t$ by the equation

$$\mathbf{u}_t = \mathbf{y}_t - \mathbf{x}_t, \tag{1}$$

so that

$$A_{\mathbf{u}}(z) = A_{\mathbf{y}}(z) + A_{\mathbf{x}}(z) - A_{\mathbf{xy}}(z) - A_{\mathbf{yx}}(z), \tag{2}$$

where $A_{\mathbf{u}}(z)$ is the ACGF of $\mathbf{u}_t$, $A_{\mathbf{xy}}(z)$ is the cross ACGF between $\mathbf{x}_t$ and $\mathbf{y}_t$, and so forth. From the right-hand side of (2), three terms are needed to calculate $A_{\mathbf{u}}(z)$. The first, $A_{\mathbf{y}}(z)$, can be consistently estimated from sample data; the second, $A_{\mathbf{x}}(z)$, is completely determined by the model; but the third, $A_{\mathbf{xy}}(z)$, is not determined by the model, and it cannot be estimated from the data (since this would require a sample drawn from the *joint* $(\mathbf{x}_t, \mathbf{y}_t)$ process). To proceed, an assumption is necessary.

A common assumption used in econometric analysis is that $A_{\mathbf{xy}}(z) = A_{\mathbf{x}}(z)$ so that $\mathbf{x}_t$ and $\mathbf{u}_t$ are uncorrelated at all leads and lags. Equation (1) can then be interpreted as the dynamic analogue of the classical errors-in-variables model. Sargent (1989) discusses this assumption and an alternative assumption, $A_{\mathbf{xy}}(z) = A_{\mathbf{y}}(z)$. He points out that under this latter assumption, $\mathbf{u}_t$ can be interpreted as signal extraction error, with $\mathbf{y}_t$ an optimal estimate of the unobserved "signal" $\mathbf{x}_t$.[1] In many applications, these covariance restrictions follow from the way the data were collected or the way expectations are formed. For example, if $\mathbf{x}_t$ represented the true value of the U.S. unemployment rate and $\mathbf{y}_t$ the value published by the U.S. Department of Labor, then $\mathbf{y}_t$ would differ from $\mathbf{x}_t$ because of the sampling error inherent in the monthly Current Population Survey from which $\mathbf{y}_t$ is derived. The sample design underlying the survey implies that the error term, $\mathbf{u}_t$, is statistically independent of $\mathbf{x}_t$. Similarly, if $\mathbf{y}_t$ denoted a rational expectation of $\mathbf{x}_t$, then the error would be uncorrelated with $\mathbf{y}_t$. Neither of these assumptions seems appropriate in the present context. The error is not the result of imprecise measurement. It is not a forecast or signal extraction error. Rather, it represents approximation or abstraction error in the economic model. Any restriction used to identify $A_{\mathbf{xy}}(z)$, and hence $A_{\mathbf{u}}(z)$, is arbitrary.[2]

It is possible, however, to calculate a lower bound for the variance of $\mathbf{u}_t$ without imposing any restrictions on $A_{\mathbf{xy}}(z)$. When this lower bound on the variance of $\mathbf{u}_t$ is large, then under any assumption on $A_{\mathbf{xy}}(z)$, the model fits the data poorly. If the lower bound on the variance of $\mathbf{u}_t$ is small, then there are possible assumptions about $A_{\mathbf{xy}}(z)$ that imply that the model fits the data well. Thus the bound is potentially useful for rejecting models on the basis of their empirical

[1] The reader familiar with work on data revisions will recognize these two sets of assumptions as the ones underlying the "news" and "noise" models of Mankiw, Runkle, and Shapiro (1984) and Mankiw and Shapiro (1986).

[2] It is interesting to note that it is possible to determine whether the dynamic errors-in-variables model or the signal extraction error model is consistent with the model and the data. The dynamic errors-in-variables model implies that $A_{\mathbf{y}}(z) - A_{\mathbf{x}}(z) \geq 0$ for $|z| = 1$, so that the spectrum of $\mathbf{y}_t$ lies everywhere above the spectrum of $\mathbf{x}_t$; the signal extraction error model implies the converse. If the spectrum of $\mathbf{x}_t$ lies anywhere above the spectrum of $\mathbf{y}_t$, the errors-in-variables model is inappropriate; if the spectrum of $\mathbf{y}_t$ lies anywhere above the spectrum of $\mathbf{x}_t$, the signal extraction model is inappropriate. If the spectra of $\mathbf{x}_t$ and $\mathbf{y}_t$ cross, neither model is appropriate.

fit. Needless to say, models that appear to fit the data well using this bound require further scrutiny.

The bound is calculated by choosing $A_{\mathbf{xy}}(z)$ to minimize the variance of $\mathbf{u}_t$ subject to the constraint that the implied joint ACGF for $\mathbf{x}_t$ and $\mathbf{y}_t$ is positive semidefinite. Equivalently, since the spectrum is proportional to the ACGF evaluated at $z = e^{-i\omega}$, the cross spectrum between $\mathbf{x}_t$ and $\mathbf{y}_t$, $(2\pi)^{-1}A_{\mathbf{xy}}(e^{-i\omega})$, must be chosen so that the spectral density matrix of $(\mathbf{x}_t' \ \mathbf{y}_t')'$ is positive semidefinite at all frequencies.

Since the measures of fit proposed in this paper are based on the solution to this minimization problem, it is useful to discuss the problem and its solution in detail. Rather than move directly to the solution of the general problem, we shall first solve two simpler problems. This helps develop intuition for the general solution. In the first problem, $\mathbf{x}_t$ and $\mathbf{y}_t$ are serially uncorrelated scalars, and the representation follows by inspection. In the second problem, $\mathbf{x}_t$ and $\mathbf{y}_t$ are serially uncorrelated $n \times 1$ vectors, and the solution is slightly more difficult to derive. Finally, in the last problem, $\mathbf{x}_t$ and $\mathbf{y}_t$ are allowed to be serially correlated.

Model 1

Suppose that x_t, y_t, and u_t are scalar serially uncorrelated random variables. The problem is to choose σ_{xy} to minimize the variance of u_t, $\sigma_u^2 = \sigma_x^2 + \sigma_y^2 - 2\sigma_{xy}$, subject to the constraint that the covariance matrix of x_t and y_t remains positive semidefinite, that is, $|\sigma_{xy}| \leq \sigma_x\sigma_y$. By inspection, the solution sets $\sigma_{xy} = \sigma_x\sigma_y$ and yields $\sigma_u^2 = (\sigma_x - \sigma_y)^2$ as the minimum. Since $\sigma_{xy} = \sigma_x\sigma_y$, x_t and y_t are perfectly correlated with

$$x_t = \gamma y_t, \tag{3}$$

where $\gamma = \sigma_x/\sigma_y$. Equation (3) is important because it shows how to calculate fitted values of x_t, given data on y_t. Variants of equation (3) will hold for all the models considered. In each model, the minimum approximation error representation makes $\{\mathbf{x}_t\}$ perfectly correlated with $\{\mathbf{y}_t\}$. In each model, the analogue of (3) provides a formula for calculating the fitted values of the variables in the model, given data from the actual economy.

Model 2

Now suppose that $\mathbf{x}_t$ and $\mathbf{y}_t$ are serially uncorrelated random vectors with covariance matrices $\boldsymbol{\Sigma}_{\mathbf{x}}$ and $\boldsymbol{\Sigma}_{\mathbf{y}}$, respectively. Let $\boldsymbol{\Sigma}_{\mathbf{u}} = \boldsymbol{\Sigma}_{\mathbf{x}} + \boldsymbol{\Sigma}_{\mathbf{y}} - \boldsymbol{\Sigma}_{\mathbf{xy}} - \boldsymbol{\Sigma}_{\mathbf{yx}}$ denote the covariance matrix of $\mathbf{u}_t$. Since $\boldsymbol{\Sigma}_{\mathbf{u}}$ is a matrix, there is not a unique way to judge how "small" it is. A convenient measure of the size of $\mathbf{u}_t$ is the trace of $\mathbf{\Sigma_u}$, $\mathrm{tr}(\mathbf{\Sigma_u}) = \Sigma_{i=1}^{n} \mathbf{\Sigma}_{\mathbf{u},ii}$, where $\mathbf{\Sigma}_{\mathbf{u},ij}$ denotes the ijth element of $\mathbf{\Sigma_u}$. While convenient, this measure is not always ideal since it weights all variables equally. Below, we shall find a representation that minimizes $\mathrm{tr}(\mathbf{W\Sigma_u})$, where $\mathbf{W}$ is a prespecified $n \times n$ matrix. When all variables are equally important, $\mathbf{W} = I_n$, and unequal weighting can be implemented by making $\mathbf{W}$ diagonal with the desired weights as the diagonal elements. The matrix $\mathbf{W}$ can also be used to focus attention on specific linear combinations of the variables that may be particularly interesting. For example, let $\mathbf{G}$ denote an $n \times n$ matrix and suppose that the researcher is primarily interested in the variables $\mathbf{Gx}_t$ and $\mathbf{Gy}_t$. Then since $\mathrm{tr}(\mathbf{G\Sigma_u G'}) = \mathrm{tr}(\mathbf{G'G\Sigma_u})$, $\mathbf{W}$ can be chosen as $\mathbf{G'G}$.

The problem then is to choose $\mathbf{\Sigma_{xy}}$ to minimize $\mathrm{tr}(\mathbf{W\Sigma_u})$ subject to the constraint that the covariance matrix of $(\mathbf{x}_t' \ \mathbf{y}_t')'$ is positive semidefinite. The solution is given below for the case in which $\mathbf{\Sigma_x}$ has rank $k \leq n$. This occurs, for example, in economic models in which the number of variables exceeds the number of shocks. The solution is summarized in the following proposition.

PROPOSITION. Assume (i) $\mathrm{rank}(\mathbf{\Sigma_x}) = k \leq n$, (ii) $\mathrm{rank}(\mathbf{W\Sigma_x W'}) = \mathrm{rank}(\mathbf{\Sigma_x})$, and (iii) $\mathrm{rank}(\mathbf{\Sigma_y}) = n$. Let $\mathbf{C_y}$ denote an arbitrary $n \times n$ matrix square root of $\mathbf{\Sigma_y}$ (i.e., $\mathbf{\Sigma_y} = \mathbf{C_y C_y'}$), and let $\mathbf{C_x}$ denote an arbitrary $n \times k$ matrix square root of $\mathbf{\Sigma_x}$ (i.e., $\mathbf{\Sigma_x} = \mathbf{C_x C_x'}$). Let $\mathbf{USV'}$ denote the singular value decomposition of $\mathbf{C_y' W C_x}$, where $\mathbf{U}$ is an $n \times k$ orthogonal matrix ($\mathbf{U'U} = I_k$), $\mathbf{S}$ is a $k \times k$ diagonal matrix, and $\mathbf{V}$ is a $k \times k$ orthonormal matrix. Then $\mathbf{\Sigma_{xy}} = \mathbf{C_x VU'C_y'}$ is the unique matrix that minimizes $\mathrm{tr}(\mathbf{W\Sigma_u})$ subject to the constraint that the covariance matrix of $(\mathbf{x}_t' \ \mathbf{y}_t')'$ is positive semidefinite.

The proof is given in the Appendix.

One important implication of this solution is that, like the scalar example, the joint covariance matrix $(\mathbf{x}_t' \ \mathbf{y}_t')'$ is singular and $\mathbf{x}_t$ can be represented as

$$\mathbf{x}_t = \Gamma \mathbf{y}_t, \tag{4}$$

where $\Gamma = \mathbf{C_x' VU'C_y^{-1}}$. (Since $\mathbf{U'U} = \mathbf{VV'} = I_k$, this simplifies to the scalar result when x_t and y_t are scalars.)

Model 3

This same approach can be used in a dynamic multivariate model with slight modifications; when $\mathbf{u}_t$ is serially correlated, the weighted trace of the spectral density matrix rather than the covariance matrix can be minimized.

To motivate the approach, it is useful to use the Cramer representations for $\mathbf{x}_t$, $\mathbf{y}_t$, and $\mathbf{u}_t$ (see, e.g., Brillinger 1981, sec. 4.6). Assume that $\mathbf{x}_t$, $\mathbf{y}_t$, and $\mathbf{u}_t$ are jointly covariance stationary with mean zero; the Cramer representation can be written as

$$\mathbf{x}_t = \int_0^{2\pi} e^{i\omega t} dz_{\mathbf{x}}(\omega),$$

$$\mathbf{y}_t = \int_0^{2\pi} e^{i\omega t} dz_{\mathbf{y}}(\omega), \tag{5}$$

$$\mathbf{u}_t = \int_0^{2\pi} e^{i\omega t} dz_{\mathbf{u}}(\omega),$$

where $dz(\omega) = (dz_{\mathbf{x}}(\omega)'\ dz_{\mathbf{y}}(\omega)'\ dz_{\mathbf{u}}(\omega)')'$ is a complex valued vector of orthogonal increments, with $E(dz(\omega)\overline{dz(\lambda)}') = \delta(\omega - \lambda)\mathbf{S}(\omega)d\omega d\lambda$, where $\delta(\omega - \lambda)$ is the dirac delta and $\mathbf{S}(\omega)$ is the spectral density matrix of $(\mathbf{x}_t'\ \mathbf{y}_t'\ \mathbf{u}_t')'$ at frequency ω. Equation (5) represents $\mathbf{x}_t$, $\mathbf{y}_t$, and $\mathbf{u}_t$ as the integral (sum) of increments $dz_{\mathbf{x}}(\omega)$, $dz_{\mathbf{y}}(\omega)$, and $dz_{\mathbf{u}}(\omega)$, which are uncorrelated across frequencies and have variances and covariances given by the spectra and cross spectra of $\mathbf{x}_t$, $\mathbf{y}_t$, and $\mathbf{u}_t$. Since the spectra are proportional to the ACGFs evaluated at $z = e^{-i\omega}$, $E(dz_{\mathbf{x}}(\omega)\overline{dz_{\mathbf{x}}(\omega)}')$ is proportional to $A_{\mathbf{x}}(e^{-i\omega})$, $E(dz_{\mathbf{x}}(\omega)\overline{dz_{\mathbf{y}}(\omega)}')$ is proportional to $A_{\mathbf{xy}}(e^{-i\omega})$, and so forth.

Now consider the problem of choosing $A_{\mathbf{xy}}(z)$ to minimize the variance of $\mathbf{u}_t$. Since $\mathbf{u}_t$ can be written as the integral of the uncorrelated increments $dz_{\mathbf{u}}(\omega)$, the variance of $\mathbf{u}_t$ can be minimized by minimizing the variance of $dz_{\mathbf{u}}(\omega)$ for each ω. Since the increments are uncorrelated across frequency, the minimization problems can be solved independently for each frequency. Thus the analysis carried out for model 2 carries over directly, with spectral density matrices replacing covariance matrices. The minimum trace problem for model 2 is now solved frequency by frequency using the spectral density matrix.

Like models 1–2, the solution yields

$$dz_{\mathbf{x}}(\omega) = \Gamma(\omega)dz_{\mathbf{y}}(\omega), \tag{6}$$

where $\Gamma(\omega)$ is the complex analogue of Γ from (4). Equation (6) implies

$$A_{\mathbf{xy}}(e^{-i\omega}) = \Gamma(\omega)A_{\mathbf{y}}(e^{-i\omega}) \tag{7}$$

and

$$A_{\mathbf{u}}(e^{-i\omega}) = A_{\mathbf{x}}(e^{-i\omega}) + A_{\mathbf{y}}(e^{-i\omega}) - A_{\mathbf{xy}}(e^{-i\omega}) - A_{\mathbf{xy}}(e^{i\omega})'. \tag{8}$$

The autocovariances of $\mathbf{u}_t$ follow directly from (8). Moreover, since $dz_{\mathbf{x}}(\omega)$ and $dz_{\mathbf{y}}(\omega)$ are perfectly correlated from (7), $\mathbf{x}_t$ can be represented as a function of leads and lags of $\mathbf{y}_t$:

$$\mathbf{x}_t = \beta(L)\mathbf{y}_t, \tag{9}$$

where $\beta(L) = \Sigma_{-\infty}^{\infty} \beta_j L^j$, with $\beta_j = \int_{-\pi}^{\pi} \Gamma(\omega)e^{i\omega j}d\omega$. Thus fitted values of $\mathbf{x}_t$ can be calculated from leads and lags of $\mathbf{y}_t$.

An Example

The model considered in the next section describes the dynamic properties of output, consumption, investment, and employment as functions of a single productivity shock. To demonstrate the mechanics of the minimum approximation error representation for that model, assume that $\mathbf{x}_t$ and $\mathbf{y}_t$ are $n \times 1$ vectors and that $\mathbf{x}_t$ is driven by a single iid(0, 1) shock ϵ_t:

$$\mathbf{x}_t = \boldsymbol{\alpha}(L)\epsilon_t, \tag{10}$$

where $\boldsymbol{\alpha}(L)$ is an $n \times 1$ matrix polynomial in the lag operator, L. Assume that the Wold representation for the data is given by

$$\mathbf{y}_t = \boldsymbol{\Theta}(L)\mathbf{e}_t, \tag{11}$$

where $\boldsymbol{\Theta}(L)$ is an $n \times n$ matrix polynomial in L, and $\mathbf{e}_t$ is an $n \times 1$ serially uncorrelated vector with mean zero and identity covariance matrix.

The minimum error representation can then be computed directly from the matrix expressions given in the proposition. From (10), $A_{\mathbf{x}}(z) = \boldsymbol{\alpha}(z)\boldsymbol{\alpha}(z^{-1})'$ and, from (11), $A_{\mathbf{y}}(z) = \boldsymbol{\Theta}(z)\boldsymbol{\Theta}(z^{-1})'$. Suppose that the weighting matrix is $\mathbf{W} = I_n$, so that the trace of the spectral density of $\mathbf{u}_t$ is to be minimized for each frequency. In terms of the matrices in the proposition, $\mathbf{C}_{\mathbf{x}}(\omega) = \boldsymbol{\alpha}(e^{-i\omega})$ and $\mathbf{C}_{\mathbf{y}}(\omega) = \boldsymbol{\Theta}(e^{-i\omega})$. Thus the cross spectrum/cross ACGF for $\mathbf{x}_t$ and $\mathbf{y}_t$ is chosen as $A_{\mathbf{xy}}(e^{-i\omega}) = \boldsymbol{\alpha}(e^{-i\omega})\mathbf{V}(\omega)\mathbf{U}(\omega)'\boldsymbol{\Theta}(e^{i\omega})'$, where $\mathbf{U}(\omega)\mathbf{S}(\omega)\mathbf{V}(\omega)'$ is the singular value decomposition of $\boldsymbol{\Theta}(e^{i\omega})'\boldsymbol{\alpha}(e^{-i\omega})$. (Since $\mathbf{U}(\omega)$ and $\mathbf{V}(\omega)$ are complex matrices, $\mathbf{V}(\omega)'$ and $\mathbf{U}(\omega)'$ denote the transpose conjugates of $\mathbf{V}(\omega)$ and $\mathbf{U}(\omega)$, respectively.) The ACGF for $\mathbf{u}_t$ follows from $A_{\mathbf{u}}(e^{-i\omega}) = A_{\mathbf{x}}(e^{-i\omega}) + A_{\mathbf{y}}(e^{-i\omega}) - A_{\mathbf{xy}}(e^{-i\omega}) - A_{\mathbf{yx}}(e^{-i\omega})$. Finally, to compute fitted values of $\mathbf{x}_t$ from the $\mathbf{y}_t$ realization, note that $dz_{\mathbf{x}}(\omega) = \Gamma(\omega)dz_{\mathbf{y}}(\omega)$, where $\Gamma(\omega) = \boldsymbol{\alpha}(e^{-i\omega})\mathbf{V}(\omega)\mathbf{U}(\omega)'\boldsymbol{\Theta}(e^{-i\omega})^{-1}$.

Relative Mean Square Approximation Error

A bound on the relative mean square approximation error for the economic model can be calculated directly from (8). The bound—analogous to a lower bound on $1 - R^2$ from a regression—is

$$r_j(\omega) = \frac{[A_{\mathbf{u}}(z)]_{jj}}{[A_{\mathbf{y}}(z)]_{jj}}, \quad z = e^{-i\omega}, \tag{12}$$

where $[A_{\mathbf{u}}(z)]_{jj}$ and $[A_{\mathbf{y}}(z)]_{jj}$ are the jth diagonal elements of $A_{\mathbf{u}}(z)$ and $A_{\mathbf{y}}(z)$, respectively. Thus $r_j(\omega)$ is the variance of the jth component of $dz_{\mathbf{u}}(\omega)$ relative to the jth component of $dz_{\mathbf{y}}(\omega)$, that is, the variance of the error relative to the variance of the data for each frequency. A plot of $r_j(\omega)$ against frequency shows how well the economic model fits the data over different frequencies. Integrating the numerator and denominator of $r_j(\omega)$ provides an overall measure of fit. (Note that since $\mathbf{u}_t$ and $\mathbf{x}_t$ are correlated, $r_j(\omega)$ can be larger than one; i.e., the R^2 of the model can be negative.)[3]

One advantage of $r_j(\omega)$ is that it is unaffected by time-invariant linear filters applied to the variables. Filtering merely multiplies both the numerator and denominator of $r_j(\omega)$ by the same constant, the squared gain of the filter. So, for example, $r_j(\omega)$ is invariant to "Hodrick-Prescott" filtering (see Hodrick and Prescott 1980; King and Rebelo 1993) or standard linear seasonal adjustment filters.[4] The integrated version of the relative mean square approximation error is not invariant to filtering since it is a ratio of averages of both the numerator and denominator across frequencies. When the data are filtered, the integrated version of $r_j(\omega)$ changes because the weights implicit in the averaging change. Frequencies for which the filter has a large gain are weighted more heavily than frequencies with a small gain.

III. Measures of Fit for a Real Business Cycle Model

In this section, a standard real business cycle model is evaluated using the measures of fit developed in the last section. The model, which derives from Kydland and Prescott (1982), is the "baseline" model of King, Plosser, and Rebelo (1988*b*). It is a one-sector neoclassical growth model driven by an exogenous stochastic trend in technology.[5]

[3] The measure $r_j(\omega)$ is not technically a metric since it does not satisfy the triangle inequality.

[4] Standard seasonal adjustment filters such as the linear approximation to Census X-11 have zeros at the seasonal frequencies, so that $r_j(\omega)$ is undefined at these frequencies for the filtered data.

[5] This model is broadly similar to the model analyzed in Kydland and Prescott (1982). While the baseline model does not include the complications of time to build, inventories, time-nonseparable utility, and a transitory component to technology contained in the original Kydland and Prescott model, these complications have been shown to be reasonably unimportant for the empirical predictions of the model (see Hansen 1985). Moreover, the King, Plosser, and Rebelo baseline model appears to fit the data better at the very low frequencies than the original Kydland and Prescott model since it incorporates a stochastic trend rather than the deterministic trend present in the Kydland and Prescott formulation.

This baseline model is analyzed, rather than a more complicated variant, for several reasons. First, the calibration/simulation exercises reported in King, Plosser, and Rebelo suggest that the model explains the relative variability of aggregate output, consumption, and investment, and it produces series with serial correlation properties broadly similar to the serial correlation properties of postwar U.S. data. Second, King, Plosser, Stock, and Watson (1991) show that the low-frequency/cointegration implications of the model are broadly consistent with similar postwar U.S. data. Finally, an understanding of where this baseline model fits the data and where it does not fit may suggest how the model should be modified.

Only a brief sketch of the model is presented; a thorough discussion is contained in King, Plosser, and Rebelo (1988*a*, 1988*b*). The details of the model are as follows:

$$\text{preferences:}\quad E_t \sum_{t=0}^{\infty} \beta^t u(C_t, L_t), \quad \text{with } u(C_t, L_t) = \log(C_t) + \theta \log(L_t);$$

$$\text{technology:}\quad Q_t = K_t^{1-\alpha}(A_t N_t)^{\alpha},$$

$$\log(A_t) \equiv a_t = \gamma_a + a_{t-1} + \epsilon_t, \quad \epsilon_t \,\text{iid}(0, \sigma_\epsilon^2),$$

$$K_t = (1 - \delta)K_{t-1} + I_t;$$

$$\text{constraints:}\quad Q_t = C_t + I_t,$$

$$1 = N_t + L_t,$$

where C_t denotes consumption, L_t is leisure, Q_t is output, K_t is capital, N_t is employment, I_t is investment, and A_t is the stock of technology, with $\log(A_t)$ assumed to follow a random walk with drift γ_a and innovation ϵ_t.

To analyze the model's empirical predictions, the equilibrium of the model must be calculated as a function of the parameters β, θ, α, γ_a, σ_ϵ^2, and δ. This equilibrium implies a stochastic process for the variables C_t, L_t, N_t, K_t, I_t, and Q_t, and these stochastic processes can then be compared to the stochastic processes characterizing U.S. postwar data. As is well known, the equilibrium can be calculated by maximizing the representative agent's utility function subject to the technology and the resource constraints. In general, a closed-form expression for the equilibrium does not exist, and numerical methods must be used to calculate the stochastic process for the variables corresponding to the equilibrium. A variety of numerical approximations have been proposed (see Taylor and Uhlig [1990] for a survey); here I use the log linearization of the Euler equations proposed by King, Plosser, and Rebelo (1987). A formal justification for approximating the equilibrium of this stochastic nonlinear model near its deterministic steady state using linear methods is provided in Woodford (1986, theorem 2).

The approximate solution yields a vector autoregression (VAR) for the logarithms of Q_t, C_t, K_t, I_t, and N_t. (As in the standard convention, these logarithms will be denoted by lowercase letters.) All of the variables except n_t are nonstationary but can be represented as stationary deviations about a_t, the logarithm of the stock of technology, which by assumption follows an integrated process. Thus q_t, c_t, i_t, and k_t are cointegrated with a single common trend, a_t. Indeed, not only are the variables in the VAR cointegrated, they are singular; the singularity follows since ϵ_t is the only shock to the system. The coefficients in the VAR are complicated functions of the structural parameters β, θ, α, γ_a, σ_ϵ^2, and δ. Values for these parameters are the same as those used by King, Plosser, and Rebelo (1988*b*): when the variables are measured quarterly, the parameter values are $\alpha = .58$, $\delta = .025$, $\gamma_a = .004$, $\sigma_\epsilon = .010$, and $\beta = .988$, and θ is chosen so that the steady-state value of N is .20. These parameter values were chosen so that the model's steady-state behavior matches postwar U.S. data.[6] With these values for the parameters, the VAR describing the equilibrium can be calculated and the ACGF of $\mathbf{x}_t = (\Delta q_t\ \Delta c_t\ \Delta i_t\ n_t)'$ follows directly.[7]

These autocovariances will be compared to the autocovariances of postwar data for the United States. The data used here are the same data used by King, Plosser, Stock, and Watson (1991). The output measure is total real private GNP, defined as total real GNP less government purchases of goods and services. The measure of consumption is total real consumption expenditures, and the measure of investment is total real fixed investment. The measure of employment is total labor hours in private nonagricultural establishments. All variables are expressed in per capita terms using the total civilian noninstitutional population over the age of 16.[8] Let $\tilde{q}_t$ denote the logarithm

[6] The choice of parameter values is described in King, Plosser, and Rebelo (1988*a*). The value of α was chosen to equal the average value of labor's share of gross national product over 1948–86. The value of γ_a was chosen as the common average quarterly rate of growth of per capita values of real GNP, consumption of nondurables and services, and gross fixed investment. The depreciation rate was chosen to yield a gross investment share of GNP of approximately 30 percent. The parameter θ was chosen so that the model's steady-state value of N matched the average workweek as a fraction of total hours over 1948–86. The discount rate β was chosen so that the model's steady-state annual interest rate matched the average rate of return on equity over 1948–81. The value of $\sigma_\epsilon = .01$ appears to have been chosen as a convenient normalization. This value is used here because it does a remarkably good job matching the very low frequency movements in output, consumption, and investment.

[7] Of course, this not the only possible definition of $\mathbf{x}_t$. The only restriction on $\mathbf{x}_t$ is covariance stationarity, so, e.g., $c_t - q_t$ and $i_t - q_t$ could be included as elements.

[8] All data are taken from Citibase. With the Citibase labels, the precise variables used were gnp82 − gge82 for output, gc82 for consumption, and gif82 for investment. The

of per capita private output, $\tilde{c}_t$ the logarithm of per capita consumption expenditures, and so forth. Then the data used in the analysis can be written as $\mathbf{y}_t = (\Delta\tilde{q}_t\ \Delta\tilde{c}_t\ \Delta\tilde{i}_t\ \tilde{n}_t)'$.

The analysis presented in the last section assumed that the ACGF/spectrum of $\mathbf{y}_t$ was known. In practice, of course, this is not the case, and the spectrum must be estimated. In this work, the spectrum of $\mathbf{y}_t$ was estimated in two different ways. First, an autoregressive spectral estimator was used, calculated by first estimating a VAR for the variables and then forming the implied spectral density matrix. As in King, Plosser, Stock, and Watson (1991), the VAR was estimated imposing a cointegration constraint between output, consumption, and investment. Thus the VAR was specified as the regression of $\mathbf{w}_t = (\Delta\tilde{q}_t,\ \tilde{q}_t - \tilde{c}_t,\ \tilde{q}_t - \tilde{i}_t,\ \tilde{n}_t)'$ onto a constant and six lags of $\mathbf{w}_t$. The parameters of the VAR were estimated using data for 1950–88. (Values before 1950 were used as lags in the regression for the initial observations.) Second, a standard nonparametric spectral estimator was also calculated. The spectrum was estimated by a simple average of 10 periodogram ordinates after prewhitening employment with the filter $1 - .95L$. These two estimators yielded similar values for the measures of fit, and to conserve space only the results for the autoregressive spectral estimator are reported.

For each variable, figure 1 presents the spectrum implied by the model, the spectrum of the data, and the spectrum of the error required to reconcile the model with the data.[9] The error process was chosen to minimize the unweighted trace of the error spectral density matrix, subject to the positive semidefiniteness constraint discussed in the last section. Thus the objective function weighted all the variables equally. For output, consumption, and investment, the model and data spectra differ little for very low frequencies (periods greater than 50 quarters) and for output and investment at high frequencies (periods less than five quarters). There are significant differences between the model and data spectra for periods typically associated with the business cycle; the largest differences occur at a frequency corresponding to approximately 20 quarters. The spectra of Δn_t and $\Delta\tilde{n}_t$ are quite different. In addition to large differences at business cycle frequencies, the spectra are also very different at low frequencies. The model implies that employment is stationary so that its

measure of total labor hours was constructed as total employment in nonagricultural establishments (lhem) less total government employment (lpgov) multiplied by average weekly hours (lhch). The population series was P16.

[9] Figure 1 is reminiscent of figures in Howrey (1971, 1972), who calculated the spectra implied by the Klein-Goldberger and Wharton models. A similar exercise is carried out in Soderlind (1993), who compares the spectra of variables in the Kydland-Prescott model to the spectra of postwar U.S. data.

growth rate has a spectrum that vanishes at frequency zero. In contrast, the data suggest significant low-frequency variation in postwar U.S. employment.[10]

The figure shows that relatively little error is needed to reconcile the model and the data for output, consumption, and investment over the very low frequencies. On the other hand, error with a variance on the order of 40–50 percent of the magnitude of the variance of the series is necessary for the components of output, consumption, and investment with periods in the 6–32-quarter range. At higher frequencies, the model is able to match the stochastic process describing investment, but not the processes describing the other series.

Table 1 provides a summary of the relative mean square approximation error (RMSAE) for a variety of weighting functions and filters. Each panel shows the RMSAE for the variables for five different minimum error representations. Column 1 presents results for the representation that obtains when the unweighted trace of the spectrum is minimized; this is the representation used to construct the error spectra shown in figure 1. Column 2 summarizes the results for the representation that minimizes the output error, with no weight placed on the other variables. Column 3 summarizes results for the representation that minimizes the consumption error, and so forth. Panel A presents the results for the differences of the data integrated across all frequencies, panel B shows results for the levels of the series detrended by the Hodrick-Prescott filter integrated across all frequencies, and panel C presents results for the levels of the series integrated over business cycle frequencies (6–32 quarters). The trade-off inherent in the different representations is evident in all panels. For example, in panel A, with the minimum output error representation, the RMSAE for output is 26 percent, and the RMSAE for consumption is 78 percent; when the minimum consumption error representation is chosen, the RMSAE for consumption falls to 21 percent but the RMSAE for output rises to 75 percent. When all the variables are equally weighted, the RMSAE is 52 percent for output and 66 percent for consumption. Panel C shows that most of this trade-off occurs at the high frequencies, at least for output, consumption, and investment; over the business cycle frequencies their RMSAEs are in the 40–60 percent range.

As explained in Section II, fitted values of the model's variables can be constructed using the minimum error representation together

[10] The figures do not include standard errors for the spectra estimated from these data. These standard errors are large—approximately one-third the size of the estimated spectra. The standard errors for the RMSAE, averaged across frequencies, are considerably smaller. These are included in tables 1 and 2 below.

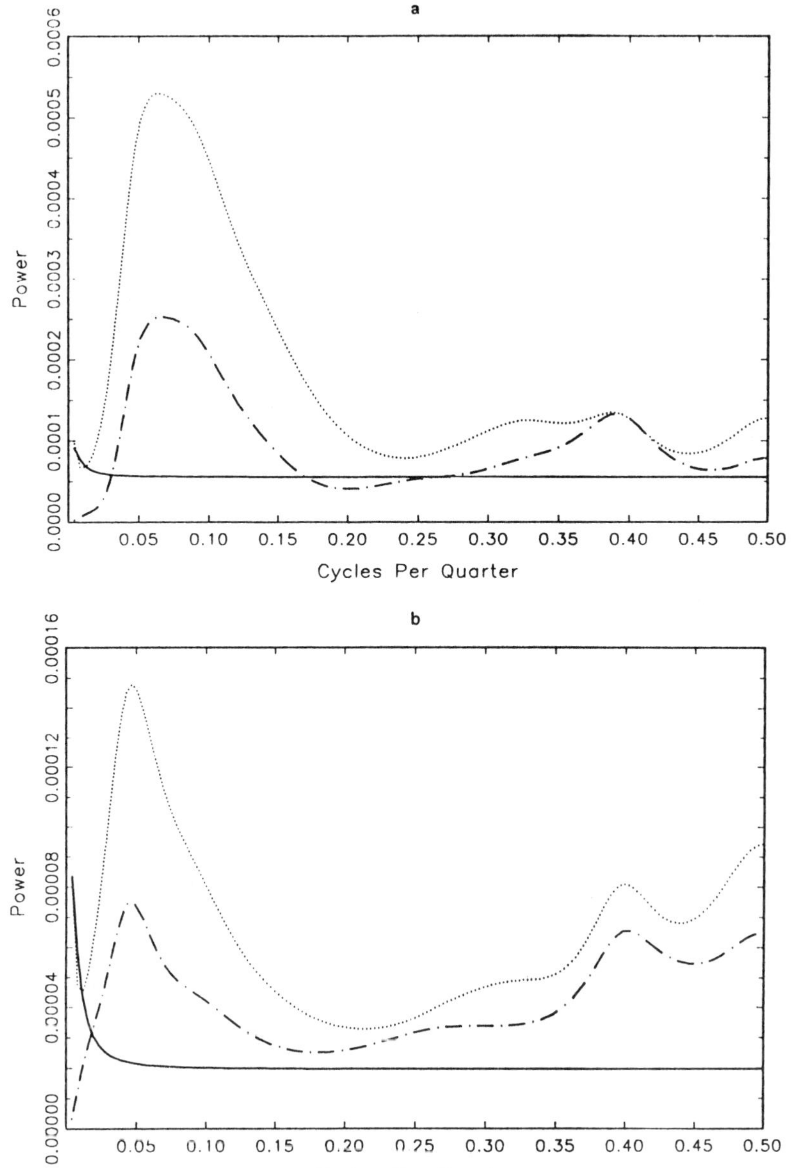

FIG. 1.—Decomposition of spectra: *a*, output; *b*, consumption; *c*, investment; *d*, employment. Dotted lines refer to the data, dashed lines to the model, and solid lines to approximation error.

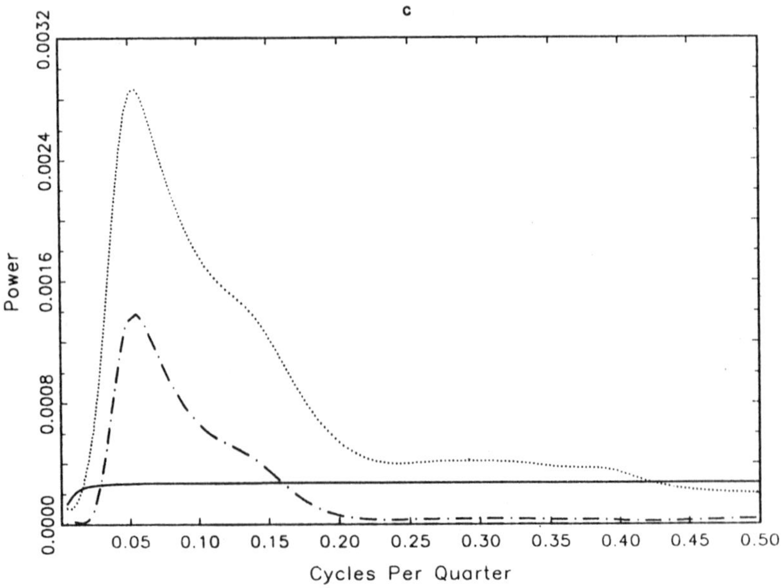

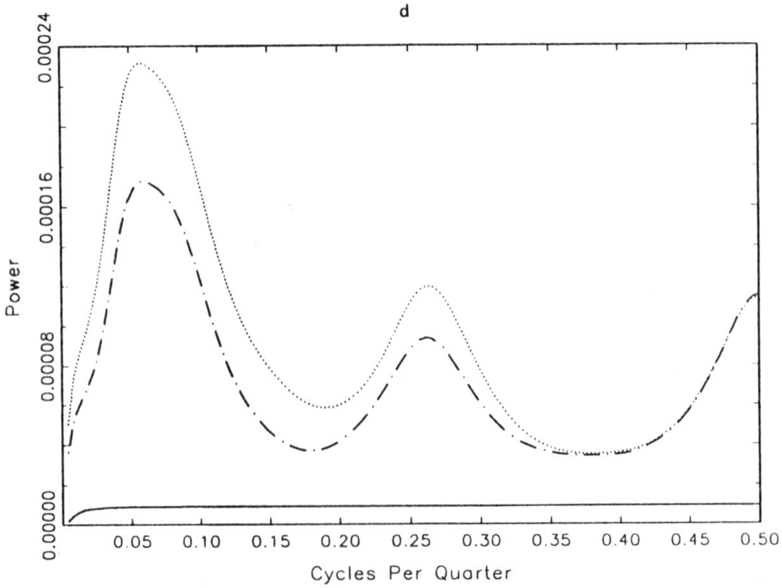

FIG. 1.—*Continued*

TABLE 1

RELATIVE MEAN SQUARE APPROXIMATION ERROR

VARIABLE	Error Minimized with Respect to: Equal Weight (1)	Output (2)	Consumption (3)	Investment (4)	Employment (5)
	A. First Differences: All Frequencies				
Output	.52 (.04)	.26 (.06)	.75 (.06)	.64 (.05)	.79 (.07)
Consumption	.66 (.06)	.78 (.08)	.21 (.05)	.75 (.08)	1.00 (.10)
Investment	.29 (.06)	.63 (.05)	.75 (.07)	.27 (.06)	.79 (.07)
Employment	.78 (.04)	.81 (.04)	.92 (.04)	.81 (.04)	.50 (.04)
	B. Hodrick-Prescott Detrended Levels: All Frequencies				
Output	.43 (.05)	.37 (.07)	.58 (.04)	.46 (.04)	.63 (.05)
Consumption	.53 (.04)	.55 (.05)	.29 (.09)	.57 (.05)	.81 (.09)
Investment	.40 (.08)	.48 (.05)	.61 (.04)	.39 (.08)	.63 (.04)
Employment	.73 (.03)	.75 (.03)	.85 (.04)	.74 (.03)	.59 (.06)
	C. Levels: 6–32 Quarters				
Output	.43 (.06)	.39 (.07)	.55 (.05)	.44 (.05)	.61 (.05)
Consumption	.51 (.05)	.51 (.06)	.32 (.09)	.53 (.05)	.77 (.08)
Investment	.42 (.08)	.46 (.06)	.59 (.04)	.42 (.08)	.61 (.05)
Employment	.72 (.03)	.74 (.03)	.84 (.04)	.73 (.03)	.61 (.06)

NOTE.—Relative mean square approximation error is the lower bound of the variance of the approximation error divided by the variance of the series. Each column represents the relative mean square approximation error of the row variable constructed from the representation that minimizes the weighted trace of the error spectrum. The weights are summarized by the column headings. For example, col. 1 is the equally weighted trace, col. 2 puts all the weight on the output error, etc. The numbers in parentheses are standard errors based on the sampling error in the estimated VAR coefficients used to estimate the data spectrum.

with the observed data. Since the measurement error model represents $\mathbf{y}_t$ as $\mathbf{x}_t$ plus error, the standard signal extraction formula can be used to extract $\{\mathbf{x}_t\}$ from $\{\mathbf{y}_t\}$. In general, of course, signal extraction methods will yield an estimate of $\mathbf{x}_t$, say $\hat{\mathbf{x}}_t$, that is not exact in the sense that $E[(\mathbf{x}_t - \hat{\mathbf{x}}_t)^2] \neq 0$. In the present context, the estimate will be exact since the measurement error process is chosen so that $dz_{\mathbf{x}}(\omega)$ and $dz_{\mathbf{y}}(\omega)$ are perfectly correlated for all ω.[11] Figure 2 shows the realizations of the data and the realizations of the variables in the model calculated from the data using the equally weighted minimum output error representation.[12]

In figure 2*a*, which shows the results for output, the model seems capable of capturing the long swings in the postwar U.S. data but not capable of capturing the cyclical variability in the data. Private per capita GNP fell by 8.4 percent from the cyclical peak in 1973 to the trough in 1975 and by 6.8 percent from the peak in 1979 to the trough in 1982. In contrast, the corresponding drops in Q_t—output in the model—were 3.1 percent and 3.0 percent, respectively. The dampened cyclical swings in consumption and investment, shown in figure 2*b* and *c*, are even more dramatic. Finally, figure 2*d* shows that the model predicts changes in employment that have little to do with the changes observed in the United States during the postwar period.[13]

One possible explanation for the relatively poor fit of the model is that the "calibrated" values of the parameters are wrong. In particular, Christiano and Eichenbaum (1990) show that the model's predictions change in an important way when the technology process changes from a random walk to a stationary AR(1). Table 2 shows how the model fares for a range of values of the AR(1) coefficient for technology, denoted by ρ_a. Panel A of the table shows the results for first differences of the variables across all frequencies, panel B presents results for the Hodrick-Prescott detrended levels of the series, and panel C shows the results for the levels of the series over the "business cycle" frequencies. From panel A, the value of ρ_a has

[11] More precisely, the estimate is exact in the sense that $\text{Proj}(\mathbf{x}_t | \mathbf{y}_{t-j}, \ldots, \mathbf{y}_{-1}, \mathbf{y}_0, \mathbf{y}_1, \ldots, \mathbf{y}_{t+j})$ converges in mean square to $\mathbf{x}_t$ as $j \to \infty$.

[12] As shown in eq. (9), $\mathbf{x}_t$ can be calculated as $\beta(L)\mathbf{y}_t$, where $\beta(L)$ is the inverse Fourier transform of $\Gamma(\omega)$. To calculate the estimates shown in the figure, $\Gamma(\omega)$ was calculated at 128 equally spaced frequencies between zero and π. Since $\beta(L)$ is two-sided, pre- and postsample values of $\mathbf{y}_t$ are required to form $\beta(L)\mathbf{x}_t$. These pre- and postsample values were replaced with the sample means of the $\mathbf{y}_t$ data. The first differences, $\mathbf{x}_t$ and $\mathbf{y}_t$, were then accumulated to form the levels series shown in the figure.

[13] The calculations required to construct figs. 1 and 2 and the results in table 1 are easily carried out. For this example, the model spectrum, data spectrum, RMSAEs, and fitted values were calculated in less than a minute on a standard desktop computer. A GAUSS program for these calculations is available from the author.

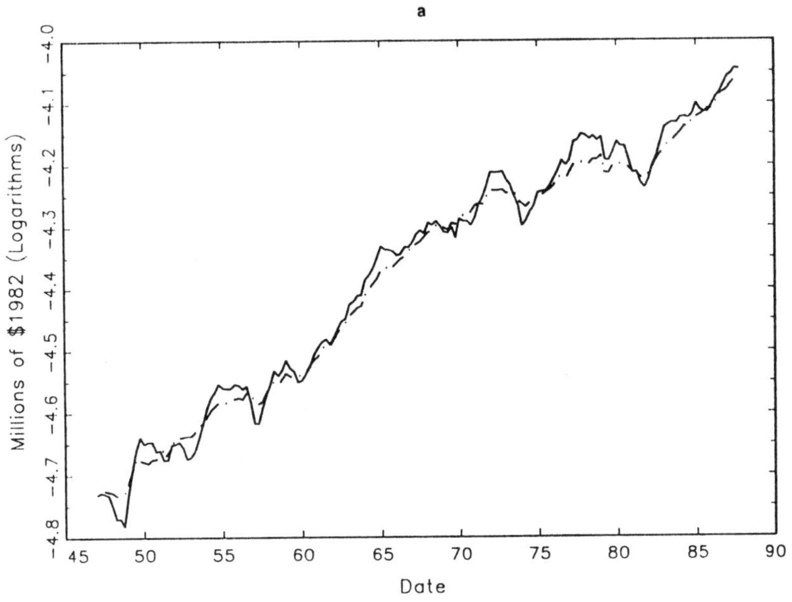

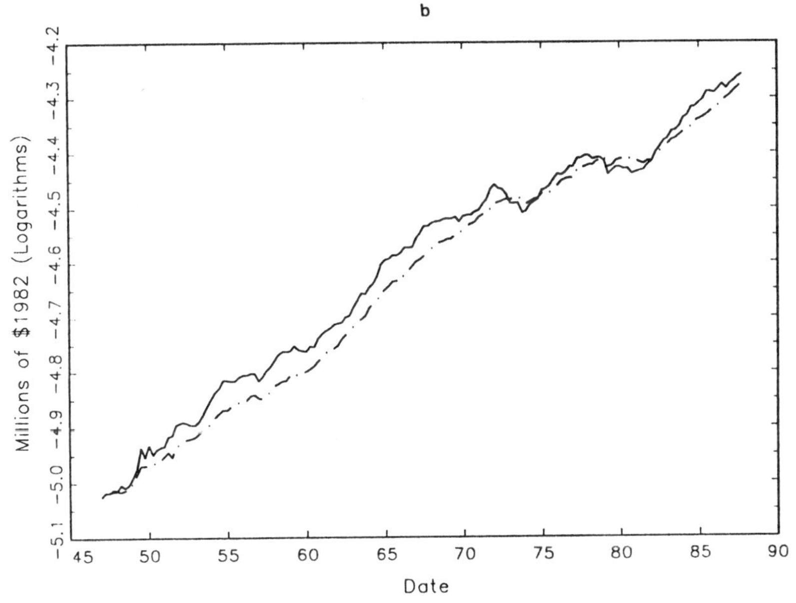

FIG. 2.—Data: *a*, output; *b*, consumption; *c*, investment; *d*, employment. Solid lines refer to U.S. data and dashed lines to realizations from the model.

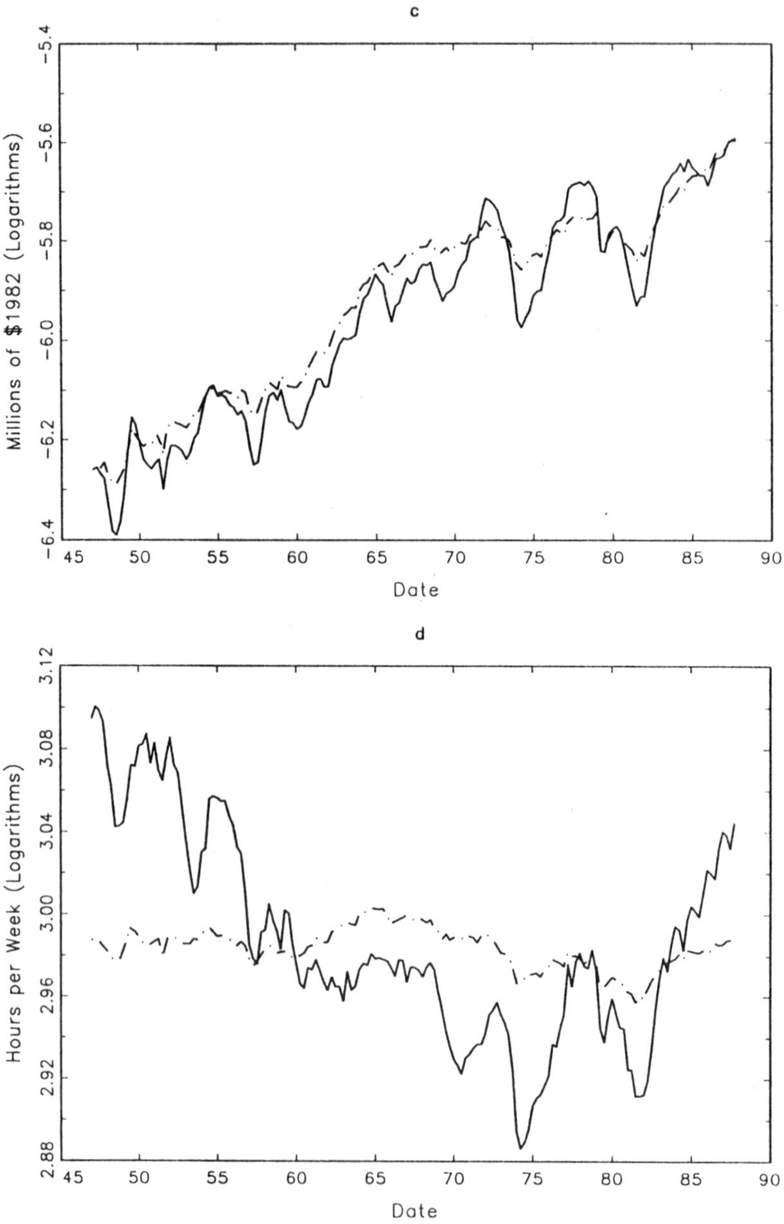

FIG. 2.—*Continued*

TABLE 2

RELATIVE MEAN SQUARE APPROXIMATION ERROR AS A FUNCTION OF THE AR(1) COEFFICIENT FOR TECHNOLOGY

	ρ_a			
VARIABLE	1.0 (1)	.98 (2)	.95 (3)	.90 (4)
	A. First Differences: All Frequencies			
Output	.52 (.04)	.52 (.04)	.53 (.05)	.54 (.06)
Consumption	.66 (.06)	.69 (.06)	.71 (.05)	.74 (.05)
Investment	.29 (.06)	.21 (.05)	.18 (.05)	.20 (.04)
Employment	.78 (.04)	.74 (.05)	.73 (.07)	.75 (.09)
	B. Hodrick-Prescott Detrended Levels: All Frequencies			
Output	.43 (.05)	.40 (.05)	.37 (.05)	.36 (.05)
Consumption	.53 (.04)	.58 (.04)	.63 (.04)	.67 (.04)
Investment	.40 (.08)	.29 (.08)	.21 (.08)	.17 (.08)
Employment	.73 (.03)	.64 (.04)	.58 (.04)	.55 (.04)
	C. Levels: 6–32 Quarters			
Output	.43 (.06)	.38 (.06)	.35 (.06)	.33 (.06)
Consumption	.51 (.05)	.56 (.05)	.61 (.05)	.66 (.05)
Investment	.42 (.08)	.30 (.09)	.22 (.09)	.17 (.09)
Employment	.72 (.03)	.63 (.04)	.56 (.05)	.52 (.05)

NOTE.—Relative mean square approximation error is the lower bound of the variance of the approximation error divided by the variance of the series. Each column represents the relative mean square approximation error of the row variable constructed from the representation that minimizes the weighted trace of the error spectrum. The column headings represent the AR(1) coefficient for the process of the logarithm of productivity in the model. For example, col. 1 represents results for the model with random walk technological progress. The numbers in parentheses are standard errors based on the sampling error in the estimated VAR coefficients used to estimate the data spectrum.

little effect on the fit of the model averaged across all frequencies. In particular, as ρ_a falls from 1.0 to .90, the RMSAE increases slightly for consumption, falls for investment, and changes little for output and employment. In contrast, the value of ρ_a has a significant effect on the fit of the model over business cycle frequencies. For example, panel C shows that as ρ_a falls from 1.0 to .90, the RMSAE falls for output (.43 to .33), for investment (.42 to .17), and for employment (.72 to .52); it increases for consumption (.52 to .66).

The source of the changes in the RMSAEs can be seen in figure 3, which plots the spectra of the variables in models with $\rho_a = 1$ and $\rho_a = .90$. The largest difference between the spectra of the models is the increase in variance in output, investment, and employment as ρ_a falls from 1.0 to .90. The economic mechanism behind this increased variance is the increase in intertemporal substitution in response to a technology shock. When $\rho_a = .90$, technology shocks are transitory, and they can be exploited only by large transitory increases in employment and investment. It is interesting to note that while this mechanism increases the variance of the growth rates in employment, investment, and output, it has little effect on their autocorrelations. That is, as ρ_a changes from 1.0 to .90, the shape of the spectra changes little.

Before we leave this section, six additional points deserve mention. First, the fitted values in figure 2 are quantitatively and conceptually similar to figures presented in Christiano (1988) and Plosser (1989). They calculated the Solow residual from actual data and then simulated the economic model using this residual as the forcing process. Implicitly, they assumed that the model and data were the same in the terms of their Solow residual, and then asked whether the model and data were similar in other dimensions. Figure 2 is constructed by making the model and data as close as possible in one dimension (in this case the trace of the variance of the implied approximation error) and then asking whether the model and data are similar in other dimensions. The difference between the two approaches can be highlighted by considering the circumstances in which they would produce exactly the same figure. If the Solow residual computed from the actual data followed exactly the same stochastic process as the change in productivity in the model, and if the approximation error representation was constructed by minimizing the variance of the difference between the Solow residual in the data and productivity growth in the model, then the two figures would be identical. Thus the figures will differ if the stochastic process for the empirical Solow residual is not the same as assumed in the model, or the approximation error representation is chosen to make the model and data close in some dimension other than productivity growth.

Second, the inability of the model to capture the business cycle properties of the data is not an artifact of the minimum measurement error representation used to form the projection of $\mathbf{x}_t$ onto $\mathbf{y}_\tau$, $\tau = 1, \ldots, n$. Rather, it follows directly from a comparison of the spectra of $\mathbf{x}_t$ and $\mathbf{y}_t$. The fitted values are constrained to have an ACGF/spectra given by the economic model. Figure 1 shows that, for all the variables, the spectral power over the business cycle frequencies is significantly less for the model than for the data. Therefore, fitted values from the model are constrained to have less cyclical variability than the data.

Third, the ability of the model to mimic the behavior of the data depends critically on the size of the variance of the technology shock. The value of σ_ϵ used in the analysis is two and one-half times larger than the drift in the series. Thus if the ϵ_t were approximately normally distributed, the stock of technology A_t would fall in one out of three quarters on average. Reducing the standard deviation of the

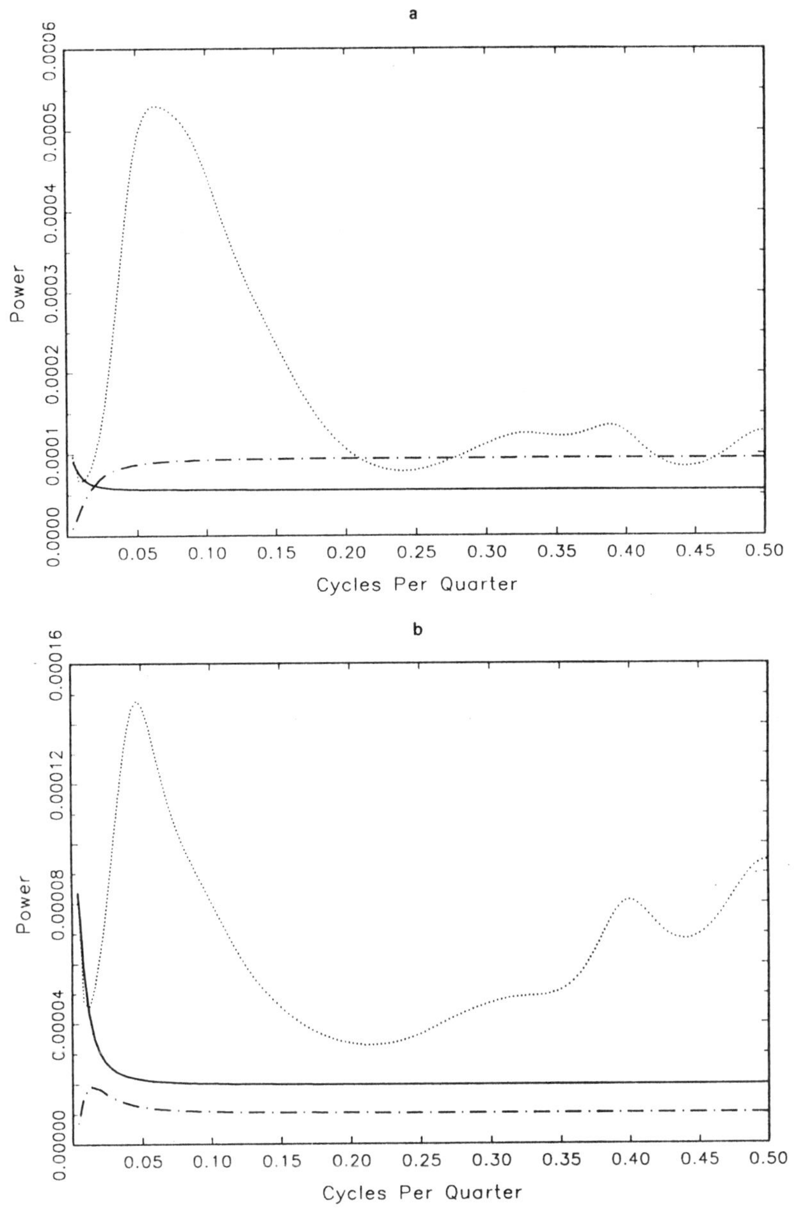

FIG. 3.—Data and model spectra: *a*, output; *b*, consumption; *c*, investment; *d*, employment. Dotted lines refer to the data, solid lines to the model with $\rho_a = 1.00$, and dashed lines to the model with $\rho_a = .90$.

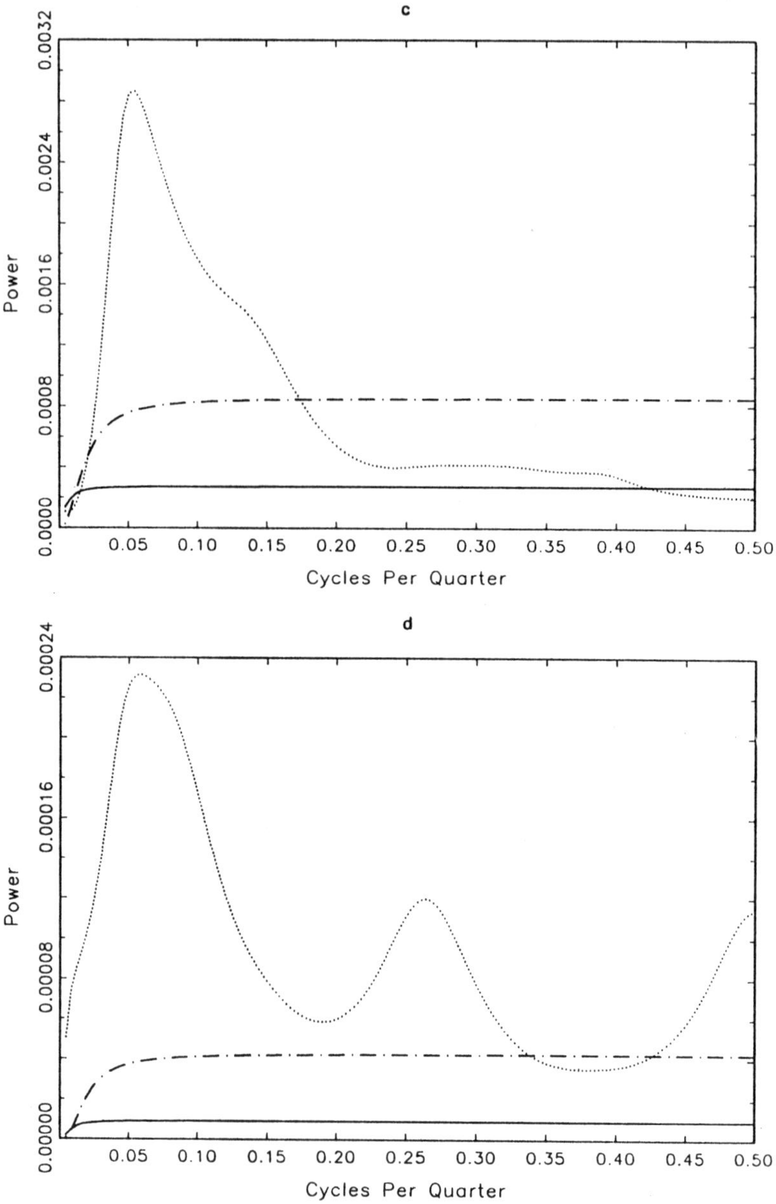

FIG. 3.—*Continued*

technology shock so that it equals the average growth in a_t drastically increases the size of the measurement error necessary to reconcile the model with the data. For example, integrated across all frequencies, the RMSAE for output increases from 52 percent to 74 percent.

Fourth, there is nothing inherent in the structure of the model that precludes the use of classical statistical procedures. Altug (1989) used maximum likelihood methods to study a version of the model that is augmented with serially correlated classical measurement errors. Singleton (1988) and Christiano and Eichenbaum (1992) pointed out that generalized method of moments procedures can be used to analyze moment implications of models like the one presented above. In the empirical work of Christiano and Eichenbaum the singularity in the probability density function of the data that is implied by the model was finessed in two ways. First, limited information estimation and testing methods were used, and second, the authors assumed that their data on employment were measured with error.

Fifth, many if not all of the empirical shortcomings of this model have been noted by other researchers. King, Plosser, and Rebelo clearly show that the model is not capable of explaining the variation in employment that is observed in the actual data. The implausibility of the large technology shocks is discussed in detail in Summers (1986), Mankiw (1989), and McCallum (1989).

Finally, the analysis above has concentrated on the ability of the model to explain the variability in output, consumption, investment, and employment across different frequencies. While it is possible to analyze the covariation of these series using the cross spectrum of the measurement error, such an analysis has not been carried out here. This is a particularly important omission since this is the dimension in which the baseline real business cycle model is typically thought to fail. For example, Christiano and Eichenbaum (1992) and Rotemberg and Woodford (1992) use the model's counterfactual implication of a high correlation between average productivity and output growth as starting points for their analysis, and the empirical literature on the intertemporal capital asset pricing model beginning with Hansen and Singleton (1982) suggests that the asset pricing implications of the model are inconsistent with the data. It would be useful to derive simple summary statistics based on the cross spectra of the measurement error and the data to highlight the ability of the model to explain covariation among the series.

IV. Discussion

The discussion thus far has assumed that the parameter values of the economic model are known. A natural question is whether the measures of fit discussed in this paper can form the basis for estimators of these parameters. Does it make sense, for example, to estimate unknown parameters by minimizing some function of the relative mean square error, $r_j(\omega)$ given in equation (12)? This certainly seems sensible. For example, a researcher may want to "calibrate" his model with a value of $\rho_a = .90$ rather than 1.0, because this value produces spectra closer to the estimated spectra of data over the business cycle frequencies. Yet dropping the standard statistical assumption that the economic model is correctly specified raises a number of important issues. Foremost among these is the meaning of the parameters. If the model does not necessarily describe the data, then what do the parameters measure? Presumably, the model is meant to describe certain characteristics of the data's stochastic process (the business cycle or the growth properties, for example), while ignoring other characteristics. It then makes sense to define the model's parameters as those that minimize the differences between the model and the data's stochastic process in dimensions that the model is attempting to explain. So, for example, it seems sensible to define the parameters of a growth model as those that minimize $r_j(\omega)$ over very low frequencies, or to define the parameters of a business cycle model as those that minimize $r_j(\omega)$ over business cycle frequencies. Given this definition of the parameters, constructing an analog estimator (see Manski 1988) by minimizing $\hat{r}_j(\omega)$ corresponds to a standard statistical practice.

Of course, the parameters may also be defined using other characteristics of the model and the stochastic process describing the data. For example, in standard "calibration" estimation exercises, many of the parameters are implicitly defined in terms of first moments of the data. Parameters are chosen so that the first moments of the variables in the model's steady state match the first moments of the data.

Two final points deserve mention. First, since the measures of fit developed in this paper are based on a representation that minimizes the discrepancy between the model and the data, they serve only as a bound on the fit of the model. Models with large RMSAEs do not fit the data well. Models with small RMSAEs fit the data well given certain assumptions about the correlation properties of the noise that separates the model and the data, but may fit the data poorly given other assumptions about the noise.

Finally, while this paper has concentrated on measures of fit motivated by a model of measurement error, other measures are certainly possible. For example, one measure, which like the measures in this paper uses only the autocovariances implied by the model and the data, is the expected log likelihood ratio using the normal probability density function (pdf) of the data and the model. More precisely, if $g(x)$ denotes the normal pdf constructed from the autocovariances of the data, $f(x)$ denotes the normal pdf constructed for the autocovariances implied by the model, and E_g is the expectation operator taken with respect to $g(x)$, the expected log likelihood ratio $I(g, f) = E_g\{\log[g(x)/f(x)]\}$ can be used to measure the distance between the densities $f(\cdot)$ and $g(\cdot)$; $I(g,f)$ is the Kullback-Leibler information criterion (KLIC), which plays an important role in the statistical literature on model selection (e.g., Akaike 1973) and quasi–maximum likelihood estimation (White 1982). Unfortunately, the KLIC will not be defined when $f(x)$ is singular and $g(x)$ is not; the KLIC distance between the two densities is infinite. Thus, for example, it would add no additional information on the fit of the real business cycle model analyzed in Section III beyond pointing out the singularity.

Arguably, one of the most informative diagnostics presented in this paper is the plot of the model and data spectra. For example, figures 1 and 2 show that the data spectra have mass concentrated around the business cycle frequencies, but the model spectra do not. Any metric comparing the data and model spectra may serve as a useful measure of fit. The RMSAE proposed here has the advantage that it can be interpreted like $1 - R^2$ from a regression, but any summary statistic discards potentially useful information contained in plots such as figures 1 and 2. Some practical advice, therefore, is to present both model and data spectra as a convenient way of comparing their complete set of second moments.

Appendix

To prove the proposition, first parameterize $\mathbf{\Sigma_x}$, $\mathbf{\Sigma_y}$, and $\mathbf{\Sigma_{xy}}$ as

$$\mathbf{\Sigma_x} = \mathbf{C_x C_x'}, \tag{A1}$$

$$\mathbf{\Sigma_y} = \mathbf{GG'} + \mathbf{\Sigma}, \tag{A2}$$

$$\mathbf{\Sigma_{xy}} = \mathbf{C_x G'}, \tag{A3}$$

where $\mathbf{C_x}$ is $n \times k$ with full column rank, $\mathbf{G}$ is $n \times k$, and $\mathbf{\Sigma}$ is positive semidefinite. Since $\mathbf{\Sigma_u} = \mathbf{\Sigma_x} + \mathbf{\Sigma_y} - \mathbf{\Sigma_{xy}} - \mathbf{\Sigma_{yx}}$, minimizing $\text{tr}(\mathbf{W\Sigma_u})$ with $\mathbf{\Sigma_x}$ and $\mathbf{\Sigma_y}$ given is equivalent to maximizing $\text{tr}(\mathbf{W\Sigma_{xy}}) = \text{tr}(\mathbf{WC_xG'})$. Given an arbitrary factorization of $\mathbf{\Sigma_x}$ of the form (A1), the problem is to find the $n \times k$ matrix $\mathbf{G}$ to maximize $\text{tr}(\mathbf{WC_xG'})$ subject to the constraint that $\mathbf{\Sigma_y} - \mathbf{GG'} = \mathbf{\Sigma}$ is positive semidefinite.

Let $\mathbf{\hat{G}} = \mathbf{C_y^{-1}G}$. Then $\mathbf{\Sigma_y} - \mathbf{GG'}$ is positive semidefinite if and only if $I_n - \mathbf{\hat{G}\hat{G}'}$ is positive semidefinite, which in turn is true if and only if all the eigenvalues of $\mathbf{\hat{G}\hat{G}'}$ are less than or equal to one. Since the eigenvalues of $\mathbf{\hat{G}\hat{G}'}$ are the same as those of $\mathbf{\hat{G}'\hat{G}}$, the problem can be written as

$$\max_{\mathbf{\hat{G}}} \text{tr}[\mathbf{\hat{G}'(C_y'WC_x)}] \quad \text{subject to} \quad \lambda_i(\mathbf{\hat{G}'\hat{G}}) \leq 1, \quad i = 1, \ldots, k, \tag{A4}$$

where $\lambda_i(\hat{\mathbf{G}}'\hat{\mathbf{G}})$ denotes the ith eigenvalue of $\hat{\mathbf{G}}'\hat{\mathbf{G}}$, and I have used the fact that $\text{tr}(\mathbf{AB}) = \text{tr}(\mathbf{BA})$ for conformable matrices **A** and **B**.

Let $\mathbf{QDR}'$ denote the singular value decomposition of $\hat{\mathbf{G}}$, where **Q** is an $n \times k$ orthogonal matrix, **R** is a $k \times k$ orthonormal matrix, and **D** is a $k \times k$ diagonal matrix with elements d_{ij}. Since $\text{tr}[\hat{\mathbf{G}}'(\mathbf{C}_y'\mathbf{W}\mathbf{C}_x)] = \text{tr}[\mathbf{RDQ}'(\mathbf{C}_y'\mathbf{W}\mathbf{C}_x)] = \text{tr}[\mathbf{DQ}'(\mathbf{C}_y'\mathbf{W}\mathbf{C}_x)\mathbf{R}]$, and since $\lambda_i(\hat{\mathbf{G}}'\hat{\mathbf{G}}) = d_{ii}^2$, the solution to (A4) is seen to require that $\lambda_i(\hat{\mathbf{G}}'\hat{\mathbf{G}}) = 1$, $i = 1, \ldots, k$. This implies that $\hat{\mathbf{G}}'\hat{\mathbf{G}} = I$. Write the singular value decomposition of $\mathbf{C}_y'\mathbf{W}\mathbf{C}_x$ as $\mathbf{USV}'$; then $\text{tr}[\hat{\mathbf{G}}'(\mathbf{C}_y'\mathbf{W}\mathbf{C}_x)] = \text{tr}(\hat{\mathbf{G}}'\mathbf{USV}') = \text{tr}(\mathbf{V}'\hat{\mathbf{G}}'\mathbf{US}) = \text{tr}(\overline{\mathbf{G}}'\mathbf{US})$, where $\overline{\mathbf{G}} = \hat{\mathbf{G}}\mathbf{V}$. Since $\overline{\mathbf{G}}'\overline{\mathbf{G}} = \mathbf{V}'\hat{\mathbf{G}}'\hat{\mathbf{G}}\mathbf{V} = I_k$, the maximization problem can be written as

$$\max_{\overline{\mathbf{G}}} \text{tr}(\overline{\mathbf{G}}'\mathbf{US}) \quad \text{subject to} \quad \overline{\mathbf{G}}'\overline{\mathbf{G}} = I_k. \tag{A5}$$

Assumptions i–iii of the proposition imply that $\mathbf{C}_y'\mathbf{W}\mathbf{C}_x$ has full column rank so that **S** is a diagonal matrix with strictly positive diagonal elements. Thus since $\mathbf{U}'\mathbf{U} = I_k$, the maximization is achieved by $\overline{\mathbf{G}} = \mathbf{U}$. Working backward, we see that $\mathbf{G} = \mathbf{C}_y\mathbf{UV}'$, so that $\mathbf{\Sigma}_{xy} = \mathbf{C}_x\mathbf{G}' = \mathbf{C}_x\mathbf{VU}'\mathbf{C}_y'$.

Uniqueness follows since this choice of $\mathbf{\Sigma}_{xy}$ does not depend on the (arbitrary) choice of the matrix square roots, $\mathbf{C}_x$ and $\mathbf{C}_y$. To see this, let $\hat{\mathbf{C}}_y$ and $\hat{\mathbf{C}}_x$ denote other matrix square roots of $\mathbf{\Sigma}_y$ and $\mathbf{\Sigma}_x$. Then $\hat{\mathbf{C}}_y = \mathbf{C}_y\mathbf{R}_y$ and $\hat{\mathbf{C}}_x = \mathbf{C}_x\mathbf{R}_x$, where $\mathbf{R}_y$ and $\mathbf{R}_x$ are orthonormal matrices. From the analysis above, this yields $\hat{\mathbf{\Sigma}}_{xy} = \hat{\mathbf{C}}_x\hat{\mathbf{V}}\hat{\mathbf{U}}'\hat{\mathbf{C}}_y'$, where $\hat{\mathbf{U}}\hat{\mathbf{S}}\hat{\mathbf{V}}'$ is the singular value decomposition of $\hat{\mathbf{C}}_y'\mathbf{W}\hat{\mathbf{C}}_x$. By inspection, $\hat{\mathbf{U}} = \mathbf{R}_y'\mathbf{U}$, $\hat{\mathbf{S}} = \mathbf{S}$, and $\hat{\mathbf{V}} = \mathbf{R}_x'\mathbf{V}$, so that $\hat{\mathbf{\Sigma}}_{xy} = \mathbf{\Sigma}_{xy}$.

References

Akaike, H. "Information Theory and an Extension of the Maximum Likelihood Principle." In *Proceedings of the Second International Symposium on Information Theory,* edited by B. N. Petrov and F. Csaki. Budapest: Akademiai Kaido, 1973.

Altug, Sumru. "Time-to-Build and Aggregate Fluctuations: Some New Evidence." *Internat. Econ. Rev.* 30 (November 1989): 889–920.

Brillinger, David R. *Time Series: Data Analysis and Theory.* San Francisco: Holden-Day, 1981.

Campbell, John Y., and Shiller, Robert J. "The Dividend-Price Ratio and Expectations of Future Dividends and Discount Factors." *Rev. Financial Studies* 1, no. 3 (1988): 195–228.

Christiano, Lawrence J. "Why Does Inventory Investment Fluctuate So Much?" *J. Monetary Econ.* 21 (March/May 1988): 247–80.

Christiano, Lawrence J., and Eichenbaum, Martin. "Unit Roots in Real GNP: Do We Know and Do We Care?" *Carnegie-Rochester Conf. Ser. Public Policy* 32 (Spring 1990): 7–61.

———. "Current Real-Business-Cycle Theories and Aggregate Labor-Market Fluctuations." *A.E.R.* 82 (June 1992): 430–50.

Cochrane, John H. "Explaining the Variance of Price-Dividend Ratios." *Rev. Financial Studies* 5, no. 2 (1992): 243–80.

Durlauf, Steven N., and Hall, Robert E. "Measuring Noise in Stock Prices." Manuscript. Stanford, Calif.: Stanford Univ., 1989.

Geweke, John. "The Dynamic Factor Analysis of Economic Time-Series Models." In *Latent Variables in Socio-economic Models,* edited by Dennis J. Aigner and Arthur S. Goldberger. Amsterdam: North-Holland, 1977.

Haavelmo, Trygve. "The Probability Approach in Econometrics." *Econometrica* 12 (suppl.; July 1944): 1–115.

Hansen, Gary D. "Indivisible Labor and the Business Cycle." *J. Monetary Econ.* 16 (November 1985): 309–27.

Hansen, Gary D., and Sargent, Thomas J. "Straight Time and Overtime in Equilibrium." *J. Monetary Econ.* 21 (March/May 1988): 281–308.

Hansen, Lars Peter, and Jagannathan, Ravi. "Implications of Security Market Data for Models of Dynamic Economies." *J.P.E.* 99 (April 1991): 255–62.

Hansen, Lars Peter, and Sargent, Thomas J. "Formulating and Estimating Dynamic Linear Rational Expectations Models." *J. Econ. Dynamics and Control* 2 (February 1980): 7–46.

Hansen, Lars Peter, and Singleton, Kenneth J. "Generalized Instrumental Variables Estimation of Nonlinear Rational Expectations Models." *Econometrica* 50 (September 1982): 1269–86.

Hodrick, Robert J., and Prescott, Edward C. "Post-War U.S. Business Cycles: An Empirical Investigation." Manuscript. Pittsburgh: Carnegie Mellon Univ., 1980.

Howrey, E. Philip. "Stochastic Properties of the Klein-Goldberger Model." *Econometrica* 39 (January 1971): 73–87.

———. "Dynamic Properties of a Condensed Version of the Wharton Model." In *Econometric Models of Cyclical Behavior,* vol. 2, edited by Bert G. Hickman. New York: Columbia Univ. Press (for NBER), 1972.

King, Robert G.; Plosser, Charles I.; and Rebelo, Sergio T. "Production, Growth, and Business Cycles: Technical Appendix." Manuscript. Rochester, N.Y.: Univ. Rochester, 1987.

———. "Production, Growth and Business Cycles: I. The Basic Neoclassical Model." *J. Monetary Econ.* 21 (March/May 1988): 195–232. (*a*)

———. "Production, Growth and Business Cycles: II. New Directions." *J. Monetary Econ.* 21 (March/May 1988): 309–41. (*b*)

King, Robert G.; Plosser, Charles I.; Stock, James H.; and Watson, Mark W. "Stochastic Trends and Economic Fluctuations." *A.E.R.* 81 (September 1991): 819–40.

King, Robert G., and Rebelo, Sergio T. "Low Frequency Filtering and Real Business Cycle Models." *J. Econ. Dynamics and Control* (1993), in press.

Kydland, Finn E., and Prescott, Edward C. "Time to Build and Aggregate Fluctuations." *Econometrica* 50 (November 1982): 1345–70.

McCallum, Bennett T. "Real Business Cycle Models." In *Modern Business Cycle Theory,* edited by Robert J. Barro. Cambridge, Mass.: Harvard Univ. Press, 1989.

McFadden, Daniel. "Econometric Models of Probabilistic Choice." In *Structural Analysis of Discrete Data with Econometric Applications,* edited by Charles Manski and Daniel McFadden. Cambridge, Mass.: MIT Press, 1981.

Mankiw, N. Gregory. "Real Business Cycles: A New Keynesian Perspective." *J. Econ. Perspectives* 3 (Summer 1989): 79–90.

Mankiw, N. Gregory; Runkle, David E.; and Shapiro, Matthew D. "Are Preliminary Announcements of the Money Stock Rational Forecasts?" *J. Monetary Econ.* 14 (July 1984): 15–27.

Mankiw, N. Gregory, and Shapiro, Matthew D. "News or Noise: An Analysis of GNP Revisions." *Survey Current Bus.* 66 (May 1986): 20–25.

Manski, Charles F. *Analog Estimation Methods in Econometrics.* New York: Chapman and Hall, 1988.

Plosser, Charles I. "Understanding Real Business Cycle Models." *J. Econ. Perspectives* 3 (Summer 1989): 51–77.

Prescott, Edward C. "Theory Ahead of Business-Cycle Measurement." *Carnegie-Rochester Conf. Ser. Public Policy* 25 (Autumn 1986): 11–44.

Rotemberg, Julio J., and Woodford, Michael. "Oligopolistic Pricing and the Effects of Aggregate Demand on Economic Activity." *J.P.E.* 100 (December 1992): 1153–1207.

Sargent, Thomas J. "Two Models of Measurements and the Investment Accelerator." *J.P.E.* 97 (April 1989): 251–87.

Sargent, Thomas J., and Sims, Christopher A. "Business Cycle Modeling without Pretending to Have Too Much *a Priori* Economic Theory." In *New Methods in Business Cycle Research,* by Christopher A. Sims et al. Minneapolis: Fed. Reserve Bank, 1977.

Singleton, Kenneth J. "Econometric Issues in the Analysis of Equilibrium Business Cycle Models." *J. Monetary Econ.* 21 (March/May 1988): 361–86.

Soderlind, Paul. "Cyclical Properties of a Real Business Cycle Model." Manuscript. Princeton, N.J.: Princeton Univ., Dept. Econ., 1993.

Summers, Lawrence H. "Some Skeptical Observations on Real Business Cycle Theory." *Fed. Reserve Bank Minneapolis Q. Rev.* 10 (Fall 1986): 23–27.

Taylor, John B., and Uhlig, H. "Solving Nonlinear Stochastic Growth Models: A Comparison of Alternative Solution Methods." *J. Bus. and Econ. Statis.* 8 (January 1990): 1–17.

White, Halbert. "Maximum Likelihood Estimation of Misspecified Models." *Econometrica* 50 (January 1982): 1–25.

Woodford, Michael. "Stationary Sunspot Equilibria: The Case of Small Fluctuations around a Deterministic Steady State." Manuscript. Chicago: Univ. Chicago, 1986.

[7]

From Causal Corrective to Calibration: Perspectives on Mimic Cycles in Macroeconomics

Robin Rowley

The interplay between economic theories and their empirical validation has a long and chequered history. Mimic cycles were first introduced 70 years ago to illustrate a difficulty in the provision of empirical support for some theories of economic fluctuations – the separation of correlation 'flukes' from genuine connections among variables (Yule, 1926). Recently they have reappeared as part of a controversy dealing with the relative primacy of theory and evidence in choice among theories. In particular, they have emerged in a debate about the appropriateness of substituting calibration for estimation of structural parameters in the display of 'real' business cycles and their theoretical rivals, usually by reference to the qualitative feature of economic cycles as established from business annals (Mitchell, 1926) and aggregate data within the framework initially associated with the National Bureau of Economic Research. In the long interval between these episodes, an awareness of potential mimic cycles affected the appraisal of economy-wide econometric models in the United States (stimulating the acceptance of stochastic simulation for such models), while a consideration of their mathematical ingredients (linearity and erratic or random shocks) provided a convenient method of demonstrating the hazards of prior data preparation, where conventional moving-average techniques for 'smoothing' data (to remove the secular trends or seasonality) may introduce 'false' cyclical phenomena for some economic time series. In this paper, we offer a brief description of these four interesting episodes – tentatively associated with an imputed causality, the numerical calibration of linear difference equations, the potential endogeneity and exogeneity of fluctuations, and the impact of linear data transformations – to illustrate a persistent awkwardness of empirical validation for simple dynamic theories. All of these episodes should be better known to macroeconomists, who are often forgetful about many historical controversies in our discipline, especially controversies which involve technical and methodological issues. This form of neglect is unfortunate when more attention to such issues might lead to a better understanding of basic causal influences and the dynamics of economic phenomena.

Causality and Mimic Cycles

By the beginning of the present century, the availability of economic data for some economic variables (over a sufficiently long time period) was encouraging prominent economists to draw firm inferences about the principal factors which might influence the frequency, amplitude and irregular impulses characterizing major economic fluctuations. Clearly, the influx of wealth from the Americas to Europe, irregular variations in sunspot activity (Jevons, 1878; Peart, 1991) and other potential influences on economic activity could be (and were) isolated by a simple inspection of these data, through a casual association of 'earlier' patterns in the experiences of a potential 'causal factor' being followed, perhaps erratically, by 'similar' patterns experienced by another 'dependent outcome' (such as in agricultural fluctuations). Some interesting illustrations, including the efforts by Herschel and Jevons, are briefly described by Davis (1941: 561ff.) in one of the first econometric textbooks. Other illustrations can readily be found in the familiar literature on the Kondratieff cycle or long wave, extending from the 1920s until the last decade – as illustrated, for example, by Kondratieff (1925, 1935), Kitchen (1923) and Forrester (1976). Almost always, this economic theorizing and its immodest attempts at empirical validation confused the presence of a (lagged) correlation with that of a fundamental causality linking variables. Nor were associations and confusions merely limited to economic phenomena. Thomas (1927) indicates the much wider literature connecting cyclical fluctuations with social data for births, deaths, marriage and infant mortality, for example. Zarnowitz (1985) offers a more recent historical account of economists' views on business cycles and their determinants. It is tempting to suggest that influential forecasts for financial markets still reflect a direct extrapolation from earlier patterns, especially those which can easily be interpreted in a graphical form!

Mimic cycles first appeared as a necessary corrective for such causal inferences. These cycles were produced by combining either summation or repeated differences with an arbitrary stream of erratic or random shocks. More formally, they arise from a linear difference equation with constant coefficients, non-homogeneous due to the stimulative impact of a 'forcing function' involving an exogenous sequence of random or 'incoherent' elements. Currently, we recognize the moving average (or moving summation) and autoregressive representations of 'linear stochastic processes' as described by Wold (1954); he had a very important role in clarifying their principal features, linking alternative representations, and outlining their historical development during the 1920s and 1930s as part of a new area of mathematical research on probability models involving ergodicity and stationarity. The two basic ingredients (linear operations and uncorrelated random shocks) of these linear stochastic processes have no economic substance. However, the 'derived' fluctuations which they can produce were similar to those often found in existing economic time series. That is, the derived fluctuations could 'mimic' actual ones. Thus if we begin with the latter fluctuations and want to infer their determinants from empirical patterns, we should *constantly* be aware that these fluctuations can be produced merely by simple mathematical operations without economic meaning, rather than by the mechanisms found in the theoretical explanations favoured by many economists. The inferential path linking data to explanation is clearly not a trivial one, simply determined by visual inspection or correlation! Everyone knows this in principle, but it is surprising how often inferential excesses appear in practice.

The earliest demonstration of mimic cycles was provided during the 1920s by Slutsky and Yule, while Frisch (1933) widened their appreciation, found a partial precursor in Wicksell (1907) and recast the discussion among economists to focus on an important choice between exogenous and endogenous explanations of persistent fluctuations. Although Yule's papers appeared in the *Journal of the Royal Statistical Society* (1921, 1926) and thus were readily accessible (at least in Britain), the very important paper of Slutsky (1927), originally written in Russian with an English summary, was little known until Schultz arranged for an English translation, subsequently printed in *Econometrica* a decade later (Allen, 1950). The history of these developments for economists, rather than for statisticians, is briefly reviewed by Morgan (1990), while Andvig (1981) describes the leading role of Frisch in business-cycle research in the interwar years. The wider context for any empirical research on fluctuations must also recognize an earlier combination of sine waves in deterministic Fourier analysis, either to generate periodic functions or to 'decompose' them into regular cyclical components, perhaps illustrated using an estimated periodogram. A later contribution of Frisch, Wiener, Wold and various members of the Russian and American 'probability' schools (such as Doob, Khinchin, Kolmogorov and Slutsky, for example) was the extension of Fourier analysis to include stochastic elements and 'changing harmonics', and thus to produce the 'spectral analysis' which is currently used by time-series analysts and econometricians – the correlations in time and spectral densities having been connected by an exploration of Fourier transform pairs in the 1930s.

How do mimic cycles differ from the dynamics found in cobweb models for agricultural commodities and in multiplier–accelerator interaction? After generating a degree of interest in the fluctuations caused by a delayed supply response to price, a general acceptance of cobweb models was undermined by assaults on the presumed myopia of producers, often dismissed as too unrealistic (Ezekiel, 1937–38). During the early 1930s, Kalecki, Tinbergen and Frisch popularized the use of lagged relationships to describe 'macrodynamic' business cycles (Koopmans, 1949). Within a decade, Hansen and Samuelson were illustrating how different values for the coefficients in difference equations reflecting multiplier–accelerator interaction could generate a variety of different cyclical patterns, most notably in Samuelson (1939; see also Samuelson, 1959). Later Hicks added multiple regimes for (explosive) upswings, ceilings, downturns and troughs to permit asymmetries in cycles. Before long, Haberler (1949) would claim that 'every sophomore is being taught how to produce any kind of cycles', although 'the more models we have, the less we seem to know of the real business cycle!'. These theoretical treatments differed from mimic cycles in two important respects. Theoretical cycles were usually deterministic rather than being affected by random shocks until the emergence of the econometric approach in the 1940s (Koopmans, 1941, 1949), and the derived difference equations were explicitly linked to economic phenomena (or associated with 'structural specifications') so that they could not be dismissed as significantly devoid of any relevant content, an essential feature of the mimic cycles. Clearly for the latter, the character of fluctuations was not a simple matter of parametric values associated with some 'reasonable' levels of a marginal propensity to consume or with an acceleration scale, for example. The parameters of any difference equations for mimic cycles were set without an economic justification.

How influential was the demonstration of mimic cycles on treatments of causality and the 'normal' path of empirical research? The visible impact of such cycles on research and advocacy was limited throughout the 1930s. Haavelmo (1943) surely exaggerates in stating that 'since the days when Yule "discovered" that correlation between time series might be "nonsense", very few economists have dared break the ban on time series as an object of statistical inference' until the prominent calculations by Tinbergen for the League of Nations. In any case, Yule's views on spurious or nonsense correlation should be placed within the context of a longer process of assimilation for the various correlation concepts by statisticians, as recently attempted by Aldrich (1995). The principal obstacles to empirical research at this time seem to have been shortages of comprehensive data, computational limitations and a lack of fashionability – rather than a better appreciation of the constant confusion of temporal correlation with causality. The impact of Frisch's theoretical treatment of exogenous and endogenous factors in persistent business cycles was much greater than its statistical counterpart in the papers of Yule and Slutsky. Nevertheless, Haavelmo (1940) still felt it necessary to remind economists of the inadequacy of 'testing' much dynamic theory by comparing the theoretical solutions of linear difference equations (with their external random shocks omitted) and observed cycles, reflecting the common practice of using deterministic theory to which shocks are simply superimposed as an afterthought! This reminder can be set against a less favourable contemporary appraisal by Tintner (1938) of the Yule–Slutsky focus on erratic shocks.

Distinguishing between propagation and impulse problems (as noted earlier by Wicksell), Frisch argued that (1) 'the majority of the economic oscillations which we encounter seem to be explained most plausibly as free oscillations' defined as depending on internal structure; (2) ' in many cases they seem to be produced by the fact that certain external impulses hit the economic mechanism and thereby initiate more or less regular oscillations'; (3) 'a more or less regular fluctuation may be produced by a cause which operates irregularly'; and (4) 'there need not be any synchronism between the initiating force or forces and the movement of the swinging system'. This perspective combines both endogenous and exogenous features, with the former assumed to affect frequency and any tendencies to dampening, and the latter to revitalize the 'energy' of economic fluctuations as erratic shocks stimulate an otherwise dampened system. It also draws on earlier treatments by Hotelling (1927) and Frisch (1928) in which the distinction between 'free' and 'forced' mechanisms is clarified and the occurrence of changing harmonics is appraised. For our purposes, the critical elements are a lack of synchronism, which must weaken any inferences primarily based on the visual inspection of time series, and the strong reliance on ill-defined external disturbances which might depend on innovation, new initiatives and whatever a researcher chooses to identify. This haphazard attribution of causality to external disturbances persists in the recent debate on calibration.

Stochastic Simulation

After the Cowles Commission successfully launched an econometric theory for simultaneous-equation models and as more data on national accounts and better computational facilities became available to economists in the 1950s, development of economy-wide models for many countries became an active 'growth' industry which enjoyed a surprising degree of commercial success. The fitted systems of economic equations (largely based on regression estimates) became a common basis for creative simulations that sought to illustrate either the potential consequences of specific governmental actions or the impact of some hypothetical changes in economic environments. Errors associated with most structural specifications were generally viewed as white noise or else generated by simple linear processes, unrelated by convention to any identifiable influences and normally assumed to satisfy a standard list of stationarity conditions rather than less convenient evolutionary ones (Haavelmo, 1954). Although simulation experiments used 'tender loving care' or ad hoc adjustments in providing potential time paths, the appreciation of such model outcomes was mixed. (Such judgmental adjustments are still prevalent in most forecasts from econometric models; see McNees, 1990.) Eventually a crisis occurred in connection with the apparent failure of these modified outcomes to yield simulated time paths that replicate the normal features assumed to characterize economic fluctuations.

Initially, this particular deficiency and the corresponding choice of some relevant criteria to evaluate dynamic 'extrapolations' were raised by Adelman and Adelman (1959) in the context of simulations over a long horizon from the large model developed for the US economy by Klein and Goldberger. Subsequently, more attention was extended by I. Adelman (from 1960 to 1965) to the simulation of long waves and to the relative importance of various endogenous and exogenous influences on business cycles. The addition of arbitrary random shocks to form 'stochastic' simulations appeared to offer a practical if partial resolution of the severe problem of inadequate 'qualitative parallelism' for the synthetic fluctuations generated by large econometric models, at least as judged by the referential NBER measures for cycles; for example, Adelman (1960) chose as measures 'the average duration of a cycle, the mean length of the expansion and contraction phases, and the degree of clustering of individual peaks and troughs around the turning points of the general business cycle'. However, much macroeconomic theory was directly embedded in specifications of such models, and however good the estimates and the empirical fit appeared to be for existing samples of data, none of the macroeconometric models was able to produce any long-run undamped fluctuations by extrapolation (to an appropriate degree) beyond those samples – unless supplemented by the introduction of arbitrary shocks and unless stochastic simulations were pursued!

The challenge of the Adelmans' findings and the relevance of the 'Yule–Slutsky effect' were given more prominence when later macroeconometric models were confronted by both traditional and spectral means of analysis at the beginning of the 1970s, as illustrated by the contributions to Hickman (1972). Stochastic simulation became commonplace – but for resistance based on cost, see Challen and Hagger (1983) – whereas the earlier disagreements over whether estimated values for coefficients were compatible with either damped or anti-damped cycles (so forcefully pursued by Frisch, Hicks and Fisher, for example) have received far less attention over the last two decades. After the mid-1970s, the Yule–Slutsky effect also disappeared from view when other theoretical challenges to macroeconometric models appeared under the banner of rational expectations and the 'Lucas critique' (Lucas, 1981), a surprising development since rational-expectations models presume that economic variables are generated by linear stochastic processes – the substance of the Yule–Slutsky challenge being drastically reformulated! Revival of interest came as a 'footnote' to newer reconsiderations of long waves, as calibration was substituted for estimation and as the proximate bases for theory choice shifted from a partial commitment to empirical testing towards the myopic primacy of fashionable 'theory'.

The methodological background for the last ingredient in this list is illustrated by a modest appeal to empirical validation in the recent survey of macroeconomics by Mankiw (1990); he offers the startling view that newer theoretical developments 'may have little practical value but ultimately they will point the way to a deeper understanding!'. (Any role for empirical validation is equally absent from the so-called theoretical *advances* outlined by contributors to Hildenbrand, 1982.) Lack of interest in the Yule–Slutsky effect is also evident in much of the recent literature on 'applied' econometric time series. Neither Yule nor Slutsky is listed in the index of Enders (1995), for example, nor in most of its rival textbooks. Further, the temporal aggregation of time series, as associated by Bentzel and Wold (1946) with a similar drawing of false inferences about economic dynamics, is also generally neglected. In the wider context of non-linear models, the importance of the Yule–Slutsky effect for stochastic simulation is diminished since the evident scope for predictability is unclear – recognized since Wiener (1949) in terms of the mathematics for non-linear operator theory and 'best' non-linear extrapolation. These models were discussed by Goodwin (1946, 1951) for their potential representation of persistent cycles, but they failed to achieve any fashionability until chaos theory (Bartlett, 1990) arrived on the scene from alternative sources in the late 1980s. The early simulation experiments with the Klein–Goldberger and similar econometric models had been 'linearized' prior to their use in generating any long-run conditional forecasts.

Data Transformations

While attempting empirical simulations, Adelman (1965) became acutely aware of a troublesome possibility that some prominent fluctuations in her generated time series might reflect 'smoothing biases' rather than inherent features of real processes for economic phenomena. Could techniques used to prepare data, before both econometric analyses and simpler methods of visual inspection, introduce spurious fluctuations which were then subsequently 'discovered' and actively promoted by economists? Could false inferences also stem from common preparation errors rather than from either specification errors or erratic shocks? These questions were also considered by Bird et al. (1965) primarily with regard to the apparent discovery of Kuznets cycles, although questionable methods of data preparation (for trend removal, in particular) have been widespread since the early 1930s. Moreover, their direct connections with linear summation, induced and excluded periodicity, and other aspects of empirical resolution have been explored and described for an equally long time – notably by Rhodes (1931) and Macaulay (1931), for example, both of whom considered methods of smoothing and the empirical consequences of using moving-average (MA) transformations; and by Kuznets (1930), who used a simple MA transformation to smooth time series for production and prices as part of his attempt to clarify the existence and character of secular movements or trends.

Attempts to remove trends and some seasonal fluctuations have a long history, going back at least to the efforts of Poynting (1884). Some of the early efforts are identified by Makridakis (1976). In a parallel development, a few economists sought to isolate, retain and measure secular trends and promote indices of 'general business conditions' (Persons, 1919) within the frameworks for various schemes to 'decompose' economic fluctuations, as illustrated in the survey by Lorenz (1935). By the end of the 1920s, simple moving averages were being used to transform raw data and thus obtain a 'smoothed' series; these were supposed to reflect some particular components of economic fluctuations. The lengths of any MA transformations could be altered according to the elimination being sought. As Davis (1941) and Tintner (1952) indicated in two novel textbooks for econometricians, the length of any chosen moving average would be some multiple of the period of the component to be removed. With constant amplitudes or ones subject to small variations, and with superimposed cyclical components, the method appeared to be quite robust. However, variations could be a severe problem, as quickly recognized by Maverick (1933); he noted that 'the great shortcoming of the moving functions is the rigidity of the period, which, even though an elaborately weighted moving function is employed, prevents the resulting curve from smoothing out fluctuations as a satisfactory trend must do'; also, 'because of the varying period in the actual data and the rigid period in the moving function, the method actually introduces spurious fluctuations in the trend or smoothing curve'.

Other illustrations of a growing awareness of the potential consequences of 'graduation' using MA and related transformations were provided by Dodd (1939, 1941), while Wald (1939) again linked the use of repeated differencing (integration) for random series to a limiting periodic function and autocorrelation. Despite the existence of critical warnings, data transformations became institutionalized for national accounts and other time series in three successive stages, as Shiskin (1958), Shiskin, Young and Musgrave (1967) and Dagum (1980) developed a computer-based software to provide adjusted data. Subsequently, the introduction of spurious periodicity and the inferential hazards of inadequate detrending or over-differencing received sporadic attention – illustrated, for example, by Nelson and Kang (1981), Prosser and Schwert (1978) and Kang (1985) – but without stimulating any general concern over basic data preparation and corresponding false signals. Clearly, many aspects of the history of data preparation have simple parallels in the earlier discovery of mimic cycles.

Calibration: Display Versus Estimation

The rapid development and assimilation of econometrics over the last half century have been characterized by a number of distinct stages. From 1940 to the mid-1950s, consistent estimation and promotion of the probability approach took centre stage. Then the practical demands of economy-wide models, including data and computational issues, attracted more attention. With the onset of the commercial success of such models, conditional simulations joined estimation as the conventional focus of debate – until weaknesses appeared to challenge the multiplier–accelerator bases of many models, as well as some wage-price specifications reflecting the Phillips curve and normal assumptions of structural stability. Supporters of the Lucas critique took advantage of these apparent weaknesses to reduce the attachment of economic theorists to macroeconometric models and to revitalize a preference for microeconomic optimization and reinstate a neglect of aggregation issues. However, preoccupations with consistent estimates were difficult to sustain in the presence of theoretical turmoil and when structural integrity was being challenged. A consequence of this unsettled situation was the pronounced shift in the 'facts' to be explained by abstract models, a shift that would eventually draw economic theorists to a modified form of mimic cycles, with arbitrary calibration replacing estimation in derived equations.

The new facts were primarily qualitative, with relative volatility, aggregate fluctuations and timing emerging as the new bases of referential criteria for theoretical models of both business cycles and growth. Kydland and Prescott (1990) illustrate the new environment for research and a rediscovery of Yule–Slutsky shocks in connection with an assertion that uniform business-cycle facts and regularities affect the qualitative co-movements of time-series data. This statement reflects the claims by Lucas (1977) that, in this regard, 'business cycles are all alike' and are governed by general laws for market economies. A drastic conversion to calibration is visible in Kydland and Prescott (1982, 1991) and Prescott (1986); a modest degree of skeptical resistance is shown by Summers (1986), and the emergence of new techniques for calibration, the appraisal of corresponding empirical fits, and interaction with conventional econometrics are reported in Pagan (1994) and Watson (1993). A valuable evaluation is provided by Hoover (1995), while Eichenbaum (1990, 1991) and Ingram, Kocherlakota and Savin (1994) demonstrate the inevitable sensitivity or empirical fragility of calibrated dynamics to the numerical values for inherent coefficients of the artificial economies which they represent, as well as a fundamental indeterminacy in resolving the relative contribution of various shocks to aggregate fluctuations. In contrast to the passive choice of coefficient values by Yule and Slutsky, calibration is now linked to a few aggregate statistics in a haphazard but self-serving manner which seems to lack sufficient discipline and provides whatever pattern is desired by uncontrolled ad hoc experimentation. The new potential for spurious findings is substantially enhanced in this movement of mimic cycles from a peripheral constraint to a central role in the display of theoretical 'stories' within the framework provided by a few theoretical equations. This ironical transformation is being driven by an eccentric commitment to the primacy of a particular approach to economic theorizing, to microeconomic optimization and unrealistic rationality, and is affected by the mysterious disappearance of the substantial obstacles to aggregation through the twin fictions of artificial economies and representative individuals.

Concluding Remarks

The emergence of theoretical models focused on rational expectations (RE) and 'real' business cycles has completed a reversion to mimic cycles with a perverse change in methodological perspectives. A critical evaluation of this development was given by Zarnowitz a decade ago. With RE models in mind, he noted an 'increasing fragmentation in the face of various theoretical problems and recalcitrant facts' as corresponding research strategies became 'mainly concerned with theoretical possibilities rather than with explanations of what actually happens', and as ingenuity was favoured over testing, confirmation and falsification. Emphases were placed on scholarly competition and on an ill-disciplined method as opposed to more substance (McCallum, 1993). In some important respects, we are back in the disappointing situation of the 1940s as described by Harberler where anyone can calibrate arbitrary models; and, the more models we have, the less we seem to know about actual economic fluctuations!

Mimic cycles have moved away from their original role as a warning against some excessive claims for the discovery of simple causal relationships. From a causal corrective, with the advent of calibration, they have become a common means of display for theoretical models in artificial economies. With a whimsical concern for the tentative specification of numerical coefficients not too remote from the arbitrariness of the initial mimic cycles but more difficult to justify 70 years later, they are often equally uninformative as to the complex nature and diversity of the external disturbances which affect economic systems. Similarly, from an empirical challenge to economic theory, mimic cycles have become supportive of theory and a challenge to conventional methods of econometric estimation. Finally, the historical dispute on 'measurement without theory' has been reconstituted with radical assertions of 'theory with less concern for measurement'.

References

Adelman, I. (1960), 'Business Cycles – Endogenous or Stochastic?', *Economic Journal*, **70**, 783–96.

Adelman, I. (1963), 'Long Cycles – A Simulation Experiment', in A.C. Hoggatt and F.E. Balderston (eds), *Symposium on Simulation Models* (Cincinatti: South-Western Publishing).

Adelman, I. (1965), 'Long Cycles – Fact or Fiction?', *American Economic Review*, **55** (3), 444–63.

Adelman, I. and F.L. Adelman (1959), 'The Dynamic Properties of the Klein–Goldberger Model', *Econometrica*, **27**, 596–625.

Aldrich, J. (1995), *Correlations Genuine and Spurious in Pearson and Yule*, Discussion Paper 9502, Department of Economics, University of Southampton.

Allen, R.G.D. (1950), 'The Work of Eugen Slutsky', *Econometrica*, **18** (3), 209–16.

Andvig, J.C. (1981), 'Ragnar Frisch and Business Cycles During the Interwar Years', *History of Political Economy*, **13** (4), 695–725.

Bartlett, M.S. (1990), 'Chance or Chaos', *Journal of the Royal Statistical Society*, **A153**, 321–47.

Bentzel, R. and H. Wold (1946), 'On Statistical Demand Analysis from the Viewpoint of Simultaneous Equations', *Skandinavisk Aktuarietidskrift*, 95–114.

Bird, R.C., M.J. Desai, J.J. Enzler and P.J. Taubman (1965), '"Kuznets Cycles" in Growth Rates: The Meaning', *International Economic Review*, **6**, 229–39.

Challen, D.W. and A.J. Haggar (1983), *Macroeconometric Systems: Construction, Validation and Applications* (London: Macmillan).

Dagum, E.B. (1980), *The X–11–ARIMA Seasonal Adjustment Method* (Ottawa: Statistics Canada).

Davis, H.T. (1941), *The Theory of Econometrics* (Bloomington, Indiana: Principia Press).

Dodd, E.L. (1939), 'The Length of the Cycles Which Result from the Graduation of Chance Elements', *Annals of Mathematical Statistics*, **10**, 254–64.

Dodd, E.L. (1941), 'The Problem of Assigning a Length to the Cycle to be Found in a Simple Moving Average and in a Double Moving Average of Chance Data', *Econometrica*, **9** (1), 25–37.

Eichenbaum, M. (1990), *Real Business Cycle Theory: Wisdom or Whimsy?*, Working Paper 3432, NBER.

Eichenbaum, M. (1991), 'Technology Shocks and the Business Cycle', *Economic Perspectives, Federal Reserve Bank of Chicago*, March/April, 14–31.

Enders, W. (1995), *Applied Econometric Time Series* (New York: Wiley).

Ezekiel, M. (1937–38), 'The Cobweb Theorem', *Quarterly Journal of Economics*, **52**, 255–80.

Fisher, G.H. (1952), 'Some Comments on Stochastic Macro-Economic Models', *American Economic Review*, **42** (4), 528–39.

Forrester, J.W. (1976), 'Business Structure, Economic Cycles and National Policy', *Business Economics*, **11** (1), 13–24.

Frisch, R. (1928), 'Changing Harmonics and Other General Types of Components in Empirical Series', *Skandinavisk Aktuarietidskrift*, 220–36.

Frisch, R. (1933), 'Propagation Problems and Impulse Problems in Dynamic Equations', in *Economic Essays in Honor of Gustav Cassel* (London: George Allen & Unwin), 117–205.

Goodwin, R.M. (1946), 'Innovations and the Irregularity of Economic Cycles', *Review of Economic Statistics*, **28**, 95–104.

Goodwin, R.M. (1951), 'The Nonlinear Accelerator and the Persistence of Business Cycles', *Econometrica*, **19** (1), 11–17.

Haavelmo, T. (1940), 'The Inadequacy of Testing Dynamic Theory by Comparing Theoretical Solutions and Observed Cycles', *Econometrica*, **8** (4), 312–21.

Haavelmo, T. (1943), 'Statistical Testing of Business-Cycle Theories', *Review of Economic Statistics*, **25** (1), 13–18.

Haavelmo, T. (1954), *A Study in the Theory of Economic Evolution* (Amsterdam: North-Holland), ch. 4.

Haberler, G. (1949), 'Comment', *American Economic Review*, **39** (3), 85.

Hickman, B.G. (ed.) (1972), *Econometric Models of Cyclical Behavior* (New York: Columbia University Press for the National Bureau of Economic Research).

Hicks, J.R. (1950), *A Contribution to the Theory of the Trade Cycle* (Oxford: Clarendon Press).

Hildenbrand, W. (ed.) (1982), *Advances in Economic Theory* (Cambridge: Cambridge University Press.

Hoover, K.D. (1995), 'Facts and Artifacts: Calibration and the Empirical Assessment of Real-Business-Cycle Models', *Oxford Economic Papers*, **47**, 24–44.

Hotelling, H. (1927), 'Differential Equations Subject to Error, and Population Estimates', *Journal of the American Statistical Association*, 283–314.

Ingram, B.F., N.R. Kocherlakota and N.E. Savin (1994), 'Explaining Business Cycles: A Multiple-Shock Approach', *Journal of Monetary Economics*, **34**, 415–28.

Jevons, W.S. (1878), 'Commercial Crises and Sunspots', *Nature*, **19**, 33–7.

Kang, H. (1985), 'The Effects of Detrending in Granger Causality Tests', *Journal of Business and Economic Statistics*, **3** (4), 344–9.

Kitchen, J. (1923), 'Cycles and Trends in Economic Factors', *Review of Economic Statistics*, **5** (1), 10–16.

Kondratieff, N.D. (1925), 'The Static and Dynamic View of Economics', *Quarterly Journal of Economics*, **39**, 575–83.

Kondratieff, N.D. (1935), 'The Long Waves in Economic Life', *Review of Economic Statistics*, **17** (6), 105–15.

Koopmans, T.C. (1941), 'The Logic of Econometric Business-Cycle Research', *Journal of Political Economy*, **19** (2), 157–81.

Koopmans, T.C. (1949), 'The Econometric Approach to Business Fluctuations', *American Economic Review*, **39** (3), 64–72.

Kuznets, S.S. (1930), *Secular Movements in Production and Prices* (New York: National Bureau of Economic Research).

Kydland, F.E. and E.C. Prescott (1982), 'Time to Build and Aggregate Fluctuations', *Econometrica*, **50**, 1345–70.

Kydland, F.E. and E.C. Prescott (1990), 'Business Cycles: Real Facts and a Monetary Myth', *Federal Reserve Bank of Minneapolis Quarterly Review*, **14** (2), 3–18.

Kydland, F.E. and E.C. Prescott (1991), 'The Econometrics of the Great Equilibrium Approach to Business Cycles', *Scandinavian Journal of Economics*, **93**, 161–78.

Lorenz, P. (1935), 'Annual Survey of Statistical Technique: Trends and Seasonal Variations', *Econometrica*, **3** (4), 456–71.

Lucas, R.E. (1977), 'Understanding Business Cycles', in K. Brunner and A.H. Meltzer (eds), *Stabilization of the Domestic and International Economy* (Amsterdam: North-Holland).

Lucas, R.E. (1981), *Studies in Business-Cycle Theory* (Cambridge, Mass.: MIT Press).

Macaulay, F.R. (1931), *Smoothing of Time Series* (New York: National Bureau of Economic Research).

Makridakis, S. (1976), 'A Survey of Time Series', *International Statistical Review*, **44** (1), 29–70.

Mankiw, N.G. (1990), 'A Quick Refresher Course in Macroeconomics', *Journal of Economic Literature*, **28** (4), 1645–60.

Maverick, L.A. (1933), 'Time Series: Their Analysis by Successive Smoothing', *Econometrica*, **1**, 238–46.

McCallum, B.T. (1993), *Macroeconomics After Two Decades of Rational Expectations*, Working Paper 4367, NBER.

McNees, S.K. (1990), 'Man Vs. Model?', *New England Economic Review*, July/August, 41–52.

Mitchell, W.C. (1926), 'Business Cycles as Revealed by Business Annals', in W.L. Thorp (ed.), *Business Annals* (New York: National Bureau of Economic Research), 15–100.

Morgan, M. (1990), 'Random Shocks Enter the Business Cycle Scene', *The History of Econometric Ideas* (Cambridge: Cambridge University Press), ch. 3.

Nelson, C.R. and H. Kang (1981), 'Spurious Periodicity in Inappropriately Detrended Time Series', *Econometrica*, **49** (3), 741–51.

Pagan, A. (1994), 'Calibration and Econometric Research: An Overview', *Journal of Applied Econometrics*, Supplement.

Peart, S.J. (1991), 'Sunspots and Expectations: W.S. Jevons's Theory of Economic Fluctuations', *Journal of the History of Economic Thought*, **13** (2), 243–65.

Persons, W.M. (1919), 'Explanation of the Data and Methods Used in the Index of General Business Conditions', *Review of Economic Statistics*, **1**.

Poynting, J.H. (1884), 'A Comparison of the Fluctuations in the Price of Wheat and in the Cotton and Silk Imports into Great Britain', *Journal of the Royal Statistical Society*, **47**, 345–64.

Prescott, E.C. (1986), 'Theory Ahead of Business Cycle Measurement', *Federal Reserve Bank of Minneapolis Quarterly Review*, **10**, Fall, 9–22.

Prosser, C.I. and G.W. Schwert (1978), 'Money, Income, and Sunspots: Measuring Economic Relationships and the Effects of Differencing', *Journal of Monetary Economics*, **4**.

Rhodes, E.C. (1931), *Smoothing*, Tracts for Computers No. 6 (Cambridge).

Samuelson, P.A. (1939), 'Interactions Between the Multiplier Analysis and the Principle of Acceleration', *Review of Economics and Statistics*, **21** (2), 75–8.

Samuelson, P.A. (1959), 'Alvin Hansen and the Interactions Between the Multiplier Analysis and the Principle of Acceleration', *Review of Economics and Statistics*, **31**, 183–4.

Shiskin, J. (1958), 'Decomposition of Economic Time Series', *Science*, **128**, 1539–46.

Shiskin, J., A.H. Young and J.C. Musgrave (1967), *The X-11 Variant of Census Method II Seasonal Adjustment Program*, Technical Paper 15, Bureau of the Census (Washington, DC: US Department of Commerce).

Slutsky, E. (1927), 'The Summation of Random Causes as the Source of Cyclic Processes', *Problems of Economic Conditions* (Moscow: The Conjuncture Institute); revised English edition, *Econometrica* (1937), 105–46.

Summers, L.H. (1986), 'Some Skeptical Observations on Real Business Cycle Theory', *Federal Reserve Bank of Minneapolis Quarterly Review*, **10**, Fall, 23–7.

Thomas, D.S. (1927), *Social Aspects of the Business Cycle* (New York: Gordon & Breach).

Tintner, G. (1938), 'A Note on Economic Aspects of the Theory of Errors in Time Series', *Quarterly Journal of Economics*, **53**, 141–9.

Tintner, G. (1952), *Econometrics* (New York: Wiley).

Wald, A. (1939), 'Long Cycles as a Result of Repeated Integration', *American Mathematical Monthly*, **46**, 136ff.

Watson, M.W. (1993), 'Measures of Fit for Calibrated Models', *Journal of Political Economy*, **101**, 1011–41.

Whittle, P. (1963), *Prediction and Regulation by Linear Least-Squares Methods* (London: English Universities Press).

Wicksell, K. (1907), 'Krisernas Gata', *Statsokonomisk Tidsskrist*, **21**, 255–86; English translation, 'The Enigma of Business Cycles', *International Economic Papers*, **3**, 255–86.

Wiener, N. (1949), *Extrapolation, Interpolation and Smoothing of Stationary Time Series* (Cambridge, Mass.: MIT Press).

Wold, H. (1954), *A Study in the Analysis of Stationary Time Series* (Stockholm: Almquist & Wiksell), second edition.

Yule, G.U. (1921), 'On the Time-Correlation Problem, with Especial Reference to the Variate-Difference Correlation Method, *Journal of the Royal Statistical Society*, **A84**, 497–526.

Yule, G.U. (1926), 'Why Do We Sometimes Get Nonsense Correlation Between Time Series?', *Journal of the Royal Statistical Society*, **A89**, 1–64: Presidential Address to the Royal Statistical Society, November 1925.

Zarnowitz, V. (1985), 'Recent Work on Business Cycles in Historical Perspective: A Review of Theories and Evidence', *Journal of Economic Literature*, **23** (2), 523–80.

Part III
Time Series Models: Estimation, Identification and Intervention

[8]

VOLUME XXXIII, PART II AUGUST 1944

ON AUTOREGRESSIVE TIME SERIES

BY M. G. KENDALL

1. The product-moment correlation coefficients obtained by correlating the members of a time-series among themselves provide a useful method of investigating the behaviour of the series, especially in regard to oscillatory movements. Consider a series of values $x_1 \ldots x_n$, measured about their mean, trend-free and defined at equal intervals of time $t = 1, \ldots, n$. The kth serial correlation r_k is defined as the correlation between members of the series k intervals apart,

$$r_k = \frac{\sum_{j=1}^{n-k} x_j x_{j+k}}{\left\{\sum_{j=1}^{n-k} x_j^2 \sum_{j=1}^{n-k} x_{j+k}^2\right\}^{\frac{1}{2}}}. \tag{1}$$

The figure obtained by plotting r_k as ordinate against k as abscissa and joining each point to the next is known as the correlation diagram or correlogram. Since $r_0 = 1$ the correlogram always starts from the point (0, 1). When the series is infinite in extent, the *serial* correlations become *auto*-correlations (denoted by a Greek ρ), and the series for which such correlations do not vanish may be said to be autocorrelated.

2. If the time series is random the correlogram presents no systematic appearance. If it consists of a simple harmonic the correlogram reproduces that harmonic. If it results from a moving average of finite extent d of a random series the correlogram will, within sampling limits, be zero after $k = d$. The correlogram thus provides a criterion for distinguishing between various kinds of oscillatory time series. In this paper I propose to consider the correlogram of a series defined by the difference equation

$$u_{t+2} + au_{t+1} + bu_t = \epsilon_{t+2}, \tag{2}$$

where a and b are constants and ϵ_{t+2} is a random variable. This equation I shall call the generating equation and the coefficients a and b generating coefficients. The generated series may be said to be autoregressive. The notion of generating series in this way was introduced by Yule (1927) in a classical paper on sunspot periodicities and has been applied to meteorological and economic series with some success. The autoregressive scheme can, in fact, explain a typical phenomenon of such series for which Fourier and periodogram analysis cannot satisfactorily account without great artificiality, namely, the continual shift in phase and variation of amplitude which occur even when the series is smooth. Accounts of the autoregressive scheme have been given in the books by Wold (1938) and Davis (1941).

3. The equation (2) may be solved by the ordinary methods appropriate to difference equations. If the roots of

$$\xi^2 + a\xi + b = 0$$

are $\alpha + i\beta$, $\alpha - i\beta$, the complementary function of (2) is

$$p^t(A \cos \theta t + B \sin \theta t), \tag{3}$$

where $p = +\sqrt{b}$, $\theta = \arctan\frac{\beta}{\alpha} = \arctan\sqrt{\left(\frac{4b}{a^2} - 1\right)}$, and A and B are arbitrary constants.

It is here assumed that b is positive and that $4b > a^2$. It is also to be assumed that $\sqrt{b} = p$ is not greater than unity. The complementary function (3) then represents a damped harmonic. I shall call $2\pi/\theta$ the fundamental period of the generated system.

Let ξ_t be a particular value of (3) such that

$$\xi_0 = 0, \quad \xi_1 = 1, \tag{4}$$

i.e. such that

$$\xi_t = \frac{2}{\sqrt{(4p^2 - a^2)}} p^t \sin\theta t. \tag{5}$$

Then a particular integral of (2) will be found to be

$$\sum_{j=0}^{\infty} \xi_j \epsilon_{t-j+1}. \tag{6}$$

The complete solution is

$$u_t = p^t(A\cos\theta t + B\sin\theta t) + \sum_{j=0}^{\infty} \xi_j \epsilon_{t-j+1}. \tag{7}$$

In practical cases we may assume that the series was 'started up' some time ago, so that the complementary function has been damped out of existence. The series is then given by

$$u_t = \sum_{j=0}^{\infty} \xi_j \epsilon_{t-j+1}. \tag{8}$$

This is a moving sum of a random series with damped harmonic weights. It has been generally assumed, apparently on the basis of experimental evidence, that the mean period of the generated series will be $2\pi/\theta$, the same as the fundamental period present in the term ξ. This, however, is not necessarily so. Something depends on what we call a period in the generated series, whether, for example, we decide to exclude small ripples on the main wave. One possibility is to define the period as the distance between successive 'upcrosses', i.e. points where the series changes sign from negative to positive. The mean distance between major peaks or major troughs will not, probably, be very different from this in the majority of practical cases.*

Some idea of the mean length of the period as so defined can be obtained for particular distributions of ϵ, though a general discussion presents great difficulties. Consider the sum, which will be required again later,

$$\begin{aligned}\sum_{j=0}^{\infty} \xi_j \xi_{j+k} &= \frac{4}{4p^2 - a^2}\Sigma\{p^{2j+k}\sin\theta j \sin\theta(j+k)\} = \frac{2p^k}{4p^2-a^2}\Sigma[p^{2j}\{\cos\theta k - \cos\theta(2j+k)\}] \\ &= \frac{2p^k}{4p^2-a^2}\left\{\frac{\cos\theta k}{1-p^2} - \frac{\cos\theta k - p^2\cos\theta(k-2)}{1-2p^2\cos 2\theta + p^4}\right\}.\end{aligned} \tag{9}$$

We have

$$\Sigma\xi_j\xi_{j+1}/\Sigma\xi_j^2 = \frac{2p\cos\theta}{1+p^2} = \frac{-a}{1+b} = \cos\phi, \text{ say.} \tag{10}$$

Now if ϵ is normally distributed, the mean period (from one upcross to the next) is $2\pi/\phi$ (Dodd, 1939). Also it is easily seen that $\cos\theta = \dfrac{-a}{2p} = \dfrac{-a}{2\sqrt{b}}$. Thus the period given by the

* Dodd (1939) points out that in series generated by moving averages of random series there sometimes occur oscillations above or below the x-axis which would not be taken into account by counting upcrosses. The difficulty is to decide which of these is not to be ignored as a 'ripple'. I think that for harmonic weights such as are given by the autoregressive scheme the method of upcrosses is satisfactory, as indicated in paragraph 4.

generating equation is not in general the same as the period in the generated series, defined as the mean difference between upcrosses. The ratio of the first to the second is

$$\frac{\arccos \dfrac{a}{1+b}}{\arccos \dfrac{a}{2\sqrt{b}}}. \tag{11}$$

4. One would expect differences of a similar kind when the variation of ϵ is not normal. Experiments indicate, for example, that rectangular variation of ϵ gives much the same periods as normal variation. It does not seem to have been previously remarked that the mean period of the generated series is not that of the fundamental, but part of the explanation is no doubt due to the fact that for ranges of b encountered in practice (say $0{\cdot}5 \leqslant b \leqslant 1{\cdot}0$) the value of the ratio (11) is not very different from unity. In the extreme case $b = 1$ (when the series becomes undamped) the ratio is exactly unity. If $b = 0{\cdot}5$, $a = -1$, the ratio is 1·07. Notwithstanding the theoretical difference exhibited by equation (11), I think we may take it that for most practical purposes a good estimate of the observed period (upcross to upcross) is that given by the generated equation, *if it is known*. Below I give examples of two artificial series of the type of equation (2) which support this conclusion.

5. Equation (9) provides one further interesting item of information, namely, the relationship between the variance of ϵ and the variance of the generated series. We have

$$\operatorname{var} u = \lim_{n\to\infty} \frac{1}{n} \sum_{t=1}^{n} \left(\sum_{j=0}^{\infty} \xi_j \epsilon_{t-j+1} \right)^2 = \sum_{j=0}^{\infty} \xi_j^2 \operatorname{var} \epsilon,$$

cross-product terms in ϵ vanishing since it is a random variable:

$$\frac{\operatorname{var} u}{\operatorname{var} \epsilon} = \Sigma \xi_j^2 = \frac{2}{4p^2 - a^2} \left\{ \frac{1}{1-p^2} - \frac{1-p^2 \cos 2\theta}{1-2p^2 \cos 2\theta + p^4} \right\} = \frac{1+b}{(1-b)\{(1+b)^2 - a^2\}}.$$

Thus
$$\frac{\operatorname{var} \epsilon}{\operatorname{var} u} = \frac{1-b}{1+b}\{(1+b)^2 - a^2\}. \tag{12}$$

In an actual series of 65 terms (referred to in detail below) with $a = -1{\cdot}1$, $b = 0{\cdot}5$, the observed ratio of variances was 0·43. The value given by (12) is 0·35. In another series of the same length for which $a = -1{\cdot}5$, $b = 0{\cdot}9$, the observed ratio was 0·04, the value given by (12) was 0·07. It is difficult to judge how good the agreement is, but to me it appears satisfactory for such short series. It is noticeable that the generated series may have a very much larger variance than the random series on which it is based.

6. Consider now the autocorrelations of the generated series. We have

$$\operatorname{cov}(u_j u_{j+k}) = \lim \frac{1}{n} \sum_t \{ \sum_j (\xi_j \epsilon_{t-j+1}) \sum_j (\xi_j \epsilon_{t+k-j+1}) \} = \operatorname{var} \epsilon \sum_{j=0}^{\infty} \xi_j \xi_{j+k}$$

$$= \operatorname{var} \epsilon \frac{2p^k}{4p^2 - a^2} \left\{ \frac{\cos \theta k}{1-p^2} - \frac{\cos \theta k - p^2 \cos \theta(k-2)}{1 - 2p^2 \cos 2\theta + p^4} \right\}.$$

Hence
$$\rho_k = \frac{p^k \{\cos \theta k + \cos \theta(k-2) - 2 \cos 2\theta \cos k\theta + p^2 \cos \theta k - p^2 \cos \theta(k-2)\}}{(1+p^2)(1-\cos 2\theta)}$$

$$= \frac{p^k \{\sin (k+1)\theta - p^2 \sin (k-1)\theta\}}{(1+p^2)\sin \theta}.$$

Writing
$$\tan\psi = \frac{1+p^2}{1-p^2}\tan\theta,$$

we have
$$\rho_k = \frac{p^k(1-2p^2\cos 2\theta + p^4)^{\frac{1}{2}}}{(1+p^2)\sin\theta}\sin(k\theta+\psi) = p^k\frac{\sin(k\theta+\psi)}{\sin\psi}. \qquad (13)$$

Apart from the constant factor, ρ_k is thus the product of the damping factor p^k and a harmonic term which has the fundamental period of the generating equation. It is noteworthy that, although the point $\rho_0 = 1$ is a peak at the beginning of the correlogram the existence of the phase angle ψ implies that the interval from $k = 0$ to the next maximum of the correlogram is not equal to the fundamental period. In judging the length of the period from the correlogram it is therefore better to measure from upcross to upcross or from trough to trough; or, if peaks are preferred, not to count the maximum at $k = 0$ as a peak.

The same result may be obtained in two other ways. Multiplying equation (2) by u_{t-k} and summing for all t we have
$$\rho_{k+2} + a\rho_{k+1} + b\rho_k = \frac{\Sigma(\epsilon_{t+2}u_{t-k})}{\operatorname{var} u}.$$

Since u_{t-k} depends only on ϵ_{t-k} and terms with lower subscripts, the expression on the right vanishes if k is not less than -1. We then have
$$\rho_{k+2} + a\rho_{k+1} + b\rho_k = 0 \quad (k \geqslant -1). \qquad (14)$$

This result is due to Walker (1931). It was pointed out by Wold that if we multiply (2) by u_{t+k+2} and sum we get
$$\rho_k + a\rho_{k+1} + b\rho_{k+2} = \frac{\Sigma(\epsilon_{t+2}u_{t+k+2})}{\operatorname{var} u}.$$

The expression on the right no longer vanishes. In fact u_{t+k+2} contains the term $\xi_{k+1}\epsilon_{t+2}$ and we have
$$\rho_k + a\rho_{k+1} + b\rho_{k+2} = \frac{\operatorname{var}\epsilon}{\operatorname{var} u}\xi_{k+1} \quad (k \geqslant -1). \qquad (15)$$

If $k = -1$ the two equations become identical, for $\rho_{-1} = \rho_1$ and we have
$$\rho_1(1+b) + a = 0, \quad \rho_1 = -\frac{a}{1+b}. \qquad (16)$$

If we now solve either of the difference equations (14) and (15), making use of the initial conditions $\rho_0 = 1$ and (16) we arrive back at equation (13).

7. The foregoing result (13) would lead us to suppose that the correlogram of an autoregressive series would be damped according to the factor p^k, and this is true for an infinite series. In a number of practical cases, however, I was puzzled by the fact that correlograms of series which appeared on the face of it to be of type (2) did not damp out in the required way. Figs. 1 and 2 show the correlograms of two series for wheat prices and sheep population. The original series were taken from the agricultural returns for England and Wales, trend eliminated by a nine-years moving average and the first thirty serial correlations computed for the resulting series of 64 or 65 terms. The data and the correlations for what prices are given in Tables 1 and 2; those for sheep have been given in a previous paper (Kendall, 1941). I found a similar effect as regards non-damping in nine other agricultural time series, though the correlograms were not so regular as in these two cases. It was always possible, however, that the failure of the fluctuations to damp out in the correlogram was due wholly or partly

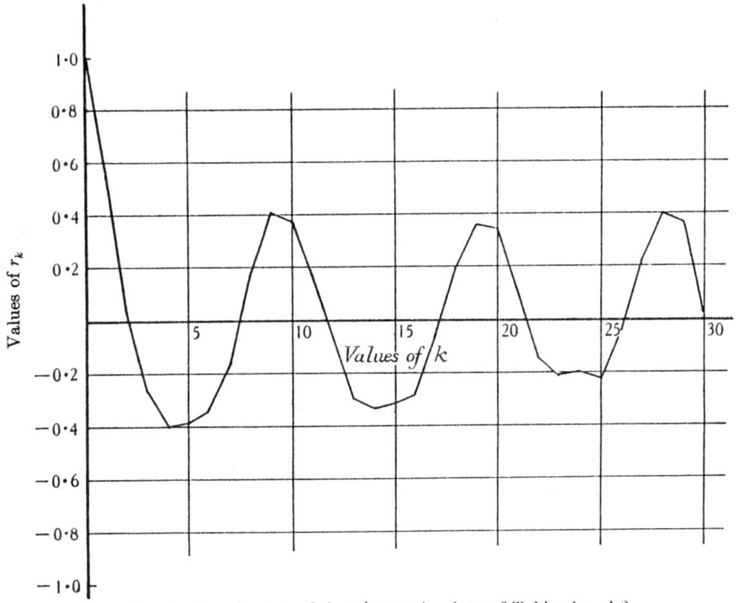

Fig. 1. Correlogram of the wheat price data of Tables 1 and 2.

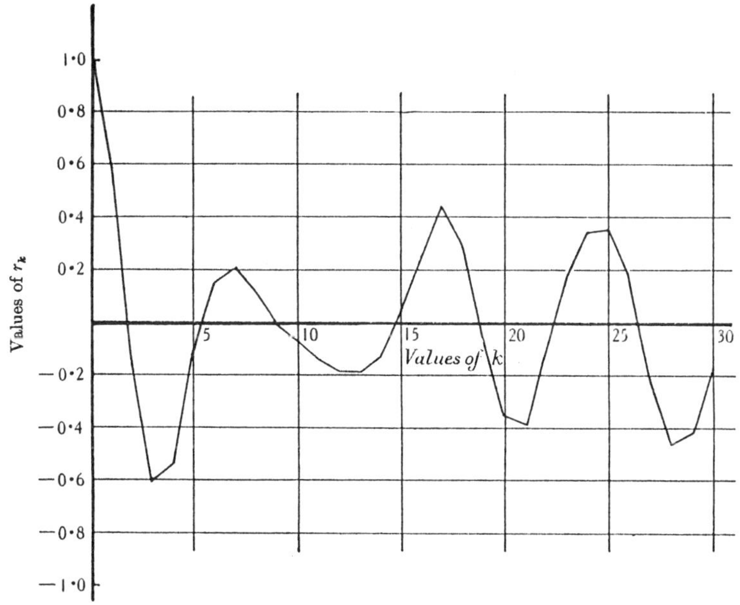

Fig. 2. Correlogram of the sheep population data referred to in paragraph 7.

to failure on the part of the original series to conform to the scheme of equation (2). To avoid such complications I constructed an artificial series with equation

$$u_{t+2} = 1{\cdot}1u_{t+1} - 0{\cdot}5u_t + \epsilon_{t+2}. \qquad (17)$$

The ϵ's were taken from tables of random numbers and consisted of positive or negative numbers ranging by units from $-9{\cdot}5$ to $+9{\cdot}5$. The series was 'started up' from zero by

Table 1. *Wheat prices, 1871–1934 inclusive, deviations from nine-years moving average in pence per hundredweight*

Year	Price	Year	Price	Year	Price
1871	−5	1893	6	1915	−3
2	−13	4	18	6	−7
3	−21	5	15	7	−40
4	−6	6	1	8	−28
5	19	7	−11	9	−27
6	11	8	−17	1920	−51
7	−20	9	5	1	−14
8	3	1900	3	2	37
9	8	1	4	3	42
1880	2	2	2	4	11
1	−6	3	3	5	−9
2	−11	4	−1	6	−17
3	−7	5	2	7	−15
4	6	6	5	8	−5
5	9	7	0	9	−10
6	9	8	−3	1930	−2
7	4	9	−9	1	19
8	3	1910	1	2	14
9	4	1	9	3	21
1890	−3	2	11	4	19
1	−20	3	32		
2	−5	4	33		

Table 2. *Serial correlations of the wheat price series of Table* 1

Order of correlation	r	Order of correlation	r	Order of correlation	r
1	+0·577	11	+0·171	21	+0·115
2	+0·025	12	−0·075	22	−0·144
3	−0·267	13	−0·302	23	−0·204
4	−0·402	14	−0·332	24	−0·195
5	−0·389	15	−0·317	25	−0·221
6	−0·340	16	−0·282	26	−0·052
7	−0·174	17	−0·049	27	+0·217
8	+0·166	18	+0·200	28	+0·404
9	+0·411	19	+0·360	29	+0·364
10	+0·372	20	+0·343	30	+0·024

assuming $u_0 = u_{-1} = 0$. The effect of assuming two consecutive terms equal to zero is not important, for the contribution to a term of the series of terms far back is very small. We are therefore entitled to expect that an artificial series constructed in this way should conform to the foregoing theory. The resultant series and the serial correlations are given in Tables 3 and 4 and the correlogram in Fig. 3. Now this series is heavily damped, p being $\sqrt{(0{\cdot}5)} = 0{\cdot}7071$.

At the twentieth serial correlation, according to equation (13), r_{20} should be less than 0·002 in absolute magnitude. Actually it is one hundred times as big.

8. The explanation lies, I think, in the shortness of the series. In arriving at equation (13) it was assumed that product sums such as $\Sigma\epsilon_j\epsilon_{j+k}$ were zero; and this is so for a series of infinite length. But when the series is short these sums may differ quite appreciably from zero. For instance, in samples from a normal population with zero correlation, the standard error of the correlation in samples of 65 is about 0·125, so that values of 0·25 are not very improbable and even values as high as 0·375 are not impossible.

Table 3. *Artificial series* $u_{t+2} = 1 \cdot 1 u_{t+1} - 0 \cdot 5 u_t + \epsilon_{t+2}$ *constructed as described in the text*

No. of term	Value of series	No. of term	Value of series	No. of term	Value of series
1	7	23	−4	45	−13
2	6	24	−5	46	1
3	−6	25	−9	47	6
4	−4	26	−4	48	4
5	3	27	−4	49	11
6	−4	28	3	50	15
7	−5	29	9	51	9
8	−1	30	4	52	8
9	10	31	−8	53	4
10	10	32	−6	54	−1
11	6	33	−3	55	4
12	−4	34	−2	56	7
13	−4	35	0	57	11
14	−7	36	−1	58	0
15	−2	37	−3	59	1
16	6	38	3	60	0
17	17	39	−1	61	−5
18	24	40	−8	62	−11
19	17	41	−3	63	−8
20	4	42	−8	64	−3
21	1	43	−10	65	5
22	−5	44	−16		

Table 4. *Serial correlations of the series of Table* 3

Order of correlation	r	Order of correlation	r	Order of correlation	r
1	+0·70	11	−0·05	21	+0·05
2	+0·29	12	−0·17	22	−0·12
3	+0·01	13	−0·27	23	−0·28
4	−0·17	14	−0·31	24	−0·43
5	−0·27	15	−0·30	25	−0·57
6	−0·25	16	−0·18	26	−0·56
7	−0·13	17	+0·12	27	−0·26
8	+0·07	18	+0·29	28	+0·02
9	+0·12	19	+0·33	29	+0·17
10	+0·05	20	+0·22	30	+0·27

Consider then the series of n terms such as

$$u_j = \xi_1\epsilon_j + \xi_2\epsilon_{j-1} + \xi_3\epsilon_{j-2} + \dots$$

The product moment of u_j and u_{j+k} will be

$$\sum_j u_j u_{j+k} = \sum_j \sum_l \xi_l \epsilon_{j-l+1} \sum_m \xi_m \epsilon_{j+k-m+1} = \sum_j \sum_{l,m} \xi_l \xi_m \epsilon_{j-l+1} \epsilon_{j+k-m+1}.$$

The terms in ϵ^2 give the expression (13). The others will be sums of products of the ξ's multiplied by the serial covariances of the ϵ's themselves. The dominating terms in these latter will be those containing the larger ξ's. These terms are themselves damped harmonics of the fundamental type and when applied to the sums $\Sigma \epsilon_j \epsilon_{j+k}$ may be expected to generate oscillatory movements of about the same period as the original series. We may therefore expect that for short series the correlogram of the autoregressive system may not decay very rapidly, but that the product terms may themselves result in a small fluctuation. This appears to be happening in both the practical and the artificial examples given above.

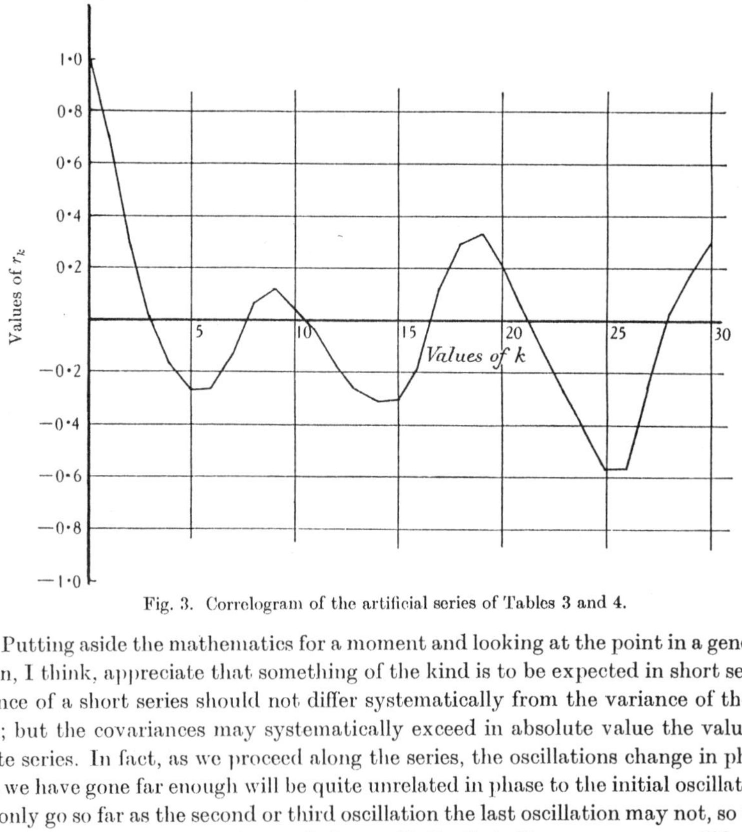

Fig. 3. Correlogram of the artificial series of Tables 3 and 4.

9. Putting aside the mathematics for a moment and looking at the point in a general way, we can, I think, appreciate that something of the kind is to be expected in short series. The variance of a short series should not differ systematically from the variance of the infinite series; but the covariances may systematically exceed in absolute value the value for the infinite series. In fact, as we proceed along the series, the oscillations change in phase, and when we have gone far enough will be quite unrelated in phase to the initial oscillations; but if we only go so far as the second or third oscillation the last oscillation may not, so to speak, have had time to get very much out of phase with the first. The consequence will be that the correlations for such a short space of time will tend to be higher than those for the series as a whole. For the generated system (and indeed for time series in general) we have to be careful not to assume too lightly that values calculated for a part of the series are typical of the corresponding values for the series as a whole; and this notwithstanding that the part of the series was chosen 'at random'.

One would like to know how long a practical series must be for the damping to show itself decisively. An exact discussion of this point presents difficulty, because in a finite series the serial covariances $\Sigma\epsilon_j\epsilon_{j+k}$ are not only non-vanishing but are correlated among themselves. Suppose, however, that we have a series with a damping factor p. Then the kth serial coefficient will not exceed p^k in absolute value, and the difference of the correlogram as a whole from expectation will not at any point exceed the error due to the sampling fluctuation of the serial correlation between u_j and u_{j+k}. This in turn will not exceed the sampling error of the correlation in samples of n from an uncorrelated series, which for large samples has a standard error $n^{-\frac{1}{2}}$. For example, if we took a series of 650 terms instead of 65, correlations up to the 30th would have a standard error not exceeding $1/\sqrt{(650-30)} = 0{\cdot}04$, and hence fluctuations of 0·10 would not be impossible. But by the 30th term in the correlogram the serial correlation has been practically damped out of existence. The fair inference is, I think, that except for the first few serial correlations of the main series, which are not damped very much, the serial correlations are seriously affected even for long series, for the sampling errors are not negligible compared with the small damped 'true' values. In general one would expect the damping effect to show itself for the first five, ten or twenty terms and then to be obliterated by the sampling effect. Whether this happens at the fifth, tenth or twentieth term depends not only on ϵ but on p, the rapidity of damping. In most of the natural series I have examined the damping is fairly rapid, so that the damping effect in the correlogram disappeared after the first few terms. The economic examples given by Wold (1938) and the meteorological examples of Walker (1931) appear to me to support this conclusion.

10. I turn now to consider another effect which may obscure the presence of the generated system of type (2) and may exert an important influence on the correlogram. The random element ϵ considered up to this point is what Yule calls a disturbance, and is integrated into the course of the series by the autoregressive scheme. There may also be a component η *superposed* on the system. This superposed element, if random, is like an error of observation in that its value at any point is unrelated to its value at other points.

If a random element with variance $\text{var}\,\eta$ is superposed on an infinite series with variance $\text{var}\,u$ the variance of the whole will be $\text{var}\,\eta + \text{var}\,u$. The autocovariances, however, will not be affected (except by sampling effects for short series). Consequently all the autocorrelations except ρ_0 will be reduced in the ratio

$$c = \frac{\text{var}\,u}{\text{var}\,u + \text{var}\,\eta}. \tag{18}$$

For short series there will still be a reduction of the same type, but the value of c may differ from its theoretical value for sampling reasons.

11. An autoregressive series of 65 terms was constructed according to the formula

$$u_{t+2} = 1{\cdot}5u_{t+1} - 0{\cdot}9u_t + \epsilon_{t+2}, \tag{19}$$

where the ϵ_{t+2} were the values of random numbers proceeding by units from $-49{\cdot}5$ to $49{\cdot}5$ with a theoretical variance of 833. On to the series so derived there were superposed (*a*) a rectangular random element $-49{\cdot}5(1)\,49{\cdot}5$ and (*b*) a further rectangular random element $-199{\cdot}5(1)\,199{\cdot}5$, additional to the first, the latter series then being divided by ten and rounded up to the nearest integer. The resultant series and serial correlations are shown in Tables 5 and 6, and the correlograms in Fig. 4.

According to (12) the variance of u for an infinite series generated by (19) should be $13{\cdot}97$ var ϵ. The values of c for the two series here considered are then, respectively,

13·97/14·963 = 0·93 and 13·97/30·963 = 0·45. In the second case the effect of the superposed variation is to halve the observed correlations. The effect on the actual series of 65 terms is somewhat irregular (see para. 14 below).

Table 5. *Artificial series* $u_{t+2} = 1{\cdot}5u_{t+1} - 0{\cdot}9u_t + \epsilon_{t+2}$, (*a*) *with small superposed element* η, (*b*) *with large element* η, *constructed as described in the text*

No. of term	Value of series		No. of term	Value of series		No. of term	Value of series	
	(*a*)	(*b*)		(*a*)	(*b*)		(*a*)	(*b*)
1	5	16	23	−215	−34	45	88	3
2	36	7	24	−219	−15	46	76	−5
3	8	10	25	−76	−17	47	93	21
4	−81	−5	26	95	−4	48	34	8
5	−89	7	27	239	15	49	60	15
6	−15	−7	28	316	23	50	−69	−13
7	35	10	29	289	21	51	−120	−10
8	112	13	30	169	13	52	−54	12
9	146	17	31	49	−7	53	−56	−13
10	100	19	32	−114	−26	54	12	7
11	1	7	33	−259	−26	55	5	−11
12	−131	1	34	−290	−26	56	13	−18
13	−195	−6	35	−208	−29	57	3	−1
14	−259	−27	36	−31	−4	58	13	11
15	−258	−37	37	21	12	59	−4	9
16	−118	−28	38	109	18	60	−71	−13
17	32	6	39	26	19	61	−94	−7
18	110	−3	40	33	−5	62	15	19
19	245	6	41	22	0	63	45	−3
20	166	24	42	−30	−10	64	138	19
21	79	15	43	51	−15	65	115	0
22	−177	−34	44	49	17			

Table 6. *Serial correlations of series* (*a*) *and* (*b*) *of Table* 5

Order of correlation	*r*		Order of correlation	*r*		Order of correlation	*r*	
	(*a*)	(*b*)		(*a*)	(*b*)		(*a*)	(*b*)
1	+0·78	+0·49	11	+0·33	+0·16	21	+0·21	+0·05
2	+0·33	+0·13	12	−0·04	−0·16	22	−0·07	−0·28
3	−0·22	−0·13	13	−0·38	−0·37	23	−0·28	−0·33
4	−0·63	−0·42	14	−0·58	−0·50	24	−0·32	−0·29
5	−0·75	−0·46	15	−0·52	−0·36	25	−0·22	−0·20
6	−0·59	−0·39	16	−0·23	−0·14	26	−0·01	−0·07
7	−0·22	−0·01	17	+0·14	+0·19	27	+0·16	+0·11
8	+0·19	+0·28	18	+0·43	+0·42	28	+0·23	+0·20
9	+0·48	+0·38	19	+0·55	+0·41	29	+0·13	+0·01
10	+0·53	+0·52	20	+0·45	+0·37	30	−0·11	−0·11

The correlograms run according to expectation. The effect of the bigger random element is to reduce the amplitude at the beginning of the series and to introduce some minor irregularities in the data, but not to affect substantially the lengths of the correlogram oscillations.

12. But here arises one important difficulty. Suppose we are given such series as these and require to estimate a and b, the constants of the generating equation. The procedure adopted by Yule was as follows: we take the observed serial correlations r_1 and r_2 as estimates of the autocorrelations. We then find the regression equation of u_{t+2} on u_{t+1} and u_t by the usual methods, assuming that the variance of the series is the same as the variance for the series less its first term and that the serial correlation r_1 for the whole series is the same as that for the series less its first term. The regression equation is

$$u_{t+2} = \frac{r_1(1-r_2)}{1-r_1^2} u_{t+1} + \frac{r_2 - r_1^2}{1-r_1^2} u_t. \tag{20}$$

The observed regression equation is then taken as an estimate of the generating equation so that we have as estimates of a and b

$$-a = \frac{r_1(1-r_2)}{1-r_1^2}, \quad -b = \frac{r_2 - r_1^2}{1-r_1^2} = \frac{r_2 - 1}{1-r_1^2} + 1. \tag{21}$$

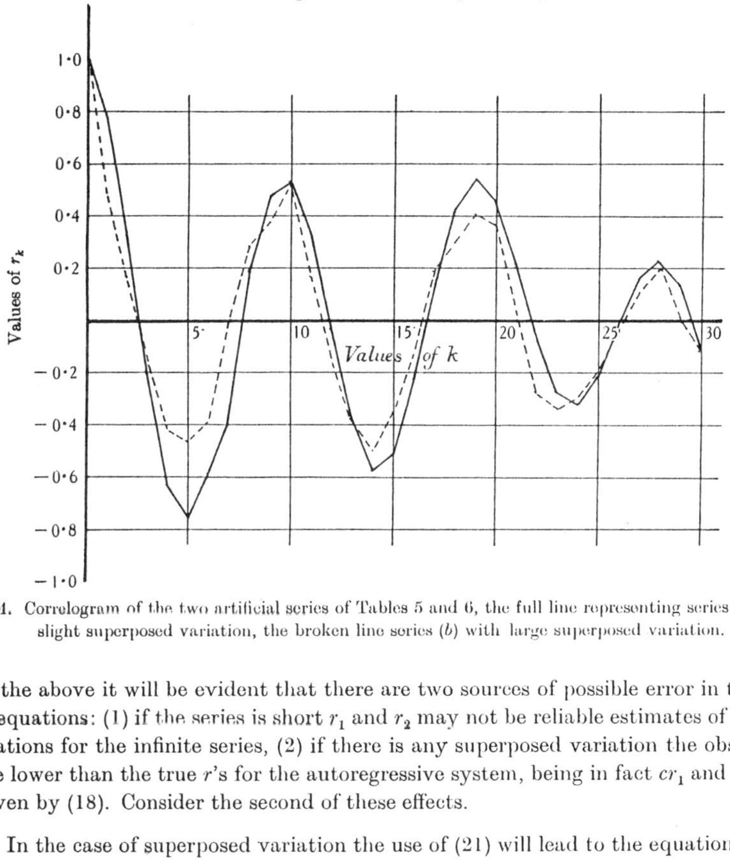

Fig. 4. Correlogram of the two artificial series of Tables 5 and 6, the full line representing series (a) with slight superposed variation, the broken line series (b) with large superposed variation.

From the above it will be evident that there are two sources of possible error in the use of these equations: (1) if the series is short r_1 and r_2 may not be reliable estimates of the auto-correlations for the infinite series, (2) if there is any superposed variation the observed r's will be lower than the true r's for the autoregressive system, being in fact cr_1 and cr_2 where c is given by (18). Consider the second of these effects.

13. In the case of superposed variation the use of (21) will lead to the equations

$$-a' = \frac{cr_1(1-cr_2)}{1-c^2r_1^2}, \quad -b' = \frac{cr_2 - c^2r_1^2}{1-c^2r_1^2}.$$

The estimated fundamental period of the generating equation is then given by

$$4\cos^2\theta' = \frac{a'^2}{b'} = \frac{cr_1^2(1-cr_2)^2}{(1-c^2r_1^2)(r_2-cr_1^2)}. \tag{22}$$

If we expand (22) in powers of $\gamma = 1-c$ we find, to first order in γ,

$$\frac{a'^2}{b'} = \frac{a^2}{b}\left\{1-\gamma\frac{(1+b)(3b^2-b-a^2)}{b\{(1+b)^2-a^2\}}\right\}.$$

Hence, if $3b^2-b-a^2>0$ the effect of a superposed variation (equivalent to positive γ) is to give

$$\frac{a'^2}{b'} < \frac{a^2}{b},$$

or in other words to result in a shortening of the observed period. The condition that $3b^2-b-a^2>0$ is equivalent to

$$b > \tfrac{1}{6}\{-1+\surd(12a^2+1)\}$$

and is not very restrictive since in any case $a^2 \leqslant 4$ and $4b \geqslant a^2$. The inequality is obeyed by all the examples I have met in practice.

We therefore reach the interesting conclusion that if there is any superposed random variation present, the period calculated from the observed regression equation according to formulae (21) will probably be too short even for long series. Yule himself found too short a period for his sunspot material and, suspecting that it was due to superposed variation, attempted to reduce that variation by graduation. The result was to give a longer period more in accordance with observation. It does not appear, however, that the superposed variation in his case was very big. In a number of agricultural time series which I have examined it is sometimes about half the variation of the series and the effect on the period as calculated from the serial correlations is very serious. For instance, in the cases of wheat prices and sheep population referred to above, formulae (21) give periods of 7·0 and 6·8 years, whereas the correlograms indicate periods of about 9·5 and 8·5 years respectively.

14. As an example, consider the second of the artificial series referred to in paragraph 11. For the observed serial correlations I find

$$r_1' = 0{\cdot}486, \quad r_2' = 0{\cdot}133,$$

giving, according to (21),

$$-a' = 0{\cdot}552, \quad b' = 0{\cdot}135, \quad \cos\theta' = \frac{-a'}{2\surd b'} = 0{\cdot}751, \quad \theta' = 41{\cdot}3^\circ,$$

which corresponds to a period of about 8·7 years, whereas we know from the construction of the series that

$$a = 1{\cdot}5, \quad b = 0{\cdot}9,$$

giving $\theta = 37{\cdot}7^\circ$ and a period of 9·5 years.

Considering the profound effect which the superposed variation has had on the first two serial coefficients, reducing r_1 from 0·78 to 0·49 and r_2 from 0·33 to 0·13, one might have expected the period to have been affected even more than appears from this result. But the example serves to bring out once again the difficulties associated with short series and the unreliability of coefficients calculated from the first two serial correlations in such cases.

If, for instance, we had found $r_2' = 0{\cdot}18$ instead of $0{\cdot}13$ we should have obtained a period of about 12 years, and if $r_2' = 0{\cdot}20$ the solution becomes impossible, for a' and b' then assume values such that $a'^2 > 4b'$ and $\cos\theta' > 1$. Furthermore, such a value as $0{\cdot}18$ for r_2' increases the period instead of decreasing it. We note, in fact, that r_2 has been reduced by $0{\cdot}13/0{\cdot}33 = 0{\cdot}40$ so that it is not legitimate to assume that r_1 and r_2 are reduced by a constant c. The errors introduced by neglect of the autocovariances of the superposed random element may be so serious as to destroy the value of calculations based on the observed regression coefficients.

15. Even in long series, when it is legitimate to suppose that r_1 and r_2 are reduced in the same proportion, the length of the period is very sensitive to superposed variation. Consider, for example, the effect of small variations in c near $c = 1$. We have from (22), differentiating logarithmically and putting $c = 1$,

$$-2\tan\theta\frac{d\theta}{dc} = 1 - \frac{2r_2}{1-r_2} + \frac{2r_1^2}{1-r_1^2} + \frac{r_1^2}{r_2 - r_1^2},$$

which on substituting $$r_1 = -\frac{a}{1+b}, \quad r_2 = -b + \frac{a^2}{1+b}$$

reduces to $$-\tan\theta\frac{d\theta}{dc} = \frac{(1+b)(3b^2+b-a^2)}{2b\{(1+b)^2-a^2\}}. \tag{23}$$

Now the period $$P = 2\pi/\theta \quad \text{and} \quad \tan\theta = \sqrt{\left(\frac{4b}{a^2} - 1\right)}.$$

Hence $$\frac{dP}{dc} = -\frac{P^2a(1+b)(3b^2+b-a^2)}{4\pi\sqrt{(4b-a^2)}\{(1+b)^2-a^2\}}. \tag{24}$$

When $a = -1{\cdot}5$, $b = 0{\cdot}9$, $P = 9{\cdot}5$, this reduces to

$$\frac{dP}{dc} = 14 \text{ intervals.}$$

Thus if $c = 0{\cdot}9$, i.e. the superposed variation is only about 10 % of the total, the period may be shortened by something of the order of one interval.

16. The position may then be summarized as follows:

(*a*) The correlogram of a generated system of the type of equation (2) will be damped according to the damping factor of the equation; but if the series is short the damping may be considerably less than the theoretical value.

(*b*) The correlogram will show a period equal, within limits of error, to that of the fundamental period of the system. The distance from the unit ordinate at $k = 0$ and the first maximum of the correlogram may not, however, be a full period and in estimating periods from the correlogram it is better to reckon from upcross to upcross.

(*c*) It does not appear that in short series the periodic movement is substantially affected, at any rate not to such an extent as the damping.

(*d*) When superposed random variation is present the fundamental period calculated from the observed regressions will be too short and may be very considerably so.

(*e*) The period of the generated series, defined as the mean distance from upcross to upcross, is not quite the same as the fundamental period: but the difference is not likely to be important in practice.

17. Armed with these results we may consider the difficult problem of determining, for a given time series, the autoregressive scheme which may have generated it.

The first step is to calculate the serial correlations and examine the correlogram. If the latter shows fairly regular oscillations there is a presumption that the series is of the autoregressive type, and this conclusion need not be rejected solely because the oscillations do not damp so rapidly in the later portion of the correlogram as at the beginning. To take the wheat price material given above, an examination of the correlogram (Fig. 1) strongly suggests a simple damped harmonic. The sheep series (Fig. 2) is not so clearly defined and there is a suggestion of more than one period in the behaviour of the correlogram. This may, however, be due to the shortness of the series and one would be inclined to consider it in the first place as a single damped harmonic.

The length of the period, as pointed out above, is best determined by the mean distances between upcrosses. In the wheat price data there are upcrosses at about 7·5 years, 17·2 years and 26·1 years, giving periods of 9·7 and 8·9 years with a mean of 9·3 years. Much the same result is arrived at by counting the periods between troughs.

18. The second step is to calculate a' and b' by equations (21) and to find the period of the fundamental harmonic as given by the observed regression equation. For wheat prices we have

$$r'_1 = 0{\cdot}5773, \quad r'_2 = 0{\cdot}0246.$$

Hence

$$a' = -0{\cdot}8446, \quad b' = 0{\cdot}4630,$$

whence

$$\cos\theta' = 0{\cdot}6206, \quad \theta' = 51{\cdot}63^\circ,$$

giving a fundamental period of 6·97 years.

This is too small, and we are immediately led to suspect the existence of superposed variation. The problem then arises of determining the variance of the superposed element. If this is random, and there are no periodic terms of very short period the variate difference method may be used. For the wheat price material, taking differences up to the 10th on the primary series (before trend was eliminated) I find for an estimate of the random variance $\operatorname{var}\eta = 27{\cdot}72$. The total variance of the series is 272·8. The constant c of equation (18) is

$$1-\frac{27{\cdot}72}{272{\cdot}8} = 0{\cdot}90.$$

The putative serial correlations of the autoregressive series will then be

$$r_1 = 0{\cdot}641, \quad r_2 = 0{\cdot}027$$

and

$$a = -1{\cdot}059, \quad b = 0{\cdot}652,$$

whence

$$\cos\theta = 0{\cdot}6551, \quad \theta = 49{\cdot}07^\circ,$$

giving a period of 7·34 years.

This is still too short. It would require a random superposed variance of about 25 % of the total, instead of the observed 10 %, to produce a period of 9·3 years.

19. This illustrates very well a constantly recurring difficulty in the theory of the variate difference method and of time series generally. The superposed variation may not be random. Indeed, we have little ground for expecting that it should be. A positive correlation between the successive values of η will reduce the variance shown as random by the variate difference method and unless we have prior reason to suppose that η is random the values given by the variate difference method are quite likely to be too small. Unfortunately we rarely have any prior knowledge of η, but from general economic considerations one would not be surprised

to find that there do exist positive correlations from one year to the next, owing to the enduring nature of some of the causes which can give rise to superposed variation. I conclude generally that discrepancies of the type here considered support the view that the period is to be determined from the correlogram, not from solution of the regression equation.

20. Two points may be mentioned incidentally. One, a matter of technique, is that the arithmetic of serial correlations and variate differences are closely linked together and the results of the one can be used to derive those of the other. This means an enormous saving in arithmetic and the method is described in the Appendix to this paper.

The second point concerns the removal of superposed random variation by graduation formulae. It will be clear that if the superposed variation is not random graduation may only make matters worse; but even if it is random, graduation formulae may induce spurious cyclical effects into the data. It seems to me that as a general rule graduation is to be undertaken with great caution.

21. Reverting to the main topic, it would seem that if the period shown by the correlogram and the period calculated from the observed regression equation disagree, and cannot be reconciled by the assumption of a superposed random element, there is little further to be done to dissect the superposed element from the autoregressive part of the system. If, however, the variate difference method supplies a variance of η which can satisfactorily explain the difference in periods, we may go forward. The constant c can be calculated and the constants of the autoregressive part of the system determined. Equation (12) then gives an estimate of the ratio between the variance of the basic random element ϵ and the variance of the generated series. If there is a superposed element it will not be possible to find the values of that element at every point and so to determine ϵ at every point; but if η is non-existent, ϵ can be explicitly determined, except for the first two terms of the series. In fact, we merely apply the generating equation to the observed series, the residuals between prediction and observation being the values of ϵ. An examination of these residuals will confirm whether they may be regarded as a random series.

22. The foregoing treatment can be extended to the case of a more general linear regressive system

$$u_{t+m} + a_1 u_{t+m-1} + \dots + a_m u_t = \epsilon_{t+m},$$

or to cases where the regression is curvilinear; and the necessity for more general schemes in representing observed data can, as shown by Yule, be discussed in terms of partial autocorrelations and scatter diagrams. A more serious problem arises if the series ϵ is itself not random, a state of affairs which one fears might be fairly common in economic series. To take the wheat price data once again, it would not be surprising to find that the wheat price oscillations were regenerated by a series of disturbances, part of which were attributable to variations in acreages, yields, or the prices of other crops. Such disturbances might themselves be oscillatory. For such cases the problem becomes exceedingly complicated. To discuss it at all satisfactorily one would require a long series or collateral evidence in the form of other series of a similar character. If there is a royal road in this subject it has not yet been discovered.

APPENDIX

Relationship between variate differences and serial correlations

If we have a series of values $x_1 \ldots x_n$ the first differences are $x_1 - x_2$, etc., the second differences $x_1 - 2x_2 + x_3$, etc., and so on. Let S_j be the sum of the squares of the jth differences and write for the product-sums

$$P_j = \sum_{k=1}^{n-j} x_k x_{k+j}. \tag{25}$$

The sums S are those appearing in variate difference analysis and the quantities P appear in serial correlation analysis. Either set can be expressed in terms of members of the other, as follows:

We have

$$S_0 = P_0, \tag{26}$$

$$S_1 = \sum (x_j - x_{j+1})^2 = \sum_{j=1}^{n-1} x_j^2 - 2\sum_{j=1}^{n-1} x_j x_{j+1} + \sum_{j=2}^{n} x_j^2 = 2P_0 - x_1^2 - x_n^2 - 2P_1, \tag{27}$$

$$\begin{aligned} S_2 = \sum (x_j - 2x_{j+1} + x_{j+2})^2 &= \sum_{j=1}^{n-2} x_j^2 + 4\sum_{j=2}^{n-1} x_j^2 + \sum_{j=3}^{n} x_j^2 - 4\sum_{j=1}^{n-2} x_j x_{j+1} + 2\sum_{j=1}^{n-2} x_j x_{j+2} - 4\sum_{j=2}^{n-1} x_j x_{j+1} \\ &= 6P_0 - 8P_1 + 2P_2 - x_1^2 - x_n^2 - (2x_1 - x_2)^2 - (2x_n - x_{n-1})^2 \end{aligned} \tag{28}$$

and so on. For the purpose of expressing the general formulae of this kind it is convenient to modify the sums S. Suppose we write the series $x_1 \ldots x_n$ preceded and followed by a number of zeros. The difference table will then appear as follows:

$$\begin{array}{lllll}
0 & & & & \\
 & 0 & & & \\
0 & & 0 & & \\
 & 0 & & -x_1 & \\
0 & & +x_1 & & \\
 & -x_1 & & 3x_1 - x_2 & \text{etc.} \\
x_1 & & -2x_1 + x_2 & & \\
 & x_1 - x_2 & & -3x_1 + 3x_2 - x_3 & \\
x_2 & & x_1 - 2x_2 + x_3 & & \\
 & x_2 - x_3 & & x_1 - 3x_2 + 3x_3 - x_4 & \\
x_3 & & x_2 - 2x_3 + x_4 & &
\end{array}$$

with a symmetrical effect at the other end. Writing now T_1, T_2, etc., for the sum of the squares of members in the first, second, etc., column of differences we see that

$$T_j = \sum_k \left\{ x_k - \binom{j}{1} x_{k+1} + \binom{j}{2} x_{k+2} \ldots \right\}^2, \tag{29}$$

where the summation now takes place over all values of x and there are no complications introduced by end effects. In fact, we have thrown the end effects into the sums T which replace the S's. In actually calculating the T's from the S's it is very little trouble to add the extra terms to the tables giving the latter; and when calculating the S's from the T's only the differences at the end of the table need be worked out.

We have then from (29), on expansion

$$T_j = P_0\left\{\binom{j}{0}^2+\binom{j}{1}^2+\dots\right\}+2(-1)^k\sum_k\left[P_k\left\{\binom{j}{0}\binom{j}{k}+\dots+\binom{j}{j-k}\binom{j}{j}\right\}\right]. \tag{30}$$

The coefficients of the various P's are easily seen to be equal to corresponding powers of t in

$$\left\{\binom{j}{0}t^0-\binom{j}{1}t+\binom{j}{2}t^2\dots\right\}\left\{\binom{j}{0}t^j-\binom{j}{1}t^{j-1}+\dots\right\},$$

i.e. in $(-1)^j(1-t)^{2j}$, and we find, on substitution in (30),

$$T_j = P_0\binom{2j}{j}-2P_1\binom{2j}{j-1}+2P_2\binom{2j}{j-2}+\dots+2(-1)^jP_j. \tag{31}$$

For example

$$\begin{aligned}
T_0 &= P_0,\\
T_1 &= 2P_0-2P,\\
T_2 &= 6P_0-8P_1+2P_2,\\
T_3 &= 20P_0-30P_1+12P_2-2P_3,\\
T_4 &= 70P_0-112P_1+56P_2-16P_3+2P_4,\\
T_5 &= 252P_0-420P_1+240P_2-90P_3+20P_4-2P_5,\\
T_6 &= 924P_0-1584P_1+990P_2-440P_3+132P_4-24P_5+2P_6,\\
T_7 &= 3432P_0-6006P_1+4004P_2-2002P_3+728P_4-182P_5+28P_6-2P_7,\\
T_8 &= 12870P_0-22880P_1+16016P_2-8736P_3+3640P_4-1120P_5+240P_6-32P_7+2P_8,\\
T_9 &= 48620P_0-87516P_1+63648P_2-37128P_3+17136P_4-6120P_5+1632P_6-306P_7\\
&\quad +36P_8-2P_9,\\
T_{10} &= 184756P_0-335920P_1+251940P_2-155040P_3+77520P_4-31008P_5+9690P_6\\
&\quad -2280P_7+380P_8-40P_9+2P_{10}.
\end{aligned} \tag{32}$$

The coefficients check in virtue of the fact that they sum to zero.

Conversely we have

$$\begin{aligned}
2P_0 &= 2T_0,\\
2P_1 &= -T_1+2T_0,\\
2P_2 &= T_2-4T_1+2T_0,\\
2P_3 &= -T_3+6T_2-9T_1+2T_0,\\
2P_4 &= T_4-8T_3+20T_2-16T_1+2T_0,\\
2P_5 &= -T_5+10T_4-35T_3+50T_2-25T_1+2T_0,\\
2P_6 &= T_6-12T_5+54T_4-112T_3+105T_2-36T_1+2T_0,\\
2P_7 &= -T_7+14T_6-77T_5+210T_4-294T_3+196T_2-49T_1+2T_0,\\
2P_8 &= T_8-16T_7+104T_6-352T_5+660T_4-672T_3+336T_2-64T_1+2T_0,\\
2P_9 &= -T_9+18T_8-135T_7+546T_6-1287T_5+1782T_4-1386T_3+540T_2-81T_1+2T_0,\\
2P_{10} &= T_{10}-20T_9+170T_8-800T_7+2275T_6-4004T_5+4290T_4-2640T_3+825T_2\\
&\quad -100T_1+2T_0.
\end{aligned} \tag{33}$$

The coefficients sum in turn to 2, 1, −1, −2, −1, 1, 2, etc. The coefficient of T_k in $2P_j$ is

$$(-1)^{j-k}\frac{2j}{j+k}\binom{j+k}{2k}.$$

REFERENCES

DAVIS, H. T. (1941). *The Analysis of Economic Time Series.* Bloomington, Indiana.

DODD, E. L. (1939). The length of the cycles which result from the graduation of chance elements. *Ann. Math. Statist.* **10**, 254.

KENDALL, M. G. (1941). The effect of the elimination of trend on oscillations in time series. *J. Roy. Statist. Soc.* **104**, 43.

YULE, G. UDNY (1927). On a method of investigating periodicities in disturbed series, with special reference to Wolfer's sunspot numbers. *Philos. Trans.* A, **226**, 267.

WALKER, SIR GILBERT (1931). On periodicity in series of related terms. *Proc. Roy. Soc.* A, **131**, 518.

WOLD, H. (1938). *A Study in the Analysis of Stationary Time-series.* Uppsala.

[9]

VOL. 13, NO. 3 WATER RESOURCES RESEARCH JUNE 1977

Advances in Box-Jenkins Modeling
1. Model Construction

KEITH WILLIAM HIPEL

Department of Systems Design, University of Waterloo, Waterloo, Ontario, Canada

ANGUS IAN MCLEOD

Department of Statistics, University of Waterloo, Waterloo, Ontario, Canada

WILLIAM C. LENNOX

Department of Civil Engineering, University of Waterloo, Waterloo, Ontario, Canada

Box-Jenkins modeling of time series data can be improved and simplified by adhering to contemporary modeling procedures. This paper gives the theory and techniques of the application of many recent advances that have been made at the identification, estimation, and diagnostic check stages of model development. The inverse autocorrelation function and the inverse partial autocorrelation function are demonstrated to be useful identification tools for both nonseasonal and seasonal models. Parameters can be estimated more efficiently by employing the modified sum of squares technique. At the estimation stage it is also possible to obtain a maximum likelihood estimate for a Box-Cox power transformation. The Akaike information criterion is introduced to formalize mathematically the concept of model parsimony. When checking for model adequacy, knowing the distribution of the residual autocorrelation allows for a sensitive test for residual whiteness. Diagnostic checks are given for verifying the assumption of homoscedasticity of the model residuals. In practice, heteroscedasticity and nonnormality of the residuals can often be removed by a Box-Cox transformation.

INTRODUCTION

In *Box and Jenkins* [1970] book on time series analysis they describe a family of linear stochastic models that are now commonly referred to as either Box-Jenkins or Arima (autoregressive integrated moving average) models. This work is in fact a culmination of the research of many prominent statisticians, starting with the pioneering work of *Yule* [1927].

When applying a Box-Jenkins model, or in general any type of stochastic model, to a particular problem it is recommended that the three stages of model development be adhered to [*Box and Jenkins*, 1970; *Box and Tiao*, 1973]. The first step is to identify the form of model that may fit the given data. At the estimation stage the model parameters are calculated by employing the method of maximum likelihood. Then the model is checked for possible inadequacies. If the diagnostic checks reveal serious anomalies, appropriate model modifications can be made by repeating the identification and estimation stage.

Since 1970 there have been numerous theoretical and technical application advances in Arima modeling. The purpose of this paper is to show recent innovations that have been made at the identification, estimation, and diagnostic check stages for both seasonal and nonseasonal Arima models. In an accompanying paper labeled part 2 [*McLeod et al.*, 1977] the utility of the methods described in this paper is illustrated by practical applications to actual time series. Although Arima models have previously been applied to hydrologic data [*Carlson et al.*, 1970; *McMichael and Hunter*, 1972; *McKerchar and Delleur*, 1974; *Tao and Delleur*, 1976], the authors maintain that the procedures outlined in this paper substantiate and simplify the modeling process and thereby further enhance the use of Box-Jenkins modeling in water resources. Furthermore, the contemporary modeling methods that are discussed are amenable for use in transfer function-noise model building and intervention analysis [*Hipel et al.*, 1975; *Hipel et al.*, 1977; *Hipel*, 1975; *Box and Tiao*, 1975].

Following a brief theoretical description of Arima difference equations, the three stages of Arima model building are discussed. Theoretical development is given where necessary, and the technique of application of all the methods considered is clearly explained for both nonseasonal and seasonal models. In the appendix the various subdivisions of the three stages of Arima modeling are summarized.

ARIMA PROCESS

Let $z_1, z_2, z_3, \cdots, z_{t-1}, z_t, z_{t+1}, \cdots, z_N$ be a discrete time series measured at equal time intervals. A seasonal Arima model for z_t is written as [*Box and Jenkins*, 1970]

$$\phi(B)\Phi(B^s)\{[(1 - B)^d(1 - B^s)^D z_t^{(\lambda)}] - \mu\} = \theta(B)\Theta(B^s)a_t \quad (1a)$$

or

$$\phi(B)\Phi(B^s)(w_t - \mu) = \theta(B)\Theta(B^s)a_t \quad (1b)$$

where

- $z_t^{(\lambda)}$ some appropriate transformation of z_t such as a Box-Cox transformation [*McLeod*, 1974; *Box and Cox*, 1964] (no transformation is a possible option);
- t discrete time;
- s seasonal length, equal to 12 for monthly river flows;
- B backward shift operator defined by $Bz_t^{(\lambda)} = z_{t-1}^{(\lambda)}$ and $B^s z_t^{(\lambda)} = z_{t-s}^{(\lambda)}$;
- μ mean level of the process, usually taken as the average of the w_t series (if $D + d > 0$ often $\mu \simeq 0$);
- a_t normally independently distributed white noise residual with mean 0 and variance σ_a^2 (written as NID $(0, \sigma_a^2)$);
- $\phi(B) = 1 - \phi_1 B - \phi_2 B^2 - \cdots - \phi_p B^p$ nonseasonal autoregressive (AR) operator or polynomial of order p such

Paper number 6W0879.

that the roots of the characteristic equation $\phi(B) = 0$ lie outside the unit circle for nonseasonal stationarity and the ϕ_i, $i = 1, 2, \cdots, p$ are the nonseasonal AR parameters;

$(1 - B)^d = \nabla^d$ nonseasonal differencing operator of order d to produce nonseasonal stationarity of the dth differences, usually $d = 0, 1$, or 2;

$\Phi(B^s) = 1 - \Phi_1 B^s - \Phi_2 B^{2s} - \cdots - \Phi_P B^{Ps}$ seasonal AR operator of order P such that the roots of $\Phi(B^s) = 0$ lie outside the unit circle for seasonal stationarity and the Φ_i, $i = 1, 2, \cdots, P$ are the seasonal AR parameters;

$(1 - B^s)^D = \nabla_s^D$ seasonal differencing operator of order D to produce seasonal stationarity of the Dth differenced data, usually $D = 0, 1$, or 2;

$w_t = \nabla^d \nabla_s^D z_t^{(\lambda)}$ stationary series formed by differencing $z_t^{(\lambda)}$ series ($n = N - d - sD$ is the number of terms in the w_t series);

$\theta(B) = 1 - \theta_1 B - \theta_2 B^2 - \cdots - \phi_q B^q$ nonseasonal moving average (MA) operator or polynomial of order q such that the roots of $\theta(B) = 0$ lie outside the unit circle for invertibility and θ_i, $i = 1, 2, \cdots, q$ are the nonseasonal MA parameters;

$\Theta(B^s) = 1 - \Theta_1 B^s - \Theta_2 B^{2s} - \cdots - \Theta_Q B^{Qs}$ seasonal MA operator of order Q such that the roots of $\Theta(B^s) = 0$ lie outside the unit circle for invertibility and the Θ_i, $i = 1, 2, \cdots, Q$ are the seasonal MA parameters.

The notation $(p, d, q) \times (P, D, Q)_s$ is used to represent the seasonal Arima model of (1). The first set of brackets contains the orders of the nonseasonal operators and the second pair of brackets has the orders of the seasonal operators. For example, a stochastic seasonal noise model of the form $(1, 1, 2) \times (0, 1, 1)_S$ with no data transformation is written as

$$(1 - \phi_1 B)\{[(1 - B)(1 - B^s)z_t] - \mu\} = (1 - \theta_1 B - \theta_2 B^2)(1 - \Theta_1 B^s)a_t \qquad (2)$$

If the model is nonseasonal, only the notation (p, d, q) is needed because the seasonal operators are not present.

When a seasonal model is stationary and requires no differencing (i.e., $D = 0$ and $d = 0$), it is often referred to simply as an Arma (autoregressive moving average) process. The notation $(p, q) \times (P, Q)_s$ is used to represent this type of model. If an Arma model is nonseasonal, the notation (p, q) is used to indicate the orders of the AR and MA operators, respectively. A pure nonseasonal AR process of order p with no differencing is often denoted by AR(p). Likewise, a nonseasonal MA process of order q is sometimes written as MA(q). Of course an AR(p) model can be represented equivalently by the notation $(p, 0)$ or $(p, 0, 0)$, while an MA(q) process can also be denoted by $(0, q)$ or $(0, 0, q)$.

METHOD OF ANALYSIS

1. *Identification*

The purpose of the identification stage is to determine the differencing required to produce stationarity and also the order of both the seasonal and the nonseasonal AR and MA operators for the w_t series. Although each identification technique is discussed separately, in practical applications the output from all the techniques is interpreted and compared together in order to design the type of model to be estimated.

If at the estimation stage it is decided that the data should be transformed by a Box-Cox transformation, in many cases this does not change the form of the model. However, this is not true in general, and as is pointed out by *Granger and Newbold* [1976], certain transformations can change the type of model to estimate. Therefore even though it is often not necessary to perform the identification stage for the transformed data, a researcher should be aware that in other instances this may not be the case. When a transformation does change the type of model to be used, diagnostic checks would detect this fact and then the transformed data can be properly identified.

In a typical Arima modeling application it is preferable that there be a minimum of about 50 data points in the w_t series in order to get reasonably accurate maximum likelihood estimates (mle) for the parameters. Therefore proceed with the identification stage only if at least the minimum required information is available.

a. Plot of the original series. A visual inspection of a plot of the time series may reveal one or more of the following characteristics: (1) seasonality, (2) trends either in the mean level or in the variance of the series, (3) persistence, (4) long-term cycles, or (5) extreme values and outliers.

b. Autocorrelation function (ACF). The ACF ρ_k measures the amount of linear dependence between observations in a time series that are separated by lag k. *Box and Jenkins* [1970, pp. 32–36] recommend a specific estimation procedure to determine an estimate r_k for ρ_k and also give approximate standard errors for the ACF estimates. To use the ACF in model identification, calculate and then plot r_k against lag k up to a maximum lag of roughly $N/4$.

The first step is to examine a plot of the ACF to detect the presence of nonstationarity in the z_t series. When the data are nonseasonal, failure of the ACF to damp out indicates that nonseasonal differencing is needed. For seasonally correlated data with the seasonal length equal to s the ACF often follows a wave pattern with peaks at s, $2s$, $3s$, and other integer multiples of s. As is shown by *Box and Jenkins* [1970, pp. 174–175], if the estimated ACF at lags that are integer multiples of the seasonal length s do not die out rapidly, this may indicate that seasonal differencing is needed to produce stationarity. Failure of other ACF estimates to damp out may imply that nonseasonal differencing is also required.

Once the data have been differenced just enough to produce nonseasonal stationarity for a nonseasonal time series and both seasonal and nonseasonal stationarity for seasonal data, then check the ACF of the w_t series to determine the number of AR and MA parameters required in the model. The w_t series is also used at the other steps of the identification procedure. Of course if no differencing is required, the w_t series is simply the z_t series. The ACF for w_t should not exceed a maximum lag of approximately $n/4$. For a seasonal model a maximum lag of about $5s$ (where $5s < n/4$) is usually sufficient.

If a series is white noise, then r_k is approximately NID $(0, 1/n)$. This result allows one to test whether a given series is white noise by checking to see if the ACF estimates are significantly different from zero. Simply plot confidence limits on the ACF diagram and see if a significant number of r_k values fall outside the chosen confidence interval.

When the w_t series is not white noise, then the following general rules may be invoked to help determine the type of model required.

Nonseasonal model: For a pure MA $(0, d, q)$ process, r_k cuts off and is not significantly different from zero after lag q. When the model is pure MA, after lag q [*Bartlett*, 1946],

$$\operatorname{Var} r_k \simeq \frac{1}{n}\left(1 + 2\sum_{l=1}^{q} r_l^2\right) \qquad k > q \tag{3}$$

If r_k tails off and does not truncate, this suggests that AR terms are needed to model the time series.

Seasonal model: When the process is a pure MA $(0, d, q) \times (0, D, Q)_s$ model, r_k truncates and is not significantly different from zero after lag $q + sQ$. For this case the variance of r_k after lag $q + sQ$ is [*Bartlett,* 1946]

$$\operatorname{Var} r_k \simeq \frac{1}{n}\left(1 + 2\sum_{l=1}^{q+sQ} r_l^2\right) \qquad k > q + sQ \tag{4}$$

If r_k attenuates at lags that are multiples of s, this implies the presence of a seasonal AR component. The failure of the ACF to truncate at other lags may imply that a nonseasonal AR term is required.

c. Partial autocorrelation function (PACF). The theoretical PACF ϕ_{kk} for an AR process of order k satisfies the Yule-Walker equations [*Box and Jenkins,* 1970, chapter 3]. For model identification calculate and plot the estimates $\hat{\phi}_{kk}$ of ϕ_{kk} against lag k. (The circumflex denotes an estimate of the theoretical statistic below it.) The $\hat{\phi}_{kk}$ are usually calculated for 20 to about 40 lags (where $40 < n/4$). For seasonal models, higher lags of the PACF may be required for identification.

The following general rules may prove helpful for interpreting the PACF of the w_t series.

Nonseasonal model: For a pure AR $(p, d, 0)$ process, $\hat{\phi}_{kk}$ truncates and is not significantly different from zero after lag p. After lag p, $\hat{\phi}_{kk}$ is approximately NID $(0, 1/n)$.

If $\hat{\phi}_{kk}$ tails off, this implies that MA terms are required.

Seasonal model: When the process is a pure AR $(p, d, 0) \times (P, D, 0)_s$ model, $\hat{\phi}_{kk}$ cuts off and is not significantly different from zero after lag $p + sP$. After lag $p + sP$, $\hat{\phi}_{kk}$ is approximately NID $(0, 1/n)$.

If $\hat{\phi}_{kk}$ damps out at lags that are multiples of s, this suggests the incorporation of a seasonal MA component into the model. The failure of the PACF to truncate at other lags may imply that a nonseasonal MA term is required.

d. Inverse autocorrelation function (IACF). Cleveland [1972] defines the IACF of a time series as the ACF associated with the inverse of the spectral density function of the series. The IACF pi_k can also be specified in an alternative equivalent manner. Consider the Box-Jenkins $(p, d, q) \times (P, D, Q)_s$ model given by (1*b*). The IACF of the w_t series is defined to be the ACF of the $(q, d, p) \times (Q, D, P)_s$ process that is written as

$$\theta(B)\Theta(B^s)(w_t - \mu) = \phi(B)\phi(B^s)a_t \tag{5}$$

To obtain an estimate ri_k for pi_k at lag k, *Cleveland* [1972] suggests employing either an AR or a smoothed periodogram estimation procedure. If the AR approach is adopted, the first step is to model the w_t series by a finite AR process of order r given by

$$(w_t - \mu) \simeq a_t + \sum_{l=1}^{r} \pi_l(w_{t-l} - \mu) \tag{6}$$

where π_l is the ith AR parameter when the model is written in inverted form. Estimates $\hat{\pi}_l$, where $i = 1, 2, \cdots, r$, for π_l can be determined from the Yule-Walker equations or from the mle of an AR process of order r. The estimates ri_k of the IACF can then be obtained from

$$ri_k = \left(-\hat{\pi}_k + \sum_{l=1}^{r-k} \hat{\pi}_l\hat{\pi}_{l+k}\right) \Big/ \left(1 + \sum_{l=1}^{r} \hat{\pi}_l^2\right) \tag{7}$$

To utilize the IACF for model identification, calculate and plot ri_k versus lag k. A recommended procedure is to choose about four values of r between 10 and about 40 (where $r < n/4$) and then to select the most representative graph from the set for use in identification. When the model is seasonal the IACF may be calculated for greater than 40 lags if more information is needed for proper identification. Because a selection procedure is required to choose an appropriate IACF plot, the authors suggest that an alternative estimation technique be developed in the future.

If the w_t series is white noise, then ri_k is approximately NID $(0, 1/n)$. When the data are correlated, the following properties of the IACF may be helpful for model identification.

Nonseasonal model: When the process is a pure AR $(p, d, 0)$ model, ri_k cuts off and is not significantly different from zero after lag p. In practice, the authors have found the IACF useful for identifying AR models which have some of the AR parameters equal to zero. At the same lags at which the AR parameters are zero the IACF often has values that are not significantly different from zero. *Cleveland* [1972, pp. 283, 284] substantiates the foregoing fact and shows by a worked example that the PACF fails to detect the AR parameters that are zero in a pure AR process.

If ri_k attenuates, this suggests the presence of a MA component.

Seasonal model: For a pure AR $(p, d, 0) \times (P, D, 0)_s$ process, ri_k truncates and is not significantly different from zero after lag $p + sP$.

If ri_k damps out but is still significant at lags s, $2s$, $3s$, etc., a seasonal MA component may be needed in the model. An additional nonseasonal MA component will cause ri_k to damp out for values between 1 and s, s and $2s$, etc., where decreasing but prominent peaks occur at s, $2s$, $3s$, etc., due to the seasonal MA term.

e. Inverse partial autocorrelation function (IPACF). The IPACF is defined in this paper as the PACF of (5). The 'inverse Yule-Walker equations' are given by

$$\begin{bmatrix} 1 & pi_1 & pi_2 & \cdots & pi_{k-1} \\ pi_1 & 1 & pi_1 & \cdots & pi_{k-2} \\ \cdot & \cdot & \cdot & & \cdot \\ \cdot & \cdot & \cdot & & \cdot \\ \cdot & \cdot & \cdot & & \cdot \\ pi_{k-1} & pi_{k-2} & pi_{k-3} & \cdots & 1 \end{bmatrix} \begin{bmatrix} \phi i_{k1} \\ \phi i_{k2} \\ \cdot \\ \cdot \\ \cdot \\ \phi i_{kk} \end{bmatrix} = \begin{bmatrix} pi_1 \\ pi_2 \\ \cdot \\ \cdot \\ \cdot \\ pi_k \end{bmatrix} \tag{8}$$

where pi_k is the IACF of the w_t series and ϕi_{kj} is the jth coefficient in a MA process of order k such that ϕi_{kk} is the last coefficient.

The coefficient ϕi_{kk} is called the IPACF. To get an estimate $\hat{\phi} i_{kk}$ for ϕi_{kk}, replace pi_k by the sample IACF ri_k and solve the inverse Yule-Walker equations for $\hat{\phi} i_{kk}$. For model identification plot $\hat{\phi} i_{kk}$ against lag k for the same number of lags as were chosen for the IACF.

Some of the inherent properties of the IPACF are listed below.

Nonseasonal model: If the process is a pure MA $(0, d, q)$ model, $\hat{\phi} i_{kk}$ truncates and is not significantly different from zero after lag q. After lag q, $\hat{\phi} i_{kk}$ is approximately NID $(0, 1/n)$.

When $\hat{\phi} i_{kk}$ dies off rather than cuts off, this suggests that AR terms are required.

Seasonal model: For a pure MA $(0, d, q) \times (0, D, Q)_s$ model, $\hat{\phi}i_{kk}$ truncates and is not significantly different from zero after lag $q + sQ$. After lag $q + sQ$, $\hat{\phi}i_{kk}$ is approximately NID $(0, 1/n)$.

If $\hat{\phi}i_{kk}$ attenuates at lags that are multiples of s, this may indicate the presence of a seasonal AR component. When the IPACF fails to cut off at other lags, this implies the need for a nonseasonal AR term.

f. Cumulative periodogram white noise test. As was mentioned previously, the ACF is an accepted means of checking whether the given data are white noise. The PACF, IACF, and IPACF can also be employed in this capacity. However, the cumulative periodogram provides another means of checking for white noise [*Bartlett*, 1966; *Box and Jenkins*, 1970, pp. 294–298].

In addition to verifying whether a series is uncorrelated, the cumulative periodogram also detects certain types of correlation. In particular, it is an effective procedure for finding hidden periodicities.

g. Summary of the identification techniques. A plot of the original data portrays an overall view of how the time series is generally behaving. However, the ACF, PACF, IACF, and IPACF transform the given information into a format whereby it is possible to detect the number of AR and MA terms required in the model. In general the ACF and the IPACF truncate for pure MA processes, while the PACF and IACF cut off for AR models. For mixed processes, all four functions attenuate.

The ACF and the IPACF possess similar general properties, while the PACF and the IACF have common attributes. However, the four functions are defined differently, and none of them behave exactly in the same fashion. In practice the authors have found that if the PACF fails to detect a certain property of the time series, then the IACF often may be more sensitive and thereby may clearly display the presence of that property and vice versa. A similar situation exists between the ACF and the IPACF. In actual applications it is necessary to consider simultaneously the output from all the functions in order to ascertain which model to estimate.

The incorporation of the IACF and the IPACF into the identification stage simplifies and substantiates this procedure because it is easier and more accurate to determine the proper Arima model to estimate. It is recommended that all the identification plots be programed for instantaneous display on a cathode ray terminal. In this way the identification stage can usually be completed in a few minutes. The capability of making an immediate copy of any results portrayed on a screen provides a convenient method of keeping a permanent record.

2. *Estimation*

a. Maximum likelihood estimates (mle) for the model parameters. *Box and Jenkins* [1970, chapter 7] suggest that the approximate mle for the Arima model parameters be obtained by employing the unconditional sum of squares method. When using this technique the unconditional sum of squares function is minimized to get least squares parameter estimates.

Recently, *McLeod* [1976*a*] has described a modified sum of squares method which provides parameter estimates that are closer approximations than those of *Box and Jenkins* [1970, chapter 7] to the exact maximum likelihood estimates. The modified sum of squares function is minimized in order to obtain the improved parameter estimates.

By utilizing simulation experiments, *McLeod* [1976*a*] demonstrates inherent assets of the modified estimation procedure. Some general conclusions regarding the advantages of the modified sum of squares method over the unconditional sum of squares technique are that (1) the modified method is more efficient, (2) the modified method gives better parameter estimates for shorter series, and (3) significantly improved parameter estimates are obtained for MA parameters. An additional advantage of the modified sum of squares method is that it is an exact mle procedure for AR processes.

Various optimization techniques are available to minimize functions such as the unconditional sum of squares function and the modified sum of squares function. Some of the optimization algorithms that have been extensively applied include (1) the Gauss linearization [*Draper and Smith*, 1966, chapter 10], (2) the steepest descent [*Draper and Smith*, 1966, chapter 10], (3) the Marquardt algorithm (combination of (1) and (2)) [*Marquardt*, 1963], and (4) conjugate directions [*Powell*, 1964, 1965]. *McLeod* [1976*a*] recommends the use of conjugate directions to minimize the modified sum of squares function. This approach is employed for obtaining parameter estimates for the applications in part 2 [*McLeod et al.*, 1977]. Improvements of the modified procedure over the unconditional sum of squares method are illustrated by the worked examples.

At the estimation stage, estimates are almost always calculated for the AR and MA parameters and σ_a^2 unless the exact value of a parameter is known in advance. For this situation the known parameter can be fixed, and only the remaining parameters are estimated. This is the usual approach taken for the parameter μ of the w_t series. In practice the mle for μ rarely differs from the arithmetic mean of the w_t series, and μ is usually assigned this value. If the data are differenced at least once either seasonally or nonseasonally, then μ usually has a value of zero. However, when it is suspected that a trend component is present, μ can be estimated [*Box and Jenkins*, 1970, pp. 91–93].

b. Box-Cox transformations. In Box-Jenkins modeling the residual a_t are assumed to be independent, homoscedastic (i.e., variance is a constant), and usually normally distributed. The independence assumption is the most important of all, and its violation can cause drastic consequences [*Box and Tiao*, 1973, p. 522]. However, if the constant variance and normality assumptions are not true, they are often reasonably well satisfied when the observations z_t are transformed by a Box-Cox transformation [*McLeod*, 1974, p. 14; *Box and Cox*, 1964].

The normality assumption of the residuals is usually not critical for obtaining good parameter estimates. As long as the a_t are independent and possess finite variance, reasonable estimates (called Gaussian estimates) of the parameters can be obtained [*Hannan*, 1970, p. 372]. *McLeod* [1974, pp. 76–85] demonstrates this fact by Monte Carlo experiments. Simulated data from specified models with known parameters are generated for the a_t distributed as uniform, double exponential, contaminated normal, and normal. For the first three cases, Gaussian estimates of the parameters for the generating model fit to the simulated data are very close to the known values. Of course this is also true for the mle of the parameters for the normal case.

In practice it is advantageous to satisfy the normality assumption reasonably well. First, it can be expected that parameter estimates will be at least slightly improved if a suitable transformation of the z_t is reflected to the a_t by causing them to become approximately normally distributed. Second, without the normality assumption, calculation of confidence intervals for the forecasted data would be impossible for practical use. Finally, if both heteroscedasticity and nonnormality of the residuals are present, then both these flaws can often be rectified simultaneously by a suitable Box-Cox transformation.

Consider power transformations of the form

$$\begin{aligned} z_t^{\lambda} &= \lambda^{-1}[(z_t + \text{const})^{\lambda} - 1] \qquad \lambda \neq 0 \\ z_t^{\lambda} &= \ln(z_t + \text{const}) \qquad \lambda = 0 \end{aligned} \tag{9}$$

where const is a constant. The log likelihood of all the AR and MA parameters, σ_a^2, μ (if this parameter is chosen to be estimated), λ, and const, is approximately [*McLeod*, 1974, p. 14]

$$Le \simeq -\frac{n}{2}\ln\frac{\text{mss}}{n} + (\lambda - 1)\sum_{t=d+sD+1}^{N}\ln(z_t + \text{const}) \tag{10}$$

where mss is the modified sum of squares [*McLeod*, 1976*a*]. When using the estimation procedure of *Box and Jenkins* [1970, chapter 7], the mss is replaced by the sum of squares.

Various approaches are available when determining the values of a Box-Cox transformation. Sometimes it is known in advance that the time series observations of a given phenomenon require a certain type of transformation. For this situation it is appropriate to specify fixed values for both λ and the constant prior to the identification and estimation stages. For example, the authors have found in practice that it is often necessary to transform average monthly river flow data by using natural logarithms. Therefore λ is set equal to zero, and the constant is also assigned a value of zero if no zero observations are present in the series. If there are one or more zero values in the series, the constant can be given a small positive value so that it is possible to take natural logarithms.

In certain instances a chosen standardized transformation, such as a natural logarithm or a square root, may fail to remove heteroscedasticity and/or nonnormality of the residuals. It may therefore be desirable to compute a mle of λ. The first step is to choose a value for the constant that causes all the values of the given series to be greater than zero. Then λ can be estimated simultaneously with the other model parameters.

Calculation of the best Box-Cox transformation for a particular model involves a significant increase in computer time in comparison with the computer time used when λ is not estimated for that model. Therefore it is not recommended that λ be estimated unless diagnostic checks for the residuals indicate that the normality and/or constant variance assumptions are not satisfied.

When it is desired to economize on computer time or when a computer package does not have the capability of estimating λ, it is still possible to select reasonable values for this parameter. Assign the constant a value such that all values of the series have magnitudes greater than zero. Then calculate the log likelihood for, say, $\lambda = 0$, ± 0.5, and ± 1.0, and choose the λ value that gives the largest likelihood.

c. Akaike information criterion (AIC). *Box and Jenkins* [1970] stress the need to use as few model parameters as possible (i.e., the model should be parsimonious) so that the model passes all the diagnostic checks. The AIC [*Akaike*, 1974] is a mathematical formulation of the parsimony criterion of model building.

When there are several competing models to choose from, select the model that gives the minimum of the AIC defined by

$$\text{AIC} = -2\ln(\text{maximum likelihood}) + 2k \tag{11}$$

where k is the number of AR and MA parameters to estimate. If μ and/or λ are also estimated, then k is increased by 1 for each extra parameter.

In certain instances the use of the AIC replaces the need for hypothesis testing. Therefore the requirement of subjective judgment for choosing the level of significance in hypothesis testing and the use of statistical tables are explicitly formulated as estimation problems. For example, in part 2 [*McLeod et al.*, 1977] it is questioned whether an AR(3) model is appropriate to model the average annual flows of the Saint Lawrence River at Ogdensburg, New York. Because mle possess a limiting normal distribution [*Pierce*, 1972], by using the estimated standard errors and subjectively choosing a level of significance, hypothesis testing can be done for the model parameters. It is shown that ϕ_2 is not significantly different from zero and therefore should be eliminated from the model. Alternatively, the AIC may be employed for this decision process. For this particular example the AIC also selects an AR model of the order of 3 with ϕ_2 constrained to zero in preference to an AR(3) model.

In the recent past the AIC has been applied to various types of stochastic problems. *Akaike* [1974, 1972*b*] has employed the AIC to select a final Arima model among competing Box-Jenkins models fit to the time series under consideration. The AIC has also been utilized to choose the number of independent variables required in a regression analysis [*Akaike*, 1972*a*], to decide upon the number of factors needed in a factor analysis [*Akaike*, 1972*a*], and to determine the order of a Markov chain process [*Tong*, 1975].

Parzen [1974] introduces a criterion for selecting the order of an AR process to fit to a time series if the series is generated by an AR scheme of finite order. However, Parzen's criterion can be shown to be asymptotically equivalent to the AIC. Because the AIC can also be used for AR processes as well as for many other types of stochastic models, the authors recommend implementation of the AIC in preference to Parzen's approach.

3. *Diagnostic Checks*

One class of diagnostic checks is devised to test model adequacy by overfitting (section 3*a*). This test assumes that the possible types of model inadequacies are known in advance.

However, most diagnostic tests deal with the residual assumptions in order to determine whether the a_t are independent (section 3*b*), homoscedastic (section 3*c*), and normally distributed (section 3*d*). Residual estimates are needed for the tests used in checking the three aforementioned residual assumptions. The estimates for a_t are automatically calculated at the estimation stage along with the mle for the parameters.

A data transformation cannot correct dependence of the residuals because the lack of independence indicates the present model is inadequate. Rather, the identification and estimation stages must be repeated in order to determine a suitable model. If the less important assumptions of homoscedasticity and normality are violated, they can often be corrected by a Box-Cox transformation of the data.

a. Overfitting. Overfitting involves fitting a more elaborate model than the one estimated to see if including one or more parameters greatly improves the fit. Extra parameters should be estimated for the more complex model only where it is feared that the simpler model may require more parameters. For example, the PACF and the IACF may possess decreasing but significant values at lags 1, 2, and 9. If an Arma (2, 0) model is originally estimated, then a model to check by overfitting the model would be

$$(1 - \phi_1 B - \phi_2 B^2 - \phi_9 B^9)(z_t - \mu) = a_t \qquad (12)$$

A mle estimate of ϕ_9 three or four times its standard error would definitely indicate that the more elaborate model should be selected. For this case the AIC and also the remaining tests in this diagnostic check stage would also point out the complex model as the best one to use. *Box and Newbold* [1971] show another interesting application of overfitting. The practitioner must take care to avoid model redundancy which could occur if the AR and MA components were simultaneously enlarged.

Another method of testing model adequacy by overfitting, which was originally suggested by *Whittle* [1952], is to fit a high-order AR model of order r (where $20 < r < 30$). Suppose the original model has $k = p + P + q + Q$ parameters estimated and estimated residual variance $\hat{\sigma}_a^2(k)$. Then it is shown [*McLeod*, 1974, p. 39] that the likelihood ratio statistic is

$$n \ln (\hat{\sigma}_a^2(k)/\hat{\sigma}_a^2(r)) \simeq \chi^2(r - k) \qquad (13)$$

where $\hat{\sigma}_a^2(r)$ is the residual variance estimate for an AR process of order r. If the calculated $\chi^2(r - k)$ from (13) is greater than $\chi^2(r - k)$ from the tables at a chosen significance level, then a model with more parameters is needed.

The likelihood ratio test in (13) can also be used to determine if a model containing fewer parameters gives as good a fit as the full model. Specific examples are given in part 2 [*McLeod et al.*, 1977] for the Saint Lawrence River data. The AIC can also be employed to decide whether a model with less parameters is preferable to a model with more parameters.

b. Tests for whiteness of the residuals. To determine whether the residual a_t are white noise, an appropriate procedure is to examine the residual autocorrelation function (RACF). Because the distribution of the RACF which is shown in the theorem below is now known, new sensitive testing techniques are available for checking the independence assumption of a_t.

The theorem for the RACF is developed as follows. The ACF $r_k(\hat{a})$ of the calculated residuals can be determined by

$$r_k(\hat{a}) = \sum_{t=k+1}^{n} \left(\hat{a}_t \hat{a}_{t-k} \Big/ \sum_{t=1}^{n} \hat{a}_t^2\right) \qquad (14)$$

Define the vector of the first L value of the RACF as

$$\mathbf{r}(\hat{a}) = [r_1(\hat{a}), r_2(\hat{a}), \cdots, r_L(\hat{a})]' \qquad (15)$$

Denote by $\psi_k(\Phi)$ the coefficient of B^k in the Maclaurin series expansion of $[\Phi(B^s)]^{-1}$ in powers of B, and similarly define $\psi_k(\phi)$, $\psi_k(\Theta)$, and $\psi_k(\theta)$. Then it can be proved for large samples [*McLeod*, 1976*b*] that

$$\mathbf{r}(\hat{a}) \simeq N[0, (1/n)\mathbf{U}] \qquad (16)$$

where $\mathbf{U} = \mathbf{1}_L - \mathbf{X}'\mathbf{I}^{-1}\mathbf{X}$, $\mathbf{1}_L$ is the identity matrix, $\mathbf{I} \simeq \mathbf{X}'\mathbf{X}$ is the large-sample information matrix, and $\mathbf{X} = [\psi_{i-js}(\Phi), \psi_{i-j}(\phi), \psi_{i-js}(\Theta), \psi_{i-j}(\theta)]$ are the i, j entries in the four partitions of the $\mathbf{X}$ matrix. The dimensions of the matrices $\mathbf{X}$, $\Psi_{i-js}(\Phi)$, $\psi_{i-j}(\phi)$, $\psi_{i-js}(\Theta)$, and $\psi_{i-j}(\theta)$ are, respectively, $L \times (P + p + Q + q)$, $L \times P$, $L \times p$, $L \times Q$, and $L \times q$.

Previously, *Box and Pierce* [1970] obtained this result for the nonseasonal AR case, but the theorem listed here is valid for a general seasonal Box-Jenkins model, transfer function-noise models, and intervention processes.

There are two useful applications of the RACF distribution theorem. A sensitive diagnostic check is first to plot the RACF along with the asymptotic significance intervals for the RACF that are obtained from the diagonal entries of the matrix $(1/n)\mathbf{U}$. If some of the RACF are significantly different from zero, this may mean that the present model is inadequate. The important RACF to examine are the RACF at the first few lags for a nonseasonal model and the RACF at the first couple of lags and also at lags that are multiples of s for a seasonal model. If the present model is insufficient, a proper model can be selected either by changing the model as suggested by *Box and Jenkins* [1970, p. 299] or by repeating the identification, estimation, and diagnostic check stages of model construction.

A second but less sensitive test is to calculate and to perform a significance test for the portmanteau statistic U_L. If L is large enough so that the weights $\psi_k(\Phi)$, $\psi_k(\phi)$, $\psi_k(\Theta)$, and $\psi_k(\theta)$ have damped out, then

$$U_L = n \sum_{l=1}^{L} r_l^2(\hat{a}) \simeq \chi^2(L - P - p - Q - q) \qquad (17)$$

where L can usually be given a value from 15 to 25 for nonseasonal models and a value of $4s$ for seasonal processes. A test of this hypothesis can be done for model adequacy by choosing a level of significance and then comparing the value of the calculated χ^2 to the actual χ^2 value from the tables. If the calculated value is greater, on the basis of the available data the present model is inadequate, and appropriate changes must be made. Note that *Box and Jenkins* [1970, p. 503] have subtracted one too many degrees of freedom.

An alternative approach that can be used to check for whiteness of the residuals is to examine the cumulative periodogram of the $\hat{a}_t$. However, when considering the residuals it should be remembered that this test is known to be inefficient. Often the cumulative periodogram test fails to indicate model inadequacy due to dependence of the residuals unless the model is a very poor fit to the given data.

c. Homoscedasticity checks of the residuals. The following tests described by *McLeod* [1974] are useful for determining whether a transformation of the data is needed by checking for changes in variance (heteroscedasticity) of the residuals. As was indicated earlier, the variance of the normally independently distributed residuals is assumed to be constant (homoscedastic). Suppose that a_t is NID $[0, \sigma_a^2(t)]$ and that the variance changes with time as $\sigma_a^2(t)$. Let the stochastic random variable ζ_t be NID $(0, \sigma^2)$ and hence have constant variance. Suppose then that

$$a_t = \exp\{(\chi/2)[K(t) - \bar{K}]\}\, \zeta_t \qquad (18)$$

where χ is some constant to be estimated, $K(t)$ is a function of time to be specified, and $\bar{K}$ is the mean of $K(t)$ and equals $n^{-1}\sum_{t=1}^{n} K(t)$. The variance of the a_t residuals is then

$$\sigma_a^2(t) = E\{\exp[\chi(K(t) - \bar{K})]\, \zeta_t^2\} = \exp\{\chi[K(t) - \bar{K}]\}\, \sigma^2 \qquad (19)$$

It can be shown [*McLeod*, 1974, p. 46] that the natural logarithm of the likelihood Lh for σ^2 and χ is

$$Lh = -\frac{n}{2} \ln \sigma^2 - \frac{1}{2\sigma^2} \sum_{t=1}^{n} \{\exp[-\chi(K(t) - \bar{K})]a_t^2\} \qquad (20)$$

and

$$\frac{\partial Lh}{\partial \chi} = \frac{1}{\sigma^2} \sum_{t=1}^{n} \{K(t) \exp[-\chi(K(t) - \bar{K})]a_t^2\} \qquad (21)$$

Solve $\partial Lh/\partial\sigma^2 = 0$ exactly for σ^2, and substitute for σ^2 into (21). Equation (21) is set equal to zero, and the residual estimates $\hat{a}_t$ obtained from the estimation stage are used for a_t. This equation is solved for a mle of χ by using the Newton-Raphson method with an initial value of $\chi = 0$.

In order to carry out a test of the hypothesis, the first step is to postulate the null hypothesis that $\chi = 0$ and therefore to assume that the residuals have constant variance. The alternative hypothesis is that the residuals are heteroscedastic and that $\chi \neq 0$. By putting $K(t) = t$ in the previous equations it is possible to test for trends in variance of the residuals over time. If $K(t) = w_t - \hat{a}_t$, then one can check for changes of variance depending on the current level of the series. A likelihood ratio test of the null hypothesis is obtained by computing the mle of χ and comparing it with its standard error. The variance for the mle $\hat{\chi}$ for χ is calculated by using the equation

$$\mathrm{Var}\ \hat{\chi} = -1/(\partial^2 Lh/\partial\chi^2) \qquad (22)$$

Because the mle for χ is asymptotically normally distributed, after a level of significance is chosen it is a straightforward procedure to determine whether to accept or to reject the null hypothesis. This test is also valid for transfer function-noise, intervention, and regression models. In regression models the test for heteroscedasticity can indicate whether an important covariate is missing [*Anscombe,* 1961; *Pierce,* 1971].

If model inadequacy is revealed by either of the tests, a simultaneous estimation procedure can be used to estimate the seasonal and nonseasonal AR and MA parameters σ^2 and χ. This would involve an enormous amount of computer time. However, in practice, the Box-Cox transformation described in the estimation stage will often stabilize the variance.

d. Tests for normality of the residuals. Many standard tests are available to check whether data are normally distributed. For instance, the graph of the cumulative distribution of the residuals should appear as a straight line when plotted on normality paper if the residuals are normally distributed [*Daniel and Wood,* 1971].

Normally distributed data should possess no significant skewness. The skewness g_1 of the residuals is calculated from

$$g_1 = \left(\frac{1}{n}\sum_{t=1}^{n}\hat{a}_t^3\right)\Big/\left(\frac{1}{n}\sum_{t=1}^{n}\hat{a}_t^2\right)^{3/2} \qquad (23)$$

It can be shown that g_1 is approximately N (0, $6/n$).

If the data are normally distributed they should not have a significant g_2 kurtosis coefficient that is given as

$$g_2 = \left(\frac{1}{n}\sum_{t=1}^{n}\hat{a}_t^4\right)\Big/\left(\frac{1}{n}\sum_{t=1}^{n}\hat{a}_t^2\right)^2 - 3 \qquad (24)$$

The statistic g_2 is approximately N (0, $24/n$). In practice a Box-Cox transformation of the data will often remove any significant skewness or pronounced kurtosis, thereby reinforcing the normality assumption of the residuals.

CONCLUSIONS

Various new procedures are now available to strengthen the three stages of Arima model construction. The IACF and the IPACF are two identification methods that allow for more versatility when designing an Arima model to estimate. All the identification techniques can be used for selecting either a nonseasonal or a seasonal Box-Jenkins model to fit to the data. By employing the modified sum of squares method, more efficient parameter estimates can be obtained. New diagnostic checks are available for checking the independence and homoscedasticity assumptions of the model residuals. If the residuals fail to satisfy the constant variance and/or the normality assumption, often a Box-Cox transformation can rectify the situation. When there are various possible models available for modeling the data, the AIC can be utilized to select the most appropriate model and at the same time to insure model parsimony.

Because of the nature of stochastic problems that occur in water resources the use of Box-Jenkins modeling in this particular field should increase dramatically in the future. The authors recommend that any researcher who deals with Arima modeling use the contemporary procedures that are outlined in this paper Since all the techniques can be programed, this means that for practical applications the methods can be implemented easily.

Often the expenses incurred when developing an Arima model are insignificant when compared to the costs of various types of applications of the model and also the penalty costs that can arise if an incorrect decision is made due to modeling nature improperly. For example, when a model is employed to simulate data for the economic design of a water resource project, it may be relatively expensive to generate on the computer a sufficient amount of synthetic data. This generated data can be used as input to the economic design of a project such as a reservoir. If the synthetic data are produced by a model that does not fit the data properly, then the final design for the project will be suspect. Furthermore, possible grave economic and social consequences could occur once the project is constructed. Therefore it is advantageous to use the best procedures possible when a model is originally fit to the historical data.

In part 2 [*McLeod et al.,* 1977], Box-Jenkins models are determined for both nonseasonal and seasonal data. The practical applications illustrate the effectiveness of the techniques given in this paper. These methods can also be used for transfer function-noise modeling and intervention analysis.

APPENDIX: STAGES IN BOX-JENKINS MODELING

1. Identification
   a. Plot of the original series
   b. Autocorrelation function (ACF)
   c. Partial autocorrelation function (PACF)
   d. Inverse autocorrelation function (IACF)*
   e. Inverse partial autocorrelation function (IPACF)*
   f. Cumulative periodogram white noise test (to see if the given series is white noise or correlated and if seasonal components are present)
2. Estimation
   a. Maximum likelihood estimates (mle) for the model parameters (modified sum of squares technique)*
   b. Box-Cox transformations*
   c. Akaike information criterion (AIC)*
3. Diagnostic Checks
   a. Overfitting*
   b. Tests for whiteness of the residuals (examination of the residual autocorrelation function (RACF) including the distribution of the RACF estimates)*
   c. Homoscedasticity checks of the residuals (test to check for changes in variance of the residuals over time and also changes depending on the current level of the series to see if a Box-Cox transformation is needed)*

d. Tests for normality of the residuals (skewness and kurtosis checks to determine if a Box-Cox transformation is required)

(Recent advances on the sections followed by asterisks are discussed in this paper.)

NOTATION

a_t white noise time series value at time t.
AR(p) AR process of order p.
B backward shift operator.
const additive constant for a Box-Cox transformation.
d order of the nonseasonal differencing operator.
D order of the seasonal differencing operator.
$E(z_t)$ expected value of z_t.
g_1 estimated residual skewness.
g_2 estimated residual kurtosis.
I large-sample information matrix.
$K(t)$ specified function of time in the homoscedasticity test for the residuals.
$\bar{K}$ mean of $K(t)$.
ln natural logarithms.
Le log likelihood for Box-Cox transformation.
Lh log likelihood in the homoscedasticity checks.
mle maximum likelihood estimates.
MA(q) MA process of order q.
mss modified sum of squares.
n length of w_t series.
NID normally independently distributed random variable.
N (a, b) normally distributed random variable with mean a and variance b.
N length of z_t time series.
p order of the nonseasonal AR operator.
(p, d) nonseasonal Arma model.
(p, d, q) nonseasonal Arima model.
$(p, d) \times (P, Q)$ seasonal Arma model.
$(p, d, q) \times (P, D, Q)_s$ seasonal Box-Jenkins Arima model.
P order of the seasonal AR operator.
q order of the nonseasonal MA operator.
Q order of the seasonal MA operator.
r_k ACF estimate at lag k.
ri_k estimate for the IACF pi_k.
$r_k(\hat{a})$ ACF of $\hat{a}_t$ at lag k.
$\mathbf{r}(\hat{a})$ vector of ACF for $\hat{a}_t$ up to lag L.
s seasonal length.
t discrete time.
U_L portmanteau statistic calculated from the estimates of the RACF up to lag L.
$(1/n)\mathbf{U}$ covariance matrix for $\mathbf{r}(\hat{a})$.
Var $\hat{\chi}$ variance of $\hat{\chi}$.
w_t stationary series formed by differencing the $z_t^{(\lambda)}$ series.
X matrix used in the calculation of the information and covariance matrix.
z_t discrete time series value at time t.
$z_t^{(\lambda)}$ transformation of z_t series.
ζ_t random variable that is NID (0, σ^2).
$\theta(B)$ nonseasonal MA operator of order q.
θ_i ith nonseasonal MA parameter.
$\Theta(B^s)$ seasonal MA operator of order Q.
Θ_i ith seasonal MA parameter.
λ exponent for Box-Cox transformation.
μ mean level of the w_t series.
π_i ith AR parameter when the model is written in inverted form.
ρ_k ACF at lag k.
pi_k IACF at lag k.
σ^2 variance of the random variable ζ_t.
σ_a^2 variance of a_t.
$\sigma_a^2(k)$ residual variance of a process with k parameters.
$\sigma_a^2(r)$ residual variance for an AR process of order r.
$\sigma_a^2(t)$ variance of a_t as a function of time.
$\phi(B)$ nonseasonal AR operator of order p.
ϕ_i ith nonseasonal AR parameter.
ϕ_{kk} PACF (kth coefficient for an AR process of order k).
ϕi_{kj} jth coefficient in a MA process of order k.
ϕi_{kk} IPACF (kth coefficient for a MA process of order k).
$\Phi(B^s)$ seasonal AR operator of order P.
Φ_i ith seasonal AR parameter.
χ constant to be estimated in the homoscedasticity test for the residuals.
$\chi^2(k)$ chi-squared random variable with k degrees of freedom.
$\psi_k(\Phi)$ coefficient of B^k in the Maclaurin series expansion of $[\Phi(B^s)]^{-1}$.
$\psi_k(\phi)$ coefficient of B^k in the expansion of $[\phi(B)]^{-1}$.
$\psi_k(\Theta)$ coefficient of B^k in the expansion of $[\Theta(B^s)]^{-1}$.
$\psi_k(\theta)$ coefficient of B^k in the expansion of $[\theta(B)]^{-1}$.
∇^d nonseasonal differencing operator of order d.
∇_s^D seasonal differencing operator of order D.
$\mathbf{I}_L$ identity matrix.

Acknowledgments. The authors appreciate advice given by T. E. Unny of the Civil Engineering Department of the University of Waterloo. The research was supported by the National Research Council of Canada.

REFERENCES

Akaike, H., Automatic data structure search by the maximum likelihood, paper presented at 5th Hawaii International Conference on System Sciences, Inform. Sci. Program, Dep. of Elec. Eng., Univ. of Hawaii, Honolulu, 1972*a*.

Akaike, H., Use of an information theoretic quantity for statistical model identification, paper presented at 5th Hawaii International Conference on System Sciences, Inform. Sci. Program, Dep. of Elec. Eng., Univ. of Hawaii, Honolulu, 1972*b*.

Akaike, H., A new look at the statistical model identification, *IEEE Trans. Automat. Contr., AC-19*(6), 716–723, 1974.

Anscombe, F. J., Examination of residuals, Paper presented at 4th Berkeley Symposium, Berkeley, Calif., 1961.

Bartlett, M. S., On the theoretical specification of sampling properties of autocorrelated time series, *J. Roy. Statist. Soc., Ser. B, 8*, 27–41, 1946.

Bartlett, M. S., *Stochastic Processes*, Cambridge University Press, New York, 1966.

Box, G. E. P., and D. R. Cox, An analysis of transformations, *J. Roy. Statist. Soc., Ser. B, 26*, 211–252, 1964.

Box, G. E. P., and G. M. Jenkins, *Time Series Analysis: Forecasting and Control*, Holden-Day Inc., San Francisco, Calif., 1970.

Box, G. E. P., and P. Newbold, Some comments on a paper of Coen, Gomme and Kendall, *J. Roy. Statist. Soc., Ser. A, 2*, 229–240, 1971.

Box, G. E. P., and D. A. Pierce, Distribution of autocorrelations in autoregressive integrated moving average time series models, *J. Amer. Statist. Ass., 65*, 1509–1526, 1970.

Box, G. E. P., and G. C. Tiao, *Bayesian Inference in Statistical Analysis*, Addison-Wesley, Reading, Mass., 1973.

Box, G. E. P., and G. C. Tiao, Intervention analysis with applications to economic and environmental problems, *J. Amer. Statist. Ass., 70*, 70–79, 1975.

Carlson, R. F., A. J. A. MacCormick, and D. G. Watts, Application of linear random models to four annual streamflow series, *Water Resour. Res., 6*(4), 1070–1078, 1970.

Cleveland, W. S., The inverse autocorrelations of a time series and their applications, *Technometrics, 14*(2), 277–298, 1972.

Daniel, C., and F. S. Wood, *Fitting Equations to Data*, Wiley-Interscience, New York, 1971.
Draper, N. R., and H. Smith, *Applied Regression Analysis*, John Wiley, New York, 1966.
Granger, C. W. J., and P. Newbold, Forecasting transformed series, *J. Roy. Statist. Soc., Ser. B, 38*, 189–203, 1976.
Hannan, E. J., *Multiple Time Series*, John Wiley, New York, 1970.
Hipel, K. W., Contemporary Box-Jenkins modelling in hydrology, Ph.D. thesis, Univ. of Waterloo, Waterloo, Ont., Canada, 1975.
Hipel, K. W., W. C. Lennox, T. E. Unny, and A. I. McLeod, Intervention analysis in water resources, *Water Resour. Res., 11*(6), 855–861, 1975.
Hipel, K. W., A. I. McLeod, and E. A. McBean, Stochastic modeling of the effects of reservoir operation, *J. Hydrol., 32*, 97–113, 1977.
Marquardt, D. W., An algorithm for least squares estimation of nonlinear parameters, *J. Soc. Ind. Appl. Math., 11*(2), 431–441, 1963.
McKerchar, A. I., and J. W. Delleur, Application of seasonal parametric linear stochastic models to monthly flow data, *Water Resour. Res., 10*(2), 246–255, 1974.
McLeod, A. I., Contributions to applied time series, masters thesis, Univ. of Waterloo, Waterloo, Ont., Canada, 1974.
McLeod, A. I., Improved Box-Jenkins estimators, report, Dep. of Statist., Univ. of Waterloo, Waterloo, Ont., Canada, 1976*a*.
McLeod, A. I., Distribution of the residual autocorrelations in seasonal Arima models, report, Dep. of Statist., Univ. of Waterloo, Waterloo, Ont., Canada, 1976*b*.
McLeod, A. I., K. W. Hipel, and W. C. Lennox, Advances in Box-Jenkins modeling, 2, Applications, *Water Resour. Res., 13*, this issue, 1977.
McMichael, F. C., and J. S. Hunter, Stochastic modeling of temperature and flow in rivers, *Water Resour. Res., 8*(1), 87–98, 1972.
Parzen, E., Some recent advances in time series modeling, *IEEE Trans. Automat. Contr., AC-19*(6), 723–730, 1974.
Pierce, D. A., Distribution of residual autocorrelation in the regression model with autoregressive moving average errors, *J. Roy. Statist. Soc., Ser. B, 33*, 140–146, 1971.
Pierce, D. A., Least squares estimation in dynamic-disturbance time series models, *Biometrika, 59*(1), 73–78, 1972.
Powell, M. J. D., An efficient method for finding the minimum of a function of several variables without calculating derivatives, *Comput. J., 7*, 155–162, 1964.
Powell, M. J. D., A method for minimizing a sum of squares of nonlinear functions without calculating derivatives, *Comput. J., 8*, 303–307, 1965.
Tao, P. C., and J. W. Delleur, Seasonal and nonseasonal Arma models in hydrology, *J. Hydraul. Div. Amer. Soc. Civil Eng., HY10*, 1541–1559, 1976.
Tong, H., Determination of the order of a Markov chain by Akaike's information criterion, *J. Appl. Probab., 12*, 488–497, 1975.
Whittle, P., Tests of fit in time series, *Biometrika, 39*, 309–318, 1952.
Yule, G. U., On a method of investigating periodicities in disturbed series, with special reference to Wolfer sunspot numbers, *Phil. Trans. Roy. Soc. London, Ser. A, 226*, 267–298, 1927.

(Received June 19, 1975;
revised November 11, 1976;
accepted November 15, 1976.)

[10]

VOL. 13, NO. 3 WATER RESOURCES RESEARCH JUNE 1977

Advances in Box-Jenkins Modeling
2. Applications

ANGUS IAN MCLEOD

Department of Statistics, University of Waterloo, Waterloo, Ontario, Canada

KEITH WILLIAM HIPEL

Department of Systems Design, University of Waterloo, Waterloo, Ontario, Canada

WILLIAM C. LENNOX

Department of Civil Engineering, University of Waterloo, Waterloo, Ontario, Canada

Recent Box-Jenkins techniques are employed to determine both nonseasonal and seasonal models for actual time series. The applied examples are carefully explained in order to demonstrate the utility of the new procedures that have been developed for use at the identification, estimation, and diagnostic check stages of model development. Even though more methods are now available for model building, it is demonstrated that this fact enhances rather than complicates the model construction phases. Furthermore, for all three applications considered, better models are obtained than it was previously possible to obtain. A new technique is described for optimal forecasting of the original time series when the data have been transformed by a nonlinear transformation.

INTRODUCTION

Improved Box-Jenkins modeling procedures are available to simplify model construction. As is explained by *Hipel et al.* [1977*a*], new methods have been developed for use at the identification, estimation, and diagnostic check stages of model development. The purpose of this paper is to demonstrate the relative ease with which improved models can be obtained in practical applications by employing recent modeling procedures.

A constrained nonseasonal autoregressive integrated moving average (Arima) model is determined for average annual river flows, a nonmultiplicative Arima process is fit to a yearly sunspot number series, and a multiplicative seasonal Box-Jenkins model is found for modeling monthly international airline passenger data. In all three cases, better models are obtained than those previously cited in the literature. It is shown at the identification stage how a simultaneous inspection of the autocorrelation function (ACF), partial autocorrelation function (PACF), inverse autocorrelation function (IACF), and inverse partial autocorrelation function (IPACF) leads to a quick but usually accurate initial design for a tentative model to estimate. All four identification procedures are used for identifying both the nonseasonal and the seasonal model. At the estimation stage, more efficient parameter estimates are procured by using the modified sum of squares method [*McLeod*, 1976*a*]. In particular, better parameter estimates than those calculated by using the unconditional sum of squares technique [*Box and Jenkins*, 1970, chapter 7] are obtained for the moving average (MA) terms of the seasonal Arima model that is fit to the airline passenger data. The Akaike information criterion (AIC) is used for model discrimination purposes [*Akaike*, 1974] for both the yearly river flow and the sunspot model. The independence assumption of the model residuals is tested by a sensitive diagnostic check. This is accomplished by calculating significance intervals [*McLeod*, 1976*b*] for the estimates of the residual autocorrelation function (RACF). Other diagnostics tests are employed to determine whether the homoscedasticity and normality assumptions are also fulfilled [*Hipel et al.*, 1977*a*; *McLeod*, 1974].

This paper clearly demonstrates for practical applications the exact use of the contemporary model-building methods discussed in an accompanying paper labeled part 1 [*Hipel et al.*, 1977*a*]. However, if necessary the reader is urged to refer to part 1 (in this issue) for an account of the general rules of the application of the modeling procedures or for a theoretical description of the techniques.

In some time series applications the given data are often transformed by a nonlinear transformation such as a Box-Cox transformation. By employing the methods of *Granger and Newbold* [1976] it is now possible to obtain minimum mean square error (mmse) forecasts of the original series when the data have been changed by a nonlinear transformation. The procedure for obtaining mmse forecasts of the untransformed data when there has been a Box-Cox square root transformation is described for the sunspot model. If there has been a natural logarithmic transformation of the data, then the technique of procuring mmse forecasts of the original observations is presented with the airline passenger model.

SAINT LAWRENCE RIVER

Average annual river flows from 1860 to 1957 for the Saint Lawrence River at Ogdensburg, New York, are available from a report by *Yevyevich* [1963]. *Carlson et al.* [1970] fit a (1, 0, 0) model to these data. However, by employing the contemporary approaches to model construction given in part 1 [*Hipel et al.*, 1977*a*] the authors derive a better model for the Saint Lawrence River flows.

In order to identify the form of the model to estimate, the plots of the ACF, PACF, IACF, and IPACF that are drawn in Figures 1–4, respectively, are examined. The ACF does not truncate but rather damps out, suggesting the presence of autoregressive (AR) terms. The 10%, 5%, and 1% significance intervals for the graph of the PACF are for values of the PACF at lags greater than p if the process is $(p, d, 0)$. Notice

Paper number 6W0880.

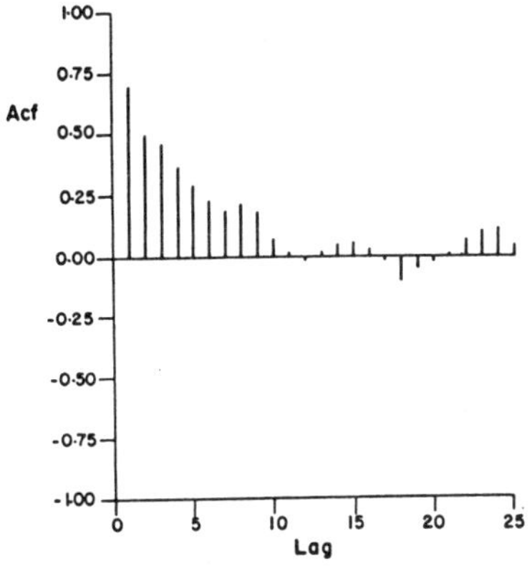

Fig. 1. ACF for the Saint Lawrence River.

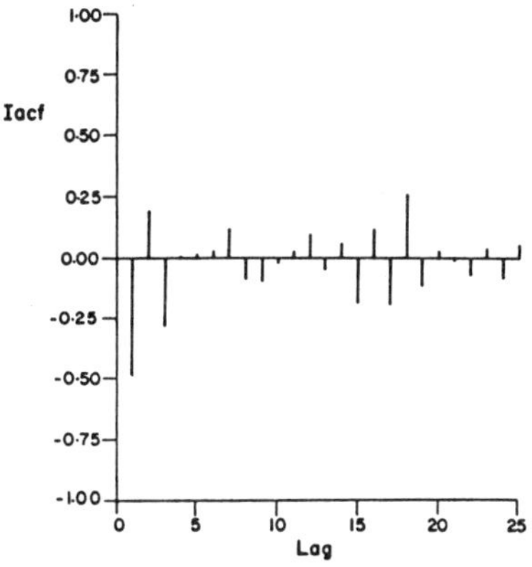

Fig. 3. IACF for the Saint Lawrence River.

that the PACF possesses a significant value at lag 1 and has a value at lag 3 that just touches the 5% significance limit. This effect is more clearly illustrated by the IACF which has definite large values at lags 1 and 3. It may therefore be appropriate to entertain a (3, 0, 0) model with ϕ_2 constrained to zero as a possible process to fit to the Saint Lawrence River data. Although there is a rather large value of the PACF at lag 19 and of the IACF at lag 18, this could be due to chance alone. The IPACF appears to be attenuating rather than truncating. However, for this particular example the ACF definitely damps out, and therefore one would suspect that the IPACF is behaving likewise, thereby indicating the need for AR terms. On the graph for the IPACF (Figure 4) the 10%, 5%, and 1% significance intervals are for values of the IPACF at lags greater than q if the process is (0, d, q).

For the case of the Saint Lawrence River data the IACF most vividly defines the type of model to estimate. However, the remaining three identification graphs reinforce the conclusions drawn from the IACF. Although it is suspected that a (3, 0, 0) model with ϕ_2 constrained to zero should be estimated, a (1, 0, 0) and a (3, 0, 0) model are examined for comparison purposes. *Carlson et al.* [1970] choose a (1, 0, 0) model to estimate for the Saint Lawrence River flows because they only employ the ACF for identification purposes. This illustrates the importance of having many identification procedures so that the proper model is not missed just because one of the identification methods does not explicitly portray the best model to fit.

Table 1 lists the maximum likelihood estimates of the parameter and the standard errors for a (1, 0, 0) model, a (3, 0, 0) model, and a (3, 0, 0) model without the ϕ_2 parameter. The parameter estimates are calculated by using the modified sum of squares technique [*McLeod,* 1976*a*].

Model discrimination can be accomplished by comparing parameter estimates to their standard errors, by using the AIC or by performing the likelihood ratio test. In order to employ the first procedure, first consider the models listed in Table 1. Notice that for both the (3, 0, 0) model and the (3, 0, 0) model without ϕ_2 the estimte $\hat{\phi}_3$ for ϕ_3 is more than twice its standard error. (The circumflex denotes an estimate of the theoretical statistic below it.) Therefore it can be argued that even at the 1% significance level, ϕ_3 is significantly different from

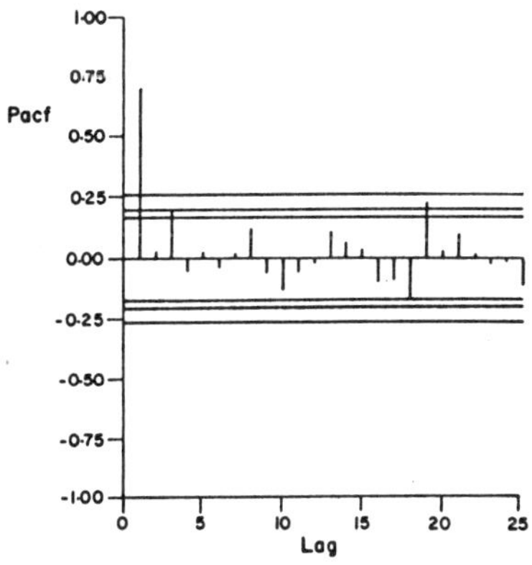

Fig. 2. PACF for the Saint Lawrence River.

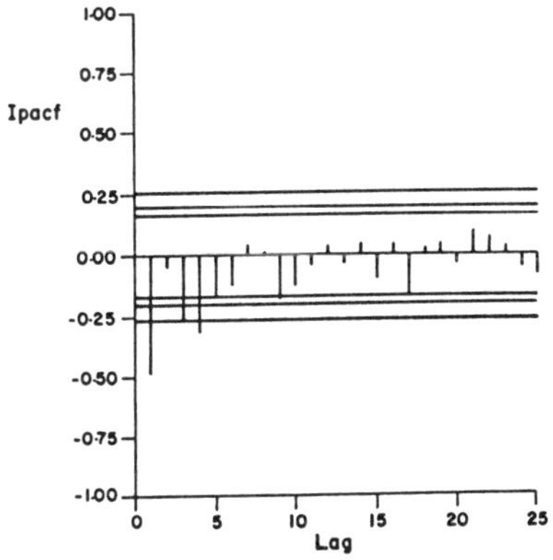

Fig. 4. IPACF for the Saint Lawrence River.

TABLE 1. Parameter Estimates for the Saint Lawrence River Arima Models

Parameter	Maximum Likelihood Estimate	Standard Error
	(1, 0, 0) Model	
ϕ_1	0.7114	0.0714
σ_a	419.66	
	(3, 0, 0) Model	
ϕ_1	0.6584	0.0991
ϕ_2	−0.0863	0.1192
ϕ_3	0.2180	0.0991
σ_a	408.94	
	(3, 0, 0) Model without ϕ_2	
ϕ_1	0.6219	0.0839
ϕ_3	0.1771	0.0840
σ_a	410.15	

zero and should be included in the model. Consequently, the (1, 0, 0) model should not be utilized to model the Saint Lawrence River flows. Furthermore, because the standard error for $\hat{\phi}_2$ for the (3, 0, 0) model is greater than $\hat{\phi}_2$, for model parsimony the (3, 0, 0) model without ϕ_2 is the proper model to select.

When the AIC is employed for model selection, it is not necessary to select subjectively a significance level, as is done in hypothesis testing. By using (11) in the paper by *Hipel et al.* [1977*a*] the AIC for the (1, 0, 0) model, the (3, 0, 0) model, and the (3, 0, 0) model without ϕ_2 are calculated, respectively, as 1176.00, 1175.50, and 1172.07. The (3, 0, 0) model without ϕ_2 has the minimum AIC, and therefore the AIC also indicates that this model should be chosen in preference to the others.

The likelihood ratio test given by *Hipel et al.* [1977*a*] in (13) can be utilized to choose between the (1, 0, 0) model and the (3, 0, 0) model with $\phi_2 = 0$. By substituting $n = 97$, $k = 1$, the residual variance of the (1, 0, 0) model for $\hat{\sigma}_a^2(k)$, $r = 2$, and the residual variance of the (3, 0, 0) model with $\phi_2 = 0$ for $\hat{\sigma}_a^2(r)$, the calculated χ^2 statistic has a magnitude of 4.58. For 1 d.f. this value is significant at the 5% significance level. Therefore this test indicates that the (3, 0, 0) model with $\phi_2 = 0$ should be selected in preference to the (1, 0, 0) model.

The likelihood ratio test can also be employed to test whether a (3, 0, 0) model without ϕ_2 gives as good a fit as the (3, 0, 0) model. Simply substitute into (13) [*Hipel et al.*, 1977*a*], $n = 97$, $k = 2$, the residual variance of the (3, 0, 0) model with $\phi_2 = 0$ for $\hat{\sigma}_a^2(k)$, $r = 3$, and the residual variance of the (3, 0, 0) model for $\hat{\sigma}_a^2(r)$. The calculated χ^2 statistic possesses a value of 0.0569. For 1 d.f. this value is certainly not significant even at the 50% significance level. Therefore the constrained model without ϕ_2 gives an adequate fit and should be used in preference to the (3, 0, 0) model in order to achieve model parsimony. The Arima difference equation for the best model is written as

$$(1 - 0.6219B - 0.1771B^3)(z_t - 6842.25) = a_t \qquad (1)$$

where 6842.25 is the mle of the mean of the z_t series.

Diagnostic checks are done to insure that the proper model is selected by checking that assumptions of Arima modeling such as independence, constant variance, and normality of the residual a_t are satisfied. The model in (1) passes all diagnostic checks. The critical assumption of independence can be checked by various methods. However, a sensitive testing procedure is to plot the RACF along with the chosen significance intervals. Figure 5 shows a plot of the RACF for the (3, 0, 0) model with $\phi_2 = 0$. As is the case for all the plots in the application section that possess significance intervals, the 10%, 5%, and 1% intervals are drawn in Figure 5. Although the RACF at lag 18 is rather large, it still lies within the 1% significance interval. This larger value could be due to inherent random variation or to the length of the time series used to estimate it. However, the important values of the RACF for the lower lags all lie well within the 10% significance interval. Therefore the RACF indicates that the chosen model for the Saint Lawrence River satisfies the independence assumption. This fact is also confirmed by the χ^2 distributed portmanteau statistic U_L that is listed in (17) by *Hipel et al.* [1977*a*]. The calculated magnitude of U_L is 13.46 for 18 d.f.

The less important modeling assumptions of homoscedasticity and normality of the residuals are also satisfied. The χ statistic for changes in variance depending on the current level of the series [*Hipel et al.*, 1977*a*] has a magnitude of 0.000081 and a standard error of 0.000341, while the χ statistic for trends in the variance over time [*Hipel et al.*, 1977*a*] possesses a value of 0.002917 with a corresponding standard error of 0.00504. Because in both instances the standard error is greater than the χ statistic, then based upon the information used, it can be assumed that the residuals are homoscedastic. The skewness statistic g_1 for the residuals [*Hipel et al.*, 1977*a*, equation (23)] has a value of −0.1482 and a standard error of 0.3046. The kurtosis statistic g_2 [*Hipel et al.*, 1977*a*, equation (24)] possesses a value of −0.3240 and a standard error of 0.4974. Due to the fact that the standard errors for both g_1 and g_2 are greater than the corresponding statistic, the normality assumption is reasonably well satisfied. Because the residuals are normally distributed and homoscedastic, a Box-Cox transformation of the given data is not required.

The flows used for the Saint Lawrence River are in cubic meters per second. However, if the flows had been in cubic feet per second and a model had been fit to these data, all the AR parameters and standard errors would have been identical with the metric model in (1). Only the mean level of the series and σ_a^2 would be different. In general, no matter what units of measurement are used the AR and the MA parameter estimates and the standard errors will remain the same (for both a nonseasonal and a seasonal model), while the mean level and σ_a^2 will be different.

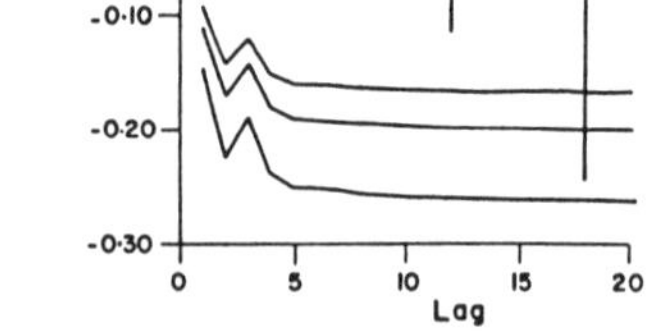

Fig. 5. RACF for the (3, 0, 0) model with $\phi_2 = 0$ for the Saint Lawrence River.

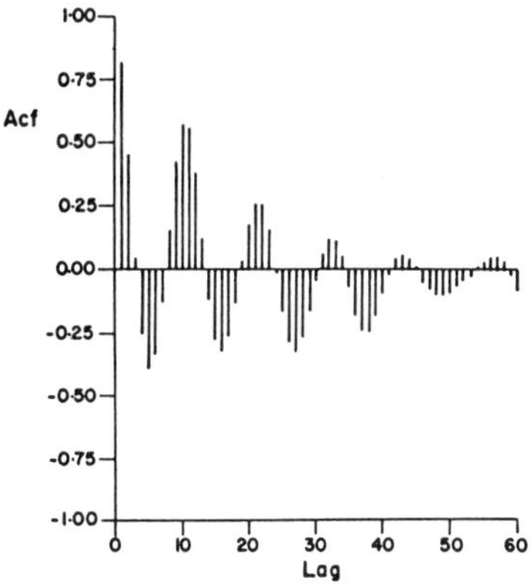

Fig. 6. ACF of the yearly sunspot numbers.

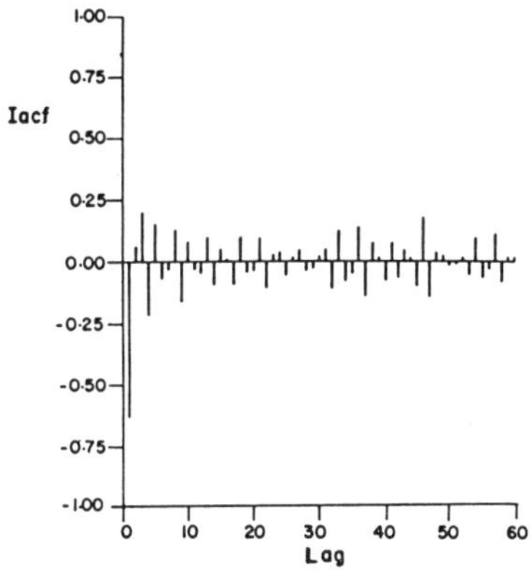

Fig. 8. IACF of the yearly sunspot numbers.

The type of model fit to the Saint Lawrence River data reflects the actual physical situation. The Great Lakes all flow into the Saint Lawrence River, and due to their immense size they are capable of over-year storage. If there is an unusually wet or an unusually dry year, the Great Lakes dampen the effect of extreme precipitation on the flows of the Saint Lawrence River. Because of this the average annual flows are correlated, and the correct model is an AR process rather than white noise.

ANNUAL SUNSPOT NUMBERS

The yearly Wolfer sunspot number series is available from 1700 to 1960 in the work of *Waldmeier* [1961]. This series is examined in this paper because of the historical controversies regarding the selection of a suitable model to fit to yearly sunspot numbers and also because sunspot data are of practical importance to geophysicists. Recently, climatologists have discovered that sunspot activity may be important for studying climatic change because of its effect upon global temperature variations [*Schneider and Mass,* 1975]. Also sunspots have long been known to affect the transmission of electromagnetic signals.

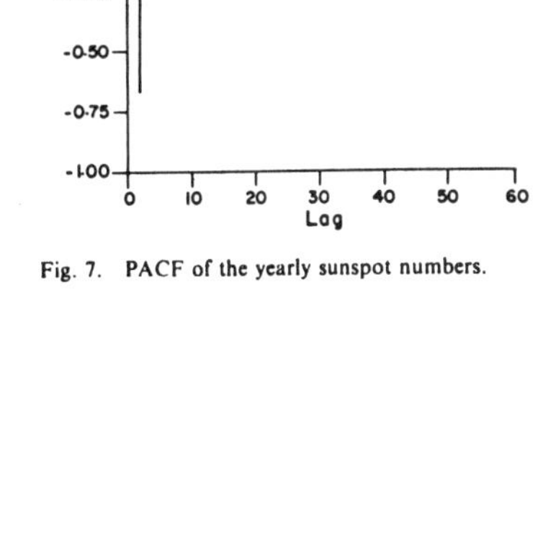

Fig. 7. PACF of the yearly sunspot numbers.

Yule [1927] was the first applied statistician who considered employing an AR process of the order of 2 to model yearly sunspot numbers. *Moran* [1954] examined various types of models for predicting annual sunspot numbers and expressed the need for a better model than an AR(2) process. *Box and Jenkins* [1970, p. 239] fit an AR(3) model to yearly sunspot data. The authors of this paper recommend an AR(9) process with ϕ_3–ϕ_8 constrained to zero to model the annual sunspot series.

Other researchers have determined stochastic sunspot models when the basic time interval is smaller than 1 year. For example, *Whittle* [1954] considered a unit of time of 6 months and developed a bivariate AR scheme to fit to the observed sunspot intensities in the northern and southern solar hemispheres. *Granger* [1957] proposed a special two-parameter curve for the monthly sunspot numbers, but unfortunately, this curve is not useful for forecasting.

The inherent stochastic characteristics of the yearly Wolfer sunspot series complicate the identification of an Arima model to fit to the data. For example, the fact that *Granger* [1957] found that the periodicity of sunspot data follows a uniform distribution with a mean of about 11 years is one reason that historically researchers have had difficulties in modeling sunspot numbers. However, an examination of the graphs of the sunspot ACF, PACF, IACF, and IPACF that are displayed, respectively, in Figures 6–9 does yield some insight into the type of model required to model the sunspot numbers. The ACF follows an attenuating sine wave pattern that reflects the random periodicity of the data and possibly indicates the need for nonseasonal and/or seasonal AR terms in the model. The behavior of the PACF could also signify the need for some type of AR model. In addition to possessing significant values at lags 1 and 2, the PACF also has rather large values at lags 6–9. The IACF has a large magnitude at lag 1, which suggests the importance of a nonseasonal AR lag 1 term in any eventual process that is chosen to estimate. The damping out effect in the first four lags of the IPACF could be a result of a nonseasonal AR component.

When an AR(2) process is fit to the yearly sunspot numbers, the independence, normality, and homoscedasticity assumptions of the residuals are not satisfied. The RACF possesses large values at lags 1, 2, 4, 9, 10, and 11, while the portmanteau statistic U_L has a magnitude of 27.42 for 9 d.f. These facts

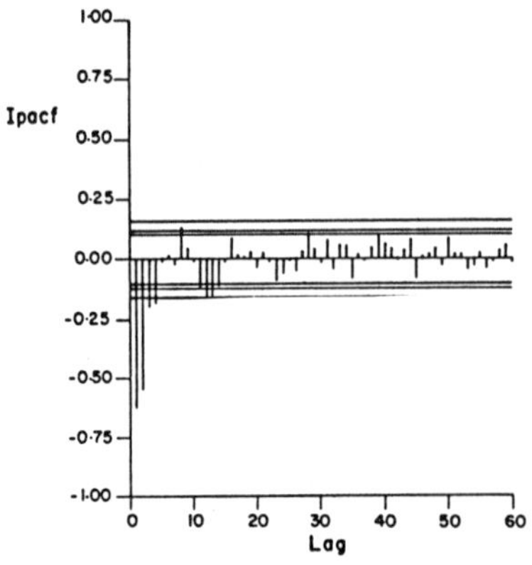

Fig. 9. IPACF of the yearly sunspot numbers.

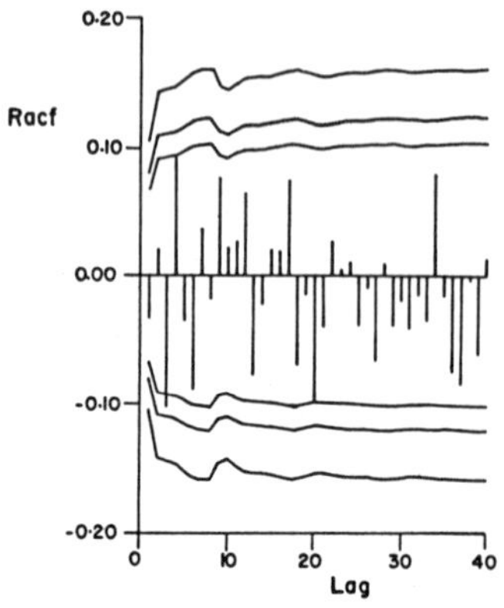

Fig. 10. RACF of the constrained sunspot model.

signify that the residuals are not uncorrelated and that a better model is therefore required. The χ statistic for changes in variance depending on the current level of the series, the χ statistic for trends in the variance over time, the skewness statistic g_1, and the kurtosis statistic g_2 all possess a magnitude that is more than twice their corresponding standard errors. This indicates that a Box-Cox transformation is needed to remove heteroscedasticity and nonnormality of the residuals. By substituting $\lambda = 0.5$ and const $= 1.0$ into (9) in the work of *Hipel et al.* [1977*a*] a Box-Cox transformation causes the residuals to be homoscedastic and approximately normally distributed. The parameter constant is set equal to 1 because there are some zero values in the sunspot time series. A data transformation usually cannot correct residual correlation, and a different type of model than an AR(2) process is therefore required to rectify the situation.

If an AR(3) model with $\lambda = 0.5$ and const $= 1.0$ is estimated, the $\hat{\phi}_3$ parameter has a magnitude of -0.1032 and a standard error of 0.0616. Because $\hat{\phi}_3$ is less than twice its standard error, for the sake of model parsimony it should not be incorporated into the model. Note that ***Box and Jenkins*** [1970, p. 239, Table 7.13] obtain a parameter estimate for ϕ_3 that is just slightly more than twice its standard error. However, Box and Jenkins do not employ a data transformation to remove heteroscedasticity and nonnormality and only use the Wolfer sunspot series from 1770 to 1869.

The RACF for the residual estimates of the AR(3) model possesses a large value at lag 9. This fact implies that it may be advisable to estimate an AR(9) process with ϕ_3–ϕ_8 constrained to zero. The estimates and standard errors for this model are listed in Table 2, while the difference equation is written in (2):

$$(1 - 1.2434B + 0.5192B^2 - 0.1954B^9) \cdot (z_t^{(\lambda)} - 11.77) = a_t \qquad (2)$$

where $z_t^{(\lambda)} = (1/0.5)[(z_t + 1.0)^{0.5} - 1.0]$ and 11.77 is the mle of the mean of the $z_t^{(\lambda)}$ series for the constrained AR(9) model.

The model in (2) satisfies all the modeling assumptions of the residuals. A plot of the RACF in Figure 10 shows that the residuals are uncorrelated. All of the estimated values of the RACF fall within the 5% significance interval. The χ^2 distributed portmanteau statistic U_L has a value of 18.85 for 22 d.f. Therefore the U_L statistic also confirms that the residuals are not correlated. The diagnostic checks for homoscedasticity and normality of the residuals reveal that these assumptions are also fulfilled. The model in (2) therefore adequately models the yearly Wolfer sunspot numbers. Other types of constained models were examined, but the AR(9) process with ϕ_3–ϕ_8 constrained to zero is the only model that was found to be satisfactory.

An alternative approach to modeling the sunspot series by a constrained model is to consider a multiplicative Box-Jenkins seasonal process. The large values of the PACF at lags 1 and 2 in Figure 7 indicate the need for the nonseasonal AR parameters ϕ_1 and ϕ_2. The behavior of the ACF in Figure 6 could be due to a seasonal AR component. On the basis of these facts and other previously mentioned information it is appropriate to estimate the parameters of a $(2, 0, 0) \times (1, 0, 0)_9$ model. The parameter estimates and standard errors for this seasonal model with $\lambda = 0.5$ and const $= 1.0$ are given in Table 3. The multiplicative seasonal Arima difference equation is written in (3):

TABLE 2. Parameter Estimates for the Constrained Sunspot Model

Parameter	Maximum Likelihood Estimate	Standard Error
ϕ_1	1.2434	0.0470
ϕ_2	−0.5192	0.0458
ϕ_9	0.1954	0.0249
σ_a	2.0569	

TABLE 3. Parameter Estimates for the Seasonal Sunspot Model

Parameter	Maximum Likelihood Estimate	Standard Error
ϕ_1	1.3783	0.0456
ϕ_2	−0.6770	0.0460
Φ_1	0.2142	0.0616
σ_a	2.1958	

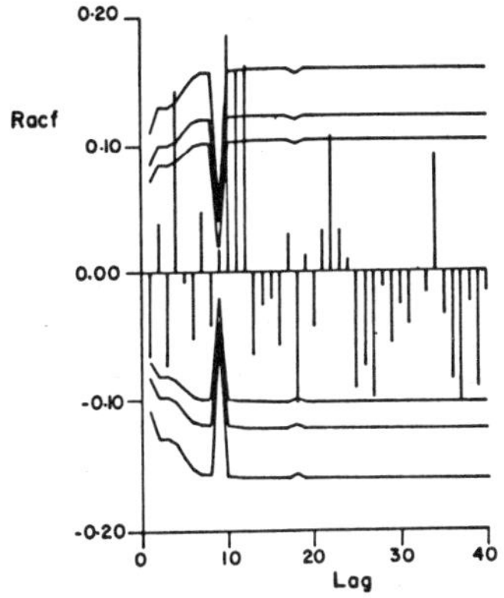

Fig. 11. RACF of the seasonal sunspot model.

$$(1 - 1.3783B + 0.6770B^2)(1 - 0.2142B^9) \cdot (z_t^{(\lambda)} - 10.62) = a_t \qquad (3)$$

where $z_t^{(\lambda)} = (1/0.5)[(z_t + 1.0)^{0.5} - 1.0]$ and 10.62 is the mle of the mean of the $z_t^{(\lambda)}$ series for the seasonal model.

Unfortunately, the seasonal model in (3) does not fare well with the whiteness checks. As is shown in Figure 11, the RACF possesses a large value at lag 10 that lies well outside the 1% significance interval. The RACF estimates at lags 4 and 12 are also outside the 1% significance interval, while the RACF at lag 11 just touches the 1% significance limit. The U_L statistic has a value of 43.35 for 22 d.f. This fact also indicates that the seasonal model is inadequate to model properly the sunspot data. Other diagnostic checks reveal that the homoscedasticity and normality assumptions are reasonably well satisfied. Although the authors examined other types of multiplicative seasonal Arima models, the process in (3) could not be improved upon by another multiplicative seasonal model.

From the foregoing discussion regarding a process to model the sunspot data it is evident that the constrained AR(9) process gives the best fit. The AIC can also be employed to verify which is the best model to select. The AIC for the AR(2), the AR(3), the seasonal Arima $(2, 0, 0) \times (1, 0, 0)_9$, and the constrained AR(9) model without ϕ_3–ϕ_8 are calculated to be, respectively, 1332.02, 1331.30, 1323.51, and 1288.63. For all four types of models the data are transformed by setting $\lambda = 0.5$ and const = 1.0. The constrained AR(9) process has the minimum AIC, and therefore according to the AIC decision-making procedure this model should be selected in preference to the other three. Because the constrained AR(9) model is chosen in preference to a seasonal model, it is also referred to as a nonmultiplicative model.

An important application of Arima models in water resources is forecasting. *Box and Jenkins* [1970, chapter 5] describe how to obtain mmse forecasts for Arima models if the original data have not been transformed by a nonlinear transformation. The same technique also applies for forecasting transformed values if the Arima model has been fit to transformed data. Recently, *Granger and Newbold* [1976] discussed a mmse method of forecasting the original series when there has also been a nonlinear transformation.

Let $z_t^{(\lambda)}(k)$ denote a mmse forecast at origin t for lead time k for the transformed series. The exponent of $z_t^{(\lambda)}(k)$ could, for example, indicate some type of Box-Cox transformation. A naive approach to obtain a forecast for the original untransformed series would be to take the inverse transformation of $z_t^{(\lambda)}(k)$. However, *Granger and Newbold* [1976] describe an optimal procedure for procuring a forecast $z_t(k)$ at origin t for lead time k for the untransformed series.

As an illustrative example, consider the sunspot series model where there is a Box-Cox transformation with $\lambda = 0.5$ and const = 1.0. This transformation is written as

$$z_t^{(\lambda)} = (1.0/\lambda)[(z_t + \text{const})^{\lambda} - 1.0] \qquad (4)$$

where $\lambda = 0.5$ and const = 1.0. *Granger and Newbold* [1976, p. 197] give the mmse forecast of the untransformed series as

$$z_t(k) = [0.5z_t^{(\lambda)}(k) + 1.0]^2 - [1.0 + \text{Var}(k)] \qquad (5)$$

where $z_t(k)$ is the mmse forecast of the original series, $z_t^{(\lambda)}(k)$ is the mmse forecast of the $z_t^{(\lambda)}$ series obtained by using the methods of *Box and Jenkins* [1970, chapter 5], and Var (k) is the variance of the forecast error of $z_t^{(\lambda)}(k)$ [*Box and Jenkins*, 1970, p. 128, equation (5.1.16)].

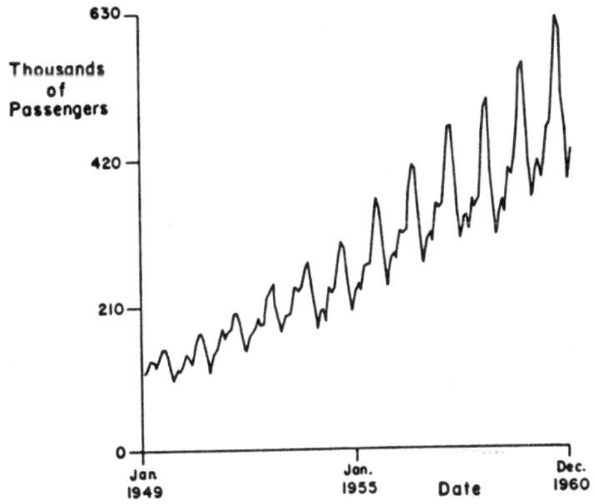

Fig. 12. Total monthly international airline passenger data.

AIRLINE PASSENGER DATA

Total monthly international airline passenger data from 1949 to 1960 are listed by *Box and Jenkins* [1970, p. 531]. Although Box and Jenkins determine a model for the airline passenger data, the same model is reformulated in this paper to demonstrate the usefulness of the contemporary methods described by *Hipel et al.* [1977*a*] for seasonal model construction.

A plot of the airline passenger data in Figure 12 reveals important information about the observations. The periodic peaks in the data reflect the seasonality of the observations. The series is seasonal due to a high travel period during the summer months and a lesser peak travel time in the spring. It is obvious from the general magnitude increase of all the data with time that there is a linear trend component present. In some instances a physical understanding of the process being analyzed allows for the incorporation of deterministic components into the model to account for seasonality and/or trends. For instance, seasonality may be modeled by a Fourier

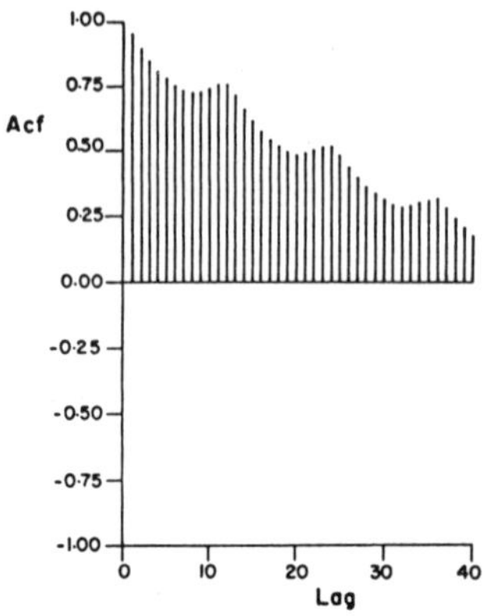

Fig. 13. ACF of the logarithmic airline data.

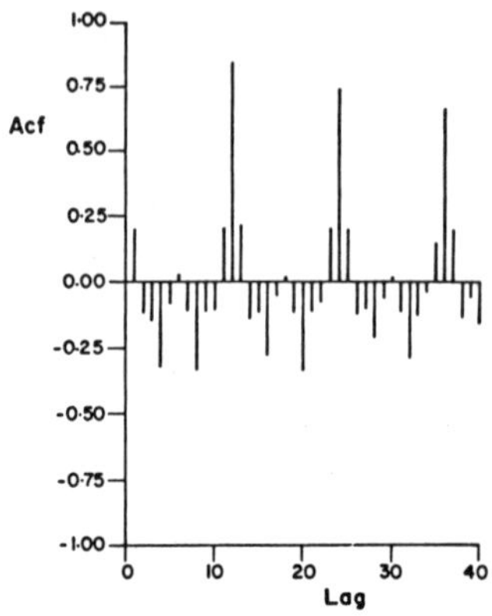

Fig. 15. ACF of the nonseasonally differenced logarithmic airline data.

series, while trend might be accounted for by a polynomial. However, for the airline passenger data a pure stochastic seasonal Arima model is fit to the data. This model stochastically accounts for the inherent properties of the given data.

Another important characteristic of the raw data is that the variance increases with time. This fact is detected by noticing the escalating amplitude of the seasonal wave pattern. A change in variance over time of the original data would eventually be mirrored by heteroscedasticity in the residuals of the model fit to the data. To rectify the situation from the start, natural logarithms are taken of the data.

The ACF of the logarithmic airline data that are plotted in Figure 13 demonstrates that the logarithmic data are seasonal due to the pronounced peaks of the ACF at lags that are multiples of 12. Because the ACF attenuates very slowly, this indicates the need for seasonal and/or nonseasonal differencing. Figure 14 illustrates that seasonal differencing removes the seasonal wave pattern in the ACF but fails to cause the ACF to damp out more rapidly than it does in Figure 13. When calculating the ACF in Figure 14, or in general when computing the ACF of any series that has been differenced, the mean of the w_t series is not removed. This procedure precludes missing any deterministic component that may still be present even after differencing. As is demonstrated in Figure 15, nonseasonal differencing of the logarithmic airline data fails to remove large but slowly decaying values of the ACF at lags that are multiples of 12. Therefore it is appropriate to difference the logarithms of the observations both seasonally and nonseasonally. Figure 16 illustrates that no further differencing of the logarithmic data is required because the ACF appears to more or less truncate after lag 12.

In order to identify the number of AR and MA terms required in the model of the nonseasonally and the seasonally differenced logarithmic airline data, the graphs of the ACF, the PACF, the IACF, and the IPACF that are shown in Figures 17–19, respectively, are interpreted simultaneously. Notice that both the ACF and the IPACF have significant values at lags 1 and 12. This indicates that possibly both a nonseasonal and a seasonal MA term are required. The IACF plot reinforces these conclusions.There are rather large values

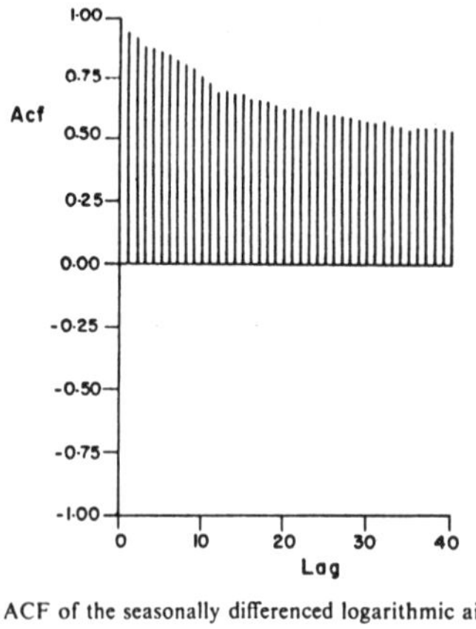

Fig. 14. ACF of the seasonally differenced logarithmic airline data.

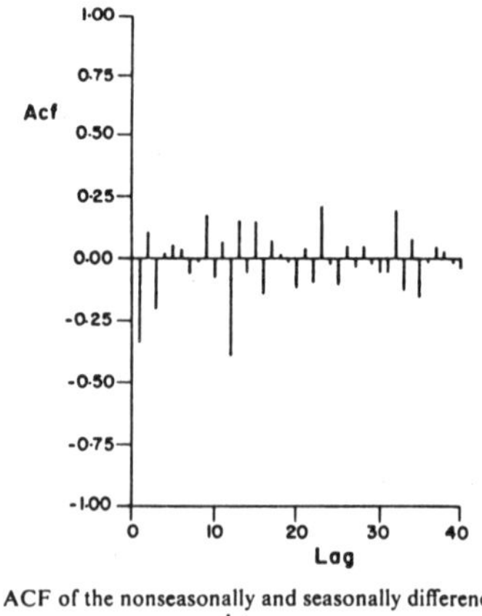

Fig. 16. ACF of the nonseasonally and seasonally differenced airline data.

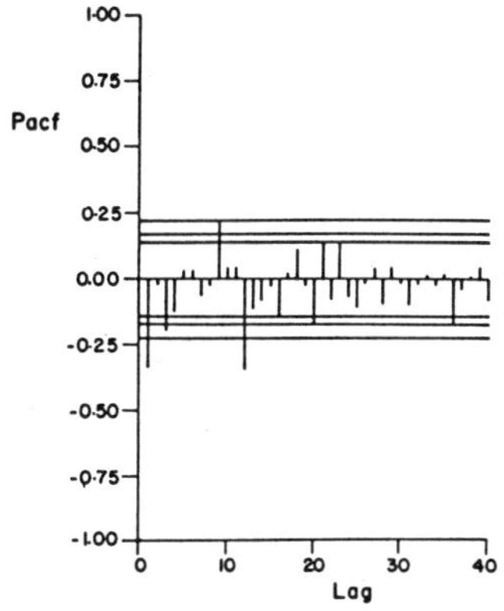

Fig. 17. PACF of the differenced logarithmic airline data.

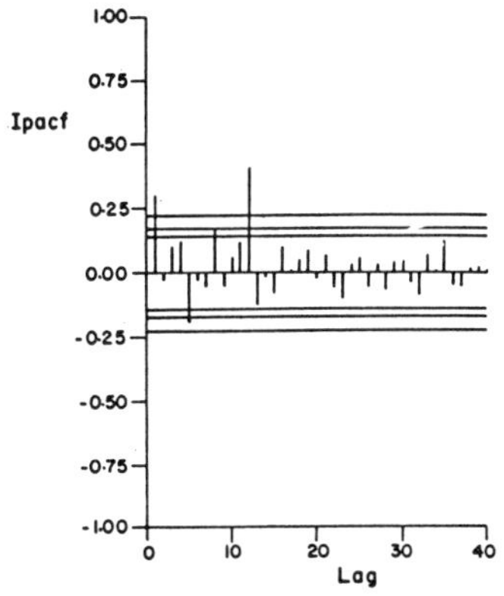

Fig. 19. IPACF of the differenced logarithmic airline data.

of the IACF for the first four lags and also some large values just after lags that are multiples of 12. This implies the presence of a nonseasonal MA component. Because the IACF attenuates at lags that are multiples of 12, this fact implies that a seasonal MA term is also needed. A possible process to try for modeling the logarithmic airline data is therefore a $(0, 1, 1) \times (0, 1, 1)_{12}$ model.

The plot of the PACF does not delineate as clearly as the other identification graphs the type of model to estimate. Because of the significant values of the PACF at lags 1 and 12 it seems that both an AR nonseasonal and an AR seasonal term are required. However, these conclusions contradict previous results. A closer inspection of the PACF reveals that some larger values at lags 3 and 4 could suggest the need for a nonseasonal MA term. There is not a significant value of the PACF at lag 24, but a rather large value at lag 36 may imply an attenuating effect due to a seasonal MA component. For this particular example the PACF contributes little to the identification and actually adds some confusion concerning which model to estimate. However, when all four graphs are examined as a unit, it is obvious that the $(0, 1, 1) \times (0, 1, 1)_{12}$ model

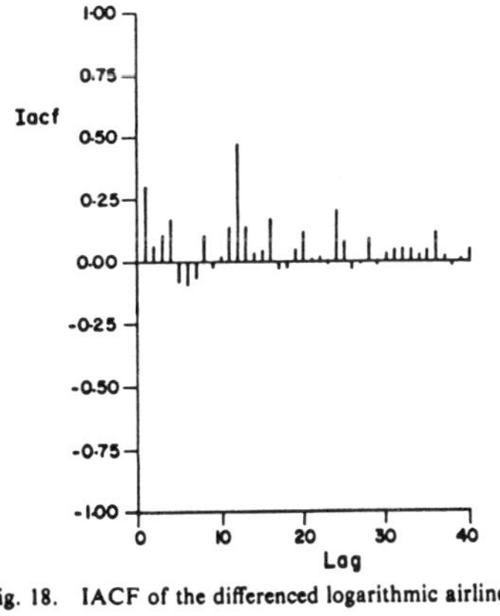

Fig. 18. IACF of the differenced logarithmic airline data.

is the proper process to estimate. When considering other time series applications the PACF usually enhances the identification procedure.

In practice, the authors have discovered that the utilization of all the identification procedures used in this paper greatly simplifies model identification, especially for seasonal Arima processes. Unfortunately, *Box and Jenkins* [1970, chapter 9] do not explain explicitly how to use the PACF for seasonal model identification. This could be the reason that *McMichael and Hunter* [1972] and *McKerchar and Delleur* [1974] fail to employ the PACF for seasonal Arima model identification and therefore appear to have some difficulty in determining which models to estimate.

Table 4 lists the parameter estimates and standard errors for a $(0, 1, 1) \times (0, 1, 1)_{12}$ model fit to the natural logarithms of the total monthly international airline passenger data. Estimates are calculated by using both the modified sum of squares technique [*McLeod,* 1976*a*] and the unconditional sum of squares method [*Box and Jenkins,* 1970, chapter 7]. Notice that the better estimates when using the modified sum of squares method do differ somewhat from the other estimates even in apparently large samples. In particular, the two estimates for Θ_1 differ by approximately 80% of their standard errors. Furthermore, the new estimation procedure involves only a slight increase in computations in comparison with the old method.

The Arima difference equation for the airline model is written as

$$(1 - B)(1 - B^{12}) \ln z_t = (1 - 0.4018B) \cdot (1 - 0.5569B^{12})a_t \qquad (6)$$

TABLE 4. Parameter Estimates for the Airline Model

	Modified Sum of Squares Method		Unconditional Sum of Squares Method	
Parameter	mle*	SE†	mle*	SE†
θ_1	0.4018	0.0800	0.3959	0.0802
Θ_1	0.5569	0.0726	0.6135	0.0690
σ_a	0.03672		0.03664	

*The mle stands for maximum likelihood estimate.
†SE stands for standard error.

A plot of the RACF in Figure 20 for the model in (6) shows that the independence assumption of the residuals is satisfied. All the values of the RACF lie within the 10% significance interval except for the RACF estimate at lag 23, which is still inside the 1% significance interval. The χ^2 distributed U_L statistic has a value of 21.45 for 22 d.f. and therefore also indicates that the residuals possess no significant nonwhiteness. Other diagnostic checks reveal that both the homoscedasticity and the normality assumption for the residuals are fulfilled. Therefore on the basis of the information used, the chosen seasonal Arima model adequately models the airline data.

Although a seasonal $(0, 1, 1) \times (0, 1, 1)_{12}$ model is determined for the logarithmic airline data in this paper, in other situations it may be advisable to design a model that avoids differencing. When a model contains differencing this means that the process is nonstationary, and therefore if the model is used for simulation purposes, the generated data are not restricted to any mean level. In engineering applications such as reservoir design, stationarity of monthly average river flows is essential in order to avoid massive overdesign. To overcome this problem, researchers often incorporate a deterministic component, or transformation, into the model to remove seasonality. Then a nonseasonal autoregressive moving average (Arma) model is fit to the remaining stochastic component. For example, *McMichael and Hunter* [1972] describe how to eliminate seasonality for daily water temperature and discharge data by employing a Fourier series and other periodic polynomials for the deterministic component. *McKerchar and Delleur* [1974] standardize the data for each month to eliminate seasonality in average monthly river flow observations. *Hipel* [1975] discusses standardization and other methods of removing seasonality and then explains the proper procedure for determining an Arma model for the stochastic component. *Tao and Delleur* [1976] describe harmonic and standardization procedures for removing the seasonal component from time series.

Forecasting is an important application of airline passenger data. In many types of time series applications it is often appropriate to compute the transformation given by

$$z_t^{(\lambda)} = \ln (z_t + \text{const}) \quad (7)$$

where $z_t^{(\lambda)}$ is the transformed z_t series and const is a constant that is chosen large enough to make all values of the $z_t^{(\lambda)}$ series positive. For the case of the airline passenger model, the constant is given a value of zero because no zero or negative values are present in the original series.

When the original z_t series is changed by the transformation in (7), the mmse forecast of the untransformed series at origin t for lead time k is [*Granger and Newbold,* 1976, p. 197]

$$z_t(k) = \exp \{z_t^{(\lambda)}(k) + [\text{Var}\,(k)/2]\} - \text{const} \quad (8)$$

where $z_t(k)$ is the mmse forecast of the original series for the Arima model fit to the data, $z_t^{(\lambda)}(k)$ is the mmse of the $z_t^{(\lambda)}$ series obtained by using the approach described by *Box and Jenkins* [1970, chapter 5], and Var (k) is the variance of the forecast error of $z_t^{(\lambda)}(k)$ [*Box and Jenkins,* 1970, p. 128, equation (5.1.16)]. In order to derive (8) it is assumed that the $z_t^{(\lambda)}(k)$ forecast is approximately normally distributed. Note that the normality assumption is not invoked to obtain (4).

If the model in (6) for the airline passenger data is employed for forecasting, the first step is to obtain mmse forecasts for $z_t^{(\lambda)} = \ln z_t$ by using the methods given by *Box and Jenkins* [1970, pp. 306–313]. Then (8) is utilized to determine mmse forecasts for the original untransformed z_t series.

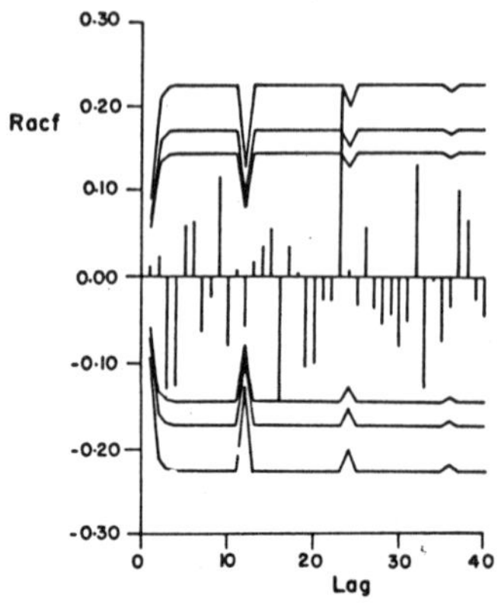

Fig. 20. RACF of the seasonal model for the airline data.

Conclusions

This paper demonstrates that in practical applications, improved Arima models can be obtained readily by using the recent modeling techniques that are described by *Hipel et al.* [1977*a*]. Although more methods are now available for use at all three stages of model construction, this does not complicate the modeling process. Rather, the model-building procedure is simplified and at the same time strengthened. Utilization of more types of identification plots allows for a fairly rapid convergence to a tentative model to estimate. At the estimation stage, better parameter estimates can be calculated by employing the modified sum of squares technique [*McLeod,* 1976*a*]. Rigorous diagnostic checks insure that an appropriate Arima model is ultimately selected, and therefore the user should have more confidence in the chosen Arima process. If problems arise due to heteroscedasticity and/or nonnormality of the residuals, these shortcomings can often be overcome by a Box-Cox transformation of the data. Finally, model parsimony can be insured by utilization of techniques such as the AIC or the likelihood ratio test.

For the case of the Saint Lawrence River model in (1) a better model is obtained here than was obtained by *Carlson et al.* [1970]. This is due to the fact that in addition to the ACF being examined, the PACF, the IACF, and the IPACF are also studied at the identification stage. The AIC and other checks confirm that a (3, 0, 0) model with ϕ_2 constrained to zero is indeed the proper model to select. Model parsimony is preserved, while simultaneously the assumptions of the residuals are not violated.

An AR(9) model without ϕ_3–ϕ_8 adequately models the annual sunspot numbers. A check for homoscedasticity of the residuals reveals that it is necessary to employ a Box-Cox transformation to remove heteroscedasticity. A square root transformation with the parameter $\lambda = 0.5$ and const $= 1.0$ rectifies the situation. Diagnostic checks and also the AIC indicate that the constrained AR(9) process should be selected in preference to an AR(2), an AR(3), or a multiplicative seasonal Box-Jenkins model.

The authors agree with the findings of *Box and Jenkins*

[1970, chapter 9] that a $(0, 1, 1) \times (0, 1, 1)_{12}$ model is the proper seasonal multiplicative process to fit to the natural logarithms of the monthly airline passenger data. However, it is clearly shown in this paper how all the identification plots can be utilized to determine a tentative seasonal model to estimate. Furthermore, as is shown in Table 4, the modified sum of squares estimation method gives better estimates for the moving average parameters than the estimates obtained from the unconditional sum of squares technique.

If the original data are changed by a nonlinear transformation, it is now possible to procure mmse forecasts of the untransformed series [*Granger and Newbold*, 1976]. This forecasting procedure is described for both a square root and a natural logarithmic transformation.

Aside from determining nonseasonal or seasonal Arima models for given data sets the contemporary model-building procedures given by *Hipel et al.* [1977*a*] can be extended for use in other types of applications. An important consideration in water resources is how to model the effects of either man-induced or natural interventions on natural hydrologic variables. For example, what are the stochastic alterations of a newly constructed reservoir on the mean level of the downstream flow regime? *Hipel et al.* [1975, 1977*b*] determine intervention models for water resource applications by employing similar modeling procedures to those used in this paper.

NOTATION

- a_t white noise time series.
- AR(p) autoregressive process of order p.
- B backward shift operator.
- const additive constant for a Box-Cox transformation.
- d order of the nonseasonal differencing operator.
- D order of the seasonal differencing operator.
- g_1 estimated residual skewness.
- g_2 estimated residual kurtosis.
- ln natural logarithm.
- mle maximum likelihood estimate.
- mmse minimum mean square error estimate.
- p order of the nonseasonal AR operator.
- (p, d, q) nonseasonal Arima model.
- $(p, d, q) \times (P, D, Q)_s$ seasonal Box-Jenkins Arima model.
- P order of the seasonal AR operator.
- q order of the nonseasonal MA operator.
- Q order of the seasonal MA operator.
- s seasonal length.
- t discrete time.
- U_L portmanteau statistic calculated from the estimates of the RACF up to lag L.
- Var (k) variance of the forecast error of $z_t^{(\lambda)}(k)$.
- z_t discrete time series value at time t.
- $z_t^{(\lambda)}$ transformation of z_t.
- $z_t(k)$ mmse forecast of z_t at origin t for lead time k.
- $z_t^{(\lambda)}(k)$ mmse forecast of $z_t^{(\lambda)}$ at origin t for lead time k.
- θ_i ith nonseasonal MA parameter.
- Θ_i ith seasonal MA parameter.
- λ exponent of a Box-Cox transformation.
- σ_a^2 variance of a_t.
- $\sigma_a^2(k)$ residual variance of a process with k parameters.
- $\sigma_a^2(r)$ residual variance for an AR process with r parameters.
- ϕ_i ith nonseasonal AR parameter.
- Φ_i ith seasonal AR parameter.
- χ constant to be estimated in the homoscedasticity test for the residuals.
- χ^2 chi-squared random variable.

Acknowledgments. The authors are grateful to T. E. Unny of the Civil Engineering Department of the University of Waterloo for his suggestions and encouragement. The cooperation of the mathematics faculty of the University of Waterloo under the auspices of W. F. Forbes and also the use of the mathematics faculty computer facility are greatly appreciated. The National Research Council of Canada contributed financial support for the research.

REFERENCES

Akaike, H., A new look at the statistical model identification, *IEEE Trans. Automat. Contr., AC-19*(6), 716–723, 1974.

Box, G. E. P., and G. M. Jenkins, *Time Series Analysis: Forecasting and Control*, Holden-Day, San Francisco, Calif., 1970.

Carlson, R. F., A. J. A. MacCormick, and D. G. Watts, Application of linear random models to four annual streamflow series, *Water Resour. Res., 6*(4), 1070–1078, 1970.

Granger, C. W. J., A statistical model for sunspot activity, *Astrophys. J., 126*, 152–158, 1957.

Granger, C. W. J., and P. Newbold, Forecasting transformed series, *J. Roy. Statist. Soc., Ser. B, 38*(2), 189–203, 1976.

Hipel, K. W., Contemporary Box-Jenkins modelling in hydrology, Ph.D. thesis, Univ. of Waterloo, Waterloo, Ont., Canada, 1975.

Hipel, K. W., W. C. Lennox, T. E. Unny, and A. I. McLeod, Intervention analysis in water resources, *Water Resour. Res., 11*(6), 855–861, 1975.

Hipel, K. W., A. I. McLeod, and W. C. Lennox, Advances in Box-Jenkins modeling, 1, Model construction, *Water Resour. Res., 13*, this issue, 1977*a*.

Hipel, K. W., A. I. McLeod, and E. A. McBean, Stochastic modelling of the effects of reservoir operation, *J. Hydrol., 32*, 97–113, 1977*b*.

McKerchar, A. I., and J. W. Delleur, Application of seasonal parametric linear stochastic models to monthly flow data, *Water Resour. Res., 10*(2), 246–255, 1974.

McLeod, A. I., Contribution to applied time series, masters thesis, Univ. of Waterloo, Waterloo, Ont., Canada, 1974.

McLeod, A. I., Improved Box-Jenkins estimators, report, Dep. of Statist., Univ. of Waterloo, Waterloo, Ont., Canada, 1976*a*.

McLeod, A. I., Distribution of the residual autocorrelations in seasonal Arima models, report, Dep. of Statist., Univ. of Waterloo, Waterloo, Ont., Canada, 1976*b*.

McMichael, F. C., and J. S. Hunter, Stochastic modeling of temperature and flow in rivers, *Water Resour. Res., 8*(1), 87–98, 1972.

Moran, P. A. P., Some experiments in the prediction of sunspot numbers, *J. Roy. Statist. Soc., Ser. B, 16*(1), 112–117, 1954.

Schneider, S. H., and C. Mass, Volcanic dust, sunspots, and temperature trends, *Science, 190*(4216), 1975.

Tao, P. C., and J. W. Delleur, Seasonal and nonseasonal Arma models in hydrology, *J. Hydraul. Div. Amer. Soc. Civil Eng., HY10*, 1541–1559, 1976.

Waldmeier, M., *The Sunspot Activity in the Years 1610–1960*, Schulthas and Company, Zurich, Switzerland, 1961.

Whittle, P., A statistical investigation of sunspot observations with special reference to H. Alfren's sunspot model, *Astrophys. J., 120*, 251-260, 1954.

Yevyevich, V. M., Fluctuation of wet and dry years, 1, Research data assembly and mathematical models, *Hydrol. Pap. 1*, Colo. State Univ., Fort Collins, Colo., 1963.

Yule, G. U., On a method of investigating periodicities in disturbed series, with special reference to Wolfer sunspot numbers, *Phil. Trans. Roy. Soc. London, Ser. A, 226*, 267–298, 1927.

(Received June 19, 1975;
revised November 11, 1976;
accepted November 15, 1976.)

[11]

INT. J. MATH. EDUC. SCI. TECHNOL., 1976, VOL. 7, NO. 2, 235–241

The backshift operator in time series analysis

by O. D. ANDERSON
Civil Service College, London, England

(*Received* 26 *November* 1975)

A time series is a set of data which develops through time in some structured manner, whose precise form is, in part, obscured by a random component. The usefulness of the backshift operator comes from the insights it gives the analyst as to the possible interpretation of a fitted model, or even in suggesting some preferable model.

1. Introduction

The use of operational methods in numerical analysis is familiar. Thus given any sequence, $\ldots, f_{i-1}, f_i, f_{i+1}, \ldots$, a typical *difference* $f_i - f_{i-1}$ is denoted by ∇f_i, where ∇ is the backward difference operator.

Associated with ∇ is the *backshift* operator B, such that $Bf_i \equiv f_{i-1}$. We can then write $\nabla f_i \equiv (1-B)f_i$ giving the connection $\nabla \equiv 1 - B$. Expressions in ∇ or B can be taken to obey the rules of elementary algebra. For instance

$$\nabla^d \equiv (1-B)^d \equiv \sum_{j=0}^{d} (-1)^j \binom{d}{j} B^j \tag{1}$$

and

$$\sum_{j=0}^{r-1} B^j \equiv (1-B^r)/(1-B) \tag{2}$$

A *time series* is a sequence of historical data; for example, the monthly unemployment figures in Britain, or the daily rainfall at a particular location. We denote such a sequence by $\{z_i\}$, and consider it to be a *realization* of a sequence of random variables, the associated stochastic process $\{Z_i\}$, which we term the parent *time process*. Thus the $\{Z_i\}$ represents the set of variables, which will possess some joint distribution, whilst the $\{z_i\}$ are the particular values observed. Consider the analogy afforded by the distinction between the heights of headmasters, H, and the height of a particular one, h. Upper and lower case letters are used, in statistics, merely to focus attention onto whether it is the ' population ', or ' individual ', which is being looked at. Though an individual can have a specific height, the population will have a distribution of heights. In the one-off situation, the population is a hypothetical conception—and so, frequently, is the time process. One cannot restart economies, or the weather, to see what other patterns they might have followed.

2. Mathematical models for time series

The simplest form of process, which we will denote by $\{A_i\}$, has the property that all the random variables A_i are identically and independently distributed with zero mean and constant variance, σ_A^2 say. Such a process is called *white noise*, as its complete randomness means that the process is completely characterless or colourless.

Recently much attention has been focused on a class of models which relate the process of interest, $\{Z_i\}$, to a white noise process, $\{A_i\}$. Thus $\{Z_i\}$ is considered to be either generated by the $\{A_i\}$ from a relation of the form

$$Z_i = \sum_{j=0}^{\infty} \theta_j A_{i-j} \tag{3}$$

or capable of being refined to give the white noise by writing

$$\sum_{j=0}^{\infty} \phi_j Z_{i-j} = A_i \tag{4}$$

where the θ_j and ϕ_j are suitable parameters.

Equations (3) and (4) might appear to be of identical form, but remember that $\{A_i\}$ is completely structureless whereas, in general, $\{Z_i\}$ is not. So there is no symmetry, except in the trivial case when

$$Z_i = A_i$$

Of course, without loss in generality, we can choose $\theta_0 = \phi_0 = 1$. The models (3) and (4) are then termed, respectively, the *Moving Average* and *Autoregressive* models. When $\theta_q \neq 0$, but $\theta_j = 0$ for all $j > q$, the process (3) is moving average of order q, which is written as MA(q). Whereas, when $\phi_p \neq 0$, $\phi_j = 0$ for $j > p$, the process (4) is autoregressive of order p, or AR(p). For instance, the annual membership of a well-established school chess club might be considered to consist of a fraction of those members it had the previous year, due to school leaving or members giving up the game – perhaps to concentrate on exams—plus those freshly taking up chess. This latter quantity might be thought of as fluctuating around an average annual number of new members, μ say. Mathematically this can be expressed as

$$M_i = \phi M_{i-1} + (\mu + A_i) \quad \phi < 1$$

with

$$E[M_i] = \mu/(1-\phi)$$

Then, working instead with

$$Z_i = M_i - E[M_i]$$

that is with deviations of $\{M_i\}$ from its mean, we have

$$Z_i = \phi Z_{i-1} + A_i \quad \phi < 1$$

which gives an AR(1) representation. For a more serious example, substitute seasonally adjusted monthly unemployment figures.

In operator form, (3) and (4) are written as, respectively,

$$Z_i = \left(\sum_{j=0}^{q} \theta_j B^j \right) A_i \tag{5}$$

and

$$\left(\sum_{j=0}^{p} \phi_j B^j \right) Z_i = A_i \tag{6}$$

A simple generalization gives the mixed autoregressive moving average process of order (p, q), or ARMA(p, q), whose model has the form

$$\left(\sum_{j=0}^{p} \phi_j B^j \right) Z_i = \left(\sum_{j=0}^{q} \theta_j B^j \right) A_i \tag{7}$$

The Box–Jenkins approach to time series analysis interests itself with studying a series $\{z_i\}$ and then seeing whether a model such as (5), (6) or (7) appears appropriate. If it does, a tentative choice of p and q is made, and then estimates of the $p+q+1$ unknowns $\phi_1,\ldots,\phi_p$; $\theta_1,\ldots,\theta_q$; and $\sigma_A{}^2$ are obtained. The resulting 'fit' is then subjected to statistical checks and, if necessary, new improved choices of p and q are made. And so on until the analyst is satisfied with the results, [2].

The properties of the polynomials in the backshift operator appearing in (5), (6) and (7) are thus important for time series analysis; and this article will be concerned with how manipulation of the operator B can contribute to the subject.

3. The interchangeability of the basic models

Evidently (3) and (4) are, subject to reservations to ensure convergence, formally equivalent. For

$$Z_i=\left(\sum_{j=0}^{\infty}\theta_jB^j\right)A_i$$

can be rewritten as

$$\left(1+\sum_{j=1}^{\infty}\theta_jB^j\right)^{-1}Z_i=A_i$$

and the expression in B on the left can then be replaced, on expansion, by one with the form

$$\left(1+\sum_{j=1}^{\infty}\phi_jB^j\right);$$

the necessary reservation being in fact that, for any ζ not outside the unit circle,

$$\left|\sum_{j=0}^{\infty}\theta_j\zeta^j\right|>0.$$

So, for instance, the MA(∞) model

$$Z_i=\left\{\sum_{j=0}^{\infty}(\alpha B)^j\right\}A_i$$

can be replaced by

$$(1-\alpha B)Z_i=A_i$$

an AR(1), since

$$(1-\alpha B)^{-1}\equiv\sum_{j=0}^{\infty}(\alpha B)^j.$$

Such simplifications are easily seen, using the backshift operator. The importance of appreciating this basic model interchangeability is that, should the analyst witness what appears to be a high-order MA process, it might be that he is really looking from the wrong angle at a low-order AR.

Again, from numerical analysis, most continuous functions on a finite domain can be closely approximated by a rational function consisting of a quotient of two low-order polynomials. Then even when, say, a high-order MA cannot be replaced or approximated by a low-order AR, its B-operator polynomial can usually be closely represented by a quotient

$$\sum_{j=0}^{q^*} \theta_j^* B^j \Big/ \sum_{j=0}^{p^*} \phi_j^* B^j$$

where q^* and p^* are small integers. It follows that, theoretically, many linear processes can be represented as models of the form (7) with $p+q$ small.

Sometimes the analyst is faced with a situation where he cannot decide whether the model is, say AR(1) or MA(1). This again is easily explained using the B-operator. Consider the model

$$(1-\alpha B)Z_i = A_i$$

where α is small. Then, equivalently, we can write

$$\begin{aligned} Z_i &= \left(\sum_{j=0}^{\infty} \alpha^j B^j\right) A_i \\ &\simeq (1+\alpha B)A_i \end{aligned}$$

neglecting terms in $\alpha^j, j \geqslant 2$.

4. Differencing to induce ' stationarity '

As yet we have not referred back to the identities (1) and (2). The processes we have been discussing possess a particular property termed *stationarity*, which means that their probabilistic structure does not vary with time. Many observed series only appear to have this property after taking differences of some low-order d. Then it is the differenced series $\{\nabla^d z_i\}$ which is modelled. For instance, a process might be ' stationary ' except for occasional random changes in its local level. Then first differencing is called for. Random changes in slope would be dealt with by taking second differences, and so on.

Note, however, that differencing should not be overdone. For instance, stock prices in general closely follow the ' random walk ' model

$$Z_i = Z_{i-1} + A_i \tag{8}$$

where there are occasional jumps in the level of $\{Z_i\}$. Then, rewriting (8) as

$$\nabla Z_i = A_i$$

we see that the first differences follow a completely structureless white noise process. However, if we difference d times further, we obtain

$$\nabla^{d+1} Z_i = \nabla^d A_i$$

and, from (1), we see that the right is now an MA(d) process. So we are overcomplicating the situation, and the extra differencing is counterproductive. Note also that we increase the variance from σ_A^2 to

$$\begin{aligned} \text{Var}\,[\nabla^d A_i] &= \sum_{j=0}^{d} \binom{d}{j}^2 \sigma_A^2 \\ &= \binom{2d}{d} \sigma_A^2 \end{aligned}$$

on comparing the coefficients of x^d in the identity

$$(1+x)^d (x+1)^d = (1+x)^{2d}.$$

Incidentally, taking statistical expectations at ' time ' $i-1$ in (8), we see that

$$E[Z_i]=Z_{i-1}+0$$

This implies that the best forecast for today's stock price that could have been made yesterday, on the basis of the past history of the stock, was just yesterday's price.

5. Autoaggregation

The identity (2) is useful when ' autoaggregating ' a series. For instance, this can occur in an attempt to smooth a series, by forming a running average of it. Thus, the classical approach to time series analysis first obtains the general ' trend ' of the series of interest, by smoothing the raw data. In such a situation, the series $\{z_i : i \geqslant 1\}$ is replaced by

$$\{s_i \equiv (z_i+z_{i-1}+\ldots+z_{i-r+1})/r \ : i \geq r\} \tag{9}$$

for some suitable choice of r. In B-operator notation, using (2), (9) can be rewritten as

$$(1-B)rs_i=(1-B^r)z_i$$

This relation can be used to deduce the model for $\{z_i\}$, after fitting one to $\{s_i\}$. Thus if, say,

$$\nabla^2 s_i=\left(\sum_{j=0}^{q} \theta_j B^j\right)a_i$$

then, denoting the *period* difference operator $(1-B^r)$ by ∇_r,

$$\nabla\nabla_r z_i=\left(\sum_{j=0}^{q} \theta_j B^j\right)ra_i$$

As a second example of autoaggregation, consider an observed time series which is obtained by accumulating a more frequent series for a number of terms, r say. For instance, annual production figures are the accumulated sums of the monthly figures, for the particular years. Then we are dealing with

$$\{rs_{ri}=(z_{ri}+z_{ri-1}+\ldots+z_{ri-r+1}) \ : i \geq 1\}$$

where $\{s_{ri}\}$ is a subsequence of $\{s_i\}$ consisting of just the rth, $2r$th, $3r$th, . . . terms. (Due to the skipped nature of such an accumulated series, we do not observe

$$B^j s_{ri}=s_{ri-j} \quad 0<j<r$$

and the analysis is in consequence a little more difficult.)

6. Improving on a tentative identification

Suppose a process $\{Z_i\}$ follows the model (7), but we try to write it as an ARMA (p^*, q^*) model

$$\left(\sum_{j=0}^{p^*} \phi_j^* B^j\right)Z_i=\left(\sum_{j=0}^{q^*} \theta_j^* B^j\right)A_i^* \tag{10}$$

Then, eliminating Z_i from (7) and (10), we see that

$$\left(\sum_{j=0}^{p} \phi_j B^j\right)\left(\sum_{j=0}^{q^*} \theta_j^* B^j\right)A_i^*=\left(\sum_{j=0}^{p^*} \phi_j^* B^j\right)\left(\sum_{j=0}^{q} \theta_j B^j\right)A_i \tag{11}$$

So $\{A_i^*\}$ cannot be a white noise process, but must follow an

$$\text{ARMA}\ (p+q^*, p^*+q) \qquad (12)$$

However, if we then realized this, eliminating A_i^* from (10) and (11) would get us back to (7).

Now (12) appears to be a more complicated model than (7); but, in practice, it will have a close low-order approximation, ARMA$(\tilde{p}, \tilde{q})$ say, given by

$$\left(\sum_{j=0}^{\tilde{p}} \tilde{\phi}_j B^j\right) A_i^* \doteqdot \left(\sum_{j=0}^{\tilde{q}} \tilde{\theta}_j B^j\right) A_i$$

This, with (10), approximately yields an ARMA$(p^*+\tilde{p}, q^*+\tilde{q})$ model for $\{Z_i\}$.

So suppose, for some series, we first identified an MA(2) model; but, after fitting this, found that the estimated $\{A_i^*\}$, instead of being white noise, was apparently AR(1), then our improved choice would be an ARMA(1, 2). Thus, even if we are mistaken in our initial identification, we have a means of homing in on a more acceptable model.

7. Interpretation

It is generally quite easy to think up explanations for why an observed pure AR or MA fit should have occurred. But mixed ARMA models were another matter; and, without a plausible explanation, many applied workers were not prepared to accept such unnatural models. However, very recently, a way round this problem has been found. Using the B-operator, it can be shown that very many mixed models do, in fact, arise from pure model situations, [1].

For instance, suppose that the chess and draughts clubs, initially with separate memberships, decided to amalgamate. It might have been that, before the amalgamation, the individual club memberships followed distinct and independent AR(1) models

$$(1-\phi B)X_i = C_i$$
$$(1-\psi B)Y_i = D_i$$

say; but that, afterwards, the joint association was found to follow an ARMA (2, 1) model. How could this be explained?

We have, for the combined club membership, $X_i + Y_i = Z_i$ say,

$$Z_i = (1-\phi B)^{-1}C_i + (1-\psi B)^{-1}D_i$$

So

$$(1-\phi B)(1-\psi B)Z_i = (1-\psi B)C_i + (1-\phi B)D_i$$

Now the right-hand side of this is the sum of two independent first-order moving average processes

$$U_i = (1-\psi B)C_i$$
$$V_i = (1-\phi B)D_i$$

There is a theorem† which states that the sum of two independent moving average processes, of orders q_1 and q_2, is also moving average of order $q \leqslant \max(q_1, q_2)$. So, in our case, we can write

$$U_i + V_i = R_i$$

where

$$R_i = (1+\theta B)A_i$$

for some suitable choice of θ and σ_A^2. We thus see that Z_i should follow an ARMA(2, 1), and we have our explanation.

† The case of the theorem used in this example is proved in the Appendix.

Similarly an AR(1) series, contaminated by an independent series of observation errors, will yield an ARMA(1, 1). And so on.

8. Conclusion

It has not been the intention, in this article, to spell out all the details, but it is hoped that we will have interested readers in the operational mathematics of time processes. From there one progresses to the statistics of time series—a subject of major practical importance. As examples of series we have mentioned production, unemployment, stock prices and rainfall, but the list is virtually unending.

The author will welcome approaches from students, who would like to carry out vacation work in this area of study in an environment where practical considerations are the motivation for theory.

Appendix

Proposition: The sum of two independent first-order moving average processes is, in general, also a first-order moving average.

Proof: Consider the two representations

$$R_i = (1-\psi B)C_i + (1-\phi B)D_i \tag{13}$$

$$R_i = (1+\theta B)A_i \tag{14}$$

Then taking ' expectations ' of $R_i R_{i-j}$, using (13), we get

$$E[R_i R_i] = (1+\psi^2)\sigma_C^2 + (1+\phi^2)\sigma_D^2$$

$$E[R_i R_{i-1}] = -\psi\sigma_C^2 - \phi\sigma_D^2$$

$$E[R_i R_{i-j}] = 0 \qquad j \geq 2$$

Using (14), we get identical expressions, provided we choose θ and σ_A^2 to satisfy

$$(1+\theta^2)\sigma_A^2 = (1+\psi^2)\sigma_C^2 + (1+\phi^2)\sigma_D^2$$

$$\theta\sigma_A^2 = -\psi\sigma_C^2 - \phi\sigma_D^2$$

which is always possible. Of course if

$$\psi\sigma_C^2 + \phi\sigma_D^2 = 0$$

(14) reduces to a zero order moving average, which is white noise.

References

[1] ANDERSON, O. D., 1975, *Time Series Analysis and Forecasting: The Box–Jenkins Approach* (Butterworth).

[2] BOX, G. E. P., and JENKINS, G. M., 1970, *Time Series Analysis, Forecasting and Control* (Hoden–Day).

[12]

Modeling Multiple Time Series With Applications

G. C. TIAO and G. E. P. BOX*

An approach to the modeling and analysis of multiple time series is proposed. Properties of a class of vector autoregressive moving average models are discussed. Modeling procedures consisting of tentative specification, estimation, and diagnostic checking are outlined and illustrated by three real examples.

KEY WORDS: Multiple time series; Vector autoregressive moving average models; Cross-correlations; Partial autoregression; Intervention analysis; Transfer function.

1. INTRODUCTION

Business, economic, engineering and environmental data are often collected in roughly equally spaced time intervals, for example, hour, week, month, or quarter. In many problems, such time series data may be available on several related variables of interest. Two of the reasons for analyzing and modeling such series jointly are

1. To understand the dynamic relationships among them. They may be contemporaneously related, one series may lead the others or there may be feedback relationships.
2. To improve accuracy of forecasts. When there is information on one series contained in the historical data of another, better forecasts can result when the series are modeled jointly.

Let

$$\{Z_{1t}\}, \ldots, \{Z_{kt}\}, \quad t = 0, \pm 1, \pm 2, \ldots \tag{1.1}$$

be k series taken in equally spaced time intervals. Writing

$$\mathbf{Z}_t = (Z_{1t}, \ldots, Z_{kt})', \tag{1.2}$$

we shall refer to the k series as a k-dimensional vector of multiple time series. Models that are of possible use in representing such multiple time series, considerations of their properties, and methods for relating them to actual data have been extensively discussed in the literature. See in particular Quenouille (1957), Whittle (1963), Hannan (1970), Zellner and Palm (1974), Brillinger (1975), Dunsmuir and Hannan (1976), Box and Haugh (1977), Granger and Newbold (1977), Parzen (1977), Wallis (1977), Chan and Wallis (1978), Deistler, Dunsmuir, and Hannan (1978), Hallin (1978), Jenkins (1979), Hsiao (1979), Akaike (1980), Hannan (1980), Hannan, Dunsmuir, and Deistler (1980), and Quinn (1980). There are, however, considerable divergences of view. The object of this article is to describe an approach to the modeling and analysis that we have developed over a considerable period of time and that we are finding effective. Our main emphasis will be on motivating, describing, and illustrating the various methods used in an iterative model building process. Much, if not all, of the underlying theory can be found in the references given and, therefore, will not be repeated. Section 2 presents a short review of the widely used univariate ($k = 1$) time series and transfer function models as developed in Box and Jenkins (1970). Section 3 discusses a class of vector autoregressive moving average models. Model building procedures are discussed in Section 4 and applied to two actual examples in Section 5. A comparison with some alternative approaches and some concluding remarks pertaining to the analysis of fitting results are given in Section 6.

2. UNIVARIATE TIME SERIES AND TRANSFER FUNCTION MODELS

When $k = 1$ we shall write $\mathbf{Z}_t = Z_t$ in (1.2). An important class of models for discrete univariate series originally proposed by Yule (1927) and Slutsky (1937) and developed by such authors as Bartlett, Kendall, Walker, Wold, and Yaglom are stochastic difference equations of the form

$$\phi_p(B)z_t = \theta_q(B)a_t, \tag{2.1}$$

where $\phi_p(B) = 1 - \phi_1 B - \cdots - \phi_p B^p$ and $\theta_q(B) = 1 - \theta_1 B - \cdots - \theta_q B^q$. In (2.1) the a_t's are independently identically and normally distributed random shocks (or white noise) with zero mean and variance σ^2; B is the back-shift operator such that $BZ_t = Z_{t-1}$; and $z_t = Z_t - \eta$ is the deviation of the observation Z_t from some convenient location η.

Relationships between k series $\{z_{1t}\}, \ldots, \{z_{kt}\}$ can sometimes be represented by linear *transfer function* models of the form

$$z_{ht} = \sum_{i \in k(h)} [\omega_{s_{hi}}(B)B^{b_{hi}}/\delta_{r_{hi}}(B)]\, z_{it} + [\theta_{q_h}(B)/\varphi_{p_h}(B)]\, a_{ht}, \quad (h = 1, 2, \ldots, k) \tag{2.2}$$

where $z_{0t} \equiv 0$, $k(h)$ is the set $(1, \ldots, h - 1)$; $\omega_{s_{hi}}(B)$, $\delta_{r_{hi}}(B)$, $\varphi_{p_h}(B)$, and $\theta_{q_h}(B)$ are polynomials in B;

* G.C. Tiao is Professor of Statistics and Business, and G.E.P. Box is Vilas Research Professor, Department of Statistics, University of Wisconsin, Madison, WI 53706. The authors are grateful to W.R. Bell, I. Chang, M.R. Grupe, G.B. Hudak, and R.S. Tsay for computing assistance. This research was partially supported by the U.S. Bureau of the Census under JSA 80-10, the Army Research Office, Durham, NC under Grant No. DAAG29-78-G00166, and the Alcoa Foundation.

© Journal of the American Statistical Association
December 1981, Volume 76, Number 376
Theory and Methods Section

the b_{hi}'s are nonnegative integers; and $\{a_{1t}\}, \ldots, \{a_{kt}\}$ are k independent Gaussian white-noise processes with zero means and variances $\sigma_1^2, \ldots, \sigma_k^2$. In particular, intervention models of this form with one or more of the z_h's indicator variables have proved useful (Box and Tiao 1975; Abraham 1980)

Transfer function models of the form (2.2), however, assume that the series, when suitably arranged, possess a triangular relationship, implying for example that z_1 depends only on its own past; z_2 depends on its own past and on the present and past of z_1; z_3 on its own past and on the present and past of z_2 and z_1; and so on. On the other hand, if z_1 depends on the past of z_2, and also z_2 depends on the past of z_1, then we must have a model that allows for this *feedback*.

3. MULTIPLE STOCHASTIC DIFFERENCE EQUATION MODELS

3.1 The Vector ARMA Model

A useful class of models obtained by direct generalization of the Yule-Slutsky ARMA models that allow for feedback relationships among the k series is obtained from (2.2) by letting $k(h)$ be the set $(1, \ldots, k)$ excluding h. These models can be alternatively expressed as the vector autoregressive moving average ARMA models (Quenouille 1957),

$$\boldsymbol{\varphi}_p(B)\mathbf{z}_t = \boldsymbol{\theta}_q(B)\mathbf{a}_t, \qquad (3.1)$$

where

$$\boldsymbol{\varphi}_p(B) = \mathbf{I} - \boldsymbol{\varphi}_1 B - \ldots - \boldsymbol{\varphi}_p B^p,$$

$$\boldsymbol{\theta}_q(B) = \mathbf{I} - \boldsymbol{\theta}_1 B - \ldots - \boldsymbol{\theta}_q B^q$$

are matrix polynomials in B, the $\boldsymbol{\varphi}$'s and $\boldsymbol{\theta}$'s are $k \times k$ matrices, $\mathbf{z}_t = \mathbf{Z}_t - \boldsymbol{\eta}$ is the vector of deviations from some origin $\boldsymbol{\eta}$ that is the mean if the series is stationary, and $\{\mathbf{a}_t\}$ with $\mathbf{a}_t = (a_{1t}, \ldots, a_{kt})'$ is a sequence of random shock vectors identically independently and normally distributed with zero mean and covariance matrix $\boldsymbol{\Sigma}$. We shall suppose that the zeros of the determinantal polynomials $|\boldsymbol{\varphi}_p(B)|$ and $|\boldsymbol{\theta}_q(B)|$ are on or outside the unit circle. The series $\mathbf{z}_t$ will be stationary when the zeros of $|\boldsymbol{\varphi}_p(B)|$ are all outside the unit circle, and will be invertible when those of $|\boldsymbol{\theta}_q(B)|$ are all outside the unit circle. Properties of such models have been discussed by, for example, Hannan (1970), Anderson (1971), and Granger and Newbold (1977).

Some Simple Examples. To illustrate the behavior of observations from these models, Figure 1 shows two series with 250 observations generated from the bivariate ($k = 2$) first order moving average [MA(1)] model, $\mathbf{z}_t = (\mathbf{I} - \boldsymbol{\theta}B)\mathbf{a}_t$, with

$$\boldsymbol{\theta} = \begin{bmatrix} .2 & .3 \\ -.6 & 1.1 \end{bmatrix} \quad \text{and} \quad \boldsymbol{\Sigma} = \begin{bmatrix} 4 & 1 \\ 1 & 1 \end{bmatrix}. \qquad (3.2)$$

Figure 2 shows two series with 150 observations generated from the bivariate first order autoregressive [AR(1)] model, $(\mathbf{I} - \boldsymbol{\varphi}B)\mathbf{z}_t = \mathbf{a}_t$, with

Figure 1. Data Generated From a Bivariate MA(1) Model With Parameter Values in (3.2)

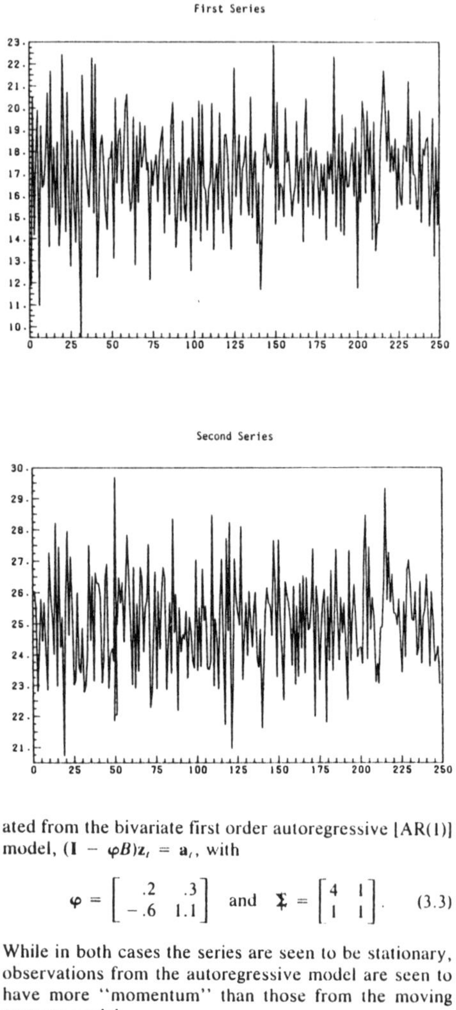

$$\boldsymbol{\varphi} = \begin{bmatrix} .2 & .3 \\ -.6 & 1.1 \end{bmatrix} \quad \text{and} \quad \boldsymbol{\Sigma} = \begin{bmatrix} 4 & 1 \\ 1 & 1 \end{bmatrix}. \qquad (3.3)$$

While in both cases the series are seen to be stationary, observations from the autoregressive model are seen to have more "momentum" than those from the moving average model.

In practice, time series often exhibit nonstationary behavior. When several such series are considered jointly, nonstationarity may be modeled by allowing the zeros of $|\boldsymbol{\varphi}(B)|$ in (3.1) to lie on the unit circle. A particular example is the model $(1 - B)\mathbf{z}_t = (\mathbf{I} - \boldsymbol{\theta}B)\mathbf{a}_t$, that is, after differencing each series we obtain a vector MA(1) model. This is a vector analog of the commonly used univariate nonstationary model $(1 - B)z_t = (1 - \theta B)a_t$. However,

Figure 2. Data Generated From a Bivariate AR(1) Model With Parameter Values in (3.3)

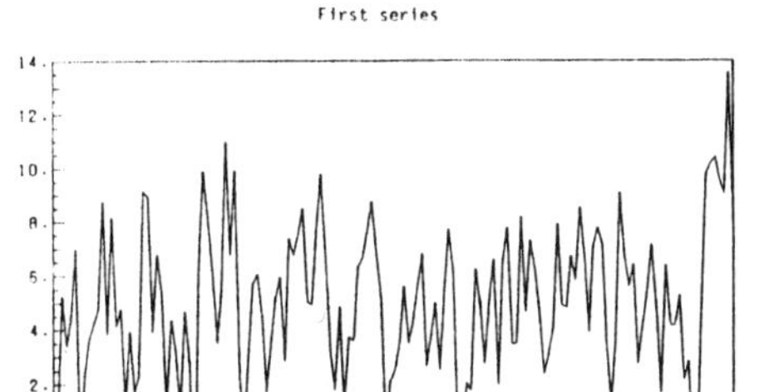

it should be noted here that for vector time series, linear combinations of the elements of $\mathbf{z}_t$ may often be stationary, and simultaneous differencing of all series can lead to unnecessary complications in model fitting. See, for example, the discussion in Box and Tiao (1977) and Hillmer and Tiao (1979).

Tranfer Function Model. For the vector model in (3.1), in general, all elements of $\mathbf{z}_t$ are related to all elements of $\mathbf{z}_{t-j}$ ($j = 1, 2, \ldots$) and there can be feedback relationships between all the series. However, if the $\mathbf{z}_t$'s can be arranged so that the coefficient matrices $\boldsymbol{\varphi}$'s and $\boldsymbol{\theta}$'s are all lower triangular, then (3.1) can be written as a transfer function model of the form (2.2). More generally, if the $\boldsymbol{\varphi}$'s and $\boldsymbol{\theta}$'s are all lower block triangular, then we obtain a generalization of the transfer function form of (2.2) in which both the input vector series and the output vector series are allowed to have feedback relationships. Furthermore, relationships between the vector transfer function model and the econometric linear simultaneous equation model have been discussed in Zellner and Palm (1974) and Wallis (1977).

3.2 Cross-Covariance and Cross-Correlation Matrices

For a stationary vector time series $\{\mathbf{Z}_t\}$ with mean vector $\boldsymbol{\eta}$, let $\boldsymbol{\Gamma}(l)$ be the lag l cross-covariance matrix

$$\boldsymbol{\Gamma}(l) = E(\mathbf{z}_{t-l}\mathbf{z}'_t) = \{\gamma_{ij}(l)\}, \quad l = 0, \pm 1, \pm 2, \ldots \quad i, j = 1, \ldots, k \tag{3.4}$$

and let $\boldsymbol{\rho}(l) = \{\rho_{ij}(l)\}$ be the corresponding cross-correlation matrix.

When the vector ARMA model in (3.1) is stationary, it is well known that

$$\boldsymbol{\Gamma}(l) = \begin{cases} \sum_{j=l-r}^{l-1} \boldsymbol{\Gamma}(j)\boldsymbol{\varphi}'_{l-j} - \sum_{j=0}^{r-l} \boldsymbol{\psi}_j \boldsymbol{\Sigma} \boldsymbol{\theta}'_{j+l}, & l = 0, \ldots, r \\ \sum_{j=1}^{r} \boldsymbol{\Gamma}(l-j)\boldsymbol{\varphi}_j', & l > r, \end{cases} \tag{3.5}$$

where the $\boldsymbol{\psi}_j$'s are obtained from the relationship

$$\boldsymbol{\psi}(B) = \boldsymbol{\varphi}^{-1}(B)\boldsymbol{\theta}(B) = (\mathbf{I} + \boldsymbol{\psi}_1 B + \cdots),$$

$\boldsymbol{\theta}_0 = -\mathbf{I}$, $r = \max(p, q)$, and it is understood that (a) if $p < q$, $\boldsymbol{\varphi}_{p+1} = \cdots = \boldsymbol{\varphi}_r = \mathbf{0}$, and (b) if $q < p$, $\boldsymbol{\theta}_{q+1} = \cdots = \boldsymbol{\theta}_r = \mathbf{0}$.

In particular, when $p = 0$, that is, we have a vector MA(q) model, then

$$\boldsymbol{\Gamma}(l) = \begin{cases} \sum_{j=0}^{q-l} \boldsymbol{\theta}_j \boldsymbol{\Sigma} \boldsymbol{\theta}'_{j+l}, & l = 0, \ldots, q \\ \mathbf{0} & l > q. \end{cases} \tag{3.6}$$

Thus, all auto- and cross-correlations are zero when $l > q$. On the other hand, for a vector autoregressive model the auto- and cross-correlations in general will decay gradually to zero as $|l|$ increases.

3.3 A Determinantal Criterion for ARMA Models and the Partial Autoregression Matrices

From the moment equations in (3.5) for a stationary ARMA (p, q) model, we see that the autocovariance matrices $\boldsymbol{\Gamma}(l)$'s and the autoregressive coefficient matrices $\boldsymbol{\varphi}_1, \ldots, \boldsymbol{\varphi}_p$ are related as follows:

$$\begin{bmatrix} \mathbf{A}(p, m) & \mathbf{b}(p, m) \\ \mathbf{g}'(p, m) & \boldsymbol{\Gamma}(m) \end{bmatrix} \begin{bmatrix} \boldsymbol{\Phi}_{p-1} \\ \boldsymbol{\varphi}'_p \end{bmatrix} = \begin{bmatrix} \mathbf{c}(p, m) \\ \boldsymbol{\Gamma}(p+m) \end{bmatrix}, \quad m = q, q+1, \ldots, \tag{3.7}$$

where

$$\mathbf{A}(p, m) = \begin{bmatrix} \Gamma(m) & \Gamma(m-1) & \cdots & \Gamma(m-p+2) \\ \Gamma(m+1) & \ddots & & \vdots \\ \vdots & & \ddots & \Gamma(m-1) \\ \Gamma(m+p-2) & \cdots & \Gamma(m+1) & \Gamma(m) \end{bmatrix},$$

$$\mathbf{b}(p, m) = \begin{bmatrix} \Gamma(m-p+1) \\ \vdots \\ \Gamma(m-1) \end{bmatrix},$$

$$\mathbf{c}(p, m) = \begin{bmatrix} \Gamma(m+1) \\ \vdots \\ \Gamma(m+p-1) \end{bmatrix},$$

$\mathbf{g}'(p, m) = [\Gamma(m+p-1), \ldots, \Gamma(m+1)]$, and $\Phi'_{p-1} = [\varphi_1, \ldots, \varphi_{p-1}]$. Consider now the $k \times k$ matrix

$$\mathbf{D}(l, m) = [d_{ij}(l, m)] \quad \begin{matrix} l = 1, 2, \ldots \\ m = 0, 1, \ldots, \end{matrix} \tag{3.8}$$

where $d_{ij}(l, m)$ is the determinant

$$d_{ij}(l, m) = \det \begin{bmatrix} \mathbf{A}(l, m) & \mathbf{c}_j(l, m) \\ \mathbf{g}'_i(l, m) & \gamma_{ij}(l+m) \end{bmatrix}, \quad i, j = 1, \ldots, k$$

$\mathbf{c}_j(l, m)$ is the jth column of $\mathbf{c}(l, m)$, $\mathbf{g}'_i(l, m)$ is the ith row of $\mathbf{g}'(l, m)$, and $\gamma_{ij}(l+m)$ is the (i, j)th element of $\Gamma(l+m)$. It follows from (3.7) that for an ARMA (p, q) model

$$\mathbf{D}(l, m) = \mathbf{0} \quad \text{for} \quad l > p \quad \text{and} \quad m \geq q. \tag{3.9}$$

This provides a multivariate generalization of the results in Gray, Kelley, and McIntire (1978) for univariate ARMA models.

In the special case $m = q = 0$, (3.7) is a multivariate generalization of the Yule-Walker equations for autoregressive models in univariate time series. Analogous to the partial autocorrelation function for the univariate case, we may define a *partial autoregression matrix function* $\mathcal{P}(l)$ having the property that if the model is AR(p), then

$$\mathcal{P}(l) = \begin{cases} \varphi_l, & l = p \\ \mathbf{0}, & l > p \end{cases}. \tag{3.10}$$

From (3.7), we define $\mathcal{P}(l)$ as

$$\mathcal{P}'(l) = \begin{cases} \Gamma^{-1}(0)\Gamma(1), \; l = 1 \\ [\Gamma(0) - \mathbf{b}'(l, 0)\mathbf{A}^{-1}(l, 0)\mathbf{b}(l, 0)]^{-1} \\ [\Gamma(l) - \mathbf{b}'(l, 0)\mathbf{A}^{-1}(l, 0)\mathbf{c}(l, 0)], \; l > 1. \end{cases} \tag{3.11}$$

4. MODEL BUILDING STRATEGY FOR MULTIPLE TIME SERIES

The models in (3.1) contain a dauntingly large number $\{k^2(p + q) + \frac{1}{2}k(k + 1)\}$ of parameters, complicating methods for model building. It is natural that attempts have been made to simplify the general form in the model building process, for example by Granger and Newbold (1977) and Wallis (1977). While we sympathize with this aspiration, we feel that so far at least these attempts have not been successful. In some comparisons made later in Section 6, we argue that they do not result in genuine simplification, nor do they provide feasible methods when k is greater than 2 or 3. We see no alternative but to provide for direct initial fitting of models of the form (3.1). It must, however, be added

1. that often models of rather low order (p and q small) provide adequate approximation,
2. that occasionally knowledge of the system might allow simplification a priori, although even here prudent checking of the adequacy of the simplifcation would be necessary (see Zellner and Palm 1974),
3. that considerable simplification is almost invariably possible after an initial model has been fitted,
4. that 2 and 3 imply that provision should be made to allow models to be fitted in which certain parameters are fixed or constrained in some other way,
5. that other methods of seeking simplifications, for example principal component analysis or canonical analysis (see Box and Tiao 1977), will often prove effective.

In brief, we feel that although the full form (3.1) needs to be fitted initially, subsequent iterations will usually lead to simplification.

In what follows we sketch an iterative approach consisting of (a) tentative specification (identification), (b) estimation, and (c) diagnostic checking for the vector ARMA models in (3.1). A computer package to carry out this analysis has been completed (Tiao et al. 1979) consisting of three main programs: (a) Preliminary Analysis, (b) Stepwise Autoregression, and (c) Estimation and Forecasting.

4.1 Tentative Specification

The aim here is to employ statistics (a) that can be readily calculated from the data and (b) that facilitate the choice of subclass of models worthy of further examination.

Sample Cross-Correlations. The sample cross-correlations $\hat{\rho}_{ij}(l)$,

$$\hat{\rho}_{ij}(l) = \sum(Z_{it} - \bar{Z}_i)(Z_{j(t+l)} - \bar{Z}_j) / \{\sum(Z_{it} - \bar{Z}_i)^2 \sum(Z_{jt} - \bar{Z}_j)^2\}^{1/2}$$

where $\bar{Z}_i$ is the sample mean of the ith component series of $\mathbf{Z}_t$, are particularly useful in spotting low order vector moving average models, since from (3.6) $\rho_{ij}(l) = 0$ for $l > q$.

For the data shown in Figure 1, which were generated from a bivariate MA(1) model, Figures 3(a)–(c) show, respectively, the sample autocorrelations $\hat{\rho}_{11}(l)$ and $\hat{\rho}_{22}(l)$, and the sample cross-correlations $\hat{\rho}_{12}(l)$. The large values occurring at $|l| = 1$ would lead to tentative specification of the model as an MA(1). However, graphs of this kind become increasingly cumbersome as the number of series is increased. Furthermore, identification is not easy from a listing of sample cross-correlation matrices $\hat{\rho}(l)$ like that in Table 1(a), particularly when k is greater than 4 or 5.

In this circumstance, we have found the following simple device of great practical value. Instead of the numerical values, a plus sign is used to indicate a value greater than $2n^{-1/2}$, a minus sign a value less than $-2n^{-1/2}$, and a dot to indicate a value inbetween $-2n^{-1/2}$ and $2n^{-1/2}$. The motivation is that if the series were white noise, for large n the $\hat{\rho}_{ij}(l)$'s would be normally distributed with mean 0 and variance n^{-1}. The symbols can be arranged either as in Table 1(b) or as in Table 1(c). We realize that the variances of the $\hat{\rho}_{ij}(l)$'s can be considerably greater than $n^{-1/2}$ when the series are highly autocorrelated, so that these indicator symbols, if taken literally, can lead to overparameterization. However, we do not interpret these indicator symbols in the sense of a formal significance test, but as a rather crude "signal-to-noise ratio" guide. Taken together they can give useful and assimilable indicators of the general correlation pattern.

Table 2 shows sample cross-correlation matrices in terms of these indicator symbols for the series in Figure 2 generated from an AR(1) model. The persistence of large correlations suggests the possibility of autoregressive behavior. In general, the pattern of indicator symbols for the cross-correlation matrices makes it very easy to identify a low order moving average model.

Figure 3. Sample Auto- and Cross-Correlations for the Data in Figure 1

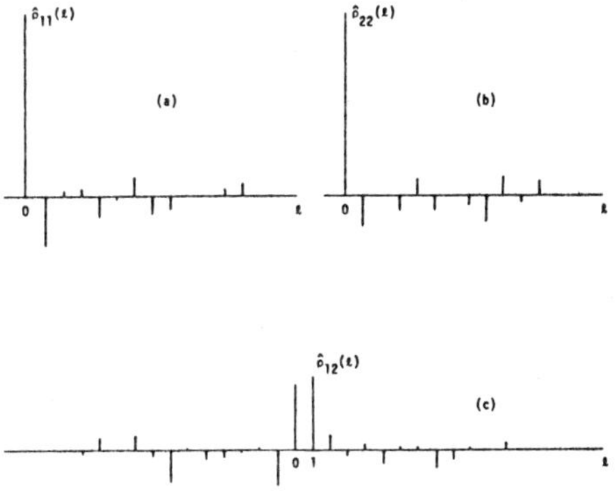

Sample Partial Autoregression and Related Summary Statistics. For an AR(p) process, the partial autoregression matrices $\mathcal{P}(l)$ in (3.11) are zero for $l > p$. They are therefore particularly useful for identifying an autoregressive model. Estimates of $\mathcal{P}(l)$ and their standard er-

Table 1. Cross-Correlations Matrices $\hat{\rho}$ (l) for the Data in Figure 1

(a) Sample cross-correlation matrices $\hat{\rho}(l)$ for the data in Figure 1

Lag 1-6

$$\begin{bmatrix} -.28 & .37 \\ -.21 & -.19 \end{bmatrix} \begin{bmatrix} .03 & .08 \\ .02 & .01 \end{bmatrix} \begin{bmatrix} .04 & -.03 \\ -.01 & -.08 \end{bmatrix} \begin{bmatrix} -.11 & .04 \\ -.03 & .09 \end{bmatrix} \begin{bmatrix} -.02 & -.09 \\ -.02 & -.08 \end{bmatrix} \begin{bmatrix} .10 & .01 \\ .01 & -.00 \end{bmatrix}$$

Lag 7-12

$$\begin{bmatrix} -.11 & .01 \\ -.17 & -.06 \end{bmatrix} \begin{bmatrix} -.09 & -.12 \\ -.03 & -.16 \end{bmatrix} \begin{bmatrix} .01 & -.06 \\ .08 & .10 \end{bmatrix} \begin{bmatrix} -.00 & .02 \\ .01 & -.04 \end{bmatrix} \begin{bmatrix} .03 & .00 \\ .08 & .08 \end{bmatrix} \begin{bmatrix} .06 & .04 \\ -.01 & .01 \end{bmatrix}$$

(b) $\hat{\rho}(l)$ in term of indicator symbols

Lag 1-6

$$\begin{bmatrix} - & + \\ - & - \end{bmatrix} \begin{bmatrix} \cdot & \cdot \\ \cdot & \cdot \end{bmatrix} \begin{bmatrix} \cdot & \cdot \\ \cdot & \cdot \end{bmatrix} \begin{bmatrix} \cdot & \cdot \\ \cdot & \cdot \end{bmatrix} \begin{bmatrix} \cdot & \cdot \\ \cdot & \cdot \end{bmatrix} \begin{bmatrix} \cdot & \cdot \\ \cdot & \cdot \end{bmatrix}$$

Lag 7-12

$$\begin{bmatrix} \cdot & \cdot \\ - & \cdot \end{bmatrix} \begin{bmatrix} \cdot & \cdot \\ \cdot & - \end{bmatrix} \begin{bmatrix} \cdot & \cdot \\ \cdot & \cdot \end{bmatrix} \begin{bmatrix} \cdot & \cdot \\ \cdot & \cdot \end{bmatrix} \begin{bmatrix} \cdot & \cdot \\ \cdot & \cdot \end{bmatrix} \begin{bmatrix} \cdot & \cdot \\ \cdot & \cdot \end{bmatrix}$$

(c) Pattern of correlations for each element in the matrix over all lags

	z_1	z_2
z_1	–	+ . . . .
z_2	– . . . . . –	– . . . . . . – . . . .

Table 2. Sample Cross-Correlation Matrices $\hat{\boldsymbol{\rho}}(l)$ for the Data in Figure 2 in Terms of Indicator Symbols

Lag 1-6

$$\begin{bmatrix} + & \cdot \\ + & + \end{bmatrix}\begin{bmatrix} \cdot & \cdot \\ + & + \end{bmatrix}\begin{bmatrix} \cdot & \cdot \\ + & + \end{bmatrix}\begin{bmatrix} \cdot & - \\ + & + \end{bmatrix}\begin{bmatrix} \cdot & \cdot \\ + & + \end{bmatrix}\begin{bmatrix} \cdot & \cdot \\ + & \cdot \end{bmatrix}$$

Lag 7-12

$$\begin{bmatrix} - & - \\ \cdot & \cdot \end{bmatrix}\begin{bmatrix} - & \cdot \\ \cdot & \cdot \end{bmatrix}\begin{bmatrix} \cdot & \cdot \\ \cdot & \cdot \end{bmatrix}\begin{bmatrix} \cdot & \cdot \\ \cdot & \cdot \end{bmatrix}\begin{bmatrix} \cdot & \cdot \\ \cdot & \cdot \end{bmatrix}\begin{bmatrix} \cdot & \cdot \\ \cdot & \cdot \end{bmatrix}$$

rors can be obtained by fitting autoregressive models of successively high order $l = 1, 2, \ldots$ by standard multivariate least squares.

It is well known (see, e.g., Anderson 1971) that for a stationary AR(p) model asymptotically the estimates $\boldsymbol{\varphi}'_1, \ldots, \boldsymbol{\varphi}'_p$ are jointly normally distributed. A useful summary of the pattern of the partials is obtained by listing indicator symbols, assigning a plus (minus) sign when a coefficient in $\hat{\boldsymbol{\mathcal{P}}}(l)$ is greater (less) than 2 (-2) times its estimated standard errors, and a dot for values in between.

To help tentatively determine the order of an autoregressive model, we may also employ the likelihood ratio statistics corresponding to testing the null hypotheses $\boldsymbol{\varphi}_l = \mathbf{0}$ against the alternative $\boldsymbol{\varphi}_l \neq \mathbf{0}$ when an AR(l) model is fitted. Let

$$\mathbf{S}(l) = \sum_{t=l+1}^{n} (\mathbf{z}_t - \hat{\boldsymbol{\varphi}}_1 \mathbf{z}_{t-1} - \ldots - \hat{\boldsymbol{\varphi}}_l \mathbf{z}_{t-l}) \times (\mathbf{z}_t - \hat{\boldsymbol{\varphi}}_1 \mathbf{z}_{t-1} - \ldots - \hat{\boldsymbol{\varphi}}_l \mathbf{z}_{t-l})' \qquad (4.1)$$

Table 3. Indicator Symbols for Partial Autoregression and Related Statistics for Data in Figure 2

Lag l	*Indicator symbols*	*M (l)*[a] $\stackrel{\sim}{\to} \chi_4^2$	*Diagonal elements of* $\hat{\boldsymbol{\Sigma}}$
1	· +	356.96	5.30
	− +		1.08
2	· ·	7.04	5.16
	· +		1.03
3	· ·	2.63	5.07
	· ·		1.03
4	· ·	4.38	5.01
	· ·		1.02
5	· ·	2.42	4.95
	· ·		1.01

[a] $\stackrel{\sim}{\to}$ means approximately distributed as.

be the matrix of residual sum of squares and cross products after fitting an AR(l). The likelihood ratio statistic is the ratio of the determinants

$$U = |\mathbf{S}(l)| \,/\, |\mathbf{S}(l-1)|. \qquad (4.2)$$

Using Bartlett's (1938) approximation, the statistic

$$M(l) = -(N - \tfrac{1}{2} - l \cdot k)\log_e U \qquad (4.3)$$

is, on the null hypothesis, asymptotically distributed as χ^2 with k^2 degrees of freedom, where $N = n - p - 1$ is the effective number of observations, assuming that a constant term is included in the model.

Finally, a measure of the extent to which the fit is improved as the order is increased is provided by the diagonal elements of the residual covariance matrices $\hat{\boldsymbol{\Sigma}}$ corresponding to the successive AR models.

For illustration, the matrices of summary symbols, the $M(l)$ statistics, and the diagonal elements of the residual covariance matrices for the series in Figure 2 are shown in Table 3 for $l = 1, \ldots, 5$. They indicate that an AR(1) or at most an AR(2) would be adequate for the data.

For the series shown in Figure 1, the pattern of the partials and related statistics are given in Table 4. Notice here that if we had confined attention to autoregressive models as is advocated in Parzen (1977), we would have needed p to be as high as 7. This is not surprising since with the MA(1) model of (3.2) written in the autoregressive form $\mathbf{z}_t = \boldsymbol{\pi}_1 \mathbf{z}_{t-1} + \boldsymbol{\pi}_2 \mathbf{z}_{t-2} + \ldots + \mathbf{a}_t$, we find

$$\boldsymbol{\pi}_1 = \begin{bmatrix} -.2 & -.3 \\ .6 & -1.1 \end{bmatrix}, \quad \boldsymbol{\pi}_2 = \begin{bmatrix} .14 & -.39 \\ .78 & -1.03 \end{bmatrix}, \ldots, \quad \boldsymbol{\pi}_6 = \begin{bmatrix} .23 & -.25 \\ .49 & -.51 \end{bmatrix}, \qquad (4.4)$$

$$|\boldsymbol{\pi}_1| = .4, \quad |\boldsymbol{\pi}_2| = .16, \quad \ldots, \quad |\boldsymbol{\pi}_6| = .0041.$$

Thus, although the determinants $|\boldsymbol{\pi}_j|$ decrease rapidly towards zero as j increases, the elements of $\boldsymbol{\pi}_j$ converge to zero very slowly so that many autoregressive terms would be needed to provide an adequate approximation.

In general, the pattern of the partial autoregression matrices, the $M(l)$ statistic, and the diagonal elements of the residual covariance matrix are useful to distinguish between moving average and low order autoregressive models and to select tentatively the appropriate order for the latter.

Table 4. Pattern of Partial Autoregression and Related Statistics for Data in Figure 1

Lag	Pattern of $\hat{\mathbf{p}}(l)$	$M(l) \dot{\rightarrow} \chi_4^2$	‡
1	− −	123.2	4.78
	+ −		1.88
2	· ·	75.9	4.75
	+ −		1.43
3	+ ·	35.2	4.63
	+ −		1.23
4	· ·	27.5	4.63
	+ ·		1.08
5	· ·	16.6	4.61
	+ ·		1.04
6	· ·	13.5	4.53
	+ ·		.98
7	· −	16.5	4.38
	+ ·		.94
8	· ·	8.1	4.31
	· −		.91

Sample Residual Cross-Correlation Matrices After AR Fit. After each AR(l) fit, $l = 1, \ldots, p$, cross-correlation matrices of the residuals $\hat{\mathbf{a}}_t$'s may be readily obtained. Table 5 shows indicator symbols for residual correlations after fitting AR(1) and AR(2) to the AR data plotted in Figure 2. Again a plus sign is used to indicate values greater than $2n^{-1/2}$, a minus sign for values less than $-2n^{-1/2}$, and a dot for in-between values. They verify that there is no need to go beyond an AR(2) model.

It is perhaps worth emphasizing here again that these indicator symbols are proposed as a rough preliminary device to help arrive at an initial model. They should not be treated as "exact significance testing." In a recent paper by Li and McLeod (1980), expressions have been obtained for the asymptotic distributions of the residual autocorrelations. As in the univariate case, the low order autocorrelations have variance considerably less than $n^{-1/2}$.

For mixed vector autoregressive moving average models in general, however, both the population cross-correlation matrices $\mathbf{p}(l)$ and the partial autoregression matrices $\mathcal{P}(l)$ decay only gradually toward $\mathbf{0}$. In some situations, the order of mixed models may be tentatively identified by inspection of patterns in residual cross-correlations after the AR fit, but in others study of residual correlations could be misleading. For illustration, consider the case of a stationary ARMA(1, 1) model

$$(\mathbf{I} - \boldsymbol{\varphi}B)\mathbf{z}_t = (\mathbf{I} - \boldsymbol{\theta}B)\mathbf{a}_t. \tag{4.5}$$

If an AR(1) model is fitted to $\{\mathbf{z}_t\}$, then the estimate $\hat{\boldsymbol{\varphi}}$ will be biased. In fact, asymptotically $\hat{\boldsymbol{\varphi}}$ converges in probability to

$$\hat{\boldsymbol{\varphi}} \rightarrow \boldsymbol{\varphi}_0 = \boldsymbol{\Gamma}'(1)\boldsymbol{\Gamma}(0)^{-1}. \tag{4.6}$$

Thus the residuals $\hat{\mathbf{a}}_t = \mathbf{z}_t - \boldsymbol{\varphi}_0\mathbf{z}_{t-1}$ approximately follow the model

$$\hat{\mathbf{a}}_t = (\mathbf{i} - \boldsymbol{\varphi}_0 B)(\mathbf{I} - \boldsymbol{\varphi}B)^{-1}(\mathbf{I} - \boldsymbol{\theta}B)\mathbf{a}_t. \tag{4.7}$$

Table 5. Indicator Symbols for Residual Cross Correlations for the AR (1) Data of Figure 2

AR (1) Lag 1-6

$$\begin{bmatrix} \cdot & \cdot \\ \cdot & - \end{bmatrix}\begin{bmatrix} \cdot & \cdot \\ \cdot & \cdot \end{bmatrix}\begin{bmatrix} \cdot & \cdot \\ \cdot & \cdot \end{bmatrix}\begin{bmatrix} \cdot & \cdot \\ \cdot & \cdot \end{bmatrix}\begin{bmatrix} \cdot & \cdot \\ \cdot & \cdot \end{bmatrix}\begin{bmatrix} + & \cdot \\ \cdot & \cdot \end{bmatrix}$$

Lag 7-12

$$\begin{bmatrix} - & \cdot \\ - & \cdot \end{bmatrix}\begin{bmatrix} \cdot & \cdot \\ \cdot & \cdot \end{bmatrix}\begin{bmatrix} \cdot & \cdot \\ \cdot & \cdot \end{bmatrix}\begin{bmatrix} \cdot & \cdot \\ \cdot & \cdot \end{bmatrix}\begin{bmatrix} \cdot & \cdot \\ \cdot & \cdot \end{bmatrix}\begin{bmatrix} \cdot & \cdot \\ \cdot & \cdot \end{bmatrix}$$

AR (2) Lag 1-6

$$\begin{bmatrix} \cdot & \cdot \\ \cdot & \cdot \end{bmatrix}\begin{bmatrix} \cdot & \cdot \\ \cdot & \cdot \end{bmatrix}\begin{bmatrix} \cdot & \cdot \\ \cdot & \cdot \end{bmatrix}\begin{bmatrix} \cdot & \cdot \\ \cdot & \cdot \end{bmatrix}\begin{bmatrix} \cdot & \cdot \\ \cdot & \cdot \end{bmatrix}\begin{bmatrix} + & \cdot \\ \cdot & \cdot \end{bmatrix}$$

Lag 7-12

$$\begin{bmatrix} \cdot & \cdot \\ \cdot & \cdot \end{bmatrix}\begin{bmatrix} \cdot & \cdot \\ \cdot & \cdot \end{bmatrix}\begin{bmatrix} \cdot & \cdot \\ \cdot & \cdot \end{bmatrix}\begin{bmatrix} \cdot & \cdot \\ \cdot & \cdot \end{bmatrix}\begin{bmatrix} \cdot & \cdot \\ \cdot & \cdot \end{bmatrix}\begin{bmatrix} \cdot & \cdot \\ \cdot & \cdot \end{bmatrix}$$

For $k = 1$, $\{\hat{a}_t\}$ follows an ARMA(1, 2) model so that the autocorrelations of $\hat{a}_t$ are

$$\rho_{\hat{a}}(j) = \varphi\rho_{\hat{a}}(j - 1), j > 2 \qquad (4.8)$$

and $\rho_{\hat{a}}(1)$ and $\rho_{\hat{a}}(2)$ are functions of φ and θ. Table 6 gives values of $\rho_{\hat{a}}(1)$ and $\rho_{\hat{a}}(2)$ for various combinations of values of φ and θ. For each combination, the first value is $\rho_{\hat{a}}(1)$ and the second $\rho_{\hat{a}}(2)$.

We see that if the true value of φ is large in magnitude, residual autocorrelations would lead to the choice of an MA(1) model for $\hat{a}_t$ and therefore the correct identification. For intermediate values of φ, a moving average of order 2 or higher might be selected, resulting in overparametrization.

In Gray, Kelley, and McIntire (1978) and Beguin, Gourieroux, and Monfort (1980), methods have been proposed to determine the order of univariate ARMA model. These methods are essentially equivalent to estimating, for $k = 1$, the determinant $D(l, m)$ in (3.8) using sample estimates of the autocovariances and selecting the orders of autoregressive and moving average polynomials on the basis of the property in (3.9). We are currently studying sampling properties of estimates of appropriate functions of $\mathbf{D}(l, m)$ in the vector case.

4.2 Estimation

Once the order of the model in (3.1) has been tentatively selected, efficient estimates of the associated parameter matrices $\boldsymbol{\varphi} = (\boldsymbol{\varphi}_1, \ldots, \boldsymbol{\varphi}_p)$, $\boldsymbol{\theta} = (\boldsymbol{\theta}_1, \ldots, \boldsymbol{\theta}_q)$, and $\boldsymbol{\Sigma}$ are determined by maximizing the likelihood function. Approximate standard errors and correlation matrix of the estimates of elements of the $\boldsymbol{\varphi}_i$'s and $\boldsymbol{\theta}_i$'s can also be obtained.

Conditional Likelihood. For the ARMA (p, q) model, we can write

$$\mathbf{a}_t = \mathbf{z}_t - \boldsymbol{\varphi}_1\mathbf{z}_{t-1} - \cdots - \boldsymbol{\varphi}_p\mathbf{z}_{t-p} + \boldsymbol{\theta}_1\mathbf{a}_{t-1} + \cdots + \boldsymbol{\theta}_q\mathbf{a}_{t-q}. \qquad (4.9)$$

As in the univariate case discussed in Box and Jenkins (1970), the likelihood function can be approximated by a "conditional" likelihood function as follows. The series is regarded as consisting of the $n - p$ vector observations

Table 6. Asymptotic Values of $\rho_{\hat{a}}(1)$ and $\rho_{\hat{a}}(2)$

φ \ θ	−.95	−.50	.50	.95
−.95	—	.265 .085	−.381 −.03	−.481 −.036
−.50	.049 −.222	—	−.223 −.201	−.321 −.267
.50	.321 −.267	.223 −.201	—	−.049 −.222
.95	.481 −.036	.381 −.03	−.265 .085	—

$\mathbf{z}_{p+1}, \ldots, \mathbf{z}_n$. The likelihood function is then determined from $\mathbf{a}_{p+1}, \ldots, \mathbf{a}_n$, using the preliminary values $\mathbf{z}_1, \ldots, \mathbf{z}_p$ and conditional on zero values for $\mathbf{a}_p, \ldots, \mathbf{a}_{p-q-1}$. Thus, as shown in Wilson (1973),

$$L_c(\boldsymbol{\varphi}, \boldsymbol{\theta}, \boldsymbol{\Sigma} \mid \mathbf{z}) \propto |\boldsymbol{\Sigma}|^{-(n-p)/2}\exp\{-\tfrac{1}{2}\operatorname{tr}\boldsymbol{\Sigma}^{-1}\mathbf{S}(\boldsymbol{\varphi}, \boldsymbol{\theta})\}, \qquad (4.10)$$

where $\mathbf{S}(\boldsymbol{\varphi}, \boldsymbol{\theta}) = \sum_{t=p+1}^{n} \mathbf{a}_t\mathbf{a}'_t$. Properties of the maximum likelihood estimates obtained from (4.10) have been discussed in Nicholls (1976, 1977) and Anderson (1980).

It has been shown in Hillmer and Tiao (1979) that this approximation can be seriously inadequate if n is not sufficiently large and one or more zeros of $|\boldsymbol{\theta}_q(B)|$ lie on or close to the unit circle. Specifically, this would lead to estimates of the moving average parameters with large bias.

Exact Likelihood Function. For univariate ARMA models, the exact likelihood function has been considered by Tiao and Ali (1971), Newbold (1974), Dent (1977), Ansley (1979), and others. For vector models, this function has been studied by Osborn (1977) for the pure moving average case and by Phadke and Kedem (1978), Nicholls and Hall (1979), and Hillmer and Tiao (1979). It takes the form

$$l(\boldsymbol{\varphi}, \boldsymbol{\theta}, \boldsymbol{\Sigma} \mid \mathbf{z}) \propto L_c(\boldsymbol{\varphi}, \boldsymbol{\theta}, \boldsymbol{\Sigma} \mid \mathbf{z})l_1(\boldsymbol{\varphi}, \boldsymbol{\theta}, \boldsymbol{\Sigma} \mid \mathbf{z}), \qquad (4.11)$$

where l_1 depends (a) only on $\mathbf{z}_1, \ldots, \mathbf{z}_p$ if $q = 0$ and (b) on all the data vectors $\mathbf{z}_1, \ldots, \mathbf{z}_n$ if $q \neq 0$. Estimation algorithms have been developed and incorporated in our computer package for the vector MA(q) model. For the general ARMA(p, q) model, it has been shown that a close approximation to the exact likelihood can be obtained by considering the transformation

$$\mathbf{w}_t = (\mathbf{I} - \boldsymbol{\varphi}_1 B - \cdots - \boldsymbol{\varphi}_p B^p)\mathbf{z}_t$$

so that $\qquad (4.12)$

$$\mathbf{w}_t = \boldsymbol{\theta}_q(B)\mathbf{a}_t$$

and then applying the results for MA(q) to $\mathbf{w}_t$, $t = p + 1, \ldots, n$.

Because estimation of moving average parameters using the exact likelihood is rather slow, we presently employ the conditional method in the preliminary stages of iterative model building and switch to the exact method towards the end.

4.3 Diagnostic Checking

To guard against model misspecification and to search for directions of improvement, a detailed diagnostic analysis of the residual series $\{\hat{\mathbf{a}}_t\}$, where

$$\hat{\mathbf{a}}_t = \mathbf{z}_t - \hat{\boldsymbol{\varphi}}_1\mathbf{z}_{t-1} - \cdots - \hat{\boldsymbol{\varphi}}_p\mathbf{z}_{t-p} + \hat{\boldsymbol{\theta}}_1\hat{\mathbf{a}}_{t-1} + \cdots + \hat{\boldsymbol{\theta}}_q\hat{\mathbf{a}}_{t-q}, \qquad (4.13)$$

is performed. Useful diagnostic checks include (a) plots of standardized residual series against time and/or other variables and (b) cross-correlation matrices of the resid-

Table 7. Pattern of Sample Cross-Correlations for the SCC Data

	Z_1 *Stocks*	Z_2 *Cars*	Z_3 *Commodities*
Z_1 Stocks	+ + + + + + + + ...	− − − − − − − − − − − − − − − − − − − −	− − − − − − − − − − − − − − − − − − − −
Z_2 Cars	. . . . + + +	+ + + + + + + + + + + + + + + ...	+ + + + + + + + + + + + + + ...
Z_3 Commodities	− − − − − − − . . . . + + + + +	+ + + + + + + + + + + + + + + + + + . .	+ + + + + + + + + + + + + + + + +

uals $\hat{\mathbf{a}}_t$. As before, the structures of the correlations are summarized by indicator symbols. Overall χ^2 tests based on the sample cross correlations of the residuals have been proposed in recent papers by Hosking (1980) and Li and McLeod (1980). However, as is noted in Box and Jenkins (1970), such overall tests are not substitutes for more detailed study of the correlation structure.

5. ANALYSES OF TWO EXAMPLES

We now apply the model building approach introduced in the preceding section to the following sets of data:

1. The Financial Time Ordinary Share Index, U.K. Car Production and the Financial Time Commodity Price Index: Quarterly Data 3/1952–4/1967, obtained from Coen, Gomme, and Kendall (1969). This will be referred to as the SCC data.
2. The Gas Furnace Data given in Box and Jenkins (1970).

5.1 The SCC Data

The three series are

Z_{1t}: Financial Time Ordinary Share Index
Z_{2t}: U.K. Car Production
Z_{3t}: Financial Time Commodity Price Index

The authors of the original study were interested in the possibility of predicting Z_{1t} from lagged values of Z_{2t} and Z_{3t} using a standard regression analysis in which Z_{1t} was treated as a dependent variable and $Z_{2(t-6)}$ and $Z_{3(t-7)}$ as regressors or independent variables. For a critical evaluation of this approach, see Box and Newbold (1970). Here we consider what structure is revealed by the present multiple time series analysis, in which the three series are jointly modeled.

Tentative Specification. We see in Table 7 that the original series show high and persistent auto- and cross-correlations. Examination of the partials and related statistics in Table 8 shows that for $l > 2$ most of the elements of $\mathcal{P}(l)$ are small compared with their estimated standard errors and the $M(l)$ statistic fails to show significant improvement. Table 9 shows that the pattern of the cross-correlations of the residuals after AR(2) is consonant with estimated white noise. However, note that there is one large residual correlation at lag 1 after the AR(1) fit, suggesting also the possibility of an ARMA(1, 1) model.

Estimation. Both an AR(2) and an ARMA(1, 1) model were fitted using the exact likelihood method* but results are given only for the ARMA(1, 1) model, which produced a marginally better representation. For this model,

$$(\mathbf{I} - \varphi B)\mathbf{Z}_t = \boldsymbol{\theta}_0 + (\mathbf{I} - \boldsymbol{\theta} B)\mathbf{a}_t, \tag{5.1}$$

where $\boldsymbol{\theta}_0$ is a vector of constants, Table 10 shows the initial unrestricted fit and also the fits for two simpler models obtained by setting to zero those coefficients whose estimates were small compared to their standard errors.

Diagnostic Checking. Table 11 suggests that the restricted ARMA(1, 1) model provides an adequate representation of the data.

Implication of the Model. The final model implies that the system is approximated by

$$(1 - .98B)Z_{1t} = a_{1t} \tag{5.2a}$$

$$(1 - .93B)Z_{2t} = .2 + a_{2t} \tag{5.2b}$$

$$(1 - .83B)Z_{3t} = 2.8 + .40a_{1(t-1)} + (1 + .41B)a_{3t}. \tag{5.2c}$$

Upon substituting (5.2a) into (5.2c), we get

$$(1 - .83B)Z_{3t} = 2.8 + .40(1 - .98B)Z_{1(t-1)} + (1 + .41B)a_{3t}. \tag{5.2d}$$

Thus all three series behave approximately as random walks with slightly correlated innovations. From the point of view of forecasting, (5.2d) is of some interest since it implies that ordinary share $Z_{1(t-1)}$ is a *leading indicator* at lag 1 for the commodity index Z_{3t}. Its effect is small, however, as can be seen for example by the improvement achieved over the corresponding best fitting univariate model, which was

$$(1 - .78B)Z_{3t} = 3.63 + (1 + .53B)a_t, \sigma^2 = .151 \tag{5.3}$$

The residual variance of .151 from the univariate model is not much larger than the value .134 for a_{3t} obtained

* For this example, estimates from the conditional likelihood for the ARMA(1, 1) case are very close to the exact results.

Table 8. Partial Autoregression and Related Statistics: SCC Data

Lag	Indicator Symbols for Partials	M(l) Statistic $\overset{a}{\sim} \chi_9^2$	Diagonal Elements of $\hat{\Sigma} \times 10$
	+ · ·		.44
1	· + ·	301.3	.89
	· · +		1.62
	− · ·		.40
2	· · ·	18.6	.84
	− + −		1.23
	· · ·		.37
3	· · ·	9.6	.81
	· · ·		1.21
	· · ·		.36
4	· · ·	3.6	.79
	· · ·		1.19
	· + ·		.32
5	· + ·	11.9	.70
	· · ·		1.11

from the final vector model. Although the multiple time series analysis fails to reveal anything very surprising for this example, it shows what is there and does not mislead.

5.2 The Gas Furnace Data

The two series consist of (a) input gas rate and (b) output as CO_2 concentration at 9-second intervals from a gas furnace. We shall let Z_{1t} = gas rate + .057 and $Z_{2t} = CO_2 - 5.35$. This set of data was employed in Box and Jenkins (1970) to illustrate a procedure of identification, fitting, and checking of a transfer function model of the form (2.3) for $k = 2$ relating two time series one of which is *known* to be input for the other. Using this approach, the following models were found for the input Z_{1t} and the output Z_{2t};

$$(1 - 1.97B + 1.37B^2 - .34B^3)Z_{1t} = a_{1t},$$

$$\hat{\sigma}^2_{a_1} = .0353 \quad (5.4a)$$

$$Z_{2t} = \frac{\omega(B)}{\delta(B)} B^b Z_{1t} + \varphi(B)^{-1} a_{2t}, \ \hat{\sigma}^2_{a_2} = .0561, \quad (5.4b)$$

Table 9. Pattern of Cross-Correlation Matrices of Residuals: SCC Data

	Lag 1	2	3	4	5	6	7	8
(a) AR(1) model								
	· · +	· · ·	· · ·	· · ·	· · ·	· · ·	· · ·	· · ·
	· · ·	· · ·	· · ·	· · ·	· · ·	· · ·	· · ·	· · ·
	· · ·	· · ·	· · ·	· · ·	· · ·	· · ·	· · +	· · ·
(b) AR(2) model								
	· · ·	· · ·	· · ·	· · ·	· · ·	· · ·	· · ·	· · ·
	· · ·	· · ·	· · ·	− · ·	· · ·	· · ·	· · ·	· · ·
	· · ·	· · ·	· · ·	· · ·	· · ·	· · ·	· · +	· · ·

Table 10. Estimation Results for the Model (5.1): SCC Data (exact likelihood)

	$\hat{\theta}_0$	$\hat{\varphi}$			$\hat{\theta}$			$\hat{\Sigma}$		
(1) Full Model	1.11	.81	.15	−.06	−.29	.23	.06	.037		
	(.64)	(.08)	(.07)	(.04)	(.15)	(.11)	(.07)			
	1.74	−.07	.98	−.09	−.45	.20	−.15	.022	.078	
	(.82)	(.10)	(.10)	(.05)	(.22)	(.17)	(.11)			
	4.08	−.32	.30	.76	−.79	.57	−.44	.013	.022	.129
	(1.47)	(.18)	(.17)	(.08)	(.28)	(.21)	(.13)			
(2) Restricted Model (intermediate)	.13	.90	.08					.042		
	(.09)	(.06)	(.06)	·	·	·	·			
	.59		.92	−.02				.022	.079	
	(.05)	·	(.04)	(.04)	·	·	·			
	2.48			.85	−.40		−.41	.017	.021	.131
	(1.10)	·	·	(.07)	(.23)	·	(.12)			
(3) Restricted Model (final)	.12	.98						.045		
	(.08)	(.03)		·	·	·	·			
	.24		.93					.024	.085	
	(.10)	·	(.04)	·	·	·	·			
	2.76			.83	−.40		−.41	.019	.023	.134
	(1.07)	·	·	(.06)	(.23)	·	(.12)			

Table 11. Pattern of Residual Cross-Correlations After Final Restricted ARMA(1,1) Model Fit: SCC Data

	$\hat{a}_1$	$\hat{a}_2$	$\hat{a}_3$
$\hat{a}_1$	. . . . – .	. . . .	. . . .
$\hat{a}_2$	. . . .	. . . .	. . . .
$\hat{a}_3$	. . . .	. . . . – .	. . . .

where $\omega(B) = -(.53 + .37B + .51B^2)$, $\delta(B) = 1 - .57B$, $\varphi(B) = 1 - 1.53B + .63B^2$, and the $\{a_{1t}\}$ and $\{a_{2t}\}$ series are assumed independent.

Particularly when we are dealing with econometric rather than engineering models, feedback relationships may not be known a priori; it is of interest, therefore, to analyze the data using the present approach where no distinction is made between an input and output variable and the fact that no feedback could occur in the system is not used.

Tentative Specification. In Table 12, we see that the auto- and cross-correlations of the original data in part (a) are persistently large in magnitude, ruling out low order moving average models; the $M(l)$ statistic (χ^2_4) in part (b) suggests that an AR(6) model might be appropriate; and the residual cross correlation pattern after an AR(6) fit in part (c) seems to verify the appropriateness of this model.

Estimation Results. Estimation results corresponding to an unrestricted AR(6) model

$$(\mathbf{I} - \varphi_1 B - \cdots - \varphi_6 B^6)\mathbf{Z}_t = \mathbf{a}_t \tag{5.5}$$

are as follows:

$$\hat{\varphi}_1 = \begin{bmatrix} 1.93 & -.05 \\ (.06) & (.05) \\ .06 & 1.55 \\ (.08) & (.06) \end{bmatrix} \quad \hat{\varphi}_2 = \begin{bmatrix} -1.20 & .10 \\ (.13) & (.08) \\ -.14 & -.59 \\ (.16) & (.11) \end{bmatrix}$$

$$\hat{\varphi}_3 = \begin{bmatrix} .17 & -.08 \\ (.15) & (.09) \\ -.44 & -.17 \\ (.19) & (.11) \end{bmatrix} \quad \hat{\varphi}_4 = \begin{bmatrix} -.16 & .03 \\ (.15) & (.09) \\ .15 & .13 \\ (.19) & (.11) \end{bmatrix}$$

$$\hat{\varphi}_5 = \begin{bmatrix} .38 & -.04 \\ (.14) & (.08) \\ -.12 & .06 \\ (.18) & (.10) \end{bmatrix} \quad \hat{\varphi}_6 = \begin{bmatrix} -.22 & .03 \\ (.08) & (.03) \\ .25 & -.04 \\ (.11) & (.04) \end{bmatrix}$$

$$\hat{\Sigma} = \begin{bmatrix} .0345 & \\ -.0023 & .0566 \end{bmatrix}, \quad \hat{\rho}(a_1, a_2) = .045 \tag{5.6}$$

If we let

$$\hat{\varphi}_l = \{\hat{\varphi}_{ij}^{(l)}\},$$

Table 12. Tentative Identification for the Gas Furnace Data

(a) Pattern of cross-correlations of the original data

	Z_{1t}	Z_{2t}
Z_{1t}	+ + + + + + + + + + +	– – – – – – – – – – –
Z_{2t}	– – – – – – – – – . .	+ + + + + + + + + + +

(b) M statistic for partial autoregression

Lag l	1	2	3	4	5	6	7	8	9	10	11
$M(l)$	1650	665	31.7	22.5	5.6	12.9	1.8	8.0	3.5	0	2.0

(c) Pattern of cross-correlations of the residuals after AR(6) fit

	$\hat{a}_{1t}$	$\hat{a}_{2t}$
$\hat{a}_{1t}$	. . . . –	. . . .
$\hat{a}_{2t}$	. . . .	. . . .

we see that $\hat{\varphi}_{12}^{(l)}$ are small compared with their standard errors over all lags, confirming (as in this case is known from the physical nature of the apparatus generating the data) that there is a unidirectional relationship between Z_{1t} and Z_{2t} involving no feedback. Also, $\hat{\varphi}_{21}^{(l)}$ is small for $l = 1, 2$, and the residuals $\hat{a}_{1t}$ and $\hat{a}_{2t}$ are essentially uncorrelated, implying a delay of 3 periods. It should be noted also that the variances for a_{1t} and a_{2t} are very close to those for a_{1t} and a_{2t} in (5.4), and their correlation is negligible.

To facilitate comparison with (5.4), we set $\varphi_{11}^{(l)} = 0$ for $l > 3$, $\varphi_{12}^{(l)} = 0$ for all l, $\varphi_{21}^{(l)} = 0$ for $l = 1, 2$, and $\varphi_{22}^{(l)} = 0$ for $l = 5, 6$. Estimation results for this restricted AR(6) model are then

$$\hat{\varphi}_1 = \begin{bmatrix} 1.98 & \cdot \\ (.06) & \\ \cdot & 1.53 \\ & (.06) \end{bmatrix} \quad \hat{\varphi}_2 = \begin{bmatrix} -1.38 & \cdot \\ (.10) & \\ \cdot & -.58 \\ & (.11) \end{bmatrix} \quad \hat{\varphi}_3 = \begin{bmatrix} .35 & \cdot \\ (.06) & \\ -.53 & -.14 \\ (.07) & (.10) \end{bmatrix}$$

$$\hat{\varphi}_4 = \begin{bmatrix} \cdot & \cdot \\ .11 & .12 \\ (.16) & (.04) \end{bmatrix} \quad \hat{\varphi}_5 = \begin{bmatrix} \cdot & \cdot \\ -.04 & \cdot \\ (.17) & \end{bmatrix} \quad \hat{\varphi}_6 = \begin{bmatrix} \cdot & \cdot \\ .21 & \cdot \\ (.11) & \end{bmatrix}$$

$$\hat{\Sigma} = \begin{bmatrix} .0359 & -.0029 \\ & .0561 \end{bmatrix}, \quad \hat{\rho}(a_1, a_2) \doteq 0 \tag{5.7}$$

Examination of the pattern of the cross-correlations of the residuals suggests that the model is adequate

Implication of the Bivariate Model. The final AR(6) model (5.7) can be written

$$\begin{bmatrix} \varphi_{11}(B) & \\ \varphi_{21}(B) & \varphi_{22}(B) \end{bmatrix} \begin{bmatrix} Z_{1t} \\ Z_{2t} \end{bmatrix} = \begin{bmatrix} a_{1t} \\ a_{2t} \end{bmatrix}, \tag{5.8}$$

where $\varphi_{11}(B) = 1 - 1.98B + 1.38B^2 - .35B^3$, $\varphi_{21}(B) = (.53 - .11B - .21B)B^3$, and $\varphi_{22}(B) = (1 - 1.53B + .58B^2 + .14B^3 - .12B^4)$. Assuming a_{1t} and a_{2t} are uncorrelated, the input model $\varphi_{11}(B)Z_{1t} = a_{1t}$ with $\text{Var}(a_{1t}) = .0359$ is essentially the same as (5.4a). Now the model relating the output Z_{2t} to the input Z_{1t} is

$$Z_{2t} = -\frac{\varphi_{21}(B)}{\varphi_{22}(B)} Z_{1t} + \frac{1}{\varphi_{22}(B)} a_{2t} \tag{5.9}$$

with $\text{Var}(a_{2t}) = .0561$. The noise model $\varphi_{22}^{-1}(B)a_{2t}$ is not very different from the corresponding one $\varphi^{-1}(B)a_{2t}$ in (5.4b), but the dynamic model $-\varphi_{21}(B)\varphi_{22}^{-1}(B)Z_{1t}$ at first sight appears markedly different from the first term on the right side of (5.4b). The reason is that in the form (5.9) the denominators of the dynamic model and of the noise model are constrained to be identical. This restriction is not present in the transfer function model (5.4b). The less restrictive form can however be written in the form of (5.9) if we set $\varphi_{22}(B) = \varphi(B)$ and $-\varphi_{21}(B) = \omega(B)B^b\{\varphi(B)\delta^{-1}(B)\}$. For this example, the factor $\varphi(B)\delta^{-1}(B) \doteq 1 - .96B$, and it is then seen that the models are in fact very similar. This may be confirmed by comparing the impulse response weights in Table 13, where $\omega(B)B^b\delta^{-1}(B) = \sum_{j=0}^{\infty} v_j B^j$ and $-\varphi_{21}(B)\varphi_{22}^{-1}(B) = \sum_{j=0}^{\infty} v^*_j B^j$.

Further Analysis of Stepwise AR Results. It is instructive to examine for this data the changes in the fitted autoregressive models as the order is increased. Using indicator symbols (and omitting the dots) Table 14 shows the situation for $p = 1, \ldots, 6$. The residual covariance matrix for each order is also given. The following observations may be made.

1. If only AR(1) or AR(2) were considered, one might be led to believe mistakenly that there was a feedback relationship between these two series.
2. The unidirectional dynamic relationship becomes clear when the order of the model, p, is increased to three. Since the input series Z_{1t} essentially follows a univariate AR(3) model, this suggests that the present procedure will correctly identify the one-sided causal dynamic relationship once the input model is appropriately selected.
3. The delay $b = 3$ emerges when the order p is increased to 4. Since only very marginal improvement in the fit occurs for $p > 4$, this is saying that the delay is correctly identified only when the model is specified essentially correctly.

Implications on General Time Series Model Building. The relative merit of the present procedure and more direct modeling of the system will depend on how much is known or how much we are prepared to assume. In some applications, particularly in engineering and most examples of intervention analysis, an adequate initial specification may be possible from knowledge of the nature of the problem. This may allow a flow diagram showing the feedback structure to be drawn and likely orders to be guessed for the various dynamic components. The resulting models can then be directly *fitted* in the manner described and illustrated in Box and MacGregor (1974, 1976) and Box and Tiao (1975). For a single input with feedback known to be absent, a prewhitening method is given in Box and Jenkins (1970) for *identifying* an unknown dynamic system, but extension of this identification method to multiple inputs is rather complex.

Particularly for economic and business examples, however, the feedback structure and orders of the multiple system are often unknown. The present multiple time series procedure has the great advantage that it allows *identification* of the feedback and dynamic structure. Furthermore,

1. A one-sided causal relationship, if it exists, will emerge in the identification process, and the stochastic structures of the input as well as the transfer function relationship between input and output will be modeled simultaneously.
2. Stochastic multiple input and multiple output situations are readily handled.
3. A useful method is provided for seeking leading indicators in economic and business applications. In this context it should be noted that a unidirectional dynamic relationship may not exist between two time series even when one variable is known to be the input for the other. One reason for this phenomenon is the effect of temporal aggregation. As shown in Tiao and Wei (1976), pseudo-feedback relationships could occur because of this temporal aggregation effect, and it would be a mistake to impose a transfer function model in such a situation.
4. However, when a simple transfer function structure of the form (2.2) *is* appropriate, the present multiple time series approach could rarely reproduce it directly—see, for example, (5.4b) and (5.9)—and some analysis of the fitted form might be necessary to reveal a more parsimonious and more easily understood structure.

6. COMPARISON WITH SOME OTHER APPROACHES AND CONCLUDING REMARKS

We have discussed various tools used in an iterative approach to modeling multiple time series and illustrated

Table 13. Impulse Response Weights for the Gas Furnace Data

	j												
	0	1	2	3	4	5	6	7	8	9	10	11	12
v_j	·	·	·	−.53	−.67	−.89	−.51	−.29	−.17	−.09	−.05	−.03	−.02
v^*_j	·	·	·	−.53	−.70	−.77	−.48	−.26	−.09	−.01	.01	.00	−.01

Table 14. Successive AR Fitting Results for the Gas Furnace Data

Order of AR	φ_1	φ_2	φ_3	φ_4	φ_5	φ_6	$\boldsymbol{\Sigma}$
1	$\begin{bmatrix} + & + \\ - & + \end{bmatrix}$						$\begin{bmatrix} .102 & .090 \\ & .346 \end{bmatrix}$
2	$\begin{bmatrix} + & - \\ + & + \end{bmatrix}$	$\begin{bmatrix} - & + \\ - & - \end{bmatrix}$					$\begin{bmatrix} .037 & -.004 \\ & .069 \end{bmatrix}$
3	$\begin{bmatrix} + & \\ & + \end{bmatrix}$	$\begin{bmatrix} - & \\ - & - \end{bmatrix}$	$\begin{bmatrix} + & \\ & + \end{bmatrix}$				$\begin{bmatrix} .036 & -.002 \\ & .063 \end{bmatrix}$
4	$\begin{bmatrix} + & \\ & + \end{bmatrix}$	$\begin{bmatrix} - & \\ & - \end{bmatrix}$	$\begin{bmatrix} & \\ - & \end{bmatrix}$	$\begin{bmatrix} & \\ + & + \end{bmatrix}$			$\begin{bmatrix} .036 & -.003 \\ & .059 \end{bmatrix}$
5	$\begin{bmatrix} + & \\ & + \end{bmatrix}$	$\begin{bmatrix} - & \\ & - \end{bmatrix}$	$\begin{bmatrix} & \\ - & \end{bmatrix}$	$\begin{bmatrix} & \\ & \end{bmatrix}$	$\begin{bmatrix} & \\ & \end{bmatrix}$		$\begin{bmatrix} .035 & -.003 \\ & .058 \end{bmatrix}$
6	$\begin{bmatrix} + & \\ & + \end{bmatrix}$	$\begin{bmatrix} - & \\ & - \end{bmatrix}$	$\begin{bmatrix} & \\ - & \end{bmatrix}$	$\begin{bmatrix} & \\ & \end{bmatrix}$	$\begin{bmatrix} + & \\ & \end{bmatrix}$	$\begin{bmatrix} - & \\ + & \end{bmatrix}$	$\begin{bmatrix} .035 & -.002 \\ & .057 \end{bmatrix}$

how they work in practice. Much further work is needed, especially in the identification of mixed autoregressive moving average models and in developing faster estimation algorithms and better tools for diagnostic checking. In spite of the imperfections of the present tools and the preliminary nature of the approach, we have felt it appropriate to present them here in order to (a) illustrate the potential usefulness of vector autoregressive moving average models in characterizing dynamic structures in the data and (b) stimulate further development of modeling procedures. Several alternative approaches to modeling multiple time series have been proposed in the literature. It may be of interest to discuss briefly those proposed by Granger and Newbold (1977), Wallis (1977), and Chan and Wallis (1978).

In the Granger and Newbold approach, one begins by fitting univariate ARMA models to each series,

$$\varphi_{p_j}(B)Z_{jt} = \theta_{q_j}(B)C_{jt}, \quad j = 1, \ldots, k \tag{6.1}$$

and then attempts to identify the dynamic structure of the k white noise residual series $\{C_{jt}\}$ by examination of their cross-correlations. A model of the form (2.2) with $k(h)$ being the set $(1, \ldots, k)$ excluding h is then fitted to the k residual series. This model and the prewhitening transformations (6.1) then determine the model for the original vector series. As the authors themselves pointed out, the procedure is complex and difficult to apply for $k > 2$. One major difficulty arises from the fact that the parameters in the model for the residuals are subject to various complicated nonlinear constraints. Also, it can be readily shown that even if the vector series $\{\mathbf{Z}_t\}$ follows a low order ARMA model (3.1), the corresponding model for the residual vector $\{\mathbf{C}_t\}$ where $\mathbf{C}'_t = (C_{1t}, \ldots, C_{kt})$ can be complex and difficult to identify in practice.

The Wallis and Chan approach uses the form (6.1) for each individual series and the fact that the model (3.1) can be written as

$$| \boldsymbol{\varphi}(B) | \mathbf{Z}_t = \mathbf{H}(B)\mathbf{a}_t, \tag{6.2}$$

where $\mathbf{H}(B) = \mathbf{A}(B)\boldsymbol{\theta}_q(B)$, $\mathbf{A}(B)$ is the adjoint matrix and $| \boldsymbol{\varphi}_p(B) |$ the determinant of $\boldsymbol{\varphi}_p(B)$. As in the G and N approach, an individual model is first constructed for each series. From the degrees of the moving average polynomials $\theta_{q_i}(B)$ of these individual models, the degree of $\mathbf{H}(B)$ is determined. Next, models of the form

$$\mathbf{D}_l(B)\mathbf{Z}_t = \mathbf{H}(B)\mathbf{a}_t, \tag{6.3}$$

where $\mathbf{D}_l(B)$ is a diagonal matrix polynomial in B of degree l, are fitted successively for $l = r, r - 1, \ldots,$ where r is some specified maximum order, to determine an appropriate value for l. A likelihood ratio test is then performed to check whether the diagonal elements of $\mathbf{D}_l(B)$ are identical, that is, of the form (6.2). Finally, from the fitted $\mathbf{H}(B)$ and $| \boldsymbol{\varphi}(B) |$ or $\mathbf{D}_l(B)$, one guesses at the values of p and q in (3.1) and then proceeds to estimate the parameters in $\boldsymbol{\varphi}_p(B)$ and $\boldsymbol{\theta}_q(B)$. The efficacy of this approach is open to question on several grounds.

1. The degree of the polynomial $\mathbf{H}(B)$ in (6.2) can be higher than the maximum degree of $\theta_{q_i}(B)$ for the individual series. For example, suppose $k = 2$,

$$\mathbf{H}(B) = \begin{pmatrix} 1 & -h_1B \\ -h_2B & 1 \end{pmatrix}$$

and the two elements of $\mathbf{a}_t$ are independent. Then $q_1 = q_2 = 0$, but it would be a mistake to infer that $\mathbf{H}(B)$ is of degree zero.

2. For vector AR or ARMA models, the representation (6.2) is certainly nonparsimonious. Apart from the covariance matrix $\boldsymbol{\Sigma}$, for k series the maximum number of parameters in the original form (3.1) is $k^2(p + q)$, while the maximum number of parameters in the form (6.2) is $kp + [(k - 1)p + q]k^2$, representing an increase

of $pk(k - 1)^2$ parameters. The increase could be even greater if the diagonal form (6.3) is employed. Thus, assuming the degree of $\mathbf{H}(B)$ is correctly specified, even for k as low as 3 or 4, a very large number of additional parameters will have to be estimated merely to identify correctly a low order vector AR model, say $p = 1$ or 2.

3. Since the correspondence between the degrees of the determinantal polynomial $|\varphi(B)|$ and $\mathbf{H}(B)$ and the values of (p, q) is not necessarily one to one, it is not clear how one determines p and q in (3.1) from the form (6.2).

4. The approach is made even more computationally burdensome because the authors propose to employ the exact likelihood method for moving average parameters throughout the processes of model building. Our experience, however, suggests that because this method converges relatively slowly it is better to use it only in the final stage of the estimation process.

The chief distinction between our approach and the two alternatives just discussed is that we believe it better to tackle the dynamic relationships of the k series in their entirety, employing tools such as the estimates of cross-correlation matrices and partial autoregression matrices to shed light directly on the structure. Simplifications of one kind or another will then often follow. At least for the tentative specification of the vector autoregressive or the vector moving average model, our procedures seem far simpler to use in practice and do not require the multitude of steps these alternative approaches need to arrive at even a simple model.

To illustrate these points, we briefly consider the mink-muskrat example which Chan and Wallis used to illustrate their methods. They treat two series $Y_{1t}{}^*$ and $Y_{2t}{}^*$ obtained after "detrending" the muskrat and mink series by first and second degree polynomials respectively. Proceeding through the various steps outlined above, they eventually arrive at an AR(1) model. However, it will be seen that this same model is suggested immediately by the simple procedures we propose. Table 15(a) shows the partial autoregression results for $l = 1, 2$ and Table 15(b) the residual cross correlations after the AR(1) fit. A very similar analysis of this set of data is given in Ansley and Newbold (1979). For various reasons, we do not wish to sanctify this AR(1) model. These include the question of whether any linear structural model is adequate for these series (see Tong and Lim 1980). Also, the validity of the detrending procedures and the suspicious behavior of a high autocorrelation at lag 10 occurring in the residuals seem suspect. Our only point is to show that the circuitous route adopted by Chan and Wallis to arrive at this model is unnecessary.

Before concluding this paper, it is worth noting that in modeling as well as analysis of vector time series one often finds it useful to perform various eigenvalue and eigenvector analyses. Specifically, writing (3.1) in the form

$$\mathbf{z}_t = \hat{\mathbf{z}}_{t-1}(1) + \mathbf{a}_t, \qquad (6.4)$$

Table 15. Identification of Muskrat-Mink Data

(a) Partial Autoregression and Related Statistics

Lag	Partials		$M(l) \sim \chi_4^2$	Diagonal elements of $\hat{\Sigma}$
1	+	−	111.7	.062
	+	+		.059
2	−	·	4.8	.0571
	·	·		.0572

(b) Cross-correlations of Residuals After AR(1) Fit

	a_1	a_2
a_1	. . . .	.−. . . . .
a_2	. . . .	. . . .+. .

where $\hat{\mathbf{z}}_{t-1}(1)$ is the one step ahead forecast of $\mathbf{z}_t$ made at time $t - 1$, and denoting, for stationary series,

$$\Gamma_z(0) = E(\mathbf{z}_t\mathbf{z}'_t)$$

and

$$\Gamma_{\hat{z}}(0) = E(\hat{\mathbf{z}}_{t-1}(1)\hat{\mathbf{z}}_{t-1}(1)'),$$

it will often be informative to compute eigenvalues and eigenvectors of estimates of the following matrices:

$$(a)\ \Gamma_z(0), \quad (b)\ \hat{\Sigma},$$

$$(c)\ \Gamma_z(0)^{-1}\Gamma_{\hat{z}}(0), \quad (d)\ \varphi_l, \text{ and } \theta_l.$$

Such analyses are described in Quenouille (1957), Box and Tiao (1977), and Tiao et al. (1979). Also, the eigenvalues and eigenvectors of the spectral density matrix of the model should also be considered (see Brillinger 1975). These techniques are useful in (a) detecting exact concurrent or lagged linear relations between series, and (b) facilitating understanding and interpretation of the fitted model. In our opinion, this is one of the most important and challenging topics for further research.

[Received January 1981. Revised June 1981.]

REFERENCES

ABRAHAM, B. (1980), "Intervention Analysis and Multiple Time Series," *Biometrika*, 67, 73–78.

ABRAHAM, B., and BOX, G.E.P. (1978), "Deterministic and Forecast-Adaptive Time Dependent Models," *Applied Statistics*, 27, 120–130.

AKAIKE, H. (1980), "On the Identification of State Space Models and Their Use in Control," in *Directions in Time Series*, eds. D.R. Brillinger and G.C. Tiao, Institute of Mathematical Statistics, 175–187.

ANDERSON, T.W. (1971), *The Statistical Analysis of Time Series*, New York: John Wiley.

——— (1980), "Maximum Likelihood Estimation for Vector Autoregressive Moving Average Models," in *Directions in Time Series*, eds. D.R. Brillinger and G.C. Tiao, Institute of Mathematical Statistics, 49–59.

ANSLEY, C. (1979), "An Algorithm for the Exact Likelihood of a Mixed Autoregressive Moving Average Process," *Biometrika*, 66, 59–65.

ANSLEY, C.F., and NEWBOLD, P. (1979), "Multivariate Partial Autocorrelations," *Proceedings of Business and Economic Statistics Section*, American Statistical Association, 349–353.

BARTLETT, M.S. (1938), "Further Aspects of the Theory of Multiple Regression," *Proceedings of the Cambridge Philosophical Society*, 34, 33–40.

BEGUIN, J.M., GOURIEROUX, C., and MONFORT, A. (1980), "Identification of a Mixed Autoregressive-Moving Average Process: The Corner Method," in *Time Series*, ed. O.D. Anderson, Amsterdam: North-Holland, 423–436.
BOX, G.E.P. and HAUGH, L. (1977), "Identification of Dynamic Regression Models Connecting Two Time Series," *Journal of the American Statistical Association*, 72, 121–130.
BOX, G.E.P., and JENKINS, G.M. (1970), *Time Series Analysis—Forecasting and Control*, San Francisco: Holden-Day.
BOX, G.E.P., and MACGREGOR, J.F. (1974), "The Analysis of Closed Loop Dynamic Stochastic Systems," *Technometrics*, 16, 391–398.
——— (1976), "Parameter Estimation with Closed-Loop Operating data," *Technometrics*, 18, 371–380.
BOX, G.E.P., and NEWBOLD, P. (1970), "Some Comments on a Paper by Coen, Gomme and Kendall," *Journal of the Royal Statistical Society*, Ser. A, 134, 229–240.
BOX, G.E.P., and TIAO, G.C. (1975), "Intervention Analysis with Applications to Environmental and Economic Problems," *Journal of the American Statistical Association*, 70, 70–79.
——— (1977), "A Canonical Analysis of Multiple Time Series," *Biometrika*, 64, 355–365.
BRILLINGER, D.R. (1975), *Time Series Data Analysis and Theory*, New York: Holt, Rinehart, and Winston.
CHAN, W.Y.T., and WALLIS, K.F. (1978), "Multiple Time Series Modelling: Another Look at the Mink-Muskrat Interaction," *Applied Statistics*, 27, 168–175.
COEN, P.G., GOMME, E.D., and KENDALL, M.G. (1969), "Lagged Relationships in Economic Forecasting," *Journal of the Royal Statistical Society*, Ser. A, 132, 133–163.
DEISTLER, M., DUNSMUIR, W., and HANNAN, E.J. (1978), "Vector Linear Time Series Models: Corrections and Extensions," *Advances in Applied Probability*, 10, 360–372.
DENT, W. (1977), "Computation of the Exact Likelihood Function of an ARIMA Process," *Journal of Statistical Computation and Simulation*, 5, 193–206.
DUNSMUIR, W., and HANNAN, E.J. (1976), "Vector Linear Time Series Models," *Advances in Applied Probability*, 8, 339–364.
GRANGER, C.W.J., and NEWBOLD, P. (1977), *Forecasting Economic Time Series*, New York: Academic Press.
GRAY, H.L., KELLEY, G.D., and McINTIRE, D.D. (1978), "A New Approach to ARMA Modelling," *Communications in Statistics*, B7, 1–77.
HALLIN, M. (1978), "Mixed Autoregressive-Moving Average Multivariate Processes with Time-Dependent Coefficients," *Journal of Multivariate Analysis*, 8, 567–572.
HANNAN, E.J. (1970), *Multiple Time Series*, New York: John Wiley.
——— (1980), "The Estimation of the Order of an ARMA Process," *Annals of Statistics*, 8, 1071–1081.
HANNAN, E.J., DUNSMUIR, W.T.M., and DEISTLER, M. (1980), "Estimation of Vector ARMAX Models," *Journal of Multivariate Analysis*, 10, 275–295.
HILLMER, S.C., and TIAO, G.C. (1979), "Likelihood Function of Stationary Multiple Autoregressive Moving Average Models," *Journal of the American Statistical Association*, 74, 652–660.
HOSKING, J.R.M. (1980), "The Multivariate Portmanteau Statistic," *Journal of the American Statistical Association*, 75, 602–607.
HSIAO, C. (1979), "Autoregressive Modeling of Canadian Money and Income Data," *Journal of the American Statistical Association*, 74, 553–560.
JENKINS, G.J. (1979), *Practical Experiences with Modelling and Forecasting Time Series*, Channel Islands: GJP Ltd.
LI, W.K., and McLEOD, A.I. (1980), "Distribution of the Residual Autocorrelations in Multivariate ARMA Time Series Models," TR-80-03, University of Western Ontario.
NEWBOLD, P. (1974), "The Exact Likelihood Function for a Mixed Autoregressive Moving Average Process," *Biometrika*, 61, 423–427.
NICHOLLS, D.F. (1976), "The Efficient Estimation of Vector Linear Time Series Models," *Biometrika*, 63, 381–390.
——— (1977), "A Comparison of Estimation Methods for Vector Linear Time Series Models," *Biometrika*, 64, 85–90.
NICHOLLS, D.F., and HALL, A.D. (1979), "The Exact Likelihood of Multivariate Autoregressive-Moving Average Models," *Biometrika*, 66, 259–264.
OSBORN, D.R. (1977), "Exact and Approximate Maximum Likelihood Estimators for Vector Moving Average Processes," *Journal of the Royal Statistical Society*, Ser. B, 39, 114–118.
PARZEN, E. (1977), "Multiple Time Series: Determining the Order of Approximating Autoregressive Schemes," in *Multivariate Analysis-IV*, ed. P. Krishnaiah, Amsterdam: North-Holland, 283–295.
PHADKE, M.S., and KEDEM, G. (1978), "Computation of the Exact Likelihood Function of Multivariate Moving Average Models," *Biometrika*, 65, 511–519.
QUENOUILLE, M.H. (1957), *The Analysis of Multiple Time Series*, London: Griffin.
QUINN, B.G. (1980), "Order Determination for a Multivariate Autoregression," *Journal of the Royal Statistical Society*, Ser. B, 42, 182–185.
SLUTSKY, E. (1937), "The Summation of Random Causes as the Source of Cyclic Processes," *Econometrika*, 5, 105–146.
TIAO, G.C., and ALI, M.M. (1971), "Analysis of Correlated Random Effects: Linear Model with Two Random Components," *Biometrika*, 58, 37–51.
TIAO, G.C., BOX, G.E.P., GRUPE, M.R., HUDAK, G.B., BELL, W.R., and CHANG, I. (1979), "The Wisconsin Multiple Time Series (WMTS-1) Program: A Preliminary Guide," Department of Statistics, University of Wisconsin, Madison.
TIAO, G.C., and WEI, W.S. (1976), "Effect of Temporal Aggregation on the Dynamic Relationship of Two Time Series Variables," *Biometrika*, 63, 513–523.
TONG, H., and LIM, K.S. (1980), "Threshold Autoregression, Limit Cycles and Cyclical Data," *Journal of the Royal Statistical Society*, Ser. B, 42, 245–292.
WALLIS, K.F. (1977), "Multiple Time Series Analysis and the Final Form of Econometric Models," *Econometrika*, 45, 1481–1497.
WHITTLE, P. (1963), "On the Fitting of Multivariate Autoregressions, and the Approximate Canonical Factorization of a Spectral Density Matrix," *Biometrika*, 50, 129–134.
WILSON, G.T. (1973), "The Estimation of Parameters in Multivariate Time Series Models," *Journal of the Royal Statistical Society*, Ser. B, 35, 76–85.
YULE, G.U. (1927), "On a Method of Investigating Periodicities in Disturbed Series, With Special Reference to Wolfer's Sunspot Numbers," *Philosophical Transactions of the Royal Society of London*, Ser. A, 226, 267–298.
ZELLNER, A., and PALM, F. (1974), "Time Series Analysis and Simultaneous Equation Econometric Models," *Journal of Econometrics*, 2, 17–54.

[13]

Intervention Analysis with Applications to Economic and Environmental Problems

G. E. P. BOX and G. C. TIAO*

This article discusses the effect of interventions on a given response variable in the presence of dependent noise structure. Difference equation models are employed to represent the possible dynamic characteristics of both the interventions and the noise. Some properties of the maximum likelihood estimators of parameters measuring level changes are discussed. Two applications, one dealing with the photochemical smog data in Los Angeles and the other with changes in the consumer price index, are presented.

1. INTRODUCTION

Data of potential value in the formulation of public and private policy frequently occur in the form of time series. Questions of the following kind often arise: "Given a known intervention,[1] is there evidence that change in the series of the kind expected actually occurred, and, if so, what can be said of the nature and magnitude of the change?"

For example, in early 1960 two events occurred, here referred to jointly as the intervention, which might have been expected to reduce the oxidant (denoted by O_3) pollution level in downtown Los Angeles. These events were the diversion of traffic by the opening of the Golden State Freeway and the coming into effect of a new law (Rule 63) which reduced the allowable proportion of reactive hydrocarbons in the gasoline sold locally. The expected effect of this intervention would be to produce a more or less immediate reduction (i.e., a step change) in the oxidant level in early 1960. Figure A shows the monthly averages of oxidant concentration level from 1955–72 in downtown Los Angeles [6]. Using this highly variable and seasonal time series, is there evidence for a change in level and, if so, what is its magnitude?

Many other problems of this kind have come to our attention in recent years. These have included the possible effect of the opening of a nuclear power station on measurements made on river samples, the possible effect of the Nixon Administration's Phases I and II on an economic indicator, and the possible effect of promotions, advertising campaigns and price changes on the sale of a product.

Available procedures such as Student's t test for estimating and testing for a change in mean have played an important role in statistics for a very long time.

A. Monthly Average of Hourly Readings of O_3 (pphm) in Downtown Los Angeles (1955–1972)[a]

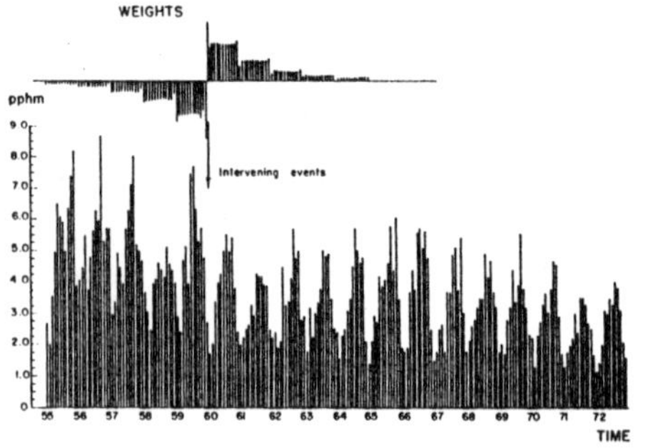

[a] With the weight function for estimating the effect of intervening events in 1960.

However, the ordinary t test would be valid only if the observations before and after the event of interest varied about means μ_1 and μ_2, not only normally and with constant variance but *independently*. In the examples quoted, however, the data are in the form of time series in which successive observations are usually serially dependent and often nonstationary, and there may be strong seasonal effects. Thus the ordinary parametric or nonparametric statistical procedures which rely on independence or special symmetry in the distribution function are not available nor are the blessings endowed by randomization.

An approach we initiated earlier [2] was to build a stochastic model which included the possibility of change of the form expected. Such model building is necessarily iterative and, as discussed, e.g., in [3], involves inferences from a tentatively entertained model alternating with criticism of the appropriate tentative analysis. The process proceeds [1] by successive use of Identification (tentative specification of the model form), Fitting, and Diagnostic Checking. Using these ideas in the present context, we come to the following general strategy:

1. Frame a model for change which describes what is expected to occur given knowledge of the known intervention;

* G.E.P. Box is R. A. Fisher professor and G. C. Tiao is professor and chairman, Department of Statistics, University of Wisconsin, Madison, Wis. 53706. This research was supported in part by a grant from the American Petroleum Institute and in part by U.S. Army Research Office under Grant DA-ARO-D-31-124-72-G162.

[1] A term introduced in [5], based on our earlier work [2].

© Journal of the American Statistical Association
March 1975, Volume 70, Number 349
Invited Paper, Theory and Methods Section

2. Work out the appropriate data analysis based on that model;
3. If diagnostic checks show no inadequacy in the model, make appropriate inferences; if serious deficiencies are uncovered, make appropriate model modification, repeat the analysis, etc.

Suppose the data . . . Y_{t-1}, Y_t, Y_{t+1}, . . . are available as a series obtained at equal time intervals. Following, e.g., [1], we will employ models of the general form

$$y_t = f(\kappa, \xi, t) + N_t \quad (1.1)$$

where:

$y_t = F(Y_t)$ is some appropriate transformation of Y_t, say $\log Y_t$, $(Y_t)^{\frac{1}{2}}$ or Y_t itself;
$f(\kappa, \xi, t)$ can allow for deterministic effects of time, t, the effects of exogenous variables, ξ, and in particular, interventions;
N_t represents stochastic background variation or noise;
κ is a set of unknown parameters.

In Section 2 we discuss a general integrated mixed autoregressive moving average model for representing the noise N_t. A class of general dynamic models capable of representing the effect of interventions is given in Section 3. The associated parameter estimation procedures are given in Section 4. In Section 5 two illustrative examples of intervention analysis are presented. The first concerns the Los Angeles oxidant data, and the second considers possible effects on the consumer price index of recent government actions. Finally, in Section 6, the nature of the maximum likelihood estimators for some specific level-change parameters is discussed in some detail.

2. A STOCHASTIC MODEL FOR THE NOISE

We suppose that the noise $N_t = y_t - f(\mathbf{k}, \xi, t)$ may be modeled by a mixed autoregressive moving average process

$$\varphi(B)N_t = \theta(B)a_t \quad (2.1)$$

where:

1. B is the backshift operator such that $By_t = y_{t-1}$;
2. . . . a_{t-1}, a_t, a_{t+1}, . . . is a sequence of independently distributed normal variables having mean zero and variance $(\sigma_a)^2$ which for brevity we refer to as "white" noise;
3. $\theta(B) = 1 - \theta_1 B - \theta_2 B^2 \cdots - \theta_q B^q$, $\varphi(B) = 1 - \varphi_1 B - \varphi_2 B^2 \cdots - \varphi_p B^p$ are "moving average" and "autoregressive" polynomials in B of degrees q and p, respectively;
4. the roots of $\theta(B)$ lie outside, and those of $\varphi(B)$ lie on or outside the unit circle.

For the representation of certain kinds of homogeneous nonstationary series, the operator $\varphi(B)$ is factored so that

$$\varphi(B) = (1 - B)^d \phi(B) \quad (2.2)$$

where the roots of $\phi(B)$ all lie outside the unit circle. This corresponds to the use of a stationary model in the dth difference. Also, for seasonal data with period s (e.g., monthly data with $s = 12$), it is often helpful to write $\varphi(B) = \varphi_1(B)\varphi_2(B^s)$ and $\theta(B) = \theta_1(B)\theta_2(B^s)$ with $\varphi_2(B^s) = (1 - B^s)^D\phi_2(B^s)$ to allow for seasonal nonstationarity.

Finally, we entertain a class of noise model of the form

$$\phi_1(B)\phi_2(B^s)(1 - B)^d(1 - B^s)^D N_t = \theta_1(B)\theta_2(B^s)a_t \quad (2.3)$$

where the polynomials $\phi_1(B)$, $\phi_2(B^s)$, $\theta_1(B)$, $\theta_2(B^s)$ are of degrees p_1, p_2, q_1, q_2, respectively.

3. A DYNAMIC MODEL FOR INTERVENTION

Frequently the effects of exogenous variables ξ can be represented by a dynamic model of the form

$$f(\mathbf{\delta}, \mathbf{\omega}, \xi, t) = \sum_{j=1}^{k} \mathcal{Y}_{tj} = \sum_{j=1}^{k} \{\omega_j(B)/\delta_j(B)\}\xi_{tj} \quad (3.1)$$

where:

1. The $\mathcal{Y}_{tj}$ represent the dynamic transfer from ξ_{tj};
2. The parameters κ previously lumped together are now denoted by $\mathbf{\delta}$ and $\mathbf{\omega}$;
3. The polynomials in B

$$\delta_j(B) = 1 - \delta_{1j}B - \cdots - \delta_{r_j j}B^{r_j} \quad \text{and}$$
$$\omega_j(B) = \omega_{0j} - \omega_{1j}B - \cdots - \omega_{s_j j}B^{s_j}$$

are of degrees r_j and s_j, respectively;
4. We shall normally assume that $\omega_j(B)$ has roots outside, and $\delta_j(B)$, outside or on, the unit circle.

In general, the individual ξ_{tj} could be exogenous time series whose influence needs to be taken into account. For the present purpose, however, some or all of them will be indicator variables taking the values 0 and 1 to denote the nonoccurrence and occurrence of intervention.

For illustration, suppose for a single exogenous variable ($k = 1$) the model is

$$y_t = \mathcal{Y}_t + N_t = (\omega(B)/\delta(B))\xi_t + (\theta(B)/\varphi(B))a_t \ ; \quad (3.2)$$

then the transfer $\mathcal{Y}_t$ to the output from ξ_t is generated by the linear difference equation

$$\delta(B)\mathcal{Y}_t = \omega(B)\xi_t \ .$$

Figures B(a), B(b) and B(c) show the response $\mathcal{Y}_t$ transmitted to the output for various simple dynamic systems by an indicator variable representing a step. We can denote such an indicator by $\xi_t = S_t^{(T)}$ where

$$S_t^{(T)} = \begin{cases} 0, & t < T \\ 1, & t \geq T \end{cases} . \quad (3.3)$$

Similarly, we use $P_t^{(T)}$ for a pulse indicator where

$$P_t^{(T)} = \begin{cases} 0, & t \neq T \\ 1, & t = T \end{cases} . \quad (3.4)$$

Referring to the figure for the case we have discussed for the Los Angeles 1960 intervention, we would expect that the change could be modelled as in Figure B(a), so that immediately following the known step change in the input, an output step change of unknown magnitude would be produced according to

$$\mathcal{Y}_t = \omega B S_t^{(T)} \ .$$

Sometimes a step change would not be expected to produce an immediate response but rather a "first order" dynamic response like that in Figure B(b). The appropriate transfer function model is then

$$\mathcal{Y}_t = \{\omega B/(1 - \delta B)\}S_t^{(T)} \ ,$$

($\delta < 1$). It is readily shown that the time constant of this system is estimated by $\{-\log_e \delta\}^{-1}$ and the steady state gain is $\omega/(1-\delta)$. When δ approaches the value unity, we have the transfer function model

$$\mathcal{Y}_t = \{\omega B/(1-B)\} S_t^{(T)}$$

in which a step change in the input produces a "ramp" response in the output (Figure B(c)).

Note that since

$$(1-B)S_t^{(T)} = P_t^{(T)} , \tag{3.5}$$

any of these transfer functions could equally well be discussed in terms of the unit pulse $P_t^{(T)}$, and sometimes matters are best thought of directly in terms of $P_t^{(T)}$. Thus, suppose we have monthly sales data and wish to represent the effect of a promotion or advertising campaign lasting less than a month. The simple first order model

$$\mathcal{Y}_t = \{\omega_1 B/(1-\delta B)\} P_t^{(T)}$$

might do this (Figure B(d)) with ω_1 indicating the initial increase in sales immediately following the intervention and δ representing the rate of decay of this increase.

This particular model implies that no lasting effect will occur as a result of the intervention. When this might not be so, the model $B(e)$

$$\mathcal{Y}_t = \{(\omega_1 B/(1-\delta B)) + (\omega_2 B/(1-B))\} P_t^{(T)}$$

could be used in which the possibility is entertained that a residual gain (or loss) in sales ω_2 persists.

B. Responses to a Step and a Pulse Input [a]

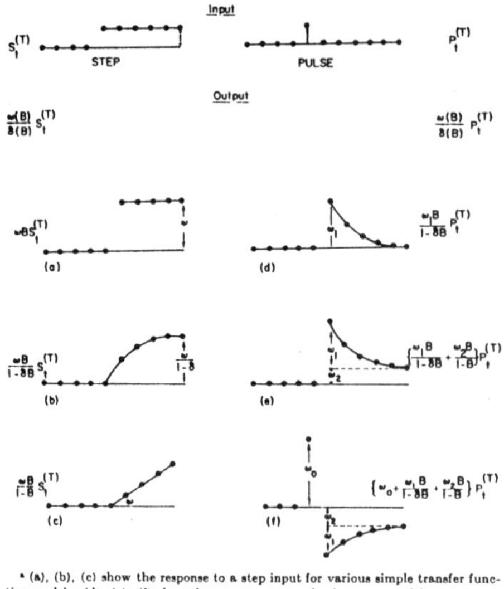

[a] (a), (b), (c) show the response to a step input for various simple transfer function models; (d), (e), (f) show the response to a pulse for some models of interest.

If it were believed that the full impact of intervention might not be felt until the second month, after which there would be a decay and possibly a residual effect as in the previous case, the model

$$\mathcal{Y}_t = \{\omega_0 B + (\omega_1 B^2/(1-\delta B)) + (\omega_2 B^2/(1-B))\} P_t^{(T)}$$

might be appropriate. This would insert a preliminary value ω_0 into the output (which in the preceding context would usually be less than ω_1). The same form of model, shifted forward and with some sign changes in the parameters, could be useful to represent the effect of price changes. In the application shown in Figure B(f), ω_0 would be positive and would represent an immediate rush of buying when a prospective price change was announced. The reduction in buying immediately after the change occurred would be represented by $\omega_1 + \omega_2$ and the final effect of the change would be represented by ω_2 which is shown as negative but, of course, could have a zero or positive value.

Obviously, these difference equation models may be readily extended to represent many situations of potential interest.

The following points are worthy of note:

(i) The function $\mathcal{Y}_t$ represents the *additional* effect of the intervention over the noise. In particular, when N_t is nonstationary, large changes could occur in the output even with no intervention. Fitting the model can make it possible to distinguish between what can and what cannot be explained by the noise.

(ii) Intervention extending over several time intervals can be represented by a series of pulses. A three month advertising campaign might be represented, for example, by three pulses whose magnitude might represent expenditure in the three months.

4. CALCULATIONS BASED ON THE LIKELIHOOD

Suppose we entertain a model of the form

$$y_t = \sum_{j=1}^{k} \mathcal{Y}_{tj} + N_t \tag{4.1}$$

where $\sum_{j=1}^{k} \mathcal{Y}_{tj}$ is the transfer function given in (3.1) associated with known interventions, N_t assumes the form in (2.3), and a time series is available of length $n + d + sD$. Then the likelihood may be obtained in terms of an n dimensional vector $\mathbf{w}$ whose tth element is $w_t = (1-B)^d(1-B^s)^D(y_t - \sum_{j=1}^{k} \mathcal{Y}_{tj})$. The corresponding model for w_t,

$$w_t = \{\theta_1(B)\theta_2(B^s)/\phi_1(B)\phi_2(B^s)\} a_t , \tag{4.2}$$

is stationary. Thus, following the argument given, e.g., in [1, p. 273], and with the vector $\boldsymbol{\beta}$ having for its g elements the stochastic and dynamic parameters in the model, the likelihood function may be written

$$L(\boldsymbol{\beta}, (\sigma_a)^2 | \mathbf{y}) = (2\pi(\sigma_a)^2)^{-(n/2)} |\mathbf{M}|^{\frac{1}{2}} \cdot \exp\{-S(\boldsymbol{\beta})/2(\sigma_a)^2\} \tag{4.3}$$

where $\mathbf{M}^{-1}(\sigma_a)^2$ is the covariance matrix of the vector w and

$$S(\boldsymbol{\beta}) = \mathbf{w}'\mathbf{M}\mathbf{w} = \sum_{t=-\infty}^{n} [a_t|\mathbf{y}, \boldsymbol{\beta}]^2 \quad (4.4)$$

with $[a_t|\mathbf{y}, \boldsymbol{\beta}]$ as the expected value of a_t conditional on $\boldsymbol{\beta}$ and $\mathbf{y}$.

If none of the roots in (4.2) is close to the unit circle, then for moderate and large n, the likelihood is dominated by the exponent. The values of the elements of $\boldsymbol{\beta}$ minimizing (4.4), which we shall call the *least squares* values, are to a close approximation also the maximum likelihood values. Alternatively, if we introduce a prior distribution such that in the neighborhood where the likelihood is nonnegligible $p(\boldsymbol{\beta}, \sigma_a) \propto p(\boldsymbol{\beta})(\sigma_a)^{-1}$, we obtain the posterior distribution

$$p(\boldsymbol{\beta}|\mathbf{y}) \propto p(\boldsymbol{\beta})|\mathbf{M}|^{\frac{1}{2}}\{S(\boldsymbol{\beta})\}^{-(n/2)} . \quad (4.5)$$

Again for moderate or large samples and for a noninformative distribution $p(\boldsymbol{\beta})$, the term involving $S(\boldsymbol{\beta})$ dominates and approximately

$$p(\boldsymbol{\beta}|\mathbf{y}) \mathrel{\dot{\propto}} \{S(\boldsymbol{\beta})\}^{-(n/2)} \quad (4.6)$$

so that the least square estimates correspond with the point of maximum posterior density.

Now if, over the region where the density is appreciable, $S(\boldsymbol{\beta})$ is approximately quadratic (and in any given case it is easy to check this numerically), then the posterior distribution is approximately a multivariate t. Then,

$$p(\boldsymbol{\beta}|\mathbf{y}) \mathrel{\dot{\propto}} \{1 + (\sum_{ij} S_{ij}(\beta_i - \hat{\beta}_i)(\beta_j - \hat{\beta}_j)/ (n-g)(s_a)^2)\}^{-(n/2)} \quad (4.7)$$

where

$$S_{ij} = \tfrac{1}{2}\partial^2\{S(\boldsymbol{\beta})\}/\partial\beta_i\partial\beta_j|_{\boldsymbol{\beta}=\hat{\boldsymbol{\beta}}}$$

and $(s_a)^2 = S(\hat{\boldsymbol{\beta}})/(n-g)$. Thus, for moderate or large n, $\boldsymbol{\beta}$ is approximately distributed as multivariate normal with mean $\hat{\boldsymbol{\beta}}$ and covariance matrix

$$V(\boldsymbol{\beta}) = (s_a)^2\{S_{ij}\}^{-1} .$$

The square roots of the diagonal elements of $V(\boldsymbol{\beta})$ will be referred to as standard errors (S.E.).

In practice we may obtain $\hat{\boldsymbol{\beta}}$, $V(\boldsymbol{\beta})$ and $(s_a)^2$ using a standard nonlinear least squares computer program for the numerical minimization of $S(\boldsymbol{\beta})$. To do this we need only to be able to compute the quantities $[a_t|\mathbf{y}, \boldsymbol{\beta}]$ for any $\boldsymbol{\beta}$ and we may proceed as follows. Since the model for w_t is stationary, $[a_t|\mathbf{y}, \boldsymbol{\beta}]$ will be negligible for values $t \leq -Q$ where Q is some suitably chosen positive number. We, therefore, replace $S(\boldsymbol{\beta})$ by the finite sum $\sum_{t=-Q}^{n} [a_t|\mathbf{y}, \boldsymbol{\beta}]^2$. It is shown in [1] that the initial values $[a_0]$, $[a_{-1}]$, $\cdots$, $[a_{-Q}]$ may often be obtained conveniently by a process of "back forecasting" which also indicates an appropriate value for Q.

5. TWO ILLUSTRATIVE EXAMPLES

The theory developed here is illustrated in this section by two examples, one employing the Los Angeles oxidant data and the other, the rate of change in the United States consumer price index, to determine the effect of known interventions.

5.1 Example 1: The Los Angeles Oxidant Data

Monthly averages of the oxidant (O_3) level in Downtown Los Angeles from January 1955 to December 1972 are shown in Figure A.

Identification (Specification) of the Model. The periods 1955–60 and 1960–65 were regarded as containing no major intervention which would affect the O_3 level. The series themselves and the sample autocorrelation functions within these periods suggest nonstationary and highly seasonal behavior. The autocorrelation functions of such differences $(1 - B^{12})y_t$ taken twelve months apart show significant correlations only at lags 1 and 12. This suggests the following model for the noise N_t:

$$(1 - B^{12})N_t = (1 - \theta_1 B)(1 - \theta_2 B^{12})a_t . \quad (5.1)$$

Interventions I_1 and I_2 of potential major importance are:

I_1: In 1960 the opening of the Golden State Freeway and the coming into effect of a new law (Rule 63) reducing the allowable proportion of reactive hydrocarbons in locally sold gasoline.

I_2: From 1966 onwards regulations required engine design changes in new cars which would be expected to reduce the production of O_3.

As already argued, I_1 might be expected to produce a step change in the O_3 level at the beginning of 1960. The effect of I_2 might be most accurately represented if we knew, for example, the proportion of new cars having specified engine changes which were in the pool of all cars driven at any point in time. Unfortunately, such data are not available to us presently. We have, therefore, represented the possible effect of intervention as a constant intervention change from year to year reflecting the increased proportion of "new design vehicles" in the car population. As explained more fully in [6], the engine changes would be expected to slow down the photochemical reactions which produce O_3 and, because of the summer-winter atmospheric temperature inversion differential and the difference in the intensity of sunlight, the net effect would be different in winter when oxidant pollution is low from that in summer when it is high.

A model form was, therefore, tentatively entertained for all the available monthly O_3 data from January 1955 to December 1972, which may be conveniently written as:

$$y_t = \omega_{01}\xi_{t1} + \omega_{02}\frac{\xi_{t2}}{1 - B^{12}} + \omega_{03}\frac{\xi_{t3}}{1 - B^{12}} + \frac{(1 - \theta_1 B)(1 - \theta_2 B^{12})}{(1 - B^{12})}a_t \quad (5.2)$$

where

$$\xi_{t1} = \begin{cases} 0, & t < \text{January, 1960} \\ 1, & t \geq \text{January, 1960} \end{cases}$$

$$\xi_{t2} = \begin{cases} 1, & \text{"summer" months June–October beginning 1966} \\ 0, & \text{otherwise} \end{cases}$$

$$\xi_{t3} = \begin{cases} 1, & \text{"winter" months November–May beginning 1966} \\ 0, & \text{otherwise.} \end{cases}$$

This allows for a step change in the level of O_3 beginning in 1960 of size ω_{01} associated with I_1 and for progressive yearly increments in the O_3 level beginning 1966 of ω_{02} and ω_{03} units, respectively, for the summer and the winter months. This representation is admittedly somewhat crude, and we hope to improve on it as more data become available.

Estimation Results. The maximum likelihood estimates and the associated standard errors are as follows:

Parameter	*MLE*	*S.E.*
ω_{01}	−1.09	.13
ω_{02}	−0.25	.07
ω_{03}	−0.07	.06
θ_1	−0.24	.03
θ_2	0.55	.04

Since examination of residuals $\hat{a}_t$ fails to show any obvious inadequacies in the model, we interpret the results as follows. The marginal distributions *a posteriori* of ω_{01}, ω_{02} and ω_{03} are very nearly normal and centered at the maximum likelihood estimate values with the approximate standard deviations shown.

Thus, there is evidence that

(i) associated with I_1 is a step change of approximately $\hat{\omega}_0 = -1.09$ units in the level of O_3;

(ii) associated with I_2 there is a progressive reduction in O_3. Over the period studied, there is a yearly increment of approximately $\hat{\omega}_{02} = -.25$ in the summer months, but the increment (if any) in the winter is slight.

5.2 Example 2: The Rate of Change in the U.S. Consumer Price Index

A second example supplies further intuitive appreciation for the kind of calculations being performed.

Figure C shows the latter part of a record of the monthly rate of change in the consumer price index (CPI) given more completely in [4]. The complete (July 1953 to December 1972) data include 234 successive values, 218 of which occurred prior to the institution of controls in August 1971. As indicated in the figure, in the three months beginning September 1971, Phase I control was applied; and after that to the end of the recorded period, Phase II was in effect.

C. Monthly Rate of Inflation of the U.S. Consumer Price Index: January 1964–December 1972

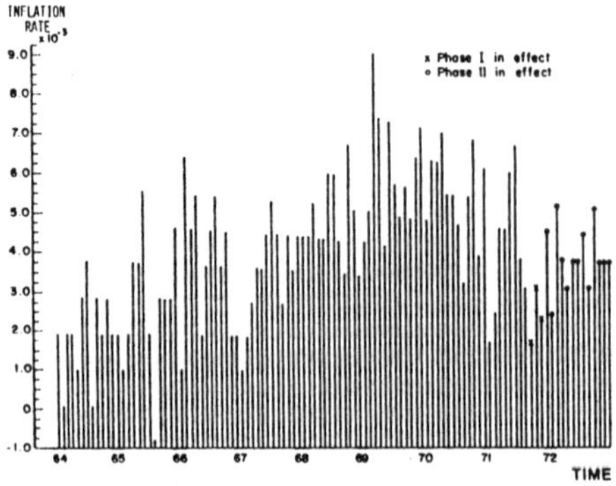

Inspection of the autocorrelation functions of the first 218 observations and their differences prior to Phase I suggests a noise model of the form

$$(1 - B)N_t = (1 - \theta B)a_t \ . \tag{5.3}$$

The maximum likelihood values for the parameters are:

Parameter	*MLE*	*S.E.*
θ	0.84	.04
σ_a	0.0019	

Inspection of the residuals and their autocorrelations reveals no obvious inadequacies of this model, so we adopt it.

We now ask the question, "What are the possible effects of Phases I and II?" To answer, we suppose:

(i) that Phases I and II can be expected to produce changes in level of the rate of change of the CPI,

(ii) that the form of the noise model remains essentially the same.

On these assumptions, the approximate model (ignoring estimation errors in the noise structure) is

$$y_t = \omega_{01}\xi_{t1} + \omega_{02}\xi_{t2} + \{(1 - .84B)/(1 - B)\}a_t \tag{5.4}$$

where

$$\xi_{t1} = \begin{cases} 1, & t = \text{September, October and November 1971} \\ 0, & \text{otherwise} \end{cases}$$

$$\xi_{t2} = \begin{cases} 1, & t \geq \text{December 1971} \\ 0, & \text{otherwise} \end{cases}$$

which may be written

$$z_t = \omega_{01}x_{t1} + \omega_{02}x_{t2} + a_t \ . \tag{5.5}$$

The sequences $\{z_t\}$, $\{x_{t1}\}$, $\{x_{t2}\}$ may be readily calculated from the equations

$$(1 - .84B)z_t = (1 - B)y_t$$
$$(1 - .84B)x_{t1} = (1 - B)\xi_{t1}$$
$$(1 - .84B)x_{t2} = (1 - B)\xi_{t2}$$

using, e.g., the initial approximation $z_1 = x_{11} = x_{12} = 0$.

Also, since

$$(1 - B)/(1 - \theta B) = 1 - B(1 - \theta)(1 + \theta B + \theta^2 B^2 + \cdots) \ ,$$

we have

$$z_t = y_t - \bar{y}_{t-1} \ , \quad x_{t1} = \xi_{t1} - \bar{\xi}_{t-1,1} \ , \quad x_{t2} = \xi_{t2} - \bar{\xi}_{t-1,2}$$

where $\bar{y}_{t-1}$, $\bar{\xi}_{t-1,1}$ and $\bar{\xi}_{t-1,2}$ are exponentially weighted moving averages of values prior to time t, e.g.,

$$\bar{y}_{t-1} = (1 - \theta)(y_{t-1} + \theta y_{t-2} + \theta^2 y_{t-3} + \cdots) \ .$$

We see that (5.5) is very much like the regression equations we are all familiar with in which the deviation of y_t from its average is related to the deviations of ξ_{t1} and ξ_{t2} from their averages. Notice, however, that the model copes with nonstationarity by using not the usual arithmetic averages, but local exponentially weighted averages which change as the series progresses.

Using (5.5), the constants ω_{01} and ω_{02} may now be estimated by ordinary linear least squares as

Parameter	*MLE*	*SE*
ω_{01}	−0.0022	0.0010
ω_{02}	−0.0007	0.0009

Alternatively, a nonlinear least squares program may be employed to estimate ω_{01}, ω_{02} and θ simultaneously from the complete set of 234 data values yielding the estimates (essentially as before):

Parameter	*MLE*	*SE*
θ	0.85	.05
ω_{01}	−0.0022	0.0010
ω_{02}	−0.0008	0.0009

The analysis suggests that a real drop in the rate of increase of the CPI is associated with Phase I, but the effect of Phase II is less certain.

6. NATURE OF THE MAXIMUM LIKELIHOOD ESTIMATORS FOR SOME LEVEL CHANGE PARAMETERS

The maximum likelihood estimators of parameters such as ω_{01}, ω_{02} and ω_{03} in (5.2) and (5.4) which measure level changes are functions of the data. It is instructive to consider the nature of these functions. Several results in the summation of series useful in the following discussion are given in the appendix.

6.1 One Parameter "Linear" Dynamic Model

Consider first the dynamic model in (3.2). Formally, it can be written

$$Q(B)y_t = (\varphi(B)/\theta(B))(\omega(B)/\delta(B))\xi_t + a_t \quad (6.1)$$

where $Q(B) = \varphi(B)/\theta(B)$, even though in practice the y_t are only available for $t = 1, \cdots, n$. Since the roots of $\theta(B)$ all lie outside the unit circle, $Q(B)$ can be expressed as a power series in B which converges for $|B| = 1$.

Here we discuss the situation where

$$(\varphi(B)/\theta(B))(\omega(B)/\delta(B)) = \beta R(B) \quad (6.2)$$

and investigate the nature of the maximum likelihood estimator of β, assuming that (i) the coefficients in $Q(B)$ and $R(B)$ are known and (ii) the power series $R(B)$ converges for $|B| = 1$.

Letting

$$z_t = Q(B)y_t \quad \text{and} \quad x_t = R(B)\xi_t ,$$

we can write (6.1) in the form of the usual linear model

$$z_t = \beta x_t + a_t \quad (6.3)$$

so that the maximum likelihood estimator of β is

$$\hat{\beta} = \sum_{t=1}^{n} z_t x_t / \sum_{t=1}^{n} (x_t)^2$$

with (6.4)

$$\text{Var}(\hat{\beta}) = (\sigma_a)^2 (\sum_{t=1}^{n} (x_t)^2)^{-1}.$$

For large n, we apply the results (A.6) and (A.7) in the appendix to obtain

$$\sum_{t=1}^{\infty} z_t x_t = \sum_{t=1}^{\infty} Q(B)y_t R(B)\xi_t = \sum_{t=1}^{\infty} \xi_t R(F)Q(B)y_t = R(F)Q(B)C_{\xi y}(0)$$

where $F = B^{-1}$ and

$$\sum_{t=1}^{n} (x_t)^2 = \sum_{t=1}^{\infty} R(B)\xi_t R(B)\xi_t = R(F)R(B)C_{\xi\xi}(0) ,$$

where

$$C_{\alpha\beta}(k) = \sum_{t=1}^{\infty} \beta_t \alpha_{t-k} , \quad k = 0, \pm 1, \pm 2, \cdots ,$$

and for a given k

$$B^l C_{\alpha\beta}(k) = C_{\alpha\beta}(k - l) , \quad l = 0, \pm 1, \pm 2, \cdots .$$

Thus,

$$\hat{\beta} = R(F)Q(B)C_{\xi y}(0)/R(F)R(B)C_{\xi\xi}(0) \quad (6.5)$$

and

$$\text{Var}(\hat{\beta}) = (\sigma_a)^2/R(F)R(B)C_{\xi\xi}(0) .$$

Making use of (A.10) in the appendix, we can write $R(B)R(F)$ as

$$R(B)R(F) = r_0 + \sum_{l=1}^{\infty} r_l(B^l + F^l) . \quad (6.6)$$

Suppose that $\xi_t = P_t^{(T)}$ is a pulse at time T, and a large number of observations are available before and after T. In this case

$$C_{\xi\xi}(k) = \begin{cases} 1, & k = 0 \\ 0, & k \neq 0 \end{cases} \quad \text{and} \quad C_{\xi y}(k) = y_{T-k} , \quad (6.7)$$

so that

$$\hat{\beta} = (r_0)^{-1} R(F)Q(B)y_T \quad \text{and} \quad \text{Var}(\hat{\beta}) = (\sigma_a)^2 (r_0)^{-1} \quad (6.8)$$

where it is understood that B is operating on T.

Now, nonstationarity in time series data can often be removed by differencing. In what follows we suppose that the polynomial $\varphi(B)$ in (6.1) is divisible by $(1 - B)$. We consider two special cases of interest.

Case (i). $\omega(B)/\delta(B) = \beta B$, (6.9)

that is, the pulse input $P_t^{(T)}$ gives rise to a response at time $(T + 1)$ measured by β which dissipates completely after the $(T + 1)$th period. It should be noted that with any number of periods of pure delay, the response will follow the same pattern but be appropriately shifted. In this case, $Q(B) = R(B)F$ so that, from (6.6) and (6.8),

$$\hat{\beta} = y_{T+1} - \tfrac{1}{2} \sum_{l=1}^{\infty} \lambda_l (y_{T+1+l} + y_{T+1-l}) , \quad (6.10)$$

where $\lambda_l = -2r_l/r_0$. Also, since $\varphi(B)$ is assumed divisible by $(1 - B)$, $r_0 + 2\sum_{l=1}^{\infty} r_l = 0$, and hence $\sum_{l=1}^{\infty} \lambda_l = 1$.

As an example, consider the integrated moving average model of order one for the noise term N_t for which

$$\varphi(B) = 1 - B \quad \text{and} \quad \theta(B) = 1 - \theta B \ . \tag{6.11}$$

Since

$$R(B)R(F) = \frac{(1 - B)(1 - F)}{(1 - \theta B)(1 - \theta F)}$$

$$= (1 + \theta)^{-1} \cdot [2 - (1 - \theta) \sum_{l=1}^{\infty} \theta^{l-1}(B^l + F^l)] \ ,$$

we find that

$$\lambda_l = (1 - \theta)\theta^{l-1} \ . \tag{6.12}$$

Thus, $\hat{\beta}$ represents a comparison between y_{T+1} and the mean of two exponentially weighted averages, one of the observations before time $(T + 1)$ and the other after, with the magnitude of the weights $(1 - \theta)\theta^{l-1}$ monotonically decreasing as l increases.

This formulation is applicable to situations where the response to the pulse input is expected to be short-lived, e.g., the effect on the demand for electricity during a sudden heat wave in the summer or the sale of beer in Wisconsin should the Packers win the Super Bowl. Essentially, we are comparing the observation y_{T+1} with the neighboring ones to determine if y_{T+1} is an "aberrant" or "outlying" observation. The results in (6.10) and (6.12) are appealing since, in forming the comparison, more weight is given to observations close to the intervening event and less and less weight to observations remote from the time of the event.

Case (ii). $\quad \omega(B)/\delta(B) = \beta B/(1 - B) \ . \qquad (6.13)$

Here, the response to the pulse $P_t^{(T)}$ is a step change in the level of the observations measured by β. Thus

$$Q(B) = (1 - B)R(B)F \tag{6.14}$$

and, from (6.6), (6.8) and (A.11), we have that

$$\hat{\beta} = (r_0)^{-1}R(B)R(F)(1 - B)y_{T+1}$$

$$= \sum_{l=0}^{\infty} \alpha_l y_{T+1+l} - \sum_{l=0}^{\infty} \alpha_l y_{T-l} \tag{6.15}$$

where $\alpha_l = (r_0)^{-1}(r_l - r_{l+1})$ so that $\sum_{l=0}^{\infty} \alpha_l = 1$.

The quantity $\hat{\beta}$ is, therefore, a contrast between two weighted averages, one of observations before the intervening pulse $P_t^{(T)}$ and the other afterward, where the weights are symmetrical.

As a first example, consider again the integrated moving average model in (6.11). We find

$$\hat{\beta} = (1 - \theta) \sum_{l=0}^{\infty} \theta^l y_{T+1+l} - (1 - \theta) \sum_{l=0}^{\infty} \theta^l y_{T-l} \tag{6.16}$$

as obtained in [2].

As a second example, we return to the model in (5.2) for the monthly averages of ozone in downtown Los Angeles. For illustration, we shall ignore the effect of interventions after 1966 and discuss the step change

$$(\beta B/(1 - B))P_t^{(T)} = \omega_{01}\xi_{t1} \ , \quad T = \text{December 1959}$$

in the level of the series due to the intervening events around that time. In this case, the noise model is such that

$$\varphi(B) = (1 - B^{12})$$

and

$$\theta(B) = (1 - \theta_1 B)(1 - \theta_2 B^{12}) \ .$$

Thus,

$$R(B)R(F) = \frac{(\sum_{j=0}^{11} B^j)(\sum_{j=0}^{11} F^j)}{(1 - \theta_1 B)(1 - \theta_2 B^{12})(1 - \theta_1 F)(1 - \theta_2 F^{12})}$$

$$= (\sum_{j=0}^{\infty} \pi_j B^j)(\sum_{j=0}^{\infty} \pi_j F^j) \tag{6.17}$$

so that from (A.10),

$$r_l = \sum_{j=0}^{\infty} \pi_j \pi_{j+l} \ .$$

The π_j can be obtained from the relationship

$$(1 - \theta_1 B)(1 - \theta_2 B^{12}) \sum_{j=0}^{\infty} \pi_j B^j = \sum_{j=0}^{11} B^j \ .$$

By writing $\pi_j = 12n + m$, we find

$$\pi_{12n+m} = (1 - \theta_1)^{-1}(\phi - \theta_2)^{-1}[(\theta_1)^{m+1}\{(1 - \phi)\phi^n - (1 - \theta_2)(\theta_2)^n\} + (\phi - \theta_2)(\theta_2)^n] \ ,$$
$$m = 0, \cdots, 11;\ n = 0, \cdots, \infty \tag{6.18}$$

where $\phi = (\theta_1)^{12}$.

From (6.18) and after some algebraic reduction, we obtain, on setting $l = 12k + s$,

$$r_{12k+s} = (1 - \theta_1)^{-2}(1 - (\theta_2)^2)^{-1} \cdot \left[12 - s(1 - \theta_2) + \frac{\theta_1(1 - \theta_2)^2}{1 - (\theta_1)^2} \cdot \left(\frac{\phi(\theta_1)^{-s}}{1 - \phi\theta_2} - \frac{(\theta_1)^s}{\phi - \theta_2}\right)\right](\theta_2)^k + (1 - \theta_1)^{-2} \cdot (\phi - \theta_2)^{-1}(1 - \phi\theta_2)^{-1}(1 - (\theta_1)^2)^{-1} \cdot (1 - \phi)^2(\theta_1)^{s+1}\phi^k \ , \tag{6.19}$$

$$s = 0, \cdots, 11; \quad k = 0, \cdots, \infty \ .$$

The resulting weight function for the Los Angeles data is shown in Figure A above the observations.

6.2 The General "Linear" Dynamic Model

The result in (6.5) can be readily extended to the case of more than one parameter. In the general dynamic model with k inputs in (4.1), letting

$$(\varphi(B)/\theta(B))(\omega_j(B)/\delta_j(B)) = \beta_j R_j(B) \tag{6.20}$$

we can write

$$Q(B)y_t = \sum_{j=1}^{k} \beta_j R_j(B)\xi_{tj} + a_t, \quad t = 1, \cdots, n \tag{6.21}$$

where, as before in (6.1), $Q(B) = \varphi(B)/\theta(B)$. Assuming that all the coefficients in $Q(B)$ and $R_j(B)$ are known and these $k+1$ power series converge for $|B| = 1$, the model is then linear in the k parameters $\boldsymbol{\beta} = (\beta_1, \cdots, \beta_k)'$. It readily follows that, for large n, the maximum likelihood estimator $\hat{\boldsymbol{\beta}}$ satisfies the normal equations

$$\mathbf{A}\hat{\boldsymbol{\beta}} = \mathbf{b} \tag{6.22}$$

where $\mathbf{A}$ is a $k \times k$ matrix and $\mathbf{b}$ a $k \times 1$ vector such that

$$\mathbf{A} = [a_{ij}] \,, \quad a_{ij} = R_i(F)R_j(B)C_{\xi_i\xi_j}(0)$$
$$\mathbf{b} = (b_1, \cdots, b_k)'$$

with

$$b_j = R_j(F)Q(B)C_{\xi_j y}(0) \,; \quad i, j = 1, \cdots, k \,.$$

In what follows, we investigate the special case having two parameters,

$$y_t = \{\beta_1\eta(B)B + \beta_2(1-B)^{-1}B\}P_t^{(T)} + (\theta(B)/\varphi(B))a_t \,. \tag{6.23}$$

In this model, $\beta_1\eta(B)BP_t^{(T)}$, where $\eta(B)$ is assumed to converge for $|B| = 1$, measures the transient effect, and β_2 represents the eventual change in the level of the observations induced by the pulse input $P_t^{(T)}$ (see Figure B(e) for the special case $\eta(B) = (1-\delta B)^{-1}$). When $\beta_1 = 0$, the model reduces to that considered in (6.13). It is, therefore, of particular interest to know to what extent the nature and precision of the estimator of β_2 is affected by the presence of β_1. We again suppose that the noise term is nonstationary so that $\varphi(B)$ is divisible by $(1-B)$.

To facilitate comparison with the model (6.13) we again define a quantity $R(B)$ such that

$$Q(B) = (1-B)R(B)F \,,$$

so that in (6.22)

$$R_1(B) = Q(B)\eta(B)B = R(B)\eta(B)(1-B)$$

and

$$R_2(B) = R(B) \,.$$

It follows that, provided $|\mathbf{A}| \neq 0$,

$$\hat{\beta}_1 = |\mathbf{A}|^{-1}\{a_{22}b_1 - a_{12}b_2\} \,, \qquad \hat{\beta}_2 = |\mathbf{A}|^{-1}\{a_{11}b_2 - a_{12}b_1\} \tag{6.24}$$

where

$$|\mathbf{A}| = a_{11}a_{22} - (a_{12})^2 \,,$$
$$b_1 = R(B)R(F)(1-F)\eta(F)(1-B)y_{T+1} \,,$$
$$b_2 = R(B)R(F)(1-B)y_{T+1} \,,$$

and a_{11}, a_{12} and a_{22} are, respectively, the coefficients of B^0 in the power series

$$R(B)R(F)\eta(B)\eta(F)(1-B)(1-F) \,,$$
$$R(B)R(F)\eta(B)(1-B) \,,$$
$$R(B)R(F) \,.$$

Some Properties of $\hat{\beta}_1$ and $\hat{\beta}_2$.

(i) Both b_1 and b_2 are linear functions of the observations y_t. By setting $B = F = 1$, the sum of the coefficients associated with y_t is zero for both of these functions. Thus, $\hat{\beta}_1$ and $\hat{\beta}_2$ are linear contrasts in y_t.

(ii) The estimator $\hat{\beta}_2$ can be expressed in the form

$$\hat{\beta}_2 = \sum_{l=0}^{\infty} \alpha_{1l}y_{T+1+l} - \sum_{l=0}^{\infty} \alpha_{2l}y_{T-l}$$

where

$$\sum_{l=0}^{\infty} \alpha_{1l} = \sum_{l=0}^{\infty} \alpha_{2l} = 1 \,, \tag{6.25}$$

i.e., a contrast between two weighted averages, one of observations on or before the pulse input and the other afterward. To see this, since $\hat{\beta}_2$ is a linear contrast, it suffices to show that $\sum_{l=0}^{\infty} \alpha_{1l} = 1$.

From the expression for b_2 in (6.24), letting

$$G(B) = R(B)R(F) \,, \quad H(B) = 1 - B$$

and

$$b_2 = \sum_{l=-\infty}^{\infty} d_l y_{T+1-l}$$

it follows from (A.11) that $\sum_{l=-\infty}^{0} d_l = a_{22}$.

Further, making use of (A.12) and (A.13), we see that a_{12} in (6.24) is also the coefficient of B^0 in $R(B)R(F)\cdot(1-F)\eta(F)$. If we now set

$$G_1(B) = R(B)R(F)(1-F)\eta(F) \,, \quad H_1(B) = 1 - B$$

and

$$b_1 = \sum_{l=-\infty}^{\infty} d_l^* y_{T+1-l} \,,$$

we then have $\sum_{l=-\infty}^{0} d_l^* = a_{12}$. The desired result follows since

$$\sum_{l=0}^{\infty} \alpha_{1l} = |\mathbf{A}|^{-1}\{a_{11}\sum_{l=-\infty}^{0} d_l - a_{12}\sum_{l=-\infty}^{0} d_l^*\} = 1 \,.$$

This property is similar to that of $\hat{\beta}$ in (6.15) for the model (6.13), except that the weight functions are no longer symmetrical. From least squares theory, we have

$$\hat{\beta}_2 = \hat{\beta} - (a_{12}/|\mathbf{A}|)(b_1 - a_{12}\hat{\beta}) \,, \tag{6.26}$$

and the second term on the right side measures the effect of the presence of the term $\beta_1\eta(B)BP_t^{(T)}$ in the model.

(iii) One would expect that addition of the parameter β_1 to the model would reduce the precision with which β_2 could be estimated. A useful measure of the loss of information is the variance ratio $\mathrm{Var}(\hat{\beta}_2)/\mathrm{Var}(\hat{\beta})$ where it is understood that the denominator corresponds to the model in (6.13). Now

$$\mathrm{Var}(\hat{\beta}_2)/\mathrm{Var}(\hat{\beta}) = (1-\rho^2)^{-1}$$

where

$$\rho = a_{12}/(a_{11}a_{22})^{\frac{1}{2}} \,. \tag{6.27}$$

We illustrate these results in terms of a specific example. Consider the case of (6.23) in which

$$\eta(B) = (1-\delta B)^{-1}, \quad \varphi(B) = 1 - B \text{ and } \theta(B) = 1 - \theta B.$$

We find

$$\hat{\beta}_2 = \hat{\beta} - \frac{(1-\theta)(1+\delta)}{(\theta-\delta)} \sum_{l=0}^{\infty} [(1-\delta)\delta^l - (1-\theta)\theta^l] y_{T+1+l} , \quad (6.28)$$

where $\hat{\beta}$ is given in (6.16). In this case only the weights associated with the observations after the intervening pulse $P_t^{(T)}$ are affected by the presence of $\beta_1(1-\delta B)^{-1}BP_t^{(T)}$ in the model. The weight function is shown in Figure D for $\theta = .5$ and $\delta = .25$.

D. Comparison of Weights Associated with y_{T+1+l}, $\hat{\beta}_2$ and for $\hat{\beta}$ ($\theta = .05$, $\delta = .25$, $l = 0, 1, 2, \ldots$)

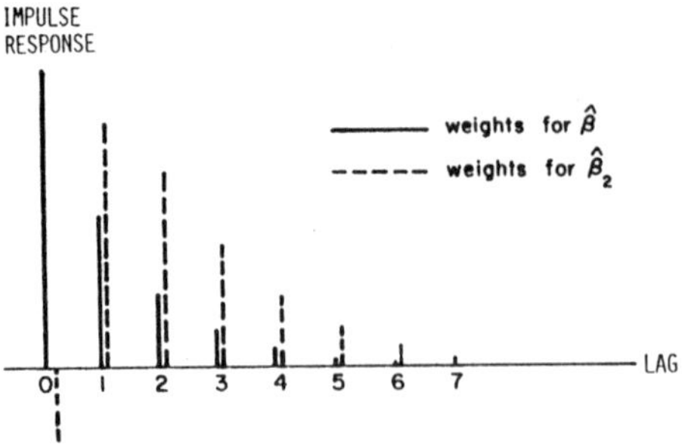

Also, for this model the variance ratio is

$$V = \text{Var}(\hat{\beta}_2)/\text{Var}(\hat{\beta}) = 1 + ((1-\theta)(1+\delta)/(1+\theta)(1-\delta)) . \quad (6.29)$$

The value of this ratio for various values of θ and δ is shown in the following tabulation:

	δ				
θ	−.5	−.25	0	.25	.5
−.5	2.00	2.80	4.00	6.00	10.00
−.25	1.56	2.00	2.67	3.78	6.00
0	1.33	1.60	2.00	2.67	4.00
.25	1.20	1.36	1.60	2.00	2.80
.5	1.11	1.20	1.33	1.56	2.00

Thus, the presence of β_1 in the model can cause large increases in the variance of $\hat{\beta}_2$, compared with $\hat{\beta}$, when θ is negative and δ is positive.

7. CONCLUDING REMARKS

In the past, much attention has been given to statistical analysis linking phenomena which are coincidental in time. In practice, it is perhaps more often the case that a response at a given point of time depends on events, both known and unknown, which have occurred not necessarily coincidentally but over the recent past. Statistical methods have, in a word, "lacked memory." The dynamic characteristics of both the transfer function and the noise parts of the model have tended to be ignored. The application of time series methods can amend this situation. This is illustrated in this article in the particular case where the object is to study the possible effect of interventions in the presence of dependent noise structure.

APPENDIX

We here state some useful results in the summation of series.

Lemma 1: Let $\{v_k\}_0^\infty$ be a sequence of numbers and let $\{x_t\}_{-\infty}^\infty$ and $\{y_t\}_{-\infty}^\infty$ be two sequences of numbers such that $x_t = y_t = 0$ for $t \leq 0$. If one of the following three double sums is absolutely convergent,

$$S_1 = \sum_{t=1}^{\infty}\sum_{k=0}^{\infty} x_t v_k y_{t-k} , \quad S_2 = \sum_{u=1}^{\infty}\sum_{k=0}^{\infty} y_u v_k x_{u+k} , \quad (A.1)$$

$$S_3 = \sum_{k=0}^{\infty}\sum_{u=1}^{\infty} v_k y_u x_{u+k} ,$$

the other two are absolutely convergent and

$$S_1 = S_2 = S_3 .$$

Proof of the lemma can be found in any standard text on infinite series.

It is convenient to express S_1, S_2 and S_3 in terms of the backshift operator B and its reciprocal, the forward shift operator $F = B^{-1}$. Letting

$$V(B) = \sum_{k=0}^{\infty} v_k B^k \quad \text{and} \quad V(F) = \sum_{k=0}^{\infty} v_k F^k \quad (A.2)$$

we can then write

$$S_1 = \sum_{t=1}^{\infty} x_t V(B) y_t \quad \text{and} \quad S_2 = \sum_{t=1}^{\infty} y_t V(F) x_t . \quad (A.3)$$

Further, suppose we define

$$C_{xy}(k) = \sum_{t=1}^{\infty} y_t x_{t-k} , \quad C_{yx}(k) = \sum_{t=1}^{\infty} x_t y_{t-k} , \quad k = 0, \pm 1, \pm 2, \cdots$$

so that

$$C_{xy}(k) = C_{yx}(-k) . \quad (A.4)$$

The quantity S_3 in (6.1) can be expressed as

$$S_3 = \sum_{k=0}^{\infty} v_k C_{xy}(-k) ,$$

and, by letting $C_{xy}(-k) = B^k C_{xy}(0)$, we have

$$S_3 = V(B) C_{xy}(0) . \quad (A.5)$$

It follows that when the conditions of Lemma 1 hold,

$$\sum_{t=1}^{\infty} x_t V(B) y_t = \sum_{t=1}^{\infty} y_t V(F) x_t = V(B) C_{xy}(0) . \quad (A.6)$$

This result can be readily extended to the following:

Lemma 2: Suppose $W(B) = V_1(B) + V_2(F)$ where $V_1(B)$ and $V_2(F)$ are two power series in B and F, respectively, such that the sum $\sum_{t=1}^{\infty} x_t W(B) y_t$ is absolutely convergent. Then

$$\sum_{t=1}^{\infty} x_t W(B) y_t = W(B) C_{xy}(0) . \quad (A.7)$$

Lemma 3: Let $G(B) = \sum_{j=-\infty}^{\infty} g_j B^j$ and $H(B) = \sum_{k=-\infty}^{\infty} h_k B^k$ be two power series in B and converge for $|B| = 1$, and let $D(B)$

$= G(B)H(B)$. Then

$$D(B) = \sum_{l=-\infty}^{\infty} d_l B^l \quad (A.8)$$

where

$$d_l = \sum_{j=-\infty}^{\infty} g_j h_{l-j} \ .$$

In particular

(i) if $g_j = g_{-j}$ and $h_k = h_{-k}$, then

$$d_l = d_{-l} = \sum_{u=0}^{\infty} h_u g_{u+l} + \sum_{u=1-l}^{\infty} g_u h_{u+l} \ , l = 0, \cdots, \infty \ ; \quad (A.9)$$

(ii) if $g_j = 0, j \leq -1$ and $H(B) = G(F)$, then

$$d_l = d_{-l} = \sum_{j=0}^{\infty} g_j g_{j+l} \ , \quad l = 0, \cdots, \infty \ ; \quad (A.10)$$

(iii) if $H(B) = 1 - B$, then

$$d_l = g_l - g_{l-1} \quad l = 0, \pm 1, \cdots, \pm \infty \ , \quad (A.11)$$

so that $\sum_{l=1}^{\infty} d_l = -g_0$ and $\sum_{l=-\infty}^{0} d_l = g_0$;

(iv) if $g_j = g_{-j}$ and $h_j = 0 \quad j \leq -1$, then

$$d_0 = \sum_{j=0}^{\infty} h_j g_j \ ; \quad (A.12)$$

(v) if $g_j = g_{-j}$ and $h_j = 0 \quad j \geq 1$, then

$$d_0 = \sum_{j=-\infty}^{0} h_j g_j \ . \quad (A.13)$$

[Received October 1973. Revised August 1974.]

REFERENCES

[1] Box, G.E.P. and Jenkins, G.M., *Time Series Analysis, Forecasting and Control*, San Francisco: Holden-Day, Inc., 1970.

[2] ——— and Tiao, G.C., "A Change in Level of a Non-stationary Time Series," *Biometrika*, 52 (June 1965), 181–92.

[3] ——— and Tiao, G.C., *Bayesian Inference in Statistical Analysis*, Reading, Mass.: Addison-Wesley Publishing Co., 1973.

[4] Feige, E. and Pearce, D.K., "Inflation and Income Policy: An Application of Time Series Models," Report #7318, Social Systems Research Institute, University of Wisconsin, Madison, 1973.

[5] Glass, G.V., "Estimating the Effects of Intervention into a Nonstationary Time Series," *American Educational Research Journal*, 9, No. 3 (1972), 463–77.

[6] Tiao, G.C., Box, G.E.P. and Hamming, W.J., "Analysis of Los Angeles Photochemical Smog Data: A Statistical Overview," *Journal of Air Pollution Control Association*, 25 (March 1975).

[14]

J. R. Statist. Soc. A
(1976), **139**, *Part* 2, p. 246

Time Series Modelling and Interpretation

By C. W. J. Granger and M. J. Morris

University of California, San Diego *University of East Anglia, U.K.*

Summary

By considering the model generating the sum of two or more series, it is shown that the mixed *ARMA* model is the one most likely to occur. As most economic series are both aggregates and are measured with error it follows that such mixed models will often be found in practice. If such a model is found, the possibility of resolving the series into simple components is considered both theoretically and for simulated data.

Keywords: TIME SERIES; MIXED AUTOREGRESSIVE-MOVING AVERAGE MODEL; AGGREGATION; MEASUREMENT ERROR; PARSIMONIOUS MODELS

1. Introduction

The recent publication of the book by Box and Jenkins has greatly increased interest by time series analysts and econometricians in more complicated, even if more "parsimonious", time series models. However, the intuitive interpretation of the models that arise is not always simple and an applied research worker may well ask how such a model could have arisen in practice. In this paper, the possibility that a complicated looking model could have arisen from a simpler situation is explored and some suggestions made about the possible interpretation of some models that appear to arise in practice.

The only series to be considered are those with zero means and generated by models with time-invariant parameters. Thus, possibly after an appropriate linear transformation, the series will be taken to be second-order stationary. Let X_t be such a series, so that

$$E\{X_t\} = 0, \quad \text{all } t.$$

Initially, suppose that X_t is second-order stationary, so that the kth autocovariance

$$\mu_k = E\{X_t X_{t-k}\} \tag{1.1}$$

is time invariant. The series will be said to be a white noise process if

$$\mu_k = 0, \quad \text{all } k \neq 0.$$

Use will be made of the backward operator B, defined so that

$$B^j X_t = X_{t-j}. \tag{1.2}$$

A series with the representation

$$a(B)\, X_t = \varepsilon_t, \tag{1.3}$$

where

$$a(B) = \sum_{j=0}^{p} a_j B^j, \quad a \neq 0, \quad a_0 = 1, \tag{1.4}$$

and ε_t is white noise, will be said to be generated by an autoregressive model of order p, and denoted by $X_t \sim AR(p)$.

Suppose further that

$$a(B) = \prod_{j=1}^{p} (1 - \theta_j B) \tag{1.5}$$

so that $\theta_j^{-1}, j = 1, \ldots, p$, are the roots of the equation $a(z) = 0$. If $|\theta_j^{-1}| > 1$, all j, then X_t will be stationary. In this case

$$\mu_k = \sum_{j=1}^{p} \lambda_j \theta_j^k. \tag{1.6}$$

A series will be said to be generated by a moving average of order q if it can be represented by

$$X_t = b(B)\, \varepsilon_t,$$

where

$$b(B) = \sum_{j=0}^{q} b_j B^j \tag{1.8}$$

and ε_t is white noise. This is denoted by $X_t \sim MA(q)$. A necessary but not sufficient condition that such a representation is possible is

$$\mu_k = 0, \quad k > q. \tag{1.9}$$

The fact that this condition is not sufficient may be seen from the result that the maximum value of the first serial correlation coefficient $\rho_1 = \mu_1/\mu_0$ achievable from an $MA(q)$ process is

$$\rho_1(\max) = \cos\left(\frac{\pi}{q+2}\right). \tag{1.10}$$

It follows, for example, that if $\rho_1 = 0{\cdot}8$, $\mu_k = \rho_k = 0$, all $k > 1$, then there is no corresponding $MA(1)$ process which has these values. Davies *et al.* (1974) have found more general inequalities on autocorrelations for MA processes.

A necessary and sufficient condition that there exists an $MA(q)$ model corresponding to a specific set of autocorrelation coefficients u_j, $j = 0, 1, \ldots, q$, has been given by Wold (1953, p. 154).

Let

$$u(x) = 1 + \sum_{j=1}^{q} u_j (x^j + x^{-j}).$$

Applying the transformation $z = x + x^{-1}$, let $u(x)$ be transformed into the qth order polynomial $v(z)$. The required necessary and sufficient condition is then that $v(z)$ has no zero of odd multiplicity in the interval $-2 < z_0 < 2$. Note that

$$v(2) = u(1) = f(0) \geqslant 0 \quad \text{and} \quad v(-2) = u(-1) = f(\pi) \geqslant 0,$$

where $f(\omega)$ is the spectrum of the moving average process. It follows that if $v(z)$ obeys the above condition, then $v(z) \geqslant 0$ for all z in the interval $(-2, 2)$.

An $MA(q)$ process, with $q < \infty$, is always stationary.

A stationary $AR(p)$ process can always be represented by an $MA(\infty)$ process (as can any stationary, purely non-deterministic process). If the roots of the equation $b(z) = 0$ all have absolute value greater than one, then the corresponding $MA(q)$ process may be inverted and be equally represented by an $AR(\infty)$ process.

Ever since their introduction by Yule (1921), the autoregressive and moving average models have been greatly favoured by time series analysts. It is not difficult to convince oneself that both models are intuitively reasonable and could well occur in practice. Simple expectations models or a momentum effect in a random variable can lead to AR models. Similarly, a variable in equilibrium but buffeted by a sequence of unpredictable events with a delayed or discounted effect will give MA models, for example.

A fairly obvious generalization of these models is the mixed autoregressive-moving average process generated by

$$a(B)\,X_t = b(B)\,\varepsilon_t, \tag{1.11}$$

where ε_t is again white noise and $a(B)$ and $b(B)$ are polynomials in B of order p and q respectively. Such a process is denoted by $X_t \sim ARMA(p,q)$ and has an autocovariance sequence given by (1.6) for $k>q$. An $ARMA(p,q)$ process can always be represented by an $MA(\infty)$ model and, with the same invertibility condition for $MA(q)$, it can also be represented in an $AR(\infty)$ form.

In practice, the *ARMA* model is more difficult to fit to data than for example an *AR* model, but in other ways the *ARMA* model may be the statistically more efficient of the two. Box and Jenkins suggest that if one fits both an $AR(p)$ model and an $ARMA(p',q')$ model, then one will generally need fewer coefficients in this second model to get a satisfactory fit, i.e. $p'+q'<p$. As there are good reasons to prefer a model with as few parameters as possible, their principle of parsimony then suggests that the *ARMA* will often be preferable.

Although the *ARMA* model may involve the estimation of fewer coefficients than alternative models, it is certainly more difficult to comprehend, interpret or explain how it might occur in the real world. Chatfield and Prothero (1973) comment on the difficulty in the interpretation of many Box–Jenkins models. In the following sections a number of ways are suggested in which such an *ARMA* model can arise from simpler models. It will be concluded that a mixed model is the one that is most likely to arise in practice.

2. THE SUM OF TWO INDEPENDENT SERIES

If X_t and Y_t are two independent, zero-mean, stationary series, then in this section statements of the following kind will be considered:

$$\text{if} \quad X_t \sim ARMA(p,m), \quad Y_t \sim ARMA(q,n)$$
$$\text{and} \quad Z_t = X_t + Y_t$$
$$\text{then} \quad Z_t \sim ARMA(x,y).$$

Such a statement will be *denoted* by

$$ARMA(p,m)+ARMA(q,n) = ARMA(x,y).$$

Lemma.

$$MA(m)+MA(n) = MA(y), \tag{2.1}$$

where

$$y \leqslant \max(m,n). \tag{2.2}$$

Necessity follows directly from (1.9) and the inequality from the fact that there may be an inter-reaction between the two *MA* processes which reduces the order of the *MA* process of the sum. This latter point will be discussed in greater detail below.

To prove that the sufficiency condition holds, let $v_1(z), v_2(z)$ be the $v(z)$ functions for $MA(m)$ and $MA(n)$ respectively, as defined after equation (1.10). As $v_1(z)$ and $v_2(z)$ do correspond to moving averages, they will both be non-negative over the interval $-2 \leqslant z \leqslant 2$. If $v_s(z)$ is the function for $MA(m)+MA(n)$, it follows that as $v_s(z) = v_1(z)+v_2(z)$ it will also be non-negative in the interval $-2 \leqslant z \leqslant 2$ and so $v_s(z)$ cannot have a root of odd multiplicity in this interval, so the truth of the lemma holds. Note that if $m \neq n$ then there must be equality in (2.2).

Basic Theorem.

$$ARMA(p,m)+ARMA(q,n) = ARMA(x,y), \tag{2.3}$$

where

$$x \leqslant p+q \quad \text{and} \quad y \leqslant \max(p+n, q+m). \tag{2.4}$$

(This is a form of the theorem proved by Box and Jenkins in their Appendix to Chapter 4.)

Proof. Let

$$a(B)\,X_t = c(B)\,\varepsilon_t \tag{2.5}$$

and

$$b(B)\,Y_t = d(B)\,\eta_t, \tag{2.6}$$

where a, b, c, d are polynomials in B of order p, q, m, n respectively and ε_t, η_t are two independent, white noise series.

As $Z_t = X_t + Y_t$, it follows that

$$a(B)\,b(B)\,Z_t = b(B)\,a(B)\,X_t + a(B)\,b(B)\,Y_t = b(B)\,c(B)\,\varepsilon_t + a(B)\,d(B)\,\eta_t. \tag{2.7}$$

The first term on the right-hand side is $MA(q+m)$ and the second term is $MA(p+n)$ and so, from the lemma, the right-hand side is $MA(y)$ where

$$y \leqslant \max(p+n, q+m).$$

The order of the polynomial $a(B)\,b(B)$ is not more than $p+q$, and so the theorem is established.

(The assumption of independence may be weakened to allow for contemporaneous correlation between the noise series. The sum would still be of the form (2.3) but the parameters of the representation would be different.)

The need for the inequalities in the expressions for x and y partly arise from the fact that the polynomials $a(B)$ and $b(B)$ may contain common roots and so part of the operator need not be applied twice. For example, if

$$(1-\alpha_1 B)\,X_t = \varepsilon_t, \quad \text{i.e. } X_t \sim AR(1)$$

and

$$(1-\alpha_1 B)(1-\alpha_2 B)\,Y_t = \eta_t, \quad \text{i.e. } Y_t \sim AR(2)$$

then with $Z_t = X_t + Y_t$ we have $(1-\alpha_1 B)(1-\alpha_2 B) Z_t = (1-\alpha_2 B)\,\varepsilon_t + \eta_t$, i.e. $Z_t \sim ARMA\ (2, 1)$. In general, if the polynomials $a(B), b(B)$ have just k roots in common, the inequalities (2.4) become

$$x = p+q-k \quad y \leqslant \max(p+n-k, q+m-k). \tag{2.8}$$

That the inequality for y in (2.8) is still necessary is seen from the following example. Suppose

$$(1-\alpha B)\,X_t = \varepsilon_t, \quad \text{i.e. } X_t \sim AR(1)$$

$$(1+\alpha B)\,Y_t = \eta_t, \quad \text{i.e. } Y_t \sim AR(1)$$

and also $\text{var}(\varepsilon) = \text{var}(\eta) = \sigma^2$.

If $Z_t = X_t + Y_t$, then $(1-\alpha B)(1+\alpha B) Z_t = (1+\alpha B)\,\varepsilon_t + (1-\alpha B)\,\eta_t$. Denote the right-hand side of the last equation by $\zeta_t = \varepsilon_t + \alpha\varepsilon_{t-1} + \eta_t - \alpha\eta_{t-1}$; then $\text{var}(\zeta_t) = 2(1+\alpha^2)\,\sigma^2$ and $E\{\zeta_t\,\zeta_{t-k}\} = 0$, all $k > 0$, so ζ_t is a white noise process and $Z_t \sim AR(2)$ rather than $ARMA(2, 1)$ which would generally occur when two independent $AR(1)$ processes are added together. Those situations in which a simpler model arises than might generally be expected will be called "coincidental situations".

If X_t and Y_t are both stationary, then any case in which x and y in (2.4) take values less than the maximum ones might well be considered coincidental. However, a more general model proposed by Box and Jenkins for marginally non-stationary processes suggests that common roots might well be expected, this common root being unity. They suggest that many series met with in practice obey a simple kind of non-stationary model:

$$(1-B)^f a(B) X_t = b(B)\varepsilon_t,$$

where $a(B)$ is a polynomial of order p and with all roots of $a(z)=0$ lying outside the unit circle and $b(B)$ is of order m. In this case X_t is said to obey an integrated autoregressive-moving average model, denoted by $ARIMA(p,f,m)$. Newbold and Granger (1974) found such models fitted a large number of economic time series, although possibly with the addition of seasonal terms. If two independent series X_t and Y_t both obey such a model, i.e. $X_t \sim ARIMA(p,f_1,m)$, $Y_t \sim ARIMA(q,f_2,n)$, then their sum will be $ARIMA(x,f',y)$ where $x \leqslant p+q; f' = \max(f_1,f_2); y \leqslant \max(p+n+f_1-f_2, q+m)$, if $f_1 \geqslant f_2$; $y \leqslant \max(p+n, q+m+f_2-f_1)$, if $f_2 \geqslant f_1$.

Similar considerations apply to the method of taking seasonal effects into account suggested by Box and Jenkins.

Given the basic theorem there is, of course, no difficulty in generalizing it to cover the sum of any number of independent series. Using an obvious generalization of the previous notation, the theorem becomes

$$\sum_{j=1}^{N} ARMA(p_j, m_j) = ARMA(x,y),$$

where

$$x \leqslant \sum_{j=1}^{N} p_j \quad \text{and} \quad y \leqslant \max(x-p_j+m_j, j=1,\ldots,N).$$

3. SERIES AGGREGATION AND OBSERVATIONAL ERROR MODELS

Two situations where series are added together are of particular interpretational importance. The first is where series are aggregated to form some total, and the second is where the observed series is the sum of the true process plus observational error, corresponding to the classical "signal plus noise" situation. Most macroeconomic series, such as G.N.P., unemployment or exports, are aggregates and there is no particular reason to suppose that all of the component series will obey exactly the same model. Virtually any macroeconomic series, other than certain prices or interest rates, contain important observation errors. It would be highly coincidental if the "true" series and the observational error series obeyed models having common roots, apart possibly from the root unity, or that the parameters of these models should be such that the cancelling out of terms produces a value of y in (2.4) less than the maximum possible.

It is interesting to consider a number of special cases of the basic theorem, concentrating on those situations in which coincidental reductions of parameters do not occur. In the cases considered the interpretations given will assume that aggregates are of independent components, an assumption almost certainly not true in practice, and that the observational error is white noise and independent of the true process, an assumption of debatable reality but on which little empirical work is available from which to form an opinion.

(i) $AR(p)$ + *white noise* = $ARMA(p,p)$

This corresponds to an $AR(p)$ signal as true process plus a simple white noise observational error series.

(ii) $AR(p)+AR(q) = ARMA(p+q, \max(p,q))$ *and in particular* $AR(1)+AR(1) = ARMA(2,1)$

This situation might correspond to a series which is aggregated from two independent AR series. A further case of possible interest is: the sum of k $AR(1)$ series is $ARMA(k,k-1)$. Case (ii) with an $AR(p)$ signal and $AR(q)$ noise was the subject of a paper by Bailey (1965).

(iii) $MA(p)+MA(q) = MA(\max(p,q))$ *and in particular* $MA(p)+$ *white noise* $= MA(p)$.

Thus if a true process follows an *MA* model then the addition of a white noise observation error will not alter the class of model, although the parameter values will change.

(iv) $ARMA(p,m)+$ *white noise* $= ARMA(p,p)$ *if* $p>m = ARMA(p,m)$ *if* $p<m$.

Thus the addition of an observational error may alter the order of an *ARMA* model but need not do so.

(v) $AR(p)+MA(n) = ARMA(p, p+n)$.

Again, this is possibly relevant to the aggregation case, or to the observation error case with noise not being white noise.

If one accepts the belief that time series, particularly in economics, obey either *AR* or *MA* models, both of which can be explained fairly easily in terms of the working of the economy, then the above special cases have a number of possible implications.

Cases (ii) and (v) suggest that a series that is an aggregate of several series, some of which are *AR* series, will be very likely to be an *ARMA* process, although from case (iii) an *MA* process is possible. The independence of the components can be relaxed in a realistic fashion with the same conclusion being reached. If each component consists of two parts, the first a factor common to all components representing the influence of the whole economy on them and the second a factor relating just to the particular component and independent of the economy-wide factor, then simple models can be assumed for each factor and on aggregation the more general form of the basic model involving the sum of several series will apply. Such factor models have been successfully used with series of stock market prices and firms' earnings.

The observational error or signal plus noise situation is also likely to produce an *ARMA* model, from cases (i) and (iv), although case (iii) again suggests that an *MA* model is possible.

Thus both of the realistic situations considered in this section are quite likely to produce *ARMA* models. These situations are discussed further in Sections 5 and 6. Other situations that also produce *ARMA* models are considered in the following section.

4. TIME AGGREGATION, NON-INTEGER LAGS AND FEEDBACK MODELS

Three other situations that might occur in practice lead either exactly, or approximately, to *ARMA* models. These are:

(i) A variable that obeys a simple model such as $AR(1)$ if it were recorded at an interval of K units of time but which is actually observed at an interval of M units. Details may be found in Amemiya and Wu (1972). The variable considered has to be an accumulated one, that is of the type called a stock variable by economists.

(ii) If X_t is an instantaneously recorded variable, called a flow variable by economists, and suppose that it obeys the model

$$X_t - \alpha X_{t-b} = \varepsilon_t, \quad |\alpha| < 1,$$

where b may be a non-integer multiple or fraction of the observation period, then it is easily shown (see Granger, 1964) that this is equivalent to the $AR(\infty)$ model

$$\sum_{j=0}^{\infty} h_j X_{t-j} = \varepsilon_t,$$

where $h_j = \{\sin(j-b)\pi\}/(j-b)\pi$ and doubtless this model could well be approximated by an *ARMA* model.

(iii) If X_t, Y_t are generated by the bivariate autoregressive scheme with feedback:

$$a(B)X_t + b(B)Y_t = \varepsilon_t, \quad c(B)X_t + d(B)Y_t = \eta_t,$$

where ε_t, η_t are uncorrelated white noise series and $b(0) = c(0) = 0$, then the model obeyed by X_t alone is found by eliminating Y_t in the equations to be

$$[a(B)\,d(B) - c(B)\,b(B)]\,X_t = d(B)\,\varepsilon_t + b(B)\,\eta_t$$

and so the $ARMA(p,q)$ model occurs once more, and it is easily shown that generally $p>q$.

The results of this and the previous section suggest that a number of real data situations are all likely to give rise to $ARMA$ models. Combining these situations will only reinforce this conclusion. In fact, one might well conclude that the model most likely to be found in practice is the mixed autoregressive moving-average model.

5. Realizability of Simple Models

Given a specific $ARMA(p,q)$ model it is interesting to ask whether or not this could have arisen from some simpler model. On occasions an answer can be found immediately: if $p<q$ then a feedback model is not appropriate for example. To merely illustrate the problem of realizability, a few examples from Section 3 are considered. As will be seen simplifications are not always possible, as conditions on the coefficients of the $ARMA$ model need to be satisfied for a simpler model to be realizable.

(i) *Can* $ARMA(1,1) = AR(1) +$ *white noise?*

Suppose $(1+aB)\,X_t = \varepsilon_t$ and $Y_t = \eta_t$, where both ε_t and η_t are white noise series, independent of each other, then if $Z_t = X_t + Y_t$ it was seen that Z_t is $ARMA(1,1)$ given by

$$(1+aB)\,Z_t = (1+aB)\,\eta_t + \varepsilon_t. \tag{5.1}$$

Now suppose that the given $ARMA(1,1)$ process is

$$(1+cB)\,Z_t = (1+dB)\,\zeta_t, \tag{5.2}$$

where ζ_t is a white noise series.

Let μ_0, μ_1 denote the variance and first autocovariance of the $MA(1)$ process on the right-hand side of (5.2). For (5.1) and (5.2) to be equivalent one needs

$$c = a, \tag{5.3(i)}$$

$$\mu_0 = (1+d^2)\,\sigma_\zeta^2 = (1+a^2)\,\sigma_\eta^2 + \sigma_\varepsilon^2, \tag{5.3(ii)}$$

$$\mu_1 = d\sigma_\zeta^2 = a\sigma_\eta^2. \tag{5.3(iii)}$$

The realizability conditions may then be written in the form

$$\frac{1}{1+c^2} > \frac{\rho_1}{c} \geqslant 0, \tag{5.3(iv)}$$

where

$$\rho_1 = \frac{\mu_1}{\mu_0} = \frac{d}{1+d^2},$$

the first inequality coming from (5.3(ii)) and the condition $\sigma_\varepsilon^2 > 0$, the second inequality from (5.3(iii)) and (5.3(i)).

(ii) *Can* $ARMA(2,2) = AR(2) +$ *white noise?*

Suppose $(1+a_1B+a_2B^2)\,X_t = \varepsilon_t$ and $Y_t = \eta_t$, where both ε_t and η_t are white noise series, independent of each other; then if $Z_t = X_t + Y_t$, Z_t is ARMA(2, 2) given by

$$(1+a_1B+a_2B^2)\,Z_t = (1+a_1B+a_2B^2)\,\eta_t + \varepsilon_t. \tag{5.4}$$

Now suppose that the given *ARMA*(2, 2) process is

$$(1+c_1 B+c_2 B^2) Z_t = (1+d_1 B+d_2 B^2)\,\zeta_t, \tag{5.5}$$

where ζ_t is a white noise series.

Let μ_0, μ_1, μ_2 denote the variance, first and second autocovariance of the *MA*(2) process on the right-hand side of (5.5). For (5.4) and (5.5) to be equivalent one needs

$$c_1 = a_1, \qquad (5.6(\text{i}))$$

$$c_2 = a_2, \qquad (5.6(\text{ii}))$$

$$\mu_0 = (1+d_1^2+d_2^2)\,\sigma_\zeta^2 = (1+a_1^2+a_2^2)\,\sigma_\eta^2+\sigma_\varepsilon^2, \qquad (5.6(\text{iii}))$$

$$\mu_1 = d_1(1+d_2)\,\sigma_\zeta^2 = a_1(1+a_2)\,\sigma_\eta^2, \qquad (5.6(\text{iv}))$$

$$\mu_2 = d_2\,\sigma_\zeta^2 = a_2\,\sigma_\eta^2. \qquad (5.6(\text{v}))$$

These realizability conditions may be written in the form

$$\frac{1}{1+c_1^2+c_2^2} > \frac{\rho_2}{c_2} \geqslant 0 \qquad (5.6(\text{vi}))$$

and

$$\frac{\rho_1}{c_1(1+c_2)} = \frac{\rho_2}{c_2}, \qquad (5.6(\text{vii}))$$

where

$$\rho_1 = \frac{\mu_1}{\mu_0} = \frac{d_1(1+d_2)}{1+d_1^2+d_2^2} \quad \text{and} \quad \rho_2 = \frac{\mu_2}{\mu_0} = \frac{d_2}{1+d_1^2+d_2^2}.$$

As an equality is involved, the realizability of the simple model may be classified as being coincidental.

(iii) *Can ARMA*(2, 2) = *ARMA*(2, 1) + *white noise?*

With the same notation as in (ii), the realizability conditions are

$$\frac{1}{1+c_1^2+c_2^2} > \frac{\rho_2}{c_2} \geqslant 0. \tag{5.7}$$

These examples illustrate the fact that some models are not capable of simplification and that the realizability conditions will usually be rather complicated. The conditions will also be coincidental if the number of parameters, or "degrees of freedom", are less than the parameters in the initial *ARMA* model.

The problem considered here is only of theoretical interest and is not realistic. An *ARMA* model will generally have been estimated from some data. A more realistic question, and one of considerable interpretational importance, is whether a simple model would have a level of fit that is not significantly different from that achieved by the *ARMA* model. This question is briefly considered in the next section, using simulated time series.

6. SIMULATION OF OBSERVATION ERROR MODELS

Two examples are considered:

Example 1: Can a given *ARMA*(1, 1) be expressed as *AR*(1) + white noise?
Example 2: Can a given *ARMA*(2, 2) be expressed as *AR*(2) + white noise?

Example 1

Two series, each of 200 terms, are generated from $AR(1)$ and white noise processes.

Series 1: $(1-0\cdot 8B)X_t = \varepsilon_t, \quad t = 1,\ldots,N \quad (N=200).$

Series 2: $Y_t = \eta_t, \quad t = 1,\ldots,N \quad (N=200)$

with $\sigma_\varepsilon^2 = 4$, $\sigma_\eta^2 = 1$.

The two series added together gives the series $Z_t = X_t + Y_t$, $t = 1,\ldots,N$, which may be regarded as being generated by the process

$$(1-0\cdot 8B)Z_t = (1-0\cdot 8B)\eta_t + \varepsilon_t$$

and this, from (5.3(i)), (5.3(ii)) and (5.3(iii)) may be written as

$$(1-0\cdot 8B)Z_t = (1-0\cdot 14B)\zeta_t \tag{6.1}$$

with $\sigma_\zeta^2 = 5\cdot 52$.

Using the maximum likelihood estimation method described in Box and Jenkins (1970) the model

$$(1+cB)Z_t = (1+dB)\zeta_t$$

fitted to the series Z_t, $t = 1,\ldots,N$, gives estimates $c = -0\cdot 76$, $d = -0\cdot 04$.

The residual sum of squares is 1,273·0, giving an estimate of $\sigma_\zeta^2 = 6\cdot 43$.

Now we take the given $ARMA(1,1)$ series to be

$$(1+cB)Z_t = (1+dB)\zeta_t$$

with

$$c = -0\cdot 76, \quad d = -0\cdot 04, \quad \sigma_\zeta^2 = 6\cdot 43. \tag{6.2}$$

Can this be expressed as $AR(1)$+white noise? Realizability conditions (5.3(iv)) are satisfied since

$$\frac{1}{1+c^2} = 0\cdot 63$$

and

$$\frac{\rho_1}{c} = \frac{d}{c(1+d^2)} = 0\cdot 05.$$

The realizability conditions (5.3(i)), (5.3(ii)) and (5.3(iii)) may be solved to give

$$a = -0\cdot 76, \quad \sigma_\eta^2 = 0\cdot 34, \quad \sigma_\varepsilon^2 = (1+d^2)\sigma_\zeta^2 - (1+a^2)\sigma_\eta^2 = 5\cdot 90.$$

Thus, the series (6.2) is exactly equivalent to the series

$$(1-0\cdot 76B)X_t = \varepsilon_t, \quad Y_t = \eta_t, \quad Z_t = X_t + Y_t \tag{6.3}$$

with $\sigma_\eta^2 = 0\cdot 34$, $\sigma_\varepsilon^2 = 5\cdot 90$, both (6.2) and (6.3) fitting the given series equally well.

It is therefore seen that if one were given the datum Z_t, one would not know if it were generated by an $ARMA(1,1)$ model of if it were the sum of two components, one of which is $AR(1)$ and the other is white noise. This is, of course, true of any $ARMA(1,1)$ model for which the realizability condition holds.

Example 2

Two series, each of 200 terms, are generated from $AR(2)$ and white noise processes.

Series 1: $(1-0\cdot 8B+0\cdot 4B^2)X_t = \varepsilon_t, \quad t = 1,\ldots,N \quad (N=200).$

Series 2: $Y_t = \eta_t, \quad t = 1,\ldots,N \quad (N=200)$

with $\sigma_\varepsilon^2 = 4$, $\sigma_\eta^2 = 1$.

The two series added together give the series $Z_t = X_t + Y_t$, $t = 1, \ldots, N$ which may be regarded as being generated by the process,

$$(1-0{\cdot}8B+0{\cdot}4B^2)Z_t = (1-0{\cdot}8B+0{\cdot}4B^2)\eta_t+\varepsilon_t$$

and this, from (5.6(i)) to (5.6(v)), may be written as

$$(1-0{\cdot}8B+0{\cdot}4B^2)Z_t = (1-0{\cdot}19B+0{\cdot}07B^2)\,\zeta_t \tag{6.4}$$

with $\sigma_\zeta^2 = 5{\cdot}59$.

The model $(1+c_1B+c_2B^2)Z_t = (1+d_1B+d_2B^2)\,\zeta_t$ fitted to the series Z_t, $t = 1, \ldots, N$, gives estimates $c_1 = -1{\cdot}01$, $c_2 = 0{\cdot}59$, $d_1 = -0{\cdot}51$, $d_2 = 0{\cdot}12$. The residual sum of squares is 988·5 giving an estimate of $\sigma_\zeta^2 = 5{\cdot}04$.

Now we take the given $ARMA(2,2)$ series to be

$$(1+c_1B+c_2B^2)Z_t = (1+d_1B+d_2B^2)\,\zeta_t \tag{6.5}$$

with $c_1 = -1{\cdot}01$, $c_2 = 0{\cdot}59$, $d_1 = -0{\cdot}51$, $d_2 = 0{\cdot}12$, $\sigma_\zeta^2 = 5{\cdot}04$.

Can this be expressed as $AR(2)$+white noise? This example is more interesting than Example 1, because it involves a reduction in the number of parameters. $ARMA(2,2)$ contains five parameters, whereas $AR(2)$ and white noise contain a total of four.

The realizability conditions (5.6(vi)) and (5.6(vii)) are not both satisfied.

Equation (5.6(vi)) is satisfied because $(1+c_1^2+c_2^2)^{-1} = 0{\cdot}42$ and

$$\frac{\rho_2}{c_2} = \frac{d_2}{c_2(1+d_1^2+d_2^2)} = 0{\cdot}16$$

but the equality (5.6(vii)) is not satisfied because

$$\frac{\rho_1}{c_1(1+c_2)} = \frac{d_1(1+d_2)}{c_1(1+c_2)(1+d_1^2+d_2^2)} = 0{\cdot}28.$$

It is therefore not possible to solve the equations (5.6(i))–(5.6(v)) to obtain a model of the form $AR(2)$+white noise which is exactly equivalent to (6.5) and which fits the data equally well. However, because the given $ARMA(2,2)$ series has been constructed as the sum of $AR(2)$ and white noise, one would hope to find a model of the form $AR(2)$+white noise which is almost as good.

We are seeking a model

$$(1+a_1B+a_2B^2)X_t = \varepsilon_t, \quad Y_t = \eta_t, \quad Z_t = X_t+Y_t \tag{6.6}$$

which may also be written as

$$(1+a_1B+a_2B^2)Z_t = (1+a_1B+a_2B^2)\eta_t+\varepsilon_t = (1+b_1B+b_2B^2)\,\zeta_t, \quad \text{say.}$$

We may proceed as follows:

Let $\gamma_{Zk} = \operatorname{cov}(Z_t, Z_{t-k})$ and $\gamma_{Xk} = \operatorname{cov}(X_t, X_{t-k})$. Because X_t and Y_t are independent, $\gamma_{Z0} = \gamma_{X0}+\sigma_\eta^2$ and $\gamma_{Zk} = \gamma_{Xk}$, $k>0$. In particular,

$$\gamma_{Z0} = \gamma_{X1}+\sigma_\eta^2, \quad \gamma_{Z1} = \gamma_{X1}, \quad \gamma_{Z2} = \gamma_{X2}.$$

The given $ARMA(2,2)$ series may be used to estimate γ_{Zk}, $k = 0,1,2$, by

$$c_{Zk} = \frac{1}{N}\sum_{t=1}^{N-k}(Z_t-\bar{Z})(Z_{t+k}-\bar{Z}).$$

Then, given an estimate of σ_η^2, γ_{Xk}, $k = 0,1,2$, may be estimated by

$$c_{X0} = c_{Z0}-\sigma_\eta^2, \quad c_{X1} = c_{Z1}, \quad c_{X2} = c_{Z2}.$$

If $r_1 = c_{X1}/x_{X0}$, $r_2 = c_{X2}/c_{X0}$, the Yule–Walker equations may be solved to give estimates of a_1, a_2,

$$a_1 = \frac{r_1(1-r_2)}{1-r_1^2}, \quad a_2 = \frac{r_1^2-r_2}{1-r_1^2}$$

and σ_ε^2 may be estimated by

$$\sigma_\varepsilon^2 = c_{X0}(1+r_1 a_1+r_2 a_2),$$

b_1 and b_2 may then be estimated using the realizability conditions (5.6(iii))–(5.6(v)) by solving the equations

$$\frac{b_2}{b_1(1+b_2)} = \frac{a_2}{a_1(1+a_2)}$$

$$\frac{b_2}{1+b_1^2+b_2^2} = \frac{a_2\sigma_\eta^2}{(1+a_1^2+a_2^2)\sigma_\eta^2+\sigma_\varepsilon^2}.$$

These equations may be written as

$$b_1 = \frac{Ab_2}{1+b_2}, \tag{6.7(i)}$$

$$1+(2-C)b_2+(2-2C+A^2)b_2^2+(2-C)b_2^3+b_2^4 = 0, \tag{6.7(ii)}$$

where

$$A = \frac{a_1(1+a_2)}{a_2}, \quad C = \frac{(1+a_1^2+a_2^2)\sigma_\eta^2+\sigma_\varepsilon^2}{a_2\sigma_\eta^2}$$

choosing the solution of (6.7(ii)) which lies between 0 and a_2 (from 5.6(v)).

The model

$$(1+a_1 B+a_2 B^2)Z_t = (1+b_1 B+b_2 B^2)\zeta_t$$

is then fitted to the given series, and the residual sum of squares obtained.

By considering a range of values of σ_η^2 it is possible to determine the parameter values which minimize the residual sum of squares.

For the given series, these values are $a_1 = -0{\cdot}91$, $a_2 = 0{\cdot}60$, $b_1 = -0{\cdot}40$, $b_2 = 0{\cdot}20$ with $\sigma_\eta^2 = 1{\cdot}62$, $\sigma_\varepsilon^2 = 2{\cdot}40$. The residual sum of squares is 994·5, giving an estimate of $\sigma_\zeta^2 = 5{\cdot}07$.

So the model (6.6) with $a_1 = -0{\cdot}91$, $a_2 = 0{\cdot}60$, $\sigma_\eta^2 = 1{\cdot}62$, $\sigma_\varepsilon^2 = 2{\cdot}40$ is almost as good as the *ARMA*(2, 2) model (6.5).

It is, of course, no surprise that the particular Z_t series here considered although it would be identified as an *ARMA*(2, 2) process it could equally well be explained as being the sum of an *AR*(2) plus white noise, since this is how it was generated. However, many series identified to be *ARMA*(2, 2) might also be equally explained by the simple sum, which is more parsimonious in the sense that it involves fewer parameters to be estimated. If a series can be so decomposed into two or more components this could help with interpretation of its generating process. One might, for example, suggest that the true series might be considered as a true *AR*(2) signal plus a white noise observation error series. If true, this decomposition would suggest the importance of the observation error measured in terms of the contribution of this error towards the variance of the optimum one-step forecasts. If this contribution is large enough it might be worth spending more to reduce observation error and thus decrease prediction error.

The technique used in our second example can easily be adapted to deal with other models and might allow the analyst to suggest the importance of the noise contribution to prediction error variance in a signal plus noise model.

REFERENCES

AMEMIYA, T. and WU, R. Y. (1972). The effect of aggregation on prediction in the autoregressive model. *J. Amer. Statist. Ass.*, **67**, 628–632.

BAILEY, M. G. (1965). Prediction of an autoregressive variable subject both to disturbances and to errors of observation. *J. Amer. Statist. Ass.*, **60**, 164–181.

BOX, G. E. P. and JENKINS, G. M. (1970). *Time Series Analysis*. San Francisco, Holden-Day.

CHATFIELD, C. and PROTHERO, D. L. (1973). Box–Jenkins seasonal forecasting: problems in a case study (with Discussion). *J. R. Statist. Soc.* A, **136**, 295–336.

DAVIES, N., PATE, M. B. and FROST, M. G. (1974). Maximum autocorrelations for moving average processes. *Biometrika*, **61**, 199–200.

GRANGER, C. W. J. and HATANAKA M. (1964). *Spectral Analysis of Economic Time Series*. Princeton University Press.

NEWBOLD, P. and GRANGER, C. W. J. (1974). Experience with forecasting univariate time series and the combination of forecasts (with Discussion). *J. R. Statistical Soc.* A, **137**, 131–164.

WOLD, H. (1953). *A Study in the Analysis of Stationary Time Series*, 2nd ed. Stockholm: Alqvist and Wiksell.

Journal of Econometrics 37 (1988) 67–86. North-Holland

CURRENT DEVELOPMENTS IN TIME SERIES MODELLING

M.B. PRIESTLEY

University of Manchester, Institute of Science and Technology, Manchester M60 1 QD, UK

In this paper a survey is given of some current developments in time series analysis. After a brief discussion of linear models, ARMA models and state–space reprentations, the discussion concentrates on a fairly general class of non-linear models called 'state-dependent models' and the applications of these to the problem of identifying general forms of non-linear structure. The effectiveness of the estimation technique is studied by means of numerical examples on simulated data. Towards the end of the paper it is indicated how these ideas may be applied to the study of systems governed by non-linear differential equations.

1. Introduction

Time series analysis is a strange subject. Its roots are firmly embedded in physics and engineering, yet its methodology is largely statistical, and its applications range from astrophysics to neurophysiology. It does not give rise to fierce arguments on the fundamental ideas of statistical inference (although Bayesian ideas do intrude from time to time), yet it has provoked some fierce battles on topics such as the Uncertainty Principle, the physical interpretation of time-dependent spectra, and the relative merits of various forecasting techniques, and it has often been said that if you present the same data to two time series analysts you will receive three different answers.

One of the areas in which time series methodology differs from that of the more conventional branches of statistics is in relation to the ideas and techniques of modelling. When we speak of a 'linear model' in conventional statistics we mean one in which the relationship between the observed variable and the explanatory variables is a linear function of the *parameters* of the model (a polynomial regression is, of course, still a linear model). However, within the context of time series modelling the term 'linear' is used in a sense which is much closer to its physical interpretation; a linear time series model is one in which the relationship between the present and the past is expressed in a linear form, i.e., the 'dynamics' of the process are of a linear form.

During the first fifty years of the development of modern methods of time series analysis linear models provided the dominant influence, and much of conventional time series analysis rests very heavily on this assumption. It may be of some interest therefore to consider some recent developments in the area of non-linear modelling, and to examine the way in which these ideas extend the well trodden areas of linear models.

Before embarking on a detailed discussion of these topics one or two general remarks may be in order. The subject of linear time series modelling has now reached a very refined state (in terms of both its theoretical structure and inferential aspects) and, by contrast, non-linear modelling is still very much in its infancy. When judged within the context of non-linear models, the subject of linear modelling appears to be almost trivial by comparison, and the availability of a complete theory is due essentially to the very neat and tidy theory of 'linear mathematics' (essentially, the theory of linear vector spaces). It is this feature which enables one to develop a very elegant theory of prediction, and which in turns leads to Akaike's superbly attractive geometrical interpretation of ideas such as 'state–space representations', 'minimal realisations' and, more importantly, the notion of the 'dimension' of a linear model [Akaike (1974a, b)]. There is of course no comparable comprehensive treatment of non-linear mathematics, and correspondingly the studies of non-linear time series models which have been conducted so far are essentially empirical in nature, although some degree of basic theory is beginning to emerge.

The subject matter of this paper is concerned with a fairly general class of non-linear models called 'state-dependent models', and the applications of these to the problem of identifying general forms of non-linear structure will be discussed in the following sections. Towards the end of the paper we will indicate a possible application of these ideas to the study of systems governed by non-linear differential equations.

2. Theory of linear models

All forms of time series modelling are based on the concept of a 'white noise' process, which henceforth we donate by $\{\varepsilon_t\}$. In this context a white noise process is defined as a sequence of zero mean random variables, with constant variancc σ_ε^2, i.c., $E\{\varepsilon_t\} = 0$, $E\{\varepsilon_t^2\} = \sigma_\varepsilon^2$, $E\{\varepsilon_s \varepsilon_t\} = 0$, $s \neq t$, $s \neq t$.

Given a general discrete parameter time series $\{X_t;\ t = 0, \pm 1, \pm 2, \dots\}$, a 'model' is specified by finding that function of future, present, and past observations which transforms the given series into a white noise process. Thus, we seek a function h which is such that

$$h(\dots, X_{t-2}, X_{t-1}, X_t, X_{t+1}, X_{t+2}, \dots) = \varepsilon_t. \tag{2.1}$$

In particular, the class of *linear* models corresponds to the case where the function h is *linear*, so that (2.1) then takes the form

$$\sum_{u=-\infty}^{\infty} h_u X_{t-u} = \varepsilon_t. \tag{2.2}$$

This is the general form of the non-linear model, but here X_t is allowed to depend on future values as well as on past values. In practice we would usually require X_t to depend only on past values, i.e., we would set $h_u = 0$, $u < 0$, and rewrite (2.2), the 'one-sided' form, as

$$\sum_{u=0}^{\infty} h_u X_{t-u} = \varepsilon_t. \tag{2.3}$$

Introducing the backward shift operator B, defined by $BX_t = X_{t-1}$, etc., (2.3) can now be expressed in the form

$$H(B) X_t = \varepsilon_t, \tag{2.4}$$

where

$$H(z) = \sum_{u=0}^{\infty} h_u z^u. \tag{2.5}$$

Eq. (2.4) may be 'solved' to express X_t as a linear function of present and past values of ε_t. Thus, inverting (2.4) formally we may write

$$x_t = H^{-1}(B)\varepsilon_t, \tag{2.6}$$

and if $H^{-1}(z)$ can be expanded as a convergent series for $|z| < 1$ [i.e., if $H(z)$ has no zeros inside the unit circle] we may write further

$$H^{-1}(z) = g_0 + g_1 z + g_2 z^2 + \dots. \tag{2.7}$$

We may now write X_t explicitly as

$$X_t = \sum_{u=0}^{\infty} g_u \varepsilon_{t-u}, \tag{2.8}$$

or

$$X_t = \Gamma(B)\varepsilon_t, \tag{2.9}$$

where

$$\Gamma(z) = \sum_{u=0}^{\infty} g_u z^u. \tag{2.10}$$

Note that

$$\Gamma(z) \equiv H^{-1}(z) \quad \text{or} \quad \Gamma(z)H(z) \equiv 1.$$

Eq. (2.8) gives us an alternative formulation for the general (non-anticipative) linear model in which X_t is expressed as a linear combination of present and past values of a white noise process $\{\varepsilon_t\}$.

2.1. AR, MA and ARMA models

The general linear model, as given by (2.3) or (2.8), involves an infinite number of parameters and cannot therefore be fitted directly to data unless further assumptions are made. In the context of practical time series model fitting we use a standard set of finite parameter models which arise as special cases of the general linear model (2.8). Thus, if we assume that $\Gamma^{-1}(z) \equiv H(z)$ may be approximated by a finite-order polynomial, say,

$$\Gamma^{-1}(z) = 1 + \alpha_1 z + \cdots + \alpha_k z^k, \tag{2.11}$$

then (2.8) reduces to the AR(k) (*autoregressive model of order* k) form

$$X_t + \alpha_1 X_{t-1} + \cdots + \alpha_k X_{t-k} = \varepsilon_t. \tag{2.12}$$

On the other hand, if we approximate to $\Gamma(z)$ by a finite-order polynomial, say,

$$\Gamma_1(z) = 1 + \beta_1 z + \cdots + \beta_l z^l, \tag{2.13}$$

then (2.8) reduces to the MA(l) (*moving average of order* l) form

$$X_t = \varepsilon_t + \beta_1 \varepsilon_{t-1} + \cdots + \beta_l \varepsilon_{t-l}. \tag{2.14}$$

If $\Gamma(z)$ and $\Gamma^{-1}(z)$ are 'well-behaved' functions, we can, to an arbitrary degree of accuracy, approximate either by a finite polynomial of sufficiently high degree. If follows, therefore, that we can, in general, approximate a general linear model by either an AR or MA model of sufficiently high order. However, we can obtain a more 'parsimonious' finite parameter representation of $\Gamma(z)$ by approximating it by a *rational function*. If we take $\Gamma(z)$ to have the form,

$$\Gamma(z) = \frac{1 + \beta_1 z + \cdots + \beta_l z^l}{1 + \alpha_1 z + \cdots + \alpha_k z^k}, \tag{2.15}$$

then (2.8) reduces to the ARMA (k, l) [*mixed autoregressive/moving average of order* (k, l)] *model*,

$$X_t + \alpha_1 X_{t-1} + \cdots + \alpha_k X_{t-k} = \varepsilon_t + \beta_1 \varepsilon_{t-1} + \cdots + \beta_{l,t-l}. \tag{2.16}$$

This model can be written in operator form as (with an obvious notation)

$$\alpha(B)X_t = \beta(B)\varepsilon_t. \tag{2.17}$$

[The slightly more general ARIMA models, which have been studied, in particular, by Box and Jenkins (1970), correspond to the case where the operator $\alpha(B)$ in (2.17) contains a factor of the form $(1-B)^d$. In this case $\Gamma(z)=[\beta(z)/\alpha(z)]$ contains a dth-order pole at $z=1$ and consequently $\{X_t\}$ is no longer a stationary process – although its dth difference, $\Delta^d X_t$, would, in general, be stationary).

2.2. *State–space representations*

An alternative way of rewriting the general ARMA model (2.16) is based on the so-called '*state–space*' (or '*Markovian*') representation which provides a compact description of any finite-parameter linear model. The basic idea rests simply on the well-known result that any finite-order linear differential or difference equation can be expressed as a vector first-order equation. For example, if we take the AR(2) model

$$X_t + \alpha_1 X_{t-1} + \alpha_2 X_{t-2} = \varepsilon_t, \tag{2.18}$$

and write $x_t^{(2)} = X_t$, $x_t^{(1)} = -\alpha_2 X_{t-1} [= -\alpha_2 X_{t-1}^{(2)}]$, then (2.18) may be rewritten as

$$\begin{bmatrix} x_t^{(1)} \\ x_t^{(2)} \end{bmatrix} = \begin{bmatrix} 0 & -\alpha_2 \\ 1 & -\alpha_1 \end{bmatrix} \begin{bmatrix} x_{t-1}^{(1)} \\ x_{t-1}^{(2)} \end{bmatrix} + \begin{bmatrix} 0 \\ 1 \end{bmatrix} \varepsilon_t. \tag{2.19}$$

To recover X_t from the vector $[x_t^{(1)}, x_t^{(2)}]'$, we now write

$$X_t = (0,1) \begin{bmatrix} x_t^{(1)} \\ x_t^{(2)} \end{bmatrix}. \tag{2.20}$$

The pair (2.18), (2.20) is completely equivalent to (2.18), but whereas (2.18) involves a two-stage dependence so that X_t is non-Markovian, (2.19) involves only a one-stage dependence so that $[x_t^{(1)}, x_t^{(2)}]'$ is a vector Markov process. [The device of expressing (2.18) in the form (2.19) may be viewed alternatively as a special case of the technique of writing certain types of non-Markov processes involving only finite-stage dependence as vector Markov processes.]

Exactly the same approach may be used to write the general ARMA model in the state–space form. Thus, assuming that $l \leq (k-1)$ in (2.16), we first write (2.16) as

$$X_t + \alpha_1 X_{t-1} + \cdots + \alpha_k X_{t-k} = \varepsilon_t + \beta_1 \varepsilon_{t-1} + \cdots + \beta_{k-1} \varepsilon_{t-k+1}, \tag{2.21}$$

where $\beta_j = 0$ $(j > l)$, and it is then easy to verify that (2.21) can be written in state–space form as

$$\boldsymbol{x}(t+1) = \boldsymbol{F}\boldsymbol{x}(t) + \boldsymbol{G}\varepsilon_t, \tag{2.22}$$

$$X_t = \boldsymbol{H}\boldsymbol{x}(t), \tag{2.23}$$

where the $k \times k$ matrix $\boldsymbol{F}$ is given by

$$\boldsymbol{F} = \begin{bmatrix} 0 & 0\ldots0 & -\alpha_k \\ 1 & 0\ldots0 & -\alpha_{k-1} \\ 0 & 1\ldots0 & -\alpha_{k-2} \\ \cdots & \cdots & \cdots \\ 0 & 0\ldots1 & -\alpha_1 \end{bmatrix},$$

the $k \times 1$ matrix G by

$$\boldsymbol{G}' = [\beta_{k-1}, \beta_{k-2}, \ldots, \beta_1, 1],$$

the $1 \times k$ matrix $\boldsymbol{H}$ by

$$\boldsymbol{H} = (0, 0, \ldots, 0, 1),$$

and the $k \times 1$ vector $x(t)$ is partitioned as

$$x'(t) = (x_1(t), x_2(t), \ldots, x_k(t)).$$

[In fact, $x_k(t)$ is simply the variable X_t in (2.21), and $x_{k-1}(t)$, $x_{t-2}(t)$, ... are defined recursively in terms of $x_k(t)$.] In this formulation $\boldsymbol{x}(t)$ is called the *state vector*, $\boldsymbol{F}$ is called the *system matrix*, **G** the *input matrix*, and $\boldsymbol{H}$ the *observation matrix*. [Note that the condition for (2.21) to represent a stationary process is that $\alpha(z)$ has no zeros inside or on the unit circle – in which case the matrix $\boldsymbol{F}$ is 'stable', i.e., all its eigenvalues have modulus less than one, and consequently the process $\boldsymbol{x}(t)$ is stationary.]

Akaike (1974a) has given a very general treatment of finite-order linear models and has shown, using a geometrical approach, that a *minimal* realisation (i.e., a state–space representation with $\boldsymbol{x}(t)$ having the smallest possible dimension) can be derived by selecting the state vector $\boldsymbol{x}(t)$ as any basis of the 'predictor space at time t', $R(t+|t-1)$, namely the space spanned by the linear least squares predictors of $X_t, X_{t+1}, X_{t+2}, \ldots,$ given $\varepsilon_t, \varepsilon_{t-1}, \varepsilon_{t-2}, \ldots$. The crucial feature of this space is that, for models described by finite-order difference equations, it has *finite dimensions*, k. A minimal realisation can now be constructed by choosing the state vector (at time t) as *any* basis of $R(t+|t-)$. If we think of the model as a physical system with ε_t as the 'input' and X_t as the 'output', the above specification of the state vector is in complete accord with the physical interpretation of the 'state' of the system at time t_0 as that set of quantities which, together with the input for all time points $\geq t_0$, uniquely determines the output for all time points $\geq t_0$. (When, e.g., the relationship between input and output is described by a finite-order difference or differential equation, the 'state' at time t_0 is simply the set of 'initial conditions' required to determine the solution of the difference or differential equation for all $t \geq t_0$.) Intuitively, therefore, we may think of the state at any time point as the totality of information on the future output contained within the past input, and this is precisely the information contained within the set of predictors $\{X_t, X_{t+1|t}, X_{t+2|t}, \ldots\}$ or, equivalently, within any set of basis variables of the space spanned by these predictors.

3. General non-linear models

We now return to the general model (2.1). If we impose the condition of 'physical realisability' on (2.1), we obtain a model of the form

$$h(X_t, X_{t-1}, X_{t-2}, \ldots) = \varepsilon_t, \tag{3.1}$$

and if we assume that this model is 'invertible' [i.e., that (3.1) may be 'solved' to yield an expression for X_t in terms of $\varepsilon_t, \varepsilon_{t-1}, \varepsilon_{t-2}, \ldots$], we then obtain, say,

$$X_t = f(\varepsilon_t, \varepsilon_{t-1}, \varepsilon_{t-2}, \ldots\}. \tag{3.2}$$

From the standpoint of statistical analysis (3.2) is just as intractable as (2.1), but we may attempt to 'parametrise' (3.2) by assuming further that the function f is analytic, so that it can be expanded about some fixed point – say about the point $\mathbf{0} = (0, 0, 0, \ldots)$. This yields the formal expansion

$$X_t = \mu + \sum_{u=0}^{\infty} g_u \varepsilon_{t-u} + \sum_{u=0}^{\infty} \sum_{v=0}^{\infty} g_{uv} \varepsilon_{t-u} \varepsilon_{t-v} \times \sum_{u=0} \sum_{v=0} \sum_{w=0} g_{uvw} \varepsilon_{t-u} \varepsilon_{t-v} \varepsilon_{t-w} + \cdots, \tag{3.3}$$

where we have written $\mu = f(\mathbf{0})$, $g_u = [\partial f / \partial \varepsilon_{t-u}]_{\mathbf{0}}, \ldots$. This expansion is known as a *Volterra series* and was used by Wiener (1958) in his pioneering study of non-linear systems. Wiener's objective was to construct transformations of these series in which the successive terms are 'orthogonal' (i.e., uncorrelated) – rather like the use of orthogonal polynomials in regression analysis. However, there is clearly no possibility of fitting such a Volterra series to a finite stretch of data since the first term contains an infinite sequence of parameters, the second term a doubly infinite sequence of parameters, and so on. To circumvent this difficulty we may assume either (a) that the Fourier transforms of the sequences $\{g_u\}, \{g_{uv}\}, \ldots$ possess certain 'smoothness' properties, or (b) that each of these transforms has a known functional form involving only a finite number of unknown parameters. Approach (a) leads to 'polyspectral analysis' [the Fourier analysis of the higher-order moments – see, e.g., Brillinger (1970)], but is feasible only when (3.3) is of 'homogeneous form' with only one term present. On the other hand, (b) leads to the development of special forms of non-linear schemes, three particularly important types being (i) *bi-linear models* [Granger and Andersen (1978), Subba Rao (1981)], (ii) *threshold autoregressive models* [Tong and Lim (1980)], and (iii) *exponential autoregressive models* [Haggan and Ozaki (1981)]. For example, a bilinear model takes the form

$$X_t + a_1 X_{t-1} + \cdots + a_k X_{t-k}$$
$$= \varepsilon_t + b_1 \varepsilon_{t-1} + \cdots + b_l \varepsilon_{t-l} + \sum_{i=1}^{m} \sum_{j=1}^{p} c_{ij} \varepsilon_{t-i} X_{t-j}, \tag{3.4}$$

and is thus seen to be a generalisation of the (linear) ARMA model (2.16) in which a bi-linear form in $\{\varepsilon_{t-i}\}, \{X_{t-j}\}$ has been added to the right-hand side. Threshold AR models are constructed by starting with the (linear) AR model (2.12) and allowing each of the coefficients $a_1, \ldots, a_k$ to 'switch' between two different values according as to whether some past observation X_{t-d} falls below or above a given 'threshold' level. Exponential AR models are constructed by again starting with the AR model (2.12) and replacing each of the coefficients by exponential functions of X_{t-1}. Each of the special non-linear schemes describes, in its own way, a specific type of non-linearity; the threshold AR models can (with suitably chosen parameters) given rise to 'limit cycle' behaviour, while the exponential AR model can reproduce certain well-known features of non-linear random vibrations theory – such as 'amplitude-dependent frequency' and 'jump phenomena'. However, in practice it may be difficult to decide which, if any, of these special models is best suited to a given set of data. In the next section we describe a more general class of non-linear models, called '*state-dependent models*', which includes the bi-linear, threshold autoregressive, and exponential regressive models as special cases, but allows much greater flexibility in the characterisation of the non-linear structure. Although these 'state-dependent models' are of a general nature they are nevertheless amenable to statistical analysis and may be fitted to data.

This approach offers two major advantages, namely (a) state-dependent models may be used directly in connection with, e.g., the prediction of future values, and (b) since they can be fitted to data without any specific prior assumptions about the form of non-linearity, they may be used to give us an 'overview' of the character of the non-linearity inherent in the data and thus indicate whether, e.g., a bi-linear threshold AR or exponential AR model is appropriate.

4. State-dependent models

In developing the approach outlined at the end of the preceding section the basic difficulty which we encounter is that of striking a judicious balance between generality and tractability. To highlight this point we may note that the model (3.1) is completely general but totally intractable (as far as statistical analysis is concerned), whereas, e.g., the bilinear model (3.4) is certainly tractable but constrains us to a particular form of non-linear structure. Our approach is to start from the general model (3.1), and then impose further restrictions until we have reached the point at which statistical analysis may commence.

As it stands, the model (3.1) is 'infinite-dimensional' – in the sense that it involves a relationship between infinitely many variables. We now reduce this to a 'finite-dimensional' form by assuming that the relationship between X_t and the 'past history' of the series can be described in terms of finitely many values of past X_t's and ε_t's, so that we may write, say,

$$X_t = h'(X_{t-1},\dots X_{t-k}, \varepsilon_{t-1},\dots,\varepsilon_{t-l}) + \varepsilon_t. \tag{4.1}$$

In this formulation ε_t plays the role of the 'innovations' process for X_t, and the function h describes the information on X_t contained in its past history. In the language of probability theory we may interpret h' as the 'projection' (i.e., conditional expectation) of X_t on $\mathscr{B}^{\varepsilon}_{t-1}$, the Borel field generated by $\varepsilon_{t-1}, \varepsilon_{t-2},\dots$. In postulating the model (4.1) we are saying, in effect, that *this 'projection' can be expressed* in terms of a finite number of functions of $\varepsilon_{t-1}, \varepsilon_{t-2},\dots$. (Recall that, for each u, X_{t-u} is itself a function of $\varepsilon_{t-1}, \varepsilon_{t-2},\dots$.)

Assuming further that the function h' in (4.1) is analytic, we may expand the right-hand side of (4.1) about an arbitrary but fixed time point t_0. Using only a first-order expansion, we obtain

$$X_t = h'(x_{t_0}) + \sum_{u=1}^{k} f_u(x_{t-1})(X_{t-u} - X_{t_0-u})$$
$$+ \sum_{u=1}^{l} g_u(x_{t-1})(\varepsilon_{t-u} - \varepsilon_{t_0-u}), \quad \text{say,} \tag{4.2}$$

where $\boldsymbol{x}_t$ denotes the 'state vector'

$$\boldsymbol{x}_t = (\varepsilon_{t-l+1}, \dots \varepsilon_t, X_{t-k+1}, \dots X_t)', \tag{4.3}$$

and f_u and g_u depend on the first-order partial derivatives of h'. We can now rewrite (4.2) in the form

$$X_t + \sum_{u=1}^{k} \phi_u(\boldsymbol{x}_{t-1}) X_{t-u} = \mu(\boldsymbol{x}_{t-1}) + \varepsilon_t + \sum_{u=1}^{l} \psi_u(\boldsymbol{x}_{t-1}) \varepsilon_{t-u}. \tag{4.4}$$

This is the basic model with which we now work, and we call (4.4) a '*state-dependent model of order* (k, l)'. It has a natural interpretation as a *locally linear* ARMA model in which the evolution of the series at time $(t-1)$ is governed by a set of AR coefficients $\{\phi_u\}$, a set of MA coefficients $\{\psi_u\}$, and a local mean μ, all of which depend on the 'state' of the series at time $(t-1)$.

For each $\boldsymbol{x}_{t-1}$, (4.4) may be interpreted geometrically as the *tangent plane* to the surface generated by $h'(\boldsymbol{x}_{t-1})$. In this sense we may regard the SDM model as being formed by 'bending' the linear model around each point in the state-space.

It is easily seen that (4.4) includes as special cases all the special non-linear models described in the previous section. Thus, if we take μ and $\{\phi_u\}$ as constants and set

$$\psi_u(\boldsymbol{x}_{t-1}) = b_u + \sum_{i=1}^{p} c_{uj} X_{t-j},$$

then (4.4) reduces to the bi-linear model (3.4) [with the value of l in (4.4) chosen as $\max(m, l)$, m and l being the corresponding parameters in (3.4)]. Similarly, if we take all the ψ_u to be zero, and let μ and the ϕ_u take the form of step functions, each switching between two levels, then (4.4) reduces to the AR threshold model, while setting all the ϕ_u to zero and taking each ϕ_u to be an exponential function of X_{t-1} gives the AR exponential model.

A formal state-space representation of the SDM model is easily obtained by augmenting the vector (4.3) with the additional element unity in the leading position. Specifically, if we re-define $\boldsymbol{x}_t$ as

$$\boldsymbol{x}_t = (1, \varepsilon_{t-l+1}, \dots \varepsilon_t, X_{t-k+1}, \dots X_t)',$$

then it is not difficult to show that, with suitably defined matrices $\boldsymbol{F}$ and $\boldsymbol{H}$, we can rewrite (4.4) as

$$\boldsymbol{x}_{t+1} = \boldsymbol{F}(\boldsymbol{x}_t)\boldsymbol{x}_t + \boldsymbol{\varepsilon}_{t+1},$$

$$x_t = \boldsymbol{H}\boldsymbol{x}_t. \tag{4.5}$$

If μ, ϕ_u, μ_u are each analytic functions of x_{t-1}, then (4.5) is a special case of the class of 'linear analytic' systems studied in the control theory literature [see, e.g., Brockett (1976)].

4.1. *Identification of SDM's*

We now consider the problem of estimating or 'identifying' the functional forms of the parameters $\mu(x_t)$, $\phi_u(x_t)$, $\mu_u(x_t)$ from observational data. The simplest assumption we can make about these parameters is that each is a linear function of the components of x_t so that, for example, we may write

$$\psi_u(x_t) = \psi_u^{(0)} + x_t'\beta_u,$$

$$\phi_u(x_t) = \phi_u^{(0)} + x_t'\gamma_u.$$

This form would be appropriate to bi-linear models (with $\gamma_u = \mathbf{0}$, all u), but it is unreasonable to suppose that all non-linear models can be approximated with sufficient accuracy with ψ_u and ϕ_u set as linear functions of x_t. However, if ψ_u and ϕ_u are 'smooth' functions of x_t, it would be reasonable to suppose that they may be represented *locally* as linear functions. This means that we can obtain a fairly general representation of these parameters by allowing both β_u and γ_u to be themselves state-dependent. We are then faced with the problem of specifying the functional forms of β_u and γ_u, but we can avoid this difficulty by simply letting β_u and γ_u 'wander' over time, i.e., we allow $\beta_u = \beta_u^{(t)}$ and $\gamma_u = \gamma_u^{(t)}$ to depend purely on the time parameters. This gives the SDM considerable flexibility, and if we now allow $\beta_u^{(t)}$ and $\gamma_u^{(t)}$ to 'wander' in the form of random walks, we can construct an estimation procedure which, for each t, determines those values of $\beta_u^{(t)}, \gamma_u^{(t)}$ which, in effect, minimises the discrepancy between X_{t+1} and its predictor $\tilde{X}_{t+1}$, computed from the model. The estimation procedure is thus based on a sequential type of algorithm, similar in nature to the '*Kalman filter*' algorithm.

The estimation algorithm involves some rather technical statistical features, and here we illustrate its operation simply by reference to the 'pure AR' SDM type of model. [For a full description, see Haggan, Heravi and Priestley (1984).] We consider the SDM model (4.4) in which $\psi_u = 0$, all u, and rewrite this in a different state–space form in which the state vector no longer represents the state of the series but now represents the current state of all the relevant parameters. Specifically, we defined the vector θ_t by

$$\theta_t = \left(\mu_{t-1}, \phi_{1,t-1}, \dots, \phi_{k,t-1}, \alpha'^{(t)}, \gamma_1'^{(t)}, \dots, \gamma_k'^{(t)}\right)',$$

where, for brevity, we have written $\phi_{1,t-1}$ in place of $\phi_1(x_{t-1})$, and similarly for other parameters. Writing $H_t^* = (1, -X_{t-1}, \dots, -X_{t-k}, 0, 0, \dots, 0)$, we may now express (4.4) in the form

$$X_t = \boldsymbol{H}_t{}^*\boldsymbol{\theta}_t + \varepsilon_t, \tag{4.6}$$

where $\boldsymbol{\theta}_t$ satisfies an evolution equation of the form

$$\boldsymbol{\theta}_t = \boldsymbol{F}^*_{t-1}\boldsymbol{\theta}_{t-1} + \boldsymbol{W}_t. \tag{4.7}$$

Eqs. (4.6) and (4.7) are now of the standard form to which the (extended) Kalman filter can be applied. If, on the basis of observations up to time $(t-1)$, we have constructed an estimate $\hat{\boldsymbol{\theta}}_{t-1}$ of $\hat{\boldsymbol{\theta}}_{t-1}$, then given the next observation X_t, the updating equation for $\hat{\boldsymbol{\theta}}_t$ takes the form

$$\hat{\boldsymbol{\theta}}_t = \boldsymbol{F}_{t-1}\hat{\boldsymbol{\theta}}_{t-1} + \boldsymbol{K}_t^*\left[X_t - \boldsymbol{H}_t{}^*\boldsymbol{F}_{t-1}\hat{\boldsymbol{\theta}}_{t-1}\right],$$

where $\boldsymbol{K}_t{}^*$, the 'Kalman gain' matrix, may be evaluated from the standard recursive algorithm for the Kalman filter [see, e.g., Jazwinski (1970)]. Thus, at each time point we obtain a new estimate of each of the parameters $\mu, \phi_1, \ldots, \phi_k$, and these estimates can then be plotted against the corresponding state vector $\boldsymbol{x}_t$. In this way we gradually build up a set of ordinates for each of the parameter functions and these ordinates can then be transformed into smooth surfaces by applying one of the standard non-parametric function fitting routines [e.g., Priestley and Chao (1972)]. Once these surfaces have been constructed, we can then examine their shapes to gain insight into the non-linear structure of the model.

5. Numerical examples on simulated data

In order to examine the effectiveness of the SDM estimation technique, the application of the algorithm to simulated time series data of differing non-linear forms was studied. In all the cases, the estimated parameters were smoothed using the non-parametric function fitting technique of Priestley and Chao (1972) which employs a Gaussian smoothing kernel. This method is usually used to smooth equally-spaced ordinates into some functional form. However, in the SDM case, the ordinates are no longer equally spaced, since estimated parameter values are obtained at values of successive *states*, not successive time points. This can mean that if there are one or two outlying states in any set of data, excessive importance is attached to the parameter values at these states by the Gaussian smoothing kernel and spurious end effects can result. Difficulties can also arise from the 'transient effect' at the start of the recursion, where some anomalous parameter values may be obtained before the recursion settles down to a stable state. For these reasons, the first few parameter values in the recursion and the extreme edges of the parameter curves are ignored in the following analysis. Erratic behaviour at the ends of the range can arise also due to the presence of outliers in the original time series data. When an outlier occurs the algorithm tries to accommodate this observation by making large changes in the model parameters – which, in turn, leads to 'outliers' in the graphs of the estimated parameters.

5.1. Bilinear model simulation

The SDM algorithm was first applied to data simulated using a bi-linear scheme. The model chosen was

$$X_t + 0.4X_{t-1} = 0.5 + 0.4X_{t-1}\varepsilon_{t-1} + \varepsilon_t.$$

In all the models, $\{\varepsilon_t\}$ is a sequence of independent N(0, 1) variables, and 500 observations were simulated on each series. This type of model was chosen for simplicity, because the functional forms of most of the parameters are functions of one variable only. Hence, the shape of the parameter surface, being merely a curve, is much easier to determine. For each model, the recursion procedure described in section 4 is carried out, fitting a linear ARMA model to the first 50 observations and starting the recursion at time origin $t = 25$. The original model fitting gave preliminary estimates,

$$\hat{\hat{\mu}} = 0.8800, \quad \hat{\hat{\phi}}_1 = 0.1777, \quad \hat{\hat{\psi}}_1 = -0.1427, \quad \hat{\hat{\sigma}}_\varepsilon^2 = 1.7663,$$

the variance–covariance matrix of $(\hat{\hat{\mu}}_1, \hat{\hat{\psi}}_1, \hat{\hat{\theta}}_1)$ being

$$\hat{\underline{R}} = \begin{bmatrix} 0.1197 & 0.1147 & 0.1134 \\ 0.1147 & 0.1157 & 0.1540 \\ 0.1134 & 0.1540 & 0.1711 \end{bmatrix}.$$

Figs. 1 and 2 show the resulting graphs of the estimated parameters $\hat{\psi}_1$ and $\hat{\phi}_1$, respectively. The straight lines in these figures represent the true functional forms of ψ_1 and ϕ_1 for comparison.

As may be seen, the slopes of the graphs of the estimated parameters are very close to the slopes of the true parameters, and the intercept of $\hat{\phi}_1$ is also very close to the true value. The intercept of the graph of $\hat{\psi}_1$ is not so close to the true value, but both graphs clearly indicate linear trends in the parameters, and hence provide strong evidence that the series is generated by a bi-linear model.

It should be emphasised that the *SDM algorithm operates purely on the data* and has no a priori knowledge of the underlying model. Thus, based on the data only, the SDM algorithm has here pointed us very clearly in the direction of bi-linear models.

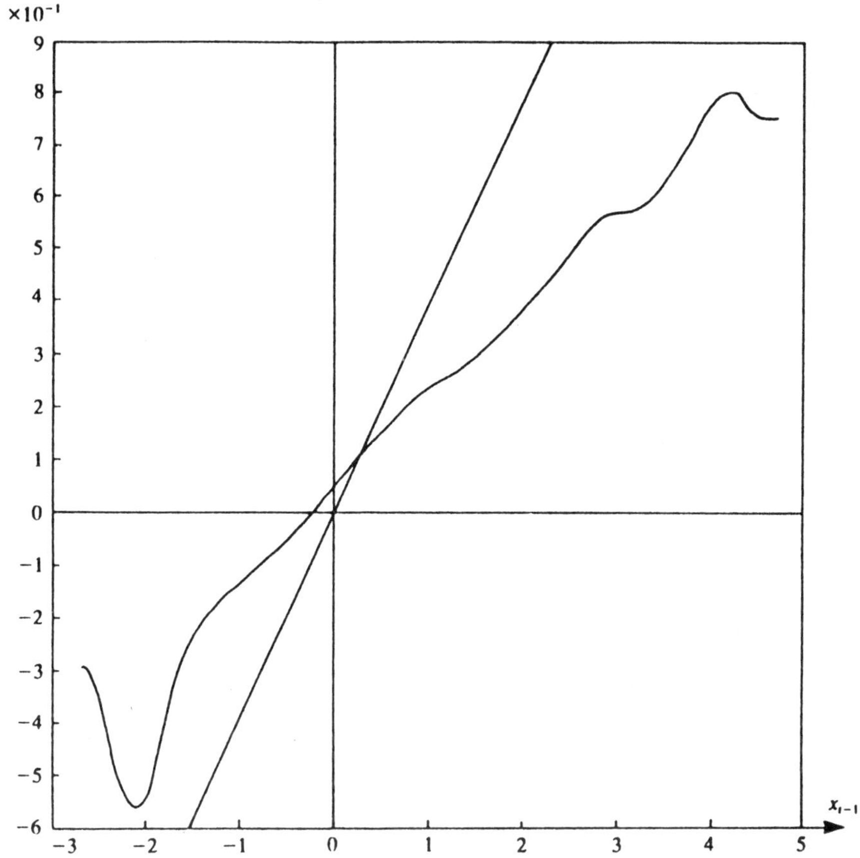

Fig. 1. Graph of the parameter $\hat{\psi}_1$ for bi-linear model.

5.2. Exponential AR model simulation

The procedure becomes slightly easier in this case in that only an AR model fitting procedure is needed for the estimation of initial values. This means that, in general, it is relatively easy to obtain sufficiently accurate initial values using only a small number of observations at the start of the data set. 500 observations were simulated on the model

$$X_t + (-0.9 - 0.1e^{-X_{t-1}^2})X_{t-1} + (0.2 + 0.1e^{-X_{t-1}^2})X_{t-2} = \varepsilon_t,$$

where $\{\varepsilon_t\}$ is a sequence of independent N(0, 1) variables. To initialise the recursive estimation procedure, a linear AR model was fitted to the first 20

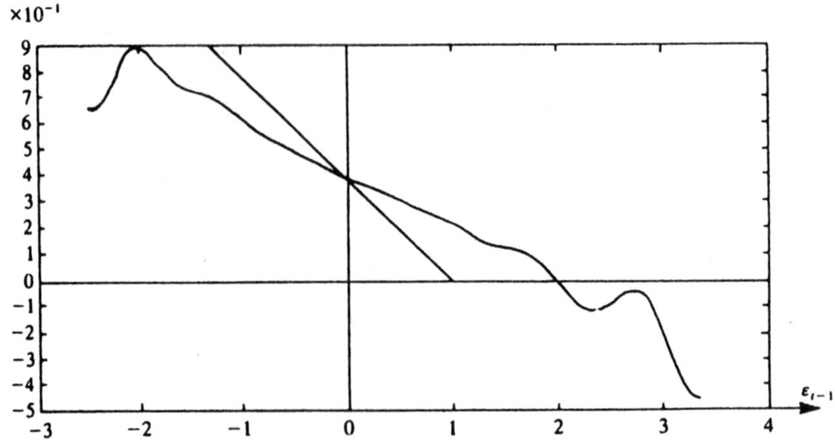

Fig. 2. Graph of the parameter $\hat{\phi}_1$ against ε_{t-1} for bi-linear model.

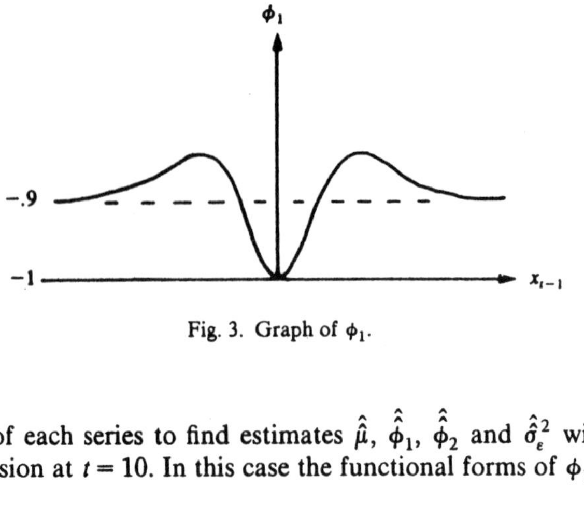

Fig. 3. Graph of ϕ_1.

observations of each series to find estimates $\hat{\mu}$, $\hat{\hat{\phi}}_1$, $\hat{\hat{\phi}}_2$ and $\hat{\hat{\sigma}}_\varepsilon^2$ with which to start the recursion at $t = 10$. In this case the functional forms of ϕ_1 and ϕ_2 are given by

$$\phi_1 = -\frac{\partial h}{\partial X_{t-1}} = -0.9 - 0.1\mathrm{e}^{-X_{t-1}^2} + 0.2X_{t-1}\mathrm{e}^{-X_{t-1}^2},$$

and

$$\phi_2 = -\frac{\partial h}{\partial X_{t-2}} = 0.2 + 0.1\mathrm{e}^{-X_{t-1}^2}.$$

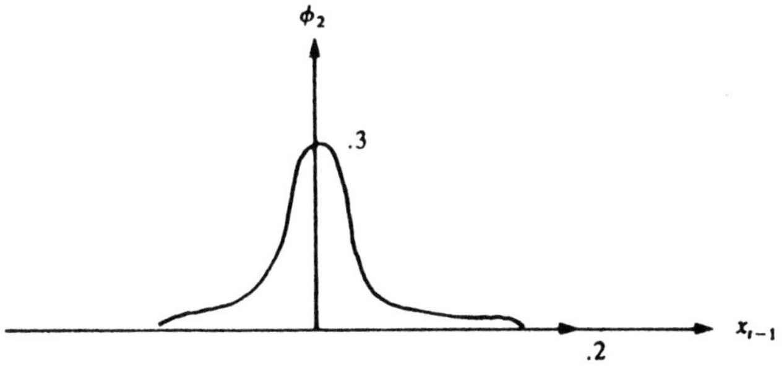

Fig. 4. Graph of ϕ_2.

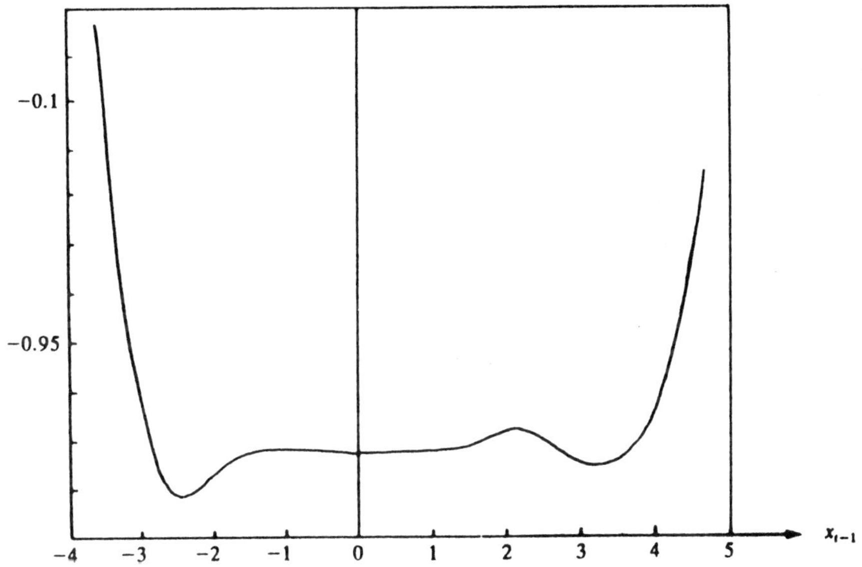

Fig. 5. $\hat{\phi}_1$ for exponential model.

The functional forms of ϕ_1 and ϕ_2 are shown graphically in figs. 3 and 4, respectively.

Preliminary estimates were

$$\hat{\hat{\mu}} = 0.2879, \quad \hat{\hat{\phi}}_1 = -0.7001, \quad \hat{\hat{\phi}}_2 = -0.0330, \quad \hat{\hat{\sigma}}_\varepsilon^2 = 1.0087,$$

with variance–covariance matrix

$$\hat{\hat{R}} = \begin{bmatrix} 0.0622 & 0.0160 & -0.0066 \\ 0.0160 & 0.0559 & -0.0418 \\ -0.0066 & -0.0418 & 0.0491 \end{bmatrix}.$$

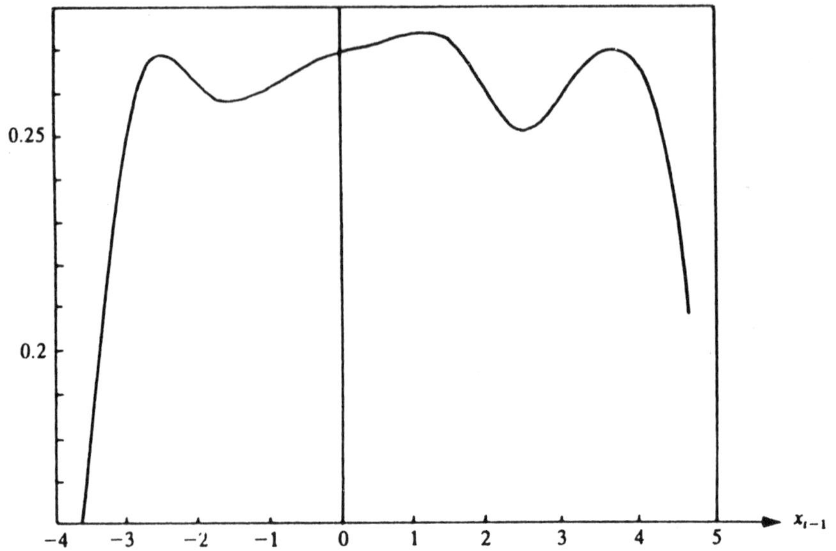

Fig. 6. $\hat{\phi}_2$ for exponential model.

The graphs of the estimated values $\hat{\phi}_1$ and $\hat{\phi}_2$ are shown in figs. 5 and 6, respectively. As can be seen, the values of the estimated parameters are approximately correct and the shapes of the graphs are of a similar form to those of the true graphs. $\hat{\phi}_1$ and $\hat{\phi}_2$ are clearly conspicuously different from what might be expected from a bi-linear model simulation. Similar results were obtained from several other simulations on this model. A particular feature of the estimated parameters is their approximately symmetric appearance.

6. SDM schemes for non-linear systems

It is well-known that a conventional linear time series model may be interpreted as a 'dynamical systems' model in which the observed series is regarded as the output of a linear system 'driven' by an (unobservable) white-noise input, $\{\varepsilon_t\}$. Thus, if we are dealing with a physical system in which the input $\{U_t\}$ and the output $\{X_t\}$ are both observable, we may adapt a linear time series model to this situation by replacing the white-noise process $\{\varepsilon_t\}$ by the observable input process $\{U_t\}$ [see, e.g., Priestley (1981, ch. 10)]. The same approach may be applied to the non-linear SDM schemes. Consider the single-input/single-output system shown schematically in the diagram below:

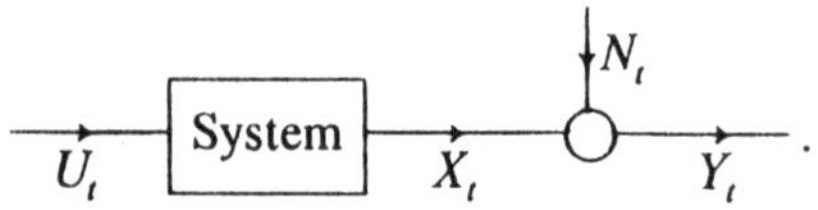

Here U_t denotes the input, X_t the 'uncorrupted' output, N_t is an additive noise disturbance, and Y_t is the observed output. We assume that the system is operating in 'open-loop' form, so that it is reasonable to assume that $\{N_t\}$ and $\{U_t\}$ are uncorrelated processes. The 'systems' model corresponding to (4.1) takes the form

$$X_t = h(X_{t-1}, X_{t-2}, \dots, X_{t-k}, U_{t-1}, U_{t-2}, \dots, U_{t-l})$$

$$+ g(X_{t-1}, X_{t-2}, \dots, X_{t-k}, U_{t-1}, U_{t-2}, \dots, U_{t-l})U_t, \tag{6.1}$$

together with the observation equation

$$Y_t = X_t + N_t. \tag{6.2}$$

Eq. (6.1) may now be re-written in SDM form as

$$X_t + \phi_1(\boldsymbol{x}_{t-1})X_{t-1} + \cdots + \phi_k(\boldsymbol{x}_{t-1})X_{t-k}$$

$$= \mu(\boldsymbol{x}_{t-1}) + \psi_0(\boldsymbol{x}_{t-1})U_t + \psi_1(\boldsymbol{x}_{t-1})U_{t-1} + \cdots + \psi_l(\boldsymbol{x}_{t-1})U_{t-l}, \tag{6.3}$$

where the state vector at time $t-1$ is here given by

$$\boldsymbol{x}_{t-1} = (U_{t-l}, \dots, U_{t-1}, X_{t-k}, \dots, X_{t-1})'. \tag{6.4}$$

(Note that since U_t is an observable process, the coefficient of U_t, ψ_0, is no longer unity but is now an additional parameter of the model.) If we augment the state vector by including the constant unity as an additional element; i.e., if we now write

$$\boldsymbol{x}_{t-1} = (1, U_{t-l}, \dots, U_{t-1}, X_{t-k}, \dots, X_{t-1})', \tag{6.5}$$

then we can write (6.2) and (6.3) in the following state–space form:

$$\boldsymbol{x}_{t+1} = \{\boldsymbol{F}(\boldsymbol{x}_t)\}\boldsymbol{x}_t + \{\boldsymbol{G}(\boldsymbol{x}_t)\}U_{t+1}, \tag{6.6}$$

$$Y_t = \boldsymbol{H}\boldsymbol{x}_t + N_t, \tag{6.7}$$

where the system matrix $\boldsymbol{F}$ is given by

$$\boldsymbol{F}=\left(\begin{array}{ccccc:cccc}
1 & 0 & 0 & \cdots & 0 & 0 & 0 & \cdots & 0 \\
0 & 0 & 1 & \cdots & 0 & 0 & 0 & \cdots & 0 \\
\hdashline
0 & 0 & 0 & \cdots & 1 & 0 & 0 & \cdots & 0 \\
0 & 0 & 0 & \cdots & 0 & 0 & 0 & \cdots & 0 \\
\hdashline
0 & 0 & 0 & \cdots & 0 & 0 & 1 & \cdots & 0 \\
0 & 0 & 0 & \cdots & 0 & 0 & 0 & 1\cdots & 0 \\
\hdashline
0 & 0 & 0 & \cdots & 0 & 0 & 0 & 0\cdots & 1 \\
\mu & \psi_l & \psi_{l-1} & \cdots\cdots & \psi_1 & -\phi_k & -\phi_{k-1} & \cdots\cdots & -\phi_1
\end{array}\right),$$

the input matrix $\boldsymbol{G}$ by

$$\boldsymbol{G}=(0,0,\ldots,1\,\vdots\,0,\ldots,\psi_0)',$$

and the observation matrix $\boldsymbol{H}$ by

$$\boldsymbol{H}=(0,0,\ldots,0\,\vdots\,0,\ldots,1).$$

Assuming, as previously, that the coefficients μ, $\{\phi_u\}$ and $\{\psi_u\}$ may be represented as locally linear function of x_t, the 'up-dating' equations then take a similar form to that used for the 'pure' time series case.

6.1. Numerical example

We illustrate the SDM systems model fitting procedure described above by applying this approach to simulated input/output data. In the simulation studies 500 observations were generated for the input and output processes. In each case the input process $\{U_t\}$ was generated from the stationary AR(1) model

$$U_t+0.5U_{t-1}=\varepsilon_t,$$

$\{\varepsilon_t\}$ being a sequence of independent N(0,1) variables, and the noise disturbance $\{N_t\}$ was also generated from a Gaussian white-noise process, with zero mean and unit variance.

The system chosen was generated by the bi-linear model

$$X_t-0.4X_{t-1}=0.8+0.4X_{t-1}U_t,$$

$$Y_t=X_t+N_t.$$

If X_t is written in the form (6.1), it can be seen that the functional form of ϕ_1

is given by

$$\phi_1 = -\frac{\partial h}{\partial X_{t-1}} = -0.4,$$

and the functional form of ψ_0 is

$$\psi_0 = g(X_{t-1}) = 0.4X_{t-1}.$$

The preliminary estimates were

$$\hat{\hat{\mu}} = 1.301, \quad \hat{\hat{\phi}}_1 = -0.3436, \quad \hat{\hat{\psi}}_0 = -0.8391, \quad \hat{\hat{\sigma}}_N^2 = 1.768,$$

with

$$\hat{\hat{R}} = \begin{bmatrix} 0.1276 & 0.0496 & 0.0200 \\ 0.0496 & 0.0273 & 0.0143 \\ 0.0200 & 0.0143 & 0.0326 \end{bmatrix}.$$

Graphs of ϕ_1 and ψ_0 (as functions of X_{t-1}) are given in Haggan et al. (1984), figs. 7 and 8, respectively. The straight line in fig. 8 represents the time functional form of ψ_0. Again, apart from the end effects, the estimated values of $\hat{\phi}_1$ are constant and very close to the value of -0.4 expected for this parameter. The graph of $\hat{\psi}_0$ shows a clear linear trend, with the slope very close to that of the expected functional form.

References

Akaike, H., 1974a, Markovian representation of stochastic processes and its application to the analysis of autoregressive moving average processes, Ann. Inst. Math. 26, 363–387.

Akaike, H., 1974b, Stochastic theory of minimal realisations, IEEE Transactions on Automatic Control AC-19, 667–673.

Box, G.E.P. and G.M. Jenkins, 1970, Time series analysis, forecasting and control (Holden-Day, San Francisco, CA).

Brillinger, D.R., 1970, The identification of polynomial systems by means of higher order spectra, Journal of Sound Vib. 12, 301–313.

Brockett, R.W., 1976, Volterra series and geometric control theory, Automatica 12, 167–172.

Granger, C.W.J. and A.P. Andersen, 1978, An introduction to bilinear time series models (Vandenhoek and Ruprecht, Göttingen).

Haggan, V. and T. Ozaki, 1981, Modelling non-linear random vibrations using an amplitude-dependent autoregressive time series model, Biometrika 68, 189–196.

Haggan, V., S.M. Heravi and M.B. Priestley, 1984, A study of the application of state-dependent models in non-linear time series analysis, Journal of Time Series Analysis 5, 69–102.

Jazwinski, A.J., 1970, Stochastic processes and filtering theory (Academic Press, New York).

Priestley, M.B., 1981, Spectral analysis and time series (Academic Press, London).

Priestley, M.B. and M.T. Chao, 1972, Non-parametric function fitting, Journal of the Royal Statistical Society B 34, 385–392.

Subba Rao, T., 1981, On the theory of bilinear time series models Journal of the Royal Statistical Society B 43, 244–255.

Tong, H. and K.-S. Lim, 1980, Threshold autoregression, limit cycles and cyclical data, Journal of the Royal Statistical Society B 42, 245–292.

Wiener, N., 1958, Non-linear problems in random theory (M.I.T. Press, Cambridge, MA).

[16]

Estimating Vector Autoregressions Using Methods Not Based on Explicit Economic Theories

Thomas J. Sargent

Adviser, Research Department
Federal Reserve Bank of Minneapolis
and
Professor of Economics
University of Minnesota

This paper describes procedures for analyzing interrelated time series[1] which are mainly intended as an alternative to using structural econometric models as forecasting devices. Alternatives to the structural models have been sought because of increasingly compelling suspicions that the a priori restrictions used in existing structural models are not implied by good dynamic economic theory and that the interpretations and policy conclusions based on those faulty a priori restrictions are worth little. The techniques described in this paper are not based on economic theory. Instead, the idea is to estimate vector autoregressions with many free parameters and to introduce restrictions not directly motivated by economic theory but rather aimed simply at forecasting better, that is, delivering estimators with small mean squared errors.

Because these techniques are not based on economic theory, they do not completely substitute for structural models. They cannot appropriately be used to analyze the range of policy interventions that structural models were designed to evaluate. The techniques are not appropriate for conditional forecasting, for predicting the behavior of the system under what may be a drastic change from the historical pattern in a feedback rule for a policy variable, for example. Instead, these techniques are designed mainly for unconditional forecasting and for compactly summarizing data. Thus, users of the statistical models described in this paper must acknowledge from the start that they are vulnerable to Lucas' (1976) criticism of econometric policy evaluation methods, and they often must restrict the domain of the questions to which answers are sought if Lucas' criticism is not to be operative.

Vector Autoregressions

For the purposes of making forecasts and displaying its operating characteristics, a linear econometric model is often represented as a particular set of random difference equations called a *vector autoregression*.[2] Thus, let z_t be an $(N \times 1)$ vector of variables, including both all of the endogenous and all of the exogenous variables in the model. Let z_t be measured in terms of deviations from means. Further, assume that z_t is a wide-sense stationary stochastic process[3] which has matrix covariogram $Ez_t z'_{t-k} = C_z(k)$. Then the Mth

[1]These procedures have been developed and applied to macroeconomic data by Christopher Sims of the University of Minnesota and Robert Litterman, now of M.I.T. but until recently an analyst in the Research Department at the Federal Reserve Bank of Minneapolis. The key references are Sims 1975, 1977; Sargent and Sims 1977; and Litterman 1979. [Author names and years refer to the works listed at the end of this paper.] This paper is intended only as an introduction to the work of Sims and Litterman and makes no claim for originality of any of the ideas discussed.

[2]Good general references on the time series methods described here are Anderson 1971, Box and Jenkins 1970, Fuller 1976, Granger and Newbold 1977, and Nerlove, Grether, and Carvalho 1979. For an introduction to vector autoregressions and some of their uses in macroeconomics, see Sargent 1979, chapter XI.

[3]A vector stochastic process z_t is said to be *wide-sense stationary* if the vector of means Ez_t is a constant vector independent of time t and if the matrix covariogram $Ez_t z'_s$ depends on only the difference $(t-s)$ and not only t and s separately. Wide-sense stationarity is also referred to as *second-order stationarity* and *covariance stationarity*.

order vector autoregression for the z_t process is

$$(1) \qquad z_t = \sum_{j=1}^{M} D_j^M z_{t-j} + \eta_t^M$$

where the D_j^M's are $(N \times N)$ matrices and the $(N \times 1)$ stochastic error process η_t^M satisfies the orthogonality conditions[4]

$$(2) \qquad E\eta_t^M z'_{t-k} = 0 \qquad k = 1, \ldots, M.$$

Post-multiplying (1) by z'_{t-k} and using (2) gives the least squares normal equations (or Yule-Walker equations)

$$(3) \qquad C_z(k) - \sum_{j=1}^{M} D_j^M C_z(k-j) = 0 \qquad k = 1, \ldots, M.$$

The normal equations (3), in general, uniquely determine the matrices D_j^M in terms of the population values of the second-moment matrices $C_z(k)$, $k = 0, 1, \ldots, M$.

Under the assumptions given here, least squares estimates of the D_j^M's are known to be statistically consistent.[5] But the vector autoregressive system (1) has $(N^2 \times M)$ free parameters in the D_j^M matrices, so that for even moderate sizes of M and N, least squares estimation either is simply not feasible due to exhaustion of degrees of freedom or else is unwise due to the large sampling errors present when the number of parameters to be estimated nearly exhausts all degrees of freedom. For this reason, systems of vector autoregressions with the sizes N and M usually encountered in economics have typically been estimated by methods other than least squares.

Until recently, the most popular method of estimating vector autoregressions was to apply classical simultaneous equation estimators to the structural model that presumably underlay the vector autoregression.[6] Simultaneous equation estimators have the virtue of permitting the model builder to bring to bear a priori information of certain kinds to produce parameter estimates with smaller sampling errors of the D_j^M's than can be produced by least squares. In statistical jargon, use of this prior information produces more "efficient estimators." In the present context, these techniques can be viewed as a device for reducing the number of parameters that have to be estimated from $(N^2 \times M)$ to a much smaller number of theoretically more fundamental parameters of which the D_j^M's are functions. The argument is that the vector autoregression is a "profligately parameterized" representation[7] and that estimation proceeds much more efficiently by focusing on the structural parameters about which something is known in advance of estimation.

To make this argument more precise, we use the representation of a linear econometric model described by Lucas and Sargent (1979). The *structural equations* are

$$(4) \qquad A_0 y_t + A_1 y_{t-1} + \ldots + A_m y_{t-m} = B_0 x_t + B_1 x_{t-1} + \ldots + B_n x_{t-n} + \epsilon_t.$$

The random error generating equations are

$$(5) \qquad R_0 \epsilon_t + R_1 \epsilon_{t-1} + \ldots + R_r \epsilon_{t-r} = u_t \qquad R_0 = I.$$

Here y_t is an $(L \times 1)$ vector of *endogenous* variables, x_t is a $(K \times 1)$ vector of *exogenous* variables, and ϵ_t and u_t are each $(L \times 1)$ vectors of random disturbances. The matrices A_j are each $(L \times L)$, the B_j's are $(L \times K)$, and the R_j's are each $(L \times L)$. We assume that $L + K = N$. The $(L \times 1)$ disturbance process u_t is assumed to be serially uncorrelated with $Eu_t = 0$ and with contemporaneous covariance matrix $Eu_t u_t' = \Sigma$ and $Eu_t u_s' = 0$ for $t \neq s$.

The defining characteristic of the exogenous variables x_t is that they are uncorrelated with the ϵ's at all lags so that $Eu_t x_s'$ is an $(L \times K)$ matrix of zeros for all t and s. The x_t process is itself assumed to be generated by the vector autoregression

$$(6) \qquad x_t = C_1 x_{t-1} + \ldots + C_p x_{t-p} + a_t$$

[4]These orthogonality conditions uniquely identify $\sum_{j=1}^{M} D_j^M z_{t-j}$ as the least squares projection of z_t onto the linear vector space spanned by $\{z_{t-1}, \ldots, z_{t-M}\}$.

[5]For proofs, see Ljung 1976 and Anderson and Taylor 1976.

[6]The classical simultaneous equation model and estimators are described in any good book on econometrics; for example, Goldberger 1964 or Maddala 1977.

[7]This is Sims' terminology.

where $Ea_t = 0$ and $Ea_t x_{t-j} = 0$ for $j \geq 1$.

As in Lucas and Sargent 1979, the *reduced form* of this system is

$$(7) \quad y_t = -P_1 y_{t-1} - \ldots - P_{r+m}\, y_{t-r-m} + Q_0 x_t + \ldots + Q_{r+n}\, x_{t-n-r} + A_0^{-1} u_t$$

where

$$(8) \quad P_s = A_0^{-1} \sum_{j=-\infty}^{\infty} R_j A_{s-j}$$
$$Q_s = A_0^{-1} \sum_{j=-\infty}^{\infty} R_j B_{s-j}.$$

In these expressions for P_s and Q_s, it is to be understood that matrices not previously defined (for example, any with negative subscripts) are zero. Substituting the right side of (6) for x_t in (7) gives the component of the vector autoregression for y_t:[8]

$$(9) \quad y_t = -P_1 y_{t-1} - \ldots - P_{r+m}\, y_{t-r-m} + [Q_0 C_1 + Q_1]\, x_{t-1} + [Q_0 C_2 + Q_2]\, x_{t-2} + \ldots + [Q_0 C_p + Q_p]\, x_{t-p} + Q_{p+1}\, x_{t-p-1} + \ldots + Q_{r+n}\, x_{t-n-r} + \{Q_0 a_t + A_0^{-1} u_t\}$$

$$(6) \quad x_t = C_1 x_{t-1} + \ldots + C_p\, x_{t-p} + a_t.$$

Notice that in the representation (9) and (6), y_t is written as a function of lagged y's and lagged x's, while the exogenous variables x_t only depend on lagged x_t's.

Equations (9) and (6) are the vector autoregressive representation of the structural model consisting of the structural equations (4) and (5). Equations (9) and (6) are a special case of the vector autoregression (1) with $z_t = [y_t\ x_t]'$. It is to be noted that (8) implies that the parameters of (9), the P_j's and Q_j's, are themselves complicated functions of the structural parameters, the A_j's, B_j's, and R_j's that appear in (4) and (5). Standard simultaneous equation estimators, as applied in economics, typically bring prior information to bear in the form of certain kinds of restrictions directly on the A_j's, B_j's, and R_j's. The notion is that the A_j's, B_j's, and R_j's are the parameters about which economic theory has something directly to say. Generally, the restrictions used take the form of sets of simple linear restrictions on the A_j's, B_j's, and R_j's. Most often, these assume the form simply of setting many, indeed most, of the coefficients in A_j, B_j, and R_j to zero a priori. Another set of exclusion restrictions is evident in (6), in which lagged y_j's are assumed not to appear. The asymmetrical treatment of lagged x's and y's in (6) and (9) is what distinguishes between endogenous and exogenous variables. For now, we simply note that the exclusion of lagged y's from (6) in most applications is done on an entirely a priori basis.

From the somewhat narrow viewpoint of estimating vector autoregressions, the virtue of using this body of a priori exclusion restrictions on lagged y's in (6) and on the A_j's, B_j's, and R_j's is that to the extent that the restrictions are approximately correct and numerous enough, more efficient estimates can be obtained of the parameters of the vector autoregression (6) and (9). That is, the D_j^M's of (1) can be estimated more precisely by constructing the model and introducing prior information in terms of the fundamental objects, the A_j's, B_j's, and R_j's. There is a presumption that these more efficient[9] estimates produced by a simultaneous equation estimator will lead to better predictions when the vector autoregression is used for forecasting.

Were there agreement that the a priori restrictions on the A_j's, B_j's, and R_j's described above are approximately correct, there would be no quarrel with the preceding case for using existing structural estimators as devices for estimating vector autoregressions for use in unconditional forecasting. However, over the last decade or so it has become increasingly evident that dynamic economic theories typically do not lead to prior information about the A_j's, B_j's, and R_j's of the kind described above. This argument is developed in some detail by Lucas and Sargent (1979), who argue that dynamic economic theory gives rise to restrictions of a very different form than those that

[8]We have assumed that $p < (n+r)$. The reader can readily derive the appropriate formula where $p \geq (n+r)$.

[9]More efficient than ordinary least squares estimates.

are currently implemented or even implementable in existing computer econometric procedures. The upshot is that there is little reason from good dynamic economic theory to believe that the restrictions on the A_j's, B_j's, and R_j's imposed by existing structural macroeconometric[10] models are even approximately correct. As Sims (1977) has described the situation, the identifying restrictions used in existing macroeconometric models are "incredible."

While this argument substantially weakens the case for using structural estimators as a device ultimately to estimate vector autoregressions, it does not entirely destroy the case. For some device restricting the number of free parameters in vector autoregressions must be adopted if the estimation of systems with sizable ($N^2 \times M$) is to be practical. Sims (1977) has argued that even though the standard identifying restrictions are incredible and most likely to be false from the viewpoint of dynamic economic theory, they may still be valuable from the instrumental point of view of helping to estimate vector autoregressions by effectively reducing the dimensionality of the space of free parameters. Loosely, the idea is that even wrong prior restrictions may prove useful by permitting one to trade reduced variance of estimates for increased bias. This line of argument is Sims' defense of existing structural macroeconometric models, at least as a device for estimating vector autoregressions.[11] The argument is by imperfect analogy to the Stein paradox in statistics.[12]

This line of argument leads one to ask whether there are alternatives to the standard simultaneous equation modeling procedures that can be used to restrict the dimensionality of the free parameter space in vector autoregressions. Current research, much of it being done at the University of Minnesota and the Federal Reserve Bank of Minneapolis, is exploring several alternative lines.

One main line is much in the spirit of the classical structural or simultaneous equation procedures. The key idea underlying this work is to estimate structural models of the form (4), (5), and (6), but to use identifying restrictions on the A_j's, B_j's, C_j's, and R_j's that are motivated by dynamic economic theory. As emphasized by Lucas and Sargent (1979), these restrictions typically come in the form of complicated nonlinear restrictions across the parameters of A_j and B_j, on the one hand, and C_j, on the other. These restrictions are of a form quite different from and more complicated than the linear or exclusion restrictions implemented in standard applications of existing simultaneous equation methods. Econometric methods are currently being developed for using dynamic economic theory to impose such restrictions in estimating time series models. To the extent that these restrictions approximately reflect valid dynamic economic theory, these methods hold out the promise of being useful devices for estimating vector autoregressions.[13] From a statistical point of view, the argument is identical with the argument made above in favor of estimating at the level of the structural objects, the A_j's, B_j's, and R_j's; the disagreement is over the form taken by the prior information supplied by the appropriate dynamic theory.

While methods for implementing cross-equation restrictions delivered by dynamic theory are now being developed,[14] they are not yet readily available and certainly have not yet proved to be successful in terms of delivering good estimates of the D_j^M's for vector autoregressions of sizable dimension. Further, there remain many controversial points about what are the most appropriate assumptions for dynamic economic theories. Partly for these reasons, other alternatives to using standard simultaneous equation methods for estimating vector autoregressions are being actively explored.

---

[10]Or microeconometric models, for that matter.

[11]It is hardly a defense that the model builders could welcome, since it acknowledges at the outset that those models are inappropriate for analyzing the effects on the economy of changes in feedback rules governing monetary and fiscal policy variables under the authorities' control.

[12]An instructive background to Sims' (1977) argument is the discussion of Leamer (1978) on ridge and Stein-James estimators.

[13]However, this is not the sole reason these techniques are being developed. A more important reason is that the techniques are in principle capable of isolating structural parameters (that is, parameters of preferences and technologies) that will remain invariant in the face of changes in feedback rules for policy variables. That will, in principle, overcome the objections against using econometric models as devices for evaluating monetary and fiscal policy or rules originally made by Lucas (1976) and summarized by Lucas and Sargent (1979).

[14]For example, see Hansen and Sargent 1979 and Nerlove, Grether, and Carvalho 1979.

A major alternative was initiated by Sims (1975) and is directed at introducing restrictions on vector autoregressions which are frankly admitted at the outset to have no formal basis in dynamic economic theory. The aim is to restrict the dimensionality of the free parameters of the D_j^M's while leaving room for substantial dynamic interactions across variables. Two general strategies for restricting the D_j^M's in this way have been proposed.

One method employs one of the index models described by Sargent and Sims (1977), Brillinger (1975, chapters 9, 10), and Priestly, Rao, and Tong (1974). The idea here is that the dynamic interactions among all N variables are forced to be entirely intermediated through a small number of k variables termed *indexes*; k is thought to be small, no larger than 2 or 3. Sargent and Sims (1977) describe two versions of this model which differ according to whether the index is observable or unobservable. Sargent and Sims (1977) and Litterman and Sargent (1979) describe and illustrate how these methods can be used to estimate vector autoregressions. While typically not based on a fully specified economic theory, index models do seem to faithfully represent a long-standing intuition in macroeconomics that movements in many important economic aggregates can be viewed as reflecting one underlying hidden index. This idea was present in the work of Mitchell (1951).[15] Further, a recent theory of the business cycle (see Lucas 1975) seems at least to suggest statistical models of the index form.

The restrictions on vector autoregressions implied by both observable and unobservable index models are rather complicated and involve technical intricacies in implementation. Partly for this reason, Litterman (1979) has developed procedures for introducing restrictions directly on the D_j^M's themselves. Even more so than with index models, these restrictions are admitted at the outset not to be based on dynamic economic theory. These restrictions are implemented via a version of Theil's mixed estimator,[16] a procedure for mixing data-based information about the D_j^M's with nondata-based information in the form of restrictions on the D_j^M's, which are represented as statements that known linear combinations of the parameters equal random terms with mean zero and known variance. The mixed estimation procedure has a Bayesian interpretation, but it is not really formally justified in the context used by Litterman.[17] The reason is that the implicit priors imposed by Litterman are not representations of prior beliefs about the D_j^M's that economic theorizing has led to. Instead, what is represented as prior information is being imposed simply on the hunch that by imposing it, estimators of the D_j^M's with better sampling properties can be obtained. For example, a common implicit prior used by Litterman is one with a mean which states that

$$D_1^M = I, \text{ and } D_j^M = 0 \qquad j = 2, \ldots, M$$

so that the system is one with N variables, each taking a random walk and being correlated only to the extent that the contemporaneous covariance matrix $E\eta_t^M\eta_t^{M\prime}$ is not diagonal. In effect, Litterman's procedure selects D_j^M by moving some distance along Dickey's "curve décolletage" from the least squares estimates to the point described by the priors.[18]

Litterman has generated a variety of examples that indicate that his procedures generate forecasts outside of the estimation period that strongly outperform forecasts from least squares estimates. Further, though there are difficulties in putting things on a comparable basis, there is evidence that Litterman's procedures produce forecasts of many macroeconomic variables that are competitive with those produced outside of the estimation periods by various of the better known of the large structural macroeconometric models.[19] To the ex-

[15] Robert E. Lucas, Jr., pointed out to me Mitchell's (1951) statement, which is quite clear on this point.

[16] See Theil 1963 or Goldberger 1964.

[17] Shiller (1973) and Leamer (1972) describe Bayesian procedures for bringing prior information to bear on distributed lags. However, as Nerlove has long emphasized (see, for example, the discussion in Nerlove, Grether, and Carvalho 1979), smoothness priors of the form imposed by Shiller and Leamer typically have no basis in dynamic economic theory. Reasoning similar to Nerlove's can be used to criticize Litterman's implicit priors as representations of information provided by dynamic economic theory.

[18] See the useful discussion of the "curve décolletage" in Leamer 1978.

[19] McNees (1975) and Fair (1978b) present evidence describing the predictive accuracy of several macroeconometric models. Fair (1978a,b) raises a number of issues involved in comparing forecasts from different models.

tent that this result holds up, it is an important one, since it suggests that good performance of a structural macroeconometric model in generating unconditional forecasts is not necessarily evidence in favor of the particular a priori theory used to overidentify and to estimate the model.

Uses of Vector Autoregressions

Let us rewrite the vector autoregression (1) in the form

$$(1') \qquad z_t = \sum_{j=1}^{M} D_j z_{t-j} + \eta_t$$

where we have omitted M superscripts from the D_j's and from η_t. So-called unconditional forecasts, that is, what are really forecasts of z_{t+k}, $k \geq 1$ conditioned on $\{z_t, z_{t-1}, \ldots, z_{t-M+1}\}$, can be made as follows. Let $\hat{E}_t z_{t+k}$ be the linear least squares forecast of z_{t+k} conditioned on $\{z_t, z_{t-1}, \ldots, z_{t-M+1}\}$. Then the $\hat{E}_t z_{t+k}$'s can be generated recursively from

$$\hat{E}_t z_{t+1} = \sum_{j=1}^{M} D_j z_{t+1-j}$$

$$\hat{E}_t z_{t+2} = D_1 \hat{E}_t z_{t+1} + \sum_{j=2}^{M} D_j z_{t+2-j}$$

$$\vdots$$

The general expression is

$$(10) \qquad \hat{E}_t z_{t+k} = \sum_{j=1}^{m} D_j \hat{E}_t z_{t+k-j} \qquad k \geq 1$$

where in (10) it is understood that $\hat{E}_t z_{t-j} \equiv z_{t-j}$ for $j \geq 0$. Formula (10) is called the *chain rule of forecasting*. Typically, vector autoregressions are used to forecast by substituting estimated values of the D_j's in (10).[20]

There is reason to expect that use of (10) will generate relatively good forecasts to the extent that the D_j's have been estimated with small sampling errors and to the extent that future z's will depend on current and recently past z's in the same way that current and past z's depended on previous z's during the estimation period. If there are structural changes or policy interventions that change some of the equations presumably underlying (1')—for example, equations (4), (5), and (6)—use of (10) is likely to give poor forecasts.

One use to which the vector autoregression (1') cannot be put is to evaluate the effects of policy interventions in the form of changes in the feedback rule governing a monetary or fiscal policy variable, say, the money supply or monetary base. Thus, suppose that one of the z_t's, say z_{it}, is the money supply. It is not appropriate to substitute a new i^{th} equation describing z_{it} under a new proposed policy regime, leave the remaining $(N-1)$ equations unchanged, and then produce forecasts using (10) in an attempt to forecast how differently the system would behave under the alternative policy rule. The reason it is not appropriate is to be found in the dynamic economic theory alluded to above and described by Lucas and Sargent (1979). That body of theory delivers a set of cross-equation restrictions which imply that when one equation of (1') describing a policy authority's feedback rule changes, in general, all of the remaining equations will also change.

While vector autoregressions can't be used to predict the effects of changes in policy feedback rules, they can be used to characterize the response to unexpected shocks in policy and other variables. Thus, if we solve the difference equation system (1') and ignore transient terms, we obtain the vector moving average representation

$$(11) \qquad z_t = \sum_{j=0}^{\infty} H_j \eta_{t-j} \qquad H_0 = I$$

where the H_j's are $(N \times N)$ matrices.

Since $\eta_t = z_t - \hat{E}_{t-1} z_t$, equation (11) permits the analyst to trace out the likely effects of unexpected shocks to the ith variable z_{it} on subsequent

[20] When the D_j's are not known with certainty but are subject to sampling error, (10) is not the correct formula for the minimum mean square error forecasts (see Chow 1973). In general, closed form formulas have not been obtained for the least squares forecasts where the D_j's are subject to sampling error. Better approximations to the least squares forecasts than are given by using estimated values as they are known in (10) can be obtained by using stochastic simulation methods (see Fair 1978b). Fair (1978b) presents evidence that in certain contexts, stochastic simulation methods do not provide much of an improvement over forecasts generated by simply using estimated values of the D_j's in (10).

values of all of the variables. By studying the H_j's together with the covariance matrix $E\eta_t\eta_t'$, the relative persistence in effects and the cross-variable effects of unexpected changes in the z_{it}'s can be characterized.

A final use of vector autoregressions is to make probabilistic statements about events in the future which depend on complicated features of sample paths. For example, one might want to know the probability of the event that, given $\{z_t, z_{t-1},...\}$, a recession begins in period $t + k$, where a recession is defined as beginning at the date of a third consecutive quarter decline in the variable z_{it}, say, real GNP. The probability of this event is complicated to compute analytically. Following the proposal of Wecker (1979), Litterman (1979) uses a Monte Carlo method to generate a large number of artificial sample paths of z_{t+k}, $k > 0$, given the historical initial conditions $\{z_t, z_{t-1}, ...\}$. The paths are generated by drawing realizations of the sequence of disturbances $\{\eta_{t+1}, \eta_{t+2}, ...\}$ using a pseudorandom number generator. The resulting realizations of $\{z_{t+1}, z_{t+2}, ...\}$ are then recorded, and frequency distributions for various events, such as the onset of a recession at date $t + k$, are recorded. In this way, economists at the Federal Reserve Bank of Minneapolis have been using vector autoregressions to make probabilistic statements about various interesting details of sample path behavior that are inadequately summarized by the point forecasts $\hat{E}_t z_{t+k}$, $k \geq 1$.

Conclusions

The techniques described in this article are still in the early stages of development, so they cannot yet be regarded as having proved themselves useful in a wide variety of contexts. Further, while the techniques were developed partly in response to criticisms of standard simultaneous equation macroeconometric models, they are not intended to remedy all the defects in the standard models pointed out by critics like Lucas. Indeed, builders of statistical models constructed along the lines described in this paper admit at the outset that the models will not be capable of analyzing the range of alternative policy interventions which the standard existing macroeconometric models were designed to analyze. Users of the techniques described here must recognize that the range of uses of these models is more limited than the range of uses that would be possessed by a truly structural simultaneous equation model.

References

Anderson, T. W. 1971. *The statistical analysis of time series.* New York: Wiley.

Anderson, T. W., and Taylor, John B. 1976. Conditions for strong consistency of least squares estimates in linear models. institute for Mathematical Studies in the Social Sciences Technical Report 213. Stanford University.

Box, G. E. P., and Jenkins, G. M. 1970. *Time series analysis: forecasting and control.* San Francisco: Holden-Day.

Brillinger, David R. 1975. *Time series: data analysis and theory.* New York: Holt, Rinehart and Winston.

Brunner, K., and Meltzer, A. H., eds. 1976. *The Phillips curve and labor markets.* Carnegie-Rochester Conference Series on Public Policy, vol. 1. Amsterdan: North Holland.

Chamberlain, Gary, and Leamer, Edward E. 1976. Matrix weighted averages and posterior bounds. *Journal of the Royal Statistical Society* Series B: 73-84.

Chow, Gregory C. 1973. Multiperiod predictions from stochastic difference equations by Bayesian methods. *Econometrica* 41 (January): 109-18.

Fair, Ray C. 1978a. Estimating the expected prediction accuracy of econometric models. Cowles Foundation for Research in Economics Discussion Paper 480. Yale University. Also forthcoming, *International Economic Review.*

———. 1978b. An analysis of the accuracy of four macroeconometric models. Cowles Foundation for Research in Economics Discussion Paper 492. Yale University. Also forthcoming, *Journal of Political Economy.*

Fuller, Wayne A. 1976., *Introduction to statistical time series.* New York: Wiley.

Goldberger, Arthur S. 1964. *Economic theory.* New York: Wiley.

Granger, C. W. J., and Newbold, P. 1977. *Forecasting economic time series.* New York: Academic Press.

Hansen, Lars P., and Sargent, Thomas J. 1979. Formulating and estimating dynamic linear rational expectations models: 1. Research Department Working Paper 127. Federal Reserve Bank of Minneapolis, Minnesota. Also forthcoming, *Journal of Economic Dynamics and Control.*

Hoerl, Arthur E., and Kennard, Robert W. 1970. Ridge regression: biased estimation for nonorthogonal problems. *Technometrics* 12(1): 55-67.

Leamer, Edward E. 1972. A class of informative priors and distributed lag analysis. *Econometrica* 40 (November): 1059-81.

———. 1978. *Specification searches: ad hoc inference with nonexperimental data.* New York: Wiley.

Litterman, Robert B. 1979. Techniques of forecasting using vector autoregressions. Research Department Working Paper 115. Federal Reserve Bank of Minneapolis, Minnesota.

Litterman, Robert B., and Sargent, Thomas J. 1979. Detecting neutral price level changes and effects of aggregate demand with index models. Research Department Working Paper 125. Federal Reserve Bank of Minneapolis, Minnesota.

Ljung, Lennart. 1976. Consistency of the least-squares identification method. *IEEE Transactions on Automatic Control* AC-21 (October): 779-81.

Lucas, Robert E., Jr. 1975. An equilibrium model of the business cycle. *Journal of Political Economy* 83 (December): 1113-44.

———. 1976. Econometric policy evaluation: a critique: In *The Phillips curve and labor markets.* ed. K. Brunner and A. H. Meltzer. Carnegie-Rochester Conference Series on Public Policy 1: 19-46. Amsterdam: North Holland.

Lucas, Robert E., Jr., and Sargent, Thomas J. 1979. After Keynesian macroeconomics. *Federal Reserve Bank of Minneapolis Quarterly Review* 3 (Spring): 1-16.

Maddala, G. S. 1977. *Econometrics.* New: York: McGraw-Hill.

McNees, Stephen K. 1975. An evaluation of economic forecasts. *New England Economic Review* (November/December): 3-39.

Mitchell, Wesley C. 1951. *What happens during business cycles: A progress report.* Studies in Business Cycles 5. New York: National Bureau of Economic Research.

Nerlove, Marc; Grether, David M.; and Carvalho, José L. 1979. *Analysis of economic time series: a synthesis.* New York: Academic Press.

Priestly, M. B.; Rao, T.S.; and Tong, H. 1974. Applications of principal components and factor analysis in the identification of multivariable systems. *IEEE Transactions on Automatic Control* AC-19 (December): 730-34.

Sargent, Thomas J. 1979. *Macroeconomic theory.* New York: Academic Press.

Sargent, Thomas J., and Sims, Christopher A. 1977. Business cycle modeling without pretending to have too much a priori economic theory. In *New methods in business cycle research: proceedings from a conference*, ed. C. A. Sims, pp. 45-109. Federal Reserve Bank of Minneapolis, Minnesota.

Shiller, Robert J. 1973. A distributed lag estimator derived from smoothness priors. *Econometrica* 41 (July): 775-88.

Sims, Christopher A. 1972. Money, income, and causality. *American Economic Review* 62 (September): 540-52.

———. 1975. Strategies for controlling dimensionality in models of multivariate time series. Paper presented to Third World Congress of the Econometrics Society, August 1975. Toronto.

———. 1977. Macroeconomics and reality. Center for Economic Research Discussion Paper 77-91. University of Minnesota. Also forthcoming, *Econometrica.*

———, ed. 1977. *New methods in business cycle research: proceedings from a conference.* Federal Reserve Bank of Minneapolis, Minnesota.

Thiel, Henri. 1963. On the use of incomplete prior information in regression analysis. *Journal of the American Statistical Association* 58 (June): 401-14.

Wecker, William E. 1979. Predicting the turning points of a time series. *Journal of Business* 52 (January): 35-50.

Part IV
Causality and Exogeneity

[17]

Econometrica, Vol. 28, 2 (April 1960)

RECURSIVE *VS.* NONRECURSIVE SYSTEMS: AN ATTEMPT AT SYNTHESIS

(PART I OF A TRIPTYCH ON CAUSAL CHAIN SYSTEMS)

BY ROBERT H. STROTZ AND H. O. A. WOLD

This paper, which in part serves as a common introduction to the two papers following in this issue, attempts to define the meaning of the "causal interpretability of a parameter" in a system of simultaneous linear relationships. It attempts, moreover, to expound a basis for interpreting the parameters of a nonrecursive or interdependent system causally. This is done in terms of an underlying causal chain system to which the interdependent system is either an approximation or a description of the equilibrium state.

OVER THE PAST fifteen years there has been an extended discussion of the meaning and applicability of nonrecursive as distinct from recursive systems in econometrics, and throughout this discussion there has been a marked divergence of views as to the merits of the two types of models. It is not the purpose of this note to extend that controversy further, but rather to attempt a constructive statement of the relationship between the two approaches and the circumstances under which each is applicable.

We assume that the reader is generally familiar with the past discussion[1] and that it will suffice here simply to recall that a recursive, or causal-chain, system has the formal property that the coefficient matrix of the non-lagged endogenous variables is triangular (upon suitable ordering of rows and columns) whereas a nonrecursive, or interdependent, system is one for which this is not the case. While the triangularity of the coefficient matrix is a formal property of recursive models, the essential property is that each relation is provided a causal interpretation in the sense of a stimulus-response relationship. The question of whether and in what sense nonrecursive systems allow a causal interpretation is the main theme of this paper.

1. FUNDAMENTAL PRINCIPLES

Much controversy can, in our opinion, be resolved once there is agreement on some initial points of principle.

(1) The first thing to consider when constructing an economic model is its purpose, that is, how it is to be applied in dealing with economic facts. We want to distinguish in this connection between descriptive and explanatory models. A descriptive model simply sets forth a set of relationships which have "bound together" different variables in situations in which they have

[1] See references appended at end. An extensive bibliography is included in [8].

previously been observed. More generally, these relationships may be described in probability terms, certain terms in these relationships representing the "disturbances" which in fact occurred. One can in this way describe given observations as a random drawing from a joint conditional probability distribution. Methodologically, the estimation of such a distribution is an exercise in n-dimensional "curve fitting." A descriptive model is thus cognate to the notion of a vector *function* such as (in the linear case)

$$Ax' = u' \tag{1}$$

where A is a (not necessarily square) matrix of constants, x' is a column vector of the variables in question, and u' is a vector of zeros in the exact case or of stochastic variables in the case of a probability model. Whatever the validity of such a specification, the validity of any other model obtained by applying any linear transformation is the same. If a priori restrictions are imposed upon the sort of distribution which is to be used for this descriptive model, this may, of course, circumscribe the acceptable transformations.

Explanatory models, by contrast, are causal. This means that each relation (equation) in the model states something about "directions of influence" among the variables. (But see Section 3(b) below.) In the case of explanatory models, then, the theorist asserts more than functional relationships among the variables; he also invests those relationships with a special interpretation, that is, with a causal interpretation. But what is a "causal interpretation" to mean?

(2) No one has monopoly rights in defining "causality." The term is in common parlance and the only meaningful challenge is that of providing an explication of it. No explication need be unique, and some may prefer never to use the word at all. For us, however, the word in common scientific and statistical-inference usage has the following general meaning.[2] z is a cause of y if, by hypothesis, it is or "would be" possible by *controlling* z indirectly to control y, at least stochastically. But it may or may not be possible by controlling y indirectly to control z. A causal relation is therefore in essence asymmetric, in that in any instance of its realization it is asymmetric. Only in special cases may it be reversible and symmetric in a causal sense. These are the cases in which sometimes a controlled change in z may cause a change in y and at other times a controlled change in y may cause a change in z, but y and z cannot both be subjected to simultaneous controlled changes independently of one another without the causal relationship between them being violated.

The asymmetry of causation in any instance of its realization has the following probability counterpart. It may make sense to talk about the

[2] H. O. A. Wold has elaborated his views in [6, 7].

probability distribution of y as being ***causally conditional*** on z, but not make sense to talk about the probability distribution of z as being ***causally conditional*** on y. This asymmetry is classical in statistical theory. It appears in the difference between a sample statistic and a population parameter. We speak of the probability that the sample frequency of successes will be 0.5 conditional upon the population frequency being 0.4. We do not speak of the probability that the population frequency is 0.4 conditional upon the sample frequency being 0.5.[3] Thus if we wish to estimate (by the maximum likelihood method) a population parameter knowing a sample of observations, we write the likelihood function as the conditional probability distribution of the *sample.*

Suppose we were to estimate by the maximum likelihood method the nth value of a causal variable (population parameter) $z(n)$ on the basis of the nth value of a resultant variable (a sample observation) $y(n)$ by use of a regression fitted to $n - 1$ previous observations in all of which z has been causal. We should use the regression of y on z—not of z on y—over the previous observations, although this point is occasionally misunderstood.[4] Causality as used here is an essential notion in the statistical inference of population parameters by the maximum likelihood method. We must hypothesize how the sample observations are *generated* (i.e., caused) in order to proceed.

The concept of causality presented here is intended to be that of the everyday usage in the laboratory and emphasizes mainly the notion of control. Now, others may present a different explication of causality. Other versions may involve strange and seemingly unnatural notions, two of which are of particular interest to us. (a) The first involves accepting simultaneously the two statements: (1) "y has the value 100 because of (by cause of) z having the value 50" and (2) "z has the value 50 because of (by cause of) y having the value of 100." (b) The second involves accepting simultaneously the two statements: (1) "z causes y in accordance with the function $y = f(z)$" and (2) "z causes y in accordance with the function $y = g(z) \neq f(z)$." Usage (a) we shall describe as a "causal circle" and discuss in Section 3(c). Usage (b) we describe as "bicausality" and discuss in Section 3(d).

Whether such notions of causality seem weird or not, whether or not

[3] "Probability" is used here in the "relative frequency," not in the "degree of belief" sense.

[4] For what we regard as the correct treatment, see A. Mood, [2, Sec. 13.4]. For the contrary view see F. V. Waugh [5]. A qualification is needed: one must not have any constraining a priori knowledge about the possible values of z, or, if z is itself a random variable, about its probability distribution. The model we have in mind is given by $y = \alpha + \beta z + u$, with u and z statistically independent. Otherwise, the likelihood function is $f(y(1), \ldots, y(n)|z(1), \ldots z(n))\cdot g(z(n))$, rather than the f function alone, where f and g are probability density functions.

they conform to usage in the scientific workshop, there is nothing to prevent their use in theory construction. Argument for the interpretation of causality presented by us is not an argument for "strait-jacketing" the freedom of the theorist and econometrician to use other interpretations. But we would (and will) argue that the notion of causality in economics is the one we have presented. Examples are: "Income is the cause of consumer expenditure (the consumption function)," "Price is a cause of quantity demanded," and "Price is a cause of quantity supplied." Most of the problems in assessing this claim arise in equilibrium models.

2. THE CAUSAL INTERPRETATION OF A RECURSIVE SYSTEM

It was not our purpose in the previous section to provide a precise definition of "causation." The term enters our discussion essentially as a "primitive," and what efforts we have made at definition have been ostensive: we have pointed to the familiar usage of the word in the laboratory. With reference to this primitive meaning of "causation," however, we wish to define the concept of "the causal interpretability of a parameter." This is what will occupy us next.

Suppose a recursive system is written in the form

$$
(2)\quad
\begin{aligned}
y_1 + \beta_{11}y_2 + \ldots + \beta_{1g}y_g + \beta_{1,g+1}y_{g+1} + \ldots + \beta_{1G}y_G + \sum_k \gamma_{1k}z_k &= u_1\,, \\
y_2 + \ldots + \beta_{2g}y_g + \beta_{2,g+1}y_{g+1} + \ldots + \beta_{2G}y_G + \sum_k \gamma_{2k}z_k &= u_2\,, \\
\ldots\ldots\ldots\ldots\ldots\ldots\ldots\ldots\ldots\ldots & \\
y_g + \beta_{g,g+1}y_{g+1} + \ldots + \beta_{gG}y_G + \sum_k \gamma_{gk}z_k &= u_g\,, \\
\ldots\ldots\ldots\ldots\ldots\ldots\ldots\ldots\ldots\ldots & \\
y_G + \sum_k \gamma_{Gk}z_k &= u_G\,,
\end{aligned}
$$

where the y's are causally dependent variables, the z's predetermined variables, and the u's stochastic variables statistically independent of the z's. Each u_g is assumed, moreover, to be statistically independent of y_{g+1}, $y_{g+2}, \ldots, y_G$.[5] In each equation the y variable with unit coefficient is regarded as the resultant variable and the other y variables and the z's are regarded as causal variables. We now consider the possibility that we gain direct control over y_g, that is, we can manipulate y_g by use of variables

[5] Although Wold has imposed this specification in his definition of a causal chain system, Strotz feels it may be too restrictive and would classify causal chain systems under two headings: those that are causal chains in their stochastic form (Wold's case) and those that are causal chains only in their exact part. In the latter case the covariance matrix of the u_g's need not be diagonal. For further discussion of this, see Strotz, *infra*, p. 430, fn. 6.

other than the z's appearing in the model. In this case we now need a new model. It can be obtained, however, by a single change in the old one. We merely strike out the gth equation and reclassify y_g as an exogenous (predetermined) variable rather than as a dependent variable. The coefficients of y_g in the $G - 1$ equations of the new model will be the same as they were before, namely, $\beta_{1g}, \ldots, \beta_{g-1,g}$, and zeros. It is in this sense that each non-unit coefficient in a recursive system has a causal interpretation. It describes the influence of the variable whose coefficient it is on the resultant variable, irrespective of whether the causal variable is dependent or exogenous in the system. Such a parameter has causal interpretability.

3. THE CAUSAL INTERPRETATION OF NONRECURSIVE SYSTEMS

We now turn our attention to nonrecursive systems. What is the possibility of causal interpretation in these systems?

(a) *No causal interpretation.* It may be that no causal interpretation of a nonrecursive system is intended. The relations in the system may be asserted only to define the joint probability distribution of the dependent variables conditional upon the predetermined variables. The coefficients to be estimated are then simply parameters in the joint conditional distribution of y given z. With nothing further claimed, there is no objection to such a model or to efforts to estimate the parameters of the distribution.

(b) *Vector causality.* It may be asserted for the *nonrecursive* model

$$\mathrm{B}y' + \Gamma z' = u' \tag{3}$$

that the vector z *causes* the vector y. Causality in this sense goes beyond the definition of "causality" given in Wold [**6, 7**]. It may readily be accepted, however, as an abstract terminological extension of the more usual notion of causation and may be employed in the everyday sense of the statement, "The food supply causes the fish population." An example may be useful. Suppose z is a vector whose elements are the amounts of various fish feeds (different insects, weeds, etc.) available in a given lake, and that y is a vector whose elements are the numbers of fish of various species in the lake. The reduced form $y' = -\mathrm{B}^{-1}\Gamma z' + \mathrm{B}^{-1}u'$ would tell us specifically how the number of fish of any species depends on the availabilities of different feeds. The coefficient of any z is the partial derivative of a species population with respect to a food supply. It is to be noted, however, that the reduced form tells us nothing about the interactions among the various fish populations—it does not tell us the extent to which one species of fish feeds on another species. Those are causal relations among the y's.[6]

[6] Indeed, even though $\partial y_g/\partial z_k > 0$, this does not imply that fish species g consumes food supply k. It may be that species g consumes species h which consumes food supply k.

Suppose, in another situation, we continuously restock the lake with species g, increasing y_g by any desired amount. How will this affect the values of the other y's? If the system were recursive and we had estimates of the elements of B, we would simply strike the gth equation out of the model and regard y_g, the number of fish of species g, as exogenous—as a food supply or, when appearing with a negative coefficient, as a poison. It will be the purpose of subsections (c) and (d) to determine whether if the model is not recursive the problem can be dealt with in this same way. The nonrecursive model does, in any case, enable us to predict the effects on the y's of controlled variations in the z's.

Herbert Simon in developing a sense of causality for econometric models [**3**] has used this notion of vector causality. He defines causal relations among *subsets* of dependent variables by using a model recursive in these subsets. Partition y' into three subsets, that is, into three column vectors, y_1', y_2', and y_3', so that $y' = (y_1, y_2, y_3)'$ and partition B conformally. Consider the system (3) in which B may be written as

$$B = \begin{pmatrix} B_{11} & B_{12} & B_{13} \\ 0 & B_{22} & B_{23} \\ 0 & 0 & B_{33} \end{pmatrix} \tag{4}$$

consisting of nine submatrices. Then y_3' is caused by z'; y_2' is caused by y_3' and z'; and y_1' is caused by y_2', y_3', and z'. In the previous sentence the word "caused" is used in the sense of vector causation, and B is "block triangular." No causal relations among the variables *within* a subset are defined. Press this logic further. If each subset consists of but a single endogenous variable, and a causal sequence is established among subsets, B is triangular and the system is recursive.

If, by way of contrast with vector causality, each effect variable is given as an explicit function of only variables that are its causes, we may speak of *explicit causality*.

(c) *Causal Circles, Mutual Causation, and Equilibrium Conditions.* By a "causal circle" we shall mean a system such as

$$p(t) = \alpha_1 + \beta_1 q(t) + \gamma_1 z_1(t) + u_1(t)\,, \tag{5a}$$

$$q(t) = \alpha_2 + \beta_2 p(t) + \gamma_2 z_2(t) + u_2(t)\,, \tag{5b}$$

where $z_1(t)$ and $z_2(t)$ are exogenous and for which the following two statements are asserted: (1) In equation (5a) $q(t)$ is a cause of $p(t)$; (2) In equation (5b) $p(t)$ is a cause of $q(t)$. Causation is here used in a sense not allowed by the operative meaning that causation has in an experimental laboratory. To accept a causal circle is, in the laboratory meaning of the word "cause," to suppose that the value of one variable is determined by the value of another variable whose value cannot be determined until that of the first has been determined. To assume that the values of the two variables determine each other makes sense only in an equilibrium system, and such a system provides no explanation of how the equilibrium comes about (of change or of causal connections among the endogenous variables of the system).[7]

The familiar illustration of the three balls in the bowl mutually *causing* one another's location, which has been advanced as an example of mutual causation,[8] might be considered in this connection. For the steady state (equilibrium) there are certain mutual conditions which must be satisfied; but if the balls are displaced and then roll towards equilibrium they are either in mutual contact and roll (or slide) as a single mass or the position of each can depend on the positions of the others only when the latter are lagged in time. Indeed, mutual causation in a dynamic system can have meaning only as a limit form of the arrow schemes shown in Figure 1 where the time lag θ is reduced towards zero.[9]

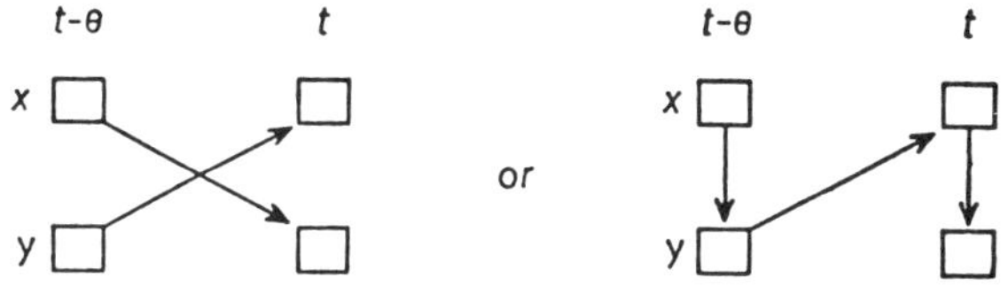

FIGURE 1

There is, however, a sense in which the coefficients of an equilibrium system may be given a causal interpretation, even though the relations in an equilibrium system may not themselves be causal relations. Let us take first an imaginary case in ecology: the balanced aquarium. Suppose there are two species of fish in an aquarium, big, b, and small, s. Their populations are y_b and y_s. The big fish feed on the small ones and on weed type a, available in quantity x_a. The small fish feed only on weed type c,

[7] If, for example, an entrepreneur wishing to produce a given amount of product at minimum cost decides simultaneously on how much of each of two factors of production, x_1 and x_2, to employ, it might be said that his decision as to x_1 causes his decision as to x_2 and his decision as to x_2 causes his decision as to x_1. We do not believe this conforms to the "laboratory" meaning of causation and we therefore reject this usage. On this, see [1].

[8] This illustration, due to Marshall, has been referred to recently by Stone [4] in this connection. Marshall spoke of mutual "determination" rather than "causation" and it is not clear whether these words are to be regarded as synonyms.

[9] In equilibrium when $x(t) = x(t-\theta)$ and $y(t) = y(t-\theta)$, these structures may be collapsed into one of apparent "mutual causation," but what are simultaneous equilibrium conditions ought not to be confused with causal relations.

available in quantity x_c. It takes time for the big fish to catch the small ones. The model is linear and stochastic, thus:

$$y_b(t) = \alpha_1 + \beta_1 y_s(t-\theta) + \gamma_1 x_a(t) + u_1(t) , \tag{6a}$$

$$y_s(t) = \alpha_2 + \beta_2 y_b(t-\theta) + \delta_2 x_c(t) + u_2(t) . \tag{6b}$$

Suppose now that every time we observe the aquarium it is in equilibrium. Moreover, we wish to estimate two numbers—are they β_1 and β_2?—so that we can answer these questions:

If we controlled the population of the big (small) fish, y_b (resp., y_s), by adding them to the aquarium or taking them out, and thereby held y_b (resp., y_s) at some arbitrary level, what would the expected value of the population of small (resp., big) fish, y_s (resp., y_b), be at the new equilibrium level, conditional upon the values of x_a and x_c?

Suppose we next formulated the model:

$$y_b(t) = \alpha_1 + \beta_1 y_s(t) + \gamma_1 x_a(t) + u_1(t) , \tag{7a}$$

$$y_s(t) = \alpha_2 + \beta_2 y_b(t) + \delta_2 x_b(t) + u_2(t) . \tag{7b}$$

To control the population of big fish is to wipe out or invalidate relation (6a) and to regard $y_b(t-\theta)$ as exogenous. To control the population of small fish is to wipe out (6b) and to regard $y_s(t-\theta)$ as exogenous. In the absence of such intervention, we certainly cannot say that $y_s(t)$ *causes* $y_b(t)$ and that $y_b(t)$ *causes* $y_s(t)$, i.e., we cannot use model (7) as a *causal* model telling us what happens through time in the uncontrolled aquarium. Nevertheless, the values of β_1 and β_2 appearing in model (7) do tell us what a second fish population will be conditional upon our specifying (controlling, manipulating) a first fish population—provided that the aquarium is then brought back to an equilibrium situation. Equilibrium models do tell us (enable us to predict) something about equilibrium values under *control.*

A comparable example in economics might well be the cobweb model. The model is:

$$p(t) = a - \beta q_h(t) + \varepsilon z_1(t) + u_1(t) \quad \text{(demand)} , \tag{8a}$$

$$q_h(t) = \gamma + \delta p(t-1) + \eta z_2(t) + u_2(t) \quad \text{(supply)} , \tag{8b}$$

where $p(t)$ is price at time t, q_h is quantity harvested, z_1 and z_2 are exogenous variables, and u_1 and u_2 are stochastic shocks. This system is recursive, but if observed in equilibrium may, by use of the equilibrium condition

$$p(t-1) = p(t) ,$$

be written as

$$p(t) = a - \beta q_h(t) + \varepsilon z_1(t) + u_1(t) \quad \text{(demand)} , \tag{9a}$$

$$q_h(t) = \gamma + \delta p(t) + \eta z_2(t) + u_2(t) \quad \text{(supply)} , \tag{9b}$$

and will be subject to the same causal interpretation as given in the previous example. The question of how β and δ are best to be estimated is left open.

(d) *Bicausality.* Suppose we confront a demand-supply model of the following sort

$$q(t) = a_{10} + a_{11}p(t) + a_{13}z_1(t) + u_1(t) \text{ (demand)}, \tag{10a}$$

$$q(t) = a_{20} + a_{21}p(t) + a_{24}z_2(t) + u_2(t) \text{ (supply)}, \tag{10b}$$

where $q(t)$ is quantity, $p(t)$ is price, $z_1(t)$ and $z_2(t)$ are exogenous variables, and $u_1(t)$ and $u_2(t)$ are stochastic shocks.

Now suppose this system is given the following causal interpretation: $p(t)$ causes $q(t)$ in accordance with equation (10a) and $p(t)$ also causes $q(t)$ in accordance with equation (10b). This notion of causality is certainly out of accord with the usual laboratory or control notion which we find so natural. Those who write such systems do not, however, really mean what they write, but introduce an ellipsis which is familiar to economists. What is meant is that

$$q_d(t) = a_{10} + a_{11}p(t) + a_{13}z_1(t) + u_1(t), \tag{11a}$$

$$q_s(t) = a_{20} + a_{21}p(t) + a_{24}z_2(t) + u_2(t), \tag{11b}$$

$$q_d(t) = q_s(t), \tag{11c}$$

where $q_d(t)$ is quantity demanded and $q_s(t)$ is quantity supplied. This is an equilibrium model (nonrecursive), and (11c) is not an *identity*, but an *equality* which is assumed to hold in fact over the observations.[10]

A somewhat far-fetched example, but in a surer context, is the following. Suppose there are two crops, d and s, whose yield is measured in bushels, and that (over the relevant range) the yield of one, q_d, is a positive linear function of rainfall, p, while the yield of the other, q_s, is a negative linear function of rainfall, and that these functions intersect within the relevant range. An amount z_1 of fertilizer 1 is applied to crop d and an amount z_2 of fertilizer 2 is applied to s. Suppose for each of N years we conduct an experiment for each crop, applying different amounts of fertilizer. Rainfall is uncontrolled. Imagine now the amazing result that each year of the experiment Nature chooses a rainfall that makes the two yields equal. We may then represent the experiment by system (11) and reduce this to system (10) simply by dropping the subscripts on q and keeping track of which equation is for which crop.

Now, while it would be remarkable for Nature to choose rainfall so as

[10] Especially for one not familiar with the economist's ellipsis, difficulty may result from the careless use of symbols in this reduction. Strictly speaking, the q in (10a and b) should be either a q_d or a q_s, or an additional equation such as $q = \min(q_d, q_s)$ or $q = q_d$ should be added to model (11). Otherwise, identity (and not simply equality) of quantities demanded and supplied is technically implied.

to give us this strange result, it may be not so remarkable for the market to choose price so that quantity demanded equals quantity supplied, at least approximately. This is because, while rainfall is independent of past crop yields, price may well depend on past quantities demanded and supplied, and, if the system is not subject to violent change, the price adjustment relation may work with great efficiency. Whether it will or not is, of course, an empirical question: the answer may vary from market to market and time to time; but this is a matter of realism which need not concern us here. When the equality holds the theoretical system (11) may be represented by system (10), although if (11c) holds only approximately, system (10) is one with errors in the variables.

The causal system which underlies the equilibrium model (11) is then one in which (11c) is replaced by some function such as

$$(11d) \qquad p(t) = f[q_d(t-\theta), q_s(t-\theta), p(t-\theta), z_1(t), z_2(t), z_1(t-\theta), z_2(t-\theta)] + u_3(t)$$

and the causal (and, in this case, dynamic) model is recursive. If $p(t)$ were now to be subject to direct control, (11d) must be abandoned and $p(t)$ must be regarded as exogenous. Equations (11a) and (11b) would then answer questions regarding the causal effect of controlled variation in $p(t)$ on $q_d(t)$ and $q_s(t)$, and a_{11} and a_{12} would be causally interpretable coefficients. They are, moreover, the same coefficients which enter the "bicausal" system (10).

What is to be concluded from all this is that equilibrium systems may appear to entail "causal circles" or "bicausality," but that this is not what is intended. The causal interpretation of a coefficient in either of these types of equilibrium models is to be found in the underlying dynamic model which, *if the laboratory notion of causality is to be sustained*, will be recursive in character.[11]

Two major questions remain: (1) Can a stochastic shock model of the sort commonly considered—i.e., equation (1)—ever be assumed to be always in equilibrium whenever observed?[12] (2) If not, must it not be said that either there are measurement errors introduced by the assumption of equilibrium (for example, ought not (11c) be regarded as an *approximate* equality) or there is a specification error? If so, this raises questions as to appropriate estimation procedure and as to the properties of estimates that ignore these model qualifications. The subsequent paper by Strotz deals with this problem.

[11] Incidentally, differential equation systems are regarded as recursive with respect to infinitesimal time intervals. See [**8**].

[12] For (11a, b, and c) to hold exactly, (11d) would need to include $u_1(t)$ and $u_2(t)$ as arguments and exclude $u_3(t)$.

Our contribution ends with a paper by Wold, who gives a brief presentation of conditional causal chains, a new type of model which is designed as an extension of ordinary (pure) causal chains in the direction of independent systems.

Northwestern University, and
the University of Uppsala

REFERENCES

[1] BENTZEL, R., AND B. HANSEN: "On Recursiveness and Interdependency in Economic Models," *Review of Economic Studies*, 22, pp. 153–168.

[2] MOOD, A.: *Introduction to the Theory of Statistics*, McGraw-Hill, 1950.

[3] SIMON, HERBERT A.: "Causal Ordering and Identifiability," in Wm. C. Hood and Tjalling C. Koopmans, eds., *Studies in Econometric Method*. Wiley & Sons, 1953.

[4] STONE, RICHARD: "Discussion on Professor Wold's Paper," *Journal of the Royal Statistical Society*, Series A, 119, I, 1956, p. 51.

[5] WAUGH, FREDERICK: "Choice of the Dependent Variable in Regression," *Journal of the American Statical Association*, 38, 22 (June, 1943), pp. 210–214.

[6] WOLD, H. O. A.: "Causality and Econometrics," *Econometrica*, 22, pp. 114 ff.

[7] ———: "On the Definition and Meaning of Causal Concepts," manuscript, submitted to *Philosophy of Science*.

[8] ———: "Ends and Means in Econometric Model Building. Basic Considerations Reviewed," in U. Grenander, ed., *Probability and Statistics* (The Harald Cramer volume), Stockholm: Almqvist & Wiksell, 1959.

[9] WOLD, H. O. A., AND L. JURÉEN, *Demand Analysis*, Almqvist & Wiksell, 1952.

[18]

Money, Income, and Causality

By CHRISTOPHER A. SIMS*

This study has two purposes. One is to examine the substantive question: Is there statistical evidence that money is "exogenous" in some sense in the money-income relationship? The other is to display in a simple example some time-series methodology not now in wide use. The main methodological novelty is the use of a direct test for the existence of unidirectional causality. This test is of wide importance, since most efficient estimation techniques for distributed lags are invalid unless causality is unidirectional in the sense of this paper. Also, the paper illustrates the estimation of long lag distributions without the imposition of the usual restrictions requiring the shape of the distribution to be rational or polynomial.

The main empirical finding is that the hypothesis that causality is unidirectional from money to income agrees with the postwar *U.S.* data, whereas the hypothesis that causality is unidirectional from income to money is rejected. It follows that the practice of making causal interpretations of distributed lag regressions of income on money is not invalidated (on the basis of this evidence) by the existence of "feedback" from income to money.

* Associate professor of economics, University of Minnesota. Work for this paper was carried out during my tenure as a research fellow at the National Bureau of Economic Research, and a more extended paper on this topic may appear as a *NBER* publication. Numerous members of the *NBER* staff provided support at various stages of the research. Special thanks are due to Philip Cagan, John Hause, Milton Friedman, the Columbia Monetary Economics Workshop, and a seminar at the Cowles Foundation, whose objections and advice have sharpened the paper's argument. Josephine Su carried out the computational work. H. I. Forman drew the charts.

I. The Causal Ordering Question for Money and Income

It has long been known that money stock and current dollar measures of economic activity are positively correlated. There is, further, evidence that money or its rate of change tends to "lead" income in some sense.[1] A body of macro-economic theory, the "Quantity Theory," explains these empirical observations as reflecting a causal relation running from money to income. However, it is widely recognized that no degree of positive association between money and income can by itself prove that variation in money causes variation in income. Money might equally well react passively and very reliably to fluctuations in income. Historically observed timing relations between turning points have also for some time been recognized not to be conclusive evidence for causal ordering. James Tobin and William Brainard and Tobin provide explicit examples of the possibilities for noncorrespondence between causal ordering and temporal ordering of turning points. People in close connection with the details of monetary policy know that some components of the money supply react passively to cyclical developments in the economy. Frank DeLeeuw and John Kalchbrenner, for example, argue that the monetary base (currency plus total reserves) is not properly treated as an exogenous variable in a regression equation because of the known dependence be-

[1] See Milton Friedman and Anna Schwartz (1963b), Friedman (1961), (1964) reprinted in chs. 10–12 of Friedman (1969).

tween certain of its components and cyclical factors.

Phillip Cagan uses an analysis of the details of money-supply determination to argue convincingly that the long-run relation between money supply and the price level cannot be due primarily to feedback from prices to money. His application of the same analytical technique to cyclical relations of money with income measures fails to yield a firm conclusion, however.

Friedman and Schwartz have argued on the basis of historical analysis that major depressions have been caused by autonomous movements in money stock.[2]

The issues between the monetarists and the skeptics are not easily defined on the basis of the literature cited in the preceding paragraphs. Probably few of the skeptics would deny *any* causal influence of money on income. But, on the other hand, leading exponents of the monetarist approach seem ready to admit that there is "clear evidence of the influence of business change on the quantity of money,"[3] at least for the mild cycles which have characterized the postwar United States.

Now if the consensus view that there is some influence of business conditions on money is correct, if this influence is of significant magnitude, and if current dollar *GNP* is a good index of business conditions,[4] then distributed lag regressions treating money as strictly exogenous are not causal relations. Since such regressions are now treated as causal relations by some economists, it is important to test the assumption of causal priority on which they rest.

As will be shown below, there is a natural analogue in a dynamic system to Wold's "causal chain" form for a static econometric model.[5] This analogue turns out to be exactly a model in which causation is unidirectional according to the criterion developed by C. W. J. Granger. But Wold's form is in general not testable in a static context; any multivariate set of data with a specified list of endogenous variables can be fit by a recursive model. The dynamic analogue is, however, easily testable: If and only if causality runs one way from current and past values of some list of exogenous variables to a given endogenous variable, then in a regression of the endogenous variable on past, current, and future values of the exogenous variables, the future values of the exogenous variables should have zero coefficients.

Application of this test to a two-variable system in a monetary aggregate and current dollar *GNP* with quarterly data shows clearly that causality does not run one way from *GNP* to money. The evidence agrees quite well with a null hypothesis that causality runs entirely from money to *GNP*, without feedback.

II. The Meaning of the Results

Before giving a rigorous explanation of the notion of causal direction and the detailed description of statistical results, it is worthwhile to consider in a nontechnical way what the results do and do not prove. That the test applied in this paper shows no feedback from y to x is a necessary condition for it to be reasonable to interpret a distributed lag regression of y on current and past x as a causal relation or to apply any of the common estimation methods involving use of lagged dependent variables or corrections for serial cor-

[2] See Friedman and Schwartz (1963b), p. 217–18 as reprinted in Friedman (1969).

[3] The quoted phrase is from Milton Friedman's introduction to Cagan, p. xxvi, and summarizes one of Cagan's main results.

[4] As I will argue below, it may be that the one-dimensional current dollar *GNP* index is so inadequate a measure of those aspects of business conditions which influence money supply that there is no feedback from current dollar *GNP* to money despite the existence of feedback from business conditions to money.

[5] See Edmond Malinvaud, p. 511 ff., for a description of causal chain models.

relation. Hence the most conservative way to state the results for money and income is that they show it to be unreasonable to interpret a least squares lag distribution for money on *GNP* as a causal relation, and that they provide no grounds for asserting that distributed lag regressions of *GNP* on money do not yield estimates of a causal relation. It is natural, and I believe appropriate, to phrase the result more positively: the data verify the null hypothesis that distributed lag regressions of *GNP* on money have a causal interpretation. However, it is possible to concoct models in which a money on *GNP* regression does not yield a causal relation and yet this paper's test would not detect feedback.

The test will fail to detect within-quarter feedback of a certain type. The "innovation" in the stochastic process x_t is that part of x_t which cannot be predicted from x_t's own past (i.e., the residual in a regression of x_t on its own past). If x_t and y_t are connected by two causal relations—one from x to y involving a distributed lag, and the other from y to x but with only the current innovation in y_t on the right-hand side—then the test used in this paper will not detect the y to x feedback.[6]

Where the data show negligible serial correlation, this failing of the test becomes important. For then y and x are their own innovations and one expects that causal relations may be purely contemporaneous. In the general case, with serially correlated data, the failing is not likely to be important. It can result in false conclusions only where there is a certain sort of exact relation between the lag distributions defining the causal structure and the autocorrelation functions of the error terms. With one important class of exceptions, there is seldom reason to suppose any relation at all between the causal structure and the properties of the error terms.

The exception arises for models in which some elements of optimal control enter. If one of the two relations in a bivariate system is chosen optimally, then the innovations in the variables become structural elements of the system. This fact is important for money and income, since it is easy to imagine that money may have been controlled to influence or to conform to income. It can be shown that in a bivariate system with optimal control of one variable, there will be in general two-way causality by the Granger criterion. The only exception is that if the information lag in the control process is just one period and if the criterion for control is minimal variance in, say, y, then causality will spuriously appear to run from y to x.[7] But then the only way optimal control would be likely to hide income-to-money feedback would be if income were controlled to hold down variance in money. This seems farfetched.

The fact that this paper finds no evidence of feedback from *GNP* to money is not direct evidence on the structure of money-supply determination. All that is necessary to allow interpretation of the money on *GNP* distributed lags as causal relations is the hypothesis that in this particular historical sample (1947–69), the determinants of money supply showed no *consistent* pattern of influence by *GNP*. Thus it would be enough if, for example, money supply were influenced quite differently by real and price components of *GNP* movements, so long as actual *GNP* movements were not dominated by one

[6] One elementary consequence is that it is possible for the test to show no feedback in either direction, despite the existence of well-defined lag distributions in both x on y and y on x regressions. This is the case where all the relation between y and x consists of contemporaneous correlation of their innovations.

[7] Proving this in any generality would require stretching the length and increasing the technical level of the paper. I expect to take up this point at greater length in a subsequent paper.

component or the other. Alternatively, a consistent pattern of feedback from *GNP* to money could have been swamped in this sample period by extraneous influences on money. The situation is analogous to that in a supply and demand estimation problem, where we have evidence that in a particular sample elements other than price dominated supply. Such evidence proves that in the sample the price-quantity relation traces the demand curve, but it does not in itself prove anything about the supply curve. Thus one can imagine that if heightened awareness of the importance of monetary policy makes money respond more consistently to the business cycle, single-equation estimates of the money-to-*GNP* relation will become unreliable.

Finally, we ought to consider whether the bivariate model underlying this paper could be mimicking a more complicated model with a different causal structure. The method of identifying causal direction employed here does rest on a sophisticated version of the *post hoc ergo propter hoc* principle. However, the method is not easily fooled. Simple linear structures with reversed causality like the one put forth by Tobin cannot be constructed to give apparent money-to-*GNP* causality. Complicated structures like that put forward by Brainard and Tobin in which both *GNP* and money are endogenous will except under very special assumptions yield a bivariate reduced form showing bidirectional causality. The special assumptions required to make endogenous money appear exogenous in a bivariate system must make money essentially identical to a truly exogenous variable. Thus, if money has in the sample been passively and quickly adjusted to match the animal spirits of bankers and businessmen, and if animal spirits is a truly exogenous variable affecting *GNP* with a distributed lag, then money might falsely appear to cause *GNP*. However, if there is substantial random error in the correspondence between animal spirits and money and that error has a pattern of serial correlation different from that of animal spirits itself, then the bivariate relation between money and *GNP* will appear to show bidirectional causality.[8]

An assumption that future values of money or income cause current values of the other, via economic actors' having forecasts of the future better than could be obtained from current and past money and *GNP*, will affect the apparent direction of causality. However, the effect is much more likely to make a truly unidirectional structure appear bidirectional than vice versa. For example, it is easy to see that if current money supply is determined in part by extraneous knowledge of *GNP* for several future quarters, past money could spuriously appear to affect current *GNP*. However, it is difficult to imagine in such a situation why past *GNP* and all the variation in future *GNP* which can be predicted from past *GNP* should *not* affect money. Without such an artificial assumption, one cannot explain a one-sided lag distribution of *GNP* on money by a "reversed-causation-with-accurate-anticipations" model.

III. Testing for the Direction of Causality[9]

In a single, static sample, the "direction of causation" connecting two related groups of variables is ordinarily not identified. That is, one can construct many different models of causal influence all of which are consistent with a given pattern

[8] This point is not obvious, but to prove it would, as in the case of the previous point about optimal control, overextend the paper. The technically sophisticated reader may easily verify the proposition for himself.

[9] It is my impression that many of the results in this section, even where they have not previously been given formal expression, are widely understood. For example, H. Akaike clearly understands that a two-sided transfer function implies the existence of feedback.

of covariances amongst the variables. If one is willing to identify causal ordering with Wold's causal chain form for a multivariate model, and if enough identifying restrictions are available in addition to those specifying the causal chain form, one can test a particular causal ordering as a set of overidentifying restrictions. The conditions allowing such a test are seldom met in practice, however.

Granger has given a definition of a testable kind of causal ordering based on the notion that absence of correlation between *past* values of one variable X and that part of another variable Y which cannot be predicted from Y's own past implies absence of causal influence from X to Y. More precisely, the time-series Y is said to "cause" X relative to the universe U (U is a vector time-series including X and Y as components) if, and only if, predictions of $X(\mathrm{t})$ based on $U(s)$ for all $s<\mathrm{t}$ are better than predictions based on all components of $U(s)$ except $Y(s)$ for all $s<\mathrm{t}$.

We will give content to Granger's definitions by assuming all time-series to be jointly covariance-stationary, by considering only linear predictors, and by taking expected squared forecast error as our criterion for predictive accuracy.

Consider the jointly covariance-stationary pair of stochastic processes X and Y. If X and Y are jointly purely linearly indeterministic (linearly regular in the terminology of Yu. S. Rozanov), then we can write

$$(1)\qquad \begin{aligned} X(\mathrm{t}) &= a^*u(\mathrm{t}) + b^*v(\mathrm{t}) \\ Y(\mathrm{t}) &= c^*u(\mathrm{t}) + d^*v(\mathrm{t}) \end{aligned}$$

where u and v are mutually uncorrelated white noise[10] processes with unit variance, a, b, c, and d all vanish for $\mathrm{t}<0$, and the notation

$$g^*f(\mathrm{t}) = \sum_{s=-\infty}^{\infty} g(s)f(\mathrm{t}-s)$$

The expression (1) is the moving average representation of the vector process $\begin{bmatrix} X \\ Y \end{bmatrix}$ and is unique up to multiplication by a unitary matrix.[11]

A useful result, not proved by Granger, is

THEOREM 1: *Y does not cause X in Granger's definition if, and only if, a or b can be chosen identically 0.*[12]

This result gives us another intuitive handle on Granger causality. If causality is from X to Y only, then of the two orthogonal white noises which make up X and Y, one is X itself "whitened" and the other is the error in predicting Y from current and past X, whitened. (A whitened variable is one which has been passed through a linear filter to make it a white noise.)

Granger has shown that if there is an autoregressive representation, given by

$$(2)\qquad B^*\begin{bmatrix} X \\ Y \end{bmatrix}(\mathrm{t}) = \begin{bmatrix} u \\ v \end{bmatrix}(\mathrm{t}),$$

$B(\mathrm{t})=0$ for $\mathrm{t}<0$, u, v defined by (1), then the absence of causality running from Y to X is equivalent to the upper right-hand element of B being zero. That is, causality runs only from X to Y if past Y does not influence current X. From this point it is not hard to show:

THEOREM 2: *When $\begin{bmatrix} X \\ Y \end{bmatrix}$ has an autore-*

[10] A "white noise" is a serially uncorrelated process.

[11] Actually, the statement that (1) is the moving average representation of $\begin{bmatrix} X \\ Y \end{bmatrix}$ is a condition for uniqueness. There will be forms of (1) for which a, b, c, and d are all 0 for $\mathrm{t}<0$ and u and v are white noises but do not yield moving average representations. These forms of (1) will not be unitary transformations of the moving average representation and can be distinguished from the true moving average representation by the fact that in a true moving average representation $a(0)u(\mathrm{t}) + b(0)v(\mathrm{t})$ is the limiting forecast error in forecasting $X(\mathrm{t})$ from all past X and Y.

[12] Proofs of both theorems appear in the Appendix.

gressive representation, Y can be expressed as a distributed lag function of current and past X with a residual which is not correlated with any values of X, past or future, if, and only if, Y does not cause X in Granger's sense.

We can always estimate a regression of Y on current and past X. But only in the special case where causality runs from X to Y can we expect that no future values of X would enter the regression if we allowed them. Hence, we have a practical statistical test for unidirectional causality: Regress Y on past and future values of X, taking account by generalized least squares or prefiltering of the serial correlation in $w(t)$. Then if causality runs from X to Y only, future values of X in the regression should have coefficients insignificantly different from zero, as a group.

An implication of Theorem 2 is that many commonly applied distributed lag estimation techniques are valid only if causality runs one way from independent to dependent variable. The condition that the independent variable X be "strictly exogenous," central to most statistical theory on time-series regression, is exactly the Theorem 2 condition that $X(t)$ be uncorrelated with the residual $U(s)$ for any t, s. For example, quasi differencing to eliminate serial correlation in residuals will produce inconsistent estimates without the one-way causality condition; and the "Koyck transformation" which is invoked to allow interpretation of regressions with autoregressive terms as estimates of infinite lag distributions depends on one-way causality. Hence in principle a large proportion of econometric studies involving distributed lags should include a preliminary test for direction of causality.

Remarks on Distributed Lag Methodology

Especially in a study of this kind, where we wish to make fairly precise use of F-tests on groups of coefficients, it is important that the assumption of serially uncorrelated residuals be approximately accurate. Therefore all variables used in regressions were measured as natural *logs* and prefiltered using the filter $1-1.5L+.5625L^2$; i.e., each logged variable $x(t)$ was replaced by $x(t)-1.5x(t-1)+.5625x(t-2)$. This filter approximately flattens the spectral density of most economic time-series, and the hope was that regression residuals would be very nearly white noise with this prefiltering.

Two problems are raised by this prefiltering. First, if the filter has failed to produce white noise residuals, it is quite unlikely to fail by leaving substantial positive first-order serial correlation. Durbin-Watson statistics are therefore of little use in testing for lack of serial correlation, and tests based on the spectral density of the residuals were used instead. Second, as I pointed out in an earlier paper (1970), prefiltering may produce a perverse effect on approximation error when lag distributions are subject to prior "smoothness" restrictions. Therefore, no Koyck, Almon, or rational lag restrictions were imposed a priori, and the length of the estimated lag distributions was kept generous.

In applying the F-tests for causal direction suggested in the previous section, one should bear in mind that the absolute size of the coefficients is important regardless of the F value. It is a truism too often ignored that coefficients which are "large" from the economic point of view should not be casually set to zero no matter how statistically "insignificant" they are. Thus, the fact that future values of the independent variable have coefficients insignificantly different from zero only shows that unidirectional causality is possible. If the estimated coefficients on future values are as large or larger than those on past values, bidirectional causality may be very important in practice, despite insignificant F's. Moreover, small coefficients on future values of the independent variable may sometimes be safely ignored even when they are statistically significant. This is especially true in the light of my observation (1971) that nonzero coefficients on future values may be generated in discrete-time data from a "one-sided" continuous-time distributed lag.[13]

All the data used in the regressions presented in this paper were seasonally adjusted at the source. This creates potential problems of a sort which has not been widely recognized heretofore. Most seasonal adjustment procedures in common use allow for a seasonal pattern which shifts slowly over time, and the rate at which the seasonal pattern is taken to shift varies from one series to another. It can be shown[14] that in distributed lag regressions relating two variables which have been deseasonalized by procedures with different assumed rates of shift in the seasonal pattern, spurious "seasonal" variation is likely to appear in the estimated lag distribution. The lag distributions estimated in this paper are long enough and free enough in form that bias from this source should be obvious wherever it is important (and it is important in one regression). However, it would be better to start from undeseasonalized data, being sure that both variables in the relation are deseasonalized in the same way. A check along these lines, using frequency-domain procedures, was carried out for this paper and is mentioned in the discussion of results below.

[13] The definition of causality given in the previous section generalized easily to continuous time. One simply reinterprets (1) as a continuous-time relation, and "Y does not cause X" still corresponds to "b identically zero."

[14] I showed this in an earlier mimeographed version of this paper. A separate short paper on this topic is in preparation.

IV. Time Domain Regression Results

The data used cover the period 1947–69, quarterly. Money was measured both as monetary base (MB)—currency plus reserves adjusted for changes in reserve requirements—and as $M1$—currency plus demand deposits. Figures for MB were taken from the series prepared by the Federal Reserve Bank of St. Louis and supplied to the National Bureau of Economic Research data bank. Results were similar for $M1$ and MB, so we sometimes use M or money to refer to both $M1$ and MB in what follows.

Regressions of the *log* of GNP (in current dollars) on future and lagged *log* M were significant, as were the reversed regressions of *log* M on future and lagged *log* GNP. (See Table 1.) Table 2 reports tests for homogeneity between the pre-1958 and post-1958 sections of the sample. No significant differences between the subsamples appeared in the regressions. Future values of GNP were highly significant in explaining the M dependent variable, but future values of M were not significant in explaining the GNP dependent variable. (See Table 3.) The largest individual coefficients in each GNP on M regression occur on past lags,

Table 1—Summary of *OLS* Regressions[a]

	F for Independent Variables	$\bar{R}^2$	Standard Error of Estimate	Degrees of Freedom
$GNP=f(M1$, 8 past lags)	1.89*	0.7927	0.01018	64
$GNP=f(M1$, 4 future, 8 past lags)	1.37	0.7840	0.01040	60
$GNP=f(MB$, 8 past lags)	2.24**	0.8004	0.00999	64
$GNP=f(MB$, 4 future, 8 past lags)	1.61	0.7924	0.01019	60
$M1=f(GNP$, 4 future, 8 past lags)	11.25**	0.8385	0.00403	60
$MB=f(GNP$, 4 future, 8 past lags)	5.89**	0.8735	0.00410	60

* Significant at 0.10 level.
** Significant at 0.05 level.
[a] All regressions were fit to the period 1949III-1968IV. $M1$ is currency plus demand deposits. MB is monetary base as prepared by the Federal Reserve Bank of St. Louis. The F-tests shown are for the null hypothesis that all right-hand side variables except trend and seasonal dummies had zero coefficients. See also notes to Table 4.

TABLE 2—F'S FOR COMPARISONS OF SUBPERIODS 1948III–1957III vs. 1957IV–1968IV[a]

Regression Equation	F	Degrees of Freedom
$GNP=f(M1$, 8 past lags)	1.44	(14, 50)
$GNP=f(MB$, 8 past lags)	0.64	(14, 50)
$M1=g(GNP$, 4 future, 8 past lags)	0.88	(18, 46)
$MB=f(GNP$, 4 future, 8 past lags)	1.01	(18, 46)

[a] Tests are for the null hypothesis that all coefficients (including trend and seasonals) remained the same in both subsamples.

TABLE 3—F-TESTS ON FOUR FUTURE QUARTERS' COEFFICIENTS[a]

Regression Equation	F
GNP on $M1$	0.36
GNP on MB	0.39
$M1$ on GNP	4.29**
MB on GNP	5.89**

** Significant at 0.05 level

[a] All tests apply to regressions run over the full sample and are assumed distributed as $F(4, 60)$.

and the estimated shapes for those regressions appear broadly reasonable on the assumption that coefficients on future lags are small and coefficients on past lags are nonzero and fairly smooth. (See Table 4 and Figures 1 and 2.)

These results allow firm rejection of the hypothesis that money is purely passive, responding to GNP without influencing it. They are consistent with the hypothesis that GNP is purely passive, responding to M according to a stable distributed lag but not influencing M.

But let us note a few statistical *caveats.* Though the estimated distribution looks like what we expect from a one-sided true distribution, the standard errors on the future coefficients are relatively high. These results are just what a unidirectional causality believer would expect, but they are not such as to necessarily force a believer in bidirectional causality to change his mind. Also, seasonality problems are

TABLE 4—LAG DISTRIBUTIONS FROM TIME-DOMAIN REGRESSIONS[a]

Coefficient on lag of:	GNP on MB past only	GNP on MB with future	MB on GNP	GNP on $M1$ past only	GNP on $M1$ with future	$M1$ on GNP
−4		−0.65	.162		−.300	.050
−3		.290	−.013		.120	.117
−2		−.088	.105		.126	.069
−1		−.110	.179		.105	.125
0	.603	.532	.171	.570	.484	.181
1	.593	.507	.015	.370	.412	.089
2	.509	.515	.052	−.034	−.017	.116
3	−.029	.080	.264	.543	.582	.107
4	−.011	.023	.107	−.242	−.363	.027
5	−.865	−.822	−.009	−.178	−.147	.027
6	−.037	−.053	.016	−.180	−.136	.025
7	−.296	−.282	.147	−.157	−.139	.123
8	.072	.039	.130	−.326	−.405	.112
Standard errors of coefficients:						
Largest s.e.	.313	.338	.052	.293	.318	.051
Smallest s.e.	.272	.276	.045	.274	.294	.044
Sum of coefficients	.540	—	—	.365	—	—
Standard error of sum	.442	—	—	.523	—	—

[a] Regressions were on *logs* of variables, prefiltered as explained in the text. Each regression included, in addition to the leading and lagging values of the independent variable for which coefficients are shown, a constant term, a linear trend term, and three seasonal dummies. Trends were in all cases significant. Seasonal dummies were insignificant. (The data were seasonally adjusted.)

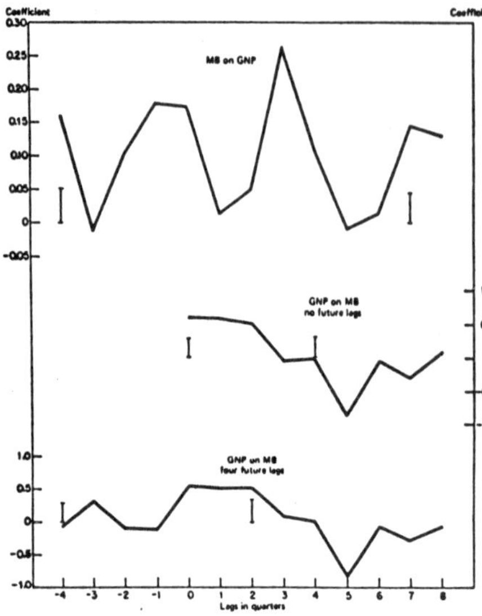

FIGURE 1. LAG DISTRIBUTIONS FOR *MB* AND *GNP*
Note: Smallest and largest standard errors are displayed as vertical lines above or below corresponding coefficients.

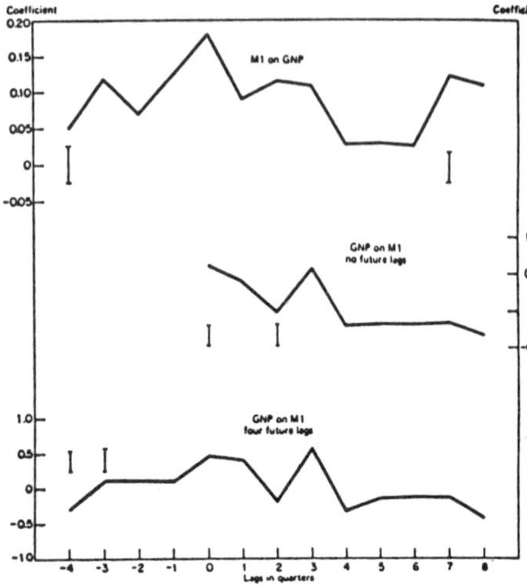

FIGURE 2. LAG DISTRIBUTIONS FOR *M*1 AND *GNP*
Note: Smallest and largest standard errors are displayed as vertical lines above or below corresponding coefficients.

clearly present in the *MB* on *GNP* regression. Seasonality effects appear to be less of a problem with *M*1 than with *MB*.

DeLeeuw and Kalchbrenner have argued, in attacking the "reduced form" money vs. *GNP* regressions put out by the St. Louis Fed, that the monetary base is not truly exogenous. We have discussed above the substance of that argument. Suffice it to say here that they claim that one could make the monetary base more "exogenous" by extracting from it borrowed reserves and (possibly) cash in hands of the public. Attempts to use these adjusted *MB* series (one of them is actually unborrowed reserves) failed, in the sense that relations were less significant statistically and *GNP* on adjusted *MB* regressions did not show one-sided lag distributions.

The same regression equations used for *GNP* and *M* were estimated also with *GNP* replaced by the *GNP* deflator (*PGNP*) and then by real *GNP* (*RGNP*) with *MB* the money variable. Quantity theory even in its modern guise does not claim to have firm implications about the way income changes divide into real and price components, but it seemed useful to examine the possibility that monetary variables would predict the components separately as well as their product. Standard errors of the (logarithmic) equations regressing *RGNP* on *MB* were slightly larger than corresponding standard errors for current dollar *GNP*. Values of coefficients and *F*-statistics were much the same with *RGNP* as dependent variable as with *GNP* the dependent variable. Future lags were again highly significant for *MB* on *GNP* regressions and highly insignificant for the reversed relation. However, with *RGNP*, current plus eight past lagged values of *MB* were not as a group significantly different from zero at the .10 level. With *PGNP*, standard errors of estimate were small, but almost every *F*-test failed to attain significance, including the test on future lags in the *MB* on *PGNP* relation.

V. Tests for Serial Correlation in Residuals

Durbin-Watson statistics for all reported regressions are close to two. This is to be expected because of the prefiltering. The test on the cumulated periodogram of the residuals, described by James Durbin, yields results in the indeterminate range for each regression.[15] The test on the cumulated periodogram is in principle capable of detecting departures from serial independence even when there is no first-order serial correlation, and in this sense is a stronger test than the Durbin-Watson for the case at hand.

The central difficulty here, though, is that a total of 17 of the available 78 degrees of freedom have been used up in the regression, so that the easily-computed bounds tests leave a wide range of indeterminancy. An alternative to the bounds tests is to use the likelihood ratio test for the null hypothesis that the periodogram of the residuals has constant expectation across a number of intervals. This test is described in E. J. Hannan (1960), p. 98.[16] In application to regression residuals this test is justified only when the number of observations is much larger than the number of independent variables, which is clearly not the case here. The statistics reported in Table 5 would be distributed as chi-square with 7 degrees of freedom if asymptotic results applied, but the true significance levels of the test will be higher than the nominal ones. Even at nominal significance levels, though, only the residuals from the regression of *GNP* on *M*1 are significantly "nonwhite" at a 5 percent level.

Table 5—Likelihood-Ratio Tests for White Noise Residuals[a]

GNP on *MB*	*GNP* on *M*1	*MB* on *GNP*	*M*1 on *GNP*
13.02	19.01	11.04	12.64

Note: .05 significance level for chi-squared with 7 degrees of freedom. 14.1

[a] The statistics shown are each distributed asymptotically as chi-square with 7 degrees of freedom on the null hypothesis of white noise residuals. As noted in the text, the asymptotic distribution is probably not a good approximation to the true distribution here. For the *GNP* on *M* equations, residuals were taken from the form with no future lags. For the *M* on *GNP* equations, residuals were taken from the form including future lags.

The conclusion from this list of approximate or inconclusive tests can only be that there is room for doubt about the accuracy of the *F*-tests on regression coefficients.

As a check on the least squares results, these same regressions were estimated also using a frequency-domain procedure, Hannan's (1963) "inefficient" procedure.[17] This procedure has some disadvantages relative to least squares, but it has the two advantages that 1) it makes it computationally simple to estimate the variance-covariance structure of the residuals and use the estimate in constructing tests on the estimated regression coefficients and 2) it makes it easy to deseasonalize raw data directly. Not all the tests for significance of groups of coefficients came out

[15] The test carried out was actually based on cumulation of the periodogram over 128 equally spaced points, instead of over the 39 harmonic frequencies as would be appropriate to get Durbin's test. This difference is, however, demonstrably asymptotically negligible (as sample size increases Durbin's test converges in distribution to any test based on more points than half the sample size) and seems unlikely to have been very important even at this particular sample size.

[16] Hannan's description includes Bartlett's small-sample correction to the likelihood ratio test. The results reported in Table 5 do not include the Bartlett correction, since it was small.

[17] The theory of these estimates has been extended in Hannan (1967) and Wahba. It is worthwhile noting that Wahba's proof that the Hannan inefficient estimates are "approximately" least squares estimates is not a proof that the Hannan inefficient estimates have the same asymptotic distribution as least squares, and their asymptotic distributions are in fact different.

the same way at the same significance levels in the frequency-domain estimates, but the general agreement with the least squares results was so close that there is no point in reproducing the frequency-domain results here.[18] Raw data for the monetary base was not readily available, but frequency-domain estimates using raw data on $M1$ and GNP, symmetrically deseasonalized, gave results very similar to those obtained with least squares on published deseasonalized data.

VI. The Form of the Lag Distribution

The lag distribution estimated here to relate GNP to M has only a loosely determined form because of the lack of prior restrictions on its shape. Still, it is worthwhile noting that it agrees in general shape with many previous estimates, and that it can be given an economic explanation. The distribution is positive at first, then becomes mostly negative beyond the fourth lag. The initial positive coefficients sum to a number greater than one, though the sum of all the coefficients is less than one. (Note, though, that the standard error on the sum of coefficients is very large. See Table 4.) The pattern of a short-run elasticity exceeding unity and a long-run elasticity below unity agrees with the theoretical speculations of Friedman (1969), pp. 138–39, concerning the effects of a demand for money dependent on permanent rather than on current income. However, note that the contemporaneous quarter response is less than unitary, and that negative response does not set in for several quarters. To explain this, one must either introduce an averaging procedure into the other side of the equation, making "permanent money" depend on permanent income, or one must introduce the possibility of transactional frictions which keep the economy off its demand curve for money in the short run. At least the latter of these elements is not novel. Alan Walters pointed out that over short enough time intervals people are likely to be off their demand curves. It seems only natural that, since individuals' money balances always fluctuate over short periods due to random timing of transactions, it should take time for changes in money balances to affect individuals' spending behavior.

[18] The frequency-domain results were presented and discussed in an earlier mimeographed version of this paper.

VII. Conclusion

The main conclusions of the paper were summarized in the introduction. I repeat them more briefly here: In time-series regression it is possible to test the assumption that the right-hand side variable is exogenous; thus the choice of "direction of regression" need not be made entirely on a priori grounds. Application of this test to aggregate quarterly data on $U.S.$ GNP and money stock variables shows that one clearly should not estimate a demand for money relation from these data, treating GNP as exogenous with money on the left-hand side; no evidence appears to contradict the common assumption that money can be treated as exogenous in a regression of GNP on current and past money.

Appendix

THEOREM 1: *Y does not cause X in Granger's definition if, and only if, in the moving average representation*

$$\text{(A)}\qquad \begin{bmatrix} X(t) \\ Y(t) \end{bmatrix} = \begin{bmatrix} a & b \\ c & d \end{bmatrix} * \begin{bmatrix} u \\ v \end{bmatrix}(t),$$

a or b can be chosen to be identically zero.

PROOF:

Following Rozanov we introduce the notation $H_z(t)$ to stand for the completion under the quadratic mean norm of the linear space of random variables spanned by $z(s)$ for $s \leq t$. Suppose b is zero. Clearly $X(t)$ then lies in $H_u(t)$. By the definition of a moving average (*m.a.*) representation, $H_{X,Y}(t)$ is identical to $H_{u,v}(t)$. But it follows from Rozanov's "Remarks" on pages 62–63 that if $H_u(t)$ and $H_X(t)$ are not identical, then with b zero the identity of $H_{X,Y}(t)$ and $H_{u,v}(t)$ fails. Therefore, $H_u(t)$ and $H_X(t)$ are identical. But then the projection of $X(t)$ on $H_{X,Y}(t-1)$ is in $H_X(t-1)$, which is to say that given past X, past Y does not help in predicting current X. One side of the double implication is proved.

In Granger's definition, Y not causing X is the same thing as the projection of $X(t+1)$ on $H_{X,Y}(t)$ lying in $H_X(t)$. Assuming this condition holds, define $u(t)$ as the difference between $X(t)$ and the projection of $X(t)$ on $H_X(t-1)$. Define $w(t)$ as the difference between $Y(t)$ and the projection of $Y(t)$ on $H_{X,Y}(t-1)$. Finally, define $v(t)$ as that part of $w(t)$ orthogonal to $u(t)$ (i.e., the residual in a regression of $w(t)$ on $u(t)$). By definition, $u(t)$ and $w(t)$ and therefore, $v(t)$ are uncorrelated with past values of each other. Also, $u(t)$ and $v(t)$ are contemporaneously uncorrelated and $H_{u,v}(t)$ is identical to $H_{X,Y}(t)$. Expressing $X(t)$ and $Y(t)$ in terms of the coordinates $u(s)$, $s \leq t$, will give us a moving average representation of the form (A).

THEOREM 2: *When* $\begin{bmatrix} X \\ Y \end{bmatrix}$ *has an autoregressive representation, Y can be expressed as a distributed lag function of current and past X with a residual which is not correlated with any $X(s)$, past or future if, and only if, Y does not cause X in Granger's sense.*

PROOF:

Suppose Y can be expressed as a distributed lag on X with a residual $w(t)$ independent of $X(s)$ for all s. Let $u(t)$ be the fundamental white noise process in the moving average representation of $X(t)$ alone and $v(t)$ be the fundamental white noise process in the *m.a.* representation of $w(t)$ alone. Write the assumed distributed lag relation

$$\text{(B)} \qquad Y(t) = \mu * X(t) + w(t)$$

Then clearly

$$\text{(C)} \qquad Y(t) = \mu * a * u(t) + d * v(t),$$

where $a*u$ and $d*v$ are the *m.a.* representations of X and w, respectively. The equation (C) together with the *m.a.* representation of X are clearly in the form (A) with $b \equiv 0$. Now we need only verify that u and v are jointly fundamental for X and Y, and for this we need only show that $H_{X,Y}(t)$ includes $H_{u,v}(t)$. $H_u(t)$ is in $H_X(t)$ by definition. $H_v(t)$ is in $H_w(t)$ which is in turn (by inspection of (B)) in $H_{X,Y}(t)$. One side of the double implication is proved. Suppose that we have the autoregressive representation

$$\text{(D)} \qquad \begin{bmatrix} \alpha & \beta \\ \gamma & \delta \end{bmatrix} * \begin{bmatrix} X \\ Y \end{bmatrix}(t) = \begin{bmatrix} u \\ v \end{bmatrix}(t)$$

and that the *m.a.* representation has the form (A) with $b \equiv 0$. Let G be the matrix on the right-hand side of (A) and H be the matrix on the left-hand side of (D). Then almost everywhere $\tilde{G}^{-1} = \tilde{H}$. (The tilde denotes a Fourier transformation.) Since $\tilde{G}$ can be written in triangular form, $\tilde{H}$ (and thus H) can be written triangular also. But then we can substitute the first equation of (D) into the second euqation of (A) to obtain

$$\text{(E)} \qquad Y(t) = c * \alpha * X(t) + d * v(t)x$$

Equation (E) has the desired properties, since X can be expressed entirely in terms of u and v is uncorrelated with u.

REFERENCES

H. Akaike, "Some Problems in the Application of the Cross-Spectral Method," in B. Harris, ed., *Advanced Seminar on Spectral Analysis of Time Series*, New York 1967.

W. Brainard, and J. Tobin, "Pitfalls of Financial Model Building," *Amer. Econ. Rev. Proc.*, May 1968, *58*, 99–122.

P. Cagan, *Determinants and Effects of Changes in the Stock of Money*, Nat. Bur. Econ. Res. *Stud. Business Cycles*, No. 13, New York 1965.

F. DeLeeuw, and J. Kalchbrenner, "Monetary and Fiscal Actions: A Test of Their Relative Stability—Comment," *Fed. Reserve Bank St. Louis Rev.*, Apr. 1969, *51*, 6–11.

J. Durbin, "Tests for Serial Correlation in Regression Analysis Based on the Periodogram of Least Squares Residuals," *Biometrika*, Mar. 1969, *56*, 1–16.

M. Friedman, "The Monetary Studies of the National Bureau," Nat. Bur. Econ. Res. *Annual Report* 1964; reprinted in Friedman (1969).

———, "The Lag in the Effect of Monetary Policy," *J. Polit. Econ.*, Oct. 1961, *69*, 447–66; reprinted in Friedman (1969).

———, *The Optimum Quantity of Money and Other Essays*, Chicago 1969.

——— and A. Schwartz, (1963a) *Monetary History of the United States 1867–1960*, Nat. Bur. Econ. Res. *Stud. Business Cycles*, No. 12, Princeton 1963.

——— and ———, (1963b) "Money and Business Cycles," *Rev. Econ. Statist.*, Feb. 1963, supp., *45*, 32–64; reprinted in Friedman (1969).

C. W. J. Granger, "Investigating Causal Relations by Econometric Models and Cross-Spectral Methods," *Econometrica*, July 1969, *37*, 424–38.

E. J. Hannan, *Time Series Analysis*, London 1969.

———, 'Regression for Time Series," in M. Rosenblatt, ed., *Time Series Analysis*, New York 1963.

———, "Estimating a Lagged Regression Relation," *Biometrika*, 1967, *54*, 409–18.

E. Malinvaud, *Statistical Methods of Econometrics*, Chicago 1965.

Y. S. Razanov, *Stationary Random Processes*, San Francisco 1967.

C. A. Sims, "The Role of Approximate Prior Restrictions in Distributed Lag Estimation," *J. Amer. Statist. Ass.*, Mar. 1972, *67*, 169–75.

———, "The Role of Approximate Prior Restrictions in Distributed Lag Estimation," mimeo 1970.

———, "Discrete Approximation to Continuous-Time Distributed Lags in Econometrics," *Econometrica*, May 1971, *39*, 545–63.

J. Tobin, "Money and Income: Post Hoc Ergo Propter Hoc?" *Quart. J. Econ.*, May 1970, *84*, 301–17.

G. Wahba, "Estimation of the Coefficients in a Multi-Dimensional Distributed Lag Model," *Econometrica*, July 1969, *37*, 398–407.

A. Walters, "Professor Friedman on the Demand for Money," *J. Polit. Econ.*, Oct. 1965, *73*, 545–55.

Scottish Journal of Political Economy, Vol. 33, No. 2, May 1986

Notes and Communications

SIMS ON CAUSALITY: AN ILLUSTRATION OF SOFT ECONOMETRICS

ROBIN ROWLEY AND RENUKA JAIN

McGill University and Worcester State College

Economists are slow to change their statistical methods when they undertake empirical research.[1] One cannot fail to be impressed with the stability of statistical practice over the last quarter century, as revealed in published papers. The increased role of econometrics in graduate programmes and the rapid expansion of computational software have widened the incidence of statistical approaches rather than changed their composition. One expects to find least-squares estimates, estimated standard errors, Durbin–Watson statistics, autoregressive corrections (Hildreth–Lu or Cochrane–Orcutt), coefficients of multiple determination, Student's t statistics, and tests of structural change. When systems of equations are used, this list can be extended but two features persist. These are the preoccupation with a very specific set of familiar techniques and the general absence of adequate discussions concerning the appropriateness of the techniques that belong to this set.

A major deviation from this picture of stability is represented by the rapid growth in the use of tests of "causality" during the last decade. Two papers by Sims (1972a,b) suggested the feasibility of such tests and provided illustrations of their application to production functions and money-income relationships. These papers appeared 20 years after Orcutt had stressed the need to check the exogeneity assumptions of the simultaneous-equations model and, also, to explore the potential interactions among exogeneous variables prior to multiplier analysis.[2] Orcutt's focus was on "exogeneity" rather than causality but Sims chose to identify the two concepts with each other. His approach seems to have been influenced by the attempt of Granger to clarify the meaning of causality in terms of predictability and, to a lesser extent, by the development of causal-chain models by Wold in a long series of papers.[3]

The significant aspect of Sims' papers was his advocacy of a very simple

[1] Rowley and Ferzandi (1984) use a survey by Hocking of advances in linear regression to demonstrate the slow assimilation of new statistical techniques by economists.

[2] Orcutt (1952) provides a valuable discussion of these topics. It is disappointing that his particular suggestions were not pursued further.

[3] See Granger (1963, 1969) for a description of his efforts to develop "testable definitions" of causality for stationary time series. Wold (1954, 1956) reflects the use of prior information from dynamic economic theory to specify causal chains.

Date of receipt of final manuscript: 19 *August* 1985.

procedure which involved a trivial extension of existing practice (the introduction of additional variables and the testing of the associated parameters relative to zero). The acceptance of his procedure was encouraged both by his fortuitous choice of applications and by its integration into the attack on Keynesian macroeconometric models by Lucas, Sargent and others. The choice of money-income relationships for determination of uni-lateral causality struck a chord among some economists especially as Sims' findings for the U.S. economy agreed with their view of monetary influences. Although less dramatic, the exploration of the exogeneity of variables in production was also important especially as it seemed to indicate means of reopening certain issues affecting the interpretation of derived demand functions for productive inputs (as, for example, those investment equations of Jorgenson). With respect to the second major element in encouraging acceptance of Sims' procedure, the development of "equilibrium business-cycle models", "new classical economics", "rational expectations" and other radical adjustments in economic theory was associated with a reappraisal of the simultaneous-equations model which has been the statistical framework of large Keynesian macroeconometric structures. Lucas and Sargent (1979) reveal three criticisms of such structures. They cite their apparent instability (possibly due to cross-equation constraints), their excessive reliance on zero restrictions, and their dependence on a fundamental partitioning of measured variables into exogenous and endogenous types. The Sims' test enters this debate as a means of testing this partition rather than depending on prior restrictions. The sensitivity of econometric structures to the particular choices involved in the partitioning of variables is apparently avoided by testing for exogeneity or causality. It should be noted that the partitioning is an essential determinant in the completeness and identification of simultaneous-equation models, in their simulation and interpretation, and in the choice of estimating procedures.[4]

The assimilation of Sims' test into general use was initially slow but has proceeded at a rapid pace recently. This has occurred despite opposition to its use by Jacobs, Leamer and Ward (1979), Feige and Pearce (1979), Zellner (1979), Conway, Swamy and Yanagida (1983) and others.[5] Our intention is not to add to this stream of opposition but rather to reconsider the contents of the two initiating papers by Sims. Since his test has become part of "standard equipment" of economists for empirical analysis and part of the debate on the adequacy of certain theoretical approaches in economics, it

[4] The methodology of the simultaneous-equations model was established by the Cowles Commission in the 1940s. It is based on the "probability approach" to econometrics that is attributed to Haavelmo (1944). He made the model represent the conditional distribution of endogenous variables relative to exogenous variables. The partition of variables is thus at the heart of this approach. The link with Keynesian models by Lucas and Sargent is due to the frequent use of Keynesian elements in construction of large economy-wide econometric models, which involve Haavelmo's approach to determine choices of estimating techniques.

[5] This list may be readily extended. Indeed it is likely that the recent work by Hendry, Richard and their associates will prove to be the biggest challenge to Sims' procedure but this work (re-expressing exogeneity in alternative ways) has little recognition outside econometric circles so far.

now seems appropriate to explore whether such prominence is deserved. It is our contention that much of econometrics can be characterized as "hard" or "soft" according to its bases in exact mathematical statements on the one hand and subjectivity, special circumstances and potential fallibility on the other.

Sims' test is usually stated with insufficient qualifications. Indeed one of our conclusions is that Sims failed to make clear to his readers the need for important supplemental assumptions to support the application of his test. Thus, although his papers treat his test as if it were hard econometrics, it should properly be recognized as soft econometrics. When such recognition is accorded to the test, its interpretation and the validity of particular applications must be reappraised. The test may still be used but loses some of its firmness as an indicator of causality and exogeneity. This undermines the arguments of Lucas, Sargent and others on the existence of suitable testing and the avoidance of prior restrictions as the basis for partitioning variables into exogenous and endogenous types. The traditional choices of Keynesian macroeconometric structures are, however, not re-instated by this conclusion. Their arbitrariness persists. (Indeed this is another illustration of soft econometrics.) Lucas and Sargent are entirely correct in dismissing the poor explanations of how exogenous variables are determined in most of the large econometric models.[6]

Our approach is to take quotations from Sims (1972a,b) and consider their implications. In doing so, we hope to move beyond Sims' test and to express concern in a wider context. The use of statistical indicators without questioning their validity is a cause of acute distress. It stems from either simple ignorance or from inadequate recognition of the softness of much econometrics in economic applications. The consequence is significant for the relevance of individual empirical papers, the reconciliation of apparently conflicting results, and the notion of progress in the level of economic understanding due to the accumulation of evidence. We touch on such matters but the modesty of this effort leaves the task of follow-up primarily in the hands of others.

The Test For Causality—Background

To identify causality with correlation is a major reversal of philosophical trends but this identification is common both in formal modelling and in casual discussions among economists. Nor is it restricted to the economic sphere, other social scientists seem just as prone to treat correlation as if it gives causal information. This is revealed, for example, in the use of path coefficients by sociologists. Here the impact of one variable on another is split into direct and indirect components with correlations between variables used as weights in the latter. Wright (1934) and Kenny (1979) described this practice whereby the causal interaction between exogenous variables is summarized by least-square coefficients and simple correlations. Read

[6] This issue is taken up in the historical context by Rowley (1984).

together, this pair of references show the remarkable persistence of path modelling, which Wright first used in 1918.

Exogeneity is simply a lack of correlation between variables and random errors of disturbances that occur in an equation of interest. This statistical characterization is essential although our textbooks often fail to make this clear by their preference for less technical language. Malinvaud (1966, p. 56–57) provides a convenient illustration of this with the following statements, which are associated with the only entry in the subject index of his book for exogenous and endogenous variables.

> The model tries to explain how certain of the quantities considered are determined. The quantities, and the variables which represent them, can be arranged in two distinct groups according to whether they are or are not to be *explained* by the model. The former, called endogenous, are considered to be determined by the phenomenon expressed in the model. The latter, called exogenous, occur in the equations but are considered to be *determined* independently.

> The importance of the assumption that the exogenous variables are determined independently of the phenomena represented must be emphasized.... In practical applications we must always ask ourselves if the assumption is admissible. It will often be allowed only as a first *approximation.*[7]

Clearly determination and explanation need not have any direct link with correlation. It is commonplace for students in statistics to be asked to demonstrate that the presence of an exact mathematical relationship between two variables is quite consistent with a zero correlation between them. Freeman (1963, p. 50) shows, for example, how y and x have a zero correlation if y is x^2 and x is a standardized symmetric random variable. The second quotation from Malinvaud, by acknowledging approximation, reveals a further source of softness. We shall note several approximations in Sims' applications of his test.

Primacy of the statistical characterization of exogeneity was established by Koopmans (1950) and persists wherever the statistical properties of estimates is a principal focus. Sims (1972a, p. 17) steps beyond this background when he makes the following assertions.

> Econometricians understand very well that, in a regression, the "right-hand-side" variables should be exogenous if the regression estimates are to be treated as reflecting a causal relation. What seems to have been understood only quite recently is that, in time series, the assumption that the right-hand-side variables are exogenous can be tested directly.

The first sentence cannot be correct. Taken at face value, it gives a strange picture of econometricians and ignores 40 years of history, during which

[7] We have added the italics. Despite this language, Malinvaud invariably uses the statistical characterization of exogeneity when he discusses estimation and inference.

econometrics has been dominated by the problems of simultaneous-equations models. Sims seems to be suggesting that an equation may only have one non-exogenous (endogenous) variable if its estimates are to be treated as reflecting a causal relation! He has thrown out the structural form of simultaneous-equations models and kept only the reduced form or the recursive form. Not only that, he indicates that econometricians understand the necessity of his action. They have revealed little of this understanding in the contents of either econometric courses or published research.

What can be done to make Sims' assertion more acceptable? Least-squares estimates will be asymptotically biased if "right-hand-side" variables are not exogenous. Their expected values, if they exist, will involve several structural parameters rather than isolated ones. Alternative estimates may be asymptotically unbiased only if the specification of exogenous variables is correct. Thus, if the initial equation has a causal interpretation, asymptotically unbiased estimates of its parameters may be obtained provided the non-exogeneity of "right-hand-side" variables is appropriately dealt with by use of instrumental variables or similar adjustments to the least-squares approach. Regression estimates (based on the least-square principle) may reflect a causal relation in a statistical sense of unbiasedness only if certain variables are exogenous. Determining the presence or absence of exogeneity is an important consideration for the statistical properties of estimates. These statements differ markedly from that of Sims but, at least, they are defensible. Unfortunately their technical character may make them less influential than Sims' erroneous statement.

The second sentence in Sims' quotation concerns the understanding that exogeneity can be tested directly. At least three issues arise here. First, does the test exist? A partial answer to this question can be based on Sims' own account as we shall attempt below. Second, if this test is used, how will the embodiment of the test in a two-stage procedure (with estimation following preliminary tests of specification) affect the properties of estimates that may be calculated ultimately? Sims did not address this issue of conditional specification which, although raised by Bancroft in the 1940s, generated little interest among economists before Bock, Judge, Yancey and their associates initiated a flood of developments in the 1970s after Sims' two papers were published. We shall briefly touch on this multi-stage issue below as a further element in softness. Finally, is the test restricted to a particular time-series context where all variables must be part of a homogeneous system of difference (or differential) equations that are structurally stable and covariance-stationary? This is again a technical issue but there are dimensions of it that are readily understood by non-specialist econometricians such as, for example, what to do about the presence of "other" variables in money-income relationships. Does the test extend to more than two variables in a practical way? Must all variables be stationary when economics often involves thresholds, changing regimes and other evolutionary perspectives? Will transformations undertaken to give stationarity also preserve clear causal linkages that can be linked with exogeneity? We are unable to treat all these dimensions but some implications of them are part of our discussion.

THE TEST ITSELF

The test of causality is introduced by Sims (1972b, pp. 540–41) with reference to efficient estimation. It is first stated in a very simple form which leaves the theoretical basis imprecise. This basis is later clarified but there is some value in beginning our commentary with Sims' initial views.

> The main methodology novelty is the use of a direct test for the existence of unidirectional causality. This test is of wide importance, since most efficient estimation techniques for distribution lags are invalid unless causality is unidirectional in the sense of this paper.

> If and only if causality runs one way from current and past values of some list of exogenous variables to a given endogenous variable, then in a regression of the endogenous variable on past, current, and future values of the exogenous variables, the future values of the exogenous variables should have zero coefficients.

The statements seem straightforward but their simplicity may be misleading. Undoubtedly such simplicity can be a significant factor in the assimilation of a new technique. As we noted above, the Sims test has rapidly been accepted by economists in their applied research. If the reader of Sims' papers fails to understand any of their technical content, these two quotations are apparently sufficient to provide both a rationale for the test and a method of undertaking it (namely, inserting future values of variables and checking whether their coefficients are zero or not).

Simplicity is achieved at some cost. The essential qualifications for the procedure are omitted and certain ambiguities prevail. Unfortunately, such ambiguities seriously constrain the use of the test although this may not be evident to everyone. Let us begin with the first quotation. Here efficiency refers to both asymptotic unbiasedness and asymptotic dispersion of estimates. The occurrence of these properties must depend on the correct identification of exogeneity but Sims' test will *not* ensure correct identification. Its use may reduce inadequacies of specification but it may also enlarge them since Sims' procedure is based on tests of significance that recognize the possibility of inaccurate decisions.[8] We cannot be sure that Sims' procedure will point us in the "right" direction. Why is this so? The answer lies in the use of a test rather than true prior specification. A test implies some inaccuracy and this leads, in turn, to the possibility of a false choice. Since the use of "significance" is not explicit in the two quotations, let us leave its implications unexplored for the moment. To complete assessment of the first quotation, we should note that the identification of exogeneity and unidirectional causality requires severe restrictions on the variables and the equations linking them. The assumption of linearity implies that the appropriate form

[8] Introductory students in statistics know of two types of errors that underly the construction of tests of significance. We know of no explorations of the "power" of Sims' procedure or of the optimal choice of critical regions. Neither type of error, in any case, can be fully eliminated.

of variables is known so there is no room for exploration of alternative functional forms. Neither is there room for inaccuracies in other transformations (such as that used by Sims to "pre-whiten" the errors in his fitted equations). The lack of awareness of exogeneity must be the sole problem.

Turning to the second quotation, it reads like a mathematical theorem and, as such, an example of "hard" econometrics. The principal ambiguity is involved with the use of the term "regression." Does Sims mean the theoretical regression (that is, the expected value of an endogeneous variable conditional on past, current, and future values of exogenous variables) or does he mean the fitted line approximating this theoretical regression? In the absence of prior knowledge (of a kind that is assumed to be unavailable here since it makes the test unnecessary), the parameters of the theoretical regression are always unknown. Thus we cannot *know* the size of the regression coefficients of future values of exogenous variables. The statement is an accurate expression of a theorem linking zero constraints in the theoretical regression with the exogeneity of variables. It does not yield a test when this exogeneity is in doubt unless supplemental assumptions are involved. Any test is thus an amalgam of elements and, clearly, may be sensitive to the appropriateness of these supplemental assumptions in a particular context. Sims' statement does not make this softness clear. Indeed nowhere in these papers does Sims provide an adequate list of these assumptions to support his test procedure. The interpretations given for his empirical results also fail to give sufficient attention to the significant step from a mathematical theorem as summarized in this quotation (and more fully in the appendix to one paper) to a test of causality.

Before pursuing this softness, we should note the restrictions introduced explicitly by Sims to provide a framework for the identification of causality with exogeneity and for the theorem given here to be valid. These are often ignored in practice but their suitability should affect interpretation of causality testing. Widespread ignorance of these restrictions must weaken the value of the tests. The causality framework is attributed to Granger by Sims (1972b, p. 544).

> More precisely, the time-series y is said to 'cause' x relative to the universe U (U is a vector time-series including x and y as components) if, and only if, predictions of $x(t)$ based on $U(s)$ for *all* $s < t$ are *better* than *predictions* based on *all components* of $U(s)$ except $y(s)$ for all $s < t$.[9]

Of course, this is not precise in any acceptable way. Sims is compelled to add further explanation.

> We give content to Granger's definitions by assuming all time-series to be jointly covariance-stationary, by considering only linear predictors, and by taking expected squared forecast error as our criterion for predictive accuracy.

[9] We have added the italics to imprecise terms (better, predictions) and to constraints violated by incomplete systems or finite samples.

How do we judge these assumptions? They certainly may permit the identification of causality with exogeneity but, in doing so, they change causality to a concept that is alien to many observers. They also restrict the application of this concept and his test to variables that have time-series characteristics consistent with the use of these assumptions. The test of causality is in fact a test only of this concept of causality. If the variables concerned are not stationary with a moving-average representation, even this concept is not to be tested.

Even when this causal framework is accepted, there are practical difficulties in testing that must be dealt with. Sims (1972b, p. 545) provides a practical test for undirectional causality as an extension of the mathematical theorem cited above.

> We can always estimate a regression of y on current and past x. But only in the special case where causality runs from x to y can we *expect that no future values of x would enter the regression if we allowed them.* Hence, we have a practical statistical test for unidirectional causality: Regress y on past and future values of x, *taking account* by generalized least squares or prefiltering of the serial correlation in $w(t)$. Then if causality runs from x to y only, future values of x in the regression *should have coefficients insignificantly different from zero*, as a group.[10]

This exhibits a host of additional elements, some of which we have already noted. Sims has moved from the theoretical regression (of the mathematical theorem) to the fitted one. He acknowledges the presence of other difficulties by introducing a transformation intended to eliminate autocorrelated errors. Then he takes significance tests as the basis for deciding whether particular regression coefficients are zero. Perhaps we should now give fuller discussion of these adjustments. Sims' practical test cannot be understood without such adjustments being present. The four sentences each reveal some softness in the test.

The practical test suggestion begins with the statement that estimates of a regression of y can always be obtained when current and past x are included. He does not point out that the number of past x to include is an important matter. No guide to determining this number is provided for the test even though test results will depend on this choice. Suppose the number of x is misspecified. Then the error on the fitted equation w will not have an expected value of zero and the remainder of the test procedure will be adversely affected. There is nothing in Sims' specifications to suggest that the appropriate number of past x is even less than the number of observations on the basic process or that enough observations are available to avoid the exhaustion of degrees of freedom due to multicollinearity. Truncation of past x values in the fitted regression is thus a major hazard. This difficulty with

[10] The italics are intended to heighten areas of difficulty in this practical test. The symbol $w(t)$ does not seem to be defined in Sims' paper but it is presumably the symbol of errors in fitted equations.

past x affects the efficiency of estimation and it may be as big a problem as non-exogeneity for the properties of estimates. Clearly the choice of past x is a major source of softness that is seldom acknowledged in tests of causality even though it has been often recognized in the distributed-lag literature.

It can be argued that we are unduly concerned about a difficulty that is common and not more severe here than elsewhere in empirical research. The defence against this argument is based on the assumptions that were used to "give content" to Granger's framework, namely homogeneity or completeness. Sims needs all variables to have joint moving-average representations and there is little room for variables that do not fit this scheme. In the money-income relationships, for example, other variables might have an influence but are excluded by the restriction to two equations, one each for the two major variables. The consequence is that such equations seem especially prone to the possible occurrence of non-zero expected values for equation errors.

Turning to the second sentence of the quotation, another issue arises. Suppose future values of x are allowed to enter into the fitted regression. Then irrespective of the estimation technique to be used, the estimated regression coefficients for these variables would not be zero. This holds whether causality runs only from x to y or not. It is the vital difference between theoretical and fitted regressions. We need a criterion for deciding where the fitted coefficients are sufficiently close to zero, which leads into the final sentences of the practical test. Sims suggests pre-filtering to eliminate autocorrelated errors or using generalized least-square estimates which amounts to about the same. However, such adjustments require knowledge of the parameters of the autocorrelation. When these secondary parameters have to be estimated too, then the adjustments have only asymptotic validity. Their impact for finite samples need not be desirable since the transformed errors have very complicated distributional properties. The final step to significance ignores these complications that we have noted. It adds further softness since it requires the errors to be normally distributed so that F-statistics can be calculated to serve as the basis for determining whether the coefficients are (statistically) significantly different from zero. Without normality and with the complications of omitted variables and incomplete adjustment for autocorrelation, the calculated F-statistics are invalid and may be poor guides in determining exogeneity and causality. Even in ideal conditions, the final sentence ignores the imprecision of significance tests. There is always a finite probability that the wrong conclusion will be drawn.

Sims (1972b, pp. 545–56) modifies this practical test anyway so that the dependence on significance tests is reduced and the softness markedly enlarged.

> It is a truism too often ignored that coefficients which are 'large' from the economic point of view should not be casually set to zero no matter how statistically 'insignificant' they are. Thus, the fact that future values of the independent variable have coefficients insignificantly different from zero

> only shows that unidirectional causality is possible. If the estimated coefficients on the future values are as large or larger than those on past values, bidirectional causality may be very important in practice, despite insignificant F's. Moreover, small coefficients on future values of the independent variable may sometimes be safely ignored even when they are statistically significant.

We are left with an awkward situation in which the test of causality seems so easy to undertake provided one closes one's eyes to the inherent softness in each step of its development and provided the "significance" of the results are agreeable to the researcher. Difficulties only arise as one recognizes the potential fallibility of instrumental assumptions, the very restricted notion of causality, the intrinsic subjectivity of choices for transformations and estimation cutoffs, and the potential sensitivity of findings to such extraneous matters.

Last Words

The views that we have expressed refer to a theoretical context and to potential difficulties in moving from this context to the practical application of the test. Clearly, if a researcher provides suitable qualifying remarks for his conclusions or attempts sensitivity experiments, then the Sims test (now revealed as potentially fallible) can still serve as a useful supplement in the struggle to extract information from economic data. Sims (1972a,b) fails to provide an example of such "good practice" either with respect to factor demand equations or to the money-output relationship. His particular treatment of transformations for seasonal adjustment, autocorrelation, and the mathematical form of measured variables is disappointing. Also his advocacy of the use of his test in a multi-stage process should be reconsidered.

To summarize, our commentary points to the following position. The Sims test is an illustration of soft econometrics however firmly its users press their conclusions. Its popularity should not distract our attention from its soft bases. With adequate recognition of these, the test might become a valuable addition to the standard list of techniques considered by economists in their empirical research. Without discussion of the soft elements and explorations of the sensitivity of results to choices among these elements, the use of the test is not likely to be defensible.

References

Conway, R. K., Swamy, P. A. V. D. and Yanagida, J. F. (1983). *The Impossibility of Causality Testing*. Special Studies Paper No. 178, Division of Research and Statistics, Federal Reserve Board, Washington.

Engle, R. F., Hendry, D. F. and Richard, J. F. (1983). "Exogeneity". *Econometrica*, 51, *pp*. 277–304.

Feige, E. and Pearce, D. K. (1979). "The Casual Causal Relationship Between Money and Income: Some Caveats for Time Series Analysis". *Review of Economics and Statistics,* 61, pp. 521–533.

FREEMAN, H. (1963). *Introduction to Statistical Inference.* Reading, Mass.: Addison-Wesley.

GRANGER, C. W. J. (1963). Economic Processes Involving Feedback. *Information and Control,* 6, pp. 28–48.

GRANGER, C. W. J. (1969). Investigating Causal Relations by Econometric Models and Cross-Spectral Methods, *Econometrica,* 37, July, pp. 424–438.

HAAVELMO, T. (1944). *The Probability Approach in Econometrics,* Supplement to *Econometrica,* 12, July.

HENDRY, D. F. AND RICHARD J.-F. (1982). On the Formulation of Empirical Models in Dynamic Econometrics. *Journal of Econometrics,* 20, 1, October, pp. 3–33.

JACOBS, R. L., LEAMER, E. E. AND WARD, M. P. (1979). Difficulties with Testing for Causation. *Economic Inquiry,* 17, pp. 401–413.

KENNY, D. A. (1979). *Correlation and Causality.* New York: John Wiley.

KOOPMANS, T. C. (1950). When is an Equation System Complete for Statistical Purposes?. In (ed.) T. C. Koopmans, *Statistical Inference in Dynamic Economic Models.* New York: John Wiley.

LUCAS, R. E., AND SARGENT, T. J. (1979). After Keynesian Macroeconomics. *Federal Reserve Bank of Minneapolis Quarterly Review,* 3, 2.

MALINVAUD, E. (1966). *Statistical Methods of Econometrics.* Amsterdam: North-Holland.

ORCUTT, G. H. (1952). Towards Partial Redirection of Econometrics. *Review of Economics and Statistics,* 34, 3, August, pp. 195–213.

ROWLEY, J. C. R. (1984). *The Demise of Structural Estimation*?. mimeo. Montreal: McGill University.

ROWLEY, J. C. R., AND FERZANDI, J. (1984). *The Assimilation of Best-Practice Statistical Procedures by Economists,* mimeo. Montreal: McGill University.

SIMS, C. A. (1972a). Are There Exogenous Variables in Short-Run Production Relations?. *Annals of Economic and Social Measurement,* 1, 1, January, pp. 17–36.

SIMS, C. A. (1972b). Money, Income, and Causality. *The American Economic Review,* 62, 4, September, pp. 540–552.

WOLD, H. O. A. (1954). Causality and Econometrics. *Econometrica,* 22, pp. 162–177.

WOLD, H. O. A. (1956). Causal Inference From Observational Data. A Review of Ends and Means. *Journal of the Royal Statistical Society,* Series A, 119, pp. 28–61.

WRIGHT, S. (1934). The Method of Path Coefficients. *Annals of Mathematical Statistics,* 5, pp. 161–215.

ZELLNER, A. (1979). Causality and Econometrics. *Carnegie-Rochester Conference Series on Public Policy,* No. 10. Amsterdam: North-Holland.

[20]

Journal of Economic Dynamics and Control 2 (1980) 329–352. © North-Holland

TESTING FOR CAUSALITY

A Personal Viewpoint

C.W.J. GRANGER

University of California, San Diego Campus, La Jolla, CA 92093, USA

Received February 1980, final version received June 1980

A general definition of causality is introduced and then specialized to become operational. By considering simple examples a number of advantages, and also difficulties, with the definition are discussed. Tests based on the definitions are then considered and the use of post-sample data emphasized, rather than relying on the same data to fit a model and use it to test causality. It is suggested that a Bayesian viewpoint should be taken in interpreting the results of these tests. Finally, the results of a study relating advertising and consumption are briefly presented.

1. The problem and a definition

Most statisticians meet the concept of causality early in their careers as, when discussing the interpretation of a correlation coefficient or a regression, most textbooks warn that an observed relationship does not allow one to say anything about causation between the variables. Of course this warning has much to recommend it, but consider the following special situation: suppose that X and Y are the only two random variables in the universe and that a strong correlation is observed between them. Further suppose that God, or an acceptable substitute, tells one that X does not cause Y, leaving open the possibility of Y causing X. In the circumstances, the strong observed correlation might lead to acceptance of the proposition that Y does cause X. This possibility occurs because of the extra structure imposed on the situation by the knowledge that X does not cause Y. As will be seen, the way structure is imposed will be important in definitions of causality.

The textbooks, having given a cautionary warning about causality, virtually never then go on with a positive statement of the form 'the procedure to test for causality is...', although a few do say that causality can be detected from a properly conducted experiment. The obvious reason for the lack of such positive statements is that there is no generally accepted procedure for testing for causality, partially because of a lack of a definition of this concept that is universally liked.

Attitudes towards causality differ widely, from the defeatist one that it is impossible to define causality, let alone test for it, to the populist viewpoint that everyone has their own personal definition and so it is unlikely that a generally acceptable definition exists. It is clearly a topic in which individual tastes predominate, and it would be improper to try to force research workers to accept a definition with which they feel uneasy. My own experience is that, unlike art, causality is a concept whose definition people know what they do not like but few know what they do like. It might therefore be helpful to present a definition that some of us appear to think has some acceptable features so that it can be publicly debated and compared with alternative definitions.

For ease of exposition, a universe is considered in which all variables are measured just at prespecified time points at constant intervals $t=1,2,\ldots$ When at time n, let all the knowledge in the universe available at that time be denoted Ω_n and denote by $\Omega_n - Y_n$ this information except the values taken by a variable Y_t up to time n, where $Y_n \in \Omega_n$. Ω_n includes no variates measured at time points $t>n$, although it may well contain expectations or forecasts of such values. However, these expectations will simply be functions of Ω_n. Ω_n will certainly be multivariate and Y_n could be, and both will be stochastic variables. To provide structure to the situation, the following axioms will be assumed to hold:

Axiom A. The past and present may cause the future, but the future cannot cause the past.

Axiom B. Ω_n contains no redundant information, so that if some variable Z_n is functionally related to one or more other variables, in a deterministic fashion, then Z_n should be excluded from Ω_n.

Thus, for example, if temperature is measured hourly at some location both in degrees Fahrenheit and degrees Centigrade, there is no point in including both of these variables in the universal information set.

Suppose that we are interested in the proposition that the variable Y causes the variable X. At time n, the value X_{n+1} will be, in general, a random variable and so can be characterized by probability statements of the form $\text{Prob}(X_{n+1} \in A)$ for a set A. This suggests the following:

General Definition. Y_n is said to cause X_{n+1} if

$$\text{Prob}(X_{n+1} \in A \mid \Omega_n) \neq \text{Prob}(X_{n+1} \in A \mid \Omega_n - Y_n) \quad \text{for some } A.$$

For causation to occur, the variable Y_n needs to have some unique information about what value X_{n+1} will take in the immediate future.

The ultimate objective is to produce an operational definition, which this is certainly not, by adding sufficient limitations. This process will be discussed in section 3, and the definition will also be defended there. In the following section some more general background material will be introduced which will, hopefully, make the defence a little easier.

2. A variety of viewpoints on causality

The obvious place to look for definitions of causality and discussions of the concept is the writings of philosophers on the topic, of which there have been plenty from Aristotle onwards. A useful discussion of parts of this literature can be found in Bunch (1963). I think that it is fair to say that the philosophers have not reached a consensus of opinion on the topic, have not found a definition that a majority can accept and, in particular, have not produced much that is useful to practising scientists. Most of the examples traditionally used by philosophers come from classical physics or chemistry, such as asking what causes the flame when a match is struck, or noting that applying heat to a metal rod causes it to become longer. Much of the literature attempts to discuss unique causes in deterministic situations, so that if A occurs then B must occur. Although most writers seem to agree with Axiom A, that causes must precede effects, even this is not universally accepted. Quite a few philosophers, at least in the past, seem to believe that causes and effects should be contiguous both in time and space, which undoubtedly reflects the pre-occupation with classical physics. Social scientists would surely want to consider the possibility that an event occurring in one part of the world could cause an event elsewhere at a later time. The philosophers are not constrained to look for operational definitions and can end up with asking questions of the ilk: 'If two people at separate pianos each strike the same key at the same time and I hear a note, which person caused the note that I hear?' The answer to such questions is, of course: 'Who cares?' For an interesting discussion of the lack of usefulness of the philosophers' contribution by a pair of lawyers, another group which clearly requires an operation definition of causation; see Hart and Honore (1959). They take the viewpoint that 'the cause is a difference to the normal course which accounts for the difference in the outcome'. They also point out that legally this difference can be not doing something, 'as the driver did not put on the brakes, the train crashed'. One interesting aspect of the philosophers' contribution is that they often try to discuss what the term causality means in 'common usage', although they make no attempt to use common usage terms in their discussion. Rather than trying to decide what the public thinks they mean by such a difficult concept as causality, it may be preferable to try to influence common usage towards a sounder definition.

The philosophers and others have provided a variety of definitions, but no attempt to review them will be made here, as most are of little relevance to statisticians. Once a definition has been presented, it is very easy for someone to say 'but that is not what I mean by causation'. Such a remark has to be taken as a vote against the particular definition, but it is entirely destructive rather than constructive. To be constructive, the critic needs to continue and provide an alternative definition. What is surely required is a menu of definitions that can be discussed and criticized but at least defended by someone. Only by providing such a menu can a debate be undertaken which, hopefully, will result in one, or a few, definitions that can receive widespread support. I believe that definitions should be allowed to evolve due to debate rather than be judged solely on a truth or not scale. It is possible, as has been suggested, that everyone has their own definition so that no convergence will occur, but this outcome does seem to be unlikely.

Before proceeding further, it is worthwhile asking if there is any need, or demand, for a testable definition of causality. It is worth noting that the Social Science Citation Index lists over 1000 papers with words such as causal, causation or causality in their titles, and in a recent five-year period the Science Citation Index lists over 3000 such articles. Papers mentioning such words in the body of the paper, not in the title, are vastly more numerous. There does therefore seem to be a need for a widely accepted definition. Statisticians already have methods for measuring relationships between variables, but causal relations may be thought of as being in some sense deeper than the ordinarily observed kind. Consider the following three time series:

X_t = number of patients entering a maternity hospital in day t,
Y_t = number of patients leaving the same hospital in day t,
Z_t = ice cream sales in the same city in day t.

It seems very likely that the series X_t is useful in forecasting Y_t, and it is also possible that Z_t may appear to be useful in forecasting Y_t, as both variables contain seasonal components. However, most people would surely expect that if a more careful analysis was conducted, using perhaps longer data series, larger information sets including more explanatory variables or more sophisticated techniques, then the observed (forecasting) relationship between X_t and Y_t is likely to continue to be found, whereas that between Z_t and Y_t may well disappear. The deeper relationship is a candidate for the title causal. There thus appears to be both a need, and a demand, for techniques to investigate causality. The possible uses of a causal relationship, if found, will be discussed below.

It has been suggested that although such deeper relations need to be named, that name should not involve words like 'cause' or 'causality', as these words are too emotion-laden, involve too much preconception and have too long a history. Alternative phrases such as 'due to', 'temporally interrelated', 'temporally prior' and 'feedback free' have been proposed, for example. To my mind, this suggestion reflects a basic misunderstanding about language and its use. Most of the components of a language are just a notation, with generally agreed meanings. If I use words such as 'apple' or 'fear', I will not need to first define them, as it is understood that most people mean approximately the same thing by them. Occasionally, with unusual or technical words, such as 'therm' or temperature', I might need to add a definition. If I start a piece of written work, or a lecture, by carefully defining something, then I can use this as a notation throughout, such as distribution, mean, or variance. If my definition is quite different from general usage, then I may be unpopular but will not be logically incorrect, as, for example, if I write $\cos x$ for what is usually denoted by x^3. As causation has no generally accepted definition, this criticism cannot apply. Provided I define what I personally mean by causation, I can use the term. I could, if I so wish, replace the word cause throughout my lecture by some other words, such as 'oshkosh' or 'snerd', but what would be gained? It is like saying that whenever I use x, you would prefer me to use z. If others wanted to refer to my definition, they can just call it 'Granger causality' to distinguish it from alternative definitions. There already exist many papers in economics which do just that, some of which are referenced later, and no misunderstanding occurs. If it is later observed that which is called 'Granger causality' is identical to the definition introduced by some earlier writer, then the name should be altered. In fact, I would be very surprised if the definition to be discussed in the next section has not been suggested many times in the past. Part of the definition was certainly proposed by Norbert Wiener (1958). It would not be a telling argument to appeal to 'common usage' in connection with the words cause or causality, as statisticians continually use words in ways different from common usage, examples being mean, variance, moments, probable, significant, normal, regression and distribution.

These remarks made so far in this section are designed to defuse certain criticisms that can be made of what is to follow. My experience suggests that I will be unsuccessful in this aim.

When discussing deterministic causation, philosophers distinguish two cases:

(a) Necessity — if A occurs, then B must occur.

(b) Sufficiency — if I observe B did occur, this means that A must have occurred.

For example, if one has a metal rod, then event A might be that one heats the rod and event B is that the rod expands. Although causality is defined for pairs of sequences, or functions, obeying axiom A in parts of mathematical science, any statistician or any worker dealing with data generated by an animal body, a person's behavior, part of an economy or an atmosphere, for example, will not be happy with these deterministic definitions. Rather than saying 'If A occurs, then B must occur', they would probably be happier with statements such as 'If A occurs, then the probability of B occurring increases (or changes)'. For example, if a person smokes, he does not necessarily get cancer, but he does increase the probability of cancer. If a person goes sailing, he does not necessarily get wet, but he does increase the probability of getting wet. It is therefore important for a useful definition to deal with stochastic events or processes. It is interesting to note that the advent of quantum physics had a big impact on the philosophical writings about causality, which had relied heavily on classical physics for examples. Bertrand Russell, in particular, dramatically changed his views of causality at that time.

There have, of course, been several attempts to introduce probabilistic theories of causality. A particularly convincing attempt, well worth reading, is that by Suppes (1970). One of his definitions is:

An event $B_{t'}$ (occurring at time t') is a prima facie cause of the event A_t if and only if (i) $t'<t$, (ii) $\mathrm{Prob}(B_{t'})>0$, and (iii) $\mathrm{Prob}(A_t\,|\,B_{t'})>P(A_t)$.

One might observe a large African population, for example, and find that the probability of not getting cholera is 0.91 but that of those inoculated against the disease, the probability of not getting cholera is 0.98. If A_t is not getting cholera and B_t is inoculation, then the evidence suggests that 'inoculation is a Suppes prima facie cause of not getting cholera'. Note that, by replacing A and B with their complements, the same evidence is also likely to lead to the conclusion 'not having inoculation is a Suppes prima facie cause of getting cholera'. There is obvious arbitrariness in practice in defining an event. If the inequality in (iii) is reversed, Suppes talks of negative causation. Nevertheless, for probabilistic events, rather than variables or processes, the discussion by Suppes is very useful and is certainly potentially applicable to a series of properly conducted random experiments.

Good (1961, 1962) has a somewhat similar definition, although he effectively hides it amongst 24 assumptions and 17 theorems combined with very little interpretation. If E and F are two events with F occurring before E, then he says that there is a tendency for F to cause E, given some state of the universe, if $\mathrm{Prob}(E\,|\,F)>\mathrm{Prob}(E\,|\,\text{not } F)$. It would be a lengthy task to critically discuss and compare such definitions, and so I will not attempt it at this time.

At the very start of this paper, the case where random variables X and Y are correlated, but God tells you that causation in one direction is impossible, was briefly discussed. Virtually all definitions of causality require some imposed structure, such as that provided here by God. In many definitions, Axiom A provides this structure, but not all definitions follow this route. The causality concepts discussed by Simon, Wold and Blalock [see Blalock (1964)] and others do not require Axiom A but do presume special knowledge about the structure of relations between two or more variables. Given this structure, the possibility of causal relationships can then be discussed, usually in terms of the vanishing or not of correlation or partial correlation coefficients. Because these definitions require a number of assumptions about structure to be true, they will be called conditional causation definitions. If the assumptions are correct, or can be accepted as being correct, these definitions may have some value. However, if the assumptions are somewhat doubtful, these definitions do not prove to be useful. Sims (1977) has discussed the Simon and Wold approach and found it not operational in practice. Certainly there has been little use made of these definitions in recent years, at least in economics. The 'path analysis' of Sewell Wright (1964) has similarities with the Wold and Simon approach, but he does state that he would prefer to use his analysis together with Axiom A, which would bring it nearer to the definition discussed in the next section. The full question of priority in these matters is a complex one and, I think, need not detain us here.

The question of whether any real statement can be made about causality based just on statistical data is clearly an important one. Naturally, as a statistician, I think that proper statements can be made, if they are carefully phrased. The link between smoking and cancer provides an example. So far the only convincing link has been a statistical one, but it is now generally accepted. The real question for most people is not 'Does smoking cause cancer?' but rather 'How does smoking cause cancer?' Before the accumulation of statistical evidence, people could be thought of as having subjective, personal probabilities that the statement 'Smoking causes cancer, in a statistical sense' is true. Since the evidence has been presented, for most people these subjective probabilities have greatly increased and may well be near one. The weight-of-evidence is certainly in favor of this causality. Smoking is certainly a prima facie cause of cancer and is probably more than that, in the opinion of the majority. A decision, such as for an individual to stop smoking or for a government to ban it, could be a wrong one, but statisticians are used to making decisions under uncertainty and realize that when properly based on the statistical evidence can be wrong but are usually correct.

There is one problem with the statistical approach which was pointed out by the philosopher Hume as applying to any testing procedure. It is always possible that the evidence from the past may be irrelevant, as causation can change from the past to the future. It is therefore necessary to introduce:

Axiom C. All causal relationships remain constant in direction throughout time.

The strength, and lags, of these relationships may change, but causal laws are not allowed to change from positive strength to zero, or go from zero to positive strength, through time. This axiom is, of course, central to the applicability of all scientific laws and so is generally accepted, even though it is not necessarily true.

3. An operational definition

The general definition introduced above is not operational, in that it cannot be used with actual data. To become operational, a number of constraints need to be introduced. To do this, it is convenient to first re-state the general definition. Suppose that one is interested in the possibility that a vector series Y_t causes another vector X_t. Let J_n be an information set available at time n, consisting of terms of the vector series Z_t, i.e.,

$$J_n : Z_{n-j}, \qquad j \geqq 0.$$

J_n is said to be a proper information set with respect to X_t if X_t is included within Z_t. Further, suppose that Z_t does not include any components of Y_t, so that the intersection of Z_t and Y_t is zero. Further, define

$$J'_n : Z_{n-j}, Y_{n-j}, \qquad j \geqq 0,$$

so that J'_n is the information set J_n plus the values in past and present Y_t.

Denote by $F(X_{n+1} \mid J_n)$ the conditional distribution function of X_{n+1} given J_n, so that this distribution has mean $E[X_{n+1} \mid J_n]$. The notation using other information sets is obvious. These expressions are used in the following definitions:

Definition 1. Y_n does *not cause* X_{n+1} with respect to J'_n if

$$F(X_{n+1} \mid J_n) = F(X_{n+1} \mid J'_n),$$

so that the extra information in J'_n has not affected the conditional distribution. A necessary condition is that

$$E[X_{n+1} \mid J_n] = E[X_{n+1} \mid J'_n].$$

Definition 2. If $J'_n \equiv \Omega_n$, the universal information set, and if

$$F(X_{n+1} \mid \Omega_n) \neq F(X_{n+1} \mid \Omega_n - Y_n),$$

then Y_n is said to *cause* X_{n+1}.

Definition 3. If

$$F(X_{n+1} \mid J'_n) \neq F(X_{n+1} \mid J'_n),$$

then Y_n is said to be a *prima facie cause* of X_{n+1} with respect to the information set J'_n.

Definition 4. Y_n is said *not to cause* X_{n+1} *in mean* with respect to J'_n if

$$\delta_{n+1}(J'_n) = E[X_{n+1} \mid J'_n] - E[X_{n+1} \mid J_n]$$

is identically zero.

Definition 5. If $\delta_{n+1}(\Omega_n)$ is not zero, then Y_n is said to *cause* X_{n+1} *in mean.*

Definition 6. If $\delta_{n+1}(J'_n)$ is not identically zero, then Y_n is said to be a *prima facie cause in mean* of X_{n+1} with respect to J'_n.

Definition 2 is equivalent to the general definition introduced in the first section, which was discussed in Granger and Newbold (1977). If a less general information set than the universal set is available, J'_n, then a prima facie cause can occur, as in Definitions 1 and 3. These definitions can be strengthened by adding phrases such as 'almost surely', or 'except on sets of measure zero' at appropriate points, but as these will not help towards the eventual aim of an operational definition capable of being tested, such niceties are ignored.

If, rather than discussing the whole distribution of X_{n+1}, one is content with just point forecasts using a least squares criterion, then the final three definitions become relevant. To ask for causality in mean is much less stringent than asking for full causality, but does provide a definition much nearer to being operational. If one wishes to use some criterion other than least squares, this can be done, but point forecasts will be made much more difficult to obtain. Definition 6 can be rephrased: Let $\sigma^2(X \mid J_n)$ be the variance of the one-step forecast error of X_{n+1} given J_n, and similarly for $\sigma^2(X \mid J_n, Y) \equiv \sigma^2(X \mid J'_n)$, then Y is a prima facie cause of X, with respect to J', if $\sigma^2(X \mid J_n, Y) < \sigma^2(X \mid J_n)$. Thus knowledge of Y_n increases one's ability to forecast X_{n+1}, in a least squares sense. This corresponds to a definition hinted at by Wiener (1958), introduced specifically in Granger (1964) and Granger and Hatanaka (1964), re-introduced in Granger (1969), amplified and applied by Sims (1972, 1977) and then used by numerous authors since, including Black (1978), Williams, Goodhart and Gowland (1976), Skoog (1976), Sargent (1976), Mehra (1977), Gordon (1977), Feige and Pearce (1976a, b), Ciccolo (1978), and Caines, Sethi and Brotherton (1977).

However, it should be said that some of the recent writers on this topic, because they have not looked at the original papers, have evolved somewhat unclear and incorrect forms of this definition. It is rather like the party game where a phrase or rumor is whispered around the room, ending up quite differently from how it started.

In this newer formulation, Axiom B becomes:

Axiom B'. $F[Y_n|J_n]$ is not a singular distribution, so that is not that of a variable taking only a constant value. This implies that Y_n is not deterministically related to the contents of J_n.

If purely time-series techniques are used to generate one-step forecasts, these forecasts will usually be linear functions of the information set because of the present state of the art, although some progress in the use of certain non-linear models is occurring; see for instance, Granger and Andersen (1978) and Swamy and Tinsley (1980). However, if forecasts are made from reduced form equations derived from a, possible non-linear, structural econometric model, then the contents of the information set may be utilized non-linearly. The definitions discussed here do not require that only linear models are used, although most of the actual applications so far and much of the theoretical discussions have concentrated on the linear case. If the available information in J_n is used only linearly, then it may be possible to observe that $\mathbf{Y}_n$ is a linear prima facie cause in mean of $\mathbf{X}_{n+1}$ with respect to J'_n and with the available modelling and forecasting techniques this provides the operational definition that is being sought. For the remainder of this paper the phrase 'linear prima facie cause' will be replaced simply by 'cause' for convenience, unless a more general case is being considered. The definition as given relates a pair of vectors, $\mathbf{Y}_n$ and $\mathbf{X}_{n+1}$, but the usual case will be concerned with just a pair of individual series, Y_n and X_{n+1}. Further, to actually model data it will usually be necessary to either assume that the series are stationary or belong to some simple class of models with time-varying parameters. Again, this is not strictly necessary for the definition but is required for practical implementation.

There are a number of important implications of the definition of cause here developed. If, for example, it is found that Y_n causes X_{n+1} with respect to some information set, then this implies no restrictions on whether or not X_n causes Y_{n+1}; this second causation may occur but need not. If both causations occur, one may say that there is feedback between the two series X_t and Y_t. A simple example is

$$X_t = \varepsilon_t + \eta_{t-1}, \qquad Y_t = \eta_t + \varepsilon_{t-1},$$

where ε_t, η_t are a pair of independent white noise series. Further, if there are three series X_t, Y_t and Z_t and it is observed that X causes Y and Y causes Z, then it is not necessarily true that X causes Z, although it can occur.

Example 1. $X_t = \varepsilon_t, \quad Y_t = \varepsilon_{t-1} + \eta_t, \quad Z_t = \eta_{t-1},$

where again ε_t, η_t are independent white noises. There are four information sets that need to be considered: $J_n(X, Y)$ — consisting of past and present X_{n-j}, Y_{n-j} $(j \geqq 0)$, and similarly, $J_n(X, Z)$, $J_n(Y, Z)$, and $J_n(X, Y, Z)$ — consisting of past and present X_{n-j}, Y_{n-j}, Z_{n-j} $(j \geqq 0)$. Then clearly X causes Y with respect to either $J_n(X, Y)$ or $J_n(X, Y, Z)$, Y causes Z with respect to $J_n(Y, Z)$ and to $J_n(X, Y, Z)$, but X does not cause Z with respect to $J_n(X, Z)$ but it does cause Z with respect to $J_n(X, Y, Z)$. This last result occurs because Z_{n+1} is completely predetermined from Y_{n-j}, X_{n-j} $(j \geqq 0)$ but not from just Y_{n-j} $(j \geqq 0)$. The importance of stating the information set being utilized is well illustrated by this example. A further example shows a different situation:

Example 2. $X_t = \varepsilon_t + \omega_t, \quad Y_t = \varepsilon_{t-1}, \quad Z_t = \varepsilon_{t-2} + \eta_t,$

where ε_t, η_t and ω_t are three independent white noises. Here X causes Z in $J_n(X, Z)$ but not in $J_n(X, Y, Z)$.

One thing that is immediately clear from the definition is that if Y_n causes X_{n+1}, then $Y'_n = a(B)Y_n$ causes $X'_{n+1} = b(B)X_{n+1}$ if $a(B)$ and $b(B)$ are each one-sided filters of the form $a(B) = \sum_{j=0}^{\infty} a_j B^j$. However, if two-sided filters are used, as occurs for example in some seasonal adjustment procedures, then causality can obviously be lost because Axiom A is disrupted.

The use of proper information sets, that is, sets including the past and present values of the series to be forecast X_t, does have the following important implication: it is impossible to find a cause for a series that is self-deterministic, that is, a series that can be forecast without error from its own past. The basic idea of the causal definition being discussed is that knowledge of the causal variable helps forecast the variable being caused. If a variable is perfectly forecastable from its own past, clearly no other variable can improve matters.

Example 3. $X_t = \alpha + bt + ct^2$ and $Y_t = dX_{t+1}$.

Then the following three equations generate X_t exactly, without error, i.e.:

$$X_t = \alpha + bt + ct^2, \quad X_t = d^{-1}Y_{t-1}, \quad X_t = 2X_{t-1} - X_{t-2} + 2c,$$

so that at first sight X_t is 'caused' by time, or by Y_{t-1}, or by its own past. If all three equations fit equally well, that is perfectly, it is clear that no kind of data analysis can distinguish between them. It is therefore obvious that in this circumstance a statistical test for causality is impossible, unless some extra structure is imposed on the situation. It may be noted that causality tests can be made with variables that contain deterministic components, as proved formally by Hosoya (1977), but with this definition one cannot say that the deterministic component of one variable causes the deterministic component of another variable.

4. Some difficulties

Virtually any sophisticated statistical procedure has some problems associated with it, and there is every reason that this will be true also with any operational definition of causality. These difficulties can either be intrinsic to the definition itself or be associated with its practical implementation.

Some of the difficulties will arise because of data inadequacies. One obvious problem arises when the data is gathered insufficiently frequently. Suppose that a change in wood prices causes a change in furniture prices one week later, but prices are only recorded monthly; then the true causal relationship will appear to be instantaneous. It is perhaps worth defining 'prima facie apparent instantaneous causality in mean', henceforth instantaneous causality, between X_{n+1} and Y_{n+1} with respect to J'_n if

$$E[X_{n+1} \mid J_n, Y_{n+1}] \neq E[X_{n+1} \mid J_n].$$

Although the phrase 'instantaneous causality' is somewhat useful on occasions, the concept is a weak one, partly because Axiom A is not being applied and because, at least in the linear case, it is not possible to differentiate between instantaneous causation of X by Y, of Y by X or of feedback between X and Y, as simple examples show. If extra structure is imposed, it may be possible to distinguish between these possibilities, as will be discussed below. If one totally accepts Axiom A, then instantaneous causality will either occur because of the data collection problem just mentioned or because both series have a common cause which is not included in the information set J'_n being used.

The problem of missing variables, and consequential mis-interpretation of one's results, is a familiar one in those parts of statistics which consider relationships between variables. A simple example of apparent causation due to a common cause is:

Example 4. $Z_t = \eta_t, \quad X_t = \eta_{t-1} + \delta_t, \quad Y_t = \eta_{t-2} + \varepsilon_t,$

where ε_t, η_t and δ_t are independent white noises. Here Z_t is causing both X_t and Y_t with respect to information sets $J_n(X, Z)$, $J_n(X, Z)$ and $J_n(X, Y, Z)$, but X_t is causing Y_t in $J_n(X, Y)$ but not $J_n(X, Y, Z)$.

This apparent causation of Y by X in $J_n(X, Y)$ may be thought of as spurious because it vanishes when the information set is expanded, something one would not expect with a true cause. Sims (1977) has studied the system

$$Y_t = c(B)Z_t + \varepsilon_t, \qquad X_t = d(B)Z_t + \eta_t,$$

and found that it is unlikely to give rise to a spurious one-way causation between X and Y based on $J_n(X, Y)$, although presumably a feedback relationship between X and Y is more likely to be found.

An important case where missing variables can lead to misleading interpretations is when one variable is measured with an error having time structure. The following example illustrates the difficulty:

Example 5. $X_t = \eta_t, \quad Y_t = \delta_t, \quad Z_t = X_t + \varepsilon_t + \beta\varepsilon_{t-1},$

where η_t and δ_t are white noises with correlation $(\eta_t, \delta_s) = 0$, $t \neq s$, but this correlation equals λ when $t = s$ and ε_t is a white noise independent of η_t and δ_t. Z_t may be thought of as X_t with an MA(1) measurement error. There is no causation between X_t and Y_t apart from instantaneous causation. As Z_t is the sum of a white noise and an MA(1) term, it will be MA(1), so that there exists a constant θ with $|\theta| < 1$ and a white noise series e_t so that

$$Z_t = (1 + \theta B)e_t.$$

It follows that

$$e_t = (1 + \theta B)^{-1}\eta_t + (1 + \theta B)^{-1}(\varepsilon_t + \beta\varepsilon_{t-1}).$$

The one-step forecast of Z_{n+1} using Z_{n-j} $(j \geqq 0)$ is just θe_n with error e_{n+1}, but this error is a function of η_{n-j} $(j \geqq 0)$ which is correlated with δ_{n-j} $(j \geqq 0)$ which is equal to Y_{n-j}. It thus follows that the Y_{n-j} will help forecast Z_{n+1}, so that apparently Y_n causes Z_{n+1} with respect to $J_n(Y, Z)$, but this would not be the case if X_{n-j} were observable, so that $J_n(X, Y, Z)$ could be considered. This result is at first sight quite worrying, as in many disciplines, such as economics, variables are almost inevitably observed with error, so that x_t — the missing variable — will always be missing. However, as the results of Sims (1977) and Newbold (1978) show, by no means does the addition of measurement error to variables necessarily produce spurious causations, as the error has to have particular time-series structure compared to the original series. Nevertheless, the possibility of mis-leading results occurring from a common type of situation has to be kept in mind when interpreting results.

Another situation which needs care in interpretation is when the time that a variable is recorded is different from the time at which the event occurred that led to the variable's value. For example, March unemployment figures in New York City and New York State may not become known to the public until April 1 and April 15, respectively. The values must be associated with March, not the time of their release, otherwise spurious causation may well occur. A further example of this problem is the relationship between lightning and thunder. As the lightning is usually observed before the thunder, because light travels faster than sound, it might seem that lightning causes thunder. However, both are manifestations of what is essentially the same event, and if the observations are placed at the time of the original electrical discharge, the spurious causation disappears. If one is being pedantic, the light-producing part of the discharge does occur before the sound-producing part, but both lightning and thunder do have a common cause.

A further interpretation problem can arise because of Axiom B. Suppose one has three variables which are related through some linear identity, such as

$$\text{Work force} = \text{Unemployed} + \text{Employed}.$$

It is clear that all three variables cannot be in the information set to be used, but it is not necessarily obvious which one should be excluded. If, for example, total consumption is caused by size of work force, but this latter variable is excluded, one may expect to find that numbers of both unemployed and employed appear to cause consumption. Once one is aware of such interpretational difficulties, it is not difficult to invent strategies for analyzing them, such as excluding different variables and repeating the analysis, or by testing equality of certain coefficients in the model, for example.

One apparently serious problem of interpretation, which is suggested by the thunder and lightning example, arises from the idea of a leading indicator. Suppose that X causes both Y and Z, but that the causal lag is shown from X to Y, then from X to Z. If now X is not observed, Y will appear to cause Z. Example 4 shows such a situation. The search for such leading indicators occurs in various fields. In economics, for example, the Bureau of the Census publishes a list of such indicators, plus an index, which are supposed to help indicate when the economy is about to experience a down-turn or an up-turn. A number of possible leading indicators for earthquakes are also being considered, an example being unusual animal behavior. If leading indicators are included in an information set, tests may well indicate prima facie causality. In most cases this will be just another example of the missing variable problem. Sometimes the missing variable will be available and, when added to the information set, the leading indicator will no longer appear to cause. In other cases the missing variable is not observable and, when this occurs, it will not always be obvious whether a variable is a cause or merely a leading indicator. This relates to the question of how to interpret the outcomes of the causality tests, which are discussed in the next section, given that the information sets used in practice will always be limited in extent. One way of viewing the test results is as an informal Bayesian. A person may start with a prior belief, or probability, that X causes Y, say, and then use the test results to alter this probability, if the test is viewed as being relevant. If the causality definition being invoked by the test is not liked, then the probability need not change. Once more, the purely personal aspect of the attitude towards causality is seen to be of real importance. For some cases, such as whether changes in animal behavior causes earthquakes, the prior probability will start at zero and will remain there despite any test results, so these changes will still be relevant leading indicators, but will not be thought of as causes. Surely no one believes that a lot of cows jumping up and down will trigger an earthquake. On the other hand, one may have a prior probability that smoking is a cause of heart failure, and, after an appropriate and well-conducted test, this probability may be changed, depending on the results of the test.

One very important aspect of forming these prior probabilities will be the availability, or otherwise, of some convincing theory for the causal situation being considered. If there exists, for example, some piece of economic theory that one strongly believes to be true, this could certainly influence, or even fully determine, one's belief about a causal relationship. In what is at present the only carefully thought out critical discussion of what has been called Granger causality, Zellner (1978) strongly proposes that causality should only be considered in the context of some accepted theory. He states: 'Perhaps a more satisfactory position would be to define causality, as Feige and others have, in terms of predictability according to well thought out economic laws.' In terms of the General Definition, or Definition 2, this approach adds nothing, as these definitions assume total knowledge of all relevant distribution functions. Any true or correct law or theory is simply an observed constraint that is found to apply to these distribution functions, and so knowledge of it does not add to the assumed available information set. However, when trying to make the definition more operative, the use of some theory may well be helpful, depending on the quality of the theory and on its nature. For example, if the theory simply tells one that certain variables need to be included in the information set to be utilized, that is extremely useful. It is also helpful to be told that certain variables can be safely omitted from the information set, as this will greatly simplify the data analysis. However, these would be rather vague theories and, I suspect, are not what Zellner had in mind. If the theory is much more specific, such as 'interest changes do not cause changes in production' or 'money supply changes do cause changes in prices', then, if true, analysis of other possible causes would again be simplified. But such theories may be precisely what the causality test is designed to verify. To impose any theory, one has conditional causality testing and, like all such situations, if the theory is correct it is helpful to use it, if it is incorrect one may well be worse off by its use. This is certainly true of any causality test that is conditional on the truth of some very specific theory. Whereas in many fields there may be theories, specific or not, that are generally accepted as being true, such theories are much more difficult to find in economics. It is interesting to note that Zellner in his paper never gives a single example of what he would consider to be a 'well thought out economic theory' nor even of a specific theory or law that is generally accepted by the majority of economists. Again, one returns to the personal belief aspect of causality testing; an individual may strongly believe some theory and is happy to test causality conditional on this theory, whereas someone else would not want to do that. One obvious place where a good theory would be particularly useful would be where extra structure is required to resolve causal directions in what appears to be instantaneous causality/feedback. For example, if sufficient structure can be put on a model to ensure identifiability — in the econometrician's sense of having a unique model — then a conditional causal test can be constructed. This is very much in the spirit of the Simon and Wold approach to causality, which is very well summarized in Zellner's article. However, it must be emphasized that only conditional causality can result, and this is potentially very much weaker than the unconditional causality definition discussed earlier.

The definitions of causation introduced in the previous section admittedly have a number of arbitrary aspects, some of which are potentially removable, others perhaps not. The data is assumed to be measurable on a cardinal scale, whereas actual data often occurs on different scales. If the data is intrinsically ordinal, I consider that it may be difficult to use these definitions, because of the lack of suitable distribution functions. However, it may be possible to build and evaluate forecasting models for such data, and so one aspect of the definitions will go through. With attribute data, without any natural order to the categories, the general definition remains unstable, but clearly the 'causality in mean' definitions are not relevant. This type of data is much nearer to the situation of one event causing another that was discussed by Suppes (1970) and Good (1961/62) and may often occur as the outcome of designed experiments. To be relevant to statisticians, a sequence of experiments will be required, as there seems to be no possibility of investigating causal relationships between unique events using statistical procedures.

A further arbitrary feature of the definitions is the use of one-step forecasts rather than h-step for any h. It is usually by no means clear what is the natural length of the step, and the pragmatic procedure is to use just the data period of the publicly available data, which can lead to the apparent instantaneous causation problem mentioned above. In the bivariate information set case, where one asks if Y causes X with respect to $J_n(X, Y)$,

Pierce (1975) has shown that if Y causes X using an h-step forecasting criterion, with $h>1$, then it will necessarily be found that Y causes X with a one-step criterion. However, this does not seem to be true in the multivariate case:

Example 6. $X_t=\varepsilon_t,\quad Y_t=\varepsilon_{t-2}+\eta_t,\quad Z_t=\varepsilon_{t-1}+\theta_t,$

where ε_t, η_t, θ_t are independent zero-mean, white noise series.

Here Z_n causes X_{n+1} with respect to $J_n(X,Z)$ and $J_n(X,Y,Z)$, Y_n causes X_{n+2} with respect to $J_n(X,Y)$ and $J_n(X,Y,Z)$, Y_n (or Y_{n-1}) causes X_{n+1} with respect to $J_n(X,Y)$ but not with respect to $J_n(X,Y,Z)$. Although some justification can be made that one-step forecasts are the most natural to consider, it will remain an arbitrary aspect of the definitions.

It is, on occasion, possible to distinguish between different types of causes by considering alternative information sets. For example, one might call Y a primary cause of X, if tests show this to be so for $J_n(X,Y)$, $J_n(X,Y,Z)$ and for all other information sets containing X and Y and any other series. A secondary cause might be one such that X causes Z in $J_n(X,Y,Z)$ but not in $J_n(X,Z)$, as illustrated in example one above. This example shows that X can cause Z, according to the definition, even though X and Z are statistically independent, provided that X can add further information to the primary cause, which in Example 1 is Y. The existence of such secondary causes may be upsetting to some readers, and so it might be relevant to alter the basic definition to deal only with primary causes. However, I personally would not, at this time, wish to emphasize such a change.

Most of the problems and difficulties discussed in this section relate not to the basic definition but with making it operational, in my opinion. Some are inherent to any statistical study using an incomplete or finite data set. Many of the difficulties become considerably reduced in inportance once care is taken with interpretation of test results.

In the following section a brief discussion of actual test procedures is presented, and in the final section some further important interpretational questions are considered, such as the relevance of control variables and the meaning of exogeneity.

5. Test procedures

There has been a lot of thought given in recent years to the question of how the above definitions can be actually tested, although the major attention has been given to the case of whether X causes Y with respect to $J_n(X,Y)$, that is, just the two-variable case. Although most empirical studies have considered this case, it is probably not a particularly important one in economics, as it is easy to suggest relevant missing variables. It is clear that more attention is needed on how to utilize bigger information sets. As the two-variable case has been well summarized recently by Pierce and Haugh (1977), only a few of the more important aspects will be discussed here. To give some structure to the discussion, consider the pair of zero-mean, jointly stationary series x_t, y_t, which are purely non-deterministic.

The moving-average, or Wold, representation can be denoted, following Pierce and Haugh, by

$$\begin{pmatrix} x_t \\ y_t \end{pmatrix} = \begin{bmatrix} \psi_{11}(B) & \psi_{12}(B) \\ \psi_{21}(B) & \psi_{22}(B) \end{bmatrix} \begin{pmatrix} a_t \\ b_t \end{pmatrix}, \tag{1}$$

where each $\psi_{ij}(B)$ is a power-series, possibly infinite in length, in the backward operator B and $(a_t, b_t)'$ is a two-element white noise vector, with zero correlation between a_t and b_s, except possibly when $t=s$. Assuming that the moving average matrix operator is invertible, the corresponding autoregressive model can be denoted by

$$\begin{bmatrix} A(B) & H(B) \\ C(B) & D(B) \end{bmatrix} \begin{pmatrix} x_t \\ y_t \end{pmatrix} = \begin{pmatrix} a_t \\ b_t \end{pmatrix}. \tag{2}$$

Rather than considering models for the actual series, one can equally well consider relationships between prewhitened series. If the filters $F(B)x_t = u_t$ and $G(B)y_t = v_t$ produce a pair of series u_t and v_t that are individually white noises, then moving average and autoregressive models will exist of the form

$$\begin{pmatrix} u_t \\ v_t \end{pmatrix} = \begin{bmatrix} \theta_{11}(B) & \theta_{12}(B) \\ \theta_{21}(B) & \theta_{22}(B) \end{bmatrix} \begin{pmatrix} a_t \\ b_t \end{pmatrix}, \tag{3}$$

and

$$\begin{bmatrix} \alpha(B) & \beta(B) \\ \gamma(B) & \delta(B) \end{bmatrix} \begin{pmatrix} u_t \\ v_t \end{pmatrix} = \begin{pmatrix} a_t \\ b_t \end{pmatrix}. \tag{4}$$

There are obviously relationships between the various operators, as described by Pierce and Haugh.

Denote the correlation between u_{t-k} and v_t by $\rho_{uv}(k)$ and consider the regression

$$v_t = \sum_{j=-\infty}^{\infty} \omega_j u_{t-j} + f_t, \tag{5}$$

where $\rho_{uv}(k) = (\sigma_u/\sigma_v)\omega_k$. Similarly, one can consider the regression

$$y_t = V(B)x_t + h_t. \tag{6}$$

Here $V(B)=(F(B)/G(B))\omega(B)$ and f_t, h_t are residuals which are uncorrelated with u_{t-j}, x_{t-j}, respectively, but are not necessarily white noises. Using this notation, Pierce and Haugh (1977) prove the following two theorems, amongst others:

Theorem 1. Instantaneous (prima facie) causality (in mean) exists if and only if the following equivalent conditions hold:

(i) *at least one of* $\operatorname{cov}(a_t, b_t), \gamma(0), \beta(0)$ *in* (4) *are non-zero, or*

(ii) *at least one of* $\operatorname{cov}(a_t, b_t), H(0), C(0)$ *in* (2) *are non-zero.*

In their 1977 paper, Pierce and Haugh had further conditions, such as $\rho_{uv}(0)\neq 0$ or $\omega_0\neq 0$, but Price (1979) and Pierce and Haugh (1979) show that these conditions are not necessarily correct when there is feedback between x and y.

Theorem 2. y is not a (prima facie) cause (in mean) of x if and only if the following equivalent conditions hold:

(1) $\psi_{12}(B)$ *[equivalently* $\theta_{12}(B)$*] can be chosen zero.*
(2) $\theta_{12}(B)$ *is either* 0 *or a constant.*
(3) $\psi_{12}(B)$ *is either* 0 *or proportional to* $\psi_{11}(B)$.
(4) $V_j=0\ (j<0)$ *in* (6).
(5) $\beta(B)$ *is either* 0 *or a constant.*
(6) $H(B)$ *is either* 0 *or proportional to* $A(B)$.
(7) $\rho_{uv}(k)=0$, *or equivalently* $\omega_k=0\ (k<0)$.

If any of these conditions do not hold, then y will be a prima facie cause of x in mean with respect to $J_n(x, y)$. (1) and (4) were pointed out by Sims (1972), the first part of (6) was mentioned in Granger (1969), and that of (7) was emphasized in Granger and Newbold (1977). Multivariate generalizations of these conditions, concerning the possibility that the vector $\boldsymbol{y}$ may cause the vector $\boldsymbol{x}$, have been discussed by Caines and Chan (1975) and elsewhere. Because of this variety of equivalent conditions, there are clearly numerous statistical tests that can be devised based on these conditions. The performance of these tests needs further investigation, either using statistical theory or Monte Carlo study, especially as some are suspected to be occasionally biased or to be lacking in power.

My own experience has largely been with the autoregressive form (2), first fitting the bivariate model with $H(B)$ constrained to be zero and then re-fitting without this constraint, to see if a significant decrease in the variance of the residual for the x_t equation can be achieved. This experience, using both simulated and actual data as, for example, in Chiang (1978), suggests that misleading results do not occur but that the power is not particularly satisfactory. However these tests are not of considerable importance for two basic reasons: (i) they deal only with the bivariate case, whereas the more important applications are likely to involve more variables; and (ii) they are not properly based on the definitions presented above. This latter point arises because these definitions are explicitly based on the extra forecasting ability schieved from one information set over another, whereas the equivalent conditions given in Theorem 2, for example, make no mention of forecasts. This makes no difference for populations, as the definition of non-causation in mean and the conditions in Theorem 2 are then equivalent. However, if only a finite sample is available, as will always occur in practice, the equivalence disappears. Suppose that a sample is used to model the relationship between x_t and y_t in the autoregressive form (2) and the estimate of $H(B)$ is found to be significantly different from zero. Then the result is essentially saying that if this fact were known at the start of the sample, it could have been used to improve forecasts of x_t. This is quite different from actually producing improved forecasts. It is generally accepted that to find a model that apparently fits better than another is much easier than to find one that forecasts better. Thus tests based on the 'equivalent conditions' in Theorem 2 are just tests of goodness of fit, whereas the original definition requires evidence of improved forecasts. To satisfy this requirement, alternative models, based on different information, can be identified and estimated using the first part of the sample and then their respective forecasting abilities compared on the later part of the sample. The best way to actually test for differences in 'post-sample' forecasting ability and the optimum way to divide the sample into a modelling part and a forecast evaluation part need further investigation, but at least a test that is in sympathy with the basis of the definition would result.

An application of these ideas, in a two-variable case, is provided by Ashley, Granger and Schmalensee (1979), who consider possible causal relationships between aggregate advertising expenditures and consumption spending. They use a five-step procedure:

(i) Using a block of data, which is called the sample, each series is prewhitened by building ARIMA models, to get u_t, v_t as above.

(ii) The cross-correlations $\rho_{uv}(k)$ are examined to see if there is evidence of possible causal relationships.

(iii) For each indicated possible causal relationship, a model is built on these residuals u_t, v_t. If a one-way cause is suggested, the transfer function methods of Box and Jenkins (1970) may be utilized, but if a two-way causality appears to be present, the method for modelling this situation suggested in Granger and Newbold (1977) can be used.

(iv) The models in stages (i) and (iii) are then put together to suggest a model for the original data, in differenced form where necessary. This model is estimated, insignificant terms dropped and a final model achieved.

(v) The forecasting ability, in terms of mean-squared one-step forecast error, of the bivariate model and the single series ARIMA model, are then compared using post-sample data. If the bivariate model forecasts significantly better, then evidence of causation is found.

These stages are somewhat biased against finding causation, as, if in stage (ii) no evidence of causes is found, then no bivariate models will be constructed. The separation of the modelling period and the evaluation period does prevent evidence for spurious causation occurring because of data mining. However, a weakness is that if an important structural change occurs between the sample and the post-sample, the test will lose power. The relevance of Axiom C is evident. Ashley, Granger and Schmalensee, using quarterly data, find evidence that consumption causes advertising, but that advertising does not cause consumption except instantaneously. These results agree with parts of the advertising literature that find advertising expenditure is determined by management from previous sales figures and that advertising has little or no long-memory ability. On the other hand, these results might well be the opposite of the pre-conceptions of many economists, which illustrates both the relevance of performing a test and also of not relying on some partly formed theory.

6. Discussion and conclusions

The definition of causation proposed and defended above essentially says that X_{n+1} will consist of a part that can be explained by some proper information set, excluding Y_{n-j} $(j \geqq 0)$, plus an unexplained part. If the Y_{n-j} can be used to partly forecast the unexplained part of X_{n+1}, then Y is said to be a prima facie cause of X. It is clear that in practice the quality of the answer one gets from a test is related to the sophistication of the analysis used in deciding what is explained and by what. The definition also relies very heavily on Axiom A, that the future cannot cause the past, as using the 'arrow of time' imposes the structure necessary for the definition to hold. It also means that the definition does emphasize forecasting. If one does not accept Axiom A, the rest of the work connected with the definition becomes irrelevant. It is important to realize that the truth of Axiom A cannot be tested using the methods discussed in this paper. I should point out that the work by physicists on 'time-reversibility' does not seem to contradict Axiom A, as a careful reading of the review article by Overseth (1967) will show. Because of the way the definition is framed, and the tests based on it are organized, it is only appropriate for use with sequences of data. It cannot say anything about unique events or contribute to topics such as whether there exists an ultimate or first cause. Such topics have to remain the province of philosophers and theologians. In interpreting the test results it has been suggested above that one thinks in terms of changing personal beliefs about whether Y causes X. There is nothing essentially new in this suggestion, as it is certainly what occurs in practice. The definition and tests based on it provide a way to organize the available data in such a way that some workers will feel is appropriate for them to need to possibly change their prior probabilities. I leave to others the discussion of the effect of this procedure, and of the whole causation testing methodology on scientific methodology.

Some of the economists writing about what is called Granger causality have related this concept to the more familiar one of exogeneity; see, for example, Sims (1977) and Geweke (1978). When econometric models are constructed it is usual to divide variables into exogenous ($\mathbf{Z}$) and endogenous ($\mathbf{Y}$), and it is assumed that components of $\mathbf{Z}$ may cause components of $\mathbf{Y}$ but not vice versa. There is thus assumed to be a one-way causal relationship from $\mathbf{Z}$ to $\mathbf{Y}$. For estimation and econometric identification purposes, it is important that this classification be correct as questions of efficiency, model uniqueness and model specification are concerned. Tests for exogeneity are with respect not only to the information set used but also to the division of variables picked. One may find, for instance, that $\mathbf{Z}$ minus W is exogenous to $\mathbf{Y}$ plus W, for some variable W. It is also possible that missing variables can disrupt the exogenous interpretation, as when $\mathbf{Z}$ is exogenous to $\mathbf{Y}$ but not to some extended $\mathbf{Y}$. The possibility of 'instantaneous causality' obviously greatly complicates the problem of how to test for exogeneity. Some of these problems have been discussed elsewhere [Granger (1980)] and so will not be followed up here. Some variables are such that prior beliefs will be strong that they are exogenous: an example is that weather is probably exogenous to the economy. However, other variables have often been considered to be exogenous yet need to be tested, the best examples being the control variables. One can argue that a government controlled interest rate is in fact partly determined by previous movements elsewhere in the economy, and so is not strictly exogenous. The true exogenous part of such a variable is that which cannot be forecast from other variables and its own past, and it follows that it is only this part that has any policy impact. The theory of rational expectations, currently attracting a lot of attention in economics, is relevant here but its discussion is not really appropriate.

The effect of the presence of control variables on causal relationships was considered by Sims (1977). It is certainly possible that the actions of a controller can lead to what appears to be a causal relationship between two variables. Equally, it is possible that two variables that would be causally related if no controls were used, would seem to be unrelated in the presence of a control. It is also worth pointing out that controlability is a much deeper property than causality, in my opinion, although some writers have confused the two concepts. If Y causes X, it does not necessarily mean that Y can be used to control X. An example is if one observes that the editorial recommendations of the New York Times about which candidates to support causes some voters to change their votes. However, if one started controlling these editorials, and this became known, the previously observed causality may well disappear. The reason is clearly that the structure has been altered by changing a previously uncontrolled variable to one that is controlled. If causation is found between a controlled variable and something else, this could be useful in deciding how to control, provided movements are kept near those observed in the past. It seems quite possible that some variables used in the past by governments to control may be so ineffectual that causation will not be found, so testing is worthwhile. The relationship between control, causation and the recent rational expectations literature is potentially an interesting one, but is too large a topic to be considered here.

There is clearly much more discussion required of this and other definitions and more experience required with the various methods of testing that have been suggested. It is my personal belief that the topic is of sufficient importance, and of interest, to justify further work in this field.

References

Ashley, R., C.W.J. Granger and R. Schmalensee, 1979, Advertising and aggregate consumption: An analysis of causality, Research report (Department of Economics, University of California, San Diego, CA).

Black, H., 1978, Inflation and the issue of unidirectional causality, Journal of Money, Credit and Banking X, Feb., 99–101.

Blalock, H.M. Jr., 1964, Causal inferences in non-experimental research (University of North Carolina Press, Chapel Hill, NC).

Box, G.E.P. and G.M. Jenkins, 1970, Time series analysis, forecasting and control (Holden Day, San Francisco, CA).

Bunch, M., 1963, Causality (Meridian Books, Cleveland, OH).

Caines, P.E. and C.W. Chan, 1975, Feedback between stationary stochastic processes, IEEE Transactions on Automatic Control AC 20, 498–508.

Caines, P.E., S.P. Sethi and T. Brotherton, 1977, Impulse response identification and causality detection for the Lydia–Pinkham data, Annals of Economic and Social Measurement 6, Spring, 147–164.

Chiang, C., 1978, An investigation of the relationship between price series, Ph.D. thesis (University of California, San Diego, CA).

Ciccolo, J.H. Jr., 1978, Money equity values and income: Tests for exogeneity, Journal of Money, Credit and Banking X, Feb., 45–64.

Feige, F.L. and D.K. Pearce, 1976a, Inflation and incomes policy: An application of time series models, Journal of Monetary Economics, Supplementary Series 2, 273–302.

Feige, E.L. and D.K. Pearce, 1976b, Economically rational expectations: Are innovations in the rate of inflation independent of innovations in measures of monetary and fiscal policy?, Journal of Political Economy 84, 499–522.

Geweke, J., 1978, Testing the exogeneity specification in the complete dynamic simultaneous equation model, Journal of Econometrics 7, no. 2, 163–186.
Good, I.J., 1961/62, A causal calculus, I/II, British Journal of Philosophical Society 11, 305/12, 43–51.
Gordon, R.J., 1977, World inflation and monetary accommodation in eight countries, Brookings Papers on Economic Activity, Part 3, 409–478.
Granger, C.W.J., 1963, Economic processes involving feedback, Information and Control 6, 28–48.
Granger, C.W.J., 1969, Investigating causal relations by econometric models and cross-spectral methods, Econometrica 37, 424–438.
Granger, C.W.J., 1980, Generating mechanisms, models and causality, Paper presented to World Econometrics Congress, Aix-en-Provence, Sept. 1980.
Granger, C.W.J. and A. Andersen, 1978, An introduction to bilinear time series models (Vandenhoeck and Ruprecht, Göttingen).
Granger, C.W.J. and M. Hatanaka, 1964, Spectral analysis of economic time series (Princeton University Press, Princeton, NJ).
Granger, C.W.J. and P. Newbold, 1977, Forecasting economic time series (Academic Press, New York).
Hart, H.L.A. and A.M. Honoré, 1959, Causation in the law (Oxford University Press, Oxford).
Hosoya, Y., 1977, On the Granger condition for non-causality, Econometrica 45, no. 7, 1735–1736.
Mehra, Y.P., 1977, Money wages, prices and causality, Journal of Political Economy 85, Dec., 1227–1244.
Newbold, P., 1978, Feedback induced by measurement errors, International Economic Review 19, 787–791.
Overseth, O.E., 1967, Experiments in time reversal, Scientific American 221, Oct., 88–101.
Pierce, D.A., 1975, Forecasting in dynamic models with stochastic regression, Journal of Econometrics 3, 349–374.
Pierce, D.A. and L.D. Haugh, 1977, The assessment and detection of causality in temporal systems, Journal of Econometrics 5, 265–293.
Pierce, D.A. and L.D. Haugh, 1979, Comment on price, Journal of Econometrics 10, 257–260.
Price, J.M., 1979, A characterization of instantaneous causality: A correction, Journal of Econometrics 10, 253–256.
Sargent, T.F., 1976, A classical macroeconometric model for the U.S., Journal of Political Economy 84, 207–238.
Sims, C.A., 1972, Money, income and causality, American Economic Review 62, 540–552.
Sims, C.A., 1977, Exogeneity and causal ordering in macroeconomic models, in: New methods in business cycle research, Proceedings of a conference (Federal Reserve Bank, Minneapolis, MN).
Skoog, G.R., 1976, Causality characterizations: Bivariate, trivariate and multivariate propositions, Staff Report no. 14 (Federal Reserve Bank, Minneapolis, MN).
Suppes, P., 1979, A probabilistic theory of causality (North-Holland, Amsterdam).
Wiener, N., 1958, The theory of prediction, in: E.F. Bec, ed., Modern mathematics for engineers, Series 1, Ch. 8.
Williams, D., C.A.E. Goodhart and D.H. Gowland, 1976, Money, income and causality: The U.K. experience, American Economic Review 66, 417–423.
Wright, S., 1964, The interpretation of multivariate systems, in: O. Kempthorne et al., Statistics and mathematics in biology, Ch. 2 (Hafner, New York).
Zellner, A., 1978, Causality and econometrics, in: Proceedings of conference held at University of Rochester, NY, forthcoming.

[21]

The Impossibility of Causality Testing

By Roger K. Conway, P. A. V. B. Swamy, John F. Yanagida, and Peter von zur Muehlen*

Abstract

Causality tests developed by Sims and Granger are fatally flawed for several reasons. First, when two variables, X and Y, are uncorrelated, X has no *linear* predictive value for Y; but X and Y may be nonlinearly related unless they are statistically independent, in which case X and Y are not related at all. The right-hand side variables in a regression equation are exogenous if they are mean independent of the disturbance term. Mean independence is stronger than uncorrelatedness. The proofs for deriving causality-exogenity tests imply weaker results than statistical or mean independence. Second, transformations such as the Box-Cox transformation and Box-Jenkins stationarity-inducing transformations are not causality preserving. Third, counterexamples constructed by Price have invalidated the Pierce-Haugh theorem on instantaneous causality. Fourth, omission of other variables influencing those tested renders any test results spurious. Finally, causality tests are inconsistent because they are based on underidentified models. We provide a logically valid method of building models which does not use causality tests.

Keywords

Causality tests, statistical independence, mean independence, uncorrelatedness, orthogonality, covariance stationarity, stationarity-inducing transformations, economic laws

"Neglect by theorists evokes malpractice by empiricists."

Arthur S. Goldberger (*30*)[1]

Introduction

Numerous recent studies in the agricultural literature use or proselytize tests of causality originally developed by Sims (*58*).[2] The theoretical basis of this test is reproduced in Sargent (*54*, pp. 285-87). (For further discussion, see (*52*).) In an earlier study, Sargent (*53*) describes a causality test procedure, attributable to Granger (*26*) which is different from Sims' procedure. Both of these tests employ the following Granger (*26*) concept of causality: A time series (x_t) Granger causes another time series (y_t) if one can predict present y better by using past values of x than by not doing so. For example, in a given bivariate covariance stationary stochastic process (y_t, x_t) possessing a vector autoregressive representation, y fails to Granger cause x if and only if the coefficient matrices of the process are upper triangular. (We use the term, "Granger cause," to refer to causality in Granger's sense.) This result holds because the upper triangularity of coefficient matrices implies that y_t

*Conway is an economist with ERS; Swamy and von zur Muehlen are senior economists at the Federal Reserve Board, Washington, D.C., and Yanagida is an associate professor of agricultural economics at the University of Nevada at Reno. Views in this article are the authors' and do not reflect those of the Federal Reserve Board or the U.S. Department of Agriculture. The authors received valuable comments and help from Lorna Aldrich, James Barth, Michael Bradley, Richard Haidacher, Charles Hallahan, Arthur Havenner, Anil Kashyap, Nadine Loften, Thomas Lutton, Lloyd Teigen, Michael Weiss, and especially J. Michael Price. The authors are also grateful to David A. Pierce whose remarks are incorporated into this article.

[1] Italicized numbers in parentheses refer to items in the References at the end of this article.

[2] For example, see (*4, 5, 6, 8, 34, 39, 60, 67*).

can be expressed as a distributed lag of current and past x's (with no future x's) with a disturbance process denoted by u_t and that past y's do not help predict x_t, given past x's. However, the disturbance u_t is uncorrelated with past, present, and future x's for only one value of ρ in the regression $a_{yt} = \rho a_{xt} + \xi_t^{\rho}$ where (a_{yt}, a_{xt}) is the vector of innovations of the process (y_t, x_t). If the coefficient matrices are not triangular, then u_t is not uncorrelated with past, present, and future x's for any value of ρ. Because the value of ρ is usually unknown, for the disturbance u_t in the regression of y_t on current and past x's to be uncorrelated with past, present, and future x's, it is necessary, but not sufficient, that y fails to Granger cause x or that the coefficient matrices of the process (y_t, x_t) are upper triangular. The null hypothesis for Granger's causality test is that the coefficient matrices of the process (y_t, x_t) are upper triangular. This hypothesis can be equivalent to Sims' hypothesis that all the coefficients of future x's in the regression of y on past, present, and future x's are zero. Thus, Sims and Granger try to test a necessary condition for Granger noncausality. These tests were formerly associated predominantly with research in macroeconomics, which tests monetarist *versus* Keynesian assumptions about the causal ordering between money and income. They have recently been used in conjunction with rational expectations hypothesis testing.[3] Various studies using the same testing procedures have produced contradictory evidence on the relationship between money and income (see (*59*)). The conflict between the conclusions of such studies were indeed heightened when different forms of causality testing procedures were employed (see (*21*)). Subsequent Monte Carlo tests offered suggestive results indicating differences in the power of various causality tests and showing that one could easily produce conflicting conclusions by employing a battery of causality tests on the same data sets (see (*25, 38*)). However, these empirical and Monte Carlo results are only symptomatic. It is now clear that there are profound problems, both theoretical and empirical, with causality tests. This viewpoint is most emphatically stated by statisticians who object to the apparent carelessness with which some economists equate correlation with causality (see (*37*)). The purpose of our article is, therefore, to alert the agricultural profession to these problems and to allow agricultural researchers to better weigh the benefits and costs of utilizing these tests.

With that purpose in mind, we establish the following points:

1. The zero correlation between u_t and past, present, and future x's is necessary, but not sufficient, for x to be strictly econometrically exogenous with respect to y. The proofs of causality and exogeneity advanced by proponents are based on weaker concepts than statistical or mean independence.

2. There is no good discriminant between stationary and nonstationary processes. Sims and Granger are testing a necessary condition for Granger noncausality only within the framework of covariance stationary processes.

3. The observed time series is necessarily finite, and the covariance stationary stochastic processes are infinite in length. Distinguishing between different stationary processes on the basis of observed time series poses fundamental difficulty. Therefore, the power of Sims' or Granger's test does not go to 1 as the sample size goes to infinity.

4. Even if we know the transformations which induce stationarity, these transformations are not causality preserving. Therefore, the causality relationships (or the lack thereof) among the transformed variables tell us nothing about the causality relationships (or the lack thereof) among the original variables.

5. Zellner (*70*) proposed a general definition of causality attributed to Feigl, according to whom the concept of causation is defined in terms of predictability according to a law. Therefore, we address a fundamental question in economics: Are there laws in economics? After answering this question, we suggest a logically valid method of building econometric models which does not use causality tests.

[3] A key requirement of rational expectations observable reduced-form equations is that all right-hand side variables be at least orthogonal to the error term (see (*17, 18*)).

In subsequent sections, we define the various notions of Granger causality and contrast them with what statisticians call statistical or mean independence. We discuss problems of forming conditional operations based on linear models. We describe and critique the characterizations of Granger causality noted by Pierce and Haugh (*41*). We consider the causality tests as Sims proposed. We offer some general remarks on causality testing. Because we refer to laws in a philosophical definition of causation, we briefly discuss the meaning of the term "law" in economic contexts.

Correct Interpretations of Granger's Definitions of Causality

Before the causality literature can be carefully critiqued, we need to understand exactly what is meant by "causality" as posited by its proponents. Therefore, we review the various forms of Granger causality defined by Granger (*26*) and extended by Pierce and Haugh (*41*). A_t is assumed to represent a stationary stochastic vector process where:

$\bar{A}_t$ = the set of past values of A_t;

$\bar{\bar{A}}_t$ = the set of past and present values of A_t;

$\bar{A}_t(k)$ = the set $(A_{t-j}, j \geq k)$;

$E_t(A|B)$ = the optimal predictor of A_t, given some set of values of B_t;[4]

$e_t(A|B)$ = the prediction error = $A_t - E_t(A|B)$;

$Var(e_t)$ = $\sigma^2(A|B)$;

U_t = the set of all information in the universe accumulated since time t-1; and

$U_t - Y_t$ = all information in the universe apart from Y_t.

With this information, we can define the various forms of causality as follows:

1. Causality: If $\sigma^2(X|\bar{U}) < \sigma^2(X|\bar{U} - \bar{Y})$, then we say Y is Granger causing X, denoted by $Y_t \Rightarrow X_t$.

2. Feedback: There is feedback between X and Y, denoted by $X_t \Leftrightarrow Y_t$, if $Y_t \Rightarrow X_t$ and if $X_t \Rightarrow Y_t$

3. Instantaneous causality: Instantaneous causality occurs when $\sigma^2(X|\bar{U}, \bar{\bar{Y}}) < \sigma^2(X|\bar{U})$.

4. Causality lag: If $Y_t \Rightarrow X_t$, we then define the causality lag m as the lowest integer value of k so that the $\sigma^2(X|U - Y(k)) < \sigma^2(X|U - Y(k+1))$.

We now show that these definitions cannot be used to discover causality relationships without their posing some serious problems. Specifically, Granger's definitions require unequal and finite mean square errors in the series being compared. These conditions may not be satisfied in practice as may be clarified if one considers two simple polar cases. Deterministic variables or components can be predicted perfectly by their own past history with zero mean square error (see (*2*, p. 420)); hence, the mean square errors of the predictions of deterministic components do not satisfy the strict inequalities stated in Granger's definitions. This limitation, however, does not mean that there are no causality relationships among deterministic components. At the other extreme, when the mean square errors of the predictions of stochastic variables are infinite (a frequent occurrence in practice), Granger's definitions stated in terms of the strict inequalities between finite mean square errors of predictions do not apply. The fundamental problems associated with Granger's definitions will be clearer once we discuss the statistician's definitions and interpretations of statistical independence, mean independence, uncorrelatedness, and orthogonality.[5]

The variable Y is said to be statistically independent of the variable X if the conditional distribution of

[4] By use of a mean square error or quadratic loss criterion.

[5] Related to this discussion are three recent papers by Chamberlain (*15*), Florens and Mouchart (*22*), and Engle, Hendry, and Richard (*19*) also expressing certain limitations of Granger's and Sims' definitions of causality. We extend their work by explicitly contrasting various notions of Granger causality with the statistician's concept of statistical independence or mean independence.

Y, given X = x, is the same as the marginal distribution of Y; that is, $F(y|x) = F(y)$, in which case:

$$F(y,x) = F(y)\,F(x) \tag{1}$$

where $F(y,x)$ is the joint distribution of Y and X, and $F(x)$ and $F(y)$ are the marginal distributions of X and Y, respectively. Then the conditional distribution of X, given Y = y, denoted by $F(x|y)$, is equal to $F(x)$; that is, X is independent of Y. These two variables, Y and X, are said to be independent if equation (1) holds, including the case where $F(y)$ or $F(x)$ is zero. It is difficult to establish the existence of $F(y|x)$ or $F(x|y)$ in the general case. The conditional probability of a set $A \in B$ (a Borel field of sets), given X = x, can be exhibited as a conditional expectation if one chooses the random variable Y as the indicator function of the set A. Thus, $P(A|x) = E(Y|x)$, as may be verified from the definition of conditional probability as given by Rao (*48*, p. 90), for example. One should note that the Radon-Nikodym theorem establishes the existence of $P(A|x)$ almost everywhere with respect to $[dF(x)]$ as a function of x for fixed A only where the exceptional x-set may depend on A. As a result, it may not be possible to define $P(A|x)$ for all A over an x-set of probability 1, unless the union of exceptional sets is of probability zero. Thus, a conditional probability distribution of Y, given X = x, may not always exist (see (*48*, p. 98)).[6] The same is true of the conditional probability distribution of X, given Y = y. Because the existence of $F(y|x)$ does not imply the existence of $F(x|y)$, if $F(y|x) = F(y)$, it need not be true that $F(x|y) = F(x)$. Nonetheless, when equation (1) is true, X and Y are said to be independent regardless of whether $F(y|x)$ or $F(x|y)$ exists.

The intuitive idea of the phrase "Y is independent of X" is roughly that a knowledge of X does not help one to infer the value of Y. If Y and X are statistically independent, then there is no causal relationship between Y and X. When $F(\cdot)$ and $F(\cdot, \cdot)$ are absolutely continuous, the probability density functions exist and equation (1) can be expressed as:

$$f(y,x) = f(y)f(x) \tag{2}$$

where $f(\cdot)$ is a density function.

As Whittle (*68*, p. 101) points out, we must live with the idea that we may know E(Y) (or E(X)) only for certain Y (or X), or that, for a given random variable Y (or X), we may know EK(Y) (or EH(X)) only for certain K (or H). Similarly, for a given pair of random variables, Y and X, we may be able to assert the validity of the independence condition:

$$EH(X)K(Y) = EH(X)EK(Y) \tag{3}$$

where the functions H and K are such that $EH(X) < \infty$ and $EK(Y) < \infty$. In this case, Y and X have only partial degrees of independence because equation (1) implies equation (3), but the converse is not true. An extreme example of this is one where we can assert the validity of the independence condition (equation (3)) only when H and K are linear functions. This essentially means we know only that:

$$EXY = EXEY \tag{4}$$

where $EX < \infty$ and $EY < \infty$. Two random variables, X and Y, are said to be uncorrelated if and only if both have finite second moments and equation (4) is true (see (*16*, p. 102)). Consequently, equation (4) is equivalent to:

$$\mathrm{Cov}\,(X,Y) = 0 \tag{5}$$

provided $EX^2 < \infty$ and $EY^2 < \infty$. Random variables that satisfy equation (5) are said to be uncorrelated. In the special case when either EX = 0 or EY = 0, so that equation (4) becomes EXY = 0, the random variables are said to be mutually orthogonal. According to Whittle (*68*, p. 102), "the concept of lack of correlation or orthogonality is important, because it is the nearest one can come to the concept of independence if one is restricted to a knowledge of second moments [as in the case of covariance stationary processes]."

[6] If the sample space has only a countable number of points, then the conditional probability measure is always defined, provided $P(X = x) \neq 0$. Alternatively, if the sample space is the n-dimensional real Euclidean space, then the conditional probability measure exists because in this case the union of exceptional sets is of zero probability measure (*48*, pp. 98-99). Our subsequent discussion further clarifies this point.

Just as independence means that X has no predictive value for Y, lack of correlation means that X has no predictive value for Y *in the linear least squares sense* (see (*68*, p. 102)). That is, suppose we consider a predictor of Y which is linear in X, $Y = \alpha + \beta X + U$, and we choose α and β so as to minimize EU^2. One can then determine the optimal value of β by Cov(Y,X)/ Var(X). Thus, if case (5) is true, the variable X will receive a zero coefficient in the prediction formula for Y. When case (5) is true, X has no *linear* predictive value for Y, but X may be nonlinearly related unless equation (1) is true, in which case X and Y are not related at all.

A case intermediate between lack of correlation and independence is that in which equation (3) holds only for linear K, so that EH(X)Y = EYEH(X) for any H assuming $EH(X) < \infty$. The relation EH(X)Y = EYEH(X) is equivalent to $E(Y|x) = EY$ because $EH(X)Y = E(E[H(X)Y|X]) = E[H(X)E(Y|X)]$ for all H so that $EH(X)Y < \infty$ (see (*68*, p. 102)).[7] Here E(Y|x) is a function of x, say G(x), which minimizes $E[Y - G(x)]^2$, at least in the case where $EY^2 < \infty$ (see (*2*, pp. 417-24)). Following Goldberger (*31*), we may say that Y is *mean independent* of X if:

$$E(Y|x) = EY \tag{6}$$

Now equation (6) holds if and only if $E(Ye^{itX}) = EYEe^{itX}$ for all real t (see (*36*, p. 10)).

It is instructive to observe that without further conditions there is no connection among the concepts (1), (5), and (6). If EY exists, it follows from the Radon-Nikodym theorem that E(Y|x) exists (see Rao (*48*, pp. 96-97)). In this case, equation (1) implies equation (6), but the converse is not true. Similarly, if EX exists, then equation (1) implies the condition, E(X|y) = EX, but the converse is not true. Because the existence of EH(X) and EK(Y) is already assumed in condition (3), partial independence condition (3) implies the mean independence condition, E(Y|x) = EY or E(X|y) = EX, but the converse is not true. It is obvious that any pair of random variables, X and Y, which are fully independent in the sense of equation (1) and which have finite variances are also uncorrelated, although the converse is not true. When X and Y have finite variances, mean independence (6) implies uncorrelatedness (5), but the converse is not true. (In the normal case, conditions (1-6) are equivalent.)

Our discussion is important as, when Granger's definitions of causality are used, some researchers have confused these statistical concepts. For example, Sargent (*52*, pp. 404-05) says that X in the following equation:

$$Y_t = \sum_{j=0}^{\infty} h_j X_{t-j} + U_t \tag{7}$$

with $\sum_{j=0}^{\infty} |h_j| < \infty$, $EU_t = 0$, $EU_t^2 = \sigma_u^2$ for all t, and $EU_tU_s = 0$ for $t \neq s$, is econometrically exogenous with respect to Y_t if and only if $EU_tX_s = 0$ for *all* integers s and t. This definition runs counter to some textbook notions of exogeneity. For example, Theil (*65*, pp. 110-11) and Goldberger (*29*, pp. 380-81) have stated that X in equation (7) is econometrically exogenous with respect to Y if $E(U_t|X_s) = EU_t = 0$ for *all* integers s and t. This condition is stronger than Sargent's condition, as shown by the direction of the implication between equations (5) and (6).[8] Furthermore, in his statement about a stricter form of the natural rate hypothesis, Sargent (*53*, p. 215) incorrectly equates condition (1) with condition (6) by saying that the unemployment rate Un_t obeys the natural rate hypothesis if, in its univariate Wold representation (without a purely deterministic component):

$$Un_t = \sum_{j=0}^{\infty} a_j U_{t-j}, \quad \sum_{j=0}^{\infty} |a_j| < \infty \tag{8}$$

where the U's are serially uncorrelated with mean zero and finite variance, σ_u^2, the innovation U_t satisfies the condition:

$$E(U_t|\theta_{t-1}) = 0 \tag{9}$$

where θ_t is a vector of the set of all variables observed at time t thought potentially to contribute to predicting unemployment, so that the innovation in the unemployment rate is statistically independent of each component of θ_{t-1}. Here some elements of θ_t represent policy instruments. Another difficulty is that Sargent's time series methods

[7] One should note that when further expectation is taken, $E(Y|x) = E(Y|X = x)$ is replaced by $E(Y|X)$ (see (*48*, p. 97)).

[8] The direction of this implication has been recognized only recently by Hayashi and Sims (*33*).

based on non-Gaussian assumptions are only capable of examining the validity of the uncorrelatedness assumption between U_t and an element of θ_{t-1} but not the validity of the mean independence assumption (9) between these two variables.

Conditional Expectations and Econometric Modeling

Note that the existence of $E(Y|x)$ does not imply the existence of $E(X|y)$.[9] Necessary and sufficient conditions for the existence of the linear population regression function, $E(Y|x) = \alpha + \beta x$, and the constant conditional variance, $\mathrm{Var}(Y|x) = \sigma_0^2$, have been established by Rao (see (*36*, p. 11, lemma 1.1.3)). Generalized conditions covering the cases of several independent variables are given by Kagan, Linnik, and Rao (*36*), hereafter referred to as KLR. Because these conditions have far-reaching implications for causality tests, we state them here:

KLR's lemma (*36*): Let $\phi(t_0, t_2,..., t_K)$ be the characteristic function of the vector variable $(Y_t^*, X_{2t}^*,..., X_{Kt}^*) = (Y_t, X_{2t},..., X_{Kt}) - E(Y_t, X_{2t},..., X_{Kt})$. Then, for the relations $E(Y_t|x_{1t},..., x_{Kt}) = \sum_{k=1}^{K} \pi_k x_{kt}$ with $x_{1t} = 1$ and $\mathrm{Var}(Y_t|x_{1t},..., x_{Kt}) = \sigma_0^2$ = a positive constant ($t = 1, 2,..., T$) to hold, it is necessary and sufficient that for $t = 1, 2,..., T$:

$$D_0\phi(t_0, t_2,..., t_K)|_{t_0=0} = \sum_{k=2}^{K} \pi_k D_k\phi(0, t_2,..., t_K),$$

$$D_0^2\phi(t_0, t_2,..., t_K)|_{t_0=0} = -\sigma_0^2\phi(0, t_2,..., t_K) + \sum_{k=2}^{K} \sum_{k'=2}^{K} \pi_k \pi_{k'} D_k D_{k'}\phi(0, t_2,..., t_K) \qquad (10)$$

where the time subscript t should be distinguished from the real arguments of $\phi(\cdot)$, $D_k\,\phi(\cdot) = \partial\phi(\cdot)/\partial t_k$, $D_k^2\,\phi(\cdot) = \partial^2\phi(\cdot)/\partial t_k^2$ and $D_k D_{k'}\phi(\cdot) = \partial^2\phi(\cdot)/\partial t_k\,\partial t_{k'}$.

If $(Y_t, X_{2t},..., X_{Kt})$ is a multivariate normal, it is well-known that the conditional expectation and conditional variance of any of these variables, given the remaining variables, are respectively linear in and independent of the conditioning vector (see (*48*, p. 523)). Although sufficient for the existence of these conditional expectations and variances, multivariate normality is by no means necessary, as KLR's lemma shows.

KLR's lemma provides conditions for the existence of a linear reduced-form equation (or a linear population regression function) between an endogenous variable, Y, and a set of exogenous variables, $X_1,..., X_K$. In light of KLR's lemma, Granger's definitions of causality and Sargent's definition of exogeneity are clearly inadequate. The inequalities between predictive variances stated in Granger's definitions and the lack of correlation between the innovation (of a covariance-stationary, purely indeterministic and invertible process) and another variable (which follows a covariance-stationary, purely indeterministic and invertible process) stated in Sargent's definition are not sufficient for the existence of conditional expectations or linear population regression functions among the economic variables.

The foregoing discussion provides the background for criticizing an econometric practice. Goldberger (*29*, pp. 380-88) reviews the reduced-form, recursive-form, and structural-form approaches to specify the population regression equations of endogenous variables on exogenous or predetermined variables. As he indicated in 1964 (*29*, pp. 386-87), each structural equation is intended to represent some aspect of the behavior of an economic unit, such as an individual, a firm, a sector, or a market. That the structural-form approach is a natural one in economics is demonstrated repeatedly in the large body of empirical literature in which models are built up equation by equation and unit by unit (see (*65*, pp. 468-83)). If the structural model is linear, under certain conditions we can derive an explicit reduced-form model (see (*29*, pp. 297-98)). Otherwise, we can only assume—incorrectly perhaps—the existence of an appropriate reduced-form model (as in (*24*)). Without sufficient *a priori* restrictions, the structural-form parameters will not be identified in either linear or nonlinear cases.

It is vital to realize that, in the linear case, KLR's lemma points to a possible danger inherent in using

[9] Conditions for the existence of these conditional expectations are given in (*48*, pp. 96-97).

a priori restrictions on the structural parameters because they may contradict the conditions of KLR's lemma and thereby prevent the existence of (1) the population regression function between each endogenous variable and a set of exogenous variables and (2) the constant conditional variance of each endogenous variable, given the exogenous variables. Thus, because the π_k's are functions of the structural parameters (*29*, p. 298), the identifying restrictions on the structural parameters may imply that some of the π_k's are restricted so that the conditions of KLR's lemma are not true. To better understand this difficulty, let us consider a simultaneous equation model which, if linear, may be expressed in the general form:

$$Y\Gamma + XB = U \tag{11}$$

where Y is a TxL matrix of observations on L endogenous variables, Γ is a LxL matrix of coefficients, X is a TxK matrix of observations on K exogenous variables, B is a KxL matrix of coefficients, and U is a TxL matrix of disturbances. The elements of Γ and B are the structural coefficients (see (*65*, p. 440)).

Assuming that Γ is nonsingular, we can derive the reduced form as:

$$Y = X\Pi + V \tag{12}$$

where $\Pi = -B\Gamma^{-1}$ is the matrix of reduced-form coefficents and $V = U\Gamma^{-1}$ is the matrix of reduced-form disturbances. Equation (12) exists if the joint characteristic functions of each endogenous variable and all the exogenous variables satisfy the conditions of KLR's lemma. In this case, we can interpret XΠ as the conditional mean of Y, given X and the covariance matrix of V as the conditional covariance matrix of Y given X. Furthermore, the covariance matrix of V will be independent of X. The reduced-form matrix of coefficients, Π, will be identified if and only if X has full-column rank. The connection between structural and reduced-form coefficients can be written as:

$$\Pi\Gamma + B = 0$$

or:

$$WC = 0 \tag{13}$$

where $W = (\Pi, I_K)$ is the K x (K+L) matrix of rank K and $C = (\Gamma', B')'$ is the (K+L) x L matrix of structural coefficients. The ith equation of (13) may be written as:

$$W\underline{c}_i = 0 \tag{14}$$

where $\underline{c}_i$ is the ith column of C. Because this is a consistent system of equations, a general solution is:

$$\underline{c}_i = (I - W^- W)\underline{z}_i \tag{15}$$

where W^- is a generalized inverse of W and where $\underline{z}_i$ is arbitrary (see (*48*, p. 25)).

A priori restrictions may be exclusion restrictions stating that certain elements of $\underline{c}_i$ are zero because the variables to which they relate do not appear in the ith equation of the structural form (11), or they may be linear homogenous restrictions involving two or more of the elements of $\underline{c}_i$. In any case, *a priori* restrictions on the elements of Γ and B do not violate the conditions of KLR's lemma if they are consistent with the class of solutions in equation (15). The vector, $\underline{c}_i$, satisfying *a priori* identifying restrictions, should belong to the null space of W. Otherwise, *a priori* restrictions used to identify a structure may invalidate an interpretation of the right-hand side of each corresponding reduced-form equation (with the disturbance suppressed) as the conditional expectation of an endogenous variable, given the exogenous variables. Nonlinear structural models, incidentally, share this problem unless the identifying restrictions imposed on them are consistent with the following alternative sets of conditions which guarantee the existence of the nonlinear population regression functions of the form $E(Y_t|x_{1t},...,x_{Kt}) = g(x_{1t},...,x_{Kt}) = g(x_t)$ (*48*, pp. 96-99).

1. If F(y,x) is the joint distribution function of $(Y, X_1,..., X_K) = (Y,X)$, then the set function $\int_{R_1 xS} y dF(y,x)$, where R_1xS is the cylinder set in the (Y,X)-plane with base S in the X-plane and $S \epsilon B_k$ (a Borel field of sets), is absolutely continuous with respect to $\int_S dF(x)$. Furthermore, $EY_t < \infty$.

or:

2. The sample space for the variable $(Y, X_1,...,X_K)$ is the (K+1) - dimensional Euclidean space.

To elaborate on these conditions, we hold that if $EY_t = \infty$, then the (sufficient) conditions of the Radon-Nikodym theorem for the existence of $g(x_t)$ are not true. However, in many economic applications, the sample space is the n-dimensional Euclidean space, in which case the conditional expectation of Y (the indicator function of a set $A \epsilon B$, a Borel field of sets), given $X_t = x_t$, denoted by $P(A|x_t) = E(Y_t|x_t)$, is defined for all A over a x_t-set of probability 1 because the union of exceptional x_t-sets over which $P(A|x_t)$ is not defined is of zero probability measure. This finding does not mean that there are no problems if $EY_t = \infty$ whenever the sample space is the n-dimensional Euclidean space because even if $g(x_t)$ exists, it may not be consistent with the marginal distribution of x_t. Roughly speaking, $F(y_t|x_t)$ and $F(x_t)$ are *consistent* if they are the conditional and marginal distributions corresponding to some joint distribution of (Y_t, X_t). This hypothesis follows from Kolmogorov's consistency theorem which is stated in (*48*, p. 108). If this consistency condition is not met, then the probability laws fail. By not specifying $F(x_t)$, econometricians typically ignore this consistency problem.

Goldberger (*29*, p. 380) points out that, by formulating a model, econometricians attempt to characterize a joint conditional probability distribution of the endogenous variables conditional on the values of the exogenous variables using available *a priori* information. In view of the preceding discussion, this task may not be feasible because econometricians' *a priori* information may prevent interpretation of each reduced-form equation as a regression equation if the information violates the conditions under which such an interpretation is valid. Thus, econometricians cannot succeed if their *a priori* information on the structural parameters is incoherent in the sense that it is inconsistent with conditions permitting the existence of the expectation of each endogenous variable, conditional on the values of the exogenous variables. This point confirms the importance of de Finetti's and Savage's coherency condition that must always be imposed on *a priori* distributions. Furthermore, a structural model is logically invalid and the attractiveness of the structural-form approach mentioned by Goldberger (*29*, pp. 386-87) is illusory if *a priori* restrictions on structural parameters do not permit the interpretation of the corresponding reduced-form equations as the population regression equations. In light of a landmark paper by Boland (*10*, p. 506), who argues that a logically valid model is necessary before one can produce "true" empirical results, one must view this conclusion as a fundamental objection to current econometric practice.

Pierce-Haugh Characterizations of Causality

Coming full circle, we return to Granger's definitions of causality, which appeared in our initial investigation of the definitions of causality. Now that we have fully discussed the direction of the implications of full independence, partial independence, mean independence, uncorrelatedness, and orthogonality, as well as KLR's conditions for the existence of a linear regression and a constant conditional variance, we rigorously appraise works by Pierce and Haugh (*41*), Sims (*58*), and Sargent (*54*) based on Granger's definitions of causality.

In their survey article, Pierce and Haugh (*41*) developed characterizations of Granger causality, using the time series approach and certain assumptions. One of these assumptions is that there exist transformations $X_t = T_x X_t^*$ and $Y_t = T_y Y_t^*$ of the observable variables X_t^* and Y_t^* so that (X_t, Y_t) is a bivariate, nonsingular, linear covariance stationary, purely indeterministic time series and so that X_t and Y_t are causally related in the same way that X_t^* and Y_t^* are.

Very often, Pierce and Haugh argue, T_x and T_y will consist of first-difference or seasonal-difference operators because this type of transformation is frequently (presumed to be) necessary and sufficient to render the observed series stationary. Because such transformations are linear and because the optimal predictions in terms of which causality was defined by Granger are now also linear, each causality event is true of (X^*, Y^*) if and only if it is true of (X, Y). Moreover, Pierce and Haugh argue that certain nonlinear transformations of individual variables, such as logarithms or those of Box and Cox (*12*), are also causality-preserving in the above sense.

Such statements, offered as assertions, have no logical proofs verifying their truth. If they are false, a study of the relationship between the transformed variables will tell us nothing about the relationship between the untransformed variables in which we are interested. Indeed, counterexamples may be constructed to show that the transformations T_x and T_y are not causality-preserving. For example, if Y_t^* is a nonstationary process with infinite mean (as would occur if Y_t^* followed a random walk), it is possible that the first difference of this series, $Y_t = Y_t^* - Y_{t-1}^*$, is stationary with a finite mean and displays causality with X_t. Yet, because Y_t^* has no finite mean, the variance of the prediction of Y_t^* may be infinite, in which case Granger's definitions of causality cannot apply. One should also remember that the Pierce-Haugh criterion assumes covariance stationarity. However, this is a condition on only the first two moments. Statistical independence, as described earlier, is concerned with the *whole* distribution. The direction of the implications between equations (5) and (6) indicates that differencing and Box-Cox transformations are not causality-preserving.

Furthermore, certain recent papers point to serious problems with the Box-Cox transformation. In their book Box and Jenkins (*13*) argue that, given $Y_t = Y_t^*$, the transformation $Y_t^{(\lambda)} = [(Y_t^\lambda - 1)/\lambda]$ gives a covariance stationary process for some λ and, under normality conditions, one may consider the model:

$$\phi(B)\, \Delta^{d_1}\, \Delta_s^{d_2}\left(\frac{Y_t^\lambda - 1}{\lambda}\right) = \theta(B)a_t,$$

$$a_t \sim N(O, \sigma_a^2) \qquad (16)$$

where B is the backward shift operator, $\Delta = I - B$, $\Delta_s = I - B^s$, $d_1 > 0$, $d_2 > 0$, $\phi(B) = 1 - \phi_1 B - \phi_2 B^2 - ... - \phi_p B^p$, $\theta(B) = 1 - \theta_1 B - \theta_2 B^2 ... - \theta_q B^q$, and the roots of $\phi(z) = 0$ and $\theta(z) = 0$ lie outside the unit circle where z is a complex variable.

A paper by Poirier (*44*) elaborates on the Box-Cox transformation. First, equation (16) requires the condition that $Y_t > 0$. Thus, if $(Y_t + \mu) > 0$ for some $\mu > 0$, the Box-Cox transformation can always be made on $(Y_t + \mu)$. However, if μ is unknown, the maximum likelihood estimates of the parameters of equation (16) for $Y_t + \mu$ may not exist, and the effects of μ on estimating λ and orders p, q, d_1, and d_2 become unknown. The question then arises how to assess the causality relationship among the original variables in equation (16) when μ is unknown.

On a related matter, Poirier and Melino (*45*) have shown that $E(Y_t^{(\lambda)}) = \infty$ if $-1 \leqslant \lambda < 0$ and $\text{Var}(Y_t^{(\lambda)}) = \infty$ if $-2 \leqslant \lambda < 0$ for the normal Y_t. Their conclusion is important because the concept of Granger causality is not appropriate if $E(Y_t^{(\lambda)}) = \infty$.

When $\lambda \neq 0$, the density for Y_t corresponding to the normal density for $Y_t^{(\lambda)}$ will usually be that of a truncated normal and Box and Cox's likelihood function will be incorrect. Recognizing this problem, Amemiya and Powell (*1*) assumed that the untransformed variable followed a two-parameter gamma distribution and then studied the limiting behavior of the Box-Cox (incorrect) maximum likelihood estimator both for the identically and independently distributed (i.i.d.) case and the regression case. Although they acknowledge that their results were based on the assumption of the gamma distribution and thus might not be universally true, "they do point to the possible danger of using the Box-Cox method." Altogether, the weight of these various studies analyzing the properties of the Box-Cox transformation cast considerable doubt on its ability to transform two time series without distorting a causal relationship between them.[10]

In another section of their paper, Pierce and Haugh (*41*) developed a test for instantaneous causality. They argued that one can determine instantaneous causality by individually prewhitening the two series of interest, using linear one-sided filters and then by analyzing the contemporaneous cross-correlation of the two created innovation series. However, Price (*46*) has constructed two counterexamples to show that the existence of instantaneous causality is neither necessary nor sufficient for a nonzero contemporaneous cross-correlation. As Price (*46*, p. 256) states, "[t]his implies that a number of the [proofs] . . . presented by Pierce and Haugh . . . concerning the relationship between

[10] See (7) for a further discussion and other limitations.

the causal patterns of two time series and the restrictions on the cross-correlations of the corresponding 'whitened' series are either invalid or in need of further justification." Replying, Pierce and Haugh (*42*) conceded their earlier mistake, but maintained that the contemporaneous cross-correlation coefficient is a useful indicator of instantaneous causality when feedback from X to Y is not present. Their argument is unclear to us as no proof is given. Furthermore, in a recent paper, Evans and Wells (*20*) amend the set of equivalent and sufficient conditions under which Y does not cause X, provided by Pierce and Haugh (*41*).

In answer to Pierce and Haugh's statement that a nonlinear transformation such as autoregressive integrated moving average (ARIMA) modeling preserves causality relationships, an important paper by Schwert (*55*) uses three counterexamples to demonstrate that causal relationships among the innovations can be quite different in pattern and magnitude from the relationships among the original variables, depending upon the ARIMA models chosen to represent the variables. By implication, the Box-Jenkins methods are also not causality-preserving.

As Schwert (*55*, p. 81) points out, the use of estimates of the residuals from ARIMA models, necessitated by lack of observations on the true innovations, is analogous to an errors-in-variables approach which leads to another problem:

> If the original variables, Y_t and X_t, are measured with error, the measurement errors will generally have a different influence on the estimators of the relationship between the innovations than on the estimators of the relationship between the original variables. . . . Thus, if the original variables are measured with random errors, causality tests based on the estimated innovations series could fail to detect relationships that would be detected using the untransformed data.

There is certainly no pat procedure for choosing the proper specification of an ARIMA model. Box and Jenkins' method is, as honest practitioners readily acknowledge, "an art form." Pindyck and Rubinfeld (*43*, p. 473) state that "it is important to realize that the specification of an ARIMA model is an art, rather than a science," while Granger and Newbold (*28*, p. 107) affirm that "it remains the case that there does not exist a clearly defined procedure leading in any given situation to a unique identification." The basic problem is that the ARIMA models are not logically valid unless specific assumptions are true (see (*61*, p. 139)). As in the case of many assumptions, the truth of assumptions underlying ARIMA models cannot be determined *a priori*.

A related problem with Box and Jenkins' methods is that the sample autocorrelation function will not accurately reflect the properties of the population autocorrelation function (see (*47*, p. 331)). As a result, a researcher could easily misidentify some model as an ARIMA process.

One should stress that, however elaborate one's assumptions (or wishes), it is impossible to ascertain whether the time series sample (or some transform thereof) is from a covariance-stationary process because samples are finite and covariance-stationary processes are infinite in length. Thus, one may choose a sample that appears to be covariance-stationary, whereas a larger sample would show this not to be the case. In this regard, Tukey (*66*, p. 50) has proved that any "finite-extent function can arise, to an arbitrarily close approximation, as a sample from a process with any spectrum." One cannot distinguish among infinite-duration processes on the basis of a finite-length time series without making strong assumptions whose truth we do not know.

Finally, there is a logical problem with Box and Jenkins' method of determining the order q of the moving-average part of an ARIMA model. The moving-average process of finite order q has an autocorrelation function which is zero beyond the order q. It is incorrect to conclude from this that, given the jth autocorrelation coefficient, $\rho_j \neq 0$ for j = 1, 2,..., q and $\rho_j = 0$ for j > q, the process has a moving-average representation. The condition that a real valued series (Y_t) has a nonzero autocorrelation of order q and no nonzero autocorrelation of order greater than q is necessary, but *not* sufficient, for Y_t to have a moving average representation (see (*51*, lemma 1)). If one looks at a sample autocorrelation function, which happens to have a cutoff after lag q and concludes that a moving average model of order q is appropriate for the series, then one would be erroneously treating a necessary condition as if it were a sufficient condition.

Sims-Granger Causality Testing

Sims (*58*) proved two theorems (also described in Sargent's book (*54*)) that provide the basis for his causality test. Theorem 1 states: Let (X_t, Y_t) be a jointly-covariance-stationary-strictly-indeterministic-process with mean zero. Then (Y_t) fails to Granger cause (X_t) if and only if there exists a vector-moving-average-representation of the form:

$$\begin{bmatrix} X_t \\ Y_t \end{bmatrix} = \begin{bmatrix} C_{11}(B) & 0 \\ C_{21}(B) & C_{22}(B) \end{bmatrix} \begin{bmatrix} \epsilon_t \\ U_t \end{bmatrix} \qquad (17)$$

where ϵ_t and U_t are serially uncorrelated processes with means zero and $E\epsilon_t U_s = 0$ for all t and s. In addition, the one-step ahead prediction errors:

$$X_t - E(X_t | X_{t-1},..., Y_{t-1},...)$$

and:

$$Y_t - E(Y_t | Y_{t-1},..., X_{t-1},...) \qquad (18)$$

are each linear combinations of ϵ_t and U_t.

Theorem 2 of Sims states: Y_t can be expressed as a distributed lag of current and past X's (with no future X's) with a disturbance process that is orthogonal to past, present, and future X's if and only if Y does not Granger cause X. That is:

$$Y_t = \sum_{j=0}^{\infty} b_j X_{t-j} + A_t \qquad (19)$$

where $E(A_t X_s) = 0 \ \forall(t,s)$ if and only if Y does not Granger cause X.[11] Sims uses these theorems to develop a test of Granger causality. His method is to regress Y_t on all X's:

$$Y_t = (...X_{t+1}, X_t, X_{t-1},...) + V_t \qquad (20)$$

A researcher then tests the joint hypothesis that coefficients of all future X's are zero.

Our first comment on this test is that equation (17) is an infinite order process. In practice, one can only estimate a model of the form (20) with a finite number of independent variables. Unfortunately, truncation of lag and lead lengths of model (20) destroys the logical validity of the model in the sense described by Boland (*10*). Indeed, in view of Boland's (*11*, p. 85) demonstration that there is no valid *approximate modus ponens*, the conclusions given by a truncated model of the form (20) cannot be approximately true, even when the truncated model is approximately true.

Second, the procedure proposed by Sims is a test of only a necessary, but not a sufficient, condition for Granger noncausality. The reason is that the lower triangularity restriction on the coefficient matrix of equation (17) only implies the condition that the coefficients of the future values of X in equation (19) are zero. The restriction does not imply the condition that $E\epsilon_t U_s = 0$ for all t and s or $E(A_t X_s) = 0 \ \forall(t,s)$ (see (*52*)). Even if we reject a necessary condition for Granger noncausality on the basis of Sims' test, the probability that Granger noncausality is false is less than 1 because conclusions of statistical tests do not hold with probability 1. A statement claiming that Granger's causality holds with probability less than 1 is thus neither absolutely true nor absolutely false!

In large samples, the situation is even worse because the power of Sims' test does not go to 1 as the sample size goes to infinity (see (*52*, p. 407)). Behind Sargent's conclusion that Sims' test may fail to reject the hypothesis in infinite samples, even when it is false, is an identification problem corresponding to an infinite duration process (see (*61*, pp. 140-41)). Gabrielsen (*23*) presented an important proof that the existence of a consistent estimator $\hat{\theta}$ for a parameter θ is a sufficient condition for its identifiability. An equivalent statement is that identifiability is a necessary condition for consistency. If a parameter is not identifiable in a model, then it has no consistent estimator, and consistent tests of hypotheses about

[11] Recall that the condition $E(A_t X_s) = 0 \ \forall(t,s)$ does not imply that $E(A_t | X_s) = EA_t = 0$ which is required to show that X_t is econometrically exogenous with respect to Y_t (see the discussion after equation (7)).

the parameter do not exist. Therefore, without additional restrictions on the coefficients and the covariance between ϵ_t and U_t, the model (20) is not identified. Tukey (*66*, p. 50) adds that:

> the existence of such a difficult connection between observables and infinite-duration processes is, for me, a good reason to doubt the adequacy of a logical structure focused on infinite duration processes to guide the analysis of data.... We cannot know precisely what the spectrum is if we know only the finite-length process, even exactly. Our fate in the real world is worse, of course, since we cannot know even the finite-length process exactly.[12]

For further discussion on spectral estimation, see (*3*).

General Remarks on Causality Testing

A common problem with any of the causality tests described is that the simple bivariate models can obscure more subtle (and not so subtle) relationships involving other variables. When two events are the effects of a third event which is the cause of them, logicians describe the causal relationship between the two events as the "*fallacy of the common cause.*" This is a problem acknowledged by proponents such as Granger (*26*), Pierce (*40*), and Sims (*56*, *57*) and is analyzed by Jacobs, Leamer, and Ward (*35*) who show that "any specification error renders the causality tests uninterpretable." Not only can causality tests reject exogeneity when the variable is exogenous because of the identification problems mentioned above, it can also accept exogeneity when the variable is, in fact, endogenous.

The stationarity assumption used by Sims (*58*) and Sargent (*53*) is inappropriate for aggregate time series. This problem can be seen from Swamy, Barth, and Tinsley (*61*, pp. 133-36) who prove that aggregation over disparate micro relations can yield models with time-varying coefficients, a result that is not always appreciated in either time series or conventional econometric literature. As shown by Swamy and Tinsley (*63*), a time-varying parameter model can accommodate a great variety of nonstationary processes. Also related to this argument is the Lucas critique; namely, when structural parameters are not invariant under alternative policy regimes, the stationarity assumptions used by Sims and Sargent are not reasonable.

Some Thoughts on Causality and Related Topics

In a wide-ranging, yet cogent, essay on the nature of causation, Zellner (*70*) argues articulately about the inadequacy of Granger's definition of causality and the superiority of the philosophical definition of causality provided by Feigl for econometric work. According to Feigl, the concept of causation is defined in terms of *predictability according to a law* (or more properly, according to a set of laws) (see (*70*, p. 12)). The reason Zellner (*70*, p. 51) prefers Feigl's definition of causation to all the other definitions he considers is that departures from Feigl's definition have produced problems, while offering little in the way of dependable and convincing results. Zellner (*70*, p. 51) further points out that in establishing and using economic laws in econometrics one can have little doubt that economic theory, data, and other subject matter considerations, as well as econometric techniques including modern time series analysis, must all play a role.

Although we agree with Zellner's views, Blaug's statement (*9*, pp. 160-62) concerning economic laws also deserves some attention. In Blaug's view, the term "law" has gradually acquired an old-fashioned ring and economists now prefer to present their most cherished general statements as "theorems" rather than as "laws." He further says:

> At any rate, if by laws we mean well-corroborated, universal relations between events or classes of events deduced from independently tested initial conditions, few modern economists would claim that economics has so far produced more than one or two laws.

[12] Other papers by Jacobs, Leamer, and Ward (*35*), Engle, Hendry and Richard (*19*), and Buiter (*14*) have discussed this subject and suggested that there is a problem of testing for exogeneity. However, none has discussed the identification problem with any degree of comprehensiveness.

The statement is accompanied by the following illuminating footnote:

> Samuelson . . . remarks that years of experience have taught him how treacherous are economic "laws" in economic life: e.g. Bowley's Law of constant relative wage share; Long's Law of constant population participation in the labor force; Pareto's Law of unchangeable inequality of incomes; Denison's Law of constant private saving ratio; Colin Clark's Law of a 25 percent ceiling on government expenditure and taxation; Modigliani's Law of constant wealth-income ratio; Marx's Law of the falling rate of real wage and/or the falling rate of profit; Everybody's Law of a constant capital-output ratio. If these be Laws Mother Nature is a criminal by nature.

As indicated earlier, some econometric assumptions have become so dear that they have assumed a power nearly as compelling as law. Thus, if stationarity for the transformation of the variable Y_t in equation (16) (given some d_1, d_2 and λ), is taken to be a law, then Mother Nature must surely be a scofflaw.

In view of these statements, a more modest, but more realistic, approach might be to define causation in terms of "predictability according to a sufficient and logically consistent explanation or theory."[13] The qualification "sufficient and logically consistent" is added to indicate that, at the very minimum, real economic theories must be logically valid if they are to provide "true" explanations of real economic phenomena. This requirement holds even though the logical validity of any explanation does not imply its truth. Nevertheless, consistency of knowledge plays a major role in how one explains the world; the *truth* of knowledge is much more difficult to ascertain (see (*10*)). A modest research program then becomes: if all the predictions of a logically valid theory pass a conventional test (of observation), then we may say without contradiction that the theory is so far confirmed.

Swamy, Barth, and Tinsley (*61*, pp. 131-36) make serious efforts to exploit economic theories in empirical research by using a minimal set of auxiliary assumptions and coherent prior information. In their expectations model, offered as an alternative to rational expectations, subjective probabilities are not carelessly equated to "objective probabilities" and all regression coefficients are allowed to vary over time as a concession to Samuelson's ironic list of so-called laws. We sometimes prefer the above model because (1) it avoids Box and Jenkins', Pierce and Haugh's, and Sims and Sargent's stationarity assumptions or stationarity-inducing transformations and (2) it is not forced to rely on econometric assumptions about *a priori* structural parameter information that may contradict necessary and sufficient conditions for the existence of the conditional expectations of endogenous variables, given the exogenous variables. Furthermore, deviating from usual practice, the model does not confine all uncertainty to the intercept term, but allocates it over all coefficients in each equation. Because the model is less restrictive, this procedure of first distributing uncertainty to all coefficients and then of letting data determine the major channels of uncertainty is less objectionable than the conventional procedure which first arbitrarily allocates all uncertainty to the intercept term and then forces the data to satisfy this restriction (see (*49*) for a survey of initial efforts in this research program and also (*50*, *63*, *64*) for some of the latest theoretical and empirical results).

In the above model, the conditions for logical validity are weaker than those which derive ARIMA and conventional econometric models. Because the problem of induction is unsolved logical validity requires that the truth of one's premises or assumptions must be assumed.[14] Under these circumstances, it is prudent to work with a minimal set of assumptions. How compelling the above advice is depends, of course, on the purpose of a model. If forecasting future events is the single object of a modeling endeavor, then predictive success is a sufficient argument in favor of the model. This view of the *role* of

[13] Perhaps by "law" Zellner (*70*) meant a "sufficient and logically consistent explanation or theory."

[14] For a demonstration that causality proponents have fallen into the trap of attempting to solve the well-known "problem of induction," see (*62*).

models is called "instrumentalism" (see *10*, p. 508)). In this case, *a priori* truth of the assumptions is not required *if* it is already known that the predictions are true or acceptable by some conventional criterion (see (*10*, p. 509)). In contrast, those economists who see the object of science as finding the *one* true theory of the economy will find their task difficult, if not impossible. On the surface, instrumentalism offers a valid guide for scientific investigation. It is unfortunate that no single model predicts all variables better than all other models for all time periods. This predictive criterion must eventually exhaust itself. Because it is impossible to foretell the time of failure, we cannot even pick a model based on instrumentalism. However, we can reject models on the grounds of logical invalidity, as we did in the preceding sections.

Given the difficulty of choosing among logically valid models, the principle of parsimony has sometimes been invoked as a tempting guide. The imposition of certain restrictions on the time-varying parameter models can lead to conventional regression models with heteroscedastic or serially correlated error terms (or the ARIMA models) (see (*63*, pp. 107-08)). Although these restrictions produce substantial economies in parameterizing a model, such economies are not without cost. Despite its tempting name, the principle of parsimony—preferring restricted specifications to more complex modeling whenever the performance of the former in prediction is *almost as good* as that of the latter—has little justification unless the conventional or ARIMA models perform *at least as well* as some more general model, for example, the alternative expectations model proposed by Swamy, Barth, and Tinsley (*61*).

The conventional models, including ARIMA models, exhibit episodic breakdowns and perform poorly in prediction. The usual practice is to repair such models by extensive respecification or, more often in the shorter run, with judgmental "add factors," dummy variables, and "ratchet" arguments. Following Lakatos (see (*9*, p. 36)), we may call this research practice "degenerating" because it involves endlessly adding *ad hoc* adjustments that merely accommodate whatever new facts become available. A positive contribution is possible only if the scientific research program is *theoretically progressive*—that is, if a successive formulation of the program contains "excess empirical content" over its predecessor, that is, the program predicts "some novel, hitherto unexpected fact" or if the program is *empirically progressive*—that is, if "this excess empirical content is corroborated." The limited evidence presented by Havenner and Swamy (*32*), Resler, Barth, Swamy, and Davis (*50*), and Swamy, Tinsley, and Moore (*64*) appears to favor the claim that the time-varying coefficient models facilitate progressive scientific research programs. Just as the philosophy of instrumentalism does not permit us to call one of the existing models the best predictor of all variables for all time periods, so the principle of parsimony does not permit us to call one model the best.

Time-varying coefficient models such as those Swamy and Tinsley (*63*) propose may be too complex to be useful. Indeed, Popper has argued that theoretical simplicity may be equated to the degree to which a theory can be falsified, in the sense that the simpler the theory, the stricter its observable implications and, hence, the greater its testability. It is because simpler theories have these properties that we aim for simplicity in science. But this principle is not universally agreed upon. Thus, Blaug (*9*, p. 25) casts his doubts about Popper's notion of simplicity as follows:

> It is doubtful that this is a convincing argument, since the very notion of simplicity of a theory is itself highly conditioned by the historical perspective of scientists. More than one historian of science has noted that the elegant simplicity of Newton's theory of gravitation, which so impressed nineteenth-century thinkers, did not particularly strike seventeenth-century contemporaries, and if modern quantum mechanics and relatively theory are true, it must be conceded that they are not very simple theories. Attempts to define precisely what is meant by a simpler theory have so far failed . . . , and Oscar Wilde may have been right when he quipped that the truth is rarely pure and never simple.

One of these statements is accompanied by the following footnote:

> As Polanyi . . . has observed, "great theories are rarely simple in the ordinary sense of the term. Both quantum mechanics and relativity theory are very difficult to understand; it takes only a few minutes to memorize the facts accounted for by relativity, but years of study may not suffice to master the theory and to see these facts in its context."

Conclusions

The term, "causality," as used by Granger and his followers, has been erroneously identified with feedback or dependence and loosely with correlation (see (*71*, p. 313)). We have contrasted this new usage with traditional approaches proposed by scientific philosophers and surveyed by Zellner (*70*). By every acceptable norm, the latter approach may still offer sharper views on the definition of causation. There is evidence (see (*71*, p. 313)) that Granger himself has altered his views since his initial article. Granger now argues: "Provided I define what I personally mean by causation, I can use the term" (*27*, pp. 333 and 337). What Granger means by causality is that knowledge of Y_t increases one's ability to forecast X_{t+1} in a least squares sense. Truth, like beauty, may be in the eyes of the beholder, but it is still fair to insist that the purpose of language is to communicate and clarify. Perhaps much of the confusion surrounding the interpretation of causality tests would not have arisen if such tests had instead been labeled "tests of relative predictive efficiencies" or some other neutral terms suggested by Schwert (*55*, p.82).

More important, the difficulty with using Granger's causality definitions, even as a measure of relative forecasting efficiency, is that the same relationship may not continue into the forecast period. There is indeed every reason to believe that such a relationship will change. One may support this belief by contemplating the numerous structural upheavals of the seventies as well as the implication of Lucas' critique suggesting that individual behavior (and hence structural coefficients) will change when policy rules change.

Zellner (*70*) recommends using Feigl's definition of causation, which we respectfully modify to read," predictability according to a sufficient and logically consistent theory." This modification is necessary because contemporary economists prefer to present their most cherished general statements as theorems rather than as laws.

Causality tests were created with the best of intentions, but one must be careful never to ask more of the data than they can deliver. It is unfortunate that these tests seem to ask for more. However, if one can find a way to avoid the contradictions between the *a priori* restrictions on the structural parameters and the conditions of KLR's lemma and if these restrictions are overidentifying, then one can invoke Wu's procedures (*69*) to examine the significance of the covariances between independent variables and the disturbances (provided we have an identifiable maintained hypothesis).[15] Unlike causality tests, Wu's procedures adhere to a law of large numbers; the powers of his tests, therefore, equal 1 in sufficiently large samples.

Where, then, is the econometrician left in devising a modeling strategy to determine causality? Zellner's fundamental argument is that the soundness of our conclusion about causality is ultimately based on the soundness of economic theory to determine causality. In our view, this advice is wise, and in the spirit of Zellner's theme, we end with a revealing conversation between Fisher and Cochran, which Zellner quotes (*72*, p. 13):

> About 20 years ago, when asked in a meeting what can be done in observational studies to clarify the step from association to causation, Sir Ronald Fisher replied: "Make your theories elaborate." The reply puzzled me at first, since by Occam's razor the advice usually given is to make theories as simple as is consistent with known data. What Sir Ronald meant, as the subsequent discussion showed, was that when constructing a causal hypothesis one should envisage as many *different* consequences of its truth as possible, and plan observational studies to discover whether each of these consequences is found to hold.

[15] Our earlier discussion indicates that in the normal case uncorrelatedness is equivalent to mean independence.

References

(1) Amemiya, T., and J. L. Powell. "A Comparison of the Box-Cox Maximum Likelihood Estimator and the Non-Linear Two-Stage Least Squares Estimator," *Journal of Econometrics*, Vol. 17, Dec. 1981, pp. 351-81.

(2) Anderson, T. W. *The Statistical Analysis of Time Series.* New York: John Wiley & Sons, 1971.

(3) Barth, J. R., and J. T. Bennett. "Cyclical Behavior Seasonality, and Trend in Economic Time Series," *Nebraska Journal of Economics and Business*, Vol. 13, No. 1, Winter 1974, pp. 48-69.

(4) Belongia, M., and D. A. Dickey. "Prefiltering and Causality Tests," *Agricultural Economics Research*, Vol. 34, No. 4, Oct. 1982, pp. 10-14.

(5) Bessler, D. A., and J. A. Brandt. "Causality Tests in Livestock Markets," *American Journal of Agricultural Economics*, Vol. 64, No. 1, Feb. 1982, pp. 140-44.

(6) Bessler, D. A., and L. F. Schrader. "Measuring, Leads and Lags Among Prices: Turkey Products," *Agricultural Economics Research*, Vol. 32, No. 1, Jan. 1980, pp. 1-7.

(7) Bickell, P. J., and K. A. Doksum. "An Analysis of Transformation Revisited," *Journal of the American Statistical Association*, Vol. 374, No. 3, June 1981, pp. 296-311.

(8) Bishop, R. V. "The Construction and Use of Causality Tests," *Agricultural Economics Research*, Vol. 31, No. 4, Oct. 1979, pp. 1-6.

(9) Blaug, M. *The Methodology of Economics.* New York: Cambridge Univ. Press, 1980.

(10) Boland, L. A. "A Critique of Friedman's Critics," *Journal of Economic Literature*, Vol. 17, No. 2, June 1979, pp. 503-22.

(11) Boland, L. A. "Satisficing in Methodology: A Reply," *Journal of Economic Literature*, Vol. 19, No. 1, Mar. 1981, pp. 84-86.

(12) Box, G. E. P., and D. R. Cox. "An Analysis of Transformations," *Journal of the Royal Statistical Society*, Series B, Vol. 26, 1964, pp. 211-52.

(13) Box, G. E. P., and G. M. Jenkins. *Time-Series Analysis: Forecasting and Control.* 2nd ed. San Francisco: Holden-Day, 1976.

(14) Buiter, W. "Granger-Causality and Stabilization Policy." NBER Technical Working Paper No. 10. 1981.

(15) Chamberlain, G. "The General Equivalence of Granger and Sims Causality," *Econometrica*, Vol. 50, No. 3, May 1982, pp. 569-82.

(16) Chung, K. L. *A Course in Probability Theory.* 2nd ed. New York: Academic Press, 1974.

(17) Conway, R. K., and J. R. Barth. "New Developments in Macroeconomic Theory: A Prospectus and Appraisal," *Agricultural Economics Research*, Vol. 35, No. 3, July 1982, pp. 23-29.

(18) Conway, R. K., and E. G. Fryar, Jr. "Rational Expectations in Agricultural Economics Research and Policy Analysis: Some Pitfalls." Univ. of Arkansas Agricultural Economics Staff Report. 1983.

(19) Engle, R. F., D. F. Hendry, and J. F. Richard. "Exogeneity," *Econometrica*, Vol. 51, No. 2, Mar. 1983, pp. 277-304.

(20) Evans, L., and G. Wells. "Pierce and Haugh on Characterizations of Causality: A Re-examination," *Journal of Econometrics*, Vol. 23, No. 3, Dec. 1983, pp. 331-36.

(21) Feige, E., and D. K. Pearce. "The Casual Causal Relationship Between Money and Income: Some Caveats for Time Series Analysis," *Review of Economics and Statistics*, Vol. 61, No. 4, Nov. 1979, pp. 521-33.

(22) Florens, J. P., and M. Mouchart. "A Note on Noncausality," *Econometrica*, Vol. 50, No. 3, May 1982, pp. 583-92.

(23) Gabrielsen, A. "Consistency and Identifiability," *Journal of Econometrics*, Vol. 8, No. 2, Oct. 1978, pp. 261-64.

(24) Gallant, A. R., and A. Holly. "Statistical Inference in An Implicit, Non-Linear, Simultaneous Equation Model in the Context of Maximum Likelihood Estimation," *Econometrica*, Vol. 48, No. 3, Apr. 1980, pp. 697-720.

(25) Geweke, J., R. Meese, and W. Dent. "Comparing Alternative Tests of Causality in Temporal Systems: Analytic Results and Experimental Evidence," *Journal of Econometrics*, Vol. 21, No. 3, Feb. 1983, pp. 161-94.

(26) Granger, C. W. J. "Investigating Causal Relations by Econometric Models and Cross-Spectral Methods," *Econometrica*, Vol. 37, No. 3, July 1969, pp. 424-38.

(27) ________. "Testing for Causality: A Personal Viewpoint," *Journal of Economic Dynamics and Control*, Vol. 2, No. 4, Nov. 1980, pp. 329-52.

(28) ________, and P. Newbold. *Forecasting Economic Time Series.* New York: Academic Press, 1977.

(29) Goldberger, A. S. *Econometric Theory.* New York: John Wiley & Sons, 1964.

(30) ________. "Structural Equation Methods in the Social Sciences," *Econometrica*, Vol. 40, No. 6, Nov. 1972, pp. 979-1002.

(31) ________. *Topics in Regression Analysis.* New York: The Macmillan Company, 1968.

(32) Havenner, A., and P. A. V. B. Swamy. "A Random Coefficient Approach to Seasonal Adjustment of Economic Time Series," *Journal of Econometrics*, Vol. 15, No. 2, Feb. 1981, pp. 177-209.

(33) Hayashi, F., and C. A. Sims. "Nearly Efficient Estimation of Time Series Models with Predetermined, But Not Exogenous, Instruments," *Econometrica*, Vol. 51, No. 3, May 1983, pp. 783-98.

(34) Heien, D. M. "Markup Pricing in a Dynamic Model of the Food Industry," *American Journal of Agricultural Economics*, Vol. 62, No. 1, Feb. 1980, pp. 10-18.

(35) Jacobs, R. L., E. E. Leamer, and M. P. Ward. "Difficulties with Testing for Causation," *Economic Inquiry*, Vol. 17, July 1979, pp. 401-13.

(36) Kagan, A. M., Y. V. Linnik, and C. R. Rao. *Characterization Problems in Mathematical Statistics.* New York: John Wiley & Sons, 1973.

(37) Ling, R. F. "Review of Correlation and Causation by David A. Kenny," *Journal of the American Statistical Association*, Vol. 77, No. 378, June 1982, pp. 488-91.

(38) Nelson, C. R., and G. W. Schwert. "Tests for Predictive Relationships Between Time Series Variables: A Monte Carlo Investigation," *Journal of the American Statistical Association*, Vol. 377, No. 1, Mar. 1982, pp. 11-18.

(39) Phipps, T. "Farmland Prices and the Return to Land: An Application of Causality Testing." Paper presented at American Agricultural Economics Association Meetings, Logan, Utah, 1982.

(40) Pierce, D. A. "Relationships—and the lack thereof—Between Economic Time Series, with Special Reference to Money and Interest Rates," *Journal of the American Statistical Association*, Vol. 72, No. 357, Mar. 1972, pp. 11-21.

(41) ________, and L. D. Haugh. "Causality in Temporal Systems: Characterizations and a Survey," *Journal of Econometrics*, Vol. 5, No. 3, May 1977, pp. 265-95.

(42) ________. "The Characterization of Instantaneous Causality: A Comment," *Journal of Econometrics*, Vol. 10, No. 2, June 1979, pp. 257-59.

(43) Pindyck, R. S., and D. L. Rubinfeld. *Econometric Models and Economic Forecasts.* New York: McGraw-Hill Book Company, 1976.

(44) Poirier, D. J. "Experience with Using the Box-Cox Transformation when Forecasting Economic Time Series—A Comment," *Journal of Econometrics*, Vol. 14, No. 2, Oct. 1980, pp. 277-80.

(45) ________, and A. Melino. "A Note on the Interpretation of Regression Coefficients Within a Class of Truncated Distributions," *Econometrica*, Vol. 46, No. 5, Sept. 1978, pp. 1207-09.

(46) Price, J. M. "The Characterization of Instantaneous Causality: A Correction," *Journal of Econometrics*, Vol. 10, No. 2, June 1979, pp. 253-6.

(47) Priestley, M. B. *Spectral Analysis and Time Series.* New York: Academic Press, 1983.

(48) Rao, C. R. *Linear Statistical Inference and Its Applications.* 2nd ed. New York: John Wiley & Sons, 1973.

(49) Rausser, G. C., Y. Mundlak, and S. R. Johnson. "Structural Change, Parameter Variation and Forecasting," *New Directions in Econometric Modeling and Forecasting in U.S. Agriculture* (ed. G. C. Rausser). New York: American Elsevier Publishing Co., 1983.

(50) Resler, D. H., J. R. Barth, P. A. V. B. Swamy, and W. D. Davis. "Detecting and Estimating Changing Economic Relationships: The Case of Discount Window Borrowings." Special Studies Paper 105. Washington, D.C.: Federal Reserve Board, 1982.

(51) Rose, D. E. "Forecasting Aggregates of Independent ARIMA Processes," *Journal of Econometrics*, Vol. 5, No. 3, May 1977, pp. 323-46.

(52) Sargent, T. J. "Causality, Exogeneity, and Natural Rate Models: Reply to C. R. Nelson and B. T. McCallum," *Journal of Political Economy*, Vol. 87, 1979, pp. 403-09.

(53) ________. "A Classicial Macroeconometric Model for the United States," *Journal of Political Economy*, Vol. 84, No. 2, Apr. 1976, pp. 207-37.

(54) ________. *Macroeconomic Theory.* New York: Academic Press, 1979.

(55) Schwert, G. W. "Tests of Causality: The Message in the Innovations," *Carnegie-Rochester Conference Series on Public Policy*, Vol. 10 (ed. Karl Brunner and Allan H. Meltzer). Supplement to *Journal of Monetary Economics.* Amsterdam: North-Holland Publishing Company, 1979, pp. 55-96.

(56) Sims, C. A. "Exogeneity and Causal Ordering in Macroeconomic Models," *New Methods in Business Cycle Research: Proceedings from a Conference* (ed. C. A. Sims). Minneapolis: Federal Reserve Bank of Minneapolis, 1977, pp. 23-43.

(57) ________. "Macroeconomics and Reality" *Econometrica*, Vol. 48, No. 1, Jan. 1980, pp. 1-49.

(58) ________. "Money, Income, and Causality" *American Economic Review*, Vol. 62, No. 4, Sept. 1972, p. 540-52.

(59) Slaugh, J. R. "Granger-Sims Causality: A Brief Survey of Its Use and Misuse." Unpublished manuscript. National Science Foundation, 1981.

(60) Spreen, T. H., and J. S. Shonkwiler. "Causal Relationships in the Fed Cattle Market," *Southern Journal of Agricultural Economics*, Vol. 13, No. 1, July 1981, pp. 149-53.

(61) Swamy, P. A. V. B., J. R. Barth, and P. A. Tinsley. "The Rational Expectations Approach to Economic Modelling," *Journal of Economic Dynamics and Control*, Vol. 4, No. 2, May 1982, pp. 125-47.

(62) Swamy, P. A. V. B., R. K. Conway, and P. von zur Muehlen. "The Foundations of Econometrics—Are There Any?" Special Studies Paper 182. Washington, D.C.: Federal Reserve Board, 1984.

(63) Swamy, P. A. V. B., and P. A. Tinsley. "Linear Prediction and Estimation Methods for Regression Models with Stationary Stochastic Coefficients," *Journal of Econometrics*, Vol. 12, No. 2, Feb. 1980, pp. 103-42.

(64) ________ , and G. Moore. "An Autopsy of a Conventional Macroeconomic Relation: The Case of Money Demand." Special Studies Paper 167. Washington, D.C.: Federal Reserve Board, 1982.

(65) Theil, H. *Principles of Econometrics.* New York: John Wiley & Sons, 1971.

(66) Tukey, J. W. "Comments on Seasonality: Causation, Interpretation, and Implications by C. W. J. Granger," *Seasonal Analysis of Economic Time Series* (ed. A. Zellner). U.S. Department of Commerce, Bureau of the Census, 1978, pp. 50-53.

(67) Ward, R. W. "Asymmetry in Retail, Wholesale, and Shipping Point Pricing for Fresh Vegetables," *American Journal of Agricultural Economics*, Vol. 64, No. 2, May 1982, pp. 205-12.

(68) Whittle, P. *Probability.* New York: John Wiley & Sons, 1976.

(69) Wu, D. M. "Alternative Tests of Independence Between Stochastic Regressors and Disturbances," *Econometrica*, Vol. 41, No. 3, July 1973, pp. 733-50.

(70) Zellner, A. "Causality and Econometrics," *Carnegie-Rochester Conference Series on Public Policy.* Vol. 10 (ed. Karl Brunner and Allan H. Meltzer). Supplement to *Journal of Monetary Economics.* Amsterdam: North-Holland Publishing Company, 1979.

(71) ________ . "Comment," *Journal of the American Statistical Association*, Vol. 77, No. 378, June 1982, pp. 313-14.

(72) ________ . *An Introduction to Bayesian Inference in Econometrics.* New York: John Wiley & Sons, 1971.

[22]

Journal of Econometrics 39 (1988) 7–21. North-Holland

CAUSALITY AND CAUSAL LAWS IN ECONOMICS*

Arnold ZELLNER

University of Chicago, Chicago, IL 60637, USA

After recognizing the wide-spread use and importance of concepts of causality and causal laws, Feigl's definition of causality is discussed. Several research approaches employed in efforts to produce causal laws in economics are considered. A preferred approach is indicated and discussed. Its use in a famous economic study is described. In conclusion, it is suggested that further use of the preferred research approach will be very helpful in efforts to produce more causal laws in economics.

1. Introduction

Many scientific workers use the concept of causality in their work, as indicated in Stigler (1949, p. 3), Simon (1953) and others. Since the concept is widely used, it is important to have a fruitful and operational definition of it. In Zellner (1979, 1984), I discussed many aspects of Feigl's (1953) definition of causality and Nelson (1979) and Sims (1979) provided thoughtful comments on my discussion. Feigl's (1953, p. 408) definition, 'predictability according to a law or set of laws', was put forward to summarize philosophers' past work on the definition of causality. See also Conway et al. (1984) and several of the papers in this issue for additional discussion of the Feigl definition. Further, there is no doubt but that establishing causality exists with a high degree of confidence, for example establishing that smoking causes cancer, is a very important matter, scientifically and practically. That is, causal laws are very useful in explaining past data and experience and in providing reliable predictions of as yet unobserved data and experience, be they the results of controlled or uncontrolled changes in initial conditions. Since these considerations are of utmost importance for the further development of economic science, the main thrusts of the present paper will be the presentation of additional clarifying thoughts on the definition and verification of causality and on how causal laws are produced with the hope that a more complete understanding of these issues will be helpful in guiding research to produce more causal laws in economics.

*Research financed in part by the National Science Foundation and in part by the H.G.B. Alexander Endowment Fund, Graduate School of Business, University of Chicago.

The plan of the paper is as follows. In section 2, selected aspects of Feigl's definition of causality and causal laws will be discussed to clarify points about them which are relevant for material presented in following sections. Section 3 briefly describes and critiques several approaches which have been put forward to produce causal laws in economics. In section 4, a particular study is considered which illustrates what the author believes is a very fruitful approach to the production of causal laws in economics. Section 5 presents a summary and some concluding remarks.

2. Discussion of causality and causal laws

In this section, further discussion of Feigl's definition of causality and of causal laws will be provided. Feigl's simple and sophisticatedly deep definition of causality is 'predictability according to a law or set of laws'. This definition is such that it is applicable in all areas of science including economics. Note that predictability means confirmed predictability not merely potential predictability. More will be said below about confirmation procedures. Further, the definition does not place any severe restrictions on the forms of laws. The laws may be deterministic or stochastic, qualitative or quantitative, micro or macro and involve simultaneous and/or non-simultaneous relations, discrete or continuous time, contiguous and/or non-contiguous effects, controlled and/or non-controlled effects, and chronologically and/or non-chronologically ordered effects. Simply put, the definition does not place any *a priori* restrictions on the forms of laws other than the mild restrictions that their structure not involve logical or mathematical contradictions and that they be capable of yielding explanations of past data and verifiable predictions of as yet unobserved data. These requirements are in agreement with Jeffreys' (1967, p. 8) rules for induction.

In Zellner (1979, 1984), Jeffreys' rules were related to issues in the previous literature on causality. Also, in Conway et al. (1984) and Swamy and von zur Muehlen's paper in the present issue, attention is given to inductive procedures used in previous analyses which violate Jeffreys' rules 1 and 2 involving the requirement of logical consistency. Such violations render these inductive procedures scientifically unacceptable. Simply put, an analysis or theory that involves logical and/or mathematical inconsistencies is not acceptable as a scientific explanation of observed phenomena. In addition to the restriction of logical and mathematical consistency, the forms of laws must be such that they are capable of explaining past data and experience and yield verifiable predictions of future data and experience. In economics, some theories are put forward which explain no past data and yield no verifiable predictions. Such 'theories' cannot achieve the status of laws because they do not meet the requirements that a law must actually explain past data and experience and actually perform well in prediction. Further, empirical regularities, for example the observed constancy of labor's share or of the long-run average propensity to save, etc., while very interesting and valuable, are obviously not laws in the sense described above. Similarly, mechanical statistical regressions or autoregressions, be they univariate or multivariate, no matter how successful they are in forecasting, are not causal laws since they generally do not provide understanding and explanation and often involve confusing association or correlation with causality. Subject matter theory and principles are needed to provide understanding and explanation as recognized by many in age-old discussions of correlation and causality. Finally, logically consistent and sufficient mathematical economic theorems do not qualify to be termed laws unless it can be shown that they actually explain a wide range of past data and experience and yield good predictions over a broad range of data and experience.

The requirement that a law *actually* perform well in explanation and prediction over a broad range of conditions cannot be emphasized too strongly. For example, this requirement rules out theories based on impossible experiments or on data that can never be produced. Little confidence would be accorded to a predictive conclusion if it related to the results of an impossible experiment or an impossible set of conditions. Perhaps the best that can be said about such a predictive conclusion is: 'How interesting!' Similarly, a theory set forth to explain a unique event may or may not be empirically valid in accord with the precept that no empirically testable proposition is ruled out on *a priori* grounds alone. However, with just one data point, the occurrence of an unusual event, it is clear that confirmation of a proferred theory is very tenuous indeed – see Keynes (1921, p. 297 ff) for further analysis of unique events and causality.

To summarize elements of the above discussion and other considerations as succinctly as possible, the schematic in fig. 1 is useful. In the figure, it is indicated that the conscious and unconscious minds interact, as well described by Hadamard (1945), Einhorn and Hogarth (1982), Hogarth (1986), and Klayman and Ha (1987), to produce ideas and combinations of ideas using as inputs at least (1) observed or known past data and experience, (2) a space of known theories, and (3) future knowable data and experience.

Initially, the conscious mind, aware of a subset of past experience and data and of a subset of theories, decides the general nature or design of an investigation. For example, many times it is very fruitful to attempt to produce an explanation or theory or extend an existing theory to explain unusual facts such as empirical regularities, anomalous empirical findings, predictive errors of existing models, facts regarding the behavior of unusual groups or unusual historical periods, and the like. Also, in an area of investigation where there is little in the way of dependable theory, fruitful 'null models' can involve the assumption that 'all variation is random' or the assumption that 'there is no effect'.

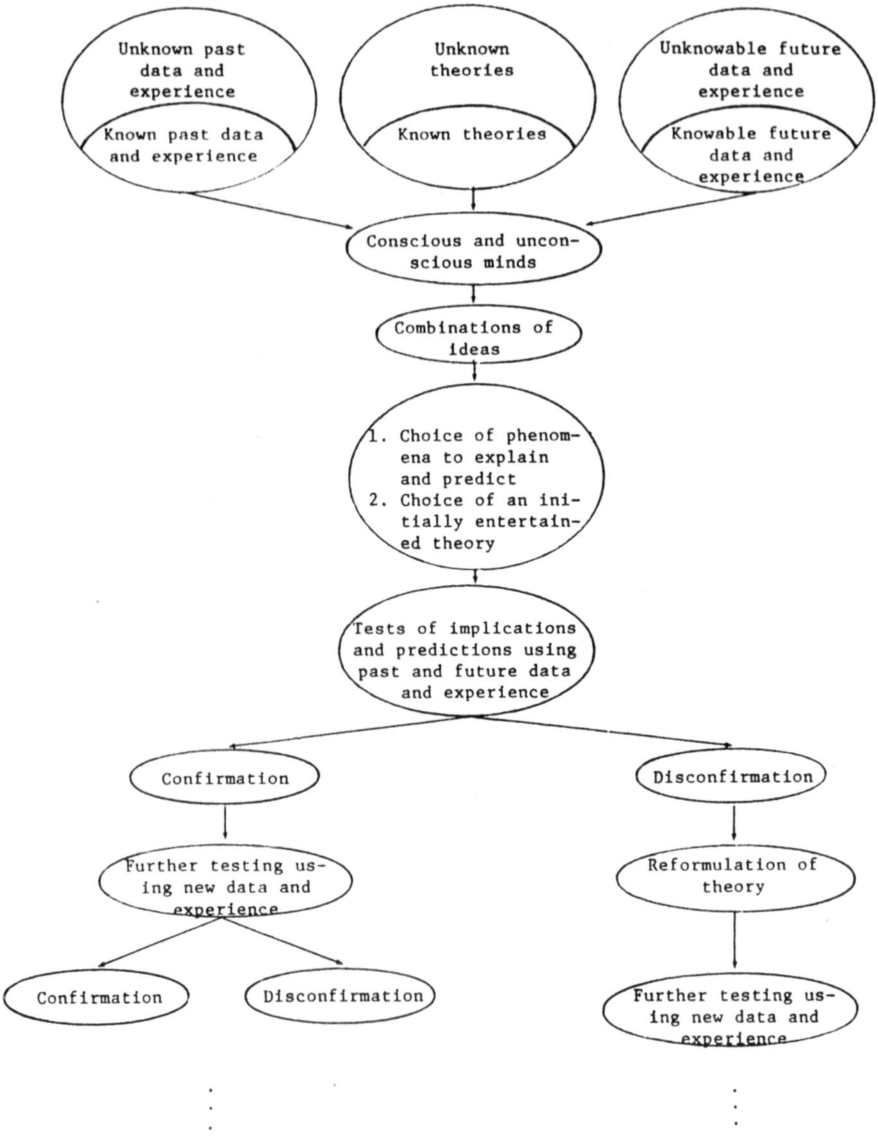

Fig. 1. Schematic of elements involved in work to produce causal laws.

When the general objective of an investigation is determined, the next problem involves getting an appropriate theory or model that is capable of explaining the phenomenon under investigation and yielding predictions. Here hard work, a breadth of empirical and theoretical knowledge, consideration of many possible combinations of ideas, luck, and a subtle interaction between the conscious and unconscious minds all play a role. Further, it is probably the case that focussing attention on sophisticatedly simple models and theories is worthwhile in accord with Ockham's Razor, the Principle of Parsimony, and the Jeffreys–Wrinch Simplicity Postulate. For example if the data, n pairs of observations on two variables, y and x fall exactly on a straight line, assuming a linear model seems natural and useful even though there are an infinity of non-linear models that can also fit the data exactly, e.g.,

$$y = \alpha + \beta x + f(x)(x_1 - x)(x_2 - x)\ldots(x_n - x),$$

where $f(x)$ is finite for $x = x_i$, $i = 1, 2, \ldots, n$. Thus for any choice of $f(x)$, the model will fit exactly. The choice of the simplest model, the linear model, suggested by considerations of simplicity, is of course not a final decision. Over the range of the observed x_i's, it may be completely adequate in explanation and prediction. However outside this range of data, new theories may suggest a need for a non-linear relation which may be approximately linear over the earlier range of the x_i's.

When the mind suggests a logically consistent model or theory to explain what has to be explained, the next step is to show that the suggested model or theory actually does explain what it purports to explain by empirical investigations using appropriate data. Further, additional implications of the model can be deduced and checked using appropriate data. To check certain implications, it is often necessary to collect new data, a very important role for empirical research. Finally, and very important in engendering further confidence in the new model or theory, it must yield a broad range of verifiable predictions about as yet unobserved experiences. If empirical research validates these predictions, then confidence in the theory increases. Continued successful explanations and predictions will elevate the theory to the status of a law and posited relations in the law would then have the status of causal relations which hold with a high degree of confidence or with high probability if the latter is regarded as a measure of the former.

Continued success in actual explanation and prediction raises confidence or reasonable belief in a theory. The degree of reasonable belief or probability associated with a theory reflects the degree to which the theory has performed successfully to date. As Jeffreys (1967), Burks (1977) and others indicate, posterior probabilities associated with alternative theories or models can be computed using Bayes' Theorem and measure degrees of confidence or reasonable belief. However, it must be realized that no theory, model or hypothesis is ever completely proved in a deductive sense. There is always room for improvement and/or the possibility that old laws may be replaced by new ones. While this is the case, the solid performance of old laws over the range of experience for which they were verified still remains. As an example, many engineers and physicists continue to use Newton's laws for low-velocity phenomena even though Einstein's more general laws cover both low- and high-velocity phenomena.

One further consideration relating to fig. 1 which seems particularly appropriate for economics is the following one. A researcher may consider explaining a complicated economic phenomenon by constructing a detailed and elaborate theory. However, it may be that data are not available for checking the explanatory and predictive aspects of the proposed theory. Given this state of affairs, it seems clear that the status of such a theory is provisional until the relevant data are produced and the theory's performance is checked using them. This is not to say that work leading to the production of such a detailed theory is without value. On the contrary, it may prompt the collection of new data appropriate for testing the new theory. On the other hand, if the required data to check the validity of the theory's explanations and predictions cannot ever be produced, then clearly the implications of the theory do not have scientific support and hence the theory's empirical validity is problematic. All of this seems obvious; yet there are many cases in which economic theorists strongly believe their theoretical constructs and econometricians believe their models to be 'true' even though they have not been subjected to extensive or even much empirical verification. Sometimes we believe what we want to believe rather than what the information in the data justifies our believing.

3. Comments on some approaches to establish causal laws

With all the work in the past two decades on definitions of causality and tests for causality, it may be asked: 'How many new causal economic laws have been produced by this work?' I believe that an honest answer is: 'Not a single one.' I shall try to indicate why this is the case in the present section.

First, with reference to fig. 1, in some analyses an initially entertained model is not well-conceived in that it may be too broad or too narrow, to mention just two possibilities. Examples of models in economics which are usually 'too broad' are unrestricted linear vector autoregressive (VAR) models and unrestricted multivariate linear autoregressive moving average (MVARMA) models. In Zellner (1979, 1984, 1985), it is pointed out that such models contain large numbers of parameters relative to the number of data points usually available and this means that parameter estimates will be imprecise, tests will not be very powerful and predictions will not be very precise – also see, e.g. Schwert (1979), Litterman (1986) and Runkle (1987). For example, in modeling a competitive industry, product price, prices of substitute and complementary products, income, consumers' liquid assets and debt, output, number of firms in operation, and factor prices are some of the variables that economic theory indicates are relevant. The above listing of variables indicates that roughly at least twelve or more variables are relevant in modeling a competitive industry. If a linear VAR model is posited for a 12×1 vector, z_t, of these variables, it would have the following form:

$$z_t = \alpha + A_1 z_{t-1} + A_2 z_{t-2} + \cdots + A_q z_{t-q} + \varepsilon_t, \qquad t = 1, 2, \ldots, T,$$

where α is a 12×1 vector of intercept terms and the A_i, $i = 1, 2, \ldots, q$, are 12×12 matrices of autoregressive coefficients. If it is assumed that the error vector has a zero mean, is serially uncorrelated and $\mathrm{E}\varepsilon_t\varepsilon_t' = \Sigma$, a 12×12 positive definite symmetric matrix with $(12)(13)/2 = 78$ distinct parameters, the total number of parameters in the system is $N = 12 + 144q + 78$ and the total number of observations is $NOBS = 12T$. With, for example, $q = 2$ and $T = 30$, $N = 378$ and $NOBS = 360$. It is seen that with only two lags ($q = 2$), the number of parameters, 378, exceeds the number of observations, 360. Thus there will be grave difficulties in implementing an unrestricted VAR approach in this instance. Also, demand, supply and entry (DSE) models for competitive industries are generally non-linear in variables and parameters – see, e.g., Veloce and Zellner (1985) and Zellner (1985) for an example involving three equations and about twenty parameters. Thus for the above reasons, and some others, a VAR approach to modeling a competitive industry is clearly one that involves entertaining too broad a model and a model that is probably inappropriate for the problem at hand. Similar arguments relate to linear MVARMA models of a competitive industry involving about twelve variables.

Many workers realize the difficulties with linear VAR and MVARMA models mentioned in the last paragraph. Some try to 'solve' these problems by modeling just a few or even just two of the variables in z_t, say $y_t' = (z_{1t}, z_{2t})$, for example price and output. Trying to understand the workings of a competitive industry by just considering price and output is clearly absurd and will not yield dependable causal inferences no matter which 'causality tests' are utilized. The problem is simply one of left-out, relevant variables. Thus a model involving two or a few of the elements of z_t will not be satisfactory from a subject matter explanatory point of view and is an example of a model that is too narrow.

Observations similar to those made in the previous paragraphs are relevant for macroeconomic modeling. Unrestricted models in the linear VAR or MVARMA forms involving the number of variables suggested by macroeconomic theories, say about ten or more, are too broad relative to available data sets and thus yield imprecise inferences and little or no understanding of macroeconomic phenomena. Since this is the case, at best analyses using them can be regarded as 'exploratory' and have not yet been capable of establishing causal laws. Even as an 'exploratory' data analysis approach, the use of linear VAR and MVARMA models may not be entirely satisfactory. A more productive and perhaps traditional approach would be to study intensively the time series properties of individual variables before trying to combine them into a multivariate model. Contrary to this advice, 'traditional' macroeconometric modelers have constructed models containing hundreds of non-linear stochastic difference equations. The mathematical, statistical and economic properties of these models are very difficult to establish. If these properties are not well understood, there is no secure basis for asserting that they can possibly be causal laws.

It is clear that in many instances workers have entertained models that are too broad or too narrow in their conception and this simple fact, I believe, has been mainly responsible for the failure to produce many or any new causal laws in economics in the past few decades by those working in the area of 'testing causality' at the macro and micro levels. It appears necessary to formulate sophisticatedly simple initial models which imply strong, testable propositions relative to the data that we do have or can reasonably expect to have within a reasonable time.

Since the use of 'sophisticatedly simple' models is strongly recommended, it is appropriate to say a few words about them in an effort to clarify what is meant by 'sophisticatedly simple', a relative term. A model is 'sophisticatedly simple' relative to other, presently known models, relative to presently available mathematical and statistical techniques and relative to available or potentially available data. If there are no effective models or theories available to explain a phenomenon, for example the variation of stock prices, a sophisticatedly simple initial hypothesis or model is that 'all variation is random unless shown otherwise', a suggestion put forward by Jeffreys (1967). This stance has proven to be very fruitful in stock market research. For example, when several researchers concluded that automobile sales could be used to forecast the British stock market price index, Box and Newbold (1971) showed that the result obtained was produced by forcing an incorrect model on the data. By analyzing a broader model containing that used by the researchers and a random walk model as special cases, Box and Newbold were able to show that the data supported the random walk hypothesis. This is not to say that the random walk model is necessarily 'true' but that it is a fruitful, sophisticatedly simple working hypothesis. Indeed, it has been the focus of much important empirical research which has uncovered departures from it, namely day-of-the-week, January, small-firm, low-frequency, and heteroskedasticity effects. These surprising and unusual effects or 'anomalies' are now the concern of much theoretical and additional empirical research designed to explain them. Such research arising from the consideration of a relatively simple hypothesis and unusual facts is most productive in my opinion and may lead to causal laws regarding stock price behavior. This point of view is in accord with that of Jeffreys (1973) who has written:

> 'The argument in this [his] book completely reverses the usual notion of causality. This started with some idea of inherent necessity. After Mach it was replaced by invariable succession, but in fact invariable successions are rare. We now see that science starts with the fact that variation is random and detecting in succession departures from randomness.' (p. 262)

When a model or models are on the scene which explain some phenomena, it is always useful to consider sophisticatedly simple modifications of them. The null hypothesis is, of course, that the modification is not needed, a hard-boiled, 'show-me' stance that is very fruitful. The Pigou effect, a modification of the Keynesian macroeconomic model, and the rational expectations hypothesis (REH) represent important examples of the modification of existing theories and have led to propositions which have been tested empirically. Both the Pigou effect and the REH are examples of sophisticatedly simple, important hypotheses with far-reaching implications. Some simple hypotheses are not sophisticated since they may not be in forms which lend themselves to analysis using known or knowable mathematical and statistical techniques and for which no data are available or will ever be available to test them. Further, given that an area of study involves much detail, it is possible to formulate a detailed, sophisticatedly simple large model to capture detail rather than a large complicated model.

It is natural to ask whether simplicity or complexity of models can be quantified. One rough index of the complexity of differential equations, put forward by Jeffreys (1967, p. 47), is stated as follows: 'We could define the complexity of a differential equation, cleared of roots and fractions, by the sum of the order, the degree, and the absolute values of the coefficients.' This rule takes account of non-linearity, the order of the equation and the number and absolute values of coefficients. The rule can also be applied to difference equations, for example the implied 'final' equations for individual variables in a linear VAR model. Since these equations are high-order autoregressive equations with many parameters, they are not very simple. While not perfect, the Jeffreys' index of complexity, discussed further in Jeffreys (1967, pp. 46–49), is a useful first approximation.

Further, with respect to sophisticatedly simple versus complicated models, the stage of development of a field must be taken into account. What appears to be sophisticatedly simple at present may not have been considered to be so years ago. For example, Schrödinger's wave equation, a partial differential equation, probably would not have been considered to be simple in the nineteenth century. But as Jeffreys (1973) has shown, relative to alternative theories which were proposed since the nineteenth century, Schrödinger's equation is probably the simplest equation which can explain the relevant empirical phenomena.

In addition, many scientists believe that sophisticatedly simple models will perform better in explanation and prediction than complicated models. Jeffreys (1967) remarks that '...the simplest law is chosen because it is most likely to give correct predictions...' (p. 4) and 'All we have to say is that simpler laws have the greater prior probabilities. This is what Wrinch and I called the *simplicity postulate*' (p. 47). In Jeffreys (1973), the important role of simplicity in science is discussed with many illustrations drawn from the history of science. In economics, the Nobel Prize winners, Arrow, Friedman, Frisch, Schultz, Stigler, Tinbergen, and Tobin all appear to appreciate the value of sophisticated simplicity in their work. In the author's opinion, a preference for complicated models and methods in economics has been a strong negative factor impeding progress in producing more economic laws. For many years in talks and papers, I have issued the following challenge: Demonstrate that a complicated model in any area of science has performed well in explanation and prediction. To date, I have not heard of any. As regards large, complicated macroeconometric models' performance, Christ (1975, p. 54) remarked that '...though the models [Wharton; Data Resources, Inc.; Bureau of Economic Analysis; St. Louis; Fair; Liu–Hwa; Hickman–Coen; and University of Michigan] forecast well over horizons of four to six quarters, they disagree so strongly about the effects of important monetary and fiscal policies that they cannot be considered reliable guides to such policy effects, until it can be determined which of them are wrong in this respect and which (if any) are right'. For more recent information regarding the forecasting performance of several large, complicated macroeconometric models and VAR models, see McNees (1986, p. 15) who concluded in his last paragraph: 'Just as conventional macroeconometric models may have been 'oversold' in the 1960s and early 1970s, leading to disappointment and rejection in the late 1970s and 1980s, there is some danger that the VAR approach to modeling and forecasting may now be oversold as a superior substitute for the more traditional approaches...' Litterman (1986) also provides interesting results on the forecasting performance of hiBayesian VAR model and that of three traditional models (Chase, Wharton and DRI). Neither McNees (1986) nor Litterman (1986) considered the models' responses to monetary and fiscal policies and their assumed causal structures.

In summary, it has been emphasized that causality and causal laws involve actually successful explanation and prediction of a wide range of data and experience. Further, posterior probabilities, explicitly or perhaps implicitly evaluated can measure degrees of confidence that are associated with theories. When such probabilities are very high, reflecting much outstanding and broad-ranging performance in explanation and prediction, a theory can be termed a causal law. The production of such laws will be facilitated by consideration of sophisticatedly simple theories and models. Some attention was given to elaboration of the concept of 'sophisticatedly simple'. Complicated theories and models, which are too broad as well as theories and models which are too narrow, utilized by many, are not satisfactory in terms of fostering the production of new economic laws. Since this process is extremely important, a review of a leading study will be presented in the next section.

4. Consideration of a specific study

In this section, a brief review of Friedman's (1957) *A Theory of the Consumption Function* is provided to illustrate some of the general points made in the previous sections of this paper.

Chapter I of Friedman's book is devoted to describing a general problem area, Keynes' (1936) consideration of consumer behavior and a serious conflict of evidence, namely, 'estimates of savings in the United States made by Kuznets for the period since 1899 revealed no rise in the percentage of income saved during the past half-century despite a substantial rise in real income' (pp. 3–4) and Kuznets' findings indicate that the marginal propensity to consume is equal to the average and is '... decidedly higher than the marginal propensities that had been computed from either time series or budget data' (p. 4, fn. omitted). Thus Kuznets' important empirical research produced unusual facts or anomalies which Friedman and others recognized required explanation, an excellent example of the vital role of measurement in economic research.

After mentioning earlier attempts by Brady and Friedman, Duesenberry, Modigliani and Tobin to explain the conflicting evidence, Friedman mentions the role of wealth in determining consumption and indicates that he will present '... yet another hypothesis to explain the observed relation between consumption expenditure and income' (p. 6). He notes that his hypothesis (1) '... seems potentially more fruitful and in some measure more general than either the relative income hypothesis or the wealth–income hypothesis taken by itself. It incorporates fully the wealth–income effect and explains why the relative income hypothesis should be valid under special circumstances' (p. 6) and (2) 'the hypothesis follows directly from the currently accepted pure theory of consumer behavior, seems consistent with existing empirical evidence, and has observable implications capable of being contradicted by additional evidence' (p. 6). In his book, Friedman analyzes a broad range of cross-section and time-series data to show that they are consistent with his theory. Also, very importantly, he proposed eight additional tests of his theory involving readily available data and predicted the outcomes of these proposed tests, many of which have been performed subsequently – see Friedman (1957, pp. 214–219).

This overview of Friedman's work indicates that attention was focussed on explaining unusual empirical findings. A range of alternative theories was considered and some were nested in this theory based on 'the currently accepted pure theory of consumer behavior', a two-period Fisherian indifference equation model in which a symmetric, homogeneous utility function $U(C_1, C_2)$ is maximized subject to a wealth constraint – see Friedman (1957, p. 7 ff). Use of this sophisticatedly simple model yielded many fruitful, testable propositions, including, among others, that current planned or permanent consumption is influenced by wealth or permanent income rather than just by current income, that the ratio of permanent consumption to permanent income is independent of wealth or permanent income and that reactions to changes in permanent income are very different from reactions to changes in transitory income.

Further, note that new unobservable, theoretical constructs, permanent and transitory income and permanent and transitory consumption are employed in Friedman's theory. This conflicts with the advice of some who recommend that science deal just with observables, an *a priori* restriction on the form of theories or models which cannot be justified. It may be that the introduction of too many unobservables can render models ineffective in explanation and prediction. However, this is a matter to be determined empirically in terms of the quality of explanation and prediction of data and not on *a priori* grounds alone. That Friedman kept his model sophisticatedly simple by not introducing too many unobservable constructs is evident and also explicit in his consideration of the possible effects of uncertainty:

> 'The introduction of uncertainty thus blurs the sharp lines of the above analysis, and suggests additional factors that may produce departures from the shape of the consumption function specified in (2.5). However, on the present level of analysis, there seems no way to judge whether these factors would tend to make consumption a larger or smaller fraction of wealth the higher the absolute level of wealth. Accordingly, this effect of uncertainty establishes no presumption against the shape assigned to the consumption function, and thus casts no shadow on the 'simplicity' that recommends it.' (p. 15)

In this quotation, there is an emphasis on the hypothesis of 'no effect' of uncertainty, unless shown otherwise, and on the consideration of simplicity, considerations mentioned in earlier sections of this paper.

Also, Friedman recognized the importance of tests of his theory using as much old and new data as possible and actually performed many tests. The nature and form of his theory indicated what tests to perform and how to perform them. Surely it is preferable to perform appropriate predictive tests implied by a theory rather than tests implied by some formal and perhaps artificial definition of causality which places important restrictions on the forms of theories and thus can lead to unsatisfactory results – see Zellner (1979, pp. 40–42) for an explicit example in which this type of 'causality testing' is applied to Friedman's theory and produces very unsatisfactory results.

While Friedman's work provides an excellent example of theory formulation and validation, as is to be expected, there are parts of the theory that are still controversial and have prompted much additional research. For example, some, including Hall (1978) have entertained multi-period stochastic optimization formulations of the theory in an effort to deal with the problem of uncertainty explicitly. Generally these works have utilized temporally separable utility functions in contrast to Friedman's non-separable two-period utility function. The assumption of temporal separability, while convenient from the point of view of obtaining mathematical solutions may not be satisfactory from an economic point of view and it is known that the properties of solutions can be very sensitive to departures from temporal separability – see, e.g., Wan (1970). Others have attempted to replace Friedman's use of an adaptive expectations hypothesis with a rational expectations formulation. In this connection, users of the rational expectations approach often assume that economic agents know 'the' true model's form and properties even when expert economists do not. Overlooking model uncertainty and use of inappropriate models may be reasons for the mixed results obtained in testing the rational expectations hypothesis – see, e.g., Lovell (1986). Finally among others, Zellner (1960), Houthakker (1965), Bhalla (1979), and Zellner and Moulton (1986) have tested Friedman's proportionality hypothesis, namely that the ratio of permanent consumption to permanent income is independent of the level of permanent income. In this work, attempts are made to investigate whether the proportionality hypothesis breaks down at very low levels of permanent income since pushing theories to extremes usually provides strong tests and often evidence that theories have to be modified.

The works cited in the previous paragraph and many more that could be cited attest to the power, breadth and fruitfulness of Friedman's sophisticatedly simple theory. Also, by bringing a wide range of data to bear on the original model and variants of it, Friedman and other economists involved in this work have set a very good example for others who wish to establish new causal laws in economics.

5. Summary and concluding remarks

As in past writings, I have emphasized that Feigl's definition of causality is a fruitful and appropriate one for work in all areas of science. It does not place undue restrictions on the forms of causal laws and is operational as indicated by a discussion of research on Friedman's theory of consumption. Several aspects of theorizing in economics were discussed with the main conclusion that sophisticatedly simple models and theories are more fruitful to consider than complicated models and theories. Some unsophisticatedly narrow models and some very broad, complicated models were mentioned and deemed unsatisfactory for efforts to establish causal laws in economics. After commenting on various aspects of the term 'sophisticatedly simple', Friedman's work on a theory of the consumption function was reviewed to indicate how the general principles have actually been applied, have yielded a wealth of useful results and can serve as a model for other research in economics aimed at the production of new causal economic laws. It involved a wholesome combination of sophisticatedly simple economic theory, extensive empirical research to establish what the facts are, and relevant testing of the theory's implications and predictions employing a broad range of data. Additional research of this type is needed to produce more causal economic laws in economics.

References

Bhalla, S.S, 1979, Measurement errors and the permanent income hypothesis: Evidence from rural India, American Economic Review 69, 295–307.

Box, G.E.P. and P. Newbold, 1971, Some comments on a paper of Coen, Gomme and Kendall, Journal of the Royal Statistical Society A 134, 229–240.

Burks, A.W., 1977, Chance, cause, reason: An inquiry into the nature of scientific evidence (University of Chicago Press, Chicago, IL).

Christ, C.F., 1975, Judging the performance of econometric models of the U.S. economy, International Economic Review 16, 54–74.

Conway, R.K., P.A.V.B. Swamy, J.F. Yanagida and P. von zur Muehlen, 1984, The impossibility of causality testing, Agricultural Economics Research 36, 1–19.

Einhorn, H.J. and R.M. Hogarth, 1982, Prediction, diagnosis, and causal thinking in forecasting, Journal of Forecasting 1, 1–14.

Feigl, H., 1953, Notes on causality, in: H. Feigl and M. Brodbeck, eds., Readings in the philosophy of science (Appleton-Century-Crofts, Inc., New York).

Friedman, M., 1957, A theory of the consumption function (National Bureau of Economic Research, Princeton University Press, Princeton, NJ).

Hadamard, J., 1945, The psychology of invention in the mathematical field (Dover Publications, New York).

Hall, R.E., 1978, Stochastic implications of the life cycle–permanent income hypothesis: Theory and evidence, Journal of Political Economy 86, 971–987.

Hogarth, R.M., 1986, Generalization in decision research: The role of formal models, IEEE Transactions on Systems, Man, and Cybernetics 16, 439–449.

Houthakker, H.S., 1965, On some determinants of saving in developed and under-developed countries, in: E.A.G. Robinson, ed., Problems in economic development (Macmillan, London) 212–227.

Jeffreys, H., 1967, Theory of probability, 3rd rev. ed. (Oxford University Press, London).

Jeffreys, H., 1973, Scientific inference, 3rd ed. (Cambridge University Press, Cambridge).

Keynes, J.M., 1921, A treatise on probability (Macmillan and Co., London).

Keynes, J.M., 1936, The general theory of employment, interest and money (Harcourt, Brace and Co., New York).

Klayman, J. and Y.-W. Ha, 1987, Confirmation, disconfirmation, and information in hypothesis testing, Psychological Review 94, 211–228.

Litterman, R.B., 1986, Forecasting with Bayesian vector autoregressions – Five years of experience, Journal of Business and Economic Statistics 4, 25–38.

Lovell, M.C., 1986, Tests of the rational expectations hypothesis, American Economic Review 76, 110–124.

McNees, S.K., 1986, Forecasting accuracy of alternative techniques: A comparison of U.S. macroeconomic forecasts (with invited discussion by C.W.J. Granger, R.B. Litterman and W.A. Spivey), Journal of Business and Economic Statistics 4, 5–23.

Nelson, C.A., 1979, Discussion of the Zellner and Schwert papers, in: K. Brunner and A.H. Meltzer, eds., Three aspects of policy and policymaking (North-Holland, Amsterdam) 97–102.

Runkle, D.E., 1987, Vector autoregressions and reality, Journal of Business and Economic Statistics 5, 437–442.

Schwert, G.W., 1979, Tests of causality: The message in the innovations, in: K. Brunner and A.H. Meltzer, eds., Three aspects of policy and policymaking (North-Holland, Amsterdam) 55–96.

Simon, H., 1953, Causal ordering and indentifiability, in: W.C. Hood and T.C. Koopmans, eds., Studies in econometric method (Wiley, New York) 49–74.

Sims, C.A., 1979, A comment on the papers by Zellner and Schwert, in: K. Brunner and A.H. Meltzer, eds., Three aspects of policy and policymaking (North-Holland, Amsterdam) 103–108.

Stigler, G.J., 1949, The theory of price (Macmillan, New York).

Swamy, P.A.V.B. and P. von zur Muehlen, 1987, Further thoughts on testing for causality with econometric models, Journal of Econometrics, this issue.

Veloce, W. and A. Zellner, 1985, Entry and empirical demand and supply analysis for competitive industries, Journal of Econometrics 30, 459–471.

Wan, H.Y., 1970, Optimal saving programs under intertemporally dependent preferences, International Economic Review 11, 521–547.

Zellner, A., 1960, Tests of some basic propositions in the theory of consumption, American Economic Review 50, 565–573.

Zellner, A., 1979, Causality and econometrics, in: K. Brunner and A.H. Meltzer, eds., Three aspects of policy and policymaking (North-Holland, Amsterdam) 9–54.

Zellner, A., 1984, Basic issues in econometrics (University of Chicago Press, Chicago, IL).

Zellner, A., 1985, Bayesian econometrics, Econometrica 53, 253–269.

Zellner, A. and B.M. Moulton, 1986, Bayesian regression diagnostics with applications to international consumption and income data, Journal of Econometrics 29, 187–211.

ECONOMETRICA

VOLUME 51 MARCH, 1983 NUMBER 2

EXOGENEITY[1]

BY ROBERT F. ENGLE, DAVID F. HENDRY, AND JEAN-FRANCOIS RICHARD

Definitions are proposed for *weak* and *strong* exogeneity in terms of the distribution of *observable* variables. The objectives of the paper are to clarify the concepts involved, isolate the essential requirements for a variable to be exogenous, and relate them to notions of predeterminedness, *strict* exogeneity and causality in order to facilitate econometric modelling. Worlds of parameter change are considered and exogeneity is related to structural invariance leading to a definition of *super* exogeneity. Throughout the paper, illustrative models are used to exposit the analysis.

1. INTRODUCTION

SINCE "EXOGENEITY" IS FUNDAMENTAL to most empirical econometric modelling, its conceptualization, its role in inference, and the testing of its validity have been the subject of extensive discussion (see inter alia, Koopmans [**21**], Orcutt [**28**], Marschak [**26**], Phillips [**29**], Sims [**38, 39**], Geweke [**13, 14**] and Richard [**32**]). Nevertheless, as perusal of the literature (and especially econometrics textbooks) quickly reveals, precise definitions of "exogeneity" are elusive and consequently, it is unclear exactly what is entailed for *inference* by the discovery that a certain variable is "exogenous" on any given definition. Moreover, the motivation underlying various "exogeneity" concepts has not always been stated explicitly so that their relationships to alternative notions of "causality" (see Wiener [**42**], Strotz and Wold [**40**], Granger [**16**], and Zellner [**45**]) remain ambiguous. This results in part because some definitions have been formulated for limited classes of models so that appropriate generalizations such as to nonlinear or non-Gaussian situations are not straightforward, while others are formulated in terms involving unobservable disturbances from relationships which contain unknown parameters. Whether or not such disturbances satisfy orthogonality conditions with certain observables may be a matter of construction or may be a testable hypothesis and a clear distinction between these situations is essential.

In this paper, definitions are proposed for *weak* and *strong* exogeneity in terms of the distributions of observable variables,[2] thereby explicitly relating these

[1] This paper is an abbreviated and substantially rewritten version of CORE Discussion Paper 80-38 (and U.C.S.D. Discussion Paper 81-1). This was itself an extensive revision of Warwick Discussion Paper No. 162, which was initially prepared during the 1979 Warwick Summer Workshop, with support from the Social Science Research Council. We are indebted to participants in the Workshop for useful discussions on several of the ideas developed in the paper and to Mary Morgan for historical references. We also greatly benefited from discussions with A. S. Deaton, J. P. Florens, S. Goldfeld, A. Holly, M. Mouchart, R. Quandt, C. Sims, and A. Ullah. Three anonymous referees made many constructive comments. Financial support from the Ford Foundation, the National Science Foundation, and the International Centre for Economics and Related Disciplines at the London School of Economics is gratefully acknowledged.

[2] The emphasis on observables does not preclude formulating theories in terms of unobservables (e.g., "permanent" components, expectations, disturbances, etc.), but these should be integrated out first in order to obtain an operational model to which our concepts may be applied.

concepts to the likelihood function and hence efficient estimation:[3] essentially, a variable z_t in a model is defined to be weakly exogenous for estimating a set of parameters λ if inference on λ conditional on z_t involves no loss of information. Heuristically, given that the joint density of random variables (y_t, z_t) always can be written as the product of y_t conditional on z_t times the marginal of z_t, the weak exogeneity of z_t entails that the precise specification of the latter density is irrelevant to the analysis, and, in particular that all parameters which appear in this marginal density are nuisance parameters. Such an approach builds on the important paper by Koopmans [**21**] using recently developed concepts of statistical inference (see e.g., Barndorff-Nielsen [**1**], and Florens and Mouchart [**10**]). If in addition to being weakly exogenous, z_t is *not caused* in the sense of Granger [**16**] by any of the endogenous variables in the system, then z_t is defined to be strongly exogenous.

The concept of exogeneity is then extended to the class of models where the mechanism generating z_t changes. Such changes could come about for a variety of reasons; one of the most interesting is the attempt by one agent to control the behavior of another. If all the parameters λ of the conditional model are invariant to any change in the marginal density of z_t, and z_t is weakly exogenous for λ, then z_t is said to be *super* exogenous. That is, changes in the values of z_t or its generating function will not affect the conditional relation between y_t and z_t. This aspect builds on the work of Frisch [**12**], Marschak [**26**], Hurwicz [**20**], Sims [**39**], and Richard [**32**].

The paper is organized as follows: formal definitions of weak, strong, and super exogeneity are introduced in Section 2; and, to ensure an unambiguous discussion, the familiar notions of predeterminedness, strict exogeneity, and Granger noncausality are also defined. These are then discussed in the light of several examples in Section 3. The examples illustrate the relations between the concepts in familiar models showing the importance of each part of the new definitions and showing the incompleteness of the more conventional notions. Special attention is paid to the impact of serial correlation. The analysis is then applied to potentially incomplete dynamic simultaneous equations systems in Section 4. The conclusion restates the main themes and implications of the paper.

1.1 *Notation*

Let $x_t \in R^n$ be a vector of *observable* random variables generated at time t, on which observations ($t = 1, \ldots, T$) are available. Let X_t^1 denote the $t \times n$ matrix:

(1) $$X_t^1 = (x_1, \ldots, x_t)'$$

and let X_0 represent the (possibly infinite) matrix of initial conditions. The analysis is conducted conditionally on X_0. For a discussion of marginalization

[3]Throughout the paper, the term "efficient estimation" is used as a shorthand for "conducting inference without loss of relevant information," and does not entail any claims as to e.g., the efficiency of particular estimators in small samples.

with respect to initial conditions, see Engle, Hendry, and Richard [**8**], hereafter EHR. The information available at time t is given by

$$(2) \qquad X_{t-1} = \begin{bmatrix} X_0 \\ X_{t-1}^1 \end{bmatrix}.$$

The process generating the T observations is assumed to be continuous with respect to some appropriate measure and is represented by the joint data density function $D(X_T^1 | X_0, \theta)$ where θ, in the interior of Θ, is an (identified) vector of unknown parameters. The likelihood function of θ, given the initial conditions X_0, is denoted by $L^0(\theta; X_T^1)$.

Below, $f_N^n(\cdot \mid \mu, \Sigma)$ denotes the n-dimensional normal density function with mean vector μ and covariance matrix Σ. The notation $x_t \sim IN(\mu, \Sigma)$ reads as "the vectors $x_1, \ldots, x_T$ are identically independently normally distributed with common mean vector μ and covariance matrix Σ." C_n denotes the set of symmetric positive definite matrices.

The vector x_t is partitioned into

$$(3) \qquad x_t = \begin{bmatrix} y_t \\ z_t \end{bmatrix}, \qquad y_t \in R^p, \quad z_t \in R^q, \quad p + q = n.$$

The matrices X_0, X_t^1, and X_t are partitioned conformably:

$$(4) \qquad X_0 = (Y_0 Z_0), \qquad X_t^1 = (Y_t^1 Z_t^1), \qquad X_t = (Y_t Z_t).$$

The expressions "$x_t \| y_t$" and "$x_t \| y_t | w_t$" read respectively as "x_t and y_t are independent (in probability)" and "conditionally on w_t, x_t and y_t are independent." In our framework it is implicit that all such independence statements are *conditional* on θ. The operator $\sum$ denotes a summation which starts at $i = 1$ and is over all relevant lags.

2. DEFINITIONS

Often the objective of empirical econometrics is to model how the observation x_t is generated conditionally on the past, so we factorize the joint data density as

$$(5) \qquad D(X_T^1 | X_0, \theta) = \prod_{t=1}^{T} D(x_t | X_{t-1}, \theta)$$

and focus attention on the conditional density functions $D(x_t | X_{t-1}, \theta)$. These are assumed to have a common functional form with a *finite*[4] dimensional parameter space Θ.

The following formal definitions must be introduced immediately to ensure an unambiguous discussion, but the examples presented below attempt to elucidate their content; the reader wishing a general view of the paper could proceed fairly rapidly to Section 3 and return to this section later.

[4] It is assumed that the dimensionality of Θ is sufficiently small relative to nT that it makes sense to discuss, e.g., "efficient" estimation.

2.1. *Granger Noncausality*

For the class of models defined by (5), conditioned throughout on X_0, Granger [16] provides a definition of noncausality which can be restated as:

DEFINITION 2.1: Y_{t-1}^1 does not Granger cause z_t with respect to X_{t-1} if and only if

(6) $$D(z_t \mid X_{t-1}, \theta) = D(z_t \mid Z_{t-1}, Y_0, \theta),$$

i.e., if and only if

(7) $$z_t \perp\!\!\!\perp Y_{t-1}^1 \mid Z_{t-1}, Y_0.$$

If condition (6) holds over the sample period, then the joint data density $D(X_T^1 \mid X_0, \theta)$ factorizes as

(8) $$D(X_T^1 \mid X_0, \theta) = \left[\prod_{t=1}^{T} D(y_t \mid z_t, X_{t-1}, \theta) \right] \left[\prod_{t=1}^{T} D(z_t \mid Z_{t-1}, Y_0, \theta) \right]$$

where the last term is $D(Z_T^1 \mid X_0, \theta)$ and the middle term is therefore $D(Y_T^1 \mid Z_T^1, X_0, \theta)$.

Where no ambiguity is likely, condition (6) is stated below as "y does not Granger cause z." Note that the definition in Chamberlain [3] is the same as 2.1.

2.2. *Predeterminedness and Strict Exogeneity*

Consider a set of $g \leq n$ behavioral relationships (whose exact interpretation is discussed in Section 4 below):

(9) $$B^* x_t + \sum C^*(i) x_{t-i} = u_t$$

where B^* and $\{C^*(i)\}$ are $g \times n$ matrix functions of θ, with rank $B^* = g$ almost everywhere in Θ, and u_t is the corresponding "disturbance."

The following definitions are adapted from Koopmans and Hood [22]—see also Christ [4, Chs. IV.4, VI.4] and Sims [39].

DEFINITION 2.2: z_t is *predetermined* in (9) if and only if

(10) $$z_t \perp\!\!\!\perp u_{t+i} \qquad \text{for all} \quad i \geq 0.$$

DEFINITION 2.3: z_t is *strictly exogenous*[5] in (9) if and only if

(11) $$z_t \perp\!\!\!\perp u_{t+i} \qquad \text{for all } i.$$

[5]We use the term "strictly exogenous" where some authors use "exogenous" to distinguish this concept from that introduced below.

The connections between strict exogeneity and Granger noncausality have been discussed by several authors—and in particular by Sims [39] and Geweke [13]—for complete dynamic simultaneous equations models. This issue is reconsidered in Section 4. See also the discussion in Chamberlain [3] and Florens and Mouchart [11].

2.3. *Parameters of Interest*

Often a model user is not interested in all the parameters in θ, so that his (implicit) loss function depends only on some functions of θ, say:

$$(12)\qquad f:\Theta\rightarrow\Psi;\qquad \theta\rightarrow\psi=f(\theta).$$

These functions are called *parameters of interest*. Parameters may be of interest, e.g., because they are directly related to theories the model user wishes to test concerning the structure of the economy. Equally, in seeking empirical econometric relationships which are constant over the sample period and hopefully over the forecast period, parameters which are *structurally invariant* (see Section 2.6), are typically of interest.

Since models can be parameterized in infinitely many ways, parameters of interest need not coincide with those which are chosen to characterize the data density (e.g., the mean vector and the covariance matrix in a normal framework). Consider, therefore, an arbitrary one-to-one transformation or reparameterization:

$$(13)\qquad h:\Theta\rightarrow\Lambda;\qquad \theta\rightarrow\lambda=h(\theta)$$

together with a partition of λ into (λ_1,λ_2). Let Λ_i denote the set of admissible values of λ_i. The question of whether or not the parameters of interest are *functions* of λ_1 plays an essential role in our analysis: that is, whether there exists a function ϕ,

$$(14)\qquad \phi:\Lambda_1\rightarrow\Psi;\qquad \lambda_1\rightarrow\psi=\phi(\lambda_1)$$

such that

$$(15)\qquad \text{for all}\quad \lambda\in\Lambda,\qquad \psi=f\left[h^{-1}(\lambda)\right]\equiv\phi(\lambda_1).$$

When (15) holds, λ_2 is often called a *nuisance* parameter.[6]

2.4. *Sequential Cuts*

Let $x_t\in R^n$ be partitioned as in (3) and let $\lambda=(\lambda_1,\lambda_2)$ be a reparameterization as in (13). The following definition is adapted from Florens and Mouchart [10]

[6]The concept of *nuisance* parameter is, however, ambiguous. Whether or not a parameter is a *nuisance* parameter critically depends on which (re)parameterization is used. If, for example, $\theta=(\alpha,\beta)$ and β is the sole parameter of interest, then α is a nuisance parameter. In contrast, a reparameterization using (α,γ) where $\gamma=\beta/\alpha$ entails that β is not a function of γ alone, and so α is not a *nuisance* parameter.

who generalized the notion of cut discussed (e.g.) by Barndorff-Nielsen [1] to dynamic models:

DEFINITION 2.4: $[(y_t \mid z_t; \lambda_1), (z_t; \lambda_2)]$ operates a (classical) *sequential cut* on $D(x_t \mid X_{t-1}, \lambda)$ if and only if

$$D(x_t \mid X_{t-1}, \lambda) = D(y_t \mid z_t, X_{t-1}, \lambda_1) D(z_t \mid X_{t-1}, \lambda_2) \tag{16}$$

where λ_1 and λ_2 are *variation free*, i.e.,

$$(\lambda_1, \lambda_2) \in \Lambda_1 \times \Lambda_2 . \tag{17}$$

Since Λ_i denotes the set of admissible values of λ_i, condition (17) requires in effect that λ_1 and λ_2 should not be subject to "cross-restrictions," whether exact or inequality restrictions, since then the range of admissible values for λ_i would vary with λ_j $(i, j = 1, 2; j \neq i)$.

2.5. *Weak and Strong Exogeneity*

The following definitions are adapted from Richard [32]. As in (12), ψ denotes the parameter of interest.

DEFINITION 2.5: z_t is *weakly exogenous* over the sample period for ψ if and only if there exists a reparameterization with $\lambda = (\lambda_1, \lambda_2)$ such that

(i) ψ is a function of λ_1 (as in (15)),

(ii) $[(y_t \mid z_t; \lambda_1), (z_t; \lambda_2)]$ operates a sequential cut.

DEFINITION 2.6: z_t is *strongly exogenous* over the sample period for ψ if and only if it is weakly exogenous for ψ and in addition

(iii) y does not Granger cause z.

When (ii) holds, $L^0(\lambda; X_T^1)$ factorizes as in

$$L^0(\lambda; X_T^1) = L_1^0(\lambda_1; X_T^1) L_2^0(\lambda_2; X_T^1), \tag{18}$$

where

$$L_1^0(\lambda_1; X_T^1) = \prod_{t=1}^{T} D(y_t \mid z_t, X_{t-1}, \lambda_1), \tag{19}$$

$$L_2^0(\lambda_2; X_T^1) = \prod_{t=1}^{T} D(z_t \mid X_{t-1}, \lambda_2), \tag{20}$$

and the two factors in (18) can be analyzed independently of each other (which, irrespective of whether or not (i) holds may considerably reduce the computational burden). If in addition (i) holds, then all the sample information concerning the parameter of interest ψ can be obtained from the partial likelihood function $L_1^0(\lambda_1; X_T^1)$. If it were known (or assumed a priori) that z_t was weakly exogenous for ψ, then the marginal process $D(z_t|X_{t-1},\lambda_2)$ would not even need to be specified. However, tests of the weak exogeneity of z_t for ψ, as described in Section 6.1 of EHR and Engle [6], evidently require that the *joint* model $D(x_t|X_{t-1},\lambda)$ be specified.

The factorization (18)–(20) does not entail that the conditional process generating $\{y_t|z_t\}$ and the marginal process generating $\{z_t\}$ can be separated from each other, i.e., for example, that z_t can be treated as "fixed" in the conditional model $D(y_t|z_t,X_{t-1},\lambda_1)$ since lagged values of y_t may still affect the process generating z_t.[7] Factorizing the joint data density $D(X_T^1|X_0,\lambda)$ requires an additional assumption and this is precisely the object of Granger noncausality. When both (ii) and (iii) hold we can factorize $D(X_T^1|X_0,\lambda)$ as in

$$(21) \qquad D(X_T^1|X_0,\lambda) = D(Y_T^1|Z_T^1,X_0,\lambda_1)D(Z_T^1|X_0,\lambda_2),$$

where

$$(22) \qquad D(Y_T^1|Z_T^1,X_0,\lambda_1) = \prod_{t=1}^{T} D(y_t|z_t,X_{t-1},\lambda_1),$$

$$(23) \qquad D(Z_T^1|X_0,\lambda_2) = \prod_{t=1}^{T} D(z_t|Z_{t-1},Y_0,\lambda_2).$$

It must be stressed that the definition of Granger noncausality as given in (6) and (8), includes *no* assumption about the *parameters*. This is precisely why it must be completed by an assumption of weak exogeneity in order to entail a complete separation of the processes generating respectively $\{y_t|z_t\}$ and $\{z_t\}$.

2.6. *Structural Invariance and Super Exogeneity*

A closely related issue of statistical inference is parameter constancy. Over time, it is possible that some of the parameters of the joint distribution may change perhaps through changing tastes, technology, or institutions such as government policy making. For some classes of parameter change or "interventions" there may be parameters which remain constant and which can be estimated without difficulty even though interventions occur over the sample period. This is a familiar assumption about parameters in econometrics which is here called invariance. Just as weak exogeneity sustains conditional inference

[7] It follows that, unless y does not Granger cause z, $L_1^0(\lambda_1; X_T^1)$ is not *sensu stricto* a likelihood function, although it is often implicitly treated as such in the econometric literature, but it is a valid basis for inferences about ψ, *provided z_t is weakly exogenous for ψ*.

within a regime, we develop the relevant exogeneity concept for models subject to a particular class of regime changes.

DEFINITION 2.7: A parameter is *invariant* for a class of interventions if it remains constant under these interventions. A model is invariant for such interventions if all its parameters are.

DEFINITION 2.8: A conditional model is *structurally invariant* if all its parameters are invariant for any change in the distribution of the conditioning variables.[8]

Since weak exogeneity guarantees that the parameters of the conditional model and those of the marginal model are variation free, it offers a natural framework for analyzing the structural invariance of parameters of conditional models. However, by itself, weak exogeneity is neither necessary nor sufficient for structural invariance of a conditional model. Note, first, that the conditional model may be structurally invariant without its parameters providing an estimate of the parameters of interest. Conversely, weak exogeneity of the conditioning variables does not rule out the possibility that economic agents change their behavior in relation to interventions. That is, even though the parameters of interest and the nuisance parameters are variation free over any given regime, where a regime is characterized by a fixed distribution of the conditioning variables, their variations between regimes may be related. This will become clear in the examples.

The concept of structurally invariant conditional models characterizes the conditions which guarantee the appropriateness of "policy simulations" or other control exercises, since any change in the distribution of the conditioning variables has no effect on the conditional submodel and therefore on the conditional forecasts of the endogenous variables. This requirement is clearly very strong and its untested assumption has been criticized in conventional practice by Lucas [23] and Sargent [35].

To sustain conditional inference in processes subject to interventions, we define the concept of *super exogeneity*.

DEFINITION 2.9: *z_t is super exogenous* for ψ if z_t is weakly exogenous for ψ and the conditional model $D(y_t \mid z_t, X_{t-1}, \lambda_1)$ is structurally invariant.

Note that Definition 2.9 relates explicitly to *conditional* submodels: since estimable models with invariant parameters but no weakly exogenous variables are easily formulated (see Example 3.2 below), super exogeneity is a sufficient but not a necessary condition for valid inference under interventions (see e.g. the discussion of feasible policy analyses under rational expectations in Wallis [41] and the formulation in Sargent [35]).

[8]The definition can always be restricted to a specific class of distribution changes. This will implicitly be the case in the examples which are discussed in Section 3.

It is clear that any assertion concerning super exogeneity is refutable in the data for past changes in $D(z_t | X_{t-1}, \lambda_2)$ by examining the behavior of the conditional model for invariance when the parameters of the exogenous process changed. For an example of this see Hendry [**18**]. However, super exogeneity for all changes in the distribution of z_t must remain a conjecture until refuted, both because nothing precludes agents from simply changing their behavior at a certain instant and because only a limited range of interventions will have occurred in any given sample period (compare the notion of nonexcitation in Salmon and Wallis [**34**]). Such an approach is, of course, standard scientific practice. When derived from a well-articulated theory, a conditional submodel with z_t super exogenous seems to satisfy the requirement for Zellner causality of "predictability according to a law" (see Zellner [**45**]).

2.7. *Comments*

The motivation for introducing the concept of weak exogeneity is that it provides a sufficient[9] condition for conducting inference conditionally on z_t without loss of relevant sample information. Our concept is a direct extension of Koopmans' [**21**] discussion of exogeneity. He shows that an implicit static simultaneous equations system which has the properties: (a) the variables of the first block of equations do not enter the second block, (b) the disturbances between the two blocks are independent, and (c) the Jacobian of the transformation from the disturbances to the observables is nowhere zero, will have a likelihood function which factors into two components as in (18), a conditional and a marginal. The variables in the second block are labeled exogenous. Implicit in his analysis is the notion that the parameters of interest are all located in the first block and that this parameterization operates a cut. The failure to state precisely these components of the definition, leads to a lack of force in the definition as is illustrated in several of the examples in this paper. Koopmans then analyzes dynamic systems in the same framework leading to a notion of exogeneity which corresponds to our strong exogeneity and predeterminedness corresponding to that concept as defined above.

Koopmans presents sufficient conditions for the factorization of the likelihood but does not discuss the case where the factorization holds but his sufficient conditions do not. Our work therefore extends Koopmans' by making precise the assumptions about the parameters of interest and by putting the definitions squarely on the appropriate factorization of the likelihood. More recent literature has in fact stepped back from Koopmans' approach, employing definitions such as that of strict exogeneity in Section 2.2. As shown in Section 4, strict exogeneity, when applied to dynamic simultaneous equations models includes condition

[9] It is also necessary for most purposes. However, since in (14) ψ need not depend on all the elements in λ_1 it might happen that ψ and λ_2 are variation free even though λ_1 and λ_2 are not in which case neglecting the restrictions between λ_1 and λ_2 *might* entail no loss of efficiency for inference on ψ. More subtly, whether or not cuts are necessary to conduct inference based on partial models without loss of information obviously very much depends on how sample information is measured. See in particular the concepts of G- and M-ancillarity in Barndorff-Nielsen [**1**].

(iii) of Definition 2.6 together with predeterminedness; condition (ii) of Definition 2.5 is not required explicitly but, at least for just identified models, is often satisfied by construction; condition (i) of Definition 2.5 is certainly absent which, in our view, is a major lacuna[10] since, unless it holds, strict exogeneity of z_t does not ensure that there is no loss of relevant sample information when conducting inference conditionally on z_t. On the other hand, if (i) and (ii) hold, then (iii) becomes irrelevant[11] since it no longer affects inference on the parameters of interest. This does not mean that condition (iii) has no merit on its own—a model user might express specific interest in detecting causal orderings and ψ should then be defined accordingly—but simply that it is misleading to emphasize Granger noncausality when discussing exogeneity. The two concepts serve different purposes: weak exogeneity validates conducting *inference* conditional on z_t while Granger noncausality validates *forecasting* z and then forecasting y *conditional* on the future z's. As is well known, the condition that y does not Granger cause z is neither necessary nor sufficient for the weak exogeneity of z. Obviously, if estimation is required before conditional predictions are made, then strong exogeneity which covers both Granger noncausality *and* weak exogeneity becomes the relevant concept.

Note that if $[(y_t \mid z_t; \lambda_1), (z_t; \lambda_2)]$ operates a sequential cut, then the information matrix, if it exists, is block-diagonal between λ_1 and λ_2. In fact for most of the examples discussed in this paper and in EHR the condition that the information matrix be block-diagonal appears to be equivalent to the condition that the parameterization should operate a sequential cut. However, at a more general level, the finding that the information matrix is block-diagonal between two sets of parameters, one of which contains all the parameters of interest, does not entail that the likelihood function factorize as in (18). Block-diagonality of the information matrix may reflect other features of the likelihood function. Therefore, it seems difficult to discuss exogeneity by means of information matrices without explicitly referring to reparameterizations in terms of conditional and marginal submodels. Further, information matrices are often difficult to obtain analytically especially in the presence of lagged endogenous variables.

Note also that some definitions seem designed to validate specific estimation methods such as ordinary least squares within a single equation framework. For example, Phillips [29, Section IV] presents conditions justifying least squares estimation in dynamic systems, which if fulfilled would allow regressors to be treated as "given," despite the presence of Granger causal feedbacks. The concept of weak exogeneity is *not directly* related to validating specific estimation methods but concerns instead the conditions under which attention may be restricted to conditional submodels without loss of relevant sample information.

[10]This criticism is hardly specific to the concept of exogeneity. For example, unless there are parameters of interest, it is meaningless to require that an estimator should be consistent since it is always possible to redefine the "parameters" such that any chosen convergent estimation method yields consistent estimates thereof (see e.g., Hendry [17]).

[11]Evidently if one wished to test the conditions under which (ii) held then overidentifying restrictions such as the ones typically implied by Granger noncausality would affect the properties of the test.

Later selection of an *inappropriate* estimator may produce inefficiency (and inconsistency) even when weak exogeneity conditions are fulfilled.

Many existing definitions of exogeneity have been formulated in terms of orthogonality conditions between observed variables and (unobservable) disturbances in linear relationships within processes which are usually required to be Gaussian. Definitions 2.5 and 2.6 apply equally well to any joint density function and therefore encompass nonlinear and non-Gaussian processes and truncated or otherwise limited dependent variables. As such nonclassical models come into more use it is particularly important to have definitions of exogeneity which can be directly applied. See for example Gourieroux, et al. **[15]** or Maddala and Lee **[25]**. For a formulation tantamount to weak exogeneity in the context of conditional logit models, see McFadden **[24**, Section 5.1]. Exogeneity also has been discussed from the Bayesian point of view by Florens and Mouchart **[10]**. The issue then becomes whether or not the posterior density of the parameters of interest as derived from a conditional submodel coincides with that derived from the complete model. Such is the case if z_t is weakly exogenous and in addition λ_1 and λ_2 in Definition 2.5 are a priori independent. However the conditions are not necessary and it may be the case that, in the absence of a sequential cut, the prior density is such that the desired result is still achieved.

3. EXAMPLES

Many of the points made in the previous section can be illustrated with the simplest of all multivariate models, the bivariate normal. Because this is a static model, the concepts of weak and strong exogeneity coincide as do the concepts of predeterminedness and strict exogeneity. The central role of the choice of parameters of interest is seen directly.

EXAMPLE 3.1: Let the data on y_t and z_t be generated by:

$$(24)\qquad \begin{bmatrix} y_t \\ z_t \end{bmatrix} \sim IN(\mu, \Omega), \qquad \mu = (\mu_i), \quad \Omega = (\omega_{ij}), \quad i,j = 1,2,$$

with the conditional distribution of y_t given z_t:

$$(25)\qquad y_t \mid z_t \sim IN(\alpha + \beta z_t, \sigma^2)$$

where $\beta = \omega_{12}/\omega_{22}$, $\alpha = \mu_1 - \beta\mu_2$, and $\sigma^2 = \omega_{11} - \omega_{12}^2/\omega_{22}$. Letting

$$(26)\qquad u_{1t} = y_t - E(y_t \mid z_t), \qquad v_{2t} = z_t - E(z_t),$$

the model is correspondingly reformulated as

$$(27)\qquad y_t = \alpha + \beta z_t + u_{1t}, \qquad u_{1t} \sim IN(0, \sigma^2),$$

$$(28)\qquad z_t = \mu_2 + v_{2t}, \qquad v_{2t} \sim IN(0, \omega_{22}),$$

where $\operatorname{cov}(z_t, u_{1t}) = \operatorname{cov}(v_{2t}, u_{1t}) = 0$ by construction. The parameters of the conditional model (27) are $(\alpha, \beta, \sigma^2)$ and those of the marginal model (28) are

(μ_2, ω_{22}). They are in one-to-one correspondence with (μ, Ω) and are variation-free since, for arbitrary choices of $(\alpha, \beta, \sigma^2)$ and (μ_2, ω_{22}) in their sets of admissible values which are respectively $R^2 \times R_+$ and $R \times R_+$, μ and Ω are given by

$$(29) \qquad \mu = \begin{bmatrix} \alpha + \beta\mu_2 \\ \mu_2 \end{bmatrix}, \qquad \Omega = \begin{bmatrix} \sigma^2 + \beta^2\omega_{22} & \beta\omega_{22} \\ \beta\omega_{22} & \omega_{22} \end{bmatrix},$$

and the constraint that Ω be positive definite is automatically satisfied (see Lemma 5.1 in Drèze and Richard [5] for a generalization of this result to multivariate regression models). It follows that z_t is weakly exogenous for $(\alpha, \beta, \sigma^2)$ or for any well-defined function thereof.

However, similar reasoning applies by symmetry to the factorization

$$(30) \qquad z_t = \gamma + \delta y_t + u_{2t}, \qquad u_{2t} \sim IN(0, \tau^2),$$

$$(31) \qquad y_t = \mu_1 + v_{1t}, \qquad v_{1t} \sim IN(0, \omega_{11}),$$

where $\delta = \omega_{12}/\omega_{11}$, $\gamma = \mu_2 - \delta\mu_1$, $\tau^2 = \omega_{22} - \omega_{12}^2/\omega_{11}$, and $\operatorname{cov}(y_t, u_{2t}) = \operatorname{cov}(v_{1t}, u_{2t}) = 0$ by construction. Therefore, y_t is weakly exogenous for (γ, δ, τ^2) or for any well-defined function thereof. In this example the choice of parameters of interest is the sole determinant of weak exogeneity which is, therefore, not directly testable.

Next, consider the concept of predeterminedness which is here equivalent to that of strict exogeneity. Regardless of the parameters of interest, z_t is predetermined in (27) by construction and so is y_t in (30). Which variable is predetermined depends upon the form of the equation, not upon the properties of the joint density function. Until some of the parameters are assumed to be more fundamental or structural (i.e., parameters of interest), the notion of predeterminedness has no force. When δ is the parameter of interest, z_t is predetermined in equation (27) but not weakly exogenous while y_t is weakly exogenous but not predetermined. Similar results hold in more complex models where the assumptions of exogeneity can be tested.

This example also illustrates the ambiguity in Koopmans' sufficient conditions as discussed in Section 2.7 since their application leads to the conclusion that z_t is exogenous in (27) and (28) while y_t is exogenous in (30) and (31), a conclusion which seems to misrepresent Koopmans' views about exogeneity.

Now consider the concepts of structural invariance and super exogeneity. Will the parameter β in (27) be invariant to an intervention which changes the variance of z? The answer depends upon the structure of the process. If β is truly a constant parameter (because, e.g., (27) is an autonomous behavioral equation) then σ_{12} will vary with σ_{22} since, given (26), $\sigma_{12} = \beta\sigma_{22}$. Alternatively it might be σ_{12} which is the fixed constant of nature in (24) and in this case β will not be invariant to changes in σ_{22}; z_t can be weakly exogenous for β within one regime with β a derived parameter which changes between regimes. By making β the parameter of interest, most investigators are implicitly assuming that it will remain constant when the distribution of the exogenous variables changes; however, this is an assumption which may not be acceptable in the light of the Lucas **[23]** critique. Similar arguments apply to α or σ^2. Therefore, if $(\alpha, \beta, \sigma^2)$ are invariant to any changes in the distribution of z_t or, more specifically in this restricted framework, to changes in μ_2 and ω_{22}, then z_t is super exogenous for $(\alpha, \beta, \sigma^2)$. If, on the other hand, β is invariant to such changes while α and σ^2 are not, e.g., because μ_1 and ω_{11} are invariant, then z_t might be weakly exogenous for β within each regime but is not super exogenous for β since the marginal process (28) now contains valuable information on the shifts of α and σ^2 between regimes.[12] It is clear from the above argument that weak exogeneity does not imply structural invariance. It is also clear that even if β is invariant to changes in the distribution of z or in fact the conditional model (27) is structurally invariant, the parameter of interest could be γ and therefore z_t would not be weakly exogenous, and thus not super exogenous either.

Finally, since weak exogeneity explicitly requires that all relevant sample information be processed, overidentifying restrictions are bound to play an essential role in a discussion of weak exogeneity assumptions.[13] This will be discussed further in Section 4 within the framework of dynamic simultaneous equations models. Example 3.2 illustrates the role of overidentifying restrictions in a simple structure.

EXAMPLE 3.2: Consider the following two-equation overidentified model:

$$(32) \qquad y_t = z_t\beta + \epsilon_{1t},$$

$$(33) \qquad z_t = z_{t-1}\delta_1 + y_{t-1}\delta_2 + \epsilon_{2t},$$

$$(34) \qquad \begin{bmatrix} \epsilon_{1t} \\ \epsilon_{2t} \end{bmatrix} \sim IN(0, \Sigma), \qquad \Sigma = \begin{bmatrix} \sigma_{11} & \sigma_{12} \\ \sigma_{12} & \sigma_{22} \end{bmatrix}.$$

Equation (33) is a typical control rule for an agent attempting to control y. For example, this could be a governmental policy reaction function or a farmer's supply decision or a worker's rule for deciding whether to undertake training. These cobweb models have a long history in econometrics. The parameter of interest is assumed to be β.

[12] This illustrates the importance of incorporating in Definition 2.9 the requirement that the conditional model $D(y_t \mid z_t, X_{t-1}, \lambda_1)$ be structurally invariant even though ψ may depend only on a subvector of λ_1.

[13] An interesting example of the complexities arising from overidentification occurs if $\omega_{11} = 1$ in (24) a priori. Then the factorization (27) and (28) no longer operates a cut as a result of the overidentifying constraint $\sigma^2 + \beta^2\omega_{22} = 1$, while the factorization (30) and (31) still does. Further, β and σ^2 are well-defined functions of (γ, δ, τ^2) since $\beta = \delta/(\delta^2 + \tau^2)$ and $\sigma^2 = \tau^2/(\delta^2 + \tau^2)$ while α is not. Therefore, z_t is no longer weakly exogenous for (β, σ^2) while y_t now is! Neither of these two variables is weakly exogenous for α.

The reduced form consists of (33) and

$$y_t = \beta\delta_1 z_{t-1} + \beta\delta_2 y_{t-1} + v_t \tag{35}$$

$$\begin{bmatrix} v_t \\ \epsilon_{2t} \end{bmatrix} \sim IN(0,\Omega), \qquad \Omega = \begin{bmatrix} \sigma_{11} + 2\beta\sigma_{12} + \beta^2\sigma_{22} & \sigma_{12} + \beta\sigma_{22} \\ \sigma_{12} + \beta\sigma_{22} & \sigma_{22} \end{bmatrix}, \tag{36}$$

and the conditional density of y_t given z_t is

$$D(y_t \mid z_t, X_{t-1}, \theta) = N(bz_t + c_1 z_{t-1} + c_2 y_{t-1}, \sigma^2) \quad \text{where} \tag{37}$$

$$b = \beta + \frac{\sigma_{12}}{\sigma_{22}}, \qquad c_i = -\delta_i \frac{\sigma_{12}}{\sigma_{22}}, \qquad \sigma^2 = \sigma_{11} - \sigma_{12}^2/\sigma_{22}, \tag{38}$$

which can be written as the regression

$$y_t = bz_t + c_1 z_{t-1} + c_2 y_{t-1} + u_t, \qquad u_t \sim IN(0,\sigma^2). \tag{39}$$

The condition which is of first concern is the value of the parameter σ_{12}. If $\sigma_{12} = 0$, then z_t is predetermined in (32) and is weakly exogenous for β since (β, σ_{11}) and $(\delta_1, \delta_2, \sigma_{22})$ operates a cut. Even so, for $\delta_2 \neq 0$, y Granger causes z and therefore z is not strongly exogenous, nor is it strictly exogenous. However, the important criterion for efficient estimation is weak exogeneity, not strong exogeneity, and tests for Granger causality have no bearing on either the estimability of (32), or the choice of estimator.

If σ_{12} is not zero, then z_t is not weakly exogenous for β because this parameter cannot be recovered from only the parameters b, c_1, c_2, σ^2 of the conditional distribution (37). In (32) z_t is also not predetermined; however, in (39) it is, again showing the ambiguities in this concept. Whether or not a variable is predetermined depends on which equation is checked, and is not an intrinsic property of a variable.

The preceding results remain unchanged if $\delta_2 = 0$, in which case y does not Granger cause z, yet z_t is still not weakly exogenous for β when $\sigma_{12} \neq 0$. Granger noncausality is neither necessary nor sufficient for weak exogeneity, or for that matter, for predeterminedness.

Suppose instead that b is the parameter of interest and $\delta_2 \neq 0$. Then OLS on (39) will give a consistent estimate. This however will not be an efficient estimate since the parameters should satisfy the restriction

$$\delta_1 c_2 = \delta_2 c_1 \tag{40}$$

and consequently joint estimation of (39) and (33) would be more efficient. The parameterization (b, c_1, c_2, σ^2), $(\delta_1, \delta_2, \sigma_{22})$ does not operate a cut because the parameter sets are not variation free so z_t is not weakly exogenous for b. If, however, $\delta_2 = 0$ so that the system becomes just identified then z_t will be weakly exogenous for b as (b, c_1, σ^2), (δ_1, σ_{22}) operates a cut. In both cases, z_t is still predetermined in (39).

Which parameter "ought" to be the parameter of interest requires further information about the behavior of the system and its possible invariants. Usually, it seems desirable to choose as parameters of interest, those parameters which are invariant to changes in the distribution of the weakly exogenous variables. Returning to the first case where β is the parameter of interest and $\sigma_{12} = 0$, the investigator might assume that (β, σ_{11}) would be invariant to changes in the distribution of z. If this were valid, z_t would be super exogenous, even though it is still Granger caused by y so it is not strongly exogenous nor strictly exogenous. Changes in the parameters of (33) or even of the distribution of z_t will not affect estimation of β nor will control of z affect the conditional relation between y_t and z_t given in (32). Conversely, if $\delta_2 = 0$, but $\sigma_{12} \neq 0$, then (b, c_1, σ^2) and (δ_1, σ_{22}) operates a cut, and z is strictly exogenous in (39) and strongly exogenous for b, yet that regression is by hypothesis not invariant to changes in either δ_1 or σ_{22}, cautioning against constructing cuts which do not isolate invariants.

The assumption of super exogeneity is testable if it is known that the parameters of the marginal distribution have changed over the sample period. A test for changes in β could be interpreted as a test for super exogeneity with respect to the particular interventions observed.

To clarify the question of structural invariance in this example, consider a derivation of the behavioral equation (32) based on the assumption that the agent chooses y to maximize his expected utility conditional on the information available to him. Let the utility function be

$$U(y, z; \beta) = -(y - z\beta)^2 \tag{41}$$

where β is a parameter which is by hypothesis completely unrelated to the distribution of z and hence is invariant to any changes in the δ's in equation (33). Allowing for a possible random error ν_t, arising from optimization, the decision rule is

$$y_t = \beta z_t^e + \nu_t \tag{42}$$

where z_t^e represents the agent's expectation of z_t conditionally on his information set I_t. In the perfect information case where z_t is contained in I_t, $z_t^e = z_t$ and (32) follows directly from (42). Hence β is structurally invariant and the assumption that $\sigma_{12} = \text{cov}(\nu_t, \epsilon_{2t}) = 0$ is sufficient for the weak exogeneity of β and, consequently, for its super exogeneity. The imperfect information case raises more subtle issues since, as argued e.g., in Hendry and Richard [**19**], z_t^e may not coincide with the expectation of z_t as derived from (33). In this example, however, we discuss only the rational expectations formulation originally proposed by Muth [**27**] whereby it is assumed that z_t^e and $E(z_t \mid \cdot)$ in (33) coincide. Hence (32) follows from (42) and

$$\epsilon_{1t} = \nu_t - \beta\epsilon_{2t} \tag{43}$$

so that $\sigma_{12} = \text{cov}(\nu_t, \epsilon_{2t}) - \beta\sigma_{22}$. Therefore, the conventional assumption that $\text{cov}(\nu_t, \epsilon_{2t}) = 0$ entails that $\sigma_{12} = -\beta\sigma_{22} \neq 0$ in which case z_t is neither weakly exogenous nor super exogenous for β even though β is invariant. On the other hand, rational expectations per se does not exclude the possibility that $\sigma_{12} = 0$ (so that z_t remains weakly exogenous for β) since, e.g.,

$$\text{cov}(\nu_t, \epsilon_{2t}) = \sigma_{22}\beta \tag{44}$$

suffices.

Under the familiar assumptions, $\text{cov}(\nu_t, \epsilon_{2t}) = 0$, the conditional expectation (37), and the reduced form, (35), coincide. No current value of z belongs in the conditional expectation of y_t given (z_t, I_t). Nevertheless, z_t is not weakly exogenous for β because the parameter β cannot be recovered from the reduced form coefficients c_1 and c_2 alone. This illustrates that even when the current value fails to enter the conditional expectation, weak exogeneity need not hold.

If the c_i were the parameters of interest, then z_t would be weakly exogenous, but these reduced form parameters are not structurally invariant to changes in the δ's. The Lucas [**23**] criticism applies directly to this equation regardless of whether y Granger causes z. The derivation and the noninvariance of these parameters suggests why they should not be the parameters of interest. Once again, testing for Granger causality has little to do with the Lucas criticism or the estimability or formulation of the parameters of interest. It is still possible to estimate β efficiently, for example by estimating (32) and (33) jointly as suggested by Wallis [**41**], but this requires specifying and estimating both equations.[14] If there is a structural shift in the parameters of the second equation, this must also be allowed for in the joint estimation. This example shows the close relationship between weak exogeneity and structural invariance and points out how models derived from rational expectations behavior may or may not have weak exogeneity and structural invariance.

EXAMPLE 3.3: This final example shows that with a slight extension of the linear Gaussian structure to include serial correlation, the concept of predeterminedness becomes even less useful.

Consider the model

$$y_t = \beta z_t + u_t, \tag{45}$$

$$u_t = \rho u_{t-1} + \epsilon_{1t}, \tag{46}$$

$$z_t = \gamma y_{t-1} + \epsilon_{2t}, \tag{47}$$

$$\begin{bmatrix} \epsilon_{1t} \\ \epsilon_{2t} \end{bmatrix} \sim IN(0, \Sigma), \qquad \Sigma = \begin{bmatrix} \sigma_{11} & \sigma_{12} \\ \sigma_{12} & \sigma_{22} \end{bmatrix}. \tag{48}$$

Although this model is unidentified in a rather subtle sense, this need not concern us here as all the special cases to be discussed will be identified. The issue is dealt with more fully in EHR.

[14] Depending on the model formulation, instrumental variables estimation of (say) (32) alone is sometimes fully efficient.

The conditional expectation of y_t given z_t and X_{t-1} implies the regression

(49) $$y_t = bz_t + cy_{t-1} + dz_{t-1} + \eta_t, \qquad \eta_t \sim IN(0,\sigma^2),$$

where

(50) $$b = \beta + \sigma_{12}/\sigma_{22}, \quad c = \rho - \gamma\sigma_{12}/\sigma_{22}, \quad d = -\beta\rho, \quad \sigma^2 = \sigma_{11} - \sigma_{12}^2/\sigma_{22}.$$

The covariance between z_t and u_t is given by

(51) $$\text{cov}(z_t, u_t) = \left(\sigma_{12} + \sigma_{11}\frac{\gamma\rho}{1-\rho^2}\right)/(1 - \gamma\rho\beta).$$

Note first that, as indicated by (51), the condition $\sigma_{12} = 0$ is *not* sufficient for the predeterminedness of z_t in (45). However, $\sigma_{12} = 0$ is sufficient for the weak exogeneity of z_t for the parameters β and ρ, as can be seen directly from (50) where the parameters of the conditional model (49) are subject to a common factor restriction but are variation free with those of the marginal model (47). Thus, the parameters of (49) could be estimated by imposing the restrictions through some form of autoregressive maximum likelihood method. Ordinary least squares estimation of β in (45) will be inconsistent whereas autoregressive least squares will be both consistent and asymptotically efficient. This example shows the advantages of formulating definitions in terms of expectations conditional on the past.

A second interesting property of this model occurs when $\sigma_{12} \neq 0$ but $\gamma = 0$. Again (51) shows that z_t is not predetermined in (45), but surprisingly, it is weakly exogenous for β and ρ. The three regression coefficients in (49) are now a nonsingular transformation of the three unknown parameters $(\beta, \rho, \sigma_{12}/\sigma_{22})$ and these operate a cut with respect to the remaining nuisance parameter σ_{22}. *Ordinary* least squares estimation of (49) provides efficient estimates of its parameters and the maximum likelihood estimate of β is $-d/c$. Both ordinary least squares and autoregressive least squares estimation of (45) would yield inconsistent estimates of β.

The case where

(52) $$(1-\rho^2)\sigma_{12} + \gamma\rho\sigma_{11} = 0$$

raises several important issues which are discussed in detail in EHR. In short, the condition (52) identifies the model but violates both conditions (i) and (ii) in Definition 2.5 so that z_t is not weakly exogenous for (β, ρ), neither is it for (b, c, d) in (49). In particular, the autoregressive least squares estimator of β in (45) and (46) is inconsistent even though, as a consequence of the predeterminedness of z_t in (45), the first step ordinary least squares estimators of β in (45) and ρ in (46) are consistent (but not efficient).

This concludes the discussion of the examples. It is hoped that these have shown the usefulness of the concepts of weak and strong exogeneity, structural invariance, and super exogeneity in analyzing familiar and possibly some unfamiliar situations. Further examples can be found in EHR including a truncated latent variable model based upon Maddala and Lee [**25**].

4. APPLICATION TO DYNAMIC SIMULTANEOUS EQUATIONS MODELS

In this section we shall apply our analysis to dynamic simultaneous equations models (DSEM). As this is the arena in which notions of exogeneity are most heavily used and tested, it is important to relate our concepts to conventional wisdom. It will be shown that the conventional definitions must be supplemented with several conditions for the concepts to have force. However, when these conditions are added, then in standard textbook models, predeterminedness becomes equivalent to weak exogeneity and strict exogeneity becomes equivalent to strong exogeneity. Finally, our framework helps clarify the connections between such (modified) concepts and the notions of Wold causal orderings (see Strotz and Wold [**40**]), "block recursive structures" (see Fisher [**9**]), and "exogeneity tests" as in Wu [**44**].

Following Richard [**31**, **32**] the system of equations need not be complete and thus the analysis is directly a generalization of the conventional DSEM. Assuming normality and linearity of the conditional expectations $\phi_t = E(x_t \mid X_{t-1}, \theta)$, let[15]

$$D(x_t \mid X_{t-1}, \theta) = f_N^n(x_t \mid \textstyle\sum \Pi(i) x_{t-i}, \Omega) \tag{53}$$

where $\{\Pi(i)\}$ and Ω are functions of a vector of unknown parameters $\theta \in \Theta$.

Define the "innovations" or "reduced form disturbances" v_t by

$$v_t = x_t - \phi_t = x_t - \textstyle\sum \Pi(i) x_{t-i}. \tag{54}$$

Then, ϕ_t being conditional on X_{t-1},

$$\operatorname{cov}(v_t, x_{t-i}) = 0 \quad \text{for all} \quad i > 0, \qquad \text{and hence} \tag{55}$$

$$\operatorname{cov}(v_t, v_{t-i}) = 0 \quad \text{for all} \quad i > 0. \tag{56}$$

We define the dynamic multipliers $Q(i)$ by the recursion

$$Q(0) = I_n \quad \text{and}$$

$$Q(i) = \sum_{j=1}^{i} \Pi(j) Q(i-j), \qquad \text{for all} \quad i \geq 1, \tag{57}$$

[15] Our framework explicitly requires that the distribution of the endogenous variables be completely specified. Normality (and linearity) assumptions are introduced here because they prove algebraically convenient. Other distributional assumptions could be considered at the cost of complicating the algebra. Furthermore, there exist distributions, such as the multivariate student distribution, for which there exist no cuts. Evidently weak exogeneity can always be achieved by construction, simply by specifying independently of each other a conditional and a marginal model, but is then no longer testable. More interestingly, conditions such as the ones which are derived below could be viewed as "approximate" or "local" exogeneity conditions under more general specifications. Given the recent upsurge of nonlinear non-Gaussian models in econometrics this is clearly an area which deserves further investigation.

and note that

(58) $\quad \mathrm{cov}(v_t, x_{t+i}) = Q(i)\Omega \qquad \text{for all} \quad i \geq 0.$

Often the specification of θ is (partially) achieved by considering sets of behavioral relationships. Such relationships can correspond to optimizing behavior given expectations about future events, allow for adaptive responses and include mechanisms for correcting previous mistakes. In our framework, where attention is focussed on the conditional densities $D(x_t | X_{t-1}, \theta)$ it is natural to specify these relationships in terms of the conditional expectations ϕ_t. Consider, therefore, a set of $g \leq n$ linear behavioral relationships of the form

(59) $\quad B\phi_t + \sum C(i)x_{t-i} = 0$

where B and $\{C(i)\}$ are $g \times n$ matrix functions of a vector of "structural" coefficients $\delta \in \Delta$, with rank $B = g$ almost everywhere in Δ. The δ's are typically parameters of interest. We can also define a g-dimensional vector of unobservable "structural disturbances:"

(60) $\quad \epsilon_t = Bx_t + \sum C(i)x_{t-i}$

which also satisfy, by construction, the properties (55), (56).

Let Σ denote the covariance matrix of ϵ_t. In all generality Σ is also treated as a function of δ. From (53), (54), (59), and (60) we must have $\epsilon_t = Bv_t$ and

(61) $\quad B\Pi(i) + C(i) \equiv 0, \qquad \text{for all} \quad i \geq 0; \qquad \Sigma = B\Omega B'.$

The identities (61) define a correspondence between Δ and Θ or, equivalently, a function h from Δ to $P(\Theta)$, the set of all subsets of Θ. To any given $\delta \in \Delta$, h associates a subset of Θ which we denote by $h(\delta)$. In the rest of the paper it is assumed that: (i) δ is *identified* in the sense that

(62) $\quad \text{for all} \quad \delta, \delta* \in \Delta, \qquad \delta \neq \delta* \rightarrow h(\delta) \cap h(\delta*) = \emptyset;$

(ii) all values in Θ are compatible with (61),

(63) $\quad \Theta = \bigcup_{\delta \in \Delta} h(\delta),$

so that $\{h(\delta)\}$ is a partition of Θ.

Let s denote the number of nonzero columns in $\{\Pi(i)\}$ and C_n the set of $n \times n$ symmetric positive definite matrices. If $\Theta = R^{sn} \times C_n$, except for the set of zero Lebesgue measure, then the model (53) is *just identified*. It is *overidentified* if Θ is a strict subset of $R^{sn} \times C_n$.

When $g < n$, it often proves convenient to define an auxiliary parameter vector, say $\bar{\theta} \in \bar{\Theta}$ of the form $\bar{\theta} = (\delta, \theta_2)$ where θ_2 is a subvector of θ defined in such a way that $\bar{\Theta}$ and Θ are in one-to-one correspondence. If, in particular, $\{\Pi(i)\}$ and Ω are subject to no other constraints than those derived from the identities (61) as implicitly assumed in this section, then we can select for θ_2 the coefficients of $n-g$ unconstrained "reduced form" equations,[16] whereby

$$\bar{\Theta}=\Delta\times\Theta_2,\quad\text{with}\quad \Theta_2=R^{s(n-g)}\times C_{n-g}. \tag{64}$$

The specification of many econometric models "allows for" serial correlation of the residuals, i.e., incorporates linear relationships of the form

$$B^*x_t+\sum C^*(i)x_{t-i}=u_t\sim N(0,\Phi) \tag{65}$$

where B^* and $\{C^*(i)\}$ are claimed to be parameters of interest (or well defined functions thereof) and u_t is seen as a g-dimensional "autonomous" process, subject to serial correlation. Note that if (65) is to be used to *derive* the distribution of x_t *from* that of u_t, then the system must be "complete", i.e., $g=n$.

Provided u_t has an autoregressive representation,

$$u_t=\sum R_i u_{t-i}+e_t,\quad\text{where}\quad e_t\sim IN(0,\Sigma), \tag{66}$$

then (65) can be transformed to have serially uncorrelated "errors" (the new parameterization being subject to common factor restrictions as in Sargan **[37]**) in which case the transformed model can be reinterpreted in terms of conditional expectations as in (53). More general specifications of u_t are not ruled out in principle, but might seriously complicate the analysis.

We can now unambiguously characterize and inter-relate the concepts of Granger noncausality, predeterminedness and strict exogeneity, as given in Definitions 2.1–2.3, for potentially overidentified and incomplete DSEM which have been transformed to have serially uncorrelated residuals. Since these concepts may apply only to a subset of the equation system (59), this is accordingly partitioned into the first $g_1\le p$ equations and the remaining $g_2=g-g_1\le q$ equations—see e.g. Fisher **[9]** on the notion of block recursive structures. We partition the Π's, Q's, and Ω conformably with the variables $x_t'=(y_t'z_t')$, B conformably with the variables and the equations and the C's and Σ conformably with the equations as:

$$\begin{aligned}
&\Pi(i)=\begin{bmatrix}\Pi_1(i)\\ \Pi_2(i)\end{bmatrix}=\begin{bmatrix}\Pi_{11}(i) & \Pi_{12}(i)\\ \Pi_{21}(i) & \Pi_{22}(i)\end{bmatrix},\\
&Q(i)=\begin{bmatrix}Q_1(i)\\ Q_2(i)\end{bmatrix}=\begin{bmatrix}Q_{11}(i) & Q_{12}(i)\\ Q_{21}(i) & Q_{22}(i)\end{bmatrix},\\
&\Omega=(\Omega_1\Omega_2)=\begin{bmatrix}\Omega_{11} & \Omega_{12}\\ \Omega_{21} & \Omega_{22}\end{bmatrix},\qquad B=\begin{bmatrix}B_1\\ B_2\end{bmatrix}=\begin{bmatrix}B_{11} & B_{12}\\ B_{21} & B_{22}\end{bmatrix},\\
&C(i)=\begin{bmatrix}C_1(i)\\ C_2(i)\end{bmatrix}\quad\text{and}\quad \Sigma=\begin{bmatrix}\Sigma_{11} & \Sigma_{12}\\ \Sigma_{21} & \Sigma_{22}\end{bmatrix}.
\end{aligned} \tag{67}$$

[16] This is current practice in the literature on so-called limited information procedures. Non-Bayesian inference procedures based on likelihood principles are invariant with respect to the choice

THEOREM 4.1: *For the class of models defined by* (53) *plus* (59): (i) *y does not Granger cause z if and only if*

$$Q_{21}(i) = 0, \qquad \text{for all} \quad i \geq 1;$$

(ii) z_t *is predetermined in the first* g_1 *equations of* (59) *if and only if*

$$B_1\Omega_2 = 0;$$

(iii) z_t *is strictly exogenous in the first* g_1 *equations of* (59) *if and only if*

$$B_1\Omega Q_2'(i) = 0, \qquad \text{for all} \quad i \geq 0.$$

(iv) *Conditions* (i) *and* (ii) *are sufficient for* (iii). *If* $g_1 = p$, *they are also necessary for* (iii).

(v) *If* $B_{21} = 0$, $\Sigma_{12} = 0$, *and rank* $B_{22} = q(= g_2)$, *then* z_t *is predetermined in the first* g_1 *equations of* (59).

PROOF: The proof follows from the Definitions 2.1–2.3 together with (57), wherefrom it can be shown by recurrence that $(\Pi_{21}(i) = 0;\ i \geq 1)$ is equivalent to $(Q_{21}(i) = 0;\ i \geq 1)$. See EHR for more details.

In order to discuss weak exogeneity the parameters of interest must be defined. In the theorems below it will be assumed that the parameters of interest are all grouped together in the first g_1 equations. Thus it is not a cavalier matter which equations are put in the first group. For example, in a control problem, the first g_1 equations might describe the behavior of the economic agents given the controlled values of z_t, while the remaining g_2 equations describe the control rules which have been operative.

Factorizing the joint density (53) also requires the introduction of an appropriate reparameterization. This is the object of Lemma 4.2 which translates into our notation results which are otherwise well-known.

LEMMA 4.2: *The joint density* (53) *factorizes into the product of the conditional density*

(68) $$D(y_t \mid z_t, X_{t-1}, \lambda_1) = f_N^p\left(y_t \mid \Delta_{12}z_t + \sum \Pi_{1.2}(i)x_{t-i}, \Omega_{11.2}\right)$$

and the marginal density

(69) $$D(z_t \mid X_{t-1}, \lambda_2) = f_N^q\left(z_t \mid \sum \Pi_2(i)x_{t-i}, \Omega_{22}\right)$$

with $\lambda_1 = (\Delta_{12}, \{\Pi_{1.2}(i)\}, \Omega_{11.2})$, $\lambda_2 = (\{\Pi_2(i)\}, \Omega_{22})$,

(70) $$\Delta_{12} = \Omega_{12}\Omega_{22}^{-1}, \quad \Omega_{11.2} = \Omega_{11} - \Omega_{12}\Omega_{22}^{-1}\Omega_{21}, \ \textit{and}\ \Pi_{1.2}(i) = \Pi_1(i) - \Delta_{12}\Pi_2(i).$$

PROOF: See e.g. Press [30, Sections 3.4 and 3.5].

of these $n - g$ reduced form equations, provided they form a nonsingular set of equations together with the g structural relationships (59). Also, in a Bayesian framework there exist prior densities on θ such that the corresponding posterior densities on δ have similar invariance properties. For details, see e.g. Drèze and Richard [5] for $g = 1$, or Richard [31] for $g > 1$.

If the model (53) is *just identified*, then λ_1 and λ_2 are variation free with respective domains of variation $\Lambda_1 = R^{p\times q} \times \{R^{p\times n}\} \times C_p$ and $\Lambda_2 = \{R^{q\times n}\} \times C_q$ and z_t is weakly exogenous for ψ if and only if ψ is a function of λ_1 only. However, in order to be operational within the framework of DSEM's, such a condition should be expressed in terms of the structural coefficients δ since these are themselves typically parameters of interest. Also, most applications involve overidentified models for which λ_1 and λ_2 are no longer variation free unless some additional conditions are satisfied. Thus, the object of Theorem 4.3 is to derive *general* conditions on δ for the weak exogeneity of z_t for ψ. By their nature, these conditions are *sufficient* and, as in Section 3, it is easy to construct examples in which they are *not necessary*. Consequently, insofar as so-called "exogeneity tests" are typically tests for such conditions, rejection on such a test does not necessarily entail that the weak exogeneity assumption is invalid (see e.g. Example 3.3 when $\sigma_{12} \neq 0$ and $\gamma = 0$).

THEOREM 4.3: *For the DSEM in* (53) *plus* (59) *consider the following conditions*:

(i) $B_1\Omega_2 = 0,$

(ii) $B_{21} = 0,$

(iii) $(B_1, \{C_1(i)\}, \Sigma_{11})$ *and* $(B_2, \{C_2(i)\}, \Sigma_{22})$ *are variation free*,

(iv) ψ *is a function of* $(B_1, \{C_1(i)\}, \Sigma_{11})$,

(v) $\Sigma_{12} = 0,$

(vi) $\text{rank}\, B_{22} = q,$

(vii) $(B_2, \{C_2(i)\}, \Sigma_{22})$ *are just identified parameters.*

The following sets of conditions are sufficient for the weak exogeneity of z_t *for* ψ:

(a) (i)(ii)(iii)(iv),

(b) (ii)(iii)(iv)(v)(vi),

(c) (i)(iii)(iv)(vii).

PROOF: The basic result (a) generalizes Theorem 3.1 in Richard [32] in that it also covers cases where restrictions are imposed on Σ. The proof in Richard extends to the more general case since, under (i) and (ii), the identity $\Sigma = B\Omega B'$ separates into the two identities $\Sigma_{11} = B_{11}\Omega_{11.2}B_{11}'$ and $\Sigma_{22} = B_{22}\Omega_{22}B_{22}'$. Result (b) follows from (a) together with condition (ii) and (v) in Theorem 4.1. Result (c) follows by applying (a) to a system consisting of the first g_1 behavioral relationships and g_2 *unrestricted* reduced form equations whose parameters are in one-to-one correspondence with $(B_2, \{C_2(i)\}, \Sigma_{22})$ and variation free with $(B_1, \{C_1(i)\}, \Sigma_{11})$ following conditions (vii) and (iii).

The major differences in the sufficient conditions for weak exogeneity and for predeterminedness are conditions (iii) and (iv) of Theorem 4.3, which assure the model builder that there are no cross equation restrictions to the second block of equations and that there are no interesting parameters in that block.

To show the importance of these conditions in any definition, consider a set of $g \leq p < n$ just identified behavioral relationships, as given by (59) such that $B\Omega_2 \neq 0$. As is well known (see, for example, Strotz and Wold [**40**]) the system (59) can be replaced by an observationally equivalent one in which z_t is predetermined, and hence is strictly exogenous if y does not Granger cause z. For example let

$$\bar{B} = \Phi(I_g : -\Omega_{12}\Omega_{22}^{-1}), \tag{71}$$

$$\bar{C}(i) = -\bar{B}\Pi(i), \qquad i \geq 1, \tag{72}$$

where Φ is an arbitrary but known $g \times g$ nonsingular matrix so that $(\bar{B}, \{\bar{C}(i)\})$ are just-identified by construction. Such transformations, with $\Phi = I_2$, have been implicitly used in the Examples 3.1–3.2. Replacing (59) by

$$\bar{B}\phi_t + \sum \bar{C}(i)x_{t-i} = 0 \tag{73}$$

leaves (53) unaffected, but now $\bar{B}\Omega_2 = 0$. Consequently, $(\bar{B}, \{\bar{C}(i)\})$ can be estimated consistently from the conditional model $D(y_t \mid z_t, X_{t-1}, \cdot)$ together with (73). These estimates would be efficient provided (59) were just-identified. However, it is essential to realize that, since $g \leq p < n$, the parameters $(B, \{C(i)\})$ are typically not functions of $(\bar{B}, \{\bar{C}(i)\})$ alone and if the former are of interest, transforming (59) to (73) does not allow valid inference conditionally on z_t.

Thus, although at first sight, in normal DSEM weak exogeneity appears to be close to the notion of a Wold causal ordering, without the concept of parameters of interest the latter lacks force since there may be no cut which separates the parameters of interest and the nuisance parameters. Nevertheless, it must be stressed that Wold and Jureen [**43**, p. 14] *explicitly* include the condition that "each equation in the system expresses a unilateral causal dependence" which, in the spirit of our use of sequential cuts, seems designed to exclude arbitrary transformations of the system (59); see also the distinction in Bentzel and Hansen [**2**] between basic and derived models.

In Wu's [**44**] analysis, where $g_1 = 1$, it is implicit that conditions (iii) and (vii) of Theorem 4.3 are satisfied in which case the condition for predeterminedness $(B_1\Omega_2 = 0)$ is indeed sufficient for the weak exogeneity of z_t for the parameters of the first behavioral equation (but not necessarily for other parameters of interest). It must be stressed, however, that if the remaining behavioral equations in the model under consideration are over-identified, then predeterminedness might no longer be sufficient on its own for the weak exogeneity of z_t. Therefore, even if the conditions (iii) and (iv) of Theorem 4.3 are incorporated in the definition of predeterminedness as is sometimes implicitly done, there would remain many situations where weak exogeneity and predeterminedness would still differ. Cases (a) and (b) in Theorem 4.3 provide *sufficient* conditions which are applicable to more general cases than the one considered in Wu. Note, however, that condition (ii) in particular is not necessary and that case (c) could be made more general at the cost of some tedious notation as hinted by the following example.[17]

EXAMPLE 4.4: Consider a (complete) DSEM with $n = 3$, $p = g_1 = 1$, $q = g_2 = 2$, and

$$B = \begin{bmatrix} 1 & b_1 & 0 \\ b_2 & 1 & 0 \\ 0 & b_3 & 1 \end{bmatrix}, \qquad C(1) = \begin{bmatrix} c_1 & 0 & 0 \\ 0 & c_2 & c_3 \\ 0 & c_4 & 0 \end{bmatrix}, \qquad C(i) = 0, \qquad i > 1.$$

The b's and c's are assumed to be variation free. The condition $B_1\Omega_2 = 0$, which is equivalent to $\sigma_{12} = b_2\sigma_{11}$ and $\sigma_{13} = 0$, is sufficient for the weak exogeneity of (y_{2t}, y_{3t}) for (b_1, c_1, σ_{11}) even though $B'_{21} = (b_2 0) \neq 0$ and the third behavioral relationship is overidentified (but does not contain y_{1t}!). Note that the predeterminedness of y_{2t} in the first behavioral relationship ($\sigma_{12} = b_2\sigma_{11}$) is sufficient for the *consistency* of OLS estimation of (b_1, c_1, σ_{11}) in that relationship but not for the weak exogeneity of (y_{2t}, y_{3t})—or y_{2t} alone—for (b_1, c_1, σ_{11}). In the absence of additional restrictions such as $\sigma_{13} = 0$ a more *efficient* estimator of (b_1, c_1, σ_{11}) is obtained e.g. by FIML estimation of the complete DSEM.

Note finally from Theorem 4.1 (v) and 4.3 (b) that the standard block-recursive model is sufficient for both (block) predeterminedness and (block) weak exogeneity (again assuming the parameterization satisfies (iii) and (iv)); this may help explain its importance in the development of the theory of simultaneous equations models.

5. SUMMARY AND CONCLUSIONS

Given the pervasive role of the concept of "exogeneity" in econometrics, it is essential to uniquely characterize the implications of claims that certain variables are "exogenous" according to particular definitions. Also, it is useful to have definitions which require minimal conditions and yet are applicable to as wide a class of relevant models as possible. Consequently, general and unambiguous definitions are proposed for *weak*, *strong*, and *super* exogeneity in terms of the joint densities of observable variables and the parameters of interest in given models, thus extending and formalizing the approach in Koopmans **[21]**. "Exogeneity" assertions are usually intended to allow the analysis of one set of variables without having to specify exactly how a second related set is deter-

[17]We are grateful to A. Holly for providing us with this example and, more generally, for pointing out several shortcomings in earlier drafts of this section.

mined and such an analysis could comprise any or all of inference, forecasting, or policy. In each case, the conclusions are conditional on the validity of the relevant "exogeneity" claims (a comment germane to theoretical models also, although we only consider observable variables) and since different conditioning statements are required in these three cases, three distinct, but inter-related, concepts of exogeneity are necessary.

The joint density of the observed variables $x_t = (y_t' z_t')'$, conditional on their past, always can be factorized as the conditional density of y_t given z_t times the marginal density of z_t. If: (a) the parameters λ_1 and λ_2 of these conditional and marginal densities are not subject to cross-restrictions (i.e., there is a cut) and, (b) the parameters of interest (denoted by ψ) can be uniquely determined from the parameters of the conditional model alone (i.e., $\psi = f(\lambda_1)$), then inference concerning ψ from the joint density will be equivalent to that from the conditional density so that the latter may be used without loss of relevant information. Under such conditions, z_t is *weakly* exogenous for ψ, and for purposes of *inference* about ψ, z_t may be treated "as if" it were determined outside the (conditional) model under study, making the analysis simpler and more robust.

Conditions (a) and (b) clearly are not sufficient to treat z_t as if it were fixed in repeated samples, since the definition of weak exogeneity is unspecific about relationships between z_t and y_{t-i} for $i \geq 1$. However, if: (c) y does not Granger cause z, then the data density of $X_t^1 = (x_1, \ldots, x_t)'$ factorizes into the conditional density of Y_t^1 given Z_t^1 times the marginal of Z_t^1 and hence $\{z_t\}$ may be treated as if it were fixed. If (a), (b), and (c) are satisfied, then z_t is *strongly exogenous* for ψ and forecasts could be made conditional on fixed future z's.

Nevertheless, strong exogeneity is insufficient to sustain conditional policy analysis since (a) does not preclude the possibility that while λ_1 and λ_2 are variation free within any *given* "regime," λ_1 might vary in response to a change in λ_2 between "regimes." The additional condition that: (d) λ_1 is invariant to changes in λ_2 (or more generally the conditional distribution is invariant to any change in the marginal distribution) is required to sustain conditional *policy* experiments for fixed λ_1, and z_t is *super exogenous* for ψ if (a), (b), and (d) are satisfied (so that (c) is not necessary either).

In fact, if the generating process of the conditioning variables is susceptible to changes over either sample or forecast periods, then the failure of (d) will invalidate inference and predictions based on the assertion that λ_1 is a constant parameter, whether or not z_t includes "policy variables." In worlds where policy parameters change, false super-exogeneity assumptions are liable to produce predictive failures in conditional models (see Lucas [**23**]). Control experiments which involve changes in λ_2 must first establish the super exogeneity of z_t for ψ under the class of interventions considered; we know of no sufficient conditions for establishing such results, but a necessary condition is that the conditional model does not experience predictive failure within sample (see Hendry [**18**]).

Even in constant parameter worlds (and certainly in worlds of parameter change), the new concepts are distinct from the more familiar notions of predeterminedness and strict exogeneity. Following precise definitions of these two concepts, it is shown through examples that their formulation in terms of *unobservable* disturbances entails ambiguous implications for inference and that strict exogeneity is neither necessary nor sufficient for inference in conditional models without loss of relevant information. Moreover, models in which predeterminedness is obtained by construction need not have invariant parameters and since predeterminedness is necessary for strict exogeneity, establishing only the latter does not provide a valid basis for conditional prediction or conditional policy. The various concepts are compared and contrasted in detail in closed linear dynamic simultaneous equations systems, and the usefulness of (a) and (b) in clarifying the debate about Wold-causal-orderings is demonstrated.

It is natural to enquire about the testable implications of alternative exogeneity assumptions. Condition (d) is indirectly testable (as noted) via tests for parameter constancy, although as with all test procedures, rejection of the null does not indicate what alternative is relevant and non-rejection may simply reflect low power (so that there are advantages in specifying the regime shift process as in Richard [**32**]). Condition (c) is common to both strong and strict exogeneity notions and may be testable in the conditional model (see Sims [**38**] and Geweke [**14**]) but may also require specification of the marginal density of z_t as in Granger [**16**]. Also, predeterminedness tests have been the subject of a large literature (see inter alia Wu [**44**]).

To test weak exogeneity, the conditional and marginal densities could be embedded in a joint density function, although the choice of the latter may or may not generate testable implications. It is somewhat paradoxical to estimate the parameters of a (potentially very complicated) marginal model just to test whether or not one needed to specify that model. Moreover, misspecifications in the marginal model may induce false rejection of the null of weak exogeneity. Nevertheless, Engle [**6, 7**] considers various weak exogeneity tests based on the Lagrange multiplier principle. Also, on a positive note, while both weak exogeneity and parameter constancy are conjectural features in a conditional modelling exercise, if the data generating process of z_t has changed, but the conditional model has not, then some credibility must attach to the latter since it was hazarded to potential rejection and survived.

Finally, we believe that the new concepts are not only general (being based explicitly on density functions and encompassing worlds of parameter change) and unambiguously characterized (thus clarifying a vital concept in econometrics) but also highlight interesting and novel aspects of familiar problems (as shown in the examples in Section 3).

University of California, San Diego,
Nuffield College, Oxford,
and
CORE, Louvain-la-Neuve, Belgium

Manuscript received November, 1979; last revision received March, 1982.

REFERENCES

[1] Barndorff-Nielsen, O.: *Information and Exponential Families in Statistical Theory*. New York: John Wiley & Sons, 1978.

[2] Bentzel, R. and B. Hansen: "On Recursiveness and Interdependency in Economic Models," *Review of Economic Studies*, 22(1955), 153–168.

[3] Chamberlain, G.: "The General Equivalence of Granger and Sims Causality," *Econometrica*, 50(1982), 569–582.

[4] Christ, C. F.: *Econometric Models and Methods*. New York: John Wiley & Sons, 1966.

[5] Drèze, J. H., and J.-F. Richard: "Bayesian Analysis of Simultaneous Equation Systems," forthcoming in the *Handbook of Econometrics*, edited by Z. Griliches and M. Intriligator. Amsterdam: North-Holland Publishing Co.

[6] Engle, R. F.: "A General Approach to the Construction of Model Diagnostics Based Upon the Lagrange Multiplier Principle," University of Warwick Discussion Paper 156, UCSD Discussion Paper 79-43, 1979.

[7] ———: "Wald, Likelihood Ratio and Lagrange Multiplier Tests in Econometrics," forthcoming in *Handbook of Econometrics*, edited by Z. Griliches and M. Intriligator. Amsterdam; North-Holland Publishing Co.

[8] Engle, R. F., D. F. Hendry, and J.-F. Richard: "Exogeneity, Causality and Structural Invariance in Econometric Modelling," CORE Discussion Paper 80-83, UCSD Discussion Paper 81-1, 1980.

[9] Fisher, F. M.: *The Identification Problem in Econometrics*. New York: McGraw Hill, 1966.

[10] Florens, J.-P., and M. Mouchart: "Initial and Sequential Reduction of Bayesian Experiments," CORE Discussion Paper 8015, Université Catholique de Louvain, Louvain-la-Neuve, Belgium, 1980.

[11] ———: "A Note on Non-Causality," *Econometrica*, 50(1982), 583–592.

[12] Frisch, R.: "Autonomy of Economic Relations," paper read at the Cambridge Conference of the Econometric Society, 1938.

[13] Geweke, J.: "Testing the Exogeneity Specification in the Complete Dynamic Simultaneous Equations Model," *Journal of Econometrics* 7(1978), 163–185.

[14] ———: "Causality, Exogeneity and Inference," Invited paper, Fourth World Congress of the Econometric Society, Aix-en Provence, 1980.

[15] Gourieroux, C., J.-J. Laffont, and A. Montfort: "Disequilibrium Econometrics in Simultaneous Equations Systems," *Econometrica*, 48(1980), 75–96.

[16] Granger, C. W. J.: "Investigating Causal Relations by Econometric Models and Cross-Spectral Methods," *Econometrica*, 37(1969), 424–438.

[17] Hendry, D. F.: "The Behavior of Inconsistent Instrumental Variables Estimators in Dynamic Systems with Autocorrelated Errors," *Journal of Econometrics*, 9(1979), 295–314.

[18] ———: "Predictive Failure and Econometric Modelling in Macroeconomics: The Transactions Demand for Money," in *Modelling the Economy*, ed. by P. Ormerod. London: Heinemann Educational Books, 1980.

[19] Hendry, D. F., and J.-F. Richard: "The Econometric Analysis of Economic Time Series," forthcoming in *International Statistical Review*.

[20] Hurwicz, L: "On the Structural Form of Interdependent Systems," in *Logic, Methodology and the Philosophy of Science*, ed. by E. Nagel et al. Palo Alto: Stanford University Press, 1962.

[21] Koopmans, T. C.: "When is an Equation System Complete for Statistical Purposes?" in *Statistical Inference in Dynamic Economic Models*, ed. by T. C. Koopmans. New York: John Wiley and Sons, 1950.

[22] Koopmans, T. C., and W. C. Hood: "The Estimation of Simultaneous Linear Economic Relationships," in *Studies in Econometric Method*, ed. by W. C. Hood and T. C. Koopmans. New Haven: Yale University Press, 1953.

[23] Lucas, R. E., Jr.: "Econometric Policy Evaluation: A Critique," in Vol. 1 of the Carnegie-Rochester Conferences on Public Policy, supplementary series to the *Journal of Monetary Economics*, ed. by K. Brunner and A. Meltzer. Amsterdam: North-Holland Publishing Company, 1976, pp. 19–46.

[24] McFadden, D.: "Econometric Analysis of Discrete Data," Fisher-Schultz Lecture, European Meeting of the Econometric Society, Athens, 1979.

[25] Maddala, G. S., and L. F. Lee: "Recursive Models with Qualitative Endogenous Variables," *Annals of Economic and Social Measurement*, 5(1976), 525–545.

[26] MARSCHAK, J.: "Economic Measurements for Policy and Prediction," in *Studies in Econometric Method*, ed. by W. C. Hood and T. C. Koopmans. New Haven: Yale University Press, 1953.
[27] MUTH, J. F.: "Rational Expectations and the Theory of Price Movements," *Econometrica*, 29(1961), 315–335.
[28] ORCUTT, G. H.: "Toward a Partial Redirection of Econometrics," *Review of Economics and Statistics*, 34(1952), 195–213.
[29] PHILLIPS, A. W.: "Some Notes on the Estimation of Time-Forms of Reactions in Interdependent Dynamic Systems," *Economica*, 23(1956), 99–113.
[30] PRESS, S. J.: *Applied Multivariate Analysis*. New York: Holt, Rinehard and Winston, Inc., 1972.
[31] RICHARD, J.-F.: "Exogeneity, Inference and Prediction in so-called Incomplete Dynamic Simultaneous Equation Models," CORE Discussion Paper 7922, Université Catholique de Louvain, Louvain-la-Neuve, Belgium, 1979.
[32] ———: "Models with Several Regimes and Changes in Exogeneity," *Review of Economic Studies*, 47(1980), 1–20.
[33] ROTHENBERG, T. J.: *Efficient Estimation with A Priori Information*. Cowles Foundation Monograph 23. New Haven: Yale University Press, 1973.
[34] SALMON, M., AND K. F. WALLIS: "Model Validation and Forecast Comparisons: Theoretical and Practical Considerations," in *Evaluating the Reliability of Macroeconomic Models*, ed. by G. C. Chow and P. Corsi. London: Wiley, 1982.
[35] SARGENT, T. J.: "Interpreting Economic Time Series," *Journal of Political Economy*, 89(1981), 213–248.
[36] SARGAN, J. D.: "The Maximum Likelihood Estimation of Economic Relationships with Autoregressive Residuals," *Econometrica*, 29(1961), 414–426.
[37] ———: "Some Tests of Dynamic Specification for a Single Equation," *Econometrica*, 48(1980), 879–897.
[38] SIMS, C. A.: "Money, Income and Causality," *American Economic Review*, 62(1972), 540–552.
[39] ———: "Exogeneity and Causal Ordering in Macroeconomic Models," in *New Methods in Business Cycle Research: Proceedings from a Conference*, ed. by C. A. Sims. Minneapolis: Federal Reserve Bank of Minneapolis, 1977.
[40] STROTZ, R. H., AND H. O. A. WOLD: "Recursive Versus Non-Recursive Systems: An Attempt at a Synthesis," *Econometrica*, 28(1960), 417–421.
[41] WALLIS, K. F.: "Econometric Implications of the Rational Expectations Hypothesis," *Econometrica*, 48(1980), 49–73.
[42] WIENER, N.: "The Theory of Prediction," in *Modern Mathematics for Engineers*, ed. by E. F. Beckenback. New York: McGraw-Hill, 1956.
[43] WOLD, H. O. A., AND L. JUREEN: *Demand Analysis—A Study in Econometrics*. New York: J. Wiley & Sons, 1955.
[44] WU, D. M.: "Alternative Tests of Independence between Stochastic Regressors and Disturbances," *Econometrica*, 41(1973), 733–750.
[45] ZELLNER, A.: "Causality and Econometrics," in *Three Aspects of Policy and Policymaking*, ed. by K. Brunner and A. H. Meltzer. Amsterdam: North-Holland, 1979.

Part V
Spectral Approaches

[24]

Econometrica, Vol. 34, No. 1 (January, 1966)

THE TYPICAL SPECTRAL SHAPE OF AN ECONOMIC VARIABLE[1]

BY C. W. J. GRANGER

In recent years, a number of power spectra have been estimated from economic data and the majority have been found to be of a similar shape. A number of implications of this shape are discussed, particular attention being paid to the reality of business cycles, stability and control problems, and model building.

1. INTRODUCTION

DURING THE past four or five years a fairly large number of power spectra have been estimated using economic data.[2] It might thus be an appropriate time to review the results obtained and to ask if the advent of spectral methods has thrown any light on the basic characteristics of economic variables. The almost unanimous result of these investigations is that the vast majority of economic variables, after removal of any trend in mean and seasonal components, have similarly shaped power spectra, the typical shape being as in Figure 1.

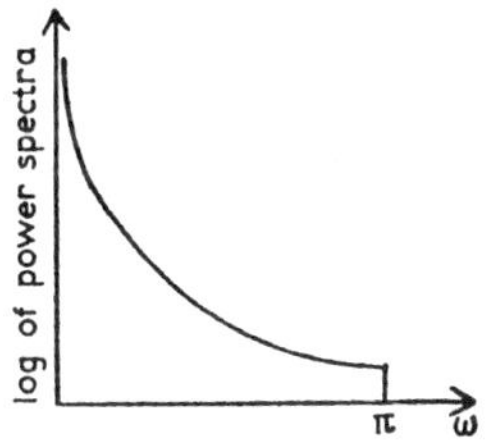

FIGURE 1.—Typical spectral shape.

It is the purpose of this paper to illustrate this result and to discuss briefly its implications both for economic theory in general and for economic model building in particular.

It is not, of course, suggested that every economic time series produce such spectra nor that nothing else is discernable from the estimated spectra other than this simple shape. Nevertheless, the fact that such a shape arises in the majority of cases does suggest that there are certain general, overall implications for economics, and, possibly, that the estimation of power spectra alone is unlikely to be a productive technique. Cross spectral methods which, in the author's opinion, are likely to prove more important and which attempt to discover and explain the relationships between economic variables, will not be considered in this paper.[3]

[1] Prepared under the auspices of National Science Foundation Grant GP-82.

[2] In addition to his own work, the author is familiar with the calculations by J. Cunnyngham, D. Fand, M. Godfrey, M. Hatanaka, M. Nerlove, E. Parzen, and M. Suzuki.

[3] For a description of cross-spectral methods and other generalizations see [3].

Spectral methods are based upon the idea of the decomposition of a stochastic process into a (possibly non-finite) number of orthogonal components, each of which is associated with a "frequency." Such a decomposition is always possible for processes that are "covariance stationary," i.e., have variances and autocovariances independent of real time. The power spectrum records the contribution of the components belonging to a given frequency band to the total variance of the process. If a band contributes a large proportion of the total variance it may be considered to be important compared to a band which contributes a smaller amount to the variance. As the introduction, interpretation, and estimation of power spectra have been dealt with in detail elsewhere,[4] it is not considered necessary to expand on these subjects further in this paper. It must be emphasized that spectral methods do not require the specification of a model but follow directly from the assumption of stationarity.[5]

2. EXAMPLES OF ESTIMATED SPECTRA

A number of power spectra of economic series displaying the "typical shape" have been published. Nerlove [**8**] shows the estimated spectra for the Federal Reserve Board index of industrial production (U.S.A., monthly, March, 1920—September, 1960, seasonally adjusted), federally inspected hog slaughter and cattle slaughter (monthly, January, 1907—December, 1960) and various U.S. employment series (monthly, July, 1947 or 1948—December, 1961, both original series and seasonally adjusted). Cunnyngham [**2**] has estimated spectra for the wholesale commodity price index (monthly, 1908–1960) and money supply (monthly, 1908–1960). It has been found that price series from the New York stock market produce the typical shape. Diagrams illustrating this may be found in Granger and Morgenstern [**4**] and in Chapter 4 of [**3**].

There also exist many unpublished estimated spectra. In the course of his studies of business cycle indicators, Hatanaka [**3**, Chapter **12**], and [**5**] has estimated the spectra of twenty-two important economic series, the large majority of which display the typical shape. Unpublished studies by Godfrey, Parzen, and Suzuki provide further examples.

It must be emphasized that many of these series contained important seasonal components so that the "typical shape" had added to it peaks at frequencies corresponding to a period of 12 months and its harmonics.

Figure 2 provides an example of a "typical" spectral shape with peaks corresponding to the seasonal component. It shows the logarithm of the estimated power spectrum for United States bank clearing data (monthly, 1875–1958) from which an exponential linear trend ($\exp(a+bt)$) has been estimated and subtracted. Despite

[4] See [**3**] or Nerlove [**8**].

[5] In fact, spectral methods can provide useful results for wider classes of process but description of these processes lies outside the scope of this paper.

this trend-removal procedure, considerable power remains at very low frequencies. In this example, roughly 99 per cent of the total power lies in the frequency band $(0, 2\pi/40)$ which illustrates the extreme subtlety of the analysis one attempts in measuring the power spectrum at higher frequencies. The fact that it is usually

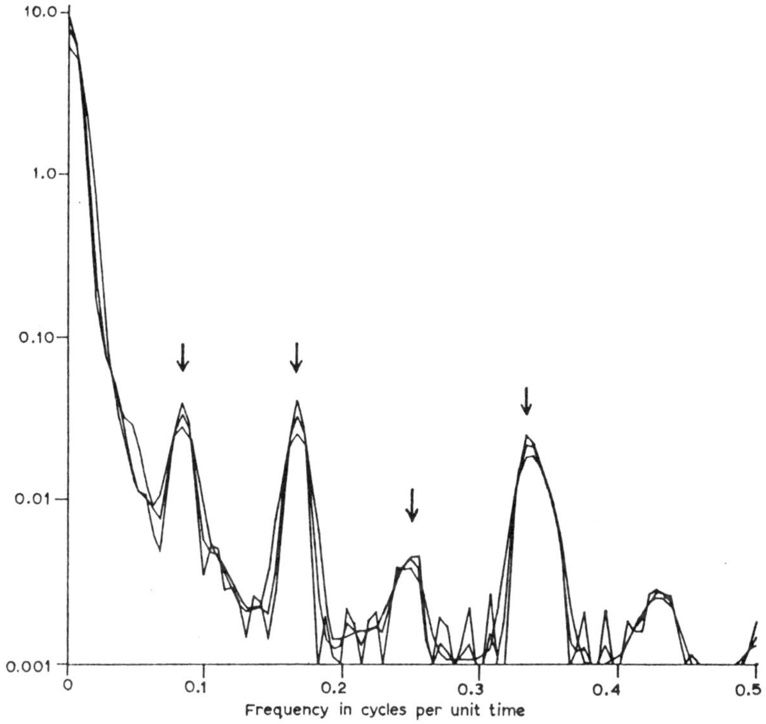

FIGURE 2.—Log of estimated spectral density functions.

possible to obtain a good estimate at all frequencies illustrates the considerable power of the available estimating procedures. The diagram shows the spectral estimates using the Parzen window and with 60, 80, and 99 lags. The consistent shape of the estimated spectrum using these different lags implies that the shape found may be accepted as being realistic with some confidence.

3. THE PROBLEM OF TREND

The most noticeable characteristic of the typical spectral shape is the overpowering importance of the low frequency components. The majority of economic time series contain important trends in mean, and it is known that such trends raise the value of the power spectrum at the low frequencies. One must thus ask if the "typical shape" is not largely due to these trends.

Before inquiring further into this possibility, one must first decide upon a definition of trend. A definition which is generally acceptable is not obvious, it being remembered that we have no reason to suppose that the trend in mean can be well approximated by a simple polynominal or exponential expression or even that it will be monotonic. It is clear that a curve that would be considered as a

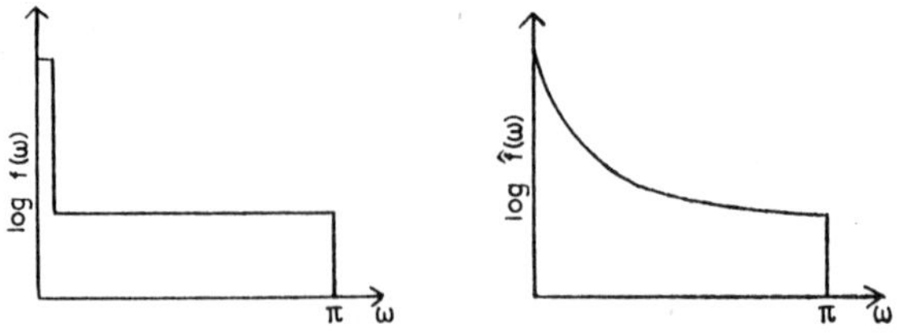

FIGURE 3

"trend" in a short series would not be so considered if the series were longer. An example of this would be temperature readings gathered every minute for four hours during the day. The known daily fluctuation would appear as a trend in such data but would not be considered as trend if the data were available for a period of three months (in which case the annual fluctuation would appear as trend). Thus the definition is likely to depend on the amount of data (n) available. In this paper "trend in mean" will be defined as comprising all frequency components with frequency equal to or less than $2\pi/n$, i.e., all components with wave length equal to or greater than the length of the series. Although, of course, this definition is to a certain extent arbitrary, it is precise and does appear to include the intuitive meaning of trend given by the majority of users of time series methods.

This definition of trend does not allow us to answer in the negative the question stated in the first paragraph of this section. The reason for this is that if the spectrum of a series containing a trend in mean is estimated directly, the resulting shape is likely to be the typical shape due to a characteristic of the estimation procedure known as leakage. If the true spectrum contains an important peak at some frequency, not only will the value of the estimated spectrum at neighboring frequency bands be raised, but up to 3 per cent of the value of the peak may also be found in the estimated value at other nearby frequency bands. This leakage, although it is a small percentage of the large value at the peak, may nevertheless introduce overwhelming biases in the estimates of the spectrum at these frequencies. As the component we have called trend will usually contribute by far the largest proportion of the total variance of the series, the value of the spectrum at the zero frequency band ($0 \leq \omega \leq \pi/2m$, if m lags used in the spectral estimating procedure) will be large and the leakage effect will make it likely that the estimated spectrum will be quickly but smoothly decreasing for the next few frequency bands.

Thus, suppose for instance that a series is constructed as the sum of white noise[6] and an important but very long cycle (with period longer than the length of the series). The theoretical spectrum will be as in Figure 3 but the leakage effect will produce an estimated spectrum as shown in this figure, on the right.

It follows from this that if one estimates the power spectrum of an economic series containing an important trend, a "typical shape" spectral estimate is likely to result. The important point about the typical shape, however, is that it still appears even if trend in mean is removed. Suppose that the trend is removed by either a filter or regression method. It is known that such methods will both effectively remove a trend in mean and that the spectrum of the residual will be (almost) unbiased for all frequencies except for very low frequencies which, in general, will lose power. In the investigations cited above, it is found that the power spectrum of the residual is basically of the form shown in Figure 4, i.e., of the typical shape

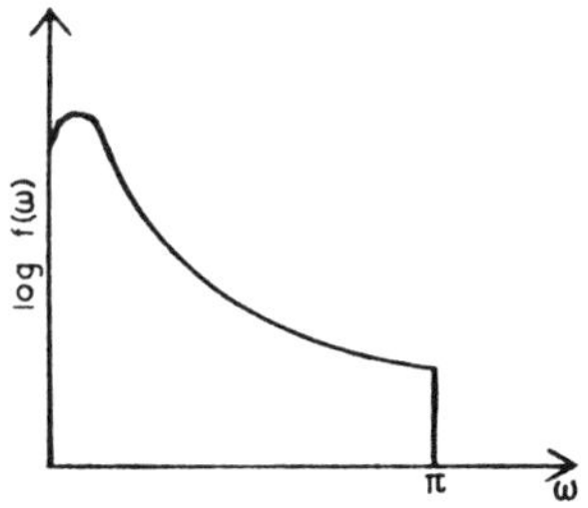

FIGURE 4

apart from the loss of power at the low frequencies. Moreover, the same basic shape is found *regardless of the length of data available*, the size of the truncation point used in the estimation procedure, or the trend removal method used. For very long series (such as pig iron production or monthly bank clearing data for the U.S., for which over a thousand recordings are available) the trend-removal techniques need affect only extremely low frequencies and the indication is consistently that the logarithm of the power spectrum increases montonically as frequency decreases for frequency bands lower than that corresponding to a 12-month period.

It is, of course, possible that the typical shape does reach an absolute peak at some low frequency; but if this is so, the peak must be at an extremely low frequency as no evidence of such a turning point has been found in studies of long series.

Studies in which the pre-whitening technique have been used, which decreases the bias due to leakage, support this finding (e.g., Nerlove **[8]**) as do analyses of data that contain no apparent trend in mean (e.g., New York Commercial Paper Rate, monthly, 1876–1914, see **[3**, Chapter **4]** and **[4]**).

[6] A series is called white noise if the covariance between the value at time t and the value at time s is zero for all $t \neq s$.

It must thus be concluded that the typical spectral shape of an economic series is as illustrated in Figure 1 and that any possible trend in mean will only accentuate this shape.

4. INTERPRETATION: BUSINESS CYCLES

The existence of a typical spectral shape suggests the following law (stated in nonrigorous but familiar terms):

The long-term fluctuations in economic variables, if decomposed into frequency components, are such that the amplitudes of the components decrease smoothly with decreasing period.[7]

One may care to associate the frequency components with various "cycles" suggested as existing in economic series by some economists prior to the Second World War, such as the Kondratieff long wave (40 to 60 years), Kuznets long wave (20 to 30 years), the building cycle (15 to 20 years), minor or Kitchin cycle (2 to 4 years), and so forth. In this case the law suggests that the amplitude of the Kondratieff long wave is greater than the amplitude of the Kuznet's long wave which is greater than the amplitude of the building cycle and so on.[8] The law also indicates, however, that the spectrum does not consist of a series of peaks of decreasing size corresponding to each of the above cycles but is rather a smooth, decreasing curve with no (significant) peaks corresponding to periods longer than 12 months.

It has, of course, long been realized that those cycles are not strictly periodic fluctuations that would correspond to jumps in the spectral distribution function but that they should be interpreted as important frequency bands. The evidence of estimated power spectra is that the peaks corresponding to these bands do, in fact, blend together to form a smooth, continuous curve. If this is the case, it might well be asked why certain fluctuations have been picked out as being of special importance, particularly the minor business cycle of roughly 30 to 50 months duration. To discuss this we first need to consider the likely properties of a sample from a process possessing a spectrum of the typical shape.

The most obvious property of such a sample would probably be a visual long-term fluctuation which would not be in any way periodic. The fluctuation need not be visible at all moments of time and would, of course, be somewhat blurred by the high frequency and seasonal components.[9] The estimated power spectrum would have essentially the correct shape but would usually also contain a number of peaks and troughs about the true spectral shape. A different sample from the same process

[7] It might be possible to restate the law as "events which affect the economy for a long period are more important than those which affect it only for a short time."

[8] If this were not the case, it is doubtful if such fluctuations could have been "seen." Thus, the existence of this early work in business cycles can be interpreted as an early discovery of this part of the "law."

[9] It would be theoretically possible to find the mean length of the long-term fluctuation but it seems doubtful if this would prove to be a useful concept.

would produce a similar estimated spectrum but with the peaks and troughs at different frequencies. This "sampling error" is due to the fact that the samples are only of finite length. The peaks found in the estimated spectra should not, of course, be significant. Suppose now that a sample is such that the most visible peak is found in the power spectrum at a frequency corresponding to 63 months, for example. In this case it appears likely that if one looks at the data with the intention of finding a cycle, the cycle one will "find" is one with a period near 63 months. In a sense, the sample does contain such a cycle but it will be only a transient feature as it is unlikely to occur in the next stretch of data from the process.

The estimated spectra for a number of economic series do, in fact, contain peaks at a frequency corresponding to roughly 40 months. Examples of such a series are certain pre-First World War short-term interest rates (illustrated in [**3**, Chapter 4] and in [**4**]) and stock price indices (illustrated in [**4**]). As Hatanaka [**5**] points out, however, similar small peaks may be found in the logarithm of other economic series such as bank clearings and pig iron production. The reason for the logarithm of the series being required to find the peaks is that these series usually contain an important trend in variance, the effect of which is to blur any small peak in the spectrum. Taking the logarithm of the series, providing it is positive, moves any trend in variance into a trend in mean, which may be removed by the usual methods.[10]

The peaks found at or near 40 months are never statistically significant and the evidence available indicates that they are more pronounced prior to 1914. The fact that the same peak occurs in several series might appear to add to the statistical significance but actually is only a reflection of the fact that most economic series follow the long-term fluctuations of the economy as a whole.

The fact that such a peak is found in long series could, of course, indicate that this is a true and permanent characteristic of the economy. The evidence, however, is not sufficiently strong for the rejection of the simple hypothesis that the true underlying spectrum is smooth and so does not contain a peak near 40 months. In any case, the size of the peak found in practice indicates that it is of little importance compared to neighboring frequency bands in terms of its contribution of the total variance of the series and so no evidence has been found that particular attention should be paid to this or any other frequency band.

5. DESCRIPTION: MODEL FITTING

Consider a process having the typical spectral shape. If we define a filter $F_\alpha(\ )$ to be such that an input of series X_t is transformed into an output series Y_t where Y_t obeys the equation

$$Y_t - \alpha Y_{t-1} = X_t ,$$

[10] It is proved in [3] that if the standard deviation of the series is small compared to the mean, the spectrum of the original series is similar in shape to the spectrum of the logarithm of the series.

it seems certain that a good representation of our process wil be $F_\alpha(\varepsilon_t)$ or $F_\alpha[F_{\alpha'}(\varepsilon_t)]$ where ε_t is white noise and α and α' have values in the range $\frac{1}{2} \leq \alpha, \alpha' \leq 1$. For example, first order autoregressive schemes were fitted to the following series with results as indicated:

	estimated α
(1) Various stock price series (see [**4**])	0.98
(2) Manufacturer's inventory (1924–1955)	0.98
(3) Bank clearings	0.95
Logarithm of bank clearings	0.97
(4) Lay-off rate (1930–1958)	0.78
(5) Average work week (1932–1958)	0.97

(the first three series are trend-adjusted, the latter two were not).

The results by Ames and Reiter [**1**], Orcutt [**9**], and unpublished results by Parzen concerning the fitting of autoregressive schemes to economic data further confirm the above suggestion. The main implication is that economic processes are almost unstable.

It must also be emphasized that these results do not preclude the possibility that the processes are best fitted by an explosive autoregressive model.

Quenouille [**10**, p. 58] points out that the simple explosive Markov process

$$Y_t - \beta Y_{t-1} = \varepsilon_t, \qquad \beta > 1$$

may be viewed as the sum of two components X_t and Z_t, where

$$Y_t = X_t + Z_t ,$$

$$X_t - \beta^{-1} X_{t-1} = \eta_t ,$$

and

$$Z_t = Z_0 \beta^t .$$

Here ε_t and η_t are both white noises.

Thus, suppose the true model is an explosive autoregressive scheme with parameter $\beta = 1.05$, for example. Then, after trend removal the residual may be represented as the output of the filter $F_\alpha(\eta_t)$ with $\alpha = 0.95$. The process of first removing the trend in mean and then analyzing the residual is essentially based upon the assumption that the trend is being generated by a different mechanism than is generating the residual.

As, however, many economic series have an exponential trend in mean and a typical spectral shape, it is not clear that the two mechanisms are unconnected. It is quite possible, in fact, that the trend contains useful information about the rest of the process and in such a case this information should be used.

It has not been felt worthwhile to attempt to fit such schemes to a large number of economic variables. This is because one must first remove efficiently any seasonal component and because of the important inaccuracies contained in the majority of economic data which tend to introduce possibly important biases into the estimates. Nerlove [8] has discussed the first of these problems and has indicated that some of the methods currently used would certainly spoil the estimate. For a complete description of the second problem see Morgenstern [7].

6. IMPLICATIONS FOR MODEL BUILDING

Let us first investigate the very simple accelerator multiplier model:

$$C_t = cY_{t-1} + \varepsilon_t',$$
$$I_t = v(Y_t - Y_{t-1}) + \eta_t',$$
$$Y_t = C_t + I_t,$$

where C is consumption, Y is national income, I is investment, and it is assumed that ε_t' and η_t' are both white noise processes.

Rearranging, we have

$$Y_t - \alpha Y_{t-1} = \varepsilon_t,$$
$$C_t - \alpha C_{t-1} = \eta_t,$$
$$I_t - \alpha I_{t-1} = \varepsilon_t - \eta_t,$$

where $(1-v)\varepsilon_t = \varepsilon_t' + \eta_t'$, $\eta_t = \varepsilon_t' + \varepsilon_{t-1}' + \dfrac{c}{1-v}(\varepsilon_{t-1}' + \eta_t')$ and $\alpha = \dfrac{v-c}{v-1}$.

Y_t, C_t, and I_t may each be considered as outputs of the filter $F_\alpha(\ )$ but with different inputs. The power spectra of Y_t and C_t are

$$f_Y(\omega) = \frac{f_\varepsilon(\omega)}{2(1-\alpha\cos\omega)},$$

$$f_C(\omega) = \frac{f_\eta(\omega)}{2(1-\alpha\cos\omega)}.$$

It should be noted that if α is near one, the term $(1-\alpha\cos\omega)$ will be dominating the values of $f_Y(\omega)$ and $f_C(\omega)$ for low frequencies and thus the typical shape will arise. It is, perhaps, interesting to record the value of α for various suggested "realistic" values for the accelerator and the multiplier.

Values of $\alpha = (v-c)/(v-1)$ for realistic combinations of c and v

c \ v	2	3	4
$\frac{1}{3}$	—	1.33	1.22
$\frac{1}{2}$	—	1.25	1.17
$\frac{2}{3}$	1.33	1.17	1.11
$\frac{3}{4}$	1.25	1.12	1.08
$\frac{4}{5}$	1.2	1.10	1.07

Thus, this simple model suggests that an explosive autoregressive scheme is appropriate and spectra of typical shape will certainly be forthcoming.

Reasoning similar to the above may be used to obtain a more general result suggesting a reason for the typical shape being obtained in practice. Let U be the shift operator such that $UX_t = X_{t-1}$. Consider the vector of exogenous variables $X' = (X_1, X_2, \ldots, X_n)$ and suppose that X_t obeys the matrix autoregressive scheme

$$P(U)X_t = Q(U)Y_t + \varepsilon_t$$

where Y_t is a $1 \times q$ vector ($q \leq m$) of endogenous variables, ε_t is a $1 \times m$ white noise vector, and $P(U)$, $Q(U)$ are $m \times m$ and $m \times q$ matrices, respectively, each element of which is a polynomial in U.

Thus, we may write (providing the inverse of P exists)

$$X_t = P^{-1}(U)Q(U)\,Y_t + P^{-1}\varepsilon_t = \frac{L(U)}{|P(U)|}\,Y_t + \frac{K(U)}{|P(U)|}\,\varepsilon_t\,.$$

The power spectrum for each component of X_t may be derived from this formula, but it should be noted that each of the power spectra will have a denominator term which is the square of the modulus of the determinant $|P(e^{i\omega})|$. Thus, if the determinant $|P(z)|$ has a root (or roots) near $z=1$ (corresponding to $\omega=0$), this denominator is likely to dominate the value of the power spectra at low frequencies. If the modulus of the determinant is not small for other values of ω, the resulting spectrum is likely to be typical, i.e., high valued at low frequencies and lower valued at other frequencies. The spectra of the components of X_t (possibly after trend removal) may vary in details but their basic shapes will be similar.

An implication of the existence of a typical spectral shape is that if a model is constructed involving economic variables, one aspect of deciding if it is reasonable is to inquire whether the power spectra derived from the model has the typical shape. An example of a simple model that does have this property is Klein's model [6]. As noted by Theil and Boot [11], "this model describes the American economy as a system which is close to instability and, in fact, leaves the question of stability open."

7. IMPLICATIONS FOR CONTROL

It has been suggested above that it might be possible to describe many economic variables in terms of one of either of two simple models:[11]

(i) an explosive scheme

$$X_t - \alpha X_{t-1} = \varepsilon_t\,,$$

with α greater than but near 1 (say $1 < \alpha \leq 1.4$), or

[11] The models are stated in terms of first-order autoregressive schemes. It is easily seen that the arguments still follow if higher-order schemes had been used.

(ii) $X_t = \text{trend in mean} + Y_t$ where

$$Y_t - \alpha Y_{t-1} = \varepsilon_t ,$$

with α less than but near 1 (say $0.7 \leq \alpha < 1$).

It was pointed out that spectral methods alone are unable to distinguish between these two models. The essential difference between them is that in (i) both the trend in mean and the long-term fluctuations of the variables are generated by the same mechanism, whereas in (ii) they need not be.

One of the possible aspects of controlling an economy might be stated as an attempt to smooth out the long-term fluctuations without affecting the (upward) trend. In spectral terms this could be described diagramatically by moving from a variable with spectral shape A to one with spectral shape B (see Figure 5), i.e., removing power in the "business cycle" band without removing power at zero frequency.

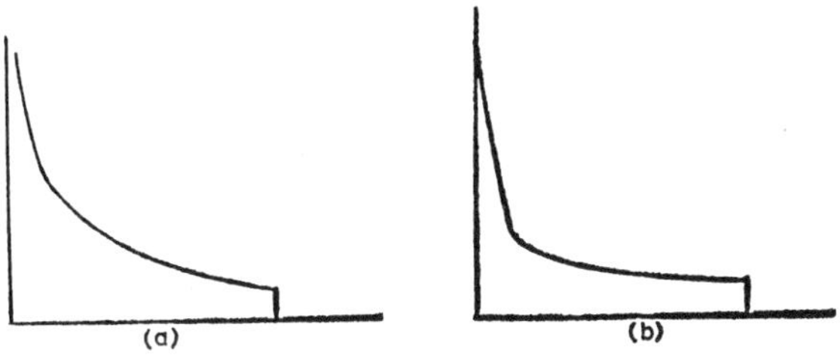

FIGURE 5

If model (i) were the correct representation it might be difficult to achieve this change without slowing down the trend. If model (ii) were correct the effect of applying such control might be to make the variable less stable, resulting in more violent, very long-term fluctuations. Either of these two effects would probably be considered undesirable. It is seen that the effect of such a control policy will be to make the process become nearer to being a random walk. The implication of this would seem to be that for a method of control to be really appropriate for use, it must be capable of controlling the whole of the low-frequency component of the variable and not just one section of this component. Thus, for instance, it can be argued that one should not use a "stop-go" policy similar to that used by the British government in recent years without at the same time implementing long-term policies that help to control the trend element. It is clear that more precise statements cannot be made on this subject using this approach without further information about the true inter-relationship between the trend and long-fluctuation elements of important economic variables.

University of Nottingham and Stanford University

REFERENCES

[1] Ames, E., and S. Reiter: "Distribution of Correlation Coefficients in Economic Time Series," *Journal of the American Statistical Association*, Vol. 56 (1961), pp. 637–656.

[2] Cunnyngham, J.: "Spectral Analysis of Economic Time Series," Working Paper No. 16, U.S. Department of Commerce, Bureau of the Census, 1963, New York.

[3] Granger, C. W. J., and M. Hatanaka: *Spectral Analysis of Economic Time Series*, Princeton, 1964.

[4] Granger, C. W. J., and O. Morgenstern: "Spectral Analysis of Stock Market Prices," *Kyklos*, Vol. 16 (1963), pp. 1–27.

[5] Hatanaka, M.: "A Spectral Analysis of Business Cycle Indicators: Lead-lag in Terms of All Time Points," Econometric Research Program, Princeton Research Memorandum No. 53, 1963.

[6] Klein, L. R.: *Economic Fluctuations in the U.S.*, 1921–1941, New York, 1950.

[7] Morgenstern, O.: *On the Accuracy of Economic Observations*, Second edition, Princeton, 1963.

[8] Nerlove, M.: "Spectral Analysis of Seasonal Adjustment Procedures," *Econometrica*, Vol. 32 (1964), pp. 241–286.

[9] Orcutt, G. H.: "A Study of the Autoregressive Nature of the Time Series Used for Tinbergen's Model of the Economic System of the United States, 1919–1932," *Journal of the Royal Statistical Society*, Vol. B10 (1948), pp. 1–45.

[10] Quenouille, M. H.: *Multivariate Time Series Analysis*, London, 1957.

[11] Theil, H., and J. C. G. Boot: "The Final Form of Econometric Equation Systems," *Review of the International Statistical Institute*, Vol. 30 (1962), pp. 136–152.

[25]

Early applications of spectral methods to economic time series

Thomas F. Cargill

> It is easy to condemn and to decry theories as impractical. The foundations of practical things of today were so decried only yesterday, and the theories which will be practical tomorrow are branded as valueless abstract games by the practical men of today.
> WILLIAM FELLER, *Probability Theory and Its Applications, Vol. I*

I. *Economics and spectral analysis*

The development of economic analysis during the nineteenth century centered on the construction of a theoretical framework or "engine of analysis." During this period there was no serious attempt to integrate deductive and inductive analysis by the application of rigorous statistical methods; however, the rise of statistical economics during the last fifty or so years has been an important characteristic of contemporary economics. According to G. Stigler, "if one seeks distinctive traits of modern economics, traits which are not shared to any important degree with the Marshallian or earlier periods, he will find only one: the development of statistical estimation of economic relationships" [40, p. 1]. The application of statistical methods to economics has had a profound impact on the roles of both economist and economics in society. Only by studying the empirical relationship among economic variables can one check economic theory against reality and employ models to make predictions. In the last analysis, economics should be a predictive science if it is to make any significant contribution to society, and the development of statistical economics is a necessary step in that direction.

While time series and cross-section data provide the working material for statistical economics, the majority of attention has been directed to time-series data, since they reflect the dynamic nature of the economic system and present challenging difficulties to statistical economics. Economists have overwhelmingly emphasized time domain meth-

THOMAS F. CARGILL *is an Associate Professor of Economics at the University of Nevada, Reno.*

ods which stress the behavior of the time series over a time axis and include such widely used techniques as regression and correlation. Relatively little attention has been directed to frequency domain methods. The frequency domain approach is based on the notion that a time series can be decomposed or divided up into components each associated with a frequency or period. The period describes the length of time required for one complete cycle in a time series, and frequency indicates the fraction of a cycle completed in one time unit. In a sense, then, frequency domain methods emphasize the behavior of the time series across a range of frequencies or periodicities. Among other terms, frequency domain analysis has been referred to as harmonic, Fourier, periodogram, or spectral analysis. The last term is currently the most widely used.

O. Morgenstern and J. von Neumann for a number of years recognized the need for a large-scale investigation of the application of spectral methods to economic time series. In the early 1960's their objective was carried out at the Time Series Project at Princeton University under the direction of Morgenstern [18] [33]. In 1964 C. W. J. Granger in association with M. Hatanaka reported the major results of the project in their well-known *Spectral Analysis of Economic Time Series* [20], thus making the techniques and computer programs[1] accessible to the general economist. Since 1964 a large number of contributions to economics literature have employed spectral analytic methods.[2] In addition, spectral methods have been extended to such areas as estimating time domain distributed lag models [25], analyzing dynamic properties of structural systems of equations [26], testing for serial correlation in regression models [11], and detecting causality in economic models [19] [36]. The large amount of space devoted to spectral analysis in a recent econometrics textbook by P. Dhrymes [10] is indicative of the increasing interest in these methods.

It is generally true that important discussions in contemporary economics have antecedents of one form or another. One can usually trace back a number of years to earlier writers who foreshadowed current developments, but their work failed to attract attention because of the

1. The availability of computer programs was indicated in the preface by Granger [20, p. xiii] and provided in a research memorandum by H. Karreman [28]. The Karreman programs are no longer generally available; however, there is ready accessibility to the BMD time series programs. More or less coinciding with the introduction of Granger and Hatanaka's book, several other studies appeared which employed spectral methods. One of the first applications was due to J. Cunnyngham [8]. Others included D. Fand [12], M. D. Godfrey, Granger, and Morgenstern [17], Granger and Morgenstern [23], M. Nerlove [34], and M. Suzuki [42].

2. A number of these studies are cited in P. Dhrymes [10, pp. 483–84].

environment in which they wrote, their style, or their specific use and formulation of the concept or problem. In the case of spectral analysis, there are several notable forerunners. The early development of statistical economics saw a number of attempts to employ frequency domain methods, most notably the periodogram, to economic data. However, these attempts failed to attract much interest, and the professional attention they did elicit was generally unfavorable. The purpose of this article is to examine what was accomplished by the early applications to economic time series and why the approach was temporarily rejected by the economics profession.

II. *Early economic applications of the periodogram*

The periodogram is the basic approach adopted in the early attempts at spectral analysis and is closely related to the modern concept of the spectral density function.[3] The periodogram is designed to determine the existence of "hidden" periodicities in a time series—that is, periodic movements that may be masked by trend or irregular movements in a time series. The concept of the periodogram is not original with the economists who applied the method to economic data, but rather has its origin in the works of J. Fourier, Sir Arthur Schuster, and H. Turner.[4] The periodogram is based on the fact that a time series at a point in time can be expressed as a weighted sum of cosine and sine functions over a range of frequencies of periodicities. Estimates of these weights at a particular frequency or period, referred to as Fourier coefficients, form an ordinate of the periodogram. The periodogram is then illustrated as a plot of the various ordinates against a range of

3. The concept of the spectrum or periodogram of an economic time series can be difficult to grasp for economists not used to thinking in terms of frequency; however, an analogy to a radio receiver suggested by Granger and Hatanaka [20, p. 52] may be informative. Consider a radio that does not emit words but rather sound or power at various frequency positions. As the dial is turned from one end of the frequency band to the other end, a constant background noise is emitted where no stations are broadcasting. The power, however, will sharply increase as the dial is centered on a broadcasting position. Thus, the behavior of the sound as the dial is turned traces out a spectrum of sorts. Likewise, the spectrum of an economic time series decomposes the power or variance of the series into many uncorrelated components, each associated with a period or frequency. The spectrum or periodogram then represents the relative importance of the periodic movements in the time series to the overall variance of the series. Two examples will help illustrate the concept of the periodogram or spectrum. First, the periodogram of a purely random process is represented by a constant for each period or frequency. Second, the periodogram of a sine wave with a single period is represented by a sharp peak in the periodogram ordinate at that periodicity, with the ordinate zero everywhere else.

4. The early foundation papers on the periodogram in chronological order are [41], [37], [38], [39], and [44].

periodicities. The ordinates describe the variation of the time series at different periodic components so that relative peaks in the periodogram represent the presence of hidden periodicities in the time series.

Shortly after the contributions of Schuster and Turner, H. L. Moore's *Economic Cycles: Their Law and Cause* [31] was published in 1914. This marked the first application of spectral analysis in economics via the periodogram. The next twenty years saw additional attempts to employ periodogram analysis; however, by the late 1930's interest had waned. In 1937 a textbook on business cycles and forecasting regarded the periodogram as "largely discredited for use with economic series" [4, p. 75].

The early applications of the periodogram and dates of publication are these:

1. Henry L. Moore, 1914 [31] and 1928 [32].
2. Sir William Beveridge, 1921 [1] and 1922 [2].
3. William L. Crum, 1923 [7].
4. Edwin B. Wilson, 1934 [45] [46].
5. Benjamin Greenstein, 1935 [24].
6. Harold T. Davis, 1941 [9].

Space limitations preclude presenting the periodograms contained in each application; however, two important periodograms drawn from Moore's and Beveridge's work are presented for illustration (Figs. 1 and 2).

Henry L. Moore

Of the small number of individuals who employed spectral analysis in economics, Moore is especially noteworthy since he is recognized as the founder of "statistical economics" [40]. Much of his statistical economics and especially that connected with spectral analysis was directed toward the study of business cycles.

Moore built his cycle analysis on earlier work by W. S. Jevons and others holding a meteorological theory. The problem of statistical economics was threefold: (i) to establish the periodicity of important characteristics of the weather and certain economic variables; (ii) to show that periodic movements in the weather induced periodic movements in yield per acre and agricultural prices; and (iii) to show that agriculture provides the main source of raw materials to manufacturing and hence induces cycles in the cost of production. Moore based the explanation of periodic movements in the weather on the relationship between the Sun, Venus and Earth [32, pp. 69–141].

In Moore's 1914 volume the periodogram was estimated for annual rainfall in the Ohio Valley from 1839 to 1910. The periodogram (Fig. 1)

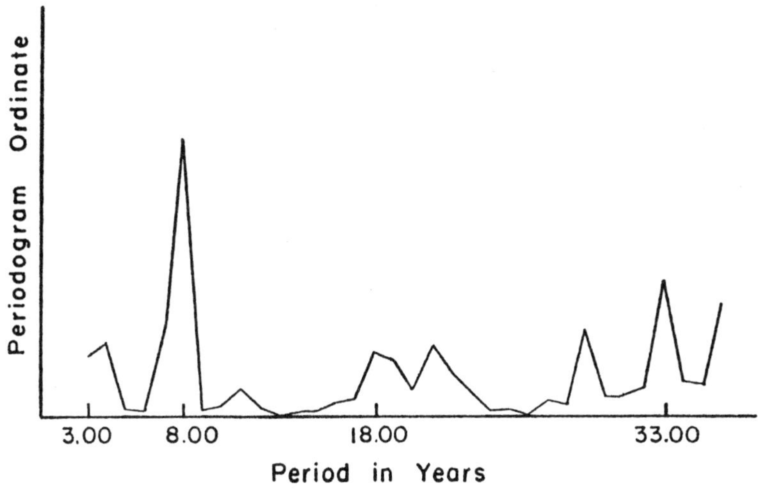

Fig. 1. Moore's periodogram of rainfall in the Ohio Valley.

was fairly well-defined, exhibiting a sharp peak at the 8-year period and the possibility of a 33-year period.[5] This was the only periodogram estimated in the 1914 volume; periodic movements were inferred in other time series on the basis of correlation analysis. In *Generating Economic Cycles,* published in 1928, additional periodograms of rainfall, yield per acre, and several economic variables were presented.

Based on evidence from the periodograms, Moore is confident of the existence of 8-year cycles in rainfall, yield per acre, production of iron and coal, and raw materials. The theory is completed by providing evidence of an inverse relationship between yield and the price of agricultural products and observing that three-fourths of the raw materials used in factories originate from farms. Thus, cycles in weather induce cycles in the cost of production and aggregate economic activity.

Sir William Beveridge

Sir William Beveridge is well-known for his contributions to the construction of historical economic time series. Beveridge and Moore both emphasized the existence of cyclical behavior in meteorological phenomena and its associated influence on the harvesting of important crops; however, there are a number of important differences between their respective periodogram analyses. (i) Beveridge confined his attention to a single wheat price series and employed secondary sources

5. The 33-year period was discarded in Moore's later work, since the periodogram ordinate at this periodicity was not prominent.

to suggest cycles in various aspects of the weather. (ii) Whereas Moore emphasized the existence of a single periodicity in the weather (rainfall), Beveridge emphasized a number of weather-related cycles, resulting in several rather than a single cycle in wheat prices. (iii) The largest time series investigated by Moore contained 96 observations, while Beveridge based his periodogram on a series of wheat prices for western and central Europe containing 300 observations. (iv) Beveridge provided a more extensive analysis of the periodogram to determine the validity of a relative peak. In fact, M. G. Kendall [29, p. 93] credited Beveridge with the most extensive application of the periodogram ever provided.

The periodogram of wheat prices is illustrated in Fig. 2. Beveridge provided an elaborate analysis of the periodogram to uncover hidden periodicities. Essentially, these involved examination of relative peaks in the periodogram, estimating separate periodograms for subperiods, and comparing periodogram peaks with well-established weather-related cycles.

In spite of the more elaborate analysis, the periodogram shown in Fig. 2 presented difficult problems of interpretation because of its extremely choppy appearance and indicated the presence of numerous

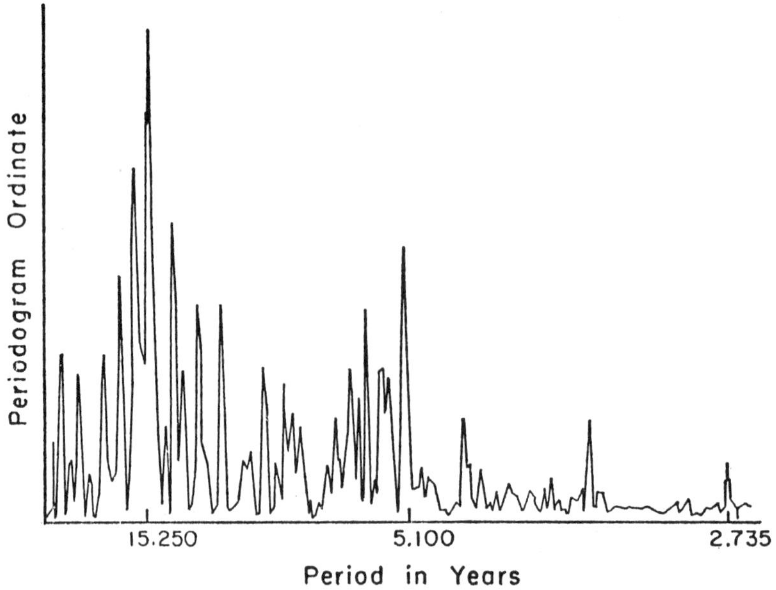

Fig. 2. Beveridge's periodogram of wheat prices in western and central Europe.

periodic movements in wheat prices. In fact, Beveridge found 19 "apparent" periods ranging from 2.735 to 68.000 years in length, and concluded that 11 of the 19 are very prominent, basing his judgment on the importance of the relative peak, subperiod periodograms, and known weather-related cycles. The large number of cycles was attributed to the complex nature of the weather.

William L. Crum

W. L. Crum applied periodogram analysis to monthly observations of the commercial paper rate over the period 1874 to 1913. Though he was one of the first to apply periodogram analysis to economic data, he was at the same time very critical and pessimistic about its usefulness in economics. In fact, the very paper applying the periodogram to interest rate data had as a major objective to "criticize the application of the periodogram method to economic statistics" [7, p. 17]. Crum concluded that the periodogram could indicate only that there may be a period of about 40 or 41 months in the interest rate series.

Edwin B. Wilson

E. B. Wilson stands out among the early users of the periodogram in that he analyzed an extremely long monthly index of business activity from January 1790 to December 1929 prepared by Leonard Ayres. Despite the unreliability of such a long and comprehensive series, it is by far the largest economic time series subjected to periodogram analysis. Unlike Moore, Beveridge, and Crum, Wilson in his study did not intend to verify a preconceived type of behavior hidden in the original time series, but rather it represented a "descriptive statistical analysis of Ayres's index in so far as that analysis throws light on the methodology of the use of the periodogram" [45, p. 376]. In this regard, Wilson devoted extensive attention to problems of interpreting the periodogram. He constructed an artificial series and illustrated the difficulty of applying the periodogram even to large amounts of data. In general, Wilson was pessimistic about the applicability of the periodogram to economic data.

Four periodograms of Ayres's index were estimated for the time periods 1790–1929, 1790–1859, 1825–1894, and 1860–1929. As might be expected, the four periodograms differed from each other. The periodogram for 1790–1859 presented the fewest difficulties of interpretation and indicated relative peaks at periods of 35, 60, 90, 120, and 232 months. Only a few of these periods were exhibited in the periodograms for the other subperiods. Wilson conducted several tests to determine whether the periodograms indicated any significant cycles in the U.S. economy and reached the negative conclusion that "there were no effective periods in American business activity" [46, pp. 195–96] over the time interval covered by the data.

Benjamin Greenstein

B. Greenstein applied the periodogram to a series of ratios of business failures to number of business firms from 1867 to 1932. The periodogram indicated relative peaks at the 9.14 and 10 year periods; however, the former was slightly larger. Greenstein then undertook an extensive analysis to determine the most representative period and concluded that there was no evidence of exact periodicity in the data; however, "9.4 years may be regarded as the typical duration of the cycle in the ratios of failures for 1867–1932, if by typical duration be understood the length which is more representative of the variable actual lengths of the cycles" [24, p. 197].

Harold T. Davis

The work of H. T. Davis represents the last major attempt to establish the priority of spectral analysis as an important tool of economic analysis. During the 1930's at the annual meetings of the newly formed Econometric Society, Davis presented several unpublished papers employing the periodogram. In 1941 he published his best-known contribution, *The Analysis of Economic Time Series* [9], in which spectral methods are given extensive emphasis and are illustrated with a large number of examples. Davis provides some brief discussion of earlier studies of the periodogram and presents a number of new periodograms of various stock prices to investigate the existence of cycles. While the other studies made few modifications in the periodogram as it was employed in non-economic areas, Davis attempted to extend the frontiers of periodogram analysis in several ways. Especially noteworthy in this regard is Davis's discussion of forecasting and the use of a "moving periodogram" [9, pp. 530–534] [14], which was designed to describe the behavior of a hidden periodic movement over time. It is only recently that the moving periodogram has received renewed interest [5] [15] [16].

III. *Professional reaction*

The reaction to the early attempts at spectral analysis by the economics profession was not enthusiastic in any sense of the word. It would be hazardous to be specific, but it is possible to set the bounds of the reaction by considering the views of W. C. Mitchell and J. A. Schumpeter, the most famous students of the business cycle.

In Mitchell's 1927 *Business Cycles: The Problem and Its Setting,* the periodogram was regarded as primarily applicable for future economists after the difficulties had been solved: "Certainly we cannot say that periodogram analysis will not play a large role in future economic work, but it seems equally certain that we cannot yet make it the standard procedure for studying cyclical fluctuations" [30, pp. 260–261]. It is doubtful whether Mitchell would be willing to accept the periodogram even on a limited scale. On the other hand, Schumpeter is critical of the periodogram but willing to admit it has some usefulness in the analysis of economic time series. Commenting on the methodological issues and difficulties raised by Wilson's analysis of Ayres's index, Schumpeter in 1939 remarked:

> Sir Arthur Schuster developed this method of finding hidden periodicities and of determining whether the results could be due to chance, for meteorological purposes. . . . Irregularities and interferences between components need not be very great to upset everything and to raise questions of interpretation which throw the findings themselves entirely into the background. It might, therefore, be asked why the writer, thinking thus, and moreover, entirely unwilling to abide by the results the analysis gives, nevertheless attaches importance to periodograms. The answer is simply that they render service in exploring the material, even if the results are negative or untrustworthy; some of our problems might be stated in terms of the periodograms we get. This importance is . . . primarily accorded to natural series or to series which, though the product of a statistical process, mean a definite thing—the commercial paper rate up to the war is an instance of the first, and the price level is an instance of the latter [35, p. 166].

The initial reaction to periodogram analysis was thus lukewarm at best.

In any event, after the 1930's and Davis's contributions, interest in the periodogram in particular and frequency domain analysis in general waned among economists. The early attempts at periodogram analysis were regarded as unsuccessful. The most devastating assessment of the periodogram was provided by Kendall [29] in 1945, who regarded the periodogram as unreliable for economic as well as other forms of data. In the same vein, J. Tukey recently stated that "the periodogram has been one of the most misleading devices . . . and . . . is dangerous rather than helpful" [43, pp. 25–26]. There are numerous factors accounting for the unfavorable response of the economics profession; however, six are especially important.

(i) The most often voiced criticism of periodogram analysis is related to the nonperiodic nature of movements in economic time series. While movements in economic time series may have a tendency to be periodic, their amplitudes, upturns, and downturns vary to such an extent that they cannot be realistically represented by a periodic function of sine and cosine terms. Mitchell expressed the criticism in the following way:

> Can we assume that the cyclical fluctuations of economic processes are, or tend to be, strictly periodic? If there are tendencies toward periodic fluctuations in given processes at a given point in economic evolution, do such tendencies maintain themselves under changing conditions over a period long enough to be revealed by periodogram analysis [30, p. 260]?

While this is a valid point, the criticism that economic phenomena are not truly periodic is one of degree. Periodic movements which have a certain degree of regularity (the extreme degree of regularity is seasonal movement) and which are fairly well isolated from other movements in the time series may be detected by the periodogram.

(ii) The high degree of accuracy attributed to the periodogram was simply unwarranted, and the attribution did a great deal to heighten a general suspiciousness of the technique. One can only read Beveridge's papers with a certain amount of amazement at the number of exact cycles in wheat prices claimed by periodogram analysis. Even Greenstein, who concluded that the periodicity in business failures could not be described by an exact mathematical formula, yet adjusted the initial cycle of 9.14 years to 9.4 years after additional analysis.

(iii) Several of the periodograms gave extremely choppy appearances indicating that a large number of periodicities were present in the data. Beveridge found no fewer than 19 apparent cycles, and Wilson found 5 for one subperiod of his data. It is difficult to accept the presence of such a large number of cycles in an economic time series. The available statistical tests were often not helpful in reducing the important peaks to only one or a few, since the ordinates were seldom independent. For example, most of Beveridge's 19 cycles were significant.

(iv) The applicability of the periodogram was questioned on the grounds of the amount and reliability of the data base. Frequency domain analysis in general required large amounts of data. Moore, Beveridge, and Greenstein used annual observations, and this necessitated extending the series back in time to obtain a sufficient number of observations. The further back in time the series was extended, however, the less reliability one could attach to individual observations. Beveridge was especially questioned on this point by A. W. Flux:

> There could hardly be, I think a greater admirer than myself of the mathematical methods of analysis applied to statistical material;

but if we are going to apply so refined a method of analysis we want to know a good deal about, and to feel a considerable amount of reliance on, our data. It is useless trying to put a fine edge upon a piece of soft steel. If you want to make a useful razor, you must have a hard piece of steel before you start grinding [2, pp. 465–66].

(v) The periodogram required an enormous amount of computation if any meaningful number of ordinates were to be estimated. Of course, computational limitation hindered the general development of statistical economics, but the problem was especially acute in the case of spectral analysis. The introduction of fast and accurate electronic computers has no doubt contributed to the growth of statistical economics in general and to spectral methods in particular.

(vi) The level of analytical and mathematical ability necessary to use the periodogram was not a common denominator among members of the economics profession. It was thus difficult to fully appraise the usefulness of the periodogram. The mathematical foundation of the periodogram tended to create mistrust for a method which claimed such accuracy as was expressed in several of the early applications.

IV. *Evaluation and concluding comments on the early applications*

The impact of these early applications of periodogram analysis on economic analysis and statistical economics is an important question that needs to be raised. Did any of these early studies make important contributions to the development of economics? There are three points that should be emphasized in answer to this question.

(i) All of the early applications represent an important part of the general rise of statistical economics. After the turn of the century, economists increasingly directed attention to the measurable aspects of economic relationships. Much of the early work in statistical economics was directed to studying business cycles or other types of cyclical behavior in the economy. All of the early applications, either directly or indirectly, were concerned with establishing the reality of cyclical movements. In spite of the controversy surrounding the use of the periodogram, they represent one of the most serious attempts to apply to a problem of great concern to professional economists statistical techniques that went far beyond the simple visual or graphical description of quantifiable economic variables.

In addition, several individuals associated with periodogram analysis played important roles in the development of statistical economics. Moore is now regarded as the father of statistical economics. In fact, his productive career stands as an example of the rigorous union of deductive and inductive analysis. Beveridge's contributions go far beyond his periodogram analysis. Especially notable is his contribution to the construction of historical economic time series. Davis played an important role in the early development of the Cowles Commission for Research in Economics and the Econometric Society.

(ii) The early applications made an important contribution to business cycle theory. The contribution is both positive and negative. Regarding the positive aspect, these early studies represent an attempt to use sophisticated techniques to establish the reality of various cycles and supplement the work of the National Bureau. Even though the periodogram is not well suited for determining the existence of cyclical behavior, several of the results of the early applications cannot simply be dismissed on this ground. It is well known that if a time series exhibits a fairly persistent and well-isolated cyclical pattern, the periodogram can indicate its presence. Several of the early periodograms are well defined and do indicate the presence of cyclical behavior. For example, recent studies of interest-rate behavior have verified the presence of a business-cycle component. Beveridge's wheat price series has also been found to contain a significant cycle of about 13 years [21]. This is very close to one of the most prominent cycles Beveridge discovered from his periodogram analysis. There are other cases in which the essential conclusions of these early studies have been borne out by other evidence.

Another and more important positive contribution of some of the early applications relates to the methodology of business cycle study. In this regard, both Davis and Moore stand out as representative of the few attempts to combine the tremendous amount of statistical data with new statistical techniques to "prove" or "refute" a theory of the business cycle. Moore set up the theoretical framework of his business-cycle theory and then used the periodogram as well as other techniques to determine whether the data were consistent with his interpretation. While not specifically concerned with a particular interpretation of the business cycle, Davis emphasized that cyclical phenomena do exist in economic time series and that the economist should formulate business cycle theory in a manner that was suspectible to statistical verification. After reviewing a number of interpretations of the business cycle, Davis writes:

> This epitome of theories clearly shows the complex nature of the problem of business cycles and the wide divergences of opinion which prevail as to the essential causes of oscillation. Where then shall we begin? The answer to this question is relatively simple. Our principal hope of discovering the dominating causes of cyclical

> fluctuations must lie in those mathematical formulations, where the assumptions are so framed that they are within the range of statistical verification [9, p. 333].

The importance of this methodology was emphasized by L. Hurwicz in a review of Davis's book:

> Professor Davis's book would have been a great contribution to our knowledge if it had merely given a systematic treatment of the available literature and techniques. However, *The Analysis of Economic Time Series* does more than that. It puts emphasis on the most essential aspects of the theory of time series; it opens new perspectives in the field of significance tests. . . . In line with the requirements of modern theory of economics and statistics it does not rigidly separate the problem of theoretical analysis from that of statistical investigation. For instance, the chapter on "The Evidence and Explanation of Cycles" could hardly be classified as either pure economics or pure statistics [27, p. 400].

The negative aspect of the contribution of these early applications of the periodogram was to highlight the need for avoiding the concept of periodicity in business cycle theory. Periodograms for many of the economic time series appeared extremely choppy and blurred because the underlying statistical model of periodogram analysis was seldom satisfied. Of course, few business cycle theorists believed that the cycle was strictly periodic, but periodicity often entered the discussion of early business cycle theory. While the term was not used in its strict mathematical meaning, it still connoted a degree of regularity in economic time series that is seldom realized in practice.

(iii) The early applications are forerunners of an important methodology in the study of economic time series and the verification of economic models. In what sense are they forerunners? Other than adopting the general approach of spectral analysis and attempting to discover hidden periodicities,[6] there are three points worth making. First, and most important, the periodogram and spectrum are uniquely related, and the spectrum underlies all of modern-day frequency domain analysis. Second, the periodogram has recently been reintroduced into economics by J. Durbin [11] as a test of serial correlation in regression analysis. Third, the last several years have witnessed a renewed interest

6. Current applications of spectral analysis extend far beyond the determination of hidden periodicities; however, this aspect of frequency domain analysis is still important. For example, the long-swing or Kuznet cycle hypothesis has been reexamined by spectral methods. References to this literature are cited in T. F. Cargill [6].

in the periodogram ordinates [3] [13] as a preliminary stage to modern frequency domain analysis.

In conclusion, the technical apparatus adopted by Moore, Beveridge, and others suffered from many difficulties. Their use and interpretation of the periodogram were often dubious at best. The techniques had to await theoretical development[7] before becoming generally applicable to economic data; however, these early students of the periodogram made important contributions to the development of economic analysis. They represented an important aspect of the rise of statistical economics, provided evidence on the reality of cyclical movement in economic time series, emphasized the importance of combining statistical technique with economic data to verify theories of the cycle, highlighted the need to avoid the concept of periodicity in business cycle theory, and can be regarded as forerunners of a methodology that is becoming an important part of the arsenal of tools available for analyzing economic time series.[8]

REFERENCES

[1] Sir William H. Beveridge. "Weather and Harvest Cycles." *Economic Journal* 31 (Dec. 1921):429–52.

[2] ———. "Wheat Prices and Rainfall in Western Europe," with discussion. *Journal of the Royal Statistical Society* 85 (May 1922):412–78.

[3] C. Bingham, M. D. Godfrey, and J. W. Tukey. "Modern Techniques of Power Spectrum Estimation." *IEEE Transactions on Audio and Electroacoustics*, vol. AU-15 (June 1967), pp. 56–66.

[4] E. C. Bratt. *Business Cycles and Forecasting*. Chicago: Business Publications, 1937.

[5] D. R. Brillinger, and M. Hatanaka. "An Harmonic Analysis of Non-Stationary Multivariate Economic Processes." *Econometrica* 37 (Jan. 1969):131–41.

[6] T. F. Cargill. "Construction Activity and Secular Change in the United States." *Applied Economics* 3 (June 1971):85–97.

[7] W. L. Crum. "Cycles of Rates on Commercial Paper." *Review of Economic Statistics* 5 (Jan. 1923):17–29.

7. Tukey [43] provides a brief survey of the theoretical and computational developments after 1945 leading up to the current application of spectral methods. Work by M. S. Bartlett, R. B. Blackman, E. J. Hannan, G. M. Jenkins, E. Parzen, J. Tukey, and others has placed spectral analysis on a firmer theoretical foundation and made the method suitable for the analysis of economic time series. The reader is referred to Tukey [43, pp. 43–46] and Fishman [13, pp. 201–6] for specific citations of this literature.

8. An earlier version of this article was presented as a paper at the Western Economic Association Meetings, August 1971, Vancouver, British Columbia. The paper has benefited from comments made on an earlier version by J. Carlson, C. W. J. Granger, M. D. Godfrey, L. Hurwicz, R. Klein, and O. Morgenstern; however, the author is responsible for any remaining errors.

[8] J. Cunnyngham. *The Spectral Analysis of Economic Time Series.* Working Paper No. 14, U.S. Bureau of the Census. Washington: Gov't Printing Office, 1963.

[9] H. T. Davis. *The Analysis of Economic Time Series.* Bloomington, Ind.: Principia Press, 1941.

[10] P. Dhrymes. *An Introduction to Econometrics.* New York: Harper and Row, 1970.

[11] J. Durbin. "Tests for Serial Correlation in Regression Analysis Based on the Periodogram of Least-Squares Residuals." *Biometrika* 56 (March 1969):1–15.

[12] D. Fand. "A Time Series Analysis of the 'Bills-Only' Theory of Interest Rates." *Review of Economics and Statistics* 48 (Nov. 1966): 361–71.

[13] G. S. Fishman. *Spectral Methods in Econometrics.* Cambridge: Harvard Univ. Press, 1969.

[14] R. Frisch. "Changing Harmonics and Other General Types of Components in Empirical Series." *Skandinavisk Aktuarietidskrift,* Haft. 4 (1928), pp. 220–36.

[15] M. D. Godfrey. "An exploratory Study of the Bi-Spectrum of Economic Time Series." *Applied Statistics,* 14 1965, pp. 48–69.

[16] ———. "The Statistical Analysis of Stochastic Processes in Economics." *Kyklos* 18, no. 1 (1967):373–86.

[17] ———, C. W. J. Granger, and O. Morgenstern. "The Random Walk Hypothesis of Stock Market Behavior." *Kyklos* 17, no. 1 (1964):1–30.

[18] C. W. J. Granger. "First Report of the Princeton Economic Time Series Project." *L'Industria* 4 (1961):194–206.

[19] ———. "Investigating Causal Relations by Econometric Models and Cross-Spectral Methods." *Econometrica* 37 (July 1969): 424–38.

[20] ———, in association with M. Hatanaka. *Spectral Analysis of Economic Time Series.* Princeton, N.J.: Princeton Univ. Press, 1964.

[21] ———, and A. O. Hughes. "A New Look at Some Old Data: The Beveridge Wheat Price Series." *Journal of the Royal Statistical Society* 134, no. 3 (1971):413–28.

[22] ———, and O. Morgenstern. *Predictability of Stock Market Prices.* Lexington, Mass.: D.C. Heath, 1970.

[23] ———, and O. Morgenstern. "Spectral Analysis of New York Stock Market Prices." *Kyklos* 16, no. 1 (1963):1–27.

[24] B. Greenstein. "Periodogram Analysis with Special Application to Business Failures in the United States, 1867–1932." *Econometrica* 3 (April 1935):170–98.

[25] E. J. Hannan. "Regression for Time Series." In *Time Series Analysis,* edited by M. Rosenblatt. New York: Wiley, 1963.

[26] E. P. Howrey. "Stochastic Properties of the Klein-Goldberger Model." *Econometrica* 39 (Jan. 1971): 73–87.

[27] L. Hurwicz. "Review of The Analysis of Economic Time Series." *American Economic Review* 33 (June 1943): 399–401.

[28] H. Karreman. *Computer Programs for Spectral Analysis of Economic Time Series.* Research Memorandum No. 59, Econometric Research Program, Princeton University, 15 July 1963.

[29] M. G. Kendall. "On the Analysis of Oscillatory Time Series." *Journal of the Royal Statistical Society* 108, nos. 1–2 (1945):93–129.

[30] W. C. Mitchell. *Business Cycles: The Problem and Its Setting*. New York: National Bureau of Economic Research, 1927.
[31] H. L. Moore, *Economic Cycles: Their Law and Cause*. New York: Augustus M. Kelley, 1967.
[32] ———. *Generating Economic Cycles*. New York: Augustus M. Kelley, 1967.
[33] O. Morgenstern. "A New Look at Economic Time Series Analysis." In *Money, Growth, and Methodology and Other Essays in Economics in Honor of Johan Akerman*, edited by H. Hegeland. C. W. K. Gleerup, Lund, Sweden: 1961.
[34] M. Nerlove. "Spectral Analysis of Seasonal Adjustment Procedures." *Econometrica* 32 (July 1964):241–86.
[35] J. A. Schumpeter. *Business Cycles*, vol. 1. New York: McGraw-Hill 1939.
[36] C. A. Sims. "Money, Income, and Causality." *American Economic Review* 62 (Sept. 1972):540–52.
[37] Sir Arthur Schuster. "On the Investigation of Hidden Periodicities with Application to a Supposed 26-Day Period of Meteorological Phenomena." *Terrestrial Magnetism and Atmospheric Electricity* 3 (1898): 13–41.
[38] ———. "On the Periodicities of Sunspots." *Philosophical Transactions of the Royal Society*, ser. A 206 (Nov. 1906):69–100.
[39] ———. "The Periodogram and Its Optical Analogy." *Proceedings of the Royal Society of London*, ser. A 77 (Feb. 1906):136–40.
[40] G. Stigler. "Henry L. Moore and Statistical Economics." *Econometrica* 30 (Jan. 1962):1–21.
[41] G. G. Stokes, "Notes." *Proceedings of the Royal Society of London* 29 (29 May 1879):122–23.
[42] M. Suzuki. "A Spectral Analysis of Japanese Economic Time Series." *Kyklos* 18, no. 2 (1965):227–58.
[43] J. W. Tukey. "An Introduction to the Calculations of Numerical Spectrum Analysis." In *Spectral Analysis of Time Series*, edited by B. Harris, pp. 25–46. New York: Wiley, 1967.
[44] H. H. Turner. "On the Expression of Sun-Spot Periodicity as a Fourier Sequence, and on the General Use of a Fourier Sequence in Similar Problems." *Royal Astronomical Society, Monthly Notices* 73 (Suppl. 1913):714–432.
[45] E. B. Wilson. "The Periodogram of American Business Activity." *Quarterly Journal of Economics* 148 (May 1934):375–417.
[46] ———. "Are There Periods in American Business Activity?" *Science* 80 (31 Aug. 1934):193–99.

[26]

Econometrica, Vol. 37, No. 3 (July, 1969)

INVESTIGATING CAUSAL RELATIONS BY ECONOMETRIC MODELS AND CROSS-SPECTRAL METHODS

BY C. W. J. GRANGER

There occurs on some occasions a difficulty in deciding the direction of causality between two related variables and also whether or not feedback is occurring. Testable definitions of causality and feedback are proposed and illustrated by use of simple two-variable models. The important problem of apparent instantaneous causality is discussed and it is suggested that the problem often arises due to slowness in recording information or because a sufficiently wide class of possible causal variables has not been used. It can be shown that the cross spectrum between two variables can be decomposed into two parts, each relating to a single causal arm of a feedback situation. Measures of causal lag and causal strength can then be constructed. A generalisation of this result with the partial cross spectrum is suggested.

1. INTRODUCTION

THE OBJECT of this paper is to throw light on the relationships between certain classes of econometric models involving feedback and the functions arising in spectral analysis, particularly the cross spectrum and the partial cross spectrum. Causality and feedback are here defined in an explicit and testable fashion. It is shown that in the two-variable case the feedback mechanism can be broken down into two causal relations and that the cross spectrum can be considered as the sum of two cross spectra, each closely connected with one of the causations. The next three sections of the paper briefly introduce those aspects of spectral methods, model building, and causality which are required later. Section 5 presents the results for the two-variable case and Section 6 generalises these results for three variables.

2. SPECTRAL METHODS

If X_t is a stationary time series with mean zero, there are two basic spectral representations associated with the series:

(i) the Cramer representation,

$$(2.1)\qquad X_t = \int_{-\pi}^{\pi} e^{it\omega}\, dz_x(\omega),$$

where $z_x(\omega)$ is a complex random process with uncorrelated increments so that

$$(2.2)\qquad \begin{aligned} E[dz_x(\omega)\,\overline{dz_x(\lambda)}] &= 0, \qquad \omega \neq \lambda, \\ &= dF_x(\omega), \quad \omega = \lambda; \end{aligned}$$

(ii) the spectral representation of the covariance sequence

$$(2.3)\qquad \mu_\tau^{xx} = E[X_t\overline{X}_{t-\tau}] = \int_{-\pi}^{\pi} e^{i\tau\omega}\, dF_x(\omega).$$

If X_t has no strictly periodic components, $dF_x(\omega) = f_x(\omega)\,d\omega$ where $f_x(\omega)$ is the power spectrum of X_t. The estimation and interpretation of power spectra have been discussed in [**4**] and [**5**]. The basic idea underlying the two spectral representations is that the series can be decomposed as a sum (i.e. integral) of uncorrelated components, each associated with a particular frequency. It follows that the variance of the series is equal to the sum of the variances of the components. The power spectrum records the variances of the components as a function of their frequencies and indicates the relative importance of the components in terms of their contribution to the overall variance.

If X_t and Y_t are a pair of stationary time series, so that Y_t has the spectrum $f_y(\omega)$ and Cramer representation

$$Y_t = \int_{-\pi}^{\pi} e^{it\omega}\, dz_y(\omega),$$

then the cross spectrum (strictly power cross spectrum) $Cr(\omega)$ between X_t and Y_t is a complex function of ω and arises both from

$$\begin{aligned} E[dz_x(\omega)\,\overline{dz_y(\omega)}] &= 0, \qquad & \omega \neq \lambda, \\ &= Cr(\omega)\,d\omega, \qquad & \omega = \lambda, \end{aligned}$$

and

$$\mu_\tau^{xy} = E[X_t \overline{Y}_{t-\tau}] = \int_{-\pi}^{\pi} e^{i\tau\omega} Cr(\omega)\,d\omega.$$

It follows that the relationship between two series can be expressed only in terms of the relationships between corresponding frequency components.

Two further functions are defined from the cross spectrum as being more useful for interpreting relationships between variables:

(i) the coherence,

$$C(\omega) = \frac{|Cr(\omega)|^2}{f_x(\omega) f_y(\omega)},$$

which is essentially the square of the correlation coefficient between corresponding frequency components of X_t and Y_t, and

(ii) the phase,

$$\phi(\omega) = \tan^{-1} \frac{\text{imaginary part of } Cr(\omega)}{\text{real part of } Cr(\omega)},$$

which measures the phase difference between corresponding frequency components. When one variable is leading the other, $\phi(\omega)/\omega$ measure the extent of the time lag.

Thus, the coherence is used to measure the degree to which two series are related and the phase may be interpreted in terms of time lags.

Estimation and interpretation of the coherence and phase function are discussed in [**4**, Chapters 5 and 6]. It is worth noting that $\phi(\omega)$ has been found to be robust under changes in the stationarity assumption [**4**, Chapter 9].

If X_t, Y_t, and Z_t are three time series, the problem of possibly misleading correlation and coherence values between two of them due to the influence on both of the third variable can be overcome by the use of partial cross-spectral methods.

The spectral, cross-spectral matrix $\{f_{ij}(\omega)\} = S(\omega)$ between the three variables is given by

$$E\begin{bmatrix} dz_x(\omega) \\ dz_y(\omega) \\ dz_z(\omega) \end{bmatrix}[\overline{dz_x(\omega)}\;\overline{dz_y(\omega)}\;\overline{dz_z(\omega)}] = \{f_{ij}(\omega)\}\,d\omega$$

where

$$\begin{aligned} f_{ij}(\omega) &= f_x(\omega) \quad \text{when} \quad i = j = x, \\ &= Cr^{xy}(\omega) \quad \text{when} \quad i = x,\, j = y, \end{aligned}$$

etc.

The partial spectral, cross-spectral matrix between X_t and Y_t given Z_t is found by partitioning $S(\omega)$ into components:

$$S = \left[\begin{array}{c|c} S_{11} & S_{12} \\ \hline S_{21} & S_{22} \end{array}\right].$$

The partitioning lines are between the second and third rows, and second and third columns. The partial spectral matrix is then

$$S_{xy.z} = S_{11} - S_{12}S_{22}^{-1}S_{21}.$$

Interpretation of the components of this matrix is similar to that involving partial correlation coefficients. Thus, the partial cross spectrum can be used to find the relationship between two series once the effect of a third series has been taken into account. The partial coherence and phase are defined directly from the partial cross spectrum as before. Interpretation of all of these functions and generalisations to the n variable case can be found in [**4**, Chapter 5].

3. FEEDBACK MODELS

Consider initially a stationary random vector $X_t = \{X_{1t}, X_{2t}, \ldots, X_{kt}\}$, each component of which has zero mean. A linear model for such a vector consists of a set of linear equations by which all or a subset of the components of X_t are "explained" in terms of present and past values of components of X_t. The part not explained by the model may be taken to consist of a white-noise random vector ε_t, such that

$$\begin{aligned} E[\varepsilon_t'\varepsilon_s] &= 0, \quad t \neq s, \\ &= I, \quad t = s, \end{aligned} \tag{3.1}$$

where I is a unit matrix and 0 is a zero matrix.

Thus the model may be written as

$$(3.2)\qquad A_0X_t = \sum_{j=1}^{m} A_jX_{t-j} + \varepsilon_t$$

where m may be infinite and the A's are matrices.

The completely general model as defined does not have unique matrices A_j as an orthogonal transformation. $Y_t = AX_t$ can be performed which leaves the form of the model the same, where A is the orthogonal matrix, i.e., a square matrix having the property $AA' = I$. This is seen to be the case as $\eta_t = A\varepsilon_t$ is still a white-noise vector. For the model to be determined, sufficient a priori knowledge is required about the values of the coefficients of at least one of the A's, in order for constraints to be set up so that such transformations are not possible. This is the so-called "identification problem" of classical econometrics. In the absence of such a priori constraints, A can always be chosen so that the A_0 is a triangular matrix, although not uniquely, thus giving a spurious causal-chain appearance to the model.

Models for which A_0 has nonvanishing terms off the main diagonal will be called "models with instantaneous causality." Models for which A_0 has no nonzero term off the main diagonal will be called "simple causal models." These names will be explained later. Simple causal models are uniquely determined if orthogonal transforms such as A are not possible without changing the basic form of the model. It is possible for a model apparently having instantaneous causality to be transformed using an orthogonal A to a simple causal model.

These definitions can be illustrated simply in the two variable case. Suppose the variables are X_t, Y_t. Then the model considered is of the form

$$(3.3)\qquad \begin{aligned} X_t + b_0Y_t &= \sum_{j=1}^{m} a_jX_{t-j} + \sum_{j=1}^{m} b_jY_{t-j} + \varepsilon'_t, \\ Y_t + c_0X_t &= \sum_{j=1}^{m} c_jX_{t-j} + \sum_{j=1}^{m} d_jY_{t-j} + \varepsilon''_t. \end{aligned}$$

If $b_0 = c_0 = 0$, then this will be a simple causal model. Otherwise it will be a model with instantaneous causality.

Whether or not a model involving some group of economic variables can be a simple causal model depends on what one considers to be the speed with which information flows through the economy and also on the sampling period of the data used. It might be true that when quarterly data are used, for example, a simple causal model is not sufficient to explain the relationships between the variables, while for monthly data a simple causal model would be all that is required. Thus, some nonsimple causal models may be constructed not because of the basic properties of the economy being studied but because of the data being used. It has been shown elsewhere [**4**, Chapter 7; **3**] that a simple causal mechanism can appear to be a feedback mechanism if the sampling period for the data is so long that details of causality cannot be picked out.

4. CAUSALITY

Cross-spectral methods provide a useful way of describing the relationship between two (or more) variables when one is causing the other(s). In many realistic economic situations, however, one suspects that feedback is occurring. In these situations the coherence and phase diagrams become difficult or impossible to interpret, particularly the phase diagram. The problem is how to devise definitions of causality and feedback which permit tests for their existence. Such a definition was proposed in earlier papers [**4**, Chapter 7; **3**]. In this section, some of these definitions will be discussed and extended. Although later sections of this paper will use this definition of causality they will not completely depend upon it. Previous papers concerned with causality in economic systems [**1**, **6**, **7**, **8**] have been particularly concerned with the problem of determining a causal interpretation of simultaneous equation systems, usually with instantaneous causality. Feedback is not explicitly discussed. This earlier work has concentrated on the form that the parameters of the equations should take in order to discern definite causal relationships. The stochastic elements and the natural time ordering of the variables play relatively minor roles in the theory. In the alternative theory to be discussed here, the stochastic nature of the variables and the direction of the flow of time will be central features. The theory is, in fact, not relevant for nonstochastic variables and will rely entirely on the assumption that the future cannot cause the past. This theory will not, of course, be contradictory to previous work but there appears to be little common ground. Its origins may be found in a suggestion by Wiener [**9**]. The relationship between the definition discussed here and the work of Good [**2**] has yet to be determined.

If A_t is a stationary stochastic process, let $\bar{A}_t$ represent the set of *past* values $\{A_{t-j}, j = 1, 2, \ldots, \infty\}$ and $\bar{\bar{A}}_t$ represent the set of *past and present values* $\{A_{t-j}, j = 0, 1, \ldots, \infty\}$. Further let $\bar{A}(k)$ represent the set $\{A_{t-j}, j = k, k + 1, \ldots, \infty\}$.

Denote the optimum, unbiased, least-squares predictor of A_t using the set of values B_t by $P_t(A|B)$. Thus, for instance, $P_t(X|\bar{X})$ will be the optimum predictor of X_t using only past X_t. The predictive error series will be denoted by $\varepsilon_t(A|B) = A_t - P_t(A|B)$. Let $\sigma^2(A|B)$ be the variance of $\varepsilon_t(A|B)$.

The initial definitions of causality, feedback, and so forth, will be very general in nature. Testable forms will be introduced later. Let U_t be all the information in the universe accumulated since time $t - 1$ and let $U_t - Y_t$ denote all this information *apart* from the specified series Y_t. We then have the following definitions.

DEFINITION 1: *Causality*. If $\sigma^2(X|U) < \sigma^2(X|\overline{U - Y})$, we say that Y is causing X, denoted by $Y_t \Rightarrow X_t$. We say that Y_t is causing X_t if we are better able to predict X_t using all available information than if the information apart from Y_t had been used.

DEFINITION 2: *Feedback*. If

$$\sigma^2(X|\bar{U}) < \sigma^2(X|\overline{U - Y}),$$

$$\sigma^2(Y|\bar{U}) < \sigma^2(Y|\overline{U - X}),$$

we say that feedback is occurring, which is denoted $Y_t \Leftrightarrow X_t$, i.e., feedback is said to occur when X_t is causing Y_t and also Y_t is causing X_t.

DEFINITION 3: *Instantaneous Causality*. If $\sigma^2(X|\overline{U}, \overline{\overline{Y}}) < \sigma^2(X|\overline{U})$, we say that instantaneous causality $Y_t \Rightarrow X_t$ is occurring. In other words, the current value of X_t is better "predicted" if the present value of Y_t is included in the "prediction" than if it is not.

DEFINITION 4: *Causality Lag*. If $Y_t \Rightarrow X_t$, we define the (integer) causality lag m to be the least value of k such that $\sigma^2(X|U - Y(k)) < \sigma^2(X|U - Y(k+1))$. Thus, knowing the values $Y_{t-j}, j = 0, 1, \ldots, m-1$, will be of no help in improving the prediction of X_t.

The definitions have assumed that only stationary series are involved. In the nonstationary case, $\sigma(X|\overline{U})$ etc. will depend on time t and, in general, the existence of causality may alter over time. The definitions can clearly be generalised to be operative for a specified time t. One could then talk of causality existing at this moment of time. Considering nonstationary series, however, takes us further away from testable definitions and this tack will not be discussed further.

The one completely unreal aspect of the above definitions is the use of the series U_t, representing *all* available information. The large majority of the information in the universe will be quite irrelevant, i.e., will have no causal consequence. Suppose that all relevant information is numerical in nature and belongs to the vector set of time series $Y_t^D = \{Y_t^i, i \in D\}$ for some integer set D. Denote the set $\{i \in D, i \neq j\}$ by $D(j)$ and $\{Y_t^i, i \in D(j)\}$ by $Y_t^{D(j)}$, i.e., the full set of relevant information except one particular series. Similarly, we could leave out more than one series with the obvious notation. The previous definitions can now be used but with U_t replaced by Y_t and $U_t - Y_t$ by $Y^{D(j)}$. Thus, for example, suppose that the vector set consists only of two series, X_t and Y_t and that all other information is irrelevant. Then $\sigma^2(X|\overline{X})$ represents the minimum predictive error variance of X_t using only past X_t and $\sigma^2(X|\overline{X}, \overline{Y})$ represents this minimum variance if both past X_t and past Y_t are used to predict X_t. Then Y_t is said to cause X_t if $\sigma^2(X|\overline{X}) > \sigma^2(X|\overline{X}, \overline{Y})$. The definition of causality is now relative to the set D. If relevant data has not been included in this set, then spurious causality could arise. For instance, if the set D was taken to consist only of the two series X_t and Y_t, but in fact there was a third series Z_t which was causing both within the enlarged set $D' = (X_t, Y_t, Z_t)$, then for the original set D, spurious causality between X_t and Y_t may be found. This is similar to spurious correlation and partial correlation between sets of data that arise when some other statistical variable of importance has not been included.

In practice it will not usually be possible to use completely optimum predictors, unless all sets of series are assumed to be normally distributed, since such optimum predictors may be nonlinear in complicated ways. It seems natural to use only linear predictors and the above definitions may again be used under this assumption of linearity. Thus, for instance, the best linear predictor of X_t using only past X_t and past Y_t will be of the form

$$P_t(X|\overline{X}, \overline{Y}) = \sum_{j=1}^{\infty} a_j X_{t-j} + \sum_{j=1}^{\infty} b_j Y_{t-j}$$

where the a_j's and b_j's are chosen to minimise $\sigma^2(X|\overline{X}, \overline{Y})$.

It can be argued that the variance is not the proper criterion to use to measure the closeness of a predictor P_t to the true value X_t. Certainly if some other criteria were used it may be possible to reach different conclusions about whether one series is causing another. The variance does seem to be a natural criterion to use in connection with linear predictors as it is mathematically easy to handle and simple to interpret. If one uses this criterion, a better name might be "causality in mean."

The original definition of causality has now been restricted in order to reach a form which can be tested. Whenever the word causality is used in later sections it will be taken to mean "linear causality in mean with respect to a specified set D."

It is possible to extend the definitions to the case where a subset of series D^* of D is considered to cause X_t. This would be the case if $\sigma^2(X|Y^D) < \sigma^2(X|Y^{D-D^*})$ and then $Y^{D^*} \Rightarrow X_t$. Thus, for instance, one could ask if past X_t is causing present X_t. Because new concepts are necessary in the consideration of such problems, they will not be discussed here in any detail.

It has been pointed out already [3] that instantaneous causality, in which knowledge of the current value of a series helps in predicting the current value of a second series, can occasionally arise spuriously in certain cases. Suppose $Y_t \Rightarrow X_t$ with lag one unit but that the series are sampled every two time units. Then although there is no real instantaneous causality, the definitions will appear to suggest that such causality is occurring. This is because certain relevant information, the missing readings in the data, have not been used. Due to this effect, one might suggest that in many economic situations an apparent instantaneous causality would disappear if the economic variables were recorded at more frequent time intervals.

The definition of causality used above is based entirely on the predictability of some series, say X_t. If some other series Y_t contains information in past terms that helps in the prediction of X_t and if this information is contained in no other series used in the predictor, then Y_t is said to cause X_t. The flow of time clearly plays a central role in these definitions. In the author's opinion there is little use in the practice of attempting to discuss causality without introducing time, although philosophers have tried to do so. It also follows from the definitions that a purely deterministic series, that is, a series which can be predicted exactly from its past terms such as a nonstochastic series, cannot be said to have any causal influences other than its own past. This may seem to be contrary to common sense in certain special cases but it is difficult to find a *testable* alternative definition which could include the deterministic situation. Thus, for instance, if $X_t = bt$ and $Y_t = c(t + 1)$, then X_t can be predicted exactly by $b + X_{t-1}$ or by $(b/c)Y_{t-1}$. There seems to be no way of deciding if Y_t is a causal factor of X_t or not. In some cases the notation of the "simplest rule" might be applied. For example, if X_t is some complicated polynomial in t and $Y_t = X_{t+1}$, then it will be easier to predict X_t from Y_{t-1} than from past X_t. In some cases this rule cannot be used, as the previous example showed. In any case, experience does not indicate that one should expect economic laws to be simple in nature.

Even for stochastic series, the definitions introduced above may give apparently silly answers. Suppose $X_t = A_{t-1} + \varepsilon_t$, $Y_t = A_t + \eta_t$, and $Z_t = A_t + \gamma_t$, where ε_t,

η_t, and γ_t are all uncorrelated white-noise series with equal variances and A_t is some stationary series. Within the set $D = (X_t, Y_t)$ the definition gives $Y_t \Rightarrow X_t$. Within the set $D' = (X_t, Y_t)$, it gives $Z_t \Rightarrow X_t$. But within the set $D'' = (X_t, Y_t, Z_t)$, neither Y_t nor Z_t causes X_t, although the sum of Y_t and Z_t would do so. How is one to decide if either Y_t or Z_t is a causal series for X_t? The answer, of course, is that neither is. The causal series is A_t and both Y_t and Z_t contain equal amounts of information about A_t. If the set of series within which causality was discussed was expanded to include A_t, then the above apparent paradox vanishes. It will often be found that constructed examples which seem to produce results contrary to common sense can be resolved by widening the set of data within which causality is defined.

5. TWO-VARIABLE MODELS

In this section, the definitions introduced above will be illustrated using two-variable models and results will be proved concerning the form of the cross spectrum for such models.

Let X_t, Y_t be two stationary time series with zero means. The simple causal model is

$$X_t = \sum_{j=1}^{m} a_j X_{t-j} + \sum_{j=1}^{m} b_j Y_{t-j} + \varepsilon_t, \tag{5.1}$$
$$Y_t = \sum_{j=1}^{m} c_j X_{t-j} + \sum_{j=1}^{m} d_j Y_{t-j} + \eta_t,$$

where ε_t, η_t are taken to be two uncorrelated white-noise series, i.e., $E[\varepsilon_t\varepsilon_s] = 0 = E[\eta_t\eta_s]$, $s \neq t$, and $E[\varepsilon_t\varepsilon_s] = 0$ all t, s. In (5.1) m can equal infinity but in practice, of course, due to the finite length of the available data, m will be assumed finite and shorter than the given time series.

The definition of causality given above implies that Y_t is causing X_t provided some b_j is not zero. Similarly X_t is causing Y_t if some c_j is not zero. If both of these events occur, there is said to be a feedback relationship between X_t and Y_t. It will be shown later that this new definition of causality is in fact identical to that introduced previously.

The more general model with instantaneous causality is

$$X_t + b_0 Y_t = \sum_{j=1}^{m} a_j X_{t-j} + \sum_{j=1}^{m} b_j Y_{t-j} + \varepsilon_t, \tag{5.2}$$
$$Y_t + c_0 X_t = \sum_{j=1}^{m} c_j X_{t-j} + \sum_{j=1}^{m} d_j Y_{t-j} + \eta_t.$$

If the variables are such that this kind of representation is needed, then instantaneous causality is occurring and a knowledge of Y_t will improve the "prediction" or goodness of fit of the first equation for X_t.

Consider initially the simple causal model (5.1). In terms of the time shift operator U—$UX_t = X_{t-1}$—these equations may be written

$$(5.3) \quad \begin{aligned} X_t &= a(U)X_t + b(U)Y_t + \varepsilon_t, \\ Y_t &= c(U)X_t + d(U)Y_t + \eta_t, \end{aligned}$$

where $a(U)$, $b(U)$, $c(U)$, and $d(U)$ are power series in U with the coefficient of U^0 zero, i.e., $a(U) = \sum_{j=1}^{m} a_j U^j$, etc.

Using the Cramer representations of the series, i.e.,

$$X_t = \int_{-\pi}^{\pi} e^{it\omega}\, dZ_x(\omega), \qquad Y_t = \int_{-\pi}^{\pi} e^{it\omega}\, dZ_y(\omega),$$

and similarly for ε_t and η_t, expressions such as $a(U)X_t$ can be written as

$$a(U)X_t = \int_{-\pi}^{\pi} e^{it\omega} a(e^{-i\omega})\, dZ_x(\omega).$$

Thus, equations (5.3) may be written

$$\int_{-\pi}^{\pi} e^{it\omega}[(1 - a(e^{-i\omega}))\, dZ_x(\omega) - b(e^{-i\omega})\, dZ_y(\omega) - dZ_\varepsilon(\omega)] = 0,$$

$$\int_{-\pi}^{\pi} e^{it\omega}[-c(e^{-i\omega})\, dZ_x(\omega) + (1 - d(e^{-i\omega}))\, dZ_y(\omega) - dZ_\eta(\omega)] = 0,$$

from which it follows that

$$(5.4) \quad A\begin{bmatrix} dZ_x \\ dZ_y \end{bmatrix} = \begin{bmatrix} dZ_\varepsilon \\ dZ_\eta \end{bmatrix}$$

where

$$A = \begin{bmatrix} 1 - a & -b \\ -c & 1 - d \end{bmatrix}$$

and where a is written for $a(e^{-i\omega})$, etc., and dZ_x for $dZ_x(\omega)$, etc.

Thus, provided the inverse of A exists,

$$(5.5) \quad \begin{bmatrix} dZ_x \\ dZ_y \end{bmatrix} = A^{-1}\begin{bmatrix} dZ_\varepsilon \\ dZ_\eta \end{bmatrix}.$$

As the spectral, cross-spectral matrix for X_t, Y_t is directly obtainable from

$$E\begin{bmatrix} dZ_x \\ dZ_y \end{bmatrix}[\overline{dZ_x}\ \overline{dZ_y}],$$

these functions can quickly be found from (5.5) using the known properties of dZ_ε and dZ_η. One finds that the power spectra are given by

$$(5.6) \quad \begin{aligned} f_x(\omega) &= \frac{1}{2\pi\Delta}(|1 - d|^2\sigma_\varepsilon^2 + |b|^2\sigma_\eta^2), \\ f_y(\omega) &= \frac{1}{2\pi\Delta}(|c|^2\sigma_\varepsilon^2 + |1 - a|^2\sigma_\eta^2), \end{aligned}$$

where $\Delta = |(1-a)(1-d) - bc|^2$. Of more interest is the cross spectrum which has the form

$$Cr(\omega) = \frac{1}{2\pi\Delta}[(1-d)\bar{c}\sigma_\varepsilon^2 + (1-\bar{a})b\sigma_\eta^2].$$

Thus, the cross spectrum may be written as the sum of two components

$$Cr(\omega) = C_1(\omega) + C_2(\omega), \tag{5.7}$$

where

$$C_1(\omega) = \frac{\sigma_\varepsilon^2}{2\pi\Delta}(1-d)\bar{c}$$

and

$$C_2(\omega) = \frac{\sigma_\eta^2}{2\pi\Delta}(1-\bar{a})b.$$

If Y_t is not causing X_t, then $b \equiv 0$ and so $C_2(\omega)$ vanishes. Similarly if X_t is not causing Y_t then $c \equiv 0$ and so $C_1(\omega)$ vanishes. It is thus clear that the cross spectrum can be decomposed into the sum of two components—one which depends upon the causality of X by Y and the other on the causality of Y by X.

If, for example, Y is not causing X so that $C_2(\omega)$ vanishes, then $Cr(\omega) = C_1(\omega)$ and the resulting coherence and phase diagrams will be interpreted in the usual manner. This suggests that in general $C_1(\omega)$ and $C_2(\omega)$ can each be treated separately as cross spectra connected with the two arms of the feedback mechanism. Thus, coherence and phase diagrams can be defined for $X \Rightarrow Y$ and $Y \Rightarrow X$. For example,

$$C_{\vec{xy}}(\omega) = \frac{|C_1(\omega)|^2}{f_x(\omega)f_y(\omega)}$$

may be considered to be a measure of the strength of the causality $X \Rightarrow Y$ plotted against frequency and is a direct generalisation of coherence. We call $C_{\vec{xy}}(\omega)$ the causality coherence.

Further,

$$\phi_{\vec{xy}}(\omega) = \tan^{-1}\frac{\text{imaginary part of } C_1(\omega)}{\text{real part of } C_1(\omega)}$$

will measure the phase lag against frequency of $X \Rightarrow Y$ and will be called the causality phase diagram.

Similarly such functions can be defined for $Y \Rightarrow X$ using $C_2(\omega)$.

These functions are usually complicated expressions in a, b, c, and d; for example,

$$C_{\vec{xy}}(\omega) = \frac{\sigma_\varepsilon^4|(1-d)c|^2}{(\sigma_\varepsilon^2|1-d|^2 + \sigma_\eta^2|b|^2)(\sigma_\varepsilon^2|c|^2 + |1-a|^2\sigma_\eta^2)}.$$

Such formulae merely illustrate how difficult it is to interpret econometric models in terms of frequency decompositions. It should be noted that $0 < |C_{\vec{xy}}(\omega)| < 1$ and similarly for $C_{\vec{yx}}(\omega)$.

As an illustration of these definitions, we consider the simple feedback system

$$(5.8)\qquad \begin{aligned} X_t &= bY_{t-1} + \varepsilon_t, \\ Y_t &= cX_{t-2} + \eta_t, \end{aligned}$$

where $\sigma_\varepsilon^2 = \sigma_\eta^2 = 1$.

In this case

$$a(\omega) = 0,$$

$$b(\omega) = b\,e^{-i\omega},$$

$$c(\omega) = c\,e^{-2i\omega},$$

$$d(\omega) = 0.$$

The spectra of the series $\{X_t\}$, $\{Y_t\}$ are

$$f_x(\omega) = \frac{1 + b^2}{2\pi|1 - bc\,e^{-3i\omega}|^2}$$

and

$$f_y(\omega) = \frac{1 + c^2}{2\pi|1 - bc\,e^{-3i\omega}|^2},$$

and thus are of similar shape.

The usual coherence and phase diagrams derived from the cross spectrum between these two series are

$$C(\omega) = \frac{c^2 + b^2 + 2bc\cos\omega}{(1 + b^2)(1 + c^2)}$$

and

$$\phi(\omega) = \tan^{-1}\frac{c\sin 2\omega - b\sin\omega}{c\cos 2\omega + b\cos\omega}.$$

These diagrams are clearly of little use in characterising the feedback relationship between the two series.

When the causality-coherence and phase diagrams are considered, however, we get

$$C_{\vec{xy}}(\omega) = \frac{c^2}{(1 + b^2)(1 + c^2)}, \qquad C_{\vec{yx}}(\omega) = \frac{b^2}{(1 + b^2)(1 + c^2)}.$$

Both are constant for all ω, and, if $b \neq 0$, $c \neq 0$, $\phi_{\vec{xy}}(\omega) = 2\omega$ (time lag of two units),[1] $\phi_{\vec{yx}}(\omega) = \omega$ (time-lag of one unit).

The causality lags are thus seen to be correct and the causality coherences to be reasonable. In particular, if $b = 0$ then $C_{\vec{yx}}(\omega) = 0$, i.e., no causality is found when none is present. (Further, in this new case, $\phi_{\vec{xy}}(\omega) = 0$.)

[1] A discussion of the interpretation of phase diagrams in terms of time lags may be found in Granger and Hatanaka [4, Chapter 5].

Other particular cases are also found to give correct results. If, for example, we again consider the same simple model (4.8) but with $\sigma_\varepsilon^2 = 1, \sigma_\eta^2 = 0$, i.e., $\eta_t \equiv 0$ for all t, then one finds

$$C_{\vec{xy}}(\omega) = 1,$$

$$C_{\vec{yx}}(\omega) = 0,$$

i.e., X is "perfectly" causing Y and Y is not causing X, as is in fact the case.

If one now considers the model (5.2) in which instantaneous causality is allowed, it is found that the cross spectrum is given by

$$Cr(\omega) = \frac{1}{2\pi\Delta'}[(1 - d)(\bar{c} - c_0)\sigma_\varepsilon^2 + (1 - \bar{a})(b - b_0)\sigma_\eta^2] \tag{5.9}$$

where

$$\Delta' = |(1 - a)(1 - d) - (b - b_0)(c - c_0)|^2.$$

Thus, once more, the cross spectrum can be considered as the sum of two components, each of which can be associated with a "causality," provided that this includes instantaneous causality. It is, however, probably more sensible to decompose $Cr(\omega)$ into three parts, $Cr(\omega) = C_1(\omega) + C_2(\omega) + C_3(\omega)$, where $C_1(\omega)$ and $C_2(\omega)$ are as in (5.7) but with Δ replaced by Δ' and

$$C_3(\omega) = \frac{-1}{2\pi\Delta}[c_0(1 - d)\sigma_\varepsilon^2 + b_0(1 - a)\sigma_\eta^2] \tag{5.10}$$

representing the influence of the instantaneous causality.

Such a decomposition may be useful but it is clear that when instantaneous causality occurs, the measures of causal strength and phase lag will lose their meaning.

It was noted in Section 3 that instantaneous causality models such as (5.2) in general lack uniqueness of their parameters as an orthogonal transformation Λ applied to the variables leaves the general form of the model unaltered. It is interesting to note that such transformations do not have any effect on the cross spectrum given by (5.9) or the decomposition. This can be seen by noting that equations (5.2) lead to

$$A\begin{bmatrix} dz_x \\ dz_y \end{bmatrix} = \begin{bmatrix} dz_\varepsilon \\ dz_\eta \end{bmatrix}$$

with appropriate A. Applying the transformation Λ gives

$$\Lambda A\begin{bmatrix} dz_x \\ dz_y \end{bmatrix} = \Lambda\begin{bmatrix} dz_\varepsilon \\ dz_\eta \end{bmatrix}$$

so that

$$\begin{bmatrix} dz_x \\ dz_y \end{bmatrix} = (\Lambda A)^{-1}\Lambda\begin{bmatrix} dz_\varepsilon \\ dz_\eta \end{bmatrix}$$

$$= A^{-1}\begin{bmatrix} dz_\varepsilon \\ dz_\eta \end{bmatrix}$$

which is the same as if no such transformation had been applied. From its definition, Δ will possess an inverse. This result suggests that spectral methods are more robust in their interpretation than are simultaneous equation models.

Returning to the simple causal model (5.3),

$$X_t = a(U)X_t + b(U)Y_t + \varepsilon_t,$$

$$Y_t = c(U)X_t + d(U)Y_t + \eta_t,$$

throughout this section it has been stated that $Y_t \not\Rightarrow X_t$ if $b \equiv 0$. On intuitive grounds this seems to fit the definition of no causality introduced in Section 4, within the set D of series consisting only of X_t and Y_t. If $b \equiv 0$ then X_t is determined from the first equation and the minimum variance of the predictive error of X_t using past X_t will be σ_ε^2. This variance cannot be reduced using past Y_t. It is perhaps worthwhile proving this result formally. In the general case, it is clear that $\sigma^2(X|\bar{X}, \bar{Y}) = \sigma_\varepsilon^2$, i.e., the variance of the predictive error of X_t, if both past X_t and past Y_t are used, will be σ_ε^2 from the top equation. If only past X_t is used to predict X_t, it is a well known result that the minimum variance of the predictive error is given by

$$\sigma^2(X|\bar{X}) = \exp \tfrac{1}{2}\pi \int_{-\pi}^{\pi} \log \tfrac{1}{2}\pi f_x(\omega)\, d\omega. \tag{5.11}$$

It was shown above in equation (5.6) that

$$f_x(\omega) = \frac{1}{2\pi\Delta}(|1 - d|^2\sigma_\varepsilon^2 + |b|^2\sigma_\eta^2)$$

where $\Delta = |(1 - a)(1 - d) - bc|^2$. To simplify this equation, we note that

$$\int_{-\pi}^{\pi} \log|1 - \alpha\, e^{i\omega}|^2\, d\omega = 0$$

by symmetry. Thus if,

$$f_x(\omega) = \alpha_0 \frac{\pi|1 - \alpha_j e^{i\omega}|^2}{\pi|1 - \beta_j e^{i\omega}|^2},$$

then $\sigma^2(X|\bar{X}) = \alpha_0$. For there to be no causality, we must have $\alpha_0 = \sigma_\varepsilon^2$. It is clear from the form of $f_x(\omega)$ that in general this could only occur if $|b| \equiv 0$, in which case $2\pi f_x(\omega) = \sigma_\varepsilon^2/|1 - a|^2$ and the required result follows.

6. THREE-VARIABLE MODELS

The above results can be generalised to the many variables situation, but the only case which will be considered is that involving three variables.

Consider a simple causal model generalising (5.1):

$$X_t = a_1(U)X_t + b_1(U)Y_t + c_1(U)Z_t + \varepsilon_{1,t},$$

$$Y_t = a_2(U)X_t + b_2(U)Y_t + c_2(U)Z_t + \varepsilon_{2,t},$$

$$Z_t = a_3(U)X_t + b_3(U)Y_t + c_3(U)Z_t + \varepsilon_{3,t},$$

where $a_1(U)$, etc., are polynomials in U, the shift operator, with the coefficient of U^0 zero. As before, $\varepsilon_{i,t}$, $i = 1, 2, 3$, are uncorrelated, white-noise series and denote the variance $\varepsilon_{i,t} = \sigma_i^2$.

Let $\alpha = a_1 - 1, \beta = b_2 - 1, \gamma = c_3 - 1$, and

$$A = \begin{bmatrix} \alpha & b_1 & c_1 \\ a_2 & \beta & c_2 \\ a_3 & b_3 & \gamma \end{bmatrix},$$

where $b_1 = b_1(e^{-i\omega})$, etc., as before. Using the same method as before, the spectral, cross-spectral matrix $S(\omega)$ is found to be given by $S(\omega) = A^{-1}k(A')^{-1}$ where

$$k = \begin{bmatrix} \sigma_1^2 & 0 & 0 \\ 0 & \sigma_2^2 & 0 \\ 0 & 0 & \sigma_3^2 \end{bmatrix}.$$

One finds, for instance, that the power spectrum of X_t is

$$f_x(\omega) = |\Delta|^{-2}[\sigma_1^2|\beta\gamma - c_2b_3|^2 + \sigma_2^2|c_1b_3 - \gamma b_1|^2 + \sigma_3^2|b_1c_2^2 - c_1\beta|^2]$$

where Δ is the determinant of A.

The cross spectrum between X_t and Y_t is

$$C_r^{xy}(\omega) = |\Delta|^{-2}[\sigma_1^2(\beta\gamma - c_2b_3)\overline{(c_2a_3 - \gamma a_2)} + \sigma_2^2(c_1b_3 - b_1\gamma)\overline{(\alpha\gamma - c_1a_3)}$$
$$+ \sigma_3^2(b_1c_2 - c_1\beta)\overline{(c_1a_2 - c_2\alpha)}].$$

Thus, this cross spectrum is the sum of three components, but it is not clear that these can be directly linked with causalities. More useful results arise, however, when partial cross spectra are considered. After some algebraic manipulation it is found that, for instance, the partial cross spectrum between X_t and Y_t given Z_t is

$$C_r^{xy,z}(\omega) = -\frac{[\sigma_1^2\sigma_2^2b_3a_3 + \sigma_1^2\sigma_2^2\beta a_2 + \sigma_2^2\sigma_3^2b_1\alpha]}{f_z'(\omega)}$$

where

$$f_z'(\omega) = \sigma_1^2|\beta\gamma - c_2b_3|^2 + \sigma_2^2|c_1b_3 - b_1\gamma|^2 + \sigma_3^2|b_1c_2 - c_1\beta|^2.$$

Thus, the partial cross spectrum is the sum of three components

$$C_r^{xy,z}(\omega) = C_1^{xy,z} + C_2^{xy,z} + C_3^{xy,z}$$

where

$$C_1^{xy,z} = -\frac{\sigma_1^2\sigma_2^2b_3a_3}{f_z'(\omega)}, \quad \text{etc.}$$

These can be linked with causalities. The component $C_1^{xy,z}(\omega)$ represents the interrelationships of X_t and Y_t *through* Z_t, and the other two components are direct generalisations of the two causal cross spectra which arose in the two variable case and can be interpreted accordingly.

In a similar manner one finds that the power spectrum of X_t, given Z_t is

$$f_{x,z}(\omega) = \frac{\sigma_1^2\sigma_2^2|b_3|^2 + \sigma_1^2\sigma_3^2|\beta|^2 + \sigma_2^2\sigma_3^2|b_1|^2}{f'_z(\omega)}.$$

The causal and feedback relationships between X_t and Y_t can be investigated in terms of the coherence and phase diagrams derived from the second and third components of the partial cross spectrum, i.e.,

$$\text{coherence}\,(\overrightarrow{xy}, z) = \frac{|C_2^{xy,z}|^2}{f_{x,y}.f_{y,z}}, \quad \text{etc.}$$

7. CONCLUSION

The fact that a feedback mechanism may be considered as the sum of two causal mechanisms and that these causalities can be studied by decomposing cross or partial cross spectra suggests methods whereby such mechanisms can be investigated. Hopefully, the problem of estimating the causal cross spectra will be discussed in a later publication. There are a number of possible approaches and accumulated experience is needed to indicate which is best. Most of these approaches are via the model-building method by which the above results were obtained. It is worth investigating, however, whether a direct method of estimating the components of the cross spectrum can be found.

The University of Nottingham

REFERENCES

[1] Basman, R. L.: "The Causal Interpretation of Non-Triangular Systems of Economic Relations," *Econometrica*, Volume 31, 1963, pp. 439–448.

[2] Good, I. J.: "A Causal Calculus, I, II," *Brit. J. Philos. Soc.*, Volume 11, 1961, pp. 305–318 and Volume 12, 1962, pp. 43–51.

[3] Granger, C. W. J.: "Economic Processes Involving Feedback," *Information and Control*, Volume 6, 1963, pp. 28–48.

[4] Granger, C. W. J., and M. Hatanaka: *Spectral Analysis of Economic Time Series*, Princeton University Press, 1964.

[5] Nerlove, M.: "Spectral Analysis of Seasonal Adjustment Procedures," *Econometrica*, Volume 32, 1964, pp. 241–286.

[6] Orcutt, G. H.: "Actions, Consequences and Causal Relations," *Review of Economics and Statistics*, Volume 34, 1952, pp. 305–13.

[7] Simon, H. A.: "Causal Ordering and Identifiability," *Studies in Econometric Method* (edited by W. C. Hood and T. C. Koopmans), Cowles Commission Monograph 14, New York, 1953.

[8] Strotz, R. H., and H. Wold: "Recursive versus Non-Recursive Systems: An Attempt at Synthesis," *Econometrica*, Volume 28, 1960, pp. 417–427.

[9] Wiener, N.: "The Theory of Prediction," *Modern Mathematics for Engineers*, Series 1 (edited by E. F. Beckenback), Chapter 8, 1956.

[27]

THE AUTOCORRELATION FUNCTION AND THE SPECTRAL DENSITY FUNCTION

By J. WISE

London School of Economics

Introduction and summary

The relationship existing between the autocorrelation function and the spectral density function of a stationary, purely non-deterministic stochastic process is well known. Discussions of the relationship have been given by Wiener (1930) and Khintchine (1934), in the case of the continuous process, and by Wold (1954, Chapter 2, § 17, pp. 66–75), and Doob (1953, Chapter 10, §§ 3 and 4, pp. 473–86) for the discrete process. The treatment in the present paper is confined to the discrete process.*

The relationship referred to also provides a fundamental connexion between the autocorrelation matrix of a process and the corresponding spectral density function of the process. Some rather ingenious manipulations on the matrix representation of the spectral function have been carried out by Whittle (1951, Chapter 4, § 2, pp. 35–6, equations (4·272) and (4·276)). However, Whittle's work contains some inaccuracies. More important still, 'exact' results exist for those cases in which Whittle gave 'asymptotic' solutions.

In the course of the derivations of these exact relationships, the author uses methods which appear to be new—though bearing some relationship to André's method of solving linear difference equations (see C. Jordan, 1947, pp. 587–99)—and are capable of wide application in the theory of discrete linear stochastic processes. The use of exact relationships does, moreover, lead to a considerable improvement in clarity and rigour.

In view of the fundamental exact relationships existing between the autocovariance matrix and the spectral density function, the former might appropriately—in the case of the stationary process—be termed the spectral density matrix of the process. Traditional terminology has, however, been adhered to in the remainder of the paper.

The main topics treated below may be classified under the following headings.

(*a*) *The circular process*

(i) The exact relationship existing between the autocovariance matrix and the spectral density function.

(ii) The latent roots of the autocovariance matrix.

(iii) The exact relationship between the canonical form of the autocovariance matrix and the spectral density function.

(*b*) *The non-circular process*

(i) The exact relationship corresponding to (*a*) (i) above.

(ii) The exact inversion of non-circular autocovariance matrices.

* This discrete process may, however, be a sample realization drawn from a continuous process.

(*a*) The circular process

Definitions

The vector of N random variables, given by $\mathbf{x}' = \{x_N, x_{N-1}, \ldots, x_1\}$, is assumed to have the following distributional properties:

$$E\mathbf{x} = \mathbf{0}, \tag{1}$$

$$Ex_s^2 = \sigma^2 \quad \{s = 1, 2, \ldots, N\}, \tag{2}$$

$$Ex_s x_{s+L} = \sigma^2 \rho_L \quad \{s = 1, 2, \ldots, N\}, \tag{3}$$

where
$$\rho_{N+L} = \rho_{N-L} = \rho_L.$$

The sequence of values $\rho_1, \rho_2, \ldots, \rho_N$ is termed the autocorrelation function of the process.

$$E\mathbf{x}\mathbf{x}' = \mathbf{V} \quad \text{(the autocovariance matrix)}$$

$$= \sigma^2 \begin{bmatrix} 1 & \rho_1 & \rho_2 & \rho_3 & \cdots & \rho_2 & \rho_1 \\ \rho_1 & 1 & \rho_1 & \rho_2 & \cdots & \rho_3 & \rho_2 \\ \rho_2 & \rho_1 & 1 & \rho_1 & \cdots & \rho_4 & \rho_3 \\ \vdots & & & & & & \vdots \\ \rho_1 & \rho_2 & \rho_3 & \rho_4 & \cdots & \rho_1 & 1 \end{bmatrix}, \tag{4}$$

an $N \times N$ matrix.

Properties

The autocovariance matrix, $\mathbf{V}$, may, from (4), be expressed in the following form:

$$\mathbf{V} = \sigma^2 \{\mathbf{I} + \rho_1(\mathbf{W} + \mathbf{W}^{-1}) + \rho_2(\mathbf{W}^2 + \mathbf{W}^{-2}) + \ldots + \rho_{\frac{1}{2}(N-1)}(\mathbf{W}^{\frac{1}{2}(N-1)} + \mathbf{W}^{-\frac{1}{2}(N-1)})\}, \tag{5}$$

where N is a positive odd integer, or, alternatively,

$$= \sigma^2 \{\mathbf{I} + \rho_1(\mathbf{W} + \mathbf{W}^{-1}) + \rho_2(\mathbf{W}^2 + \mathbf{W}^{-2}) + \ldots + \tfrac{1}{2}\rho_{\frac{1}{2}N}(\mathbf{W}^{\frac{1}{2}N} + \mathbf{W}^{-\frac{1}{2}N})\},$$

where N is a positive even integer. For all values of N, $\mathbf{I}$ denotes the $N \times N$ identity matrix, and $\mathbf{W}$ denotes the $N \times N$ circulant definition of the auxiliary identity matrix, that is to say,

$$\mathbf{W} = 0 \begin{bmatrix} 0 & 1 & 0 & 0 & \ldots & 0 \\ 0 & 0 & 1 & 0 & \ldots & 0 \\ 0 & 0 & 0 & 1 & \ldots & 0 \\ \vdots & & & & \ddots & \vdots \\ 0 & 0 & . & . & \ldots & 1 \\ 1 & 0 & . & . & \ldots & 0 \end{bmatrix}. \tag{6}$$

Since the matrices $(\mathbf{W}^L + \mathbf{W}^{-L})$ for $(L = 1, 2, \ldots, N)$ are commutative, they may all be simultaneously reduced to canonical form by a single transformation.

Thus, if we consider the matrix $\mathbf{L}$, satisfying the property

$$\mathbf{L}'\mathbf{L} = \mathbf{I}, \tag{7}$$

$$\mathbf{L}'(\mathbf{W}^L + \mathbf{W}^{-L})\,\mathbf{L} = \operatorname{diag}\{\omega_1^L + \omega_1^{-L}, \ldots, \omega_N^L + \omega_N^{-L}\}, \tag{8}$$

where $\omega_1, \omega_2, \ldots, \omega_N$ are the N values of the roots of the equation

$$y^N - 1 = 0, \tag{9}$$

then
$$\mathbf{L}'\mathbf{V}\mathbf{L} = \operatorname{diag}\{\nu_1, \nu_2, \nu_3, \ldots, \nu_N\}$$

provides the canonical form of the autocovariance matrix $\mathbf{V}$.

Furthermore, we have

$$\omega_s^L + \omega_s^{-L} = 2\cos\frac{2\pi s L}{N} \quad (s = 1, 2, \ldots, N;\ L = 1, 2, \ldots, N). \tag{10}$$

The latent roots of **V** are thus given by

$$\begin{aligned} \nu_s &= \sigma^2\{1+\rho_1(\omega_s+\omega_s^{-1})+\rho_2(\omega_s^2+\omega_s^{-2})+\ldots+\rho_{\frac{1}{2}(N-1)}(\omega_s^{\frac{1}{2}(N-1)}+\omega_s^{-\frac{1}{2}(N-1)})\} \quad (s = 1, 2, \ldots, N) \\ &= \sigma^2\left\{1+2\rho_1\cos\frac{2\pi s}{N}+2\rho_2\cos\frac{4\pi s}{N}+\ldots+2\rho_{\frac{1}{2}(N-1)}\cos\frac{(N-1)\pi s}{N}\right\} \quad (s = 1, 2, \ldots, N) \end{aligned}$$

for N odd, or by

$$\begin{aligned} \nu_s &= \sigma^2\{1+\rho_1(\omega_s+\omega_s^{-1})+\rho_2(\omega_s^2+\omega_s^{-2})+\ldots+\tfrac{1}{2}\rho_{\frac{1}{2}N}(\omega_s^{\frac{1}{2}N}+\omega_s^{-\frac{1}{2}N})\} \quad (s = 1, 2, \ldots, N) \\ &= \sigma^2\left\{1+2\rho_1\cos\frac{2\pi s}{N}+2\rho_2\cos\frac{4\pi s}{N}+\ldots+\rho_{\frac{1}{2}N}\cos\pi s\right\} \quad (s = 1, 2, \ldots, N) \end{aligned} \tag{11}$$

for N even.

The relationships given by (5) and (11) are the correct restatement of similar forms given by Whittle (1951, Chapter 4, § 2, pp. 35–6), which are incorrect even as approximations in the non-circular case.

General rules for the multiplicities of the latent roots of **V** have been incorrectly stated by both Whittle (1951, Chapter 4, § 3, p. 37) and Watson (1951*, Chapter 2, § 5, p. 50).

Results correctly obtained by R. L. Anderson (1942, § 5*a*, pp. 7–8), on the multiplicities in the values of the terms in the sequence,

$$\cos\frac{2\pi L}{N}, \quad \cos\frac{4\pi L}{N}, \quad \cos\frac{6\pi L}{N}, \quad \ldots, \quad \cos 2\pi L, \tag{12}$$

may, however, be used to derive valid statements relating to the multiplicities in the latent roots of **V**.

Let $N = nk$ and $L = lk$, where n, l and k are positive integers, n and l being prime to one another. Two cases may then be distinguished.

(i) For n odd, there are $\frac{1}{2}(n-1)$ terms in the series (12) occurring with $2k$-fold multiplicities, together with the value unity occurring with k-fold multiplicity.

(ii) For n even, there are $\frac{1}{2}(n-2)$ terms in the series (12) occurring with $2k$-fold multiplicities, together with each of the values ± 1 occurring with k-fold multiplicities. For the derivation of these results the reader is referred to R. L. Anderson's paper.

Although it is impossible to enumerate here all the possibilities in detail, a 'rule' which the author has found useful in applications of the theory to sampling problems will be given relating to the multiplicities in the latent roots of **V**. This 'rule' is adequate for most of the cases which occur in practice. The 'rule' is not, however, a theorem, since exceptions to it occur when certain relationships exist between the elements of **V**. Care must therefore be taken when it is applied. This 'rule' is as follows:

If $\rho_L \neq 0$ for at least one value of L satisfying the condition $N = nk$ and $L = lk$, n and l being prime to one another, then the multiplicities in the latent roots will be at most $2k$-fold.

Whittle's assertion that if N is odd there are $\frac{1}{2}(N-1)$ pairs of distinct roots, with a single root greater than or less than all of these others; and if N is even there are $\frac{1}{2}(N-2)$ pairs of

* Watson states here that 'real symmetric circulant matrices have at most one odd latent root, the rest being pairwise equal'. That is, of course, incorrect.

distinct roots with one root greater than and one root less than all of the other roots, is incorrect.

An example occurring in the literature on time-series analysis, demonstrating a practical instance in which the 'rule' stated above yields the correct result, whereas Whittle's assertion breaks down, is the lag $-L$ definition of the Markoff process, given by

$$x_t - \rho x_{t-L} = \epsilon_t \quad (t = 1, 2, \ldots, N), \tag{13}$$

where $x_{N+S} = x_S$, N and L not being prime to one another.

The spectral function of a circular process

The spectral density function of the circular process possessing the distributional properties (1), (2) and (3) is of the form*

$$\nu(\theta) = \sigma^2 \left\{1 + 2\rho_1 \cos\theta + 2\rho_2 \cos 2\theta + \ldots + 2\rho_{\frac{1}{2}(N-1)} \cos\frac{(N-1)\theta}{2}\right\} \quad \left\{\theta = \frac{2\pi}{N}, \frac{4\pi}{N}, \ldots, 2\pi\right\},$$

where N is odd; or of the form

$$\nu(\theta) = \sigma^2\{1 + 2\rho_1 \cos\theta + 2\rho_2 \cos 2\theta + \ldots + \rho_{\frac{1}{2}N} \cos\tfrac{1}{2}N\theta\} \quad \left\{\theta = \frac{2\pi}{N}, \frac{4\pi}{N}, \ldots, 2\pi\right\}, \tag{14}$$

where N is even.

The latent roots of $\mathbf{V}$, given by (11), are thus the values of the spectral density function, $\nu(\theta)$, taken at constant intervals of $2\pi/N$ in the values of θ.

These roots may thus be regarded as being generated by the spectral density function of the process.

The results obtained so far are, of course, exact for finite N. By considering the limiting values of the roots as N tends to infinity, asymptotic results may be obtained.

The autoregressive-moving average process

The discrete circular linear process of the autoregressive-moving average type may be written in the form

$$x_t + \alpha_1 x_{t-1} + \ldots + \alpha_k x_{t-k} = \epsilon_t + \beta_1 \epsilon_{t-1} + \ldots + \beta_h \epsilon_{t-h} \quad \{t = 1, 2, \ldots, N\}, \tag{15}$$

where $x_{N+S} = x_S$, $\epsilon_{N+S} = \epsilon_S$, and

$$\left.\begin{aligned} E\epsilon_s &= 0 \quad \{s = 1, 2, \ldots, N\}, \\ E\epsilon_s^2 &= \sigma^2 \quad \{s = 1, 2, \ldots, N\}, \\ E\epsilon_s \epsilon_t &= 0 \quad \{s \neq t\}. \end{aligned}\right\} \tag{16}$$

* Any discrete stationary purely non-deterministic process may be written in the form

$$x_t = \eta_t + \beta_1 \eta_{t-1} + \beta_2 \eta_{t-2} + \ldots,$$

where the summation extends to infinity.

The spectral density function of this process is defined as

$$\nu(\theta) = (1 + \beta_1 e^{i\theta} + \beta_2 e^{2i\theta} + \ldots)(1 + \beta_1 e^{-i\theta} + \beta_2 e^{-2i\theta} + \ldots) \operatorname{var} \eta$$

for both circular and non-circular definitions of the process, for samples consisting of any number of consecutive observations. The relation (14) is obtained by expanding $\nu(\theta)$, thus defined, as a Fourier series.

In the matrix notation the process becomes

$$(\mathbf{I}+\alpha_1\mathbf{W}+\ldots+\alpha_k\mathbf{W}^k)\,\mathbf{x} = (\mathbf{I}+\beta_1\mathbf{W}+\ldots+\beta_h\mathbf{W}^h)\,\boldsymbol{\epsilon}, \tag{17}$$

where $\mathbf{x}' = \{x_N, x_{N-1}, x_{N-2}, \ldots, x_2, x_1\}$

and $\boldsymbol{\epsilon}' = \{\epsilon_N, \epsilon_{N-1}, \epsilon_{N-2}, \ldots, \epsilon_2, \epsilon_1\}$.

Solving (17) for $\mathbf{x}$, we obtain

$$\mathbf{x} = (\mathbf{I}+\alpha_1\mathbf{W}+\ldots+\alpha_k\mathbf{W}^k)^{-1}(\mathbf{I}+\beta_1\mathbf{W}+\ldots+\beta_h\mathbf{W}^h)\,\boldsymbol{\epsilon}. \tag{18}$$

Thus, from (18), we obtain

$$E\mathbf{x} = \mathbf{0}, \tag{19}$$

and

$$\begin{aligned} E\mathbf{x}\mathbf{x}' &= \mathbf{V} \quad \text{(the autocovariance matrix)} \\ &= \sigma^2(\mathbf{I}+\alpha_1\mathbf{W}+\ldots+\alpha_k\mathbf{W}^k)^{-1}(\mathbf{I}+\beta_1\mathbf{W}+\ldots+\beta_h\mathbf{W}^h)(\mathbf{I}+\beta_1\mathbf{W}^{-1}+\ldots+\beta_h\mathbf{W}^{-h}) \\ &\qquad \times(\mathbf{I}+\alpha_1\mathbf{W}^{-1}+\ldots+\alpha_k\mathbf{W}^{-k})^{-1}. \end{aligned} \tag{20}$$

The latent roots of $\mathbf{V}$ are therefore given by

$$\begin{aligned} \nu_s &= \sigma^2\frac{(1+\beta_1\omega_s+\ldots+\beta_h\omega_s^h)(1+\beta_1\omega_s^{-1}+\ldots+\beta_h\omega_s^{-h})}{(1+\alpha_1\omega_s+\ldots+\alpha_k\omega_s^k)(1+\alpha_1\omega_s^{-1}+\ldots+\alpha_k\omega_s^{-k})} \quad (s = 1, 2, \ldots, N) \\ &= \sigma^2\frac{(1+\beta_1 e^{2i\pi s/N}+\ldots+\beta_h e^{2i\pi hs/N})(1+\beta_1 e^{-2i\pi s/N}+\ldots+\beta_h e^{-2i\pi hs/N})}{(1+\alpha_1 e^{2i\pi s/N}+\ldots+\alpha_k e^{2i\pi ks/N})(1+\alpha_1 e^{-2i\pi s/N}+\ldots+\alpha_k e^{-2i\pi ks/N})} \quad (s = 1, 2, \ldots, N). \end{aligned} \tag{21}$$

The spectral density function of the circulant process (15) may be written as

$$\begin{aligned} \nu(\theta) &= \sigma^2\frac{(1+\beta_1 e^{i\theta}+\ldots+\beta_h e^{ih\theta})(1+\beta_1 e^{-i\theta}+\ldots+\beta_h e^{-ih\theta})}{(1+\alpha_1 e^{i\theta}+\ldots+\alpha_k e^{ik\theta})(1+\alpha_1 e^{-i\theta}+\ldots+\alpha_k e^{-ik\theta})} \quad (0\leqslant\theta\leqslant 2\pi) \\ &= g(e^{i\theta}) \quad \text{(let us say)} \quad (0\leqslant\theta\leqslant 2\pi). \end{aligned} \tag{22}$$

It follows from (20) and (22) that

$$\mathbf{V} = g(\mathbf{W}), \tag{23}$$

and, in addition,

$$\nu_s = g(\omega_s) = g(e^{2i\pi s/N}) \quad (s = 1, 2, \ldots, N). \tag{24}$$

These results are exact, and are fundamental to the exact treatment of circular processes.

An asymptotic relationship between $\mathbf{V}$ (in the non-circular case, to be further discussed in § (*b*) of this paper) and $g(\mathbf{W})$ has been given by Whittle (1951). It is not at all clear in what sense this asymptotic relationship is valid, unless the exact form is used. Whittle (1952, Theorem 1, (6) and (7), pp. 49–50), and Wold (1953, Chapter 11, § 2, Theorem 1) use the following interpretation of the asymptotic relationship:

$$\lim_{N\to\infty}\frac{\mathbf{x}'\mathbf{V}\mathbf{x}}{\mathbf{x}'g(\mathbf{W})\,\mathbf{x}} = 1 \tag{25}$$

for almost all realizations of the process. This result, though valid, is difficult to work with rigorously. Whittle does not adhere to it in any of his derivations, and for a rigorous treatment it is preferable to work throughout with exact relationships. The latter are no more cumbersome than the asymptotic forms, and their use may lead to the avoidance of substantial errors.

This is abundantly illustrated in the case of the first-order autoregressive process in the circular case. The largest latent root of the autocorrelation matrix for $\alpha_1 < 0$ is given by $\frac{1-(-\alpha_1)^N}{1+(-\alpha_1)^N}\frac{1-\alpha_1}{1+\alpha_1}$. The corresponding asymptotic form of this is $\frac{1-\alpha_1}{1+\alpha_1}$, which differs substantially from the exact value when N is small and $-\alpha_1$ is close to unity. In fact, as $-\alpha_1$ tends to unity, the exact form tends in value to N, while the asymptotic form tends to infinity.

A final point which should be made on the subject of the latent roots of circulant variance matrices is that in the derivation of the values of, and of the multiplicities in these roots, it is usually more convenient to consider the spectral density function in the form (22) than in the form (14).

(b) The non-circular process

Whittle (1951, Chapter 4, § 2, relations (4·253), (4·262) and (4·28), pp. 34–6) used the 'asymptotic' form of (23) to obtain a simple method for the 'approximate' inversion of **V** in the non-circular case. For many purposes, approximate inversion is not adequate, and is not in any case necessary. It will be shown below that a very simple method of exact inversion is available. Whittle (1951, Chapter 4, § 2, relations (4·242)–(4·252), pp. 33–4) does give a cumbersome method of exact inversion based on the auxiliary identity matrix, denoted by **U**, where

$$\mathbf{U} = \begin{bmatrix} 0 & 1 & 0 & 0 & \cdots & 0 \\ 0 & 0 & 1 & 0 & \cdots & 0 \\ 0 & 0 & 0 & 1 & \cdots & 0 \\ \vdots & & & & \ddots & \vdots \\ 0 & 0 & 0 & 0 & \cdots & 1 \\ 0 & 0 & 0 & 0 & \cdots & 0 \end{bmatrix} \tag{26}$$

an $N \times N$ matrix. Unfortunately Whittle's method appears to give the required result only in the case of the first-order autoregressive process.

An exact method of inversion will be given below which utilizes a non-circular counterpart of (20), the relation between the autocovariance matrix and the spectral density function.

The non-circular discrete linear process, generated by the relationship

$$x_t + \alpha_1 x_{t-1} + \ldots + \alpha_k x_{t-k} = \epsilon_t + \beta_1 \epsilon_{t-1} + \ldots + \beta_h \epsilon_{t-h}, \tag{27}$$

will be assumed to be semi-infinite. This does not prevent us from deriving results from samples consisting of N successive terms of the process. Such results for finite samples follow immediately from the case of the semi-infinite process. This is due to the fact that the autocovariance function and the spectral density function are both completely independent of N, a property which does not hold in the circular case.

We will assume (27) to represent a purely non-deterministic stationary process. An important theorem obtained by Wold (1954, Chapter 2, § 20, pp. 84–9, especially Theorem 7, p. 89) states, furthermore, that every semi-infinite, stationary, purely non-deterministic process can be expressed in the form (27).

A condition which is both necessary and sufficient for the stationarity of the process (27) can be obtained from a result given by Doob (1953).

The spectral density function of the process (27) is given by

$$g(e^{i\theta}) = \sigma^2 \frac{(1+\beta_1 e^{i\theta}+\ldots+\beta_h e^{ih\theta})(1+\beta_1 e^{-i\theta}+\ldots+\beta_h e^{-ih\theta})}{(1+\alpha_1 e^{i\theta}+\ldots+\alpha_k e^{ik\theta})(1+\alpha_1 e^{-i\theta}+\ldots+\alpha_k e^{-ik\theta})} \quad (0 \leqslant \theta \leqslant 2\pi).$$

It may, in passing, be noted that this is the same as (22), given for the circular process.

According to Doob (1953, Chapter 10, pp. 452–506, especially § 10, pp. 501–6), the necessary and sufficient condition for a stochastic process with the spectral function (22) to be stationary in the 'wide sense' (Chapter 2, § 8, pp. 94–5) is that the equation

$$z^h+\beta_1 z^{h-1}+\ldots+\beta_h = 0$$

shall have no roots outside the unit circle, and that the roots of the equation

$$z^k+\alpha_1 z^{k-1}+\ldots+\alpha_k = 0$$

shall all lie inside the unit circle. The reader is referred to Doob's* penetrating exposition for a more detailed treatment of this topic.

The relationship (27) may be transcribed as

$$(\mathbf{I}+\alpha_1\mathbf{U}+\ldots+\alpha_k\mathbf{U}^k)\,\mathbf{x} = (\mathbf{I}+\beta_1\mathbf{U}+\ldots+\beta_h\mathbf{U}^h)\,\boldsymbol{\epsilon}, \tag{28}$$

where $\mathbf{x}$ and $\boldsymbol{\epsilon}$ are semi-infinite vectors, and $\mathbf{U}$ is the semi-infinite auxiliary identity matrix.

Solving (28) for $\mathbf{x}$, leads to

$$\mathbf{x} = (\mathbf{I}+\alpha_1\mathbf{U}+\ldots+\alpha_k\mathbf{U}^k)^{-1}(\mathbf{I}+\alpha_1\mathbf{U}+\ldots+\beta_h\mathbf{U}^h)\,\boldsymbol{\epsilon}. \tag{29}$$

From (29) we deduce $$E\mathbf{x} = \mathbf{0}, \tag{30}$$

and

$$\begin{aligned}\mathbf{V} &= E\mathbf{x}\mathbf{x}' \\ &= \sigma^2(\mathbf{I}+\alpha_1\mathbf{U}+\ldots+\alpha_k\mathbf{U}^k)^{-1}(\mathbf{I}+\beta_1\mathbf{U}+\ldots+\beta_h\mathbf{U}^h)(\mathbf{I}+\beta_1\mathbf{U}'+\ldots+\beta_h\mathbf{U}'^h) \\ &\qquad \times(\mathbf{I}+\alpha_1\mathbf{U}'+\ldots+\alpha_k\mathbf{U}'^k)^{-1},\end{aligned} \tag{31}$$

which is thus the autocovariance matrix of the process (27). This is the exact, non-circular counterpart to the relationships (20) and (23), given above for the case of the circular process.

Relationship (31) bears a close affinity to the 'autocovariance generating function' given by

$$g(z) = \sigma^2 \frac{(1+\beta_1 z+\ldots+\beta_h z^h)(1+\beta_1 z^{-1}+\ldots+\beta_h z^{-h})}{(1+\alpha_1 z+\ldots+\alpha_k z^k)(1+\alpha_1 z^{-1}+\ldots+\alpha_k z^{-k})}. \tag{32}$$

However, (31) is much more useful. From it can be obtained directly (i) the autocovariance function of the process (27), this being the property (31) shares with (32); (ii) the inverse of $\mathbf{V}$ in its exact form; (iii) the integral and rational powers of $\mathbf{V}$ and $\mathbf{V}^{-1}$.

Thus we have, from the elementary rule on the inversion of a product of several matrices,

$$\begin{aligned}\sigma^2\mathbf{V}^{-1} &= (\mathbf{I}+\alpha_1\mathbf{U}'+\ldots+\alpha_k\mathbf{U}'^k)(\mathbf{I}+\beta_1\mathbf{U}'+\ldots+\beta_h\mathbf{U}'^h)^{-1} \\ &\qquad \times(\mathbf{I}+\beta_1\mathbf{U}+\ldots+\beta_h\mathbf{U}^h)^{-1}(\mathbf{I}+\alpha_1\mathbf{U}+\ldots+\alpha_k\mathbf{U}^k),\end{aligned} \tag{33}$$

which is no more difficult to evaluate exactly than the matrix product in (31), which is the autocovariance matrix itself.

It is apparent from (31) and (33) that although $\mathbf{V}$ is a Laurent matrix, $\mathbf{V}^{-1}$ is not, a property already noted by Whittle.

* See also Wise (1955, Chapter III) for a further analysis of this problem.

The autoregressive process

To illustrate the application of the above results to problems of importance which have not been solved in the literature even in special cases, the inverse of the autocovariance matrix of the autoregressive process generated by the relation

$$x_t + \alpha_1 x_{t-1} + \ldots + \alpha_k x_{t-k} = \epsilon_t \tag{34}$$

will now be derived for the semi-infinite process.

From this result the inverses of the autocovariance matrices of N successive observations from the process (34) are then given in full for $k = 1$, $k = 2$ and $k = 3$.

From (33) we deduce for the special case (34) the result

$$\sigma^2 \mathbf{V}^{-1} = (\mathbf{I} + \alpha_1 \mathbf{U}' + \ldots + \alpha_k \mathbf{U}'^k)(\mathbf{I} + \alpha_1 \mathbf{U} + \ldots + \alpha_k \mathbf{U}^k). \tag{35}$$

Taking $k = 1$, 2 and 3 respectively, we deduce at once from (35) the matrices

(i) $k = 1$:

$$\sigma^2 \mathbf{V}^{-1} = \begin{bmatrix} 1 & \alpha_1 & 0 & \ldots & 0 & 0 \\ \alpha_1 & 1+\alpha_1^2 & \alpha_1 & \ldots & 0 & 0 \\ 0 & \alpha_1 & 1+\alpha_1^2 & \ldots & 0 & 0 \\ \vdots & & & \ddots & & \vdots \\ 0 & 0 & 0 & \ldots & 1+\alpha_1^2 & \alpha_1 \\ 0 & 0 & 0 & \ldots & \alpha_1 & 1 \end{bmatrix} \tag{36}$$

an $N \times N$ matrix.

(ii) $k = 2$:

$$\sigma^2 \mathbf{V}^{-1} = \begin{bmatrix} 1 & \alpha_1 & \alpha_2 & 0 & \ldots & 0 & 0 \\ \alpha_1 & 1+\alpha_1^2 & \alpha_1+\alpha_1\alpha_2 & \alpha_2 & \ldots & 0 & 0 \\ \alpha_2 & \alpha_1+\alpha_1\alpha_2 & 1+\alpha_1^2+\alpha_2^2 & \alpha_1+\alpha_1\alpha_2 & \ldots & 0 & 0 \\ 0 & \alpha_2 & \alpha_1+\alpha_1\alpha_2 & 1+\alpha_1^2+\alpha_2^2 & \ldots & 0 & 0 \\ \vdots & & & & \ddots & & \vdots \\ 0 & 0 & 0 & 0 & \ldots & 1+\alpha_1^2 & \alpha_1 \\ 0 & 0 & 0 & 0 & \ldots & \alpha_1 & 1 \end{bmatrix} \tag{37}$$

an $N \times N$ matrix.

(iii) $k = 3$:

$$\sigma^2 \mathbf{V}^{-1} = \begin{bmatrix} 1 & \alpha_1 & \alpha_2 & \alpha_3 & \ldots & 0 & 0 \\ \alpha_1 & 1+\alpha_1^2 & \alpha_1+\alpha_1\alpha_2 & \alpha_2+\alpha_1\alpha_3 & \ldots & 0 & 0 \\ \alpha_2 & \alpha_1+\alpha_1\alpha_2 & 1+\alpha_1^2+\alpha_2^2 & \alpha_1+\alpha_1\alpha_2+\alpha_2\alpha_3 & \ldots & 0 & 0 \\ \alpha_3 & \alpha_2+\alpha_1\alpha_3 & \alpha_1+\alpha_1\alpha_2+\alpha_2\alpha_3 & 1+\alpha_1^2+\alpha_2^2+\alpha_3^2 & \ldots & 0 & 0 \\ \vdots & & & & \ddots & & \vdots \\ 0 & 0 & 0 & 0 & \ldots & 1+\alpha_1^2 & \alpha_1 \\ 0 & 0 & 0 & 0 & \ldots & \alpha_1 & 1 \end{bmatrix}. \tag{38}$$

The result (36) confirms that obtained for $k = 1$ by Cochrane & Orcutt (1949, equation (6·14), p. 57). However, the results (37) and (38) for $k = 2$ and $k = 3$ respectively do not appear to have been given previously in the literature.* So far as the author is aware, (35) is new, and the inverses of the autocovariance matrices for $k = 4, 5, 6, \ldots$, etc., can be written down immediately from it, rendering 'approximate' methods of inversion unnecessary.

* Note, however, Champernowne (1948, p. 206, equation 3·5), which gives the inverse implicitly for the case of the autoregressive process.

REFERENCES

ANDERSON, R. L. (1942). Distribution of the serial correlation coefficient. *Ann. Math. Statist.* **13**, 1.
CHAMPERNOWNE, D. G. (1948). Sampling theory applied to autoregressive schemes. *J. R. Statist. Soc.* **10**, 204.
COCHRANE, D. & ORCUTT, G. H. (1949). Application of least squares regression to relationships containing autocorrelated error terms. *J. Amer. Statist. Ass.* **44**, 32.
DOOB, J. L. (1953). *Stochastic Processes.* New York: John Wiley and Sons.
JORDAN, C. (1947). *Calculus of Finite Differences.* New York: Chelsea Publishing Co.
KHINTCHINE, A. (1934). Korrelationstheorie der stationaren stochastischen Prozesse. *Math. Ann.* **109**, 604.
WATSON, G. S. (1951). Serial correlation in regression analysis. Unpublished Ph.D. thesis and Inst. of Stat. Mimeo. Series, North Carolina State College.
WHITTLE, P. (1951). *Hypothesis Testing in Time-Series Analysis.* Uppsala: Almquist and Wiksell.
WHITTLE, P. (1952). Some results in time-series analysis. *Skand. ActuarTidskr.* **35**, 200.
WIENER, N. (1930). Generalized harmonic analysis. *Acta-Math.* **55**, 117.
WISE, J. (1955). Ph.D. Thesis (unpublished), University of London.
WOLD, H. (1953). *Demand Analysis.* New York: John Wiley and Sons.
WOLD, H. (1954). *A Study in the Analysis of Stationary Time Series.* Uppsala: Almquist and Wiksell.

[28]

SPECTRAL PROPERTIES OF NON-STATIONARY SYSTEMS OF LINEAR STOCHASTIC DIFFERENCE EQUATIONS*

GREGORY C. CHOW AND RICHARD E. LEVITAN
International Business Machines Corporation

A method is proposed to eliminate trends from a sample from a non-stationary system of linear stochastic difference equations. The auto-covariance matrix and the spectral density matrix of the detrended component of the sample are derived. The latter matrix turns out to have the same form as the spectral density matrix for a stationary system when expressed in terms of the roots of the system. Since the parameters of the system are assumed known throughout the paper, the problem of statistical inference does not arise.

1. INTRODUCTION

In an applied field such as economics, one is often interested in the dynamic characteristics of a system of stochastic difference equations. For the purpose of analyzing a theoretical model, e.g., business cycle theory [1], or an empirical one, the parameters of the system are assumed to be known. In the latter case, only estimates of the parameters are available, but the present paper is concerned only with deducing certain measures of the dynamic properties of the system given the values of the parameters, rather than with sampling errors of the measures induced by the errors of the estimates of the parameters. The results of this paper, nevertheless, may be a step toward a solution of the latter problem.[1]

If the system is linear, i.e., the vector time series y_t satisfies

$$y_t = Ay_{t-1} + u_t \tag{1}$$

where a higher-order system is already converted to first order, and where $Eu_tu_t' = V$ and $Eu_tu_{t-k}' = 0$ for $k \neq 0$, and if it is stationary, i.e., the roots of A are all smaller than one in absolute value, its second-order behavior can be characterized by the autocovariance matrix or the spectral density matrix with a well-known expression [4, p. 29].

However, if the system (1) is non-stationary, when some roots are greater than one in absolute value, its behavior appears difficult to characterize since the autocovariances do not converge and the spectral densities are not defined. At the same time, it may be reasonable to represent a growing economy by such a non-stationary system. The cyclical characteristics of many apparently explosive economic time series have been studied, some by spectral analysis, after applying certain methods to eliminate trends from the observed series. The question then arises as to whether a method can be set forth to eliminate trends from a realization of system (1), given its parameters, so that the de-

* We would like to express our thanks to T. W. Anderson, R. K. Brayton, and B. B. Mandelbrot for helpful discussions; and to E. P. Howrey, I. R. Savage, and two referees for suggestions to improve the exposition of the original draft.

[1] Given the sampling distribution of the estimates of the parameters, one can at least use simulation to obtain the distribution of the statistics given by (33).

trended component can be characterized by an appropriate autocovariance matrix or spectral density matrix.

This paper proposes such a method for the case of an explosive or non-stationary system (1). The method is an extension of a suggestion made by Quenouille [3] applicable to system (1) when A is a scalar. Our extension to the multivariate case is fairly straightforward. However, Quenouille himself did not make use of this suggestion but recommended a different procedure for the multivariate situation.

In section 2, Quenouille's suggestion for the univariate case will be restated, and a property of the detrended sample will be derived for the purpose of adaptation to the multivariate situation. Section 3 deals with trend elimination for a realization of system (1) and derives the autocovariance and spectral properties of the detrended component. The Appendix raises some questions concerning Quenouille's method for the multivariate system, which is supposed to apply only when all roots of the system are real, and treats the case of complex roots greater than one in absolute value.

It turns out that the spectral density matrix of the detrended component of the sample from a non-stationary system of the form (1) will have the same form as the spectral density matrix for a stationary system of the form (1) when the density is expressed in terms of the roots of the system.

2. TREND ELIMINATION FOR A REALIZATION OF A NON-STATIONARY FIRST-ORDER STOCHASTIC DIFFERENCE EQUATION

Consider a series z_t in discrete time generated by

$$z_t = \lambda z_{t-1} + \epsilon_t \qquad (t = 1, \cdots, T) \tag{2}$$

where ϵ_t are mutually independent random variables with mean zero and variance w. We will be concerned with the non-stationary or explosive case ($\lambda > 1$), and will treat z_0 as given. Quenouille [3, pp. 57–58] pointed out that any particular realization $(z_1, \cdots, z_T)$ can be written as the sum of an exponential trend and a realization $(z_1^d, \cdots, z_T^d)$ of a stationary series (superscript d for detrended).

Let $(z_1^d, \cdots, z_T^d)$ satisfy

$$z_t^d = \lambda z_{t-1}^d + \epsilon_t \qquad (t = 1, \cdots, T) \tag{3}$$

where the ϵ_t are the same as in (2). The difference

$$x_t \equiv z_t - z_t^d = \lambda(z_{t-1} - z_{t-1}^d) \equiv \lambda x_{t-1} \tag{4}$$

must be an exponential trend.

To find a vector $(z_1^d, \cdots, z_T^d)$ satisfying (3) which is a sample from a stationary process, one first selects the end value z_T^d from a distribution with zero mean and independently of ϵ_T, and then works backward by equation (3), i.e.,

$$z_{t-1}^d = \lambda^{-1} z_t^d - \lambda^{-1} \epsilon_t \qquad (t = T, T-1, \cdots, 1) \tag{5}$$

The vector so chosen is a sample, going backward in time, from a stationary first-order series with coefficient λ^{-1} and independent residuals $-\lambda^{-1}\epsilon_t$. Since the variance of this series is

$$\frac{\operatorname{Var}(-\lambda^{-1}\epsilon_t)}{1-\lambda^{-2}} = \frac{w}{\lambda^2-1}, \tag{6}$$

Quenouille suggested choosing z_T^d from a distribution with variance (6).

It is easy to show that a sample from such a stationary series, going backward, can also be interpreted as a sample from the forward going scheme

$$z_t^d = \lambda^{-1} z_{t-1}^d + \eta_t \qquad (t = 1, \cdots, T). \tag{7}$$

By (5) and (7), one finds the residuals η_t of the forward scheme to be

$$\begin{aligned} \eta_t &= z_t^d - \lambda^{-1} z_{t-1}^d \\ &= (1-\lambda^{-2}) z_t^d + \lambda^{-2}\epsilon_t. \end{aligned} \tag{8}$$

By repeated applications of (5), one obtains

$$z_{t-1}^d = -\lambda^{-1}(\epsilon_t + \lambda^{-1}\epsilon_{t+1} + \cdots + \lambda^{-(T-t)}\epsilon_T - \lambda^{-(T-t)} z_T^d). \tag{9}$$

Hence, z_{t-1}^d can be regarded as a linear function of future ϵ's if the end point z_T^d is chosen from the distribution suggested by Quenouille, or is simply set equal to zero for sufficiently large T. In the latter case, the trend value x_T equals z_T. When (9) is used to substitute for z^d in (8), we have

$$\eta_t = -(1-\lambda^{-2})\lambda^{-1}(\epsilon_{t+1} + \lambda^{-1}\epsilon_{t+2} + \lambda^{-2}\epsilon_{t+3} + \cdots) + \lambda^{-2}\epsilon_t. \tag{10}$$

From (10), it will follow that the residuals η_t of the forward scheme (7) have the same autocovariance function as the residuals $-\lambda^{-1}\epsilon_t$ of the backward scheme (5). The expectation of η_t is zero; its variance is

$$\begin{aligned} E\eta_t^2 &= (1-\lambda^{-2})^2\lambda^{-2}(1+\lambda^{-2}+\lambda^{-4}+\cdots)w + \lambda^{-4}w \\ &= \lambda^{-2}w \end{aligned} \tag{11}$$

the same as the variance of $-\lambda^{-1}\epsilon_t$. Similarly, the covariance between η_t and $\eta_{t-k} (k>0)$ is

$$\begin{aligned} E\eta_t\eta_{t-k} &= E[-(1-\lambda^{-2})\lambda^{-1}(\epsilon_{t+1}+\lambda^{-1}\epsilon_{t+2}+\cdots)+\lambda^{-2}\epsilon_t] \\ &\quad\times[-(1-\lambda^{-2})\lambda^{-1}(\epsilon_{t-k+1}+\lambda^{-1}\epsilon_{t-k+2}+\cdots)+\lambda^{-2}\epsilon_{t-k}] \\ &= (1-\lambda^{-2})^2\lambda^{-2-k}(1-\lambda^{-2})^{-1}w - (1-\lambda^{-2})\lambda^{-2-k}w = 0. \end{aligned} \tag{12}$$

Equation (10) also provides all the information concerning the residuals η_t required for our extension to the multivariate case. Any sample from the non-stationary process (2), with ϵ_t as residuals, can be decomposed into an exponential trend plus a sample from the stationary series (7) whose residuals η_t are each the sum of $\lambda^{-2}\epsilon_t$ and a term independent of it. These residuals have mean zero, variance $\lambda^{-2}w$. and are uncorrelated.

3. DYNAMIC PROPERTIES OF NON-STATIONARY LINEAR SYSTEMS

In this section, we will decompose a sample from the system (1) into a sample from a stationary system plus exponential trends, and derive the autocovariance matrix and spectral density matrix of the stationary system. The square matrix A in (1) is assumed to be real and non-singular. The covariance matrix of u_t is denoted by V, assumed to be positive semi-definite, with some equations in (1) possibly being identities.

A new set of variables z_t will be defined, which are linear combinations of y_t, by diagonalizing the matrix A,

$$A = BD_\lambda B^{-1} \tag{13}$$

where D_λ is the diagonal matrix consisting of the characteristic roots of A, and the columns of B are the corresponding (right) characteristic vectors. Equations (1) and (13) imply

$$B^{-1}y_t = D_\lambda B^{-1}y_{t-1} + B^{-1}u_t \tag{14}$$

or

$$z_t = D_\lambda z_{t-1} + \epsilon_t.$$

The canonical variables z_t are defined as $B^{-1}y_t$, and the residuals $\epsilon_t = B^{-1}u_t$ in the transformed system have a covariance matrix

$$E\epsilon_t\epsilon_t' = B^{-1}VB^{-1'} = W = (w_{ij}). \tag{15}$$

If some roots are greater than one in absolute value, the system will be non-stationary. We will first treat the case of a single real root greater than one, then the case of many real roots greater than one later on in this section, leaving the case of complex roots greater than one in absolute value to the Appendix. Let $\lambda_1 > 1$. By the result of section 2, a sample of the first canonical variable

$$z_{1t} = \lambda_1 z_{1,t-1} + \epsilon_{1t} \qquad (t = 1, \cdots, T) \tag{16}$$

can be decomposed into an exponential trend

$$x_{1t} = \lambda_1 x_{1,t-1} \qquad (t = 1, \cdots, T) \tag{17}$$

plus a sample from a stationary series

$$z^d_{1t} = \lambda_1^{-1} z^d_{1,t-1} + \eta_{1t} \qquad (t = 1, \cdots, T) \tag{18}$$

where η_{1t} have zero mean and are mutually uncorrelated.

A sample from the multivariate time series (1) can be similarly decomposed. Observations on the first canonical variable are assumed to be decomposed as in the preceding paragraph. Observations on all other canonical variables will be unchanged. Let b_{ij} be the ijth element of B, and b_i be the ith row of B. The sample of the ith variable is partitioned as

$$y_{it} = b_i z^d_t + b_{i1}x_{1t} \qquad (t = 1, \cdots, T) \tag{19}$$

where z^d_t denotes the vector z_t with the first component replaced by z^d_{1t}. We will be concerned with the dynamic properties of the detrended observations

$$y^d_{it} = b_i z^d_t \qquad (t = 1, \cdots, T) \tag{20}$$

after the exponential trends $b_{i1}x_{1t} (i = 1, \cdots, p)$ have been eliminated.

Consider first the autocovariance matrix of the (detrended) canonical variables

$$\Gamma_k^{*d} = E(z_t^d z_{t-k}^{d'}) = E(z_{it}^d z_{j,t-k}^d) = (\gamma_{ij,k}^{*d}). \tag{21}$$

Here the superscript star indicates that the variables are canonical variables rather than the original variables y; and the superscript d signifies "detrended." Expectations here and elsewhere are taken under the assumption that the correct value of λ, and not an estimate of it, is used for detrending. The covariances $\gamma_{ij,k}^{*d}$ for the three cases $(i, j \neq 1)$, $(i, j = 1)$ and $(i = 1, j \neq 1$ or $i \neq 1, j = 1)$ are given respectively by expressions (22), (23), and (24).

$$\begin{aligned}
\gamma_{ij,k}^{*d} &= \gamma_{ij,k}^{*} = E z_{it} z_{j,t-k} \\
&= E(\epsilon_{it} + \lambda_i \epsilon_{i,t-1} + \lambda_i^2 \epsilon_{i,t-2} + \cdots)(\epsilon_{j,t-k} + \lambda_j \epsilon_{j,t-k-1} + \cdots) \\
&= \lambda_i^k (1 + \lambda_i \lambda_j + \lambda_i^2 \lambda_j^2 + \cdots) E \epsilon_{it} \epsilon_{jt} \qquad (22) \\
&= \frac{\lambda_i^k w_{ij}}{1 - \lambda_i \lambda_j} = \gamma_{ji,-k}^{*} \qquad (i, j \neq 1; k \geq 0).
\end{aligned}$$

$$\gamma_{11,k}^{*d} = \gamma_{11,-k}^{*d} = \frac{\lambda_1^{-k}(\lambda_1^{-2} w_{11})}{1 - \lambda_1^{-2}} \qquad (k \geq 0). \tag{23}$$

$$\begin{aligned}
\gamma_{1j,k}^{*d} &= E(z_{1,t}^d z_{j,t-k}) \\
&= -E(\lambda_1^{-1} \epsilon_{1,t+1} + \lambda_1^{-2} \epsilon_{1,t+2} + \cdots)(\epsilon_{j,t-k} + \lambda_j \epsilon_{j,t-k-1} + \cdots) \qquad (24a) \\
&= 0 = \gamma_{j1,-k}^{*d} \qquad (j \neq 1; k \geq 0)
\end{aligned}$$

and[2]

$$\begin{aligned}
\gamma_{1j,-k}^{*d} &= -E(\lambda_1^{-1} \epsilon_{1,t+1} + \lambda_1^{-2} \epsilon_{1,t+2} + \cdots)(\epsilon_{j,t+k} + \lambda_j \epsilon_{j,t+k-1} + \cdots) \\
&= -(\lambda_1^{-k} + \lambda_1^{-k+1} \lambda_j + \lambda_1^{-k+2} \lambda_j^2 + \cdots + \lambda_1^{-1} \lambda_j^{k-1}) w_{1j} \qquad (24b) \\
&= \frac{(\lambda_j^k - \lambda_1^{-k}) w_{ij}}{1 - \lambda_1 \lambda_j} = \gamma_{j1,k}^{*d} \qquad (j \neq 1; k \geq 1).
\end{aligned}$$

Using these covariances, the corresponding spectral densities can be obtained (except for a normalization constant[3]) by

$$f_{ij}^{*d}(\omega) = \sum_{k=-\infty}^{\infty} \gamma_{ij,k}^{*d} e^{-i\omega k} \qquad (i = \sqrt{-1}) \tag{25}$$

Since the key term in the covariance functions is λ_1^{-k} or λ_j^k, the weighted sum (25) can be performed by using

$$\sum_{k=0}^{\infty} \lambda_j^k e^{-i\omega k} = \frac{1}{1 - \lambda_j e^{-i\omega}} \tag{26}$$

---

[2] Here we ignore the possibility that $\lambda_1 \lambda_j = 1$, in which case $(1 - \lambda_1^k \lambda_j^k)/(1 - \lambda_1 \lambda_j)$ should be replaced by k.

[3] The purpose of normalization is to make the area under the spectral density function equal to one. Dividing the auto covariance function $\gamma_{ii,k}^{*d}$ by the product of the standard deviations $\sqrt{\gamma_{ii,0}^{*d}}$ and $\sqrt{\gamma_{jj,0}^{*d}}$ yields the autocorrelation function. If our discussion is confined to real time series in discrete time, the range of ω is only from 0 to π; thus the area under the spectral density from 0 to π has to be one, as accomplished by a further division of (25) by π. If complex time series in discrete time are considered, with ω ranging from $-\pi$ to π, then further division by 2π would make the area under the spectral density from $-\pi$ to π equal to one. When the apparatus is set up for complex time series, with the spectral density defined accordingly, any plot of the spectral density for a real time series only from 0 to π will require doubling the ordinate.

The spectral densities for the three cases are (27), (28) and (29).

$$\begin{aligned} f_{ij}^{*d}(\omega) &= \sum_{k=0}^{\infty} \gamma_{ij,k}^{*d} e^{-i\omega k} + \sum_{k=0}^{\infty} \gamma_{ij,-k}^{*d} e^{-i\omega k} - \gamma_{ij,0}^{*d} \\ &= \frac{w_{ij}}{1-\lambda_i\lambda_j}\left(\frac{1}{1-\lambda_i e^{-i\omega}} + \frac{1}{1-\lambda_j e^{i\omega}}\right) - 1 \qquad (27) \\ &= \frac{w_{ij}}{(1-\lambda_i e^{-i\omega})(1-\lambda_j e^{i\omega})} \qquad (i, j \neq 1) \end{aligned}$$

$$\begin{aligned} f_{11}^{*d}(\omega) &= \frac{\lambda_1^{-2} w_{11}}{(1-\lambda_1^{-1}e^{-i\omega})(1-\lambda_1^{-1}e^{i\omega})} \\ &= \frac{w_{11}}{(1-\lambda_1 e^{-i\omega})(1-\lambda_1 e^{i\omega})} \end{aligned} \qquad (28)$$

$$\begin{aligned} f_{1j}^{*d}(\omega) &= \sum_{k=1}^{\infty} \gamma_{1j,-k}^{*d} e^{i\omega k} \\ &= \frac{w_{1j}}{1-\lambda_1\lambda_j}\left(\frac{\lambda_j e^{i\omega}}{1-\lambda_j e^{i\omega}} - \frac{\lambda_1^{-1} e^{i\omega}}{1-\lambda_1^{-1}e^{i\omega}}\right) \qquad (29a) \\ &= \frac{w_{ij}}{(1-\lambda_1 e^{-i\omega})(1-\lambda_j e^{i\omega})} \end{aligned}$$

and

$$f_{j1}^{*d}(\omega) = \frac{w_{j1}}{(1-\lambda_j e^{-i\omega})(1-\lambda_1 e^{i\omega})}. \qquad (29b)$$

The results (28) and (29) show that even when a characteristic root λ_1 is greater than unity, or when a canonical variable z_{1t} is non-stationary, the spectral or cross-spectral density functions $f_{ij}^{*d}(\omega)$ of the canonical variables, once detrended, will have the same form as the function (27) for the stationary canonical variables. The autocovariance or cross-covariance functions (23) and (24) involving the non-stationary (but detrended) canonical variable z_{1t}^d differ in form from the function (22) for the stationary canonical variables, however, the corresponding spectral density functions have the same form. This result does not lead to mathematical inconsistency because the covariance functions (23) and (24) are defined and valid only for $\lambda_1 > 1$, whereas the covariance functions (22) are defined for $\lambda_i < 1$ and $\lambda_j < 1$.

It is easy to show that the formula (27) applies to two or more real roots greater than unity. For $\lambda_1 > 1$ and $\lambda_2 > 1$, say, one needs to check only $f_{12}^{*d}(\omega)$. Using (9), one obtains

$$\begin{aligned} \gamma_{12,k}^{*d} &= E(z_{1,t}^d z_{2,t-k}^d) \\ &= E(\lambda_1^{-1}\epsilon_{1,t+1} + \lambda^{-2}\epsilon_{1,t+2} + \cdots)(\lambda_2^{-1}\epsilon_{2,t-k+1} + \lambda_2^{-2}\epsilon_{2,t-k+2} + \cdots) \\ &= \frac{\lambda_2^{-k}(\lambda_1^{-1}\lambda_2^{-1}w_{12})}{1-\lambda_1^{-1}\lambda_2^{-1}} = \gamma_{21,-k}^{*d} \qquad (k \geq 0) \end{aligned} \qquad (30)$$

The cross-spectral density function is

$$
\begin{aligned}
\overset{*d}{f}_{12}(\omega) &= \sum_{k=0}^{\infty} \overset{*d}{\gamma}_{12,k} e^{-i\omega k} + \sum_{k=0}^{\infty} \overset{*}{\gamma}_{12,-k} e^{i\omega k} - \overset{*}{\gamma}_{12,0} \\
&= \frac{\lambda_1^{-1}\lambda_2^{-1} w_{12}}{1-\lambda^{-1}\lambda^{-1}}\left(\frac{1}{1-\lambda^{-1}e^{-i\omega}} + \frac{1}{1-\lambda_1^{-1}e^{i\omega}} - 1\right) \\
&= \frac{w_{12}}{(\lambda_2 - e^{-i\omega})(\lambda_1 - e^{i\omega})} \\
&= \frac{w_{12}}{(1-\lambda_1 e^{-i\omega})(1-\lambda_2 e^{i\omega})}
\end{aligned}
\tag{31}
$$

which has the same form as (27).

In fact, the above analysis can be applied when there are complex roots. Obviously, if the complex roots are smaller than one in absolute value, all of our derivations in this section remain valid. For the case of complex roots greater than one in absolute value, the reader is referred to the Appendix.

We have derived the autocovariance matrix $\Gamma_k^{*d} = [\gamma_{ij,k}^{*d}]$ and the spectral density matrix $F^{*d}(\omega) = [f_{ij}^{*d}(\omega)]$ of the detrended canonical variables. The corresponding matrices for the detrended original variables y_t^d, defined by equation (20), are simply

$$\Gamma_k^d = B\Gamma_k^{*d}B' \tag{32}$$

and

$$F^d(\omega) = BF^{*d}(\omega)B' = B\left(\frac{w_{ij}}{(1-\lambda_i e^{-i\omega})(1-\lambda_j e^{i\omega})}\right)B'. \tag{33}$$

The main result of this paper is summarized by the following theorem.

Theorem: Given system (1), *with* $A = BD_\lambda B^{-1}$, D_λ *being a diagonal matrix consisting of the roots* λ_j *of* A, $Eu_tu_t' = V$, $(w_{ij}) = B^{-1}VB^{-1'}$, (33) *is the spectral density matrix of*

$$\overset{d}{y}_{it} = b_i \overset{d}{z}_t$$

where b_i *is the ith row of* B, $z_t = B^{-1}y_t$, $z_{jt}^d = z_{jt}$ *for* $|\lambda_j| < 1$, $z_{jt}^d = z_{jt} - x_{jt}$ for $|\lambda_j| > 1$ *and for the exponential trend* $x_{jt} = \lambda_j x_{j,t-1}$.[4]

APPENDIX

QUENOUILLE'S METHOD OF DECOMPOSING A NON-STATIONARY SYSTEM AND THE CASE OF COMPLEX ROOTS

Instead of following up his own suggestion for the univariate case, Quenouille has recommended a different method for the multivariate system. In the para-

[4] Strictly speaking, our method breaks down when a root is *exactly* one, but this rarely happens. Even when certain theorizing, such as assuming linear equations for the first differences of some variables, could lead to roots of unity if the theory were strictly adhered to, we would still recommend using equation (33) since the theory itself is only an approximation. In an economic application [2], we have computed the spectral densities from a matrix A with .99997 and .99991 as two of its roots. The expression (27) for each of these canonical variables implies extremely high densities at very low frequencies, a phenomenon which many spectral analyses of economic time series have revealed and which our calculations [2] confirm. For a discussion of the possible relevance of the present paper to business cycle theory, the reader may refer to another paper [1], which has motivated the present paper.

graph immediately after making his former suggestion [3, p. 58], Quenouille wrote (italics ours; $F^{-1}(D)$ replacing $F(D)$ for consistency with the rest of his book),

"In general, any non-stationary autoregressive process $F^{-1}(D)x_t = \epsilon_t$, *with real roots*, may be partitioned in a similar manner [sic], the stochastic element following a stationary scheme whose terms when operated upon by $F^{-1}(D)$ gives series of random elements. To determine this stationary scheme, it is necessary to use the results of §3.2: the corresponding scheme has its u_i and w_i interchanged."

Here x_t and ϵ_t correspond respectively to our y_t and u_t in system (1). D is the lag operator, and $F_\lambda^{1-}(D)$ is a polynomial in D for an autoregressive process—$F^{-1}(D)$ equals $I - AD$ for the first order system (1). u_i corresponds to the ith column of the matrix B of right characteristic vectors. w_i had been defined [3, p. 10] as the vector

$$\sum_{j=1}^{p}\left(\frac{v_i' v_j}{\lambda_i^{-1}\lambda_j^{-1} - 1}\right) u_j$$

where v_i' corresponds to the ith row of $-D_\lambda^{-1}B^{-1}$ in our notations.

It is difficult to accept Quenouille's proposal for the multivariate case. His rationale is the statement [3, §3.2] that the 2^n autoregressive schemes given by

$$F^{-1}(D) = \prod_{i=1}^{n} (i - \lambda_i^{\pm 1} D),$$

where all permutations of the ± 1 are used, have the same autocorrelation function. This statement is based on the relationship

$$\Gamma \equiv \sum_{k=-\infty}^{\infty} (E y_t y_{t-k}') D^k = F(D)F'(D^{-1}).$$

We question the validity of this relationship for a non-stationary time series where $E y_t y_{t-k}'$ is a function of t and where $F(D)$ may not converge. For example, the scheme given by

$$F^{-1}(D) = (1 - \lambda_1 D)$$

will be non-stationary when $\lambda_1 > 1$, and

$$F(D) = 1 + \lambda_1 D + \lambda_1^2 D^2 + \cdots$$

does not converge.

Even if the above proposal were accepted, it could not deal with a process with complex roots. We will now examine the applicability of our method to the case of complex roots greater than one in absolute value. Since complex roots come in conjugate pairs, let λ_1 and λ_2 be such a pair, and the corresponding right characteristic vectors b_1 and b_2 (u_1 and u_2 in Quenouille's notation) are also complex conjugates. So are the left characteristic vectors b^1 and b^2, the first and second rows of B^{-1}. Therefore, $z_{1t}=b^1y_t$ and $z_{2t}=b^2y_t$ are conjugate complex, as are $\epsilon_{1t}=b^1u_t$ and $\epsilon_{2t}=b^2u_t$. From any sample of the pair of complex canonical time series

$$z_{1t} = \lambda_1 z_{i,t-1} + \epsilon_{1t} \qquad (t = 1, \cdots, T)$$

and

$$z_{2t} = \lambda_2 z_{2,t-1} + \epsilon_{2t}$$

we subtract the sample of the complex stationary series

$$\overset{d}{z}_{1t} = \lambda_1^{-1} \overset{d}{z}_{1,t-1} + \eta_{1t} \qquad (t = 1, \cdots, T)$$

and

$$\overset{d}{z}_{2t} = \lambda_2^{-1} \overset{d}{z}_{2,t-1} + \eta_{2t}$$

where, as before, z_{1t}^d and z_{2t}^d are generated backward in time, with z_{1T}^d and z_{2T}^d selected at random from their conjugate bivariate stationary process, or set equal to zero for sufficiently large T. The remaining "trends"

$$x_{1t} = z_{1t} - \overset{d}{z}_{1t} = \lambda_1^t x_{10} \qquad (t = 1, \cdots, T)$$

and

$$x_{2t} = z_{2t} - \overset{d}{z}_{2t} = \lambda_2^t x_{20}$$

will be conjugate complex.

For the partition of the sample of the original variables, we replace equation (19) by

$$y_{it} = b_i \overset{d}{z}_t + b_{i1}x_{1t} + b_{i2}x_{2t} \qquad (t = 1, \cdots, T). \tag{A1}$$

The contribution of λ_1 and λ_2 to the stationary part $b_i z_t^d$ is real since the sum $b_{i1}z_{1t}^d + b_{i2}z_{2t}$ is. The non-stationary part is

$$b_{i1}x_{10}\lambda_1^t + b_{i2}x_{20}\lambda_2^t$$

Letting r and θ be the absolute value and the angle of the roots, and s_i and p_i be the absolute value and the angle of the coefficients, we can write the non-stationary part as (superscript $i=\sqrt{-1}$)

$$s_i r^t (e^{i(\theta t + p_i)} + e^{-i(\theta t + p_i)}) = 2s_i r^t \cos(\theta t + p_i) \tag{A2}$$

which is an explosive cosine function of time. Although our method of decomposition is formally applicable to a pair of complex (canonical) time series, we have to keep in mind the cyclical nature of the non-stationary part eliminated from the original time series.

REFERENCES

[1] Chow, G. C., "The acceleration principle and the nature of business cycles," IBM Research Center Report, RC-1919, October 1967, *Quarterly Journal of Economics*, 82 (August, 1968) 403–418.

[2] Chow, G. C. and Levitan, R. E., "Nature of business cycles implicit in a linear economic model," IBM Research Center Report, RC-2085, May 1968.

[3] Quenouille, M. H., *The Analysis of Multiple Time-Series*. London: Charles Griffin, 1957.

[4] Whittle, P., *Prediction and Regulation by Linear Least-Square Methods*. New York: D. Van Nostrand Company, 1963.

[29]

Annals of Economic and Social Measurement, 5/1, 1976

INTERPRETING SPECTRAL ANALYSES IN TERMS OF TIME-DOMAIN MODELS

BY ROBERT F. ENGLE*

This paper derives relationships between frequency-domain and standard time-domain distributed-lag and autoregressive moving-average models. These relations are well known in the literature but are presented here in a pedogogic form in order to facilitate interpretation of spectral and cross-spectral analyses. In addition, the paper employs the conventions and discusses the estimation procedures used in the NBER's TROLL system.

1. INTRODUCTION

Although spectral analysis is a widely used tool in the statistical analysis of time series, the mathematical difficulties and the unfamiliarity of the concepts make it inaccessible to many economists. Increasing familiarity with time series models such as distributed lags and autoregressive-moving average processes (so called "Box–Jenkins" models), makes it now easy to describe and interpret spectral analysis without the use of complicated mathematics. Traditional time domain and more difficult frequency domain (spectral) analysis are just two ways of looking at the same phenomenon, but each has some advantages and the use of both can be an important aid in model building. Because frequency domain methods are more non-parametric, they are particularly useful in model specification.

The computational difficulties of performing spectral analysis have been substantially reduced through an innovative computer algorithm called the fast Fourier transform and the availability of the NBER TROLL computer system throughout the U.S. and many places abroad. The system is used by telephone and easily performs both time domain and frequency domain analysis. All the facilities to be described in this paper are available in TROLL.

The paper is intended to be a tutorial. It will develop in Sections 2 and 3 the correspondences between time and frequency domain analyses assuming only that the reader is familiar with time domain analysis. A short description of frequency domain estimation in Section 4 focuses upon confidence intervals and some adjustments which are available in TROLL. Finally, in Section 5, spectral analysis is used to provide a guide to the specification of time domain models with an example from economics.

There are many excellent reference works on spectral analysis which should be consulted for more details. Granger [6]† is perhaps the easiest to read, while Jenkins and Watts [10] is the most comprehensive. Fishman [7] focuses on some economic estimation problems and Dhrymes [3, 4] extends this direction with somewhat more mathematics. Hannan [8] gives a very rigorous treatment of the

* Research supported in part by National Science Foundation Grant GJ-1154X3 to the National Bureau of Economic Research, Inc.

† Parenthesized numerals refer to entries in the Reference section.

whole area. Relatively short and simple early expositions of the theory and practice are in Jenkins [9] and Parzen [13] with a good application to economics in Nerlove [12]. The book which is recommended as a companion to the TROLL system is Cooley, Lewis, and Welch [1] which is more application oriented and which describes, in Chapters 5 and 7, the basic concepts used in designing the system. Also see Cooley, Lewis, and Welch [2].

2. The Spectrum

Many data series can be considered successive chance observations over time called stochastic processes. Possibly, each observation is independent of the preceding ones. However, for most applications, there is some suspected dependence between the observations. Both spectral analysis (frequency domain) and the more familiar time domain analysis are ways to characterize this dependence. High correlations between neighboring observations or seasonal components might be important forms of this dependence. Once the stochastic process is characterized, it may be possible to forecast its values, improve the efficiency of a regression where this is the disturbance, or make an inference about the economic model which produced such a variable.

Both frequency domain and time domain analyses begin with stochastic processes which are covariance stationary. This means that the covariance between an observation now and one a few periods later depends only on the time interval, not the dates themselves. Mathematically this can be expressed as

$$\gamma(s)=E(x_{t+s}-\mu)(x_t-\mu) \tag{1}$$

where γ is the autocovariance function and μ is the mean. The important assumption is that neither depend upon t. While this assumption may seem strong, it is because of this condition that information from the past can be used to describe the present or future behavior.

Many economic time series appear to violate this assumption, particularly those with pronounced trends. It is generally possible, however, to create an approximately stationary series by taking first differences, or extracting a trend, thus leaving the series with a constant mean of zero. There may also be trends in variance which can often be removed by first taking logs of the series.

In the time domain the most common models are the autoregressive moving average models (ARMA). These may be purely autoregressive, purely moving average, or mixed.

A p-th order autoregressive and a q-th order moving average model are defined in equations (2) and (3), respectively, while (4) is an ARMA (p, q).

$$x_t=a_1x_{t-1}+a_2x_{t-2}+\ldots+a_px_{t-p}+\varepsilon_t \tag{2}$$

$$A(L)x_t=\varepsilon \tag{2'}$$

$$x_t=b_1\varepsilon_{t-1}+b_2\varepsilon_{t-2}+\ldots+b_q\varepsilon_{t-q}+\varepsilon_t \tag{3}$$

$$x=B(L)\varepsilon \tag{3'}$$

$$x_t=a_1x_{t-1}+\ldots+a_px_{t-p}+b_1\varepsilon_{t-1}+\ldots+b_q\varepsilon_{t-q}+\varepsilon_t; \tag{4}$$

$$A(L)x=B(L)\varepsilon \tag{4'}$$

In these equations ε is a series of independent, identically distributed random errors with ε_t independent of x_{t-i} for all i greater than zero; L is the lag operator and $A(L)$ and $B(L)$ are polynomials. These classifications are not unique since one type of process can, in general, be transformed into another. Nevertheless, they provide useful, simple models of time series which can be tested with data or used for analysis. Knowledge of $A(L)$ in (2′), $B(L)$ in (3′) or $A(L)$ and $B(L)$ in (4′) is equivalent to knowing the dynamics of the stochastic process of x.

The spectrum provides another way of characterizing time series. In this case we think of a series as being made up of a great number of sine and cosine waves of different frequencies which have just the right (random) amplitudes to make up the original series. Thus the list of how much of each frequency component was necessary is also a full description of the time series. The spectrum is a plot of the squared amplitude of each component against the frequency of that component. It is continuous and always greater than zero as long as there are no deterministic elements (that is, no exactly repeating components, or components which can be predicted exactly on the basis of the past). This is a very general way to describe a stochastic process.

The spectral density function is defined as the Fourier transform of the autocovariance function

$$(5)\quad f(\theta)=\gamma(0)+2\sum_{s=1}^{\infty}\gamma(s)\cos(2\pi\theta s)=\sum_{s=-\infty}^{\infty}\gamma(s)\,e^{-2\pi i\theta s}\qquad 0\le\theta\le 1$$

where $i=\sqrt{-1}$, $e^{i\theta}=\cos(\theta)+i\sin(\theta)$, and the last equality follows from $\gamma(s)=\gamma(-s)$. There are several important features of this definition. First, although written in complex notation, the spectrum is real valued since all the imaginary sine terms cancel exactly. Second, since the cosine is symmetric $f(\theta)=f(1-\theta)$, and only the frequencies from 0 to 1/2 are needed to describe the spectrum. Third, integrating equation (5) from 0 to 1, shows that the area under the spectrum is equal to $\gamma(0)$, the variance. The spectrum is a decomposition of the variance into the components contributed by each frequency. A strict proof of the probabilistic basis of this interpretation is provided by the spectral representation theorem. Fourth, since θ is measured in cycles per period, it appears that there are no components from less than one cycle every two periods (the Nyquist frequency). The reason for this becomes clear upon reflection. When observing monthly data, weekly fluctuations will be indistinguishable from longer oscillations which have the same value at the moment the observation is taken. The weekly component will therefore be counted with these lower frequencies.

To clarify the interpretation of a spectrum and help with the notion of frequency components, consider the spectrum in Figure 1 which has been estimated from quarterly data.

From the definition of the spectrum in equation (5), the highest frequency oscillation which can be distinguished is 0.5 cycle per period. At this frequency, it takes two quarters to complete a cycle so there are two cycles per year. There is a peak at 0.25 cycle which corresponds to a four-quarter, or annual cycle. This is most likely a seasonal component. Similarly, the peak at 0.5 also indicates a seasonal component since it has an even number of cycles per year. The peak at

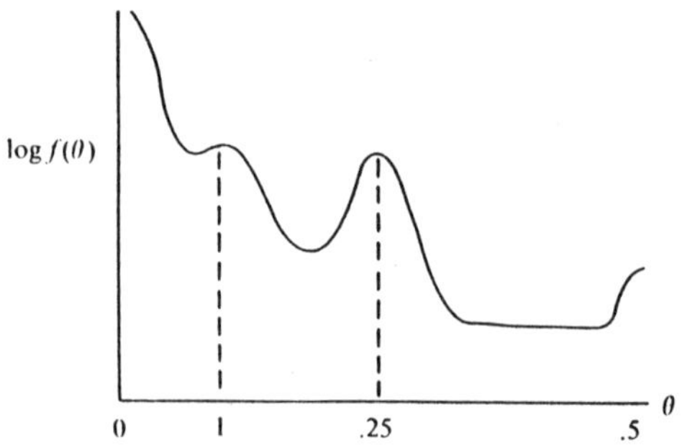

Figure 1 Typical spectrum

0.1 corresponds to a two and a half year oscillation. This might be a business cycle and economically interesting if it is significantly above its neighboring points. Generally, economic time series show behavior much like that of Figure 1.

The purpose of this paper is to emphasize the relationship between these concepts of frequency domain analysis and the more conventional time domain analysis. The first order serial correlation coefficient is easily calculated in the time domain and is generally large and positive for economic time series. This finding is easily observed in the frequency domain as well. Multiply the spectrum by $\cos(2\pi\theta)$ and integrate to obtain from equation (5) just $\gamma(1)$, the first order serial covariance. Roughly, this amounts to multiplying low frequencies by a positive number, high frequencies by a negative number, and adding. If the result is positive, there is positive first order serial correlation. Thus data series with generally downward sloping spectra have positive first order serial correlations while those with upward sloping spectra have negative serial correlations. Very important is the observation that spectra which are roughly symmetric about 0.25 will show no first order serial correlation.

A useful application of this analysis is found in interpretation of regression results. The assumption of no serial correlation in the disturbance is equivalent to the assumption that its spectrum is constant. The Durbin–Watson statistic gives a test against the possibility that there is first order serial correlation. This is a test against a general slope of the spectrum of the disturbance, whereas one would like to test against all forms of variation. In particular, notice that if the seasonality in Figure 1 were more severe, the spectrum might easily have no first order serial correlation but be far from constant. Durbin [5] formulated such a test based upon the spectrum of the residuals. In general, examination of the residual spectrum gives very useful information about the validity of the regression assumptions.

The link between time domain and frequency domain is completed by a derivation of the spectrum corresponding to the ARMA models of equations (2)–(4). The basic result is quite simple but will be established in the appendix.

Lemma 1: If x is a stochastic process generated by the model

$$A(L)x_t = B(L)\varepsilon_t$$

where ε_t is a series of independent identically distributed random variables with variance σ^2, and the polynomial $A(L)$ has all roots outside the circle, then the spectrum of x is given by

(6) $$f_x(\theta) = \sigma^2|B(z)|^2/|A(z)|^2, \qquad z = e^{(-2\pi i\theta)}$$

Notice that z is a complex function of θ.

Several examples should help to illustrate the usefulness of this result. First, notice that the spectrum of the very simple (white noise) process which has no time dependence, is just a constant. It has equal contributions from all frequencies.

Now consider the first order moving average process with parameter ρ, $x_t = \varepsilon_t + \rho\varepsilon_{t-1}$. From equation (6) the spectrum of x is

$$f_x(\theta) = |1 + \rho\varepsilon^{-2\pi i\theta}|^2\sigma^2 = \{1 + \rho^2 + 2\rho \cos(2\pi\theta)\}\sigma^2$$

Evaluating this for θ in the range (0, 1/2), gives a smooth spectrum which begins at $(1+\rho)^2$ and ends at $(1-\rho)^2$. If ρ is positive, this has the typical spectral shape which is common to most economic time series, and which implies a positive serial correlation coefficient, $\rho/(1+\rho^2)$. The first order autoregressive case is very similar but gives a somewhat steeper spectrum at low frequencies.

A very simple autoregressive model which captures the behavior of purely seasonal stochastic processes for monthly data is

$$x_t = \rho x_{t-12} + \varepsilon_t$$

From equation (6) the spectrum of this seasonal process is given by

$$f_x(\theta) = \sigma^2/|1 - \rho\varepsilon^{-24\pi i\theta}|^2 = \sigma^2/(1 + \rho^2 - 2\rho \cos(24\pi\theta))$$

which is plotted in Figure 2. There are peaks at all the harmonic frequencies: $\theta = 1/12, 2/12, 3/12, 4/12, 5/12, 6/12$, and all are equally important.

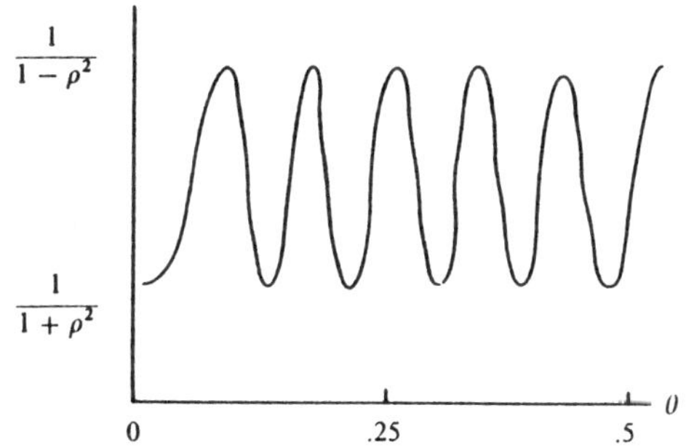

Figure 2 Spectrum of pure seasonal

3. The Cross Spectrum

The techniques used above can also be used to describe the relations between two jointly covariance-stationary time series. Both the individual behavior and the interrelations can be decomposed into basic sinusoidal elements.

The cross covariance function is a direct analogue of the autocovariance function. For two series with mean zero this is simply defined as:

(7) $$\gamma_{xy}(s) = E(x_{t+s}y_t)$$

Again, notice that it does not depend on t. The cross spectrum is similarly defined as:

(8) $$f_{xy}(\theta)=\sum_{s=-\infty}^{\infty}\gamma_{xy}(s)\,e^{-2\pi i\theta s}$$

Because γ_{xy} is no longer symmetric the cross spectrum is not a real valued function of θ but rather a complex valued function.

Although the cross spectrum summarizes all the information in the series, it cannot be plotted directly. Instead, one examines statistics called "coherence squared," "gain," and "phase." These measures are defined here and given a rather extended interpretation below, connecting these concepts with the ideas of distributed lag regression models.

The coherence squared (COH) is like a correlation coefficient and is defined as:

(9) $$\mathrm{COH}(\theta)=|f_{xy}(\theta)|^2/f_x(\theta)f_y(\theta)$$

which is clearly between 0 and 1.

The gain (G) indicates how much the spectrum of x has been amplified to approximate that component of y.

(10) $$\mathrm{G}_{xy}(\theta)=|f_{xy}(\theta)|/f_x(\theta)$$

This expression can clearly never be negative. However, if it is small, it indicates that at frequency θ, x has little effect on y.

The phase (PH) is a measure of the timing between the series. It is measured in the fraction of a cycle that y leads x.

(11) $$\mathrm{PH}(\theta)=\frac{1}{2\pi}\arctan\left(\frac{-\mathrm{Im}\,(f_{xy}(\theta))}{\mathrm{Re}\,(f_{xy}(\theta))}\right)$$

where Im and Re are the imaginary and real parts of the cross spectrum.* There is a natural ambiguity about the phase since adding or subtracting 1 whole cycle from an angle will not change its tangent. The phase is known only up to adding or subtracting an integer and therefore even the lead-lag relation is not known for sure. The plot of the phase is designed to emphasize this fact. It is possible to combine the phase and the gain in a simple expression

(12) $$f_{xy}(\theta)/f_x(\theta)=\mathrm{G}_{xy}(\theta)\,e^{-2\pi i\,\mathrm{PH}(\theta)}$$

Two other potentially useful measures of the cross spectrum are its amplitude, which is merely its absolute value, and its time lag. The latter describes the phase in terms of the number of periods y leads x rather than the fraction of a cycle. Although this seems like a useful measure, the natural ambiguity of the phase also makes the time lag ambiguous and difficult to interpret. This may not be the case at low frequencies, where these difficulties are less likely to be important.

* The appropriate quadrant for PH is chosen on the basis of the signs of the real and imaginary components of the cross spectrum.

A natural and very general way for economists to think about the relations between two time series is in terms of a bivariate distributed lag model, such as

$$y_t = \sum_{j=p}^{-p} w_j x_{t-j} + \varepsilon_t. \tag{13}$$

This is often rewritten in terms of the lag operator L as

$$y_t = \sum_{j=p}^{-p} w_j L^j x_t + u_t = w(L)x_t + \varepsilon_t \tag{14}$$

where, for generality, leads as well as lags have been allowed and L^{-1} is interpreted as a lead operator. The same techniques required for equations (5) and (6), establish frequency domain interpretations of equation (14).

Lemma 2: If y is generated by a distributed lag model

$$y = w(L)x + \varepsilon$$

where x and ε are uncorrelated covariance stationary processes, then

$$f_{xy}(\theta) = w(z^{-1})f_x(\theta), \tag{15}$$

and

$$f_y(\theta) = |w(z)|^2 f_x(\theta) + f_\varepsilon(\theta) \tag{16}$$

where $z = e^{(-2\pi i\theta)}$.

Notice from (16) that the variance of y is broken into two parts: one which is the variation due to x modified by the lag distribution and the other due to the disturbance. Equation (15) shows that f_{xy}/f_x is an estimator of $w(z)$ which is just a function of the lag coefficients. Once $w(z)$ is known, all the lag coefficients can be found by merely taking the inverse Fourier transform. This is the basis of a very useful type of distributed lag estimation which is often called Hannan's inefficient method.*

Now consider running a regression of one component of y against the same frequency component of x. The regression coefficient would be the ratio of the covariance of x and y to the variance of x. In spectral notation this would be just $f_{xy}(\theta)/f_x(\theta)$. The R-squared of this regression is one minus the unexplained variance over the total variance. Substituting (15) into equation (16) demonstrates that the coherence squared is just the R-squared of this regression.

Similarly, from (12), the regression coefficient is the gain times $e^{-2\pi i PH(\theta)}$. The regression coefficient is just the gain if there is no time lag between the independent and dependent variables. If there is a time lag, the gain can be interpreted as the regression coefficient if the series were lagged just the right amount to eliminate any phase shift, and the phase is the angle by which they would have to be shifted (or the phase over the frequency is the time shift which is necessary). As a particular example, if the series are negatively related, the gain will still be positive but the phase will be 0.5.

* It is inefficient because it does not use the properties of the disturbance to construct an estimator with the smallest possible variance. It too is available in TROLL.

In summary, the coherence squared, the gain and the phase at a particular frequency can be interpreted in terms of a regression using only data at that frequency. The coherence squared is the R^2, the gain is the regression coefficient once any delay has been eliminated, and the phase is the angular shift needed to make this delay.

From Lemma 2 it is simple to plot the gain and phase corresponding to any particular time domain distributed lag model. A variety of these plots, often called Bode plots, are presented in Figure 3. In the balance of this section these figures will be analyzed for salient characteristics; and in Section 5 these are used to help specify a distributed lag model.

1. *Simple Static Model*

$w(L) = w_0$

$w(z^{-1}) = w_0$

$G(\theta) = w_0$

$PH(\theta) = 0$

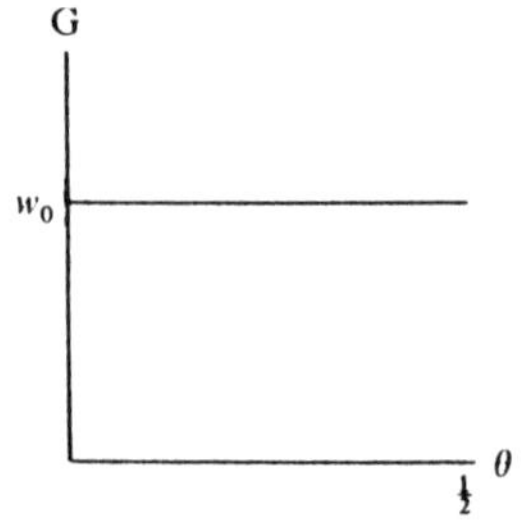

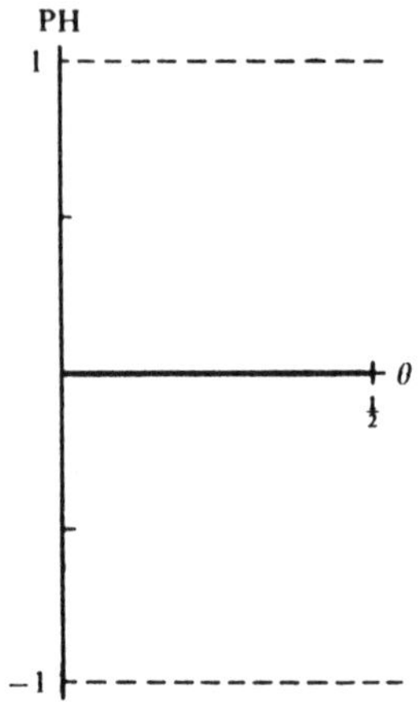

2. *Simple Delay*

$w(\theta) = w_j L^j$

$w(z^{-1}) = w_j e^{-2\pi i j \theta}$

$G(\theta) = w_j$

$PH(\theta) = -j\theta$

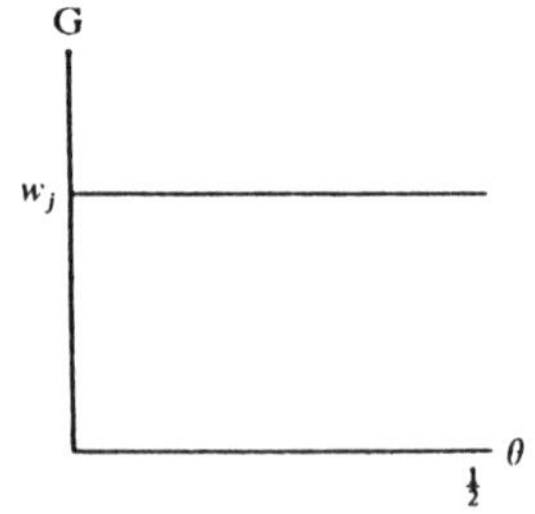

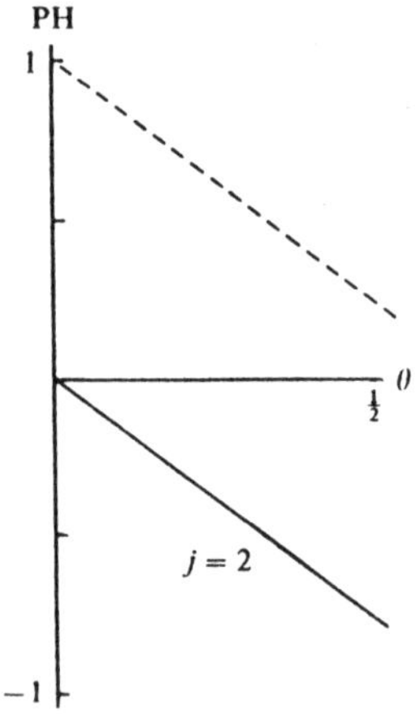

3. *One Period Lag*

$$w(L) = w_0 + w_1 L \quad w_0, w_1 > 0$$

$$w(z^{-1}) = w_0 + w_1 e^{2\pi i\theta}$$

$$G(\theta) = \sqrt{w_0^2 + w_1^2 + 2w_1 w_0 \cos 2\pi\theta}$$

$$PH(\theta) = \arctan\left(-\frac{w_1 \sin 2\pi\theta}{w_0 + w_1 \cos 2\pi\theta}\right)$$

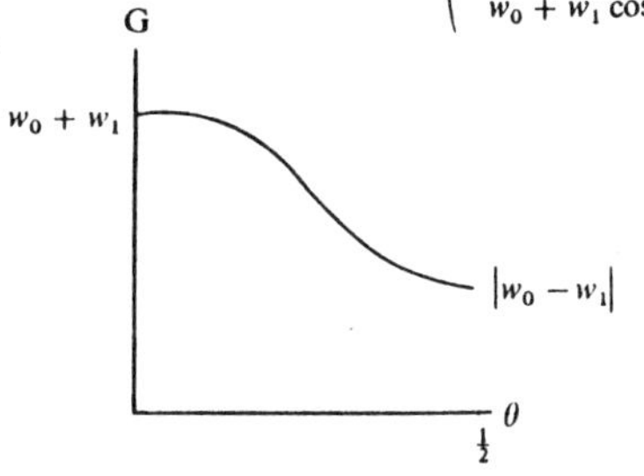

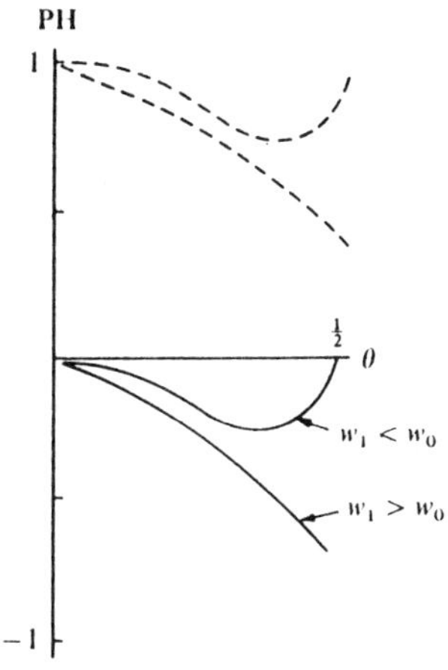

4. *Geometric Lag*

$$w(L) = \frac{w_0}{1 - w_1 L} = w_0 (1 + w_1 L + w_1{}^2 L^2 + \ldots)$$

$$0 \leq w_1 < 1$$

$$w(z^{-1}) = \frac{w_0}{1 - w_1 e^{2\pi i\theta}}$$

$$G(\theta) = w_0 \sqrt{1 + w_1^2 - 2w_1 \cos 2\pi\theta}$$

$$PH(\theta) = \arctan\left(\frac{-w_1 \sin 2\pi\theta}{1 - w_1 \cos 2\pi\theta}\right)$$

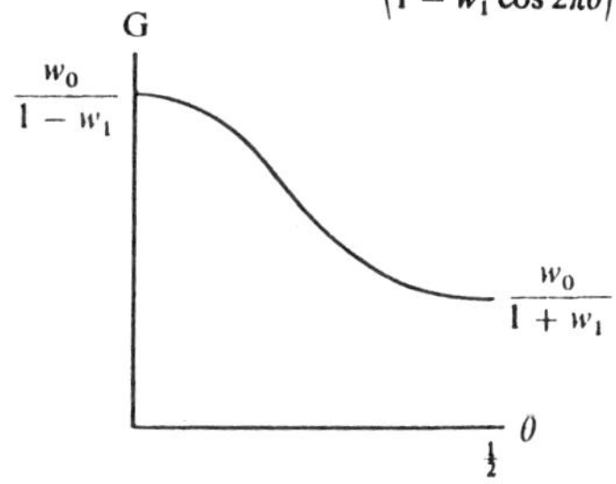

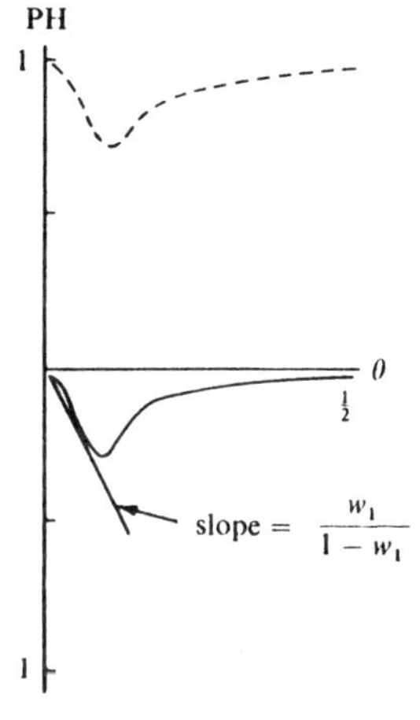

The simplest models are the static model described in (1) and the delay model shown in (2). Each has only one $w_j \neq 0$; thus

(17) $$w(z^{-1}) = w_j e^{2\pi i\theta j}.$$

The gain of these models is therefore constant and equal to w_j and the phase plot will be a straight line with slope $-j$. The (negative) slope of this line is just the delay of the dependent variable behind the independent variable. For any lag distribution, the mean lag is the slope of the phase at zero frequency (as long as the gain is non-zero). For the delay model, the slope is everywhere equal to the mean lag.

5. *First Differences*

$$w(L) = w_0 - w_1 L \quad w_0, w_1 > 0$$

$$w(z^{-1}) = w_0 - w_1 e^{2\pi i\theta}$$

$$G(\theta) = \sqrt{w_0^2 + w_1^2 - 2w_0 w_1 \cos 2\pi\theta}$$

$$PH(\theta) = \arctan\left(\frac{-w_1 \sin 2\pi\theta}{w_0 - w_1 \cos 2\pi\theta}\right)$$

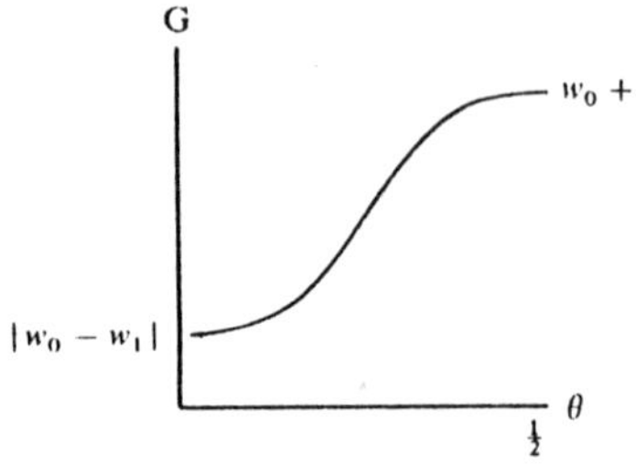

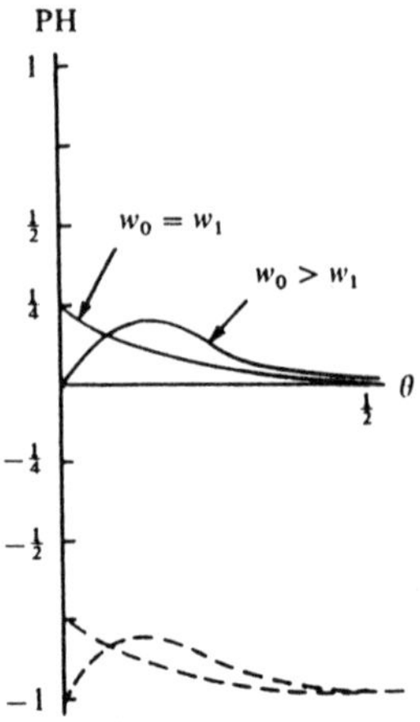

6. *Four Period Differences*

$$w(L) = w_0(1 - L^4)$$

$$w(z^{-1}) = w_0(1 - e^{8\pi i\theta})$$

$$G(\theta) = w_0\sqrt{2 - 2\cos(8\pi\theta)}$$

$$PH(\theta) = \arctan\left(\frac{-\sin 8\pi\theta}{1 - \cos 8\pi\theta}\right)$$

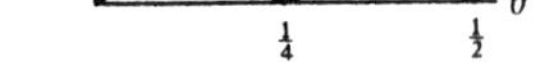

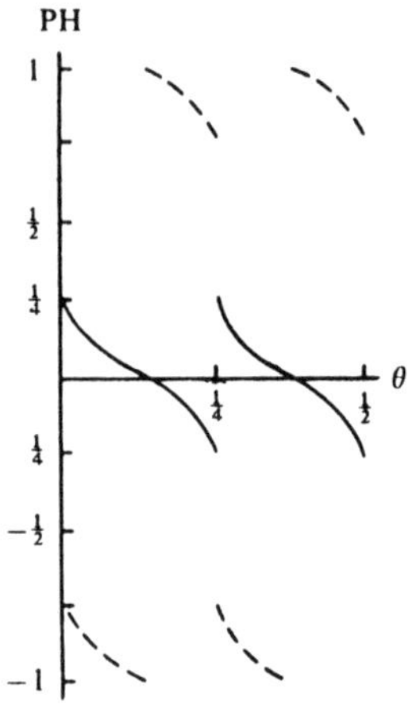

Models (3) and (4) include current and one lagged independent variable, and a lagged dependent variable, respectively. These very common types of lag distributions are used to model processes where the dependent variable only adjusts partially to a change in the independent variable in the current period. In model (3) the adjustment is completed in the second period, while in model (4) it continues forever but with geometrically declining effect.

In both of these cases, the gain is largest at low frequencies and then falls at higher frequencies. At zero frequency $z = 1$ and the gain is the sum of the lag coefficients or the long run propensity. Since z cannot exceed one, the peak of the gain function will always be at zero frequency if all the lag weights are positive. The phase will be zero at zero frequency and then will decline with a slope equal to (minus) the mean lag. For more complicated models with all positive lag weights, the phase may change sign for higher frequencies; nevertheless, the initial slope will be the mean lag.

The final two models have a different character. In these cases, the dependent variable is influenced by the rate of change of the independent variable; the lag weights change sign. The peak in the gain function can now occur at any frequency, but it will generally not be at zero. In fact, if the sum of the lag weights is zero as with first differences, the gain will be zero at the beginning. Notice the interesting double peak associated with a four period difference. A twelve period difference would of course have six peaks and a three period difference would have one and a half (the second peak would occur at $\theta = 0.5$).

The phase plots can have both positive and negative portions. If the gain is non-zero at the origin, then the slope of the phase at the origin will be algebraically equal to (minus) the mean lag of the distribution. But, the mean lag is not a useful measure when the lag weights are of different signs. In particular, a negative mean lag does not imply a lead.

Both plots can be constructed for many other lag distributions either by hand or using the computer. A simple corollary of Lemma 2 will make it easy to combine these simple forms into more complicated lag distributions.

Corollary. If a lag distribution can be written as the product of two lag distributions such as

$$w(L) = u(L)v(L),$$

then

$$G_w(\theta) = G_u(\theta)G_v(\theta)$$

$$PH_w(\theta) = PH_u(\theta) + PH_v(\theta).$$

The rule for combining lag distributions is that the gains multiply and the phases add. A special case of this is familiar from the time domain: the product of two lag distributions will have a long run propensity which is the product of the separate propensities and a mean lag which is the sum.

As an example, consider the geometric form when the independent variable is lagged two periods. This is the product of a two period delay and a lagged dependent variable. Thus the gain is the product of a constant and the geometric gain, while the phase is the sum of the constant slope of the delay and the variation shown for the geometric.

4. Spectrum Estimation

There are several distinct methods for estimating spectra and cross-spectra. The advantages and disadvantages of each have been extensively discussed. In particular, see Cooley, Lewis, and Welch [1] and Parzen [14]. Since the rediscovery of the fast Fourier transform, computational considerations suggest that periodogram averaging may be the most efficient method for spectrum estimation. In addition, it is conceptually simplest and leads to great versatility in the estimation procedures. Finally, the usefulness of the periodogram in regression and various test procedures makes it sensible to compute this as a first step. See also Jones [11] and Tick [15].

The periodogram is defined as the square of the absolute value of the Fourier transform of the data series at each frequency, all divided by m, the number of observations. The formula for the periodogram is

$$I_x(\theta_j) = \frac{1}{m}\left|\sum_{t=0}^{m-1} x_t e^{-2\pi i t\theta_j}\right|^2 \tag{18}$$

where $\theta_j = j/m$ and $j = 0, 1, 2, \ldots, m$. This quantity is an estimator of the spectrum, but it is not a very good one. The expected value of the periodogram is

$$E(I_x(\theta_j)) = \sum_{v=-m+1}^{m-1} \frac{(m-|v|)}{m} \gamma(v)\, e^{-2\pi i v\theta_j}. \tag{19}$$

For large values of m this estimator is an unbiased estimator of the spectrum, since $\gamma(v)$ is small for large v. Unfortunately, it is not a consistent estimator since the variance does not decrease as the sample approaches infinity. In fact, the periodogram at each frequency is approximately proportional to a chi squared random variable with two degrees of freedom, regardless of the number of observations. An intuitive explanation for this unusual circumstance is that as the sample becomes larger, more and more frequency points are estimated rather than obtaining better estimates of a fixed number of parameters. This explanation also suggests the solution. The average of a few neighboring points should give a better estimate of the spectrum in that neighborhood. Thus smoothing procedures must be used to obtain consistent spectrum estimators.

Two averaging or smoothing procedures, called "windows", are commonly used with periodogram averaging. A rectangular moving average gives the minimum variance for smoothing over a flat spectrum using only a certain number of points. However, when there are peaks in the spectrum, the rectangular window will lead to considerable bias and broadening of the peaks. An alternative window is a triangular window which gives the spectrum a much smoother appearance and is often better at describing the shape of peaks.

The width of the window is an important parameter in the estimation. The wider the window, the smaller is the variance of the resulting estimate; yet, the wider the window, the more serious may be the bias of smoothing over non-smooth portions of the spectrum. Two measures of width can be used to describe the windows, the bandwidth and the range. The bandwidth is the half-power width of the window. It is measured in frequency units, i.e., it is a fractional number of cycles per period. If, for example, the bandwidth is specified as 0.1, there will be five separate "bands" since the frequencies range from 0 to 0.5. For many purposes, spectral estimates separated by more than one bandwidth are considered to be independent.

The second measure is the range. This is merely the number of spectral points used in each moving average; it gives the separation between which two points are known to be completely independent. If the effective sample is 200 observations (implying 100 points in the spectrum) and the range is 20, there will be five separate window widths in the estimation. A sensible value for the range is $\sqrt{m}$, where m is the number of observations.

Near the endpoints of the spectrum, the smoothing procedures must be modified. One choice is to decrease the range so that the window does not overlap the endpoints. Because the variance increases as the window becomes narrower, the variance increases markedly at very low or very high frequencies and one must be very cautious in interpreting low frequency peaks or troughs.

An alternative endpoint procedure is to keep the range constant but take advantage of the symmetry properties of the spectrum. The smoothing windows will "wrap" around the endpoints of the spectrum since the spectrum at $+\theta$ is just the same as at $-\theta$. This method will give smaller variances but bigger biases than the first method.

The spectral estimator resulting from smoothing the periodogram is approximately proportional to another chi squared random variable, this time with more degrees of freedom. The equivalent degrees of freedom are equal to

$$\text{E.D.F.} = B \cdot m \tag{20}$$

where B is the bandwidth. This allows computation of a confidence interval for the spectrum. On the spectral plot, a 95 percent confidence interval can be constructed for each frequency separately.

Estimates of the cross spectrum are accomplished in exactly the same manner. The finite Fourier transform of one series is multiplied by the complex conjugate of the Fourier transform of the other to form the cross periodogram. The real and complex parts of this are then smoothed individually, just as for the periodogram. The sampling distributions for the various measures derived from the cross spectrum also depend only on the equivalent degrees of freedom of the estimate. With the coherence plot, the critical point for a 5 percent test of the hypothesis of zero coherence can be calculated. Approximate 50 percent confidence intervals for the gain can be plotted with the output. These depend on the sample coherence; where the coherence is small, the confidence interval is large.

When using a wide window, peaks tend to be spread out. For many series we know a priori where these peaks will be, either because the series is typical in having strong low frequencies or because it has important seasonality. In these cases "prewhitening" is often recommended. This amounts to dividing the raw periodogram by the expected or typical shape, smoothing this "prewhitened" periodogram which no longer has the large peaks, and then "recoloring" by multiplying by the typical spectral shape. A seasonal and non-seasonal version of the prewhitening filter might be important. Prewhitening can be done in connection with either spectrum or cross spectrum estimation.

A second characteristic which is likely to make the smoothing procedure badly biased in cross spectral estimation is misalignment of the series. When one series lags another by several periods, there is a peak in the cross covariance function which is not at zero. This leads to a regular oscillation in the amplitude of the cross periodogram. Smoothing this will obscure this particular bit of information as well as distorting other results. The recommended procedure is to first divide the cross periodogram by an aligning series, smooth the cross periodogram, and then remultiply it by the aligning series. To construct the alignment series one first computes the inverse Fourier transform of the cross periodogram which is exactly the cross covariance function. This could have been computed from the data directly, but such a method is apparently inferior to the computation of Fourier and inverse Fourier transforms. Searching the cross covariance function for the maximum yields the information needed to construct the alignment series. If this procedure were applied to the estimate of the spectrum or a cross spectrum which was already aligned, the maximum covariance would be the zeroth estimate and thus the alignment series would be unity and would have no effect.

The Fourier transform algorithm used in these computations is the Cooley–Tukey fast Fourier transform. In its basic form it expects a series with 2^n elements and thus each series is padded out to this length with zeros (the mean). The number of spectral points estimated is therefore 2^{n-1} which are evenly spaced between the frequencies 0 and 1/2 cycle per basic time unit of the data. Frequently it is desirable to estimate the spectrum at particular points or not to pad with zeros. In this case, it is possible to pick an integer so that the series is padded to $N = 2^s r$. Choosing $r = 3$, for example, would insure factors of 12 which would be required in order to have exact seasonal points with monthly data. This variation can make substantial difference in the results when there is strong seasonality.

5. The Use of Spectra in Specifying Models

This paper has shown that the time domain and the frequency domain are just two different ways of looking at the same models. The estimation procedures are, however, dramatically different, and it is here that the two techniques can fruitfully be combined. In order to estimate an ARMA or a distributed lag model, using time domain methods, one must first specify (or "identify" as the statisticians say) the form of the model. The process of specification usually involves a series of trial forms and statistical tests coupled with a liberal amount of good judgment. The judgment is particularly important since the tests become of questionable validity when applied in sequence.

On the other hand, the spectral methods do not require the specification of the model. The estimation procedure is independent of the form of the model. This is clearly an advantage since the first difficult step can be avoided; however, it is also a disadvantage, since in general, a very large number of parameters must be estimated and will have relatively wide confidence intervals.

The situation is exactly comparable with the choice of parametric or non-parametric statistical methods. If the parameterization is correct, the parametric procedure is far more efficient than the non-parametric procedure. However, if the parameterization is incorrect, only the non-parametric method will give a valid result. The user of non-parametric statistics gives up some efficiency for insurance against a wrong parameterization.

This discussion suggests a two step procedure for the analysis of stochastic processes. Use the spectral methods to aid in the specification of time domain models, and then use standard time domain methods to estimate them, thereby avoiding the trial and error search for an appropriate model. This is an approach which has been used by engineers for many years but has not had wide acceptance by economists. It will be illustrated by an economic model of housing expenditures in the U.S.

In Figure 4, quarterly housing expenditures and mortgage rates are plotted from 1950 through 1974. The two series are apparently non-stationary and growing exponentially. They appear to be negatively correlated as expected since higher interest rates generally discourage housing. With careful attention to the timing, it may be possible to see that declines in housing follow any interest rate increase with a lag. Questions of particular interest in this analysis might be (1) the timing of interest rate effects on housing and (2) whether the housing market overshoots so that the lag weights change sign for long lags. This is presumably the behavior of other types of investment as implied by the accelerator and neoclassical models of investment.

To calculate the cross spectrum of housing with interest rates, both series are expressed as the first difference of the logarithms, that is, the quarterly growth rates. The gain and the phase as well as the summary statistics from the one line TROLL command requesting this output are shown in Figure 5. The triangular smoothing window is used with the "wrap around" endpoint option and the bandwidth is set (by default) at 0.079. Notice that the rate is multiplied by minus one so that the phase will be centered at 0 rather than 0.5, since interest rates and housing starts are negatively related.

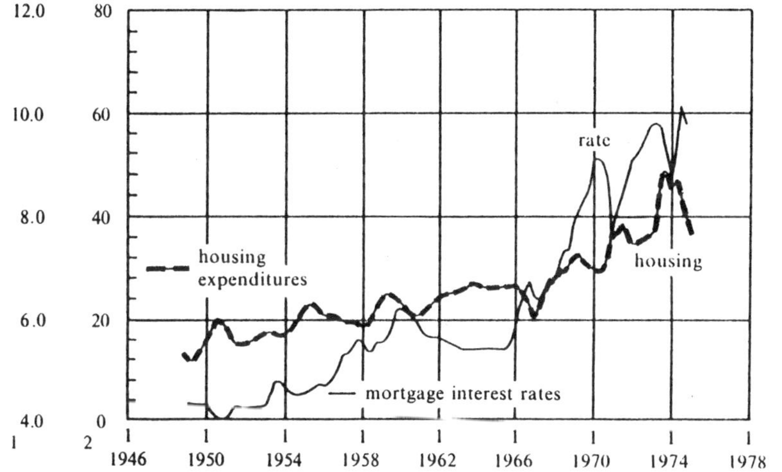

Figure 4 Housing data

Time bounds: 1946 1st to 1974 4th. Data names: Rate Hous.

The task of choosing a time domain specification for a distributed lag model is now to compare the theoretical Bode plots in Figure 3 with the observed gain and phase in Figure 5. It is clear that none of the theoretical plots are close approximations of the estimated gain and phase, but this is to be expected. Some features are, however, recognizable. The gain begins quite small and then rises to a peak at a

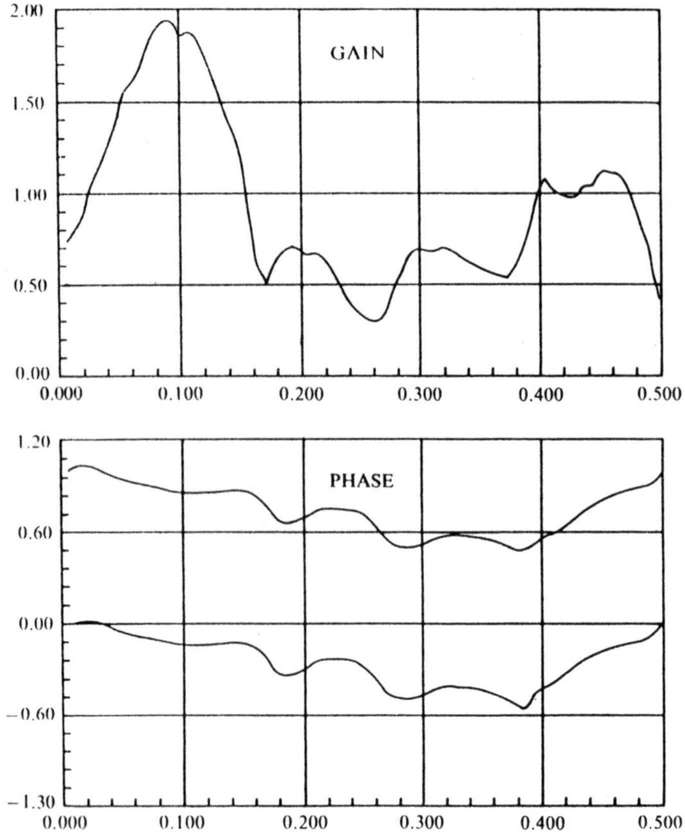

Summary statistics and options:
Type of smoothing: Wrap-triangular. Range: 10.
Type of prewhitening: None.
FFT parameter: 1.
Preprocessing: Demean.
Number of observations in data series: 100
Basis: 128.
Bandwidth: 0.079.
No alignment.
Critical coherence squared (at 5 percent level): 0.636.
−(Del(1 : Log(Rate))) variance: 0.001. Spectrum total: 0.001.
Del(1 : Log(Hous)) variance: 0.003. Spectrum total: 0.003.

Figure 5 Gain and phase between housing and interest rates

period of about 10 quarters where the interest rate elasticity is almost 2. The second most important peak is at approximately 2 quarters per cycle. These look roughly like the four quarter first difference except that the second peak is at too high a frequency and is too small. The phase looks much like a one quarter delay for the first half of the spectrum but then deviates from this in the second half.

TABLE 1

REGRESSION COEFFICIENTS FOR HOUSING AND INTEREST RATES

	Spectral Specification	Alternative 1	Alternative 2	Alternative 3
R^2	.53681	.53566	.42562	.56004
$\bar{R}^2$	.52203	.51043	.40092	.52049
H_{-1}	.51 (6.74)	.48 (5.28)	.69 (6.71)	.51 (4.86)
H_{-2}	—	—	−.07 (.58)	.03 (.23)
H_{-3}	—	—	−.12 (1.18)	.16 (1.60)
R	—	.17 (1.28)	.26 (1.94)	.08 (.60)
R_{-1}	.70 (5.71)	.55 (3.75)	—	.62 (4.11)
R_{-2}	—	.22 (1.36)	—	.15 (.91)
R_{-3}	—	−.16 (1.10)	—	.05 (.32)
R_{-4}	−.24 (1.83)	—	—	.08 (.52)
Const.	.007 (1.71)	.0 (2.19)	.006 (1.25)	.01 (2.29)

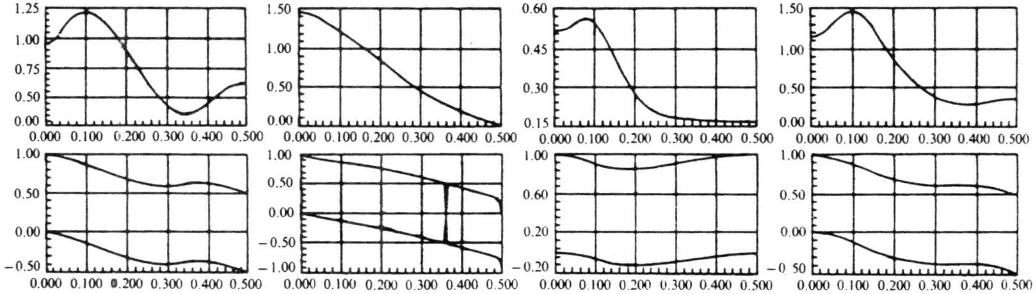

* t-statistics in parentheses. All regressions have 98 observations.

To synthesize a close approximation to Figure 5, one must remember the rules for combining lag distributions. If two lag distributions are multiplied together, the gains are multiplied and the phases are added. Multiplying a geometric distribution times a four quarter first difference will increase the gain of the first peak relative to the second. If a three quarter difference is used, then the second peak will occur at 0.5 which is closer to the observed maximum, especially recalling that the confidence intervals at the endpoints are very large. Finally, the gain at low frequencies is not exactly zero, so probably the coefficients on the third differences should be allowed to differ. In summary, a model with one lagged dependent variable and a current and three period lagged independent variable appears capable of producing approximately the observed gain pattern.

If this model is used, the phase pattern would be the sum of a negative contribution, due to the lagged dependent variable, and a positive component, due to the three period lag. Altogether, this is unlikely to produce the appropriate decline in the phase with frequency which is observed. An additional delay will not alter the gain since it has gain of unity, but will add a linearly declining phase to the others. This line of reasoning leads to consideration of the time domain model:

$$(1 - w_0 L)H = (w_1 + w_2 L^3)(L)R \tag{21}$$

where H and R are the first differences of the logs of housing and interest rates.

This model can be estimated directly with ordinary least squares.* The result is given in Table 1, along with the gain and phase plots which correspond to this set of parameters. The pictures are rather close to the calculated spectra and the time domain regression statistics are generally good with significant t-statistics. The change of sign in the regression coefficients which was anticipated for the lagged independent variable does occur and, as expected, the lagged coefficient is not as large as the current one.

To examine whether this identification procedure led to a particularly good model, both simpler and more complicated versions were estimated. Two naive ways to generate lag distributions are to successively increase the number of lagged independent or lagged dependent variables. Three models are shown in Table 1 with their associated gain and phase plots. One has the current and three quarters lag on interest rates with one lagged dependent variable, a second has three lagged dependent variables but only the current independent variable, and the third is the most general model with three lagged dependent variables and the current and four quarters of lagged independent variables. Notice that the first and second of these alternative models fail to reproduce the second peak of the gain function. The third model does show roughly the right shape, but it does so by using 9 parameters rather than the 4 required by the spectrally specified model. Furthermore, F tests for the restrictions implied by the spectral model are invariably less than one (even testing against alternative 1 when R_{-4} is included) and thus the restrictions are easily accepted.

In conclusion, the specification suggested by spectral analysis is a good specification which might have eventually been reached by time domain techniques after much trial and error. Of many models tried, it has almost the highest

* Least squares will be consistent only if the dynamic specification has eliminated serial correlation in the disturbance. A test of the hypothesis of white noise was accepted.

corrected R^2 and F tests supported the restrictions it imposed. The economic result is that there appears to be a one quarter delay before interest rates influence housing, thereafter there is a geometrically declining effect. Eventually (one year later) there is a change in the direction of housing response as the market has presumably caught up to the desired capital stock. This is easily seen in the time domain but is also apparent in the frequency domain since the gain is small for low frequencies.

This example lends credibility to the proposition that the use of both time and frequency domain techniques may enrich each and, in particular, that frequency domain methods may be very helpful in model specification.

received April 1974
revised May 1975

NBER and University of California, San Diego

Appendix

Lemma A.1: If x is a stochastic process generated by the model

$$A(L)x_t = B(L)\varepsilon_t$$

where ε_t is a series of independent identically distributed random variables with variance σ^2, and $A(L)$ has all roots outside the unit circle, then the spectrum of x is given by

$$f_x(\theta) = \sigma^2 |B(z)|^2 / |A(z)|^2$$

where $z = \varepsilon^{(-2\pi i\theta)}$.

Proof: Consider the moving average process

$$x_t = \sum_{j=0}^{q} b_j \varepsilon_{t-j}$$

where the ε are all independent. Then

$$\gamma(s) = Ex_{t+s}x_t = E \sum_{j=0}^{q} b_j \varepsilon_{t+s-j} \sum_{k=0}^{q} b_k \varepsilon_{t-k}$$

where the expectation on the right only has non-zero values where $-k = s - j$ and $0 \leq k \leq q$. Therefore for $q \geq s \geq 0$

$$\gamma(s) = \sigma^2 \sum_{j=s}^{q} b_j b_{j-s}$$

and is 0 otherwise. The spectrum of x is defined using equation (5) and the symmetry of γ by

$$f(\theta) = \sum_{s=-\infty}^{\infty} \gamma(s) z^s = \sum_{s=1}^{q} \gamma(s)(z^s + z^{-s}) + \gamma(0)$$

$$= \sigma^2 \sum_{s=1}^{q} \sum_{j=s}^{q} b_j b_{j-s}(z^s + z^{-s}) + \sigma^2 \sum_{j=0}^{q} b_j^2$$

which can be written

$$f(\theta)=\sigma^2\sum_{j=0}^{q} b_j z^j \sum_{k=0}^{q} b_k z^{-k}=\sigma^2\left|\sum_{j=0}^{q} b_j z^j\right|^2.$$

There is nothing in this proof which requires that q be finite. Since every stable ARMA process has a (possibly infinite dimensional) moving average representation, the result is true for any ARMA process.

Lemma A.2: If y is generated by a distributed lag model

$$y=w(L)x+\varepsilon$$

where x and ε are uncorrelated covariance stationary processes, then

$$f_{xy}(\theta)=w(z^{-1})f_x(\theta)$$

and

$$f_y(\theta)=|w(z)|^2 f_x(\theta)+f_\varepsilon(\theta)$$

where $z=\varepsilon^{(-2\pi i\theta)}$.

Proof: Without loss of generality take both x and y to have mean zero

$$\gamma_{xy}(s)=Ex_{t+s}y_t$$

$$=E\sum_j w_j x_{t-j}x_{t+s}+Ex_{t+s}\varepsilon_t$$

$$\gamma_{xy}(s)=\sum_j w_j\gamma(s+j)$$

$$f_{xy}(\theta)=\sum_{s=-\infty}^{\infty}\gamma_{xy}(s)z^s=\sum_j\sum_s w_j\gamma(s+j)z^{s+j}z^{-j}$$

$$=\sum_j w_j z^{-j}f_x(\theta)$$

$$f_{xy}(\theta)=w(z^{-1})f_x(\theta).$$

And

$$\gamma_y(s)=Ey_{t+s}y_t$$

$$=E\left(\sum w_j x_{t+s-j}+\varepsilon_{t+s}\right)\left(\sum w_k x_{t-k}+\varepsilon_t\right)$$

$$\gamma_y(s)=\sum_j\sum_k w_j w_k\gamma_x(s-j+k)+\gamma_\varepsilon(s)$$

$$f_y(\theta)=\sum_s\gamma_y(s)z^s$$

$$=\sum_s\sum_j\sum_k w_j w_k\gamma_x(s-j+k)z^{s-j+k}z^{-k}z^j+\sum_s\gamma_\varepsilon(s)z^s$$

$$=\sum w_j z^j\sum w_k z^{-k}f_x(\theta)+f_\varepsilon(\theta)$$

$$f_y(\theta)=|w(z)|^2 f_x(\theta)+f_\varepsilon(\theta).$$

References

[1] Cooley, J. W., P. A. W. Lewis, and P. D. Welch, *The Fast Fourier Transform Algorithm and its Applications*, IBM Research Paper RC-1743, 1967.
[2] ——— "The Application of the Fast Fourier Transform Algorithm to the Estimation of Spectra and Cross Spectra," *Journal of Sound Vibrations*, 1970.
[3] Dhrymes, P. J., *Econometrics: Statistical Foundations and Applications*. New York: Harper and Row, 1970.
[4] ——— *Distributed Lags; Problems of Estimation and Formulation*. San Francisco: Holden Day, 1971.
[5] Durbin, J., "Tests for Serial Correlation in Regression Analysis Based on the Periodogram of Least Squares Residuals," *Biometrica*, 56 (1969), pp. 1–14.
[6] Granger, C. W. J., in association with M. Hatanaka, *Spectral Analysis of Economic Time Series*. Princeton: Princeton University Press, 1964.
[7] Fishman, G. S., *Spectral Methods in Econometrics*. Cambridge: Harvard University Press, 1969.
[8] Hannan, E. J., *Multiple Time Series*. New York: J. Wiley, 1970.
[9] Jenkins, G. M., "General Considerations in the Analysis of Spectra," *Technometrics*, 3, 2 (1961), pp. 133–166.
[10] Jenkins, G. M. and D. G. Watts, *Spectral Analysis and Its Applications*. San Francisco: Holden Day, 1969.
[11] Jones, R. H., "A Reappraisal of the Periodogram in Spectral Analysis," *Technometrics*, 7 (1965), pp. 531–542.
[12] Nerlove, M., "Spectral Analysis of Seasonal Adjustment Procedures," *Econometrica*, 32 (July 1964), pp. 241–286.
[13] Parzen, E., "Mathematical Considerations in the Estimation of Spectra," *Technometrics*, 3, 2 (1961), pp. 167–190.
[14] ——— "Multiple Time Series Modeling," in *Multivariate Analysis*. P. Krishnaia editor. New York: Academic Press, 1969.
[15] Tick, L. H., Letter to the Editor, *Technometrics*, 8 (1966), pp. 559–561.

[30]

INTERNATIONAL ECONOMIC REVIEW
Vol. 19. No. 2, June, 1978

LINEAR REGRESSION IN THE FREQUENCY DOMAIN*

BY A. C. HARVEY[1]

1. INTRODUCTION

Consider the linear regression model

$$y = X\beta + u, \tag{1.1}$$

where X is an $n \times k$ matrix of fixed observations on the independent variables, β is a $k \times 1$ vector of parameters, y is an $n \times 1$ vector of observations on the dependent variable, and u is an $n \times 1$ vector of disturbance terms each with zero mean and constant variance, σ^2. The model may be expressed in terms of frequencies by applying a finite Fourier transform to the dependent and independent variables. There are a number of reasons for doing this. One is to permit the application of the technique known as 'band spectrum regression', in which regression is carried out in the frequency domain with certain wavelengths omitted. This has a number of interesting applications particularly with regard to dealing with seasonality and errors in variables. Another reason for interest in spectral regression is that if the disturbances in (1.1) are serially correlated, being generated by any stationary stochastic process, then regression in the frequency domain will yield an asymptotically efficient estimator of β.

The applications of band spectrum regression in econometrics have been explored recently by Engle [1974]. However, he takes his finite Fourier transforms in complex terms. In order to use a conventional regression package programme, he suggests that once the appropriate frequencies have been deleted the remaining transformed observations should be subjected to an inverse Fourier transform which puts them back in the time domain in real terms. Apart from requiring that the inverse Fourier transform be repeated each time a different set of frequencies are excluded from the model, this approach also leads to a minor problem with the degrees of freedom employed by a standard regression package (Engle [1974 (8)]).

If one were interested in an efficient estimator of β in the face of a general stationary disturbance term (Engle and Gardner [1976]), the use of a complex Fourier transform would also be computationally unattractive if it was felt that the estimation procedure should be iterated in order to improve small sample properties.

This article argues in favor of carrying out the finite Fourier transform in *real* terms. This circumvents the problems raised above. In addition it means that

* Manuscript received May 27, 1977.

[1] I am grateful to J. Durbin and R.F. Engle for reading through and commenting on this article. Any errors, however, are solely my responsibility.

ordinary least squares (OLS) residuals and "recursive residuals" (Brown, et al. [1975], Harvey and Phillips [1974]), may be computed in the frequency domain. Both sets of residuals are extremely useful in this context as they may be used to construct tests either to detect changing relationships between the variables at different frequencies, (cf. Granger and Rees [1968]), or to test for serial correlation in the disturbances.

2. COMPUTATIONS BASED ON THE COMPLEX FOURIER TRANSFORM

The complex finite Fourier transform is based on the $n \times n$ matrix W, in which element (t, s) is given by

$$w_{ts} = \frac{1}{\sqrt{n}} e^{i\lambda_t s}, \qquad s = 0, 1, \ldots, n-1 \tag{2.1}$$

where $\lambda_t = 2\pi t/n$, $t = 0, 1, \ldots, n-1$, and $i = \sqrt{-1}$. Pre-multiplying the observations in (1.1) by W yields

$$\dot{y} = \dot{X}\beta + \dot{u} \tag{2.2}$$

where $\dot{y} = Wy$, $\dot{X} = WX$, and $\dot{u} = Wu$.

If the disturbance vector in (1.1) obeys the classical assumptions, viz. $E[u] = 0$ and $E[uu'] = \sigma^2 I_n$, then the transformed disturbance vector, $\dot{u}$, will have identical properties. This follows because the matrix W is unitary, i.e., $WW^\dagger = I$, where $W^\dagger$ is the transpose of the complex conjugate of W. Furthermore the observations in (2.2) contain precisely the same amount of information as the untransformed observations in (1.1).

Application of OLS to (2.2) yields, in view of the properties of $\dot{u}$, the best linear unbiased estimator (BLUE) of β. This estimator is, of course, identical to the OLS estimator in (1.1), a result which follows directly on taking account of the unitary property of W.

When the relationship implied by (2.2) is only assumed to hold for certain frequencies, band spectrum regression is appropriate, and this may be carried out by omitting the observations in (2.2) corresponding to the remaining frequencies. Since the variables in (2.2) are complex, however, Engle suggests an inverse Fourier transform in order to convert everything back into real terms, thereby making the use of standard regression programmes feasible. He does this by first defining an $n \times n$ matrix A which has zeros everywhere except in the positions on the leading diagonal corresponding to included frequencies. Premultiplying $\dot{y}$ and $\dot{X}$ by A therefore removes certain of the observations, and replaces them by zeros. Transforming back into the time domain yields the real sets of observations:

$$y^* = W^\dagger A\dot{y} = W^\dagger AWy$$

and

$$X^* = W^\dagger A\dot{X} = W^\dagger AWX. \tag{2.3}$$

Regressing y^* on X^* then yields a band spectrum estimator of β identical to the estimator given by the regression of the observations in $\dot{y}$ on the corresponding observations in $\dot{X}$.

In carrying out band spectrum regression in this way, minor problems arise in the sampling statistics due to incorrect degrees of freedom. This, as Engle [1974] notes, is because in dealing with the regression of y^* on X^*, a standard package programme will assume $n-k$ degrees of freedom, whereas, in fact, the true number of degrees of freedom is only $n'-k$, where n' is the number of included frequencies. Some adjustment must therefore be made.

If spectral regression is being used to compute an asymptotically efficient estimator of β in the presence of a stationary serially correlated disturbance term, the matrix A referred to above is replaced by another diagonal matrix, V. The elements in the leading diagonal of V are set equal to estimates of $f_u^{-1/2}(\lambda)$, where $f_u(\lambda)$ is the power spectrum of the disturbance term in (1.1) at frequency λ. Again a standard regression package may be used to estimate β by making a transformation analogous to that in (2.3); see Engle and Gardner [1976]. However if the procedure were to be iterated — which could well lead to an improvement in small sample properties — the inverse Fourier transform in (2.3) would have to be carried out at each iteration. This would be computationally burdensome.

3. THE REAL FINITE FOURIER TRANSFORM

The problems which arise from the use of the complex Fourier transform may be circumvented by carrying out the Fourier transform of the data in real terms. In order to do this the observations in (1.1) are pre-multiplied by the orthogonal matrix Z whose elements are defined as follows:

$$
\begin{aligned}
z_{ts} &= n^{-1/2}, && t = 1,\\
z_{ts} &= (2/n)^{\frac{1}{2}} \cos[\pi t(s-1)/n], && t = 2, 4, 6, \ldots, n-2 \text{ or } n-1,\\
z_{ts} &= (2/n)^{\frac{1}{2}} \sin[\pi(t-1)(s-1)/n], && t = 3, 5, 7, \ldots, n-1 \text{ or } n,\\
z_{ts} &= n^{-1/2}(-1)^{s+1}, && t = n \text{ if } n \text{ is even}, \quad s = 1, \ldots, n,
\end{aligned} \tag{3.1}
$$

Duncan and Jones [1966] note a number of ways in which this transformation may be handled efficiently on a computer. The resulting frequency domain regression model is:

$$y^{**} = X^{**}\beta + v, \tag{3.2}$$

where $y^{**}=Zy$, $X^{**}=ZX$ and $v=Zu$. In view of the orthogonality of Z, $E[vv']=\sigma^2 I_n$ when $E[uu']=\sigma^2 I_n$, and the application of OLS to (3.2) gives the BLUE of β.

Since all the elements of y^{**} and X^{**} are real, model (3.2) may be treated by a standard regression package. If band spectrum regression is to be carried out, the number of rows in y^{**} and X^{**} is reduced accordingly, and so no problems arise from the use of an inappropriate number of degrees of freedom.

If the disturbances in (1.1) are serially correlated, then iterations based on (3.2) may be carried out without the need for computing additional (inverse) Fourier transforms. Once y^{**} and X^{**} have been computed the iterative procedure consists simply of applying weighted least squares to (3.2) with the weights derived from the estimated spectrum of the disturbances in (1.1). Since a consistent estimator of the spectral density may be obtained by smoothing the periodogram of the residuals in the untransformed model (1.1), and since, as is shown in the next section, the same periodogram may be obtained *directly* from the residuals of a regression based on (3.2), these iterations may be carried out at very little extra cost.

4. TESTS BASED ON RESIDUALS FROM FREQUENCY DOMAIN REGRESSION

Suppose $\hat{\beta}$ is an estimator of β. The $n \times 1$ vector of residuals is then defined by

$$\hat{u} = y - X\hat{\beta}. \tag{4.1}$$

Similarly the $n \times 1$ vector of residuals in the transformed model, (3.2), is given by

$$\begin{aligned} \hat{v} &= y^{**} - X^{**}\hat{\beta} \\ &= Z(y - X\hat{\beta}) = Z\hat{u}. \end{aligned} \tag{4.2}$$

If p_j denotes the ordinate of the periodogram[2] of $\hat{u}$ at frequency $\lambda_j = 2\pi j/n$, and $\hat{v}_j$ denotes the j-th element of $\hat{v}$, then

$$p_j = \hat{v}_{2j}^2 + \hat{v}_{2j+1}^2, \qquad j = 1,\dots\frac{n}{2} - 1 \quad (n \text{ even}) \tag{4.3}$$

$$j = 1,\dots\frac{n-1}{2} \quad (n \text{ odd}),$$

$$p_j = 2\hat{v}_{2j}^2, \qquad j = \frac{n}{2} \text{ and } n \text{ even}, \tag{4.4}$$

and

$$p_0 = 2\hat{v}_1^2. \tag{4.5}$$

Thus the squares of the elements in $\hat{v}$ may be used to form a consistent estimator of the power spectrum of $\hat{u}$ by a suitable averaging process. Furthermore, if $\hat{\beta}$ is a consistent estimator of β, then this will also be a consistent estimator of the power spectrum of the true disturbances in the model.

[2] Note that the periodogram is here being defined as the sample spectral density multiplied by a factor of 4π at all frequencies.

As regards test statistics, if $\hat{\beta}$ is the OLS estimator of β, then the elements of $\hat{v}$ may be used directly in Durbin's cumulative periodogram test. This test is based on the quantities

$$s_j = \sum_{r=1}^{j} p_r / \sum_{r=1}^{m} p_r, \qquad j=1,\dots m, \tag{4.6}$$

where $m=\frac{1}{2}n$ for n even and $\frac{1}{2}(n-1)$ for n odd. The procedure is a bounds test and upper and lower critical values may be constructed using the tables provided in Durbin [1969]. Note that p_0 does not enter into the test statistic as $p_0=\hat{v}_1=0$.

Rather than apply this test, an alternative procedure would be to carry out the OLS calculations recursively in the transformed model. This yields a set of $n-k$ recursive residuals; see Brown, Durbin and Evans [1975] and Harvey and Phillips [1974, 1976]. When the disturbances in (1.1) are $NID(0, \sigma^2)$ the recursive residuals in the frequency domain will also be $NID(0, \sigma^2)$. They may therefore be used to construct a CUSUM of squares test, which is closely related to the cumulative periodogram test, but which is not a bounds test. A very simple test, which is likely to have high power against an excess of low frequency (positive serial correlation) is a "heteroscedasticity test" based on the quantity

$$H = \sum_{t=k+1}^{k+p} \tilde{v}_t^2 / \sum_{t=n-p+1}^{n} \tilde{v}_t^2, \tag{4.7}$$

where $\tilde{v}_t$ is the t-th recursive residual in the frequency domain and p is approximately equal to $(n-k)/3$; c.f. Harvey and Phillips [1974, 1976]. Under the null hypothesis that the disturbances in (1.1) are $NID(0, \sigma^2)$, H follows an F-distribution with (p, p) degrees of freedom. Under the alternative hypothesis that the power spectrum of the disturbances declines as the frequency increases, however, (4.7) will tend to be large and so a one-sided test on the upper tail of the F-distribution is appropriate.

The above tests are all tests for serial correlation in the frequency domain. Tests for changes in the structure of the model over different frequencies may also be constructed, however, and these can be regarded as frequency domain analogues of the tests for time-varying parameters introduced by Brown, Durbin and Evans [1975] and Harvey and Phillips [1976]. Such tests included the CUSUM test, as well as the CUSUM of squares test already mentioned. In addition the ψ-test, which was suggested as a test for time-varying parameters by Harvey in the discussion to Brown, et al. [1975(179)], may also prove useful in this context. This has the form

$$\psi = \{(n-k-1)^{-1}\Sigma(\tilde{v}_t - \bar{\tilde{v}})^2\}^{-1/2}(n-k)^{-1/2}\Sigma\tilde{v}_t, \tag{4.8}$$

where $\bar{\tilde{v}}$ is the mean of the $\tilde{v}_t$'s, and it follows a t-distribution with $n-k-1$ degrees of freedom under the null hypothesis that the model is correctly specified with $NID(0, \sigma^2)$ disturbances.

Finally, it should be noted that alternative sets of recursive residuals may be obtained by re-ordering the transformed observations. An obvious possibility, for example, is to reverse the order of the transformed observations, so that those corresponding to the highest frequencies are dealt with first. For the "heteroscedasticity tests", orderings corresponding to those suggested in Harvey and Phillips [1974] may be employed. Tests based on re-orderings such as these may, in certain circumstances, have higher power, although this is a matter for empirical investigation.

5. CONCLUSION

The use of a real finite Fourier transform appears to offer significant computational advantages over a method based on a complex Fourier transform, although the latter is generally easier to handle theoretically. Furthermore, the residuals from a spectral regression calculated using a real Fourier transform may be used to detect various types of misspecification, such as serial correlation and a changing relationship over different frequencies. The residuals are therefore likely to have important applications in the context of investigating these and other hypotheses relevant to regression in the frequency domain.

University of British Columbia

REFERENCES

Brown, R. L., Durbin, J. and J. M. Evans, "Techniques for Testing the Constancy of Regression Relationships Over Time (with Discussion)," *Journal of the Royal Statistical Society, Series B*, 37, (No. 2, 1975), 149–192.

Duncan, D. B. and R. H. Jones, "Multiple Regression with Stationary Errors," *Journal of the American Statistical Association*, 61, (December, 1966), 917–928.

Durbin, J., "Tests for Serial Correlation in Regression Analysis based on the Periodogram of Least-Squares Residuals," *Biometrika*, 56, (No. 1, 1969), 1–15.

Engle, R. F., "Band Spectrum Regression," *International Economic Review*, 15, (February, 1974), 1–11.

——— and R. Gardner, "Some Finite Sample Properties of Spectral Estimators of a Linear Regression," *Econometrica*, 44, (January, 1976), 149–166.

Granger, C. W. J. and H. J. B. Rees, "Spectral Analysis of the Term Structure of Interest Rates," *Review of Economic Studies*, 35, (January, 1968), 67–75.

Harvey, A. C. and G. D. A. Phillips, "A Comparison of the Power of Some Tests for Heteroscedasticity in the General Linear Model," *Journal of Econometrics*, 2, (December, 1974), 307–316.

——— and ———, "Testing for Stochastic Parameters in Regression Models," Paper presented at the European Meeting of the Econometric Society, Helsinki, August 1976.

Name Index